mike kunkel's

HEROBEAR

and the kid

The Inheritance

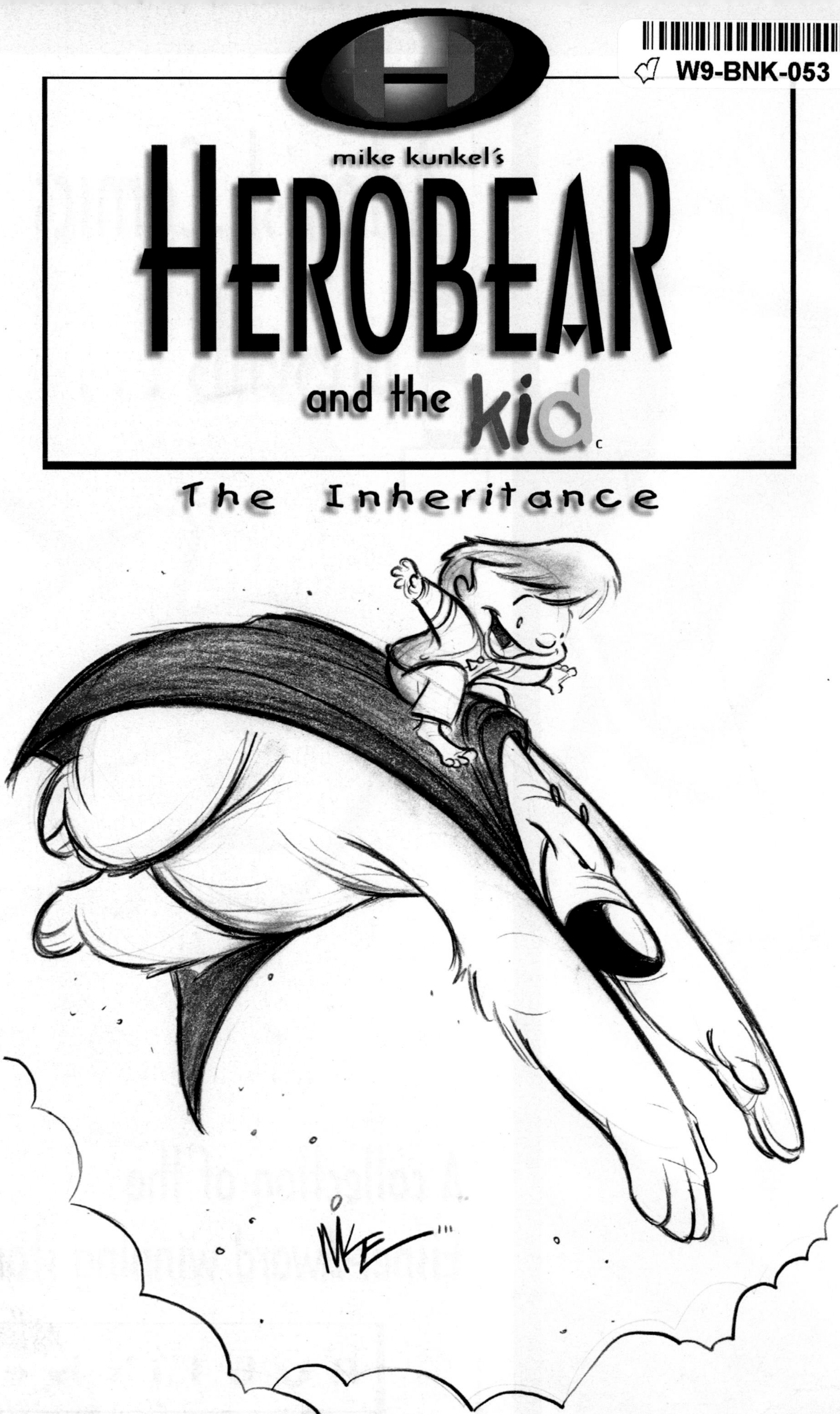

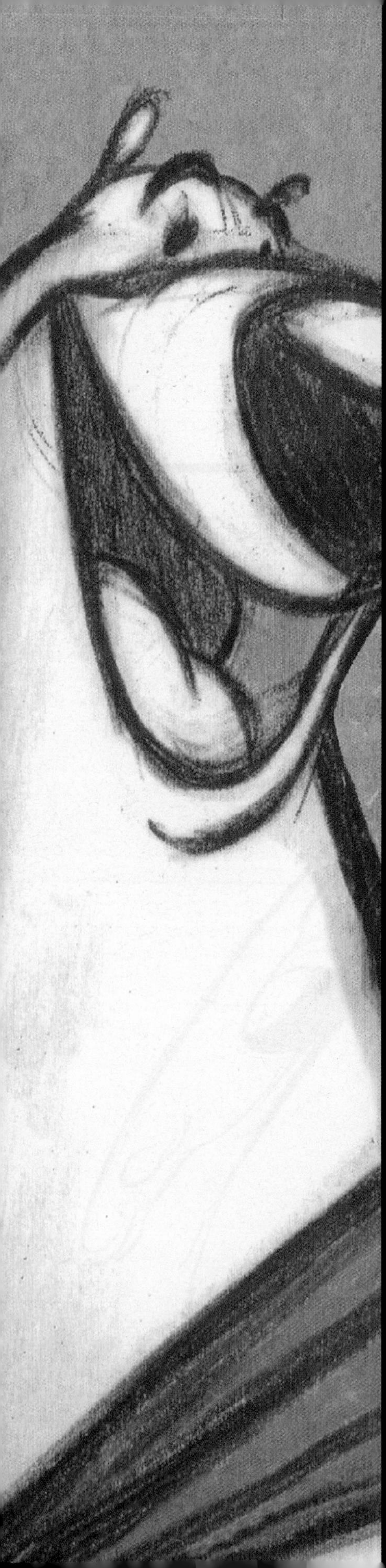

Astonish Comics presents . . .

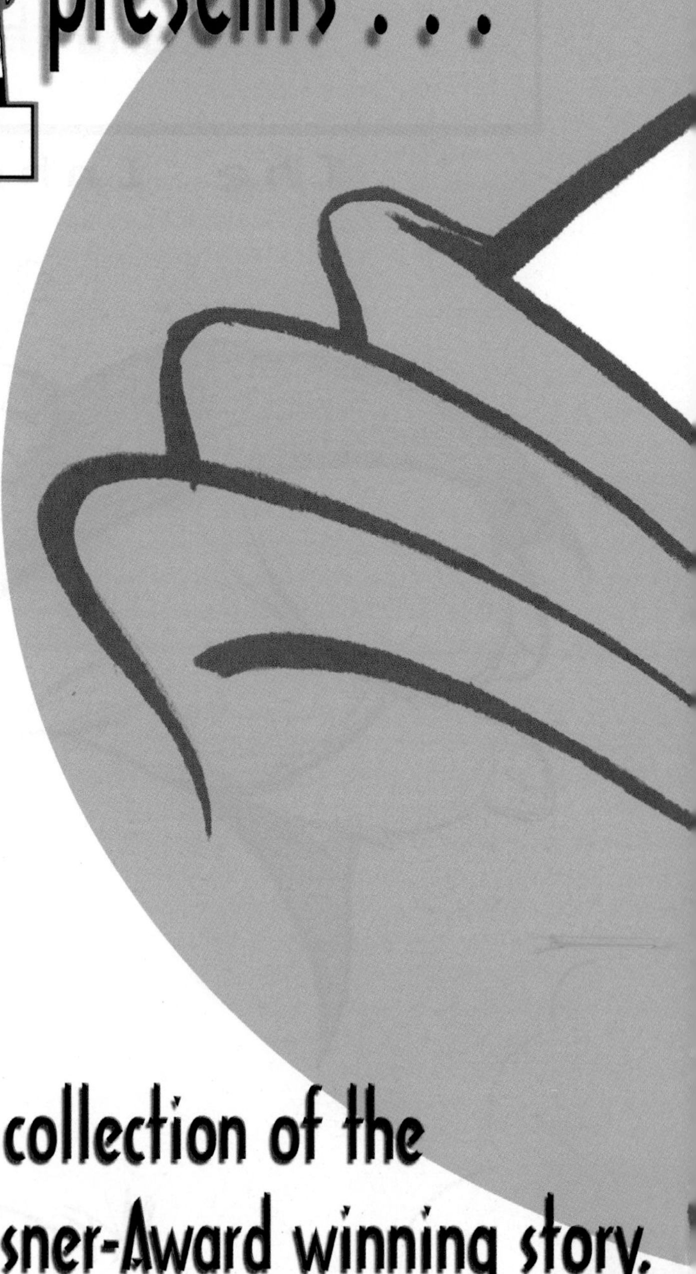

A collection of the Eisner-Award winning story.

Published

HEROBEAR
AND THE kid C&TM
the inheritance
by Mike Kunkel

With introductions by
Don Hahn and Jeph Loeb

by ASTONISH COMICS

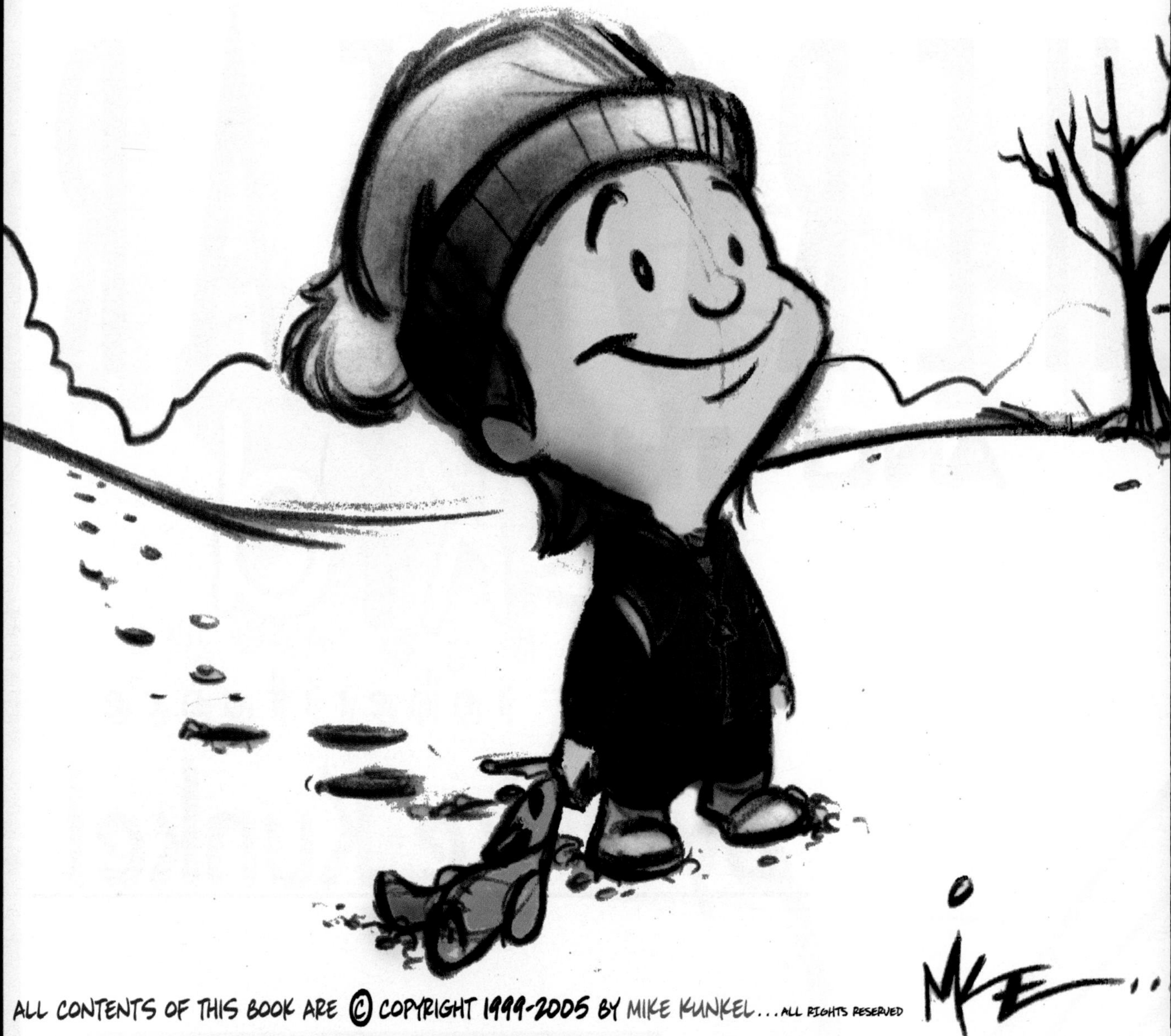

HEROBEAR AND THE KID : THE INHERITANCE.
PUBLISHED IN THE USA BY ASTONISH COMICS, 10061 RIVERSIDE DRIVE
SUITE NUMBER 785 TOLUCA LAKE, CALIFORNIA 91602

"HEROBEAR FONT" CREATED BY RICHARD STARKINGS' AMAZING COMICRAFT STUDIO

VISIT AT WWW.THEASTONISHFACTORY.COM

ORIGINALLY PUBLISHED AS HEROBEAR AND THE KID VOLUME 1 #1-5 C 1999-2005 MIKE KUNKEL

LIBRARY OF CONGRESS CATALOGING IN PUBLICATION DATA
KUNKEL, MIKE (1969-)
HEROBEAR AND THE KID VOLUME 1 : THE INHERITANCE
1. BEARS. 2. SUPER HEROES. 3. CHILDREN'S FICTION.

LIBRARY OF CONGRESS CONTROL NUMBER: 2002113738

ISBN : 0-9721259-0-6 (HARDCOVER EDITION)
ISBN : 0-9721259-1-4 (PAPERBACK EDITION)

10 9 8 7 6 5 4 3 2

2nd printing PRINTED IN TURKEY

contents

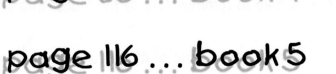

animation

introduction by Don Hahn

As a director, animator and story artist, Mike Kunkel has lent his considerable talents to projects at Sony, Warner Brothers, and of course The Walt Disney Studios on blockbuster films like Hercules and Tarzan. Even though I knew Mike as a gifted animator and storyteller, I always felt that he had something else burning inside of him.

That "something else" turned out to be a passion for comics, which eventually grew into his extraordinary Eisner-winning comic book HEROBEAR AND THE KID. It's not surprising that Herobear is one of those unique properties that brings the world of animation into the world of comic art by virtue of Mike's expressive drawing style and sense of movement, emotion and storytelling. It's a unique personal style that allows Mike to communicate to the reader in a very intimate way.

There is also a sense of magic, wonder and curiosity about Mike's work that conjures up the innocence and fun of childhood in a way that is reminiscent of the best of Charles Schultz or Bill Watterson.

If you aren't familiar with Mike's work, then you're in for a real treat. And if you're a fan like me, welcome home to the amazing world of Herobear and his creator, Mike Kunkel.

Don Hahn

Los Angeles 2002

Producer of Beauty and the Beast and The Lion King

two worlds...

introduction by Jeph Loeb

"**Remember** your childhood and pass it on." In a world where remembering your childhood often leads to years of therapy, Mike Kunkel's simple, poignant message asks you to find something...magical in your "Wonder Bread years."

So, when I agreed to write this introduction, I took him at his challenge and remembered something I had forgotten long ago.

When I was somewhere between the ages of one and yesterday, I had an imaginary friend. Friends, actually, since I guess even then, I didn't think small. They were called, "The Boys and The Bears." They followed me around, came with me in the car, and sat with me at the dinner table. On one particular day I came running into the house and my mother closed the door behind me. I burst into hysterical tears and my mother, being my mother, thought she'd somehow slammed my finger in the door. No, it was far worse. She had locked out The Boys and The Bears! So, being my mother, she opened the door and much to my relief, my friends rushed in and all was good in the world.

I don't know what it is with us human beings and those bears. We have teddy bears and beanie baby bears and Yogi Bear and Smokey The Bear. Bears just seem like they're having more fun than the rest of the animal kingdom. No matter how many times we're told "They're killers!" "Don't feed them!" "Run away!" -- we're the first ones to melt when we flip past the Discovery Channel and stop to watch two cubs wrestling around. It's like they're having a party -- a teddy bear picnic -- and maybe, if we're quiet enough, we'll get invited to stick around.

Maybe all of this is why three years ago at The San Diego Comic Book Convention I found myself noticing a huge line up to an unassuming little booth quietly off to the side. The Big Publishing Boys had their giant booths with neon signs, video screens and special guest stars, but here was this line. So, being a bit of a nosey bear myself, I wandered over and found something... wondrous.

It was HEROBEAR & THE KID. Mike Kunkel, a gentle man with a twinkle in his eye, was handing out his "black & white with a hint of red" comic book along with a small stuffed bear with a red cape. Curmudgeonly, I flipped through the pages expecting to put it down and be on my way. I got to page two and fell into one of the most imaginative stories since a certain baby was put in a rocket and sent to Earth from the doomed planet Krypton.

Here was the story of Tyler, a smart-alecky little guy who was suffering through the slings and arrows of childhood. He'd lost his grandpa, was terrified of going to a new school, lived in an old mysterious house and all he had going for him was an inheritance that made perfect sense if, as we're told, he wanted to get beat up.

But, the magic -- and that's the only word I can think of to explain it -- was that all Tyler really wanted was a friend. What he got in return was a ten foot-tall super, er, bear who would change his life forever.

And I warn you, as you read this collection, it will change yours. That's Mike Kunkel's gift.

Mike began drawing at about Tyler's age and never put down the pencil. He's grown into a world class animator which accounts for the sense you'll have while reading this collection -- that it's all moving pictures, sweeping you up and flying off into a story that has humor, pathos, and more than a few surprises. It's more than a little bit like coming downstairs on Christmas morning and finding brightly wrapped boxes.

Each one of those boxes is a page in this book, so open them slowly and have fun.

Me? Even as I'm writing this, I can hear The Boys and The Bears giggling outside somewhere, reminding me that anytime I want to rejoin them, all I have to do is open the door. I guess I've gotten back a bit of my childhood I need to pass on and for that, I'm honored that Mike asked me to extend the invitation on to you.

Jeph Loeb
Los Angeles 2002
Writer and Producer of Smallville
Writer of Superman For All Seasons, Batman: The Long Halloween, Spiderman: Blue

f o r w a r d

"Ever since I was a kid, I've loved to tell stories. I soon came to realize what kind of stories I liked. I've come to think that stories should be fun. Fun to look at, fun to read, and fun to experience ... but not only that, they should also have a quality and direction that connects with people emotionally. The audience should care about the characters and become immersed in their world. I can only hope that the art and story in this book and the others that I'm involved with will always be able to translate that.

So thank you for joining us here for the story of Herobear and the kid. A nostalgic view of childhood, complete with new schools, bullies, true love, imagination, and ... a magic bear

mike kunkel ...

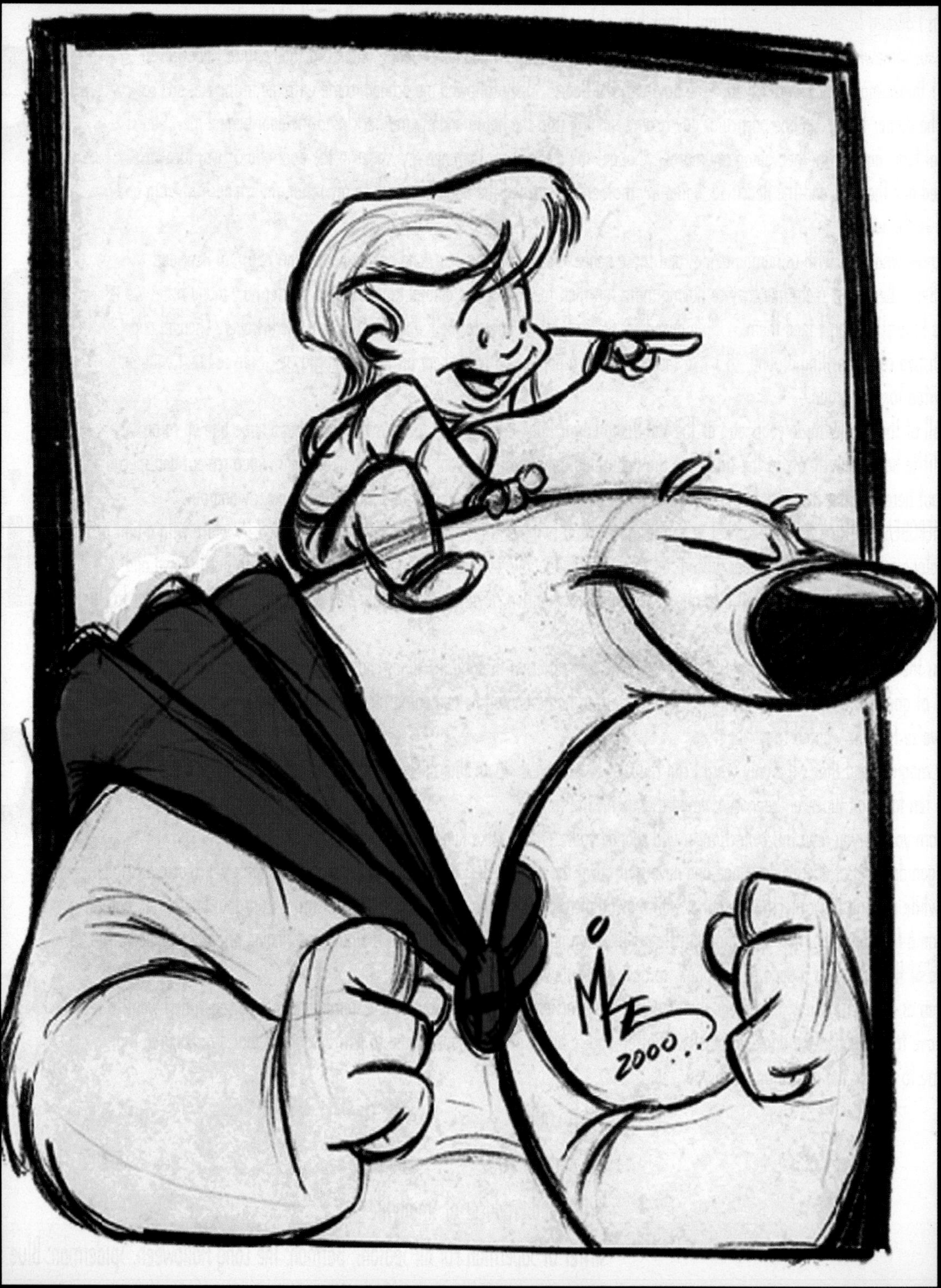

Herein follows a tale that is dedicated to Alec and Leigha ... my two most wonderful souls of inspiration.

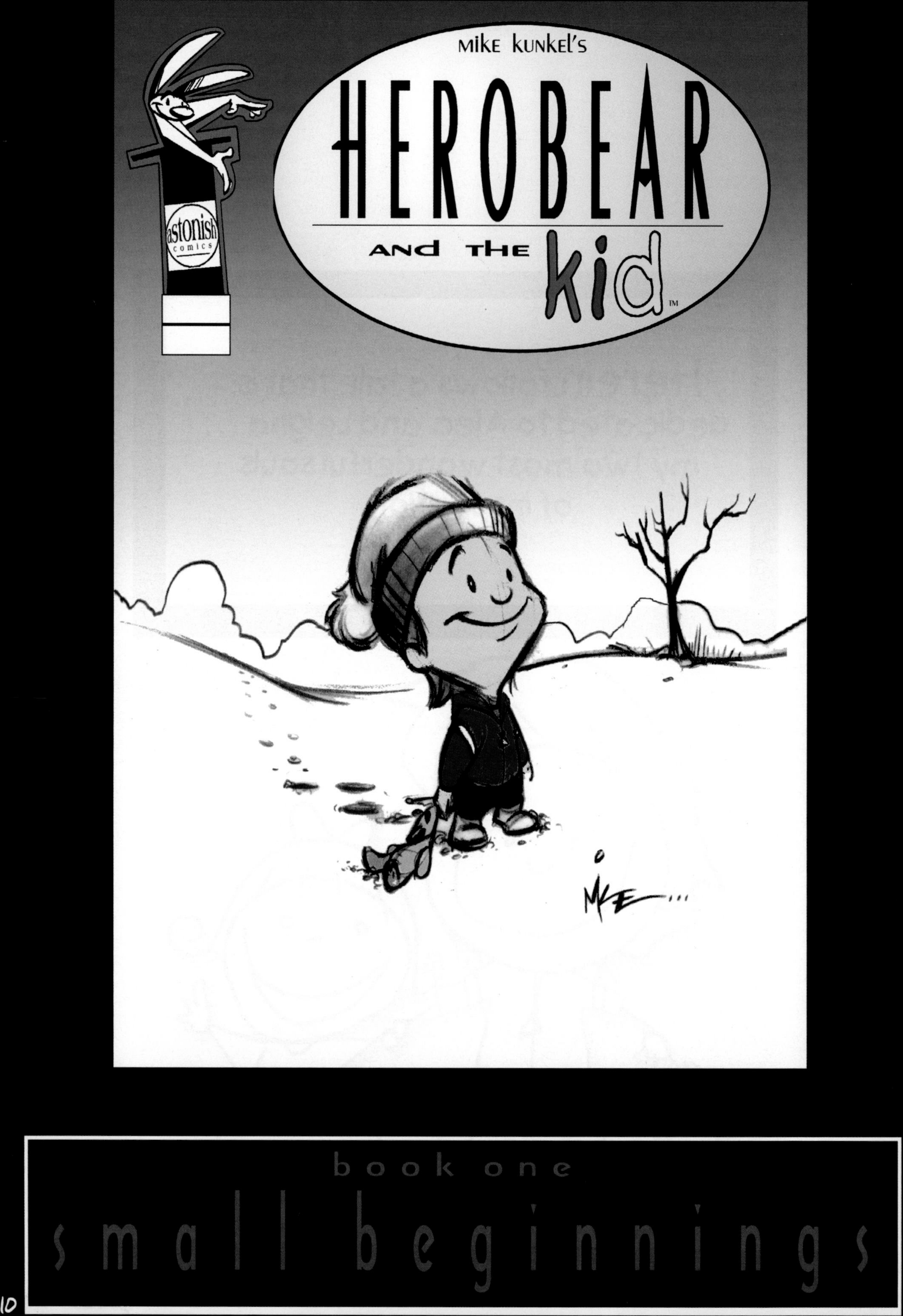
MIKE KUNKEL'S
HEROBEAR
AND THE kid™
astonish comics
MIKE...

book one
small beginnings

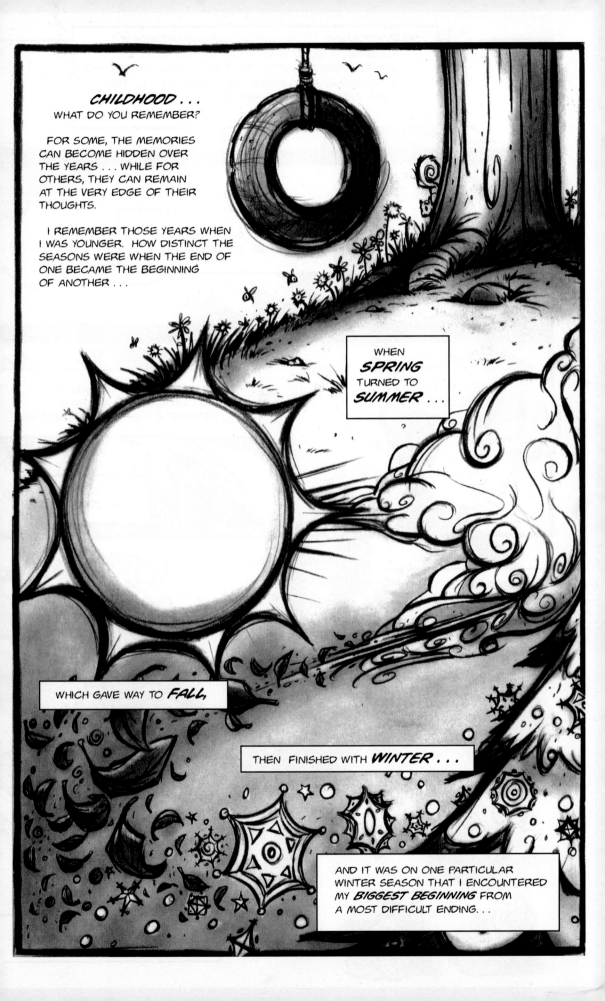

CHILDHOOD . . .
WHAT DO YOU REMEMBER?

FOR SOME, THE MEMORIES
CAN BECOME HIDDEN OVER
THE YEARS . . . WHILE FOR
OTHERS, THEY CAN REMAIN
AT THE VERY EDGE OF THEIR
THOUGHTS.

I REMEMBER THOSE YEARS WHEN
I WAS YOUNGER. HOW DISTINCT THE
SEASONS WERE WHEN THE END OF
ONE BECAME THE BEGINNING
OF ANOTHER . . .

WHEN
SPRING
TURNED TO
SUMMER . . .

WHICH GAVE WAY TO *FALL,*

THEN FINISHED WITH *WINTER* . . .

AND IT WAS ON ONE PARTICULAR
WINTER SEASON THAT I ENCOUNTERED
MY *BIGGEST BEGINNING* FROM
A MOST DIFFICULT ENDING. . .

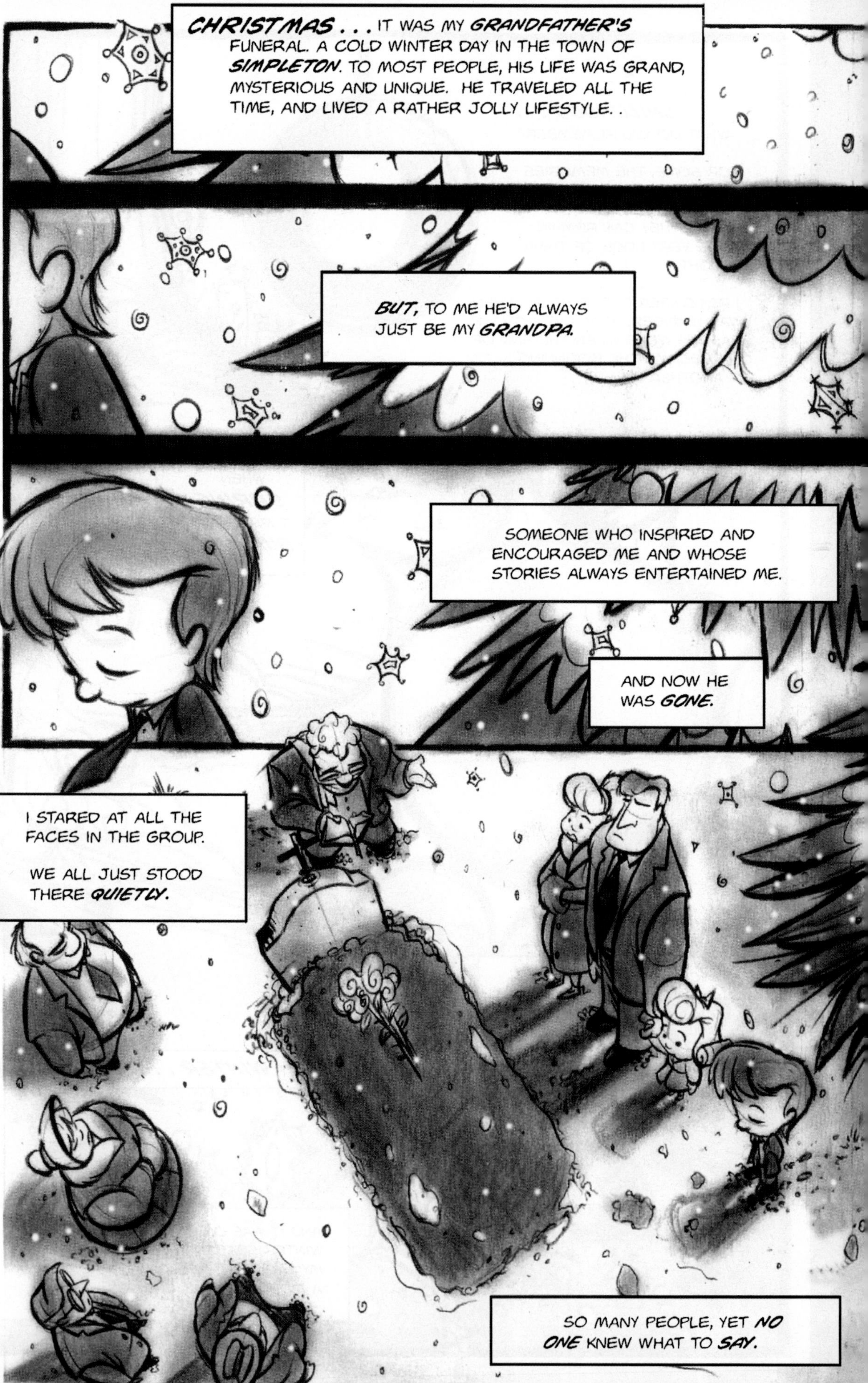
CHRISTMAS . . . IT WAS MY GRANDFATHER'S FUNERAL. A COLD WINTER DAY IN THE TOWN OF SIMPLETON. TO MOST PEOPLE, HIS LIFE WAS GRAND, MYSTERIOUS AND UNIQUE. HE TRAVELED ALL THE TIME, AND LIVED A RATHER JOLLY LIFESTYLE. .
BUT, TO ME HE'D ALWAYS JUST BE MY GRANDPA.
SOMEONE WHO INSPIRED AND ENCOURAGED ME AND WHOSE STORIES ALWAYS ENTERTAINED ME.
AND NOW HE WAS GONE.
I STARED AT ALL THE FACES IN THE GROUP.
WE ALL JUST STOOD THERE QUIETLY.
SO MANY PEOPLE, YET NO ONE KNEW WHAT TO SAY.

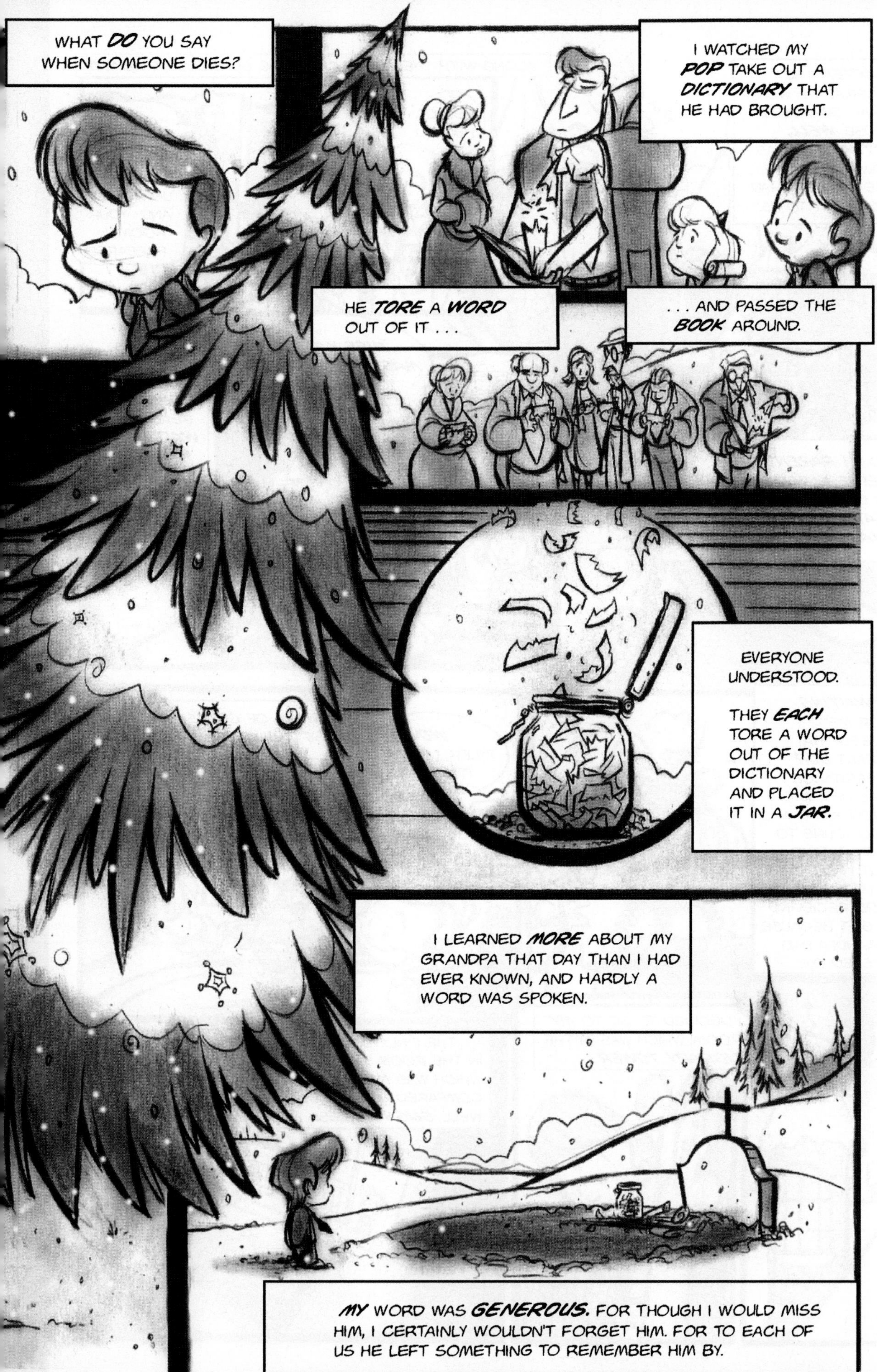
WHAT DO YOU SAY WHEN SOMEONE DIES?
I WATCHED MY POP TAKE OUT A DICTIONARY THAT HE HAD BROUGHT.
HE TORE A WORD OUT OF IT . . .
. . . AND PASSED THE BOOK AROUND.
EVERYONE UNDERSTOOD.
THEY EACH TORE A WORD OUT OF THE DICTIONARY AND PLACED IT IN A JAR.
I LEARNED MORE ABOUT MY GRANDPA THAT DAY THAN I HAD EVER KNOWN, AND HARDLY A WORD WAS SPOKEN.
MY WORD WAS GENEROUS. FOR THOUGH I WOULD MISS HIM, I CERTAINLY WOULDN'T FORGET HIM. FOR TO EACH OF US HE LEFT SOMETHING TO REMEMBER HIM BY.

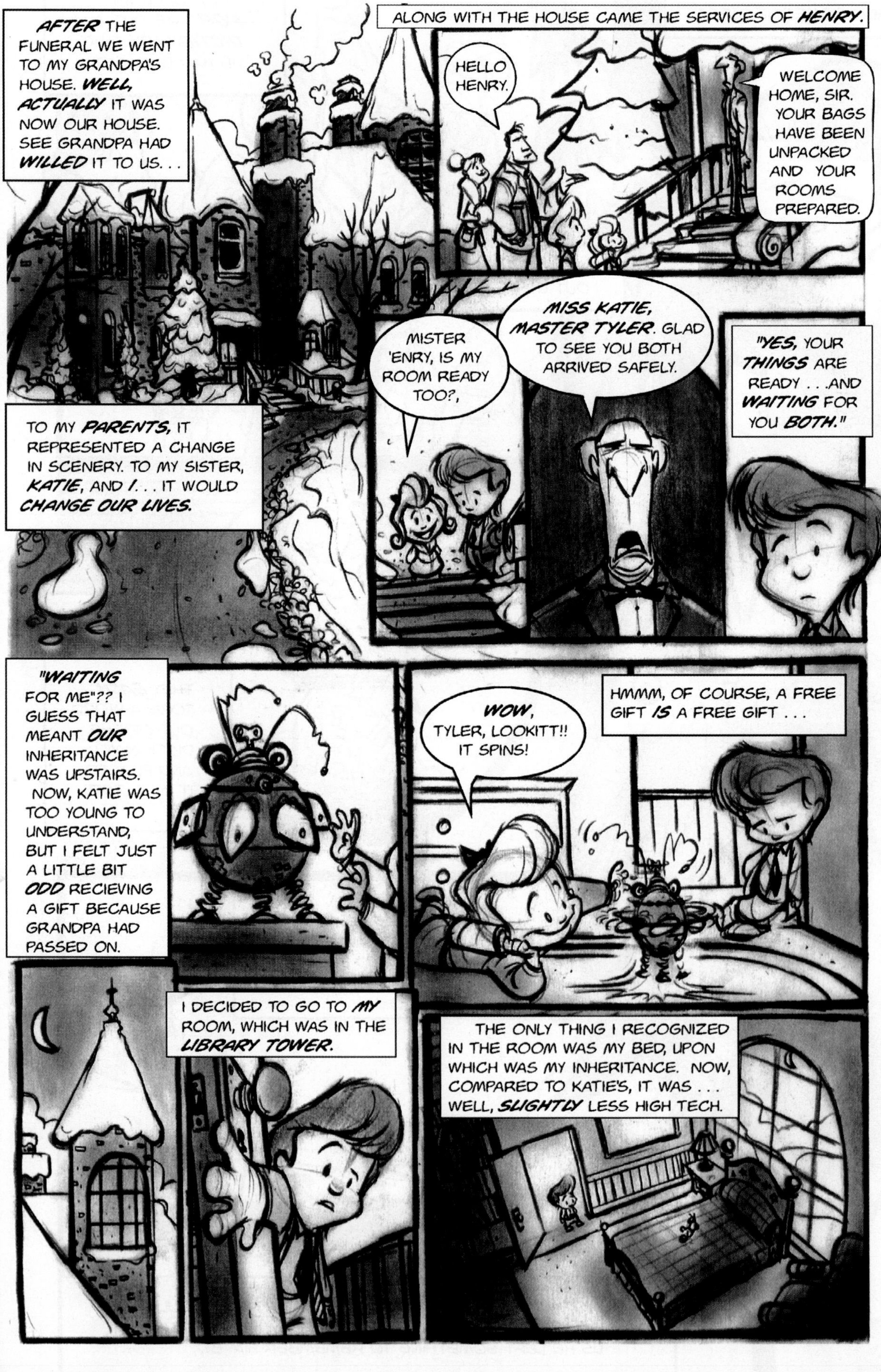
AFTER THE FUNERAL WE WENT TO MY GRANDPA'S HOUSE. WELL, ACTUALLY IT WAS NOW OUR HOUSE. SEE GRANDPA HAD WILLED IT TO US. . .
ALONG WITH THE HOUSE CAME THE SERVICES OF HENRY.
HELLO HENRY.
WELCOME HOME, SIR. YOUR BAGS HAVE BEEN UNPACKED AND YOUR ROOMS PREPARED.
TO MY PARENTS, IT REPRESENTED A CHANGE IN SCENERY. TO MY SISTER, KATIE, AND I. . . IT WOULD CHANGE OUR LIVES.
MISTER 'ENRY, IS MY ROOM READY TOO?,
MISS KATIE, MASTER TYLER. GLAD TO SEE YOU BOTH ARRIVED SAFELY.
"YES, YOUR THINGS ARE READY . . .AND WAITING FOR YOU BOTH."
"WAITING FOR ME"?? I GUESS THAT MEANT OUR INHERITANCE WAS UPSTAIRS. NOW, KATIE WAS TOO YOUNG TO UNDERSTAND, BUT I FELT JUST A LITTLE BIT ODD RECIEVING A GIFT BECAUSE GRANDPA HAD PASSED ON.
WOW, TYLER, LOOKITT!! IT SPINS!
HMMM, OF COURSE, A FREE GIFT IS A FREE GIFT . . .
I DECIDED TO GO TO MY ROOM, WHICH WAS IN THE LIBRARY TOWER.
THE ONLY THING I RECOGNIZED IN THE ROOM WAS MY BED, UPON WHICH WAS MY INHERITANCE. NOW, COMPARED TO KATIE'S, IT WAS . . . WELL, SLIGHTLY LESS HIGH TECH.

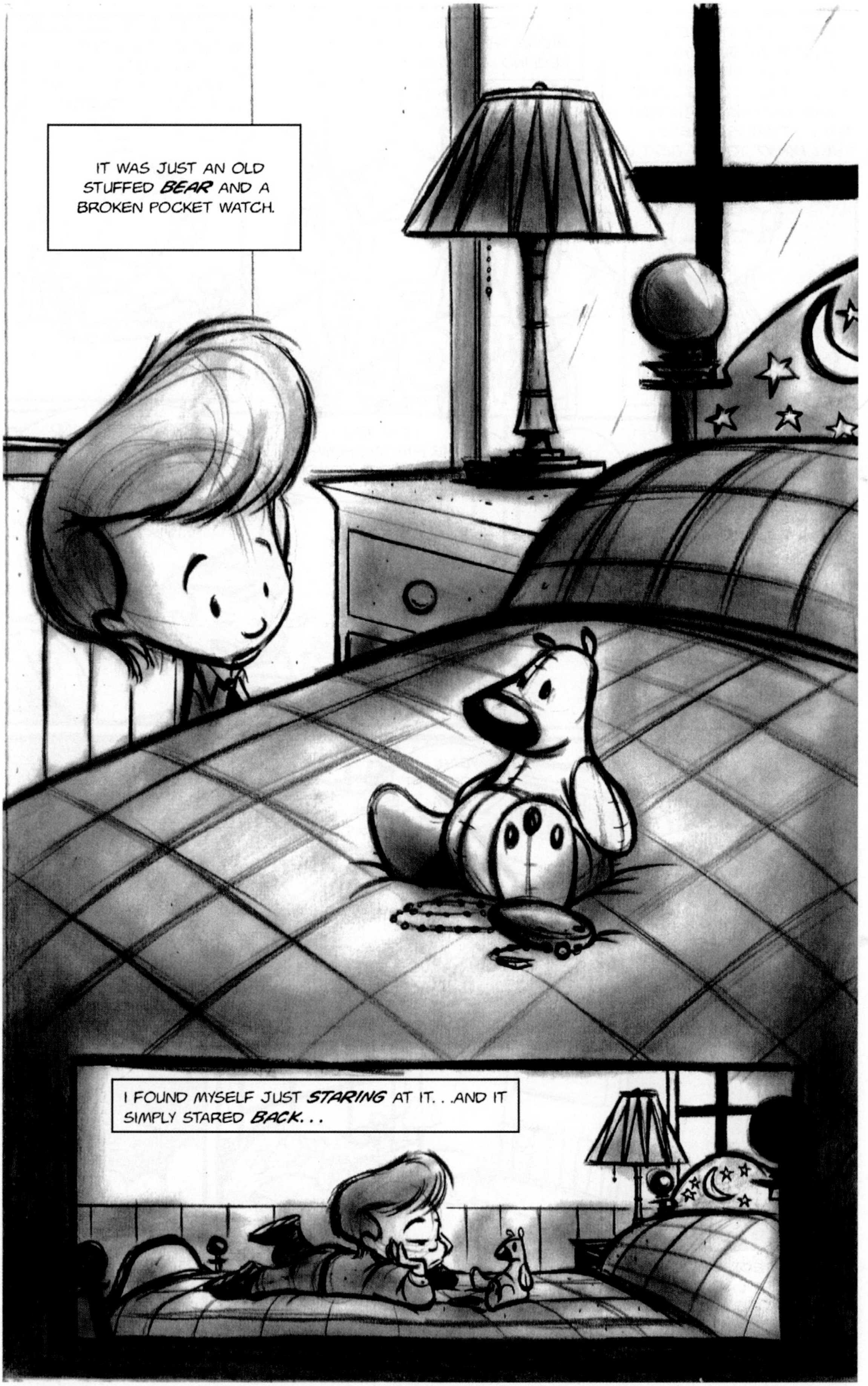
IT WAS JUST AN OLD STUFFED BEAR AND A BROKEN POCKET WATCH.
I FOUND MYSELF JUST STARING AT IT. . .AND IT SIMPLY STARED BACK. . .

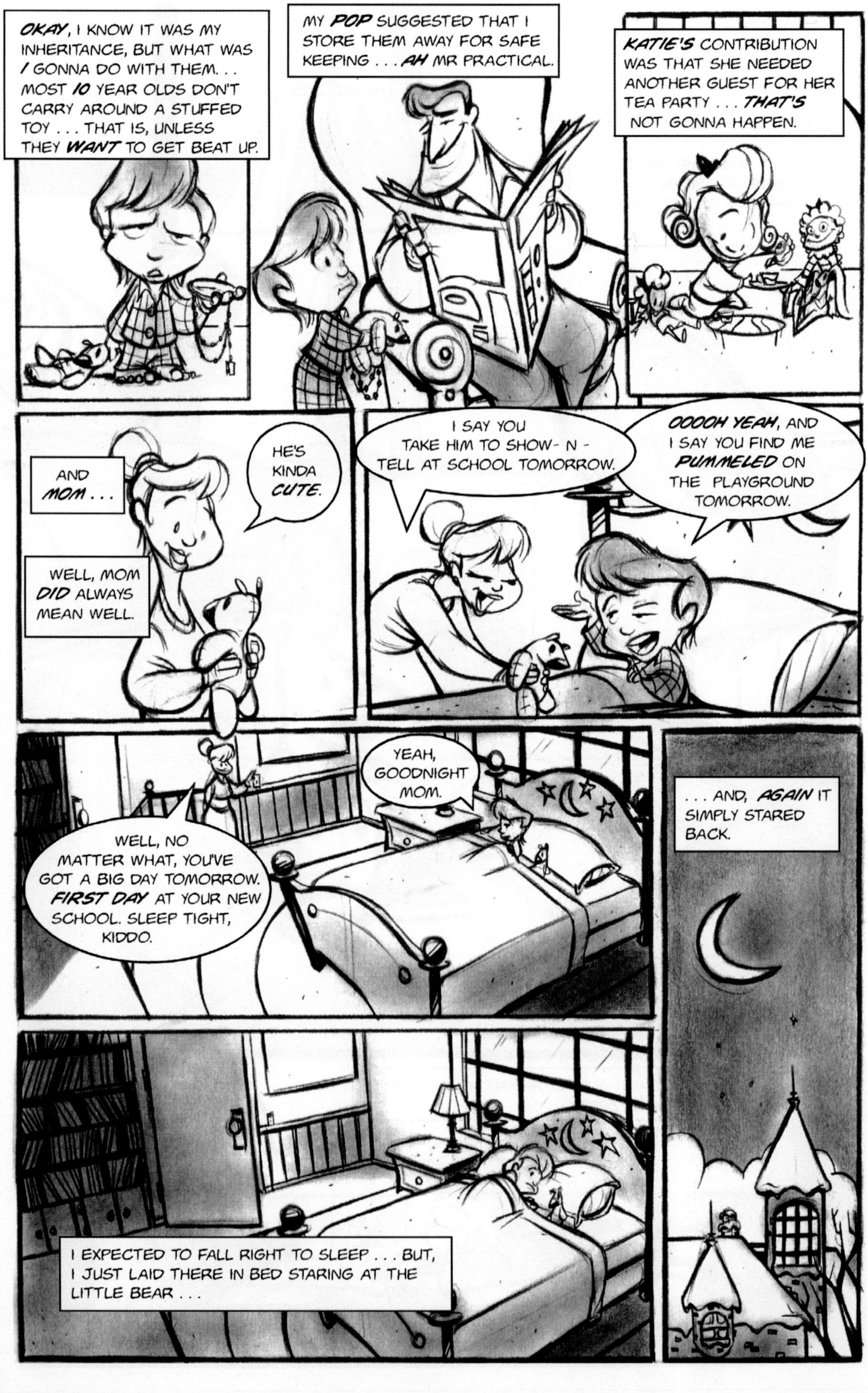
OKAY, I KNOW IT WAS MY INHERITANCE, BUT WHAT WAS I GONNA DO WITH THEM. . . MOST 10 YEAR OLDS DON'T CARRY AROUND A STUFFED TOY . . . THAT IS, UNLESS THEY WANT TO GET BEAT UP.
MY POP SUGGESTED THAT I STORE THEM AWAY FOR SAFE KEEPING . . . AH MR PRACTICAL.
KATIE'S CONTRIBUTION WAS THAT SHE NEEDED ANOTHER GUEST FOR HER TEA PARTY . . . THAT'S NOT GONNA HAPPEN.
AND MOM . . .
HE'S KINDA CUTE.
WELL, MOM DID ALWAYS MEAN WELL.
I SAY YOU TAKE HIM TO SHOW- N - TELL AT SCHOOL TOMORROW.
OOOOH YEAH, AND I SAY YOU FIND ME PUMMELED ON THE PLAYGROUND TOMORROW.
WELL, NO MATTER WHAT, YOU'VE GOT A BIG DAY TOMORROW. FIRST DAY AT YOUR NEW SCHOOL. SLEEP TIGHT, KIDDO.
YEAH, GOODNIGHT MOM.
I EXPECTED TO FALL RIGHT TO SLEEP . . . BUT, I JUST LAID THERE IN BED STARING AT THE LITTLE BEAR . . .
. . . AND, AGAIN IT SIMPLY STARED BACK.

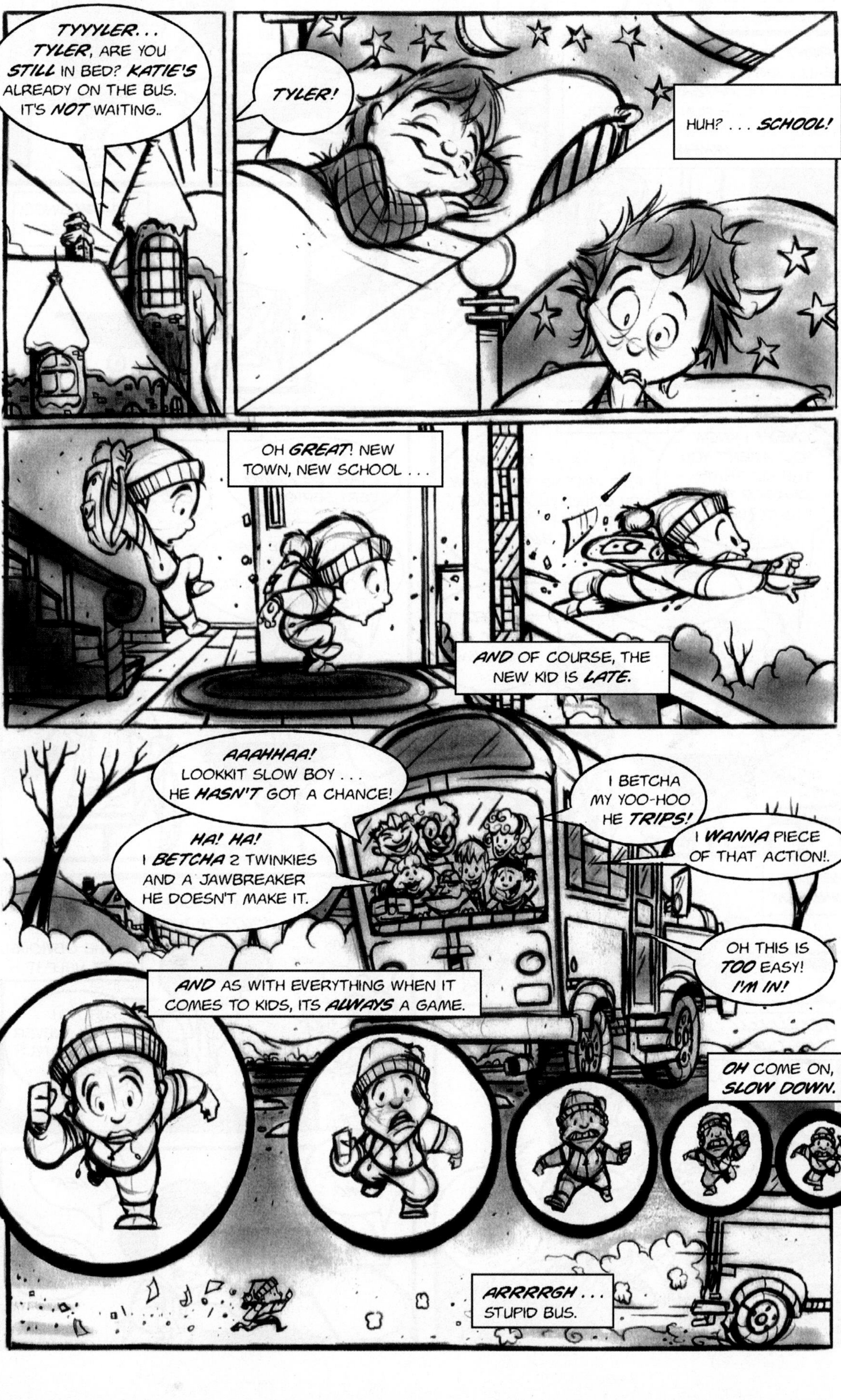
TYYYLER... TYLER, ARE YOU STILL IN BED? KATIE'S ALREADY ON THE BUS. IT'S NOT WAITING..
TYLER!
HUH? . . . SCHOOL!
OH GREAT! NEW TOWN, NEW SCHOOL . . .
AND OF COURSE, THE NEW KID IS LATE.
AAAHHAA! LOOKKIT SLOW BOY . . . HE HASN'T GOT A CHANCE!
I BETCHA MY YOO-HOO HE TRIPS!
HA! HA! I BETCHA 2 TWINKIES AND A JAWBREAKER HE DOESN'T MAKE IT.
I WANNA PIECE OF THAT ACTION!.
OH THIS IS TOO EASY! I'M IN!
AND AS WITH EVERYTHING WHEN IT COMES TO KIDS, ITS ALWAYS A GAME.
OH COME ON, SLOW DOWN.
ARRRRGH . . . STUPID BUS.

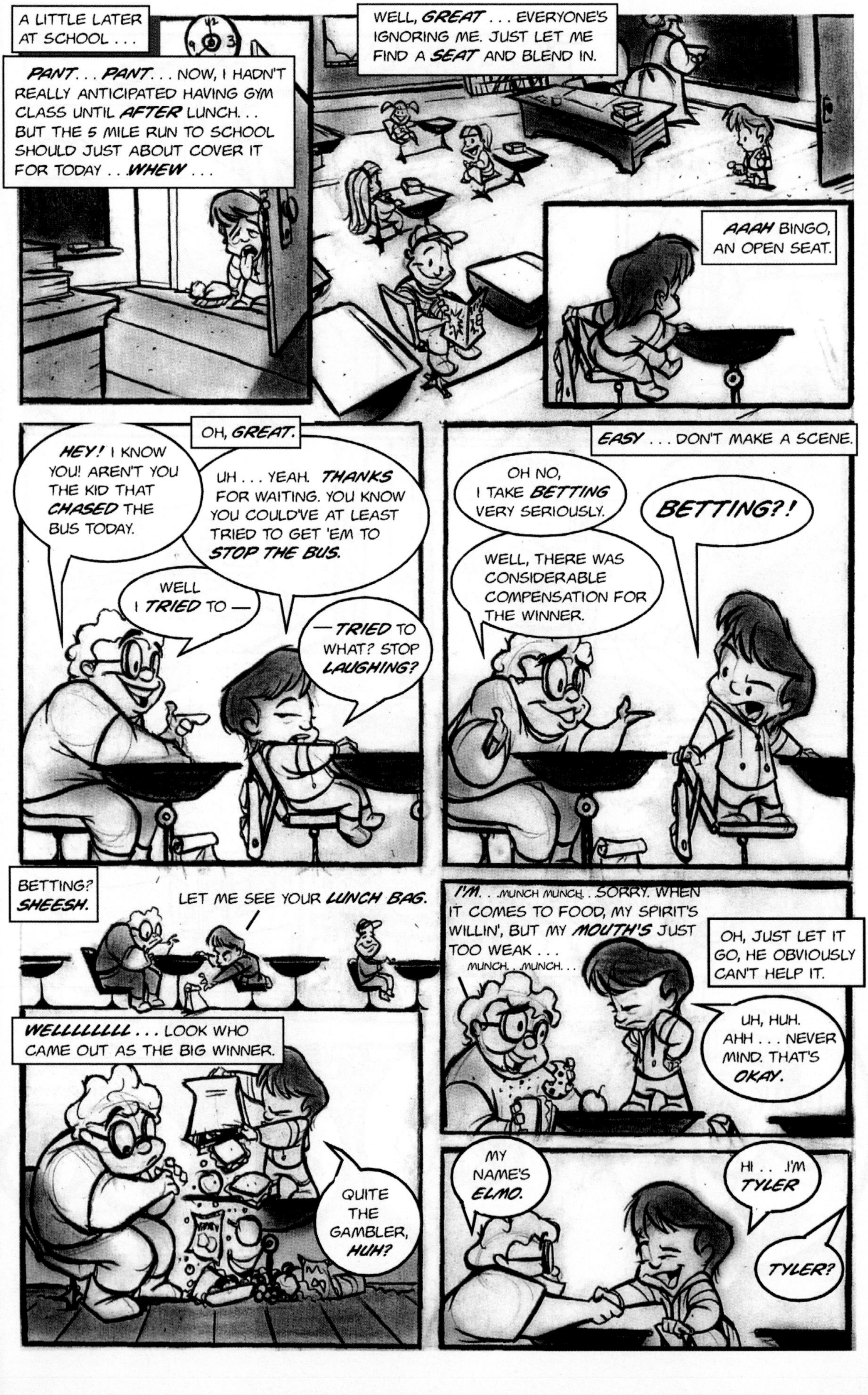

A LITTLE LATER AT SCHOOL . . .
PANT . . . PANT . . . NOW, I HADN'T REALLY ANTICIPATED HAVING GYM CLASS UNTIL AFTER LUNCH . . . BUT THE 5 MILE RUN TO SCHOOL SHOULD JUST ABOUT COVER IT FOR TODAY . . . WHEW . . .
WELL, GREAT . . . EVERYONE'S IGNORING ME. JUST LET ME FIND A SEAT AND BLEND IN.
AAAH BINGO, AN OPEN SEAT.
OH, GREAT.
HEY! I KNOW YOU! AREN'T YOU THE KID THAT CHASED THE BUS TODAY.
UH . . . YEAH. THANKS FOR WAITING. YOU KNOW YOU COULD'VE AT LEAST TRIED TO GET 'EM TO STOP THE BUS.
WELL I TRIED TO —
— TRIED TO WHAT? STOP LAUGHING?
EASY . . . DON'T MAKE A SCENE.
OH NO, I TAKE BETTING VERY SERIOUSLY.
BETTING?!
WELL, THERE WAS CONSIDERABLE COMPENSATION FOR THE WINNER.
BETTING? SHEESH.
LET ME SEE YOUR LUNCH BAG.
WELLLLLLLLL . . . LOOK WHO CAME OUT AS THE BIG WINNER.
QUITE THE GAMBLER, HUH?
I'M . . . MUNCH MUNCH . . . SORRY. WHEN IT COMES TO FOOD, MY SPIRIT'S WILLIN', BUT MY MOUTH'S JUST TOO WEAK . . .
MUNCH . . . MUNCH . . .
OH, JUST LET IT GO, HE OBVIOUSLY CAN'T HELP IT.
UH, HUH. AHH . . . NEVER MIND. THAT'S OKAY.
MY NAME'S ELMO.
HI . . . I'M TYLER
TYLER?

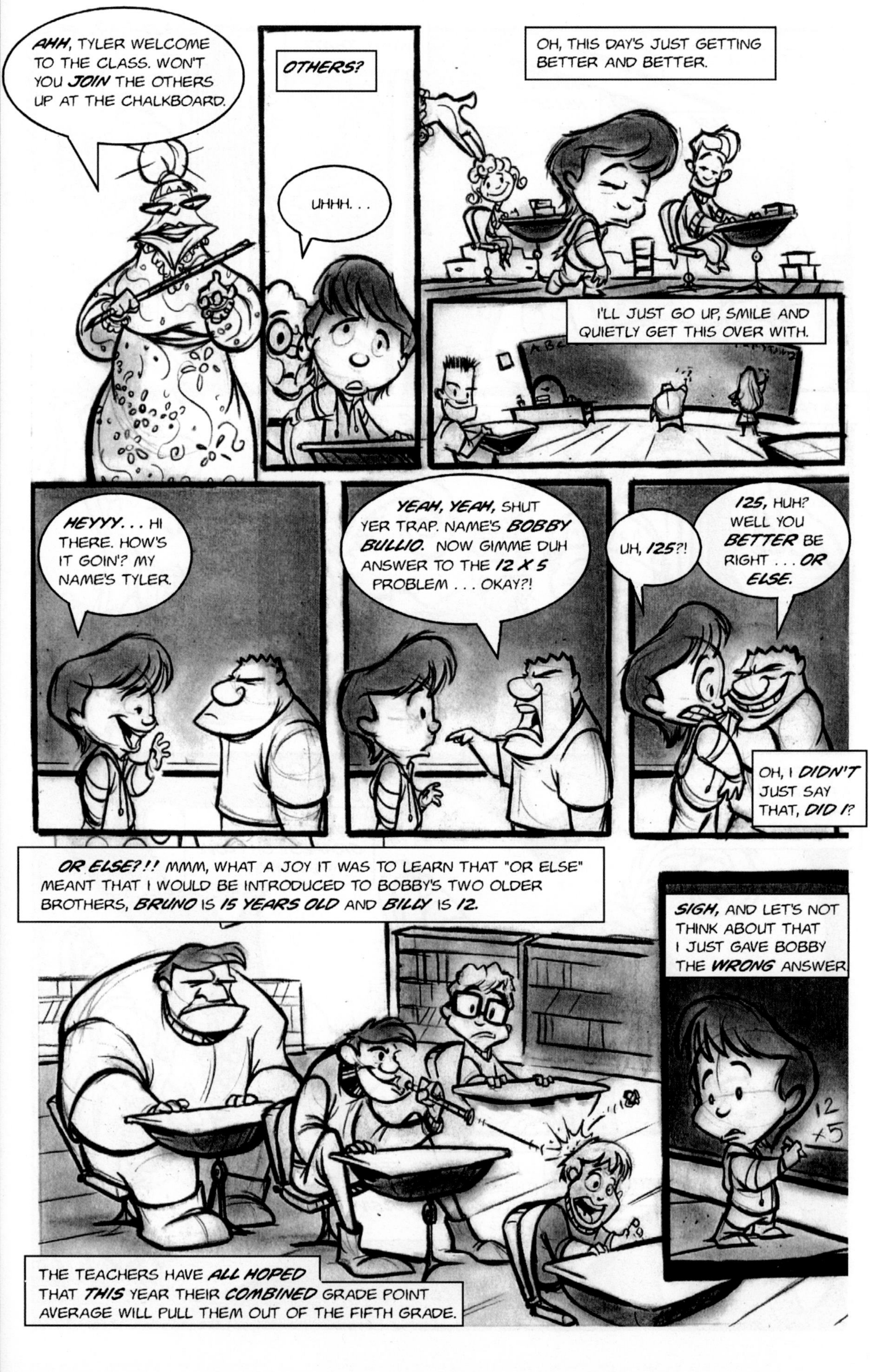
AHH, TYLER WELCOME TO THE CLASS. WON'T YOU JOIN THE OTHERS UP AT THE CHALKBOARD.
OTHERS?
UHHH. . .
OH, THIS DAY'S JUST GETTING BETTER AND BETTER.
I'LL JUST GO UP, SMILE AND QUIETLY GET THIS OVER WITH.
HEYYY. . . HI THERE. HOW'S IT GOIN'? MY NAME'S TYLER.
YEAH, YEAH, SHUT YER TRAP. NAME'S BOBBY BULLIO. NOW GIMME DUH ANSWER TO THE 12 X 5 PROBLEM . . . OKAY?!
UH, 125?!
125, HUH? WELL YOU BETTER BE RIGHT . . . OR ELSE.
OH, I DIDN'T JUST SAY THAT, DID I?
OR ELSE?!! MMM, WHAT A JOY IT WAS TO LEARN THAT "OR ELSE" MEANT THAT I WOULD BE INTRODUCED TO BOBBY'S TWO OLDER BROTHERS, BRUNO IS 15 YEARS OLD AND BILLY IS 12.
SIGH, AND LET'S NOT THINK ABOUT THAT I JUST GAVE BOBBY THE WRONG ANSWER.
12 x5
THE TEACHERS HAVE ALL HOPED THAT THIS YEAR THEIR COMBINED GRADE POINT AVERAGE WILL PULL THEM OUT OF THE FIFTH GRADE.

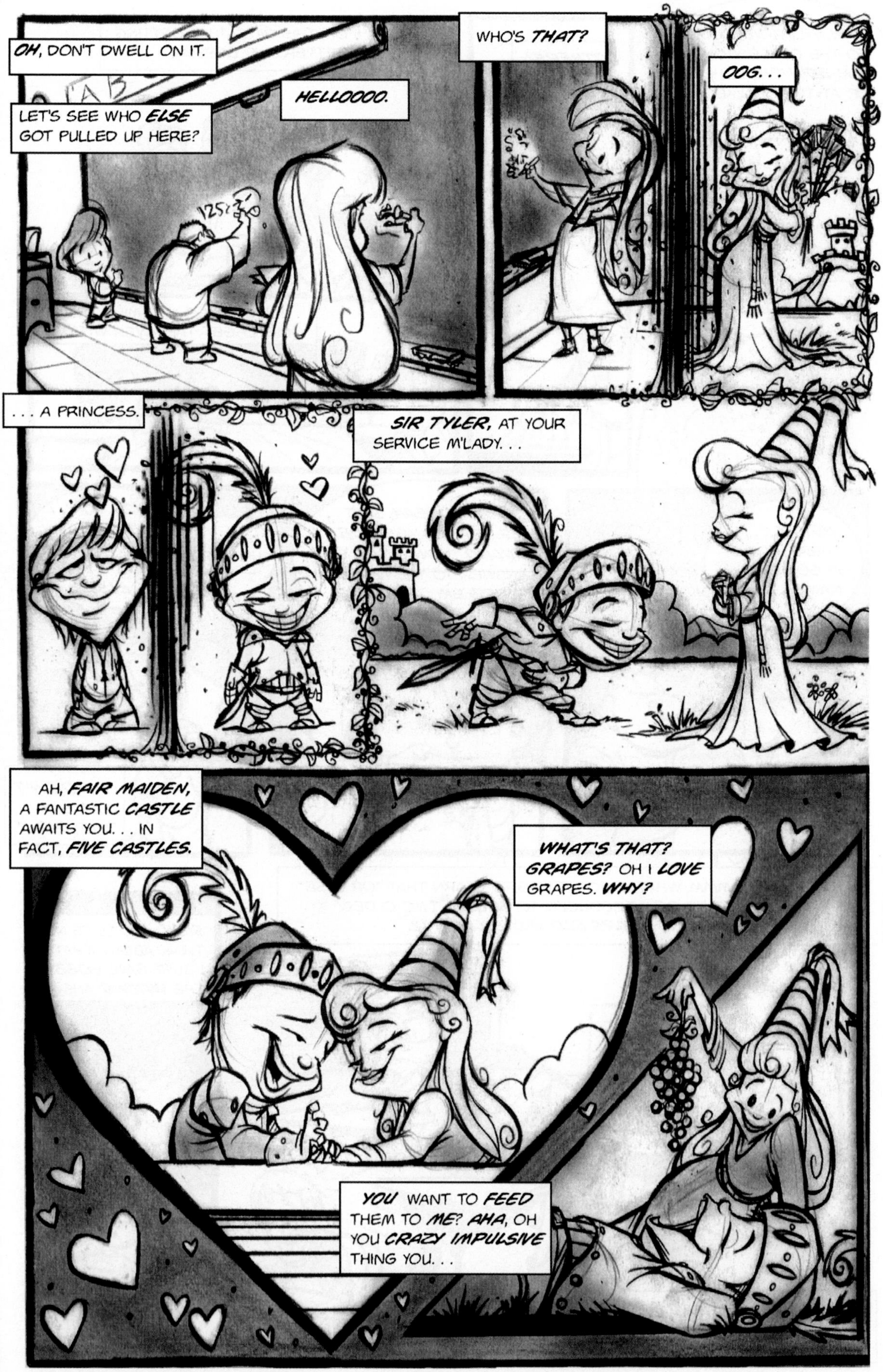
OH, DON'T DWELL ON IT.
LET'S SEE WHO ELSE GOT PULLED UP HERE?
HELLOOOO.
WHO'S THAT?
OOG. . .
. . . A PRINCESS.
SIR TYLER, AT YOUR SERVICE M'LADY. . .
AH, FAIR MAIDEN, A FANTASTIC CASTLE AWAITS YOU. . . IN FACT, FIVE CASTLES.
WHAT'S THAT? GRAPES? OH I LOVE GRAPES. WHY?
YOU WANT TO FEED THEM TO ME? AHA, OH YOU CRAZY IMPULSIVE THING YOU. . .

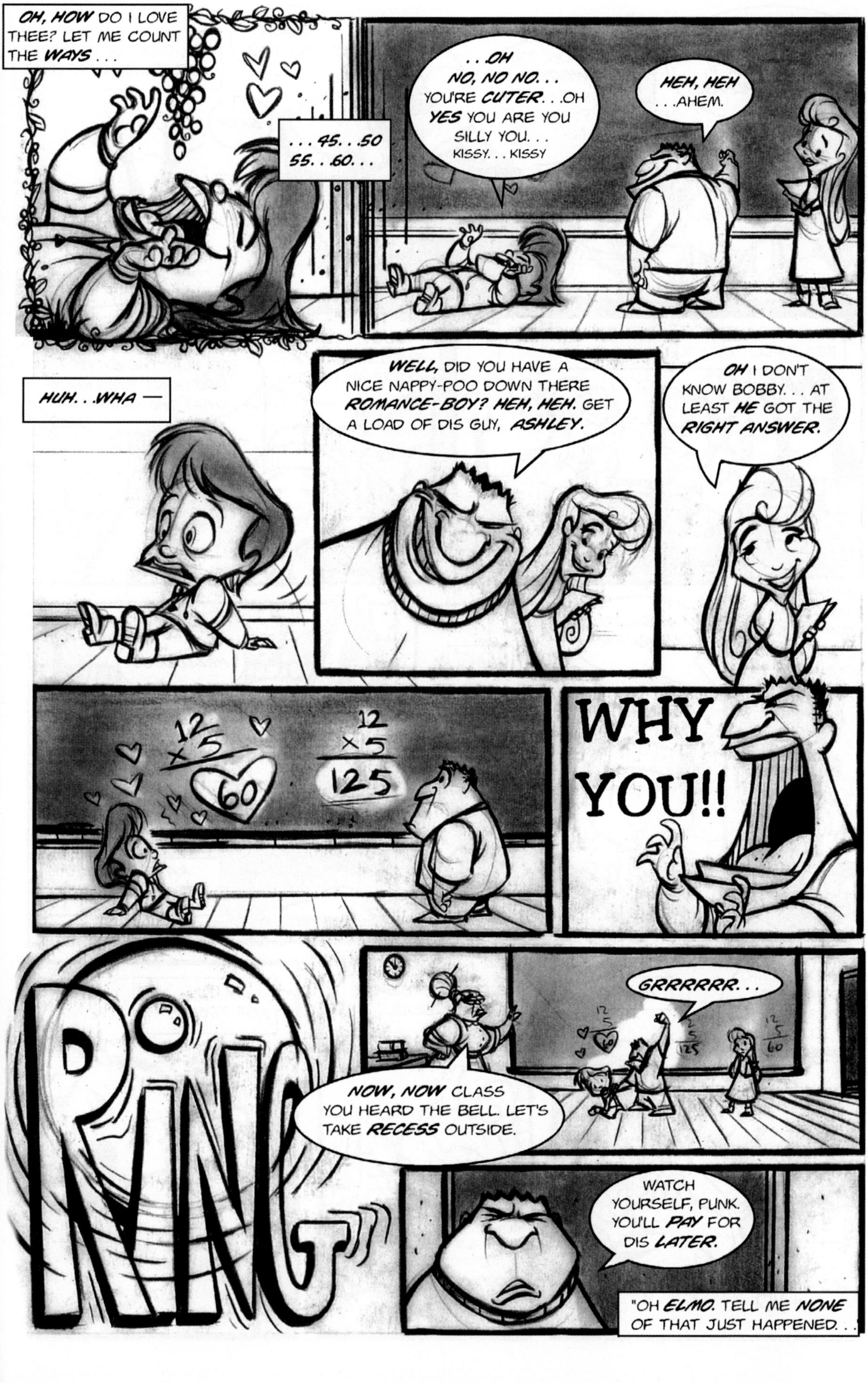
OH, HOW DO I LOVE THEE? LET ME COUNT THE WAYS . . .
. . . 45. . .50 55. . .60. . .
. . OH NO, NO NO. . . YOU'RE CUTER. . .OH YES YOU ARE YOU SILLY YOU. . . KISSY. . . KISSY
HEH, HEH . . .AHEM.
HUH. . .WHA —
WELL, DID YOU HAVE A NICE NAPPY-POO DOWN THERE ROMANCE-BOY? HEH, HEH. GET A LOAD OF DIS GUY, ASHLEY.
OH I DON'T KNOW BOBBY. . . AT LEAST HE GOT THE RIGHT ANSWER.
12 x5 60
12 x5 125
WHY YOU!!
RING
GRRRRRR. . .
NOW, NOW CLASS YOU HEARD THE BELL. LET'S TAKE RECESS OUTSIDE.
WATCH YOURSELF, PUNK. YOU'LL PAY FOR DIS LATER.
"OH ELMO. TELL ME NONE OF THAT JUST HAPPENED. . .

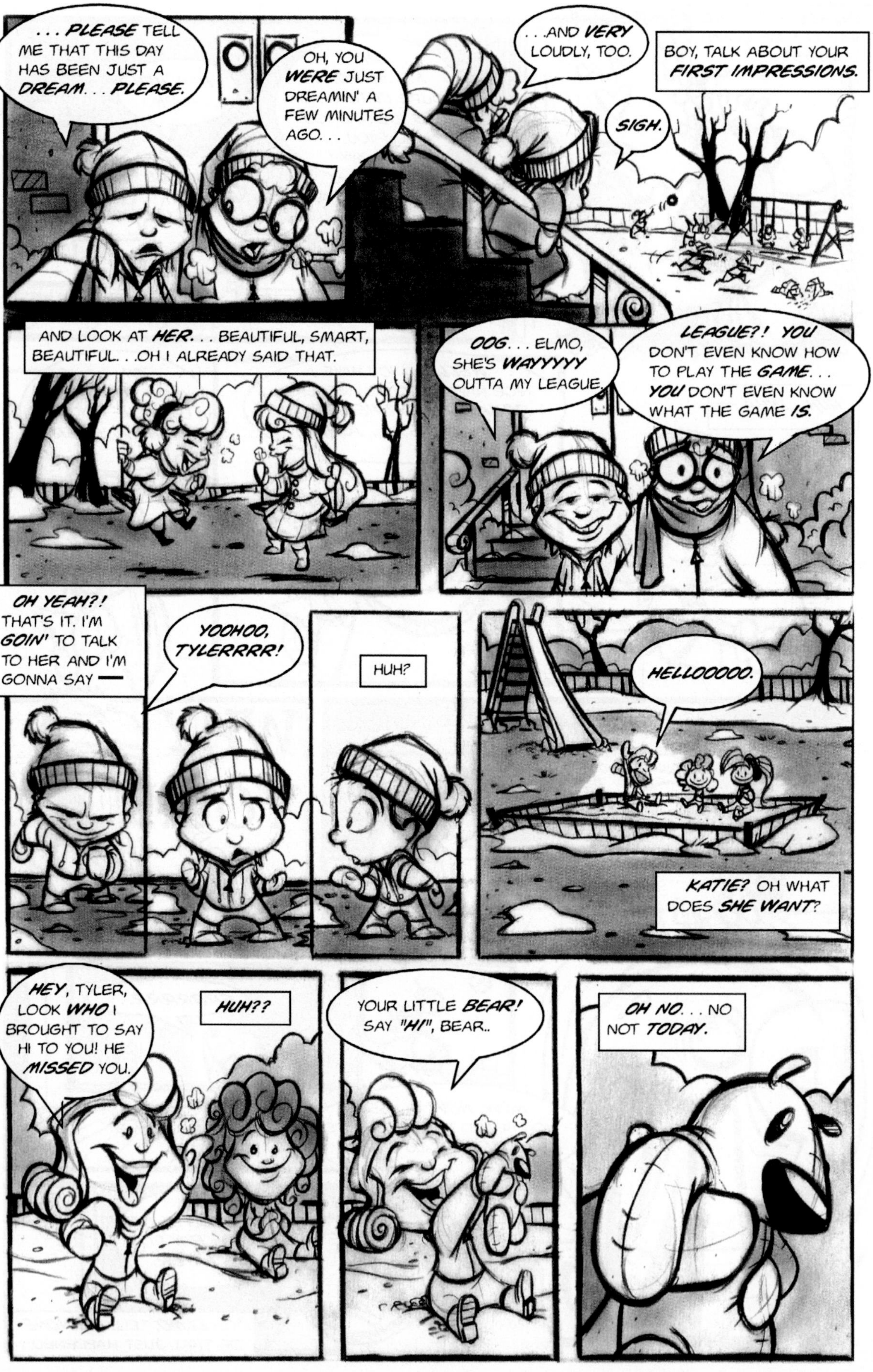
. . . PLEASE TELL ME THAT THIS DAY HAS BEEN JUST A DREAM. . . PLEASE.
OH, YOU WERE JUST DREAMIN' A FEW MINUTES AGO. . .
. . .AND VERY LOUDLY, TOO.
BOY, TALK ABOUT YOUR FIRST IMPRESSIONS.
SIGH.
AND LOOK AT HER. . . BEAUTIFUL, SMART, BEAUTIFUL. . .OH I ALREADY SAID THAT.
OOG. . . ELMO, SHE'S WAYYYYY OUTTA MY LEAGUE.
LEAGUE?! YOU DON'T EVEN KNOW HOW TO PLAY THE GAME. . . YOU DON'T EVEN KNOW WHAT THE GAME IS.
OH YEAH?! THAT'S IT. I'M GOIN' TO TALK TO HER AND I'M GONNA SAY —
YOOHOO, TYLERRRR!
HUH?
HELLOOOOO.
KATIE? OH WHAT DOES SHE WANT?
HEY, TYLER, LOOK WHO I BROUGHT TO SAY HI TO YOU! HE MISSED YOU.
HUH??
YOUR LITTLE BEAR! SAY "HI", BEAR..
OH NO. . . NO NOT TODAY.

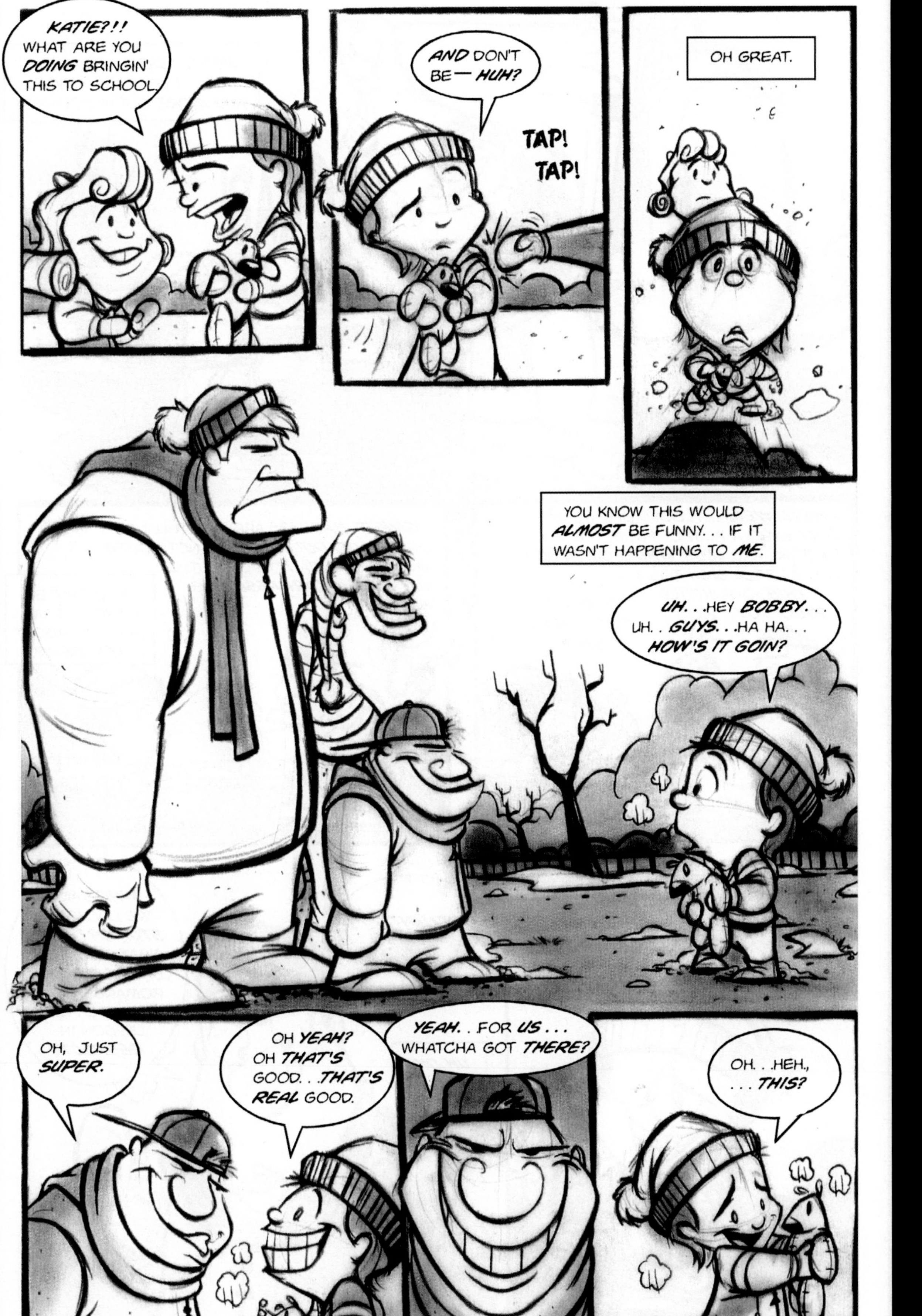
KATIE?!! WHAT ARE YOU DOING BRINGIN' THIS TO SCHOOL.
AND DON'T BE— HUH?
TAP! TAP!
OH GREAT.
YOU KNOW THIS WOULD ALMOST BE FUNNY. . . IF IT WASN'T HAPPENING TO ME.
UH. . .HEY BOBBY. . . UH. . GUYS. . .HA HA. . . HOW'S IT GOIN?
OH, JUST SUPER.
OH YEAH? OH THAT'S GOOD. . .THAT'S REAL GOOD.
YEAH. . FOR US . . . WHATCHA GOT THERE?
OH. . .HEH., . . . THIS?

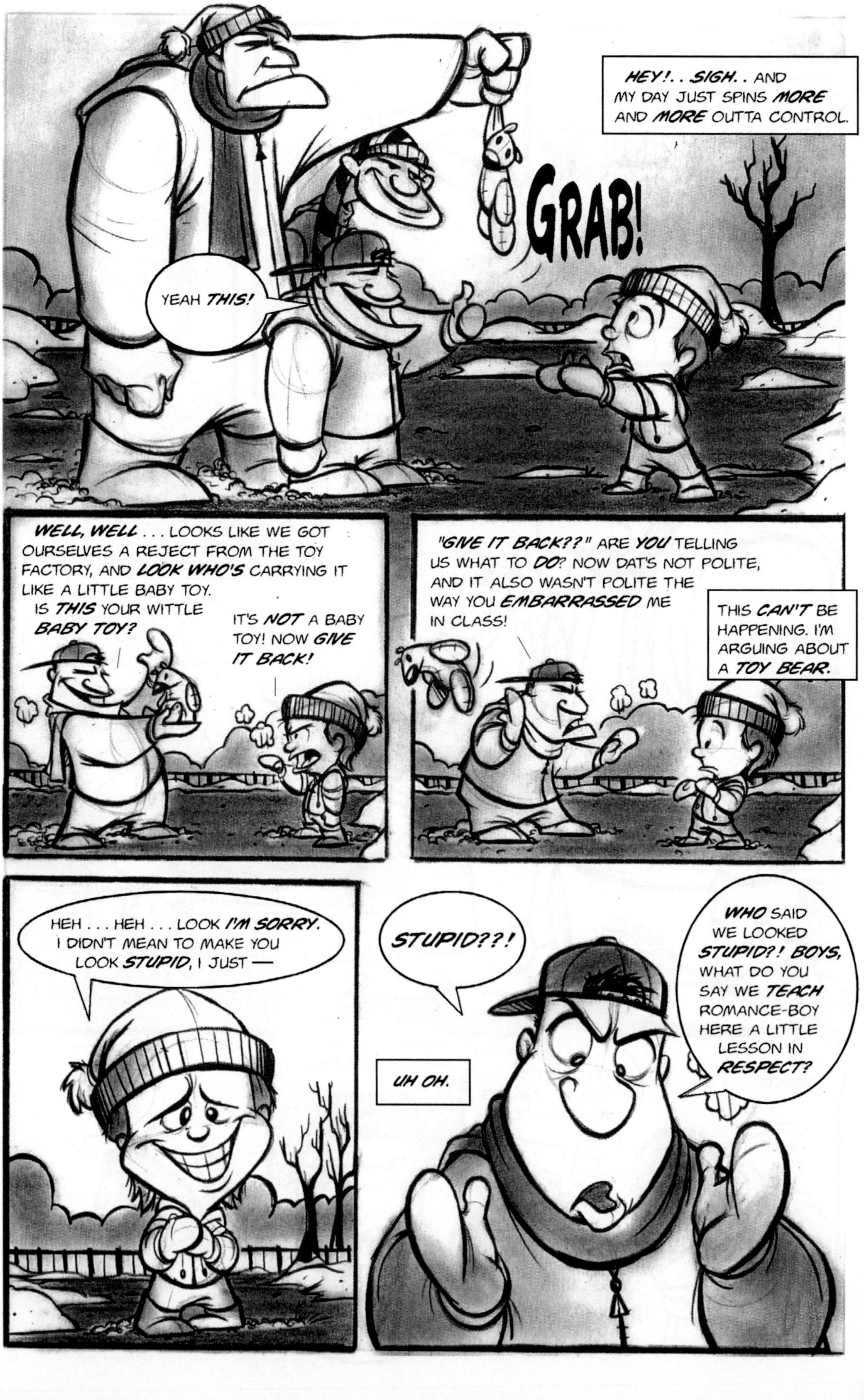
HEY!.. SIGH.. AND MY DAY JUST SPINS MORE AND MORE OUTTA CONTROL.
GRAB!
YEAH THIS!
WELL, WELL ... LOOKS LIKE WE GOT OURSELVES A REJECT FROM THE TOY FACTORY, AND LOOK WHO'S CARRYING IT LIKE A LITTLE BABY TOY.
IS THIS YOUR WITTLE BABY TOY?
IT'S NOT A BABY TOY! NOW GIVE IT BACK!
"GIVE IT BACK??" ARE YOU TELLING US WHAT TO DO? NOW DAT'S NOT POLITE, AND IT ALSO WASN'T POLITE THE WAY YOU EMBARRASSED ME IN CLASS!
THIS CAN'T BE HAPPENING. I'M ARGUING ABOUT A TOY BEAR.
HEH ... HEH ... LOOK I'M SORRY. I DIDN'T MEAN TO MAKE YOU LOOK STUPID, I JUST —
STUPID??!
UH OH.
WHO SAID WE LOOKED STUPID?! BOYS, WHAT DO YOU SAY WE TEACH ROMANCE-BOY HERE A LITTLE LESSON IN RESPECT?

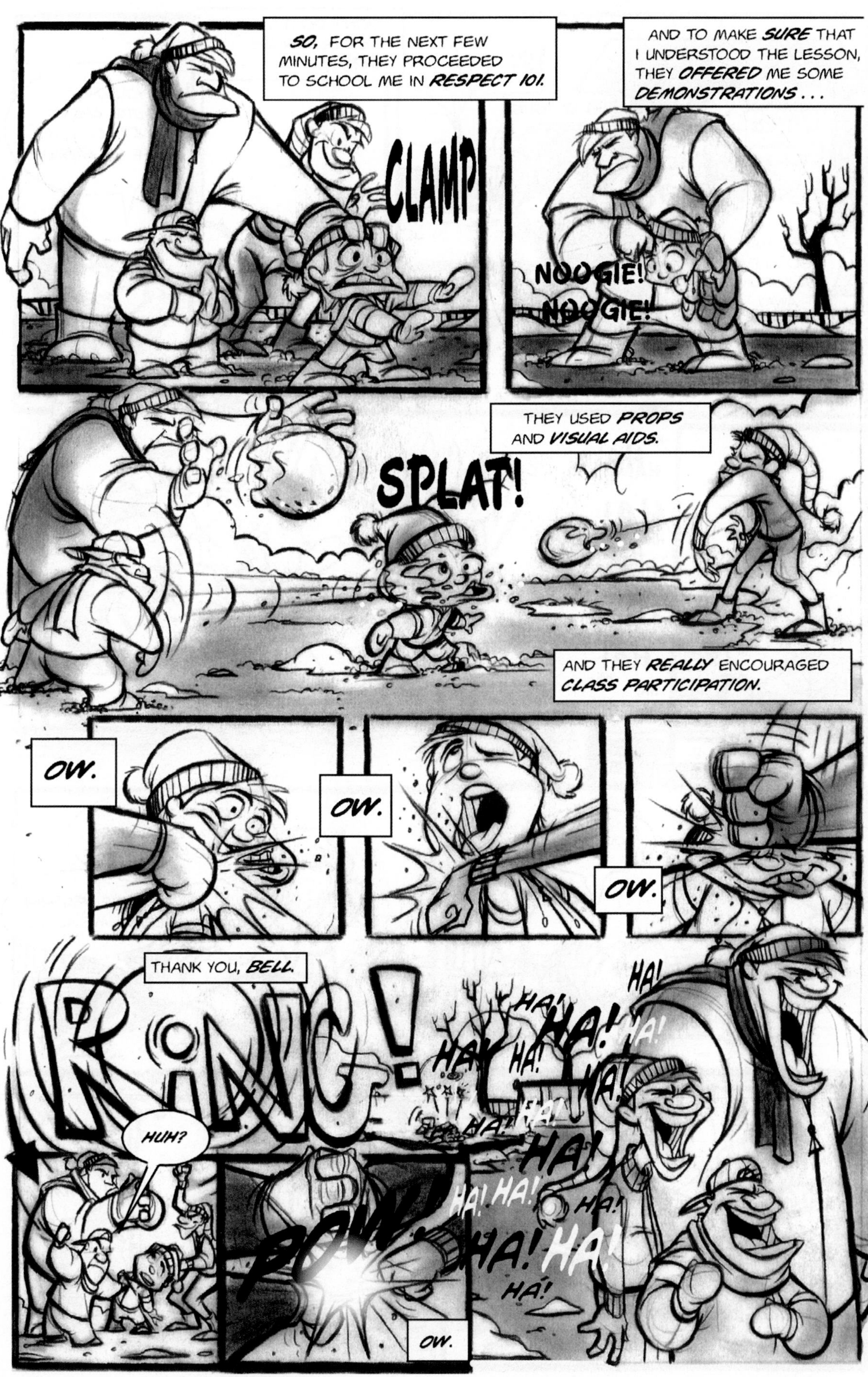

SO, FOR THE NEXT FEW MINUTES, THEY PROCEEDED TO SCHOOL ME IN RESPECT 101.
CLAMP
AND TO MAKE SURE THAT I UNDERSTOOD THE LESSON, THEY OFFERED ME SOME DEMONSTRATIONS . . .
NOOGIE! NOOGIE!
THEY USED PROPS AND VISUAL AIDS.
SPLAT!
AND THEY REALLY ENCOURAGED CLASS PARTICIPATION.
OW.
OW.
OW.
THANK YOU, BELL.
RING!
HUH?
POW
OW.
HA! HA! HA! HA! HA! HA! HA! HA! HA! HA! HA! HA! HA! HA! HA! HA!

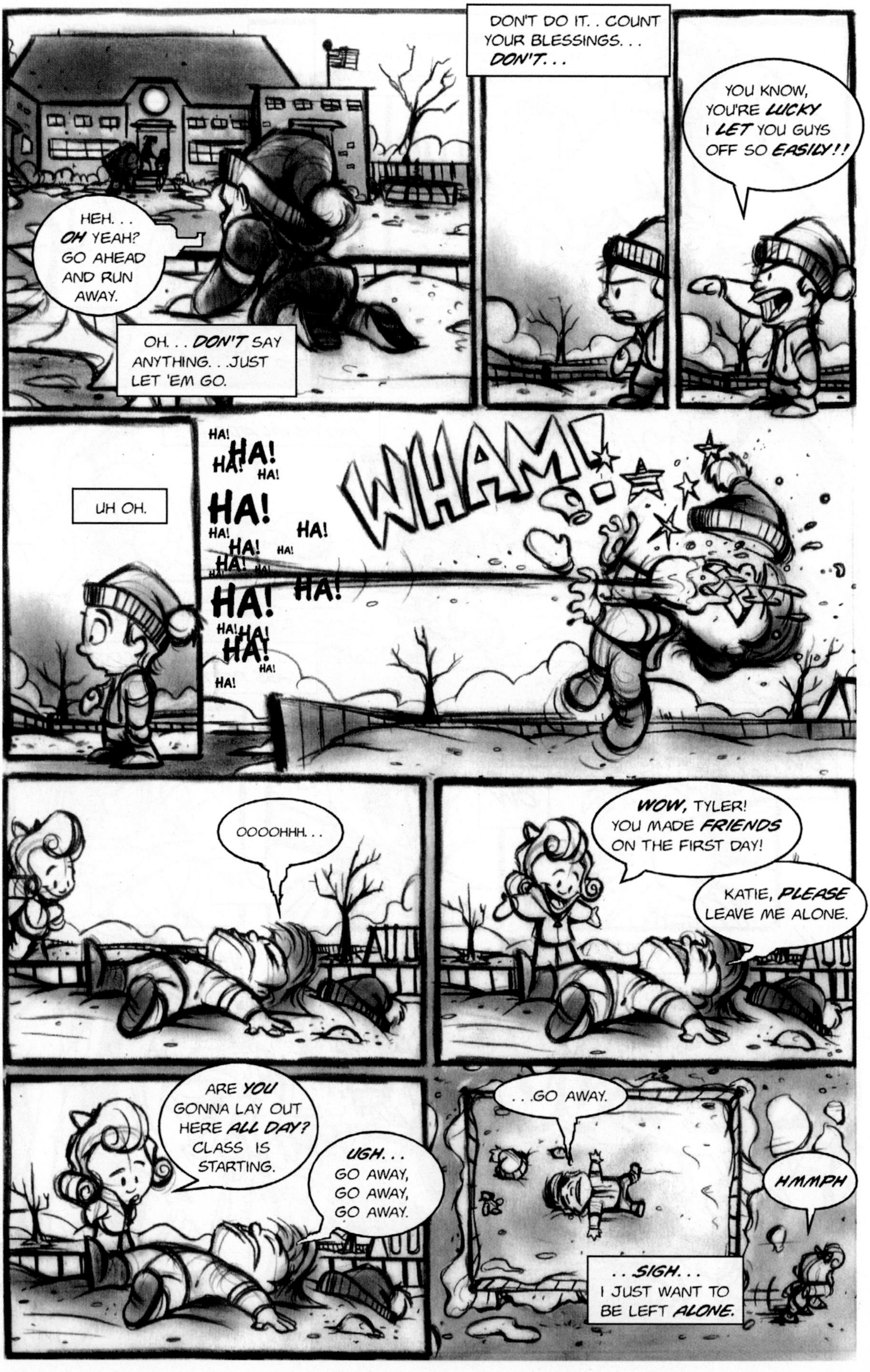
HEH. . . OH YEAH? GO AHEAD AND RUN AWAY.
OH. . . DON'T SAY ANYTHING. . .JUST LET 'EM GO.
DON'T DO IT. . COUNT YOUR BLESSINGS. . . DON'T. . .
YOU KNOW, YOU'RE LUCKY I LET YOU GUYS OFF SO EASILY!!
UH OH.
HA! HA! HA! HA! HA! HA! HA! HA! HA! HA! HA! HA! HA! HA! HA! HA! HA! HA!
WHAM!
OOOOHHH. . .
WOW, TYLER! YOU MADE FRIENDS ON THE FIRST DAY!
KATIE, PLEASE LEAVE ME ALONE.
ARE YOU GONNA LAY OUT HERE ALL DAY? CLASS IS STARTING.
UGH. . . GO AWAY, GO AWAY, GO AWAY.
. . .GO AWAY.
HMMPH
. . SIGH. . . I JUST WANT TO BE LEFT ALONE.

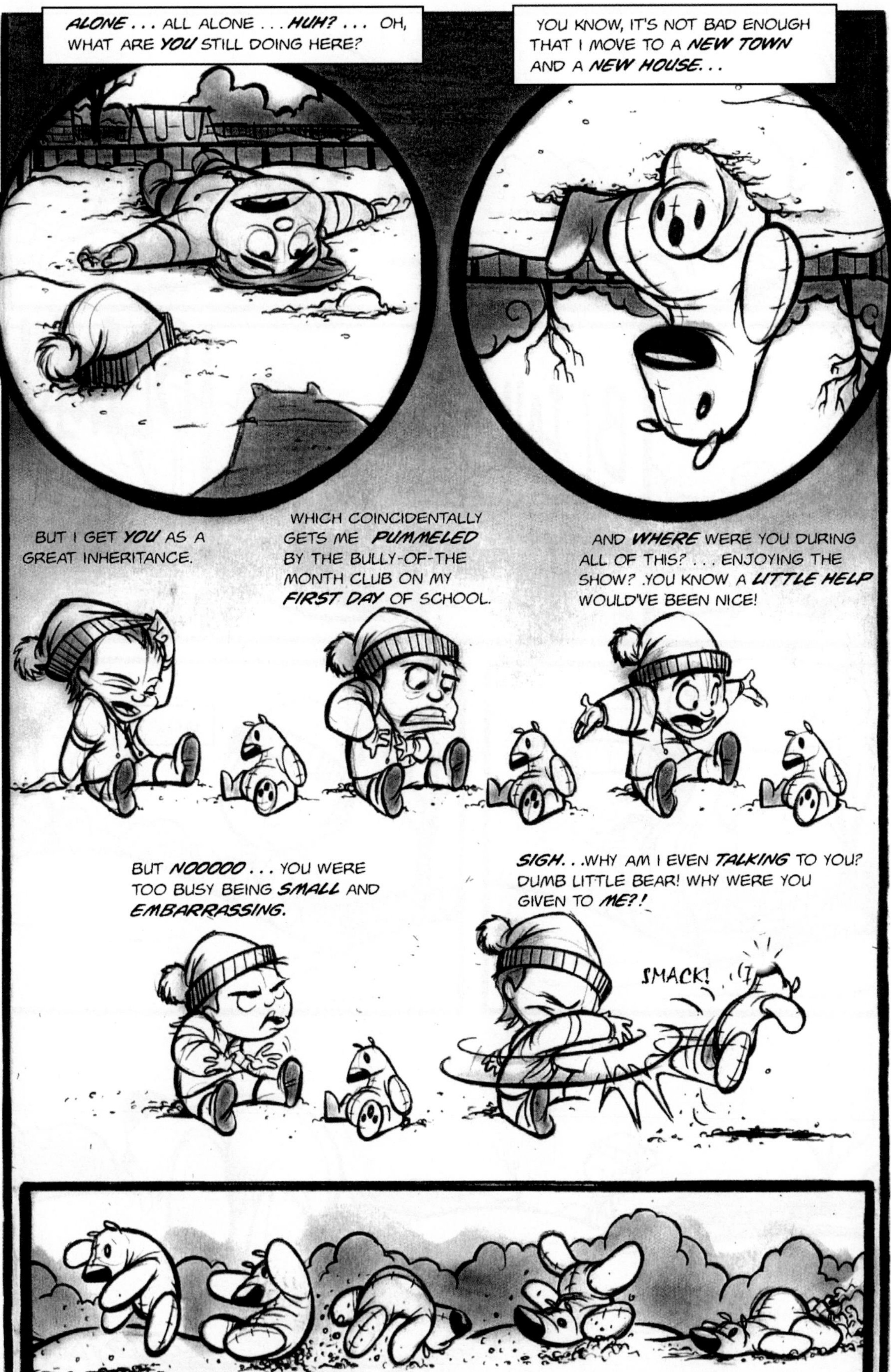

ALONE . . . ALL ALONE . . . HUH? . . . OH, WHAT ARE YOU STILL DOING HERE?
YOU KNOW, IT'S NOT BAD ENOUGH THAT I MOVE TO A NEW TOWN AND A NEW HOUSE. . .
BUT I GET YOU AS A GREAT INHERITANCE.
WHICH COINCIDENTALLY GETS ME PUMMELED BY THE BULLY-OF-THE MONTH CLUB ON MY FIRST DAY OF SCHOOL.
AND WHERE WERE YOU DURING ALL OF THIS? . . . ENJOYING THE SHOW? .YOU KNOW A LITTLE HELP WOULD'VE BEEN NICE!
BUT NOOOOO . . . YOU WERE TOO BUSY BEING SMALL AND EMBARRASSING.
SIGH. . .WHY AM I EVEN TALKING TO YOU? DUMB LITTLE BEAR! WHY WERE YOU GIVEN TO ME?!
SMACK!

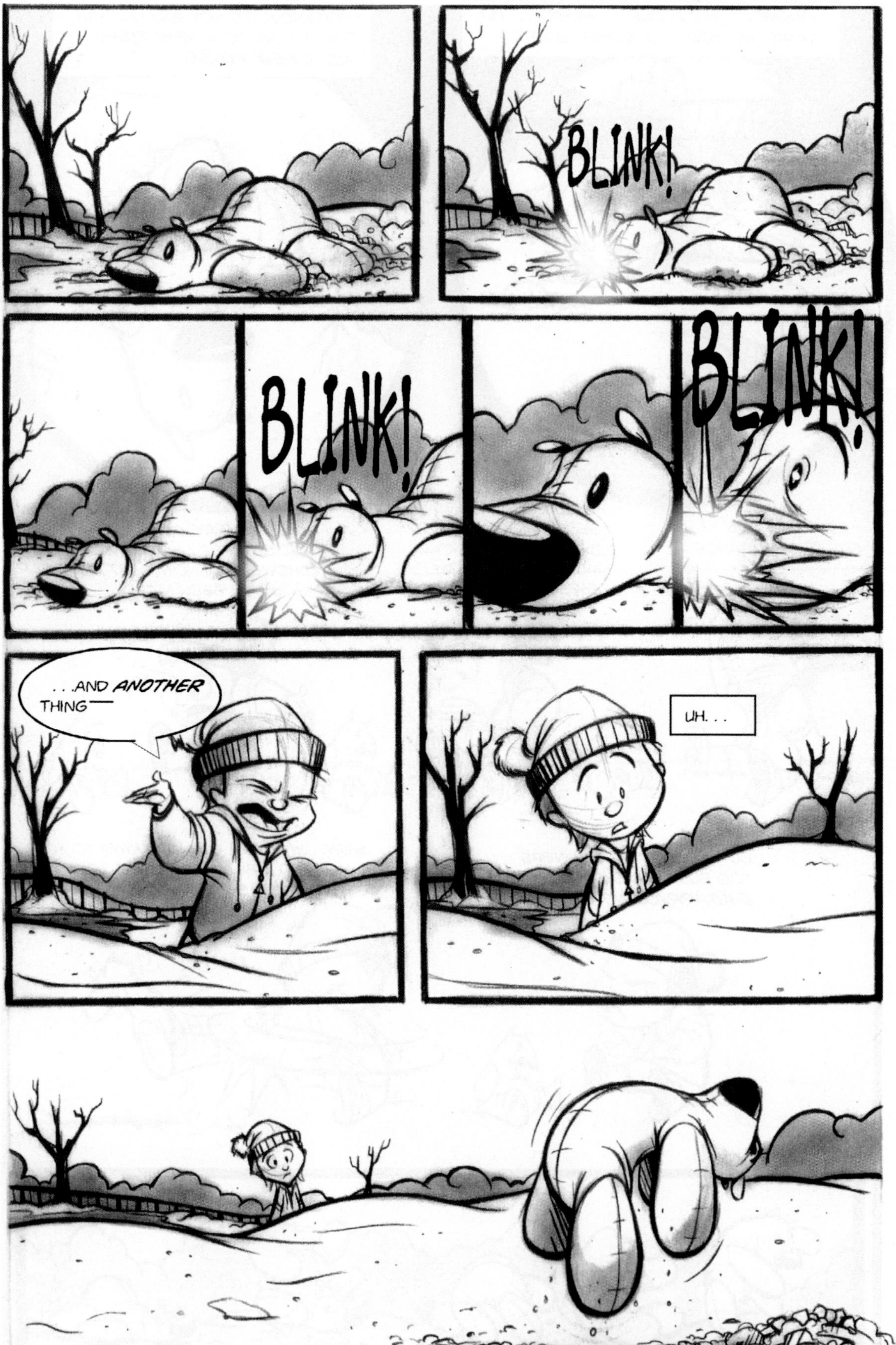
BLINK!
BLINK!
BLINK!
. . .AND ANOTHER THING—
UH. . .

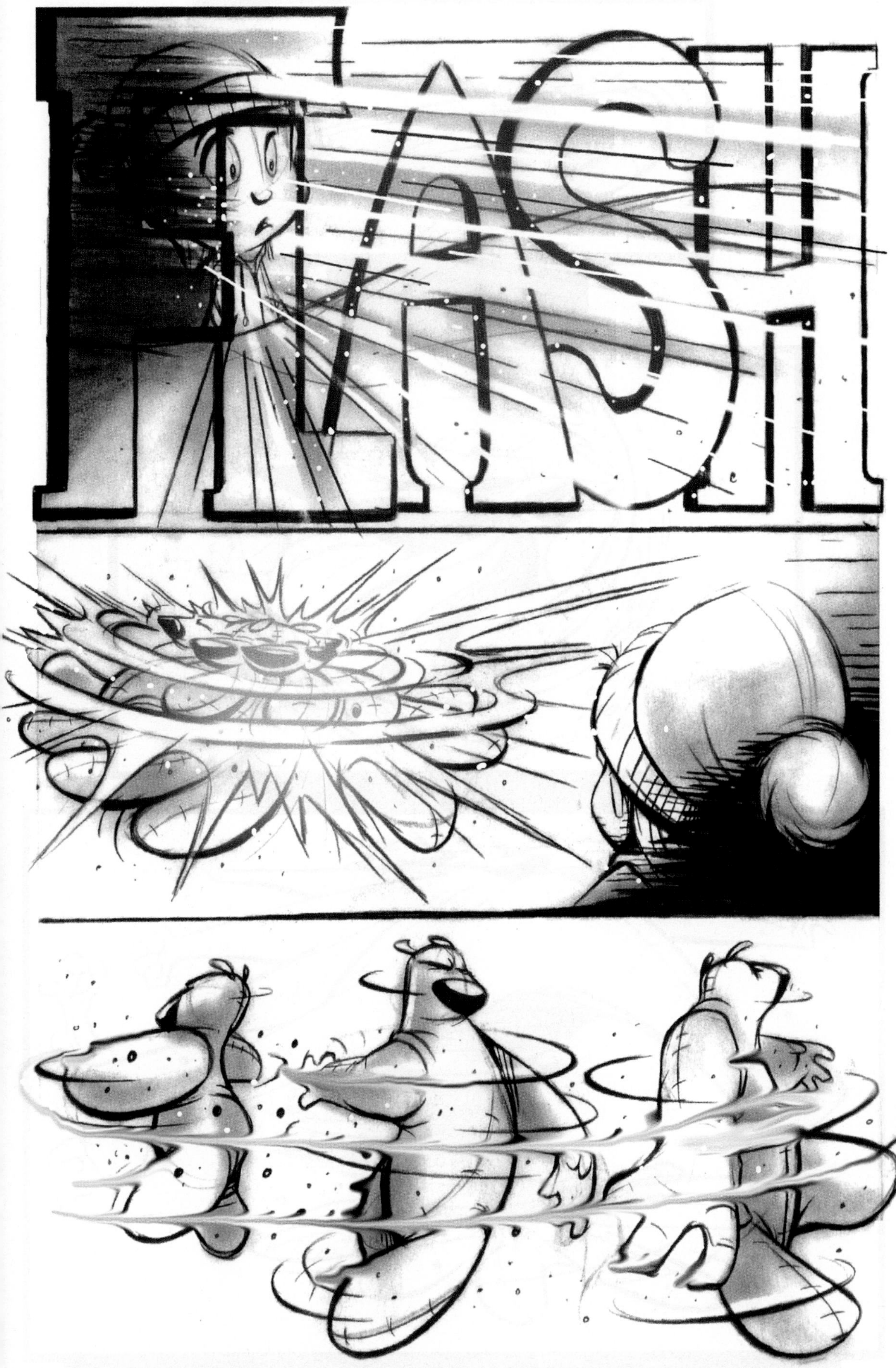
FLASH

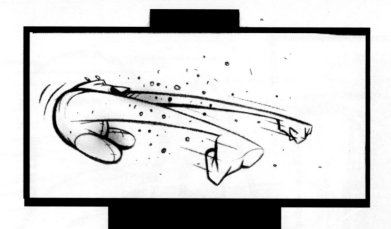

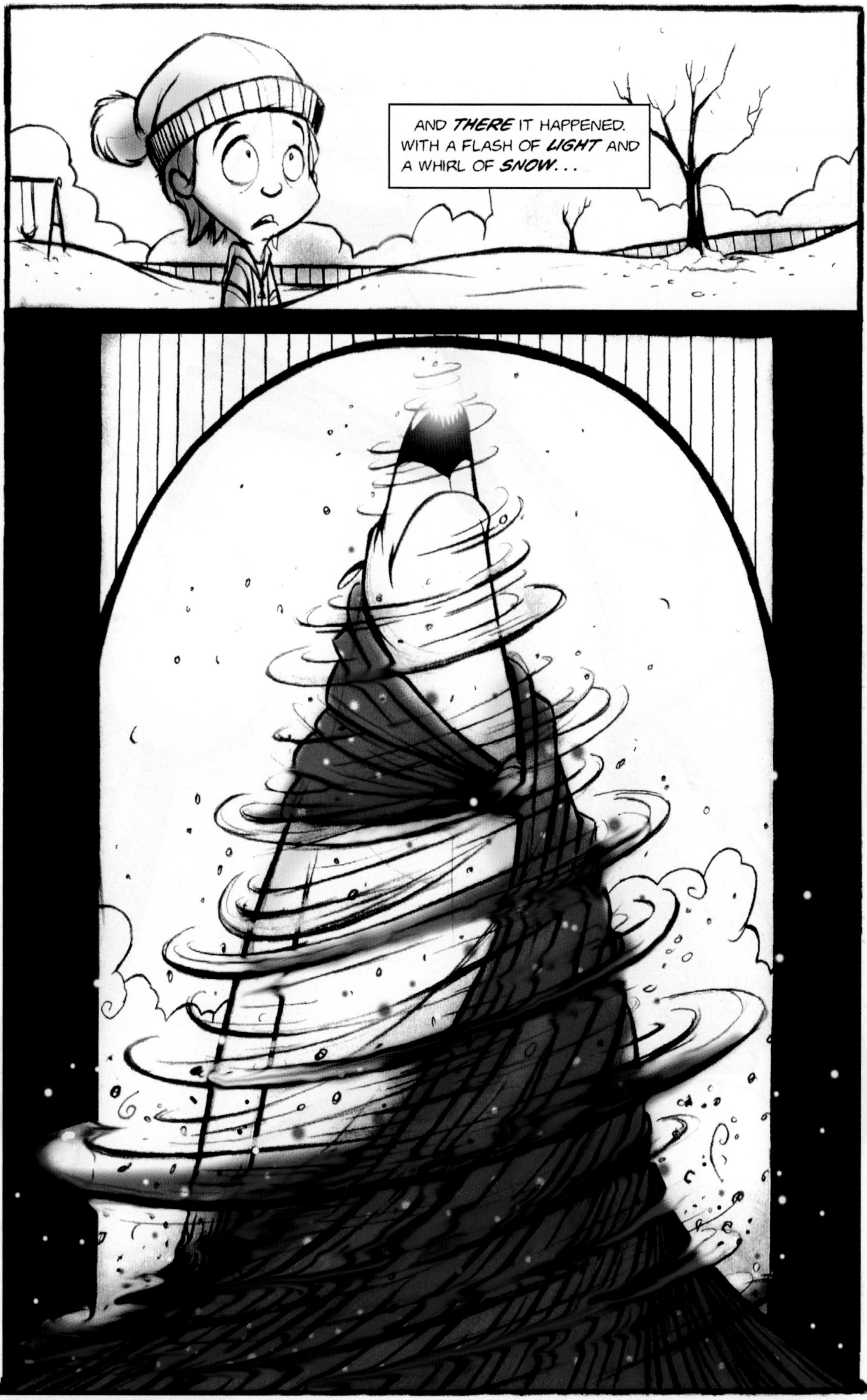
AND THERE IT HAPPENED. WITH A FLASH OF LIGHT AND A WHIRL OF SNOW...

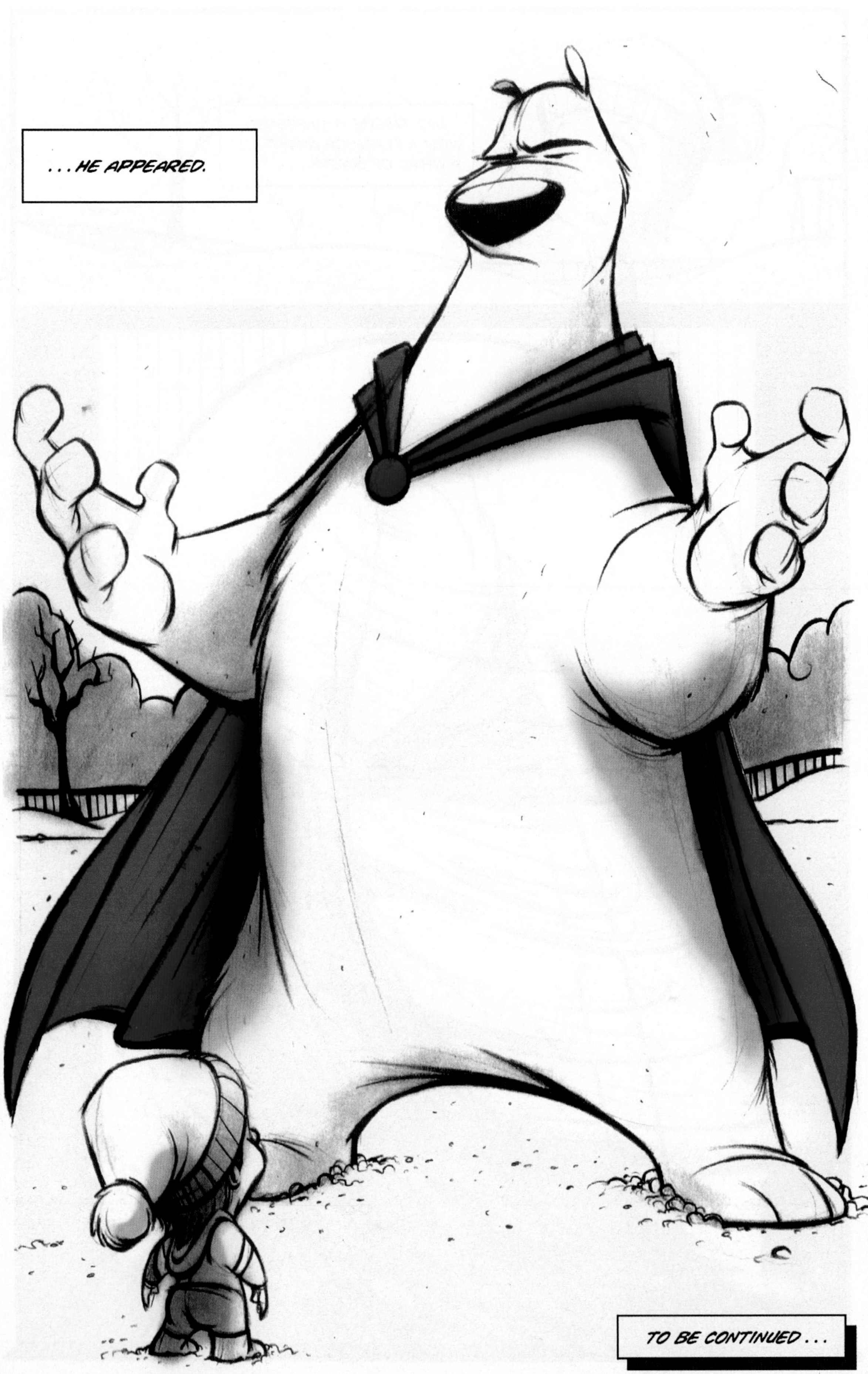
. . . HE APPEARED.
TO BE CONTINUED . . .

"**One** doesn't need to go much more beyond the first page of Mike Kunkel's Herobear and the Kid" to fall in love with this story. It has that one quality that doesn't come around very often ... its timeless."

JOE QUESADA (EDITOR-IN-CHIEF OF MARVEL COMICS)

"**HEROBEAR** AND THE KID manages to combine practically everything I like in a comic story - humor, warmth, charm, imagination, a sense of wonder inspired by childhood, and a drawing and staging style inspired by classical character animation. In the tradition of POGO, CALVIN AND HOBBES, and PEANUTS, the artwork is animated by the inner lives of the characters, all of whom are brimming with personality. All of this is brought together under the sure hand of the fabulously talented Mike Kunkel, who I sincerely hope does not get an better at this than he already is ... the bum."

ERIC GOLDBERG (FEATURE ANIMATION AND TELEVISION DIRECTOR)

"**The** movement of Jack Kirby and Chuck Jones and the unsentimental sentiment of Calvin and Hobbes wrapped up in glorious black-white-and-red. Mike Kunkel seems to have sprung fully formed from God knows where to delight us all."

TIM SALE(ARTIST OF SUPERMAN FOR ALL SEASONS, BATMAN: THE LONG HALLOWEEN, AND SPIDERMAN: BLUE)

"...**wonderfully** fun for the imagination, soothingly warm for the heart, and solid in principle and value for one's life. Mike Kunkel is a real breath of fresh air."

JOHN TOLLE (PASTOR OF THE LIGHTHOUSE CHURCH)

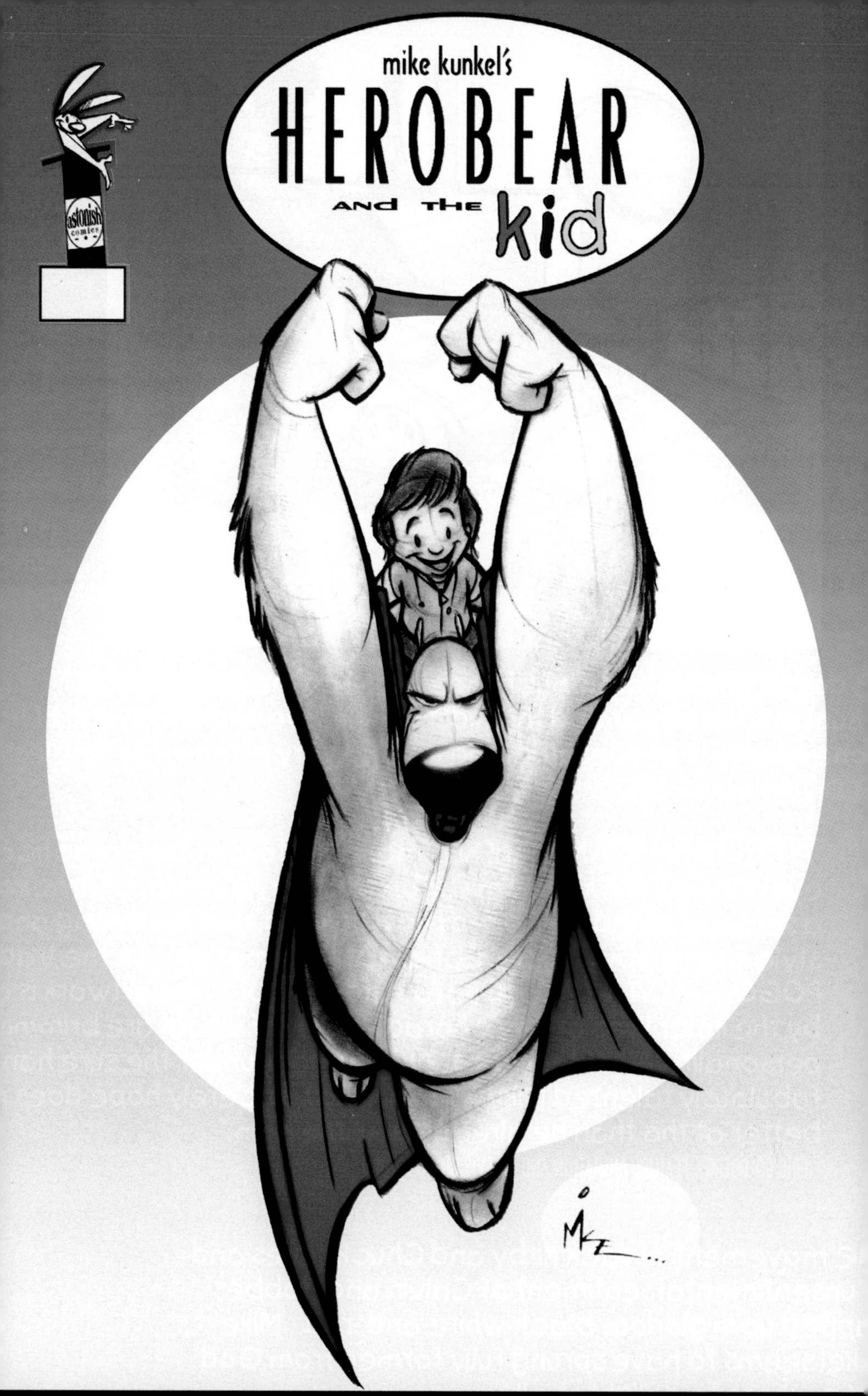
mike kunkel's
HEROBEAR
AND THE kid
astonish comics

book two

dreams

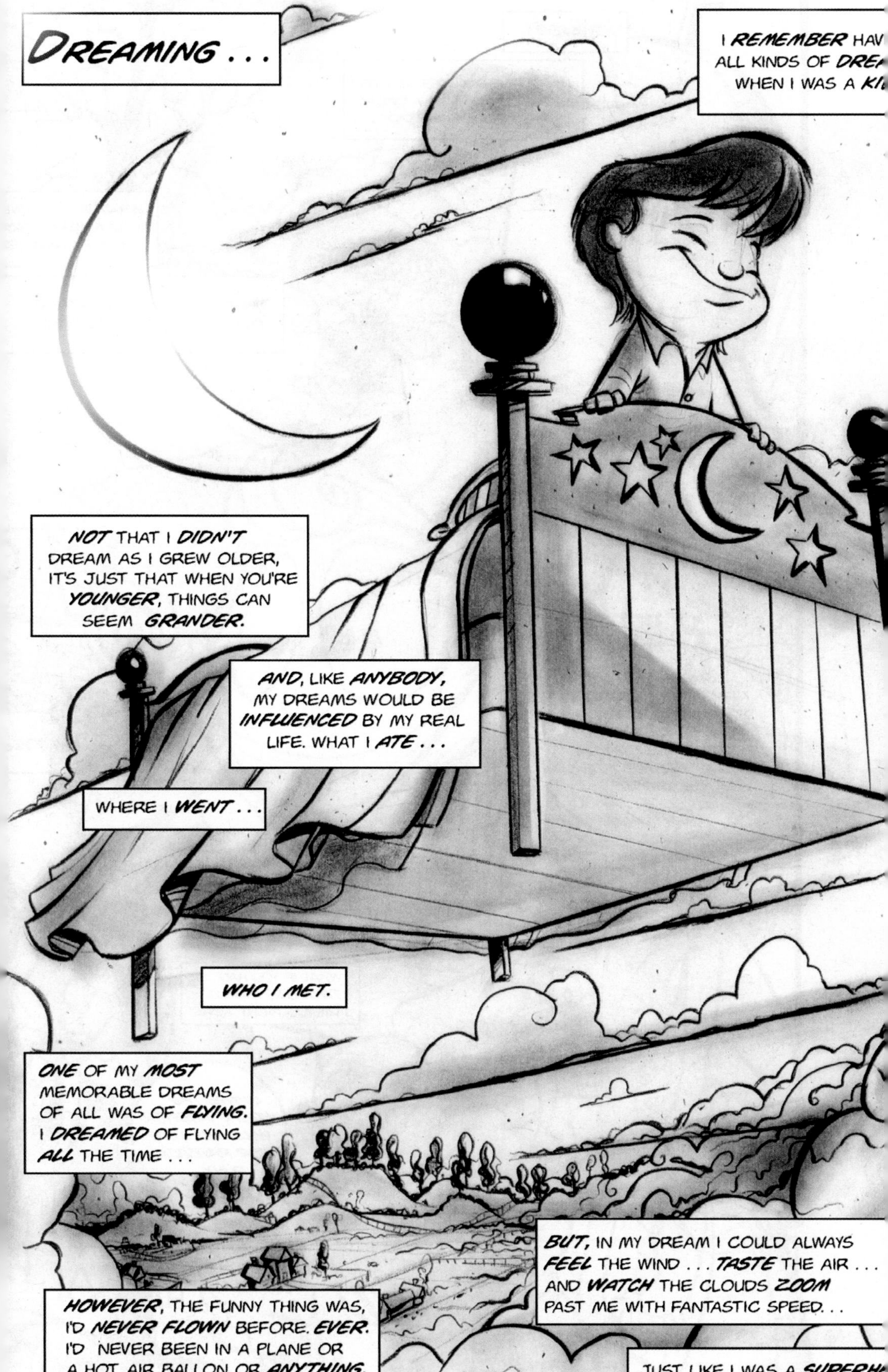
DREAMING . . .
I REMEMBER HAV
ALL KINDS OF
WHEN I WAS A
NOT THAT I DIDN'T DREAM AS I GREW OLDER, IT'S JUST THAT WHEN YOU'RE YOUNGER, THINGS CAN SEEM GRANDER.
AND, LIKE ANYBODY, MY DREAMS WOULD BE INFLUENCED BY MY REAL LIFE. WHAT I ATE . . .
WHERE I WENT . . .
WHO I MET.
ONE OF MY MOST MEMORABLE DREAMS OF ALL WAS OF FLYING. I DREAMED OF FLYING ALL THE TIME . . .
HOWEVER, THE FUNNY THING WAS, I'D NEVER FLOWN BEFORE. EVER. I'D NEVER BEEN IN A PLANE OR A HOT AIR BALLON OR ANYTHING.
BUT, IN MY DREAM I COULD ALWAYS FEEL THE WIND . . . TASTE THE AIR . . . AND WATCH THE CLOUDS ZOOM PAST ME WITH FANTASTIC SPEED. . .
JUST LIKE I WAS A

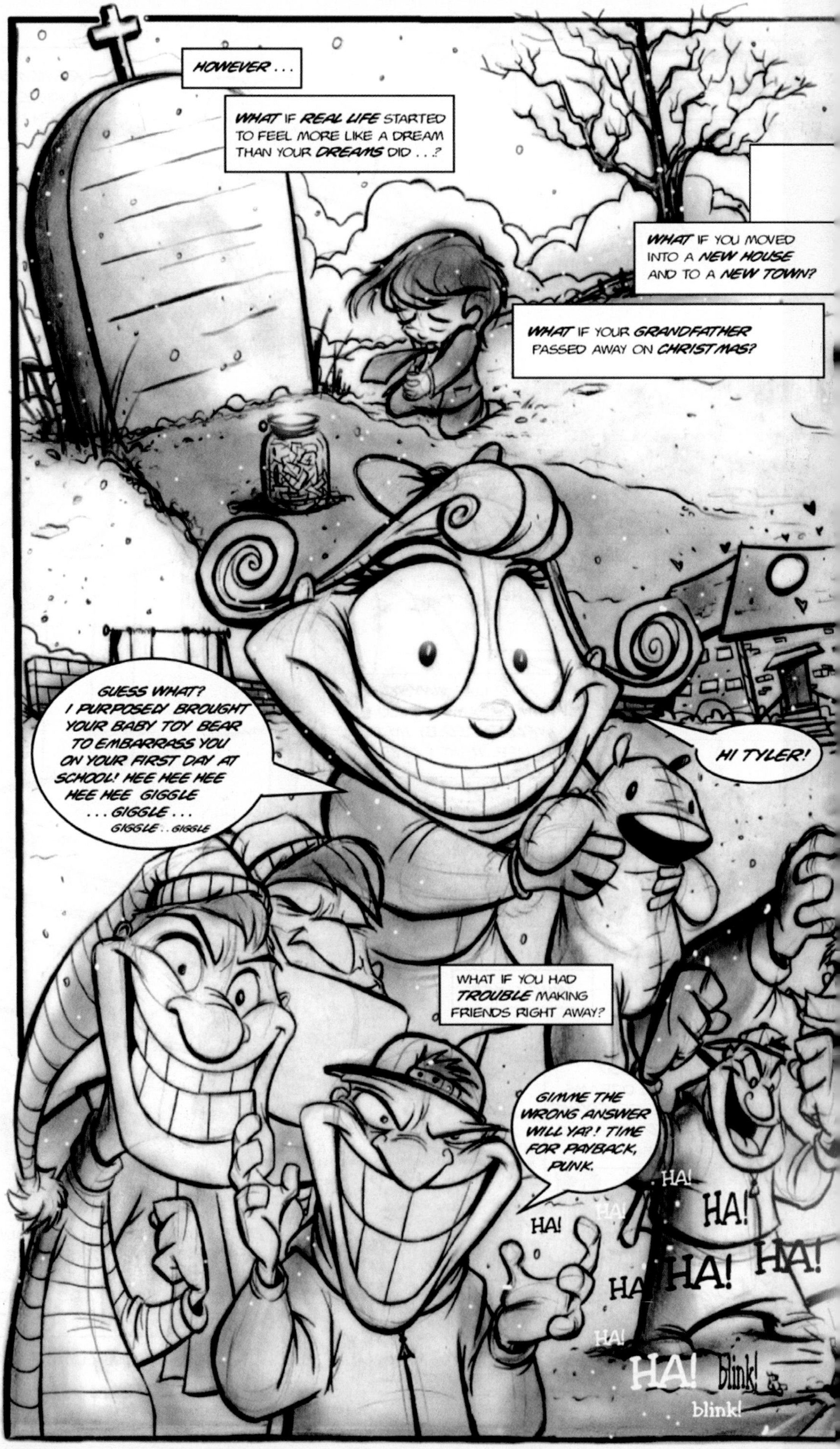
HOWEVER . . .
WHAT IF REAL LIFE STARTED TO FEEL MORE LIKE A DREAM THAN YOUR DREAMS DID . . .?
WHAT IF YOU MOVED INTO A NEW HOUSE AND TO A NEW TOWN?
WHAT IF YOUR GRANDFATHER PASSED AWAY ON CHRISTMAS?
GUESS WHAT? I PURPOSELY BROUGHT YOUR BABY TOY BEAR TO EMBARRASS YOU ON YOUR FIRST DAY AT SCHOOL! HEE HEE HEE HEE HEE GIGGLE . . . GIGGLE . . . GIGGLE . . GIGGLE
HI TYLER!
WHAT IF YOU HAD TROUBLE MAKING FRIENDS RIGHT AWAY?
GIMME THE WRONG ANSWER WILL YA?! TIME FOR PAYBACK, PUNK.
HA! HA! HA! HA! HA! HA! HA! HA! HA!
blink! blink!

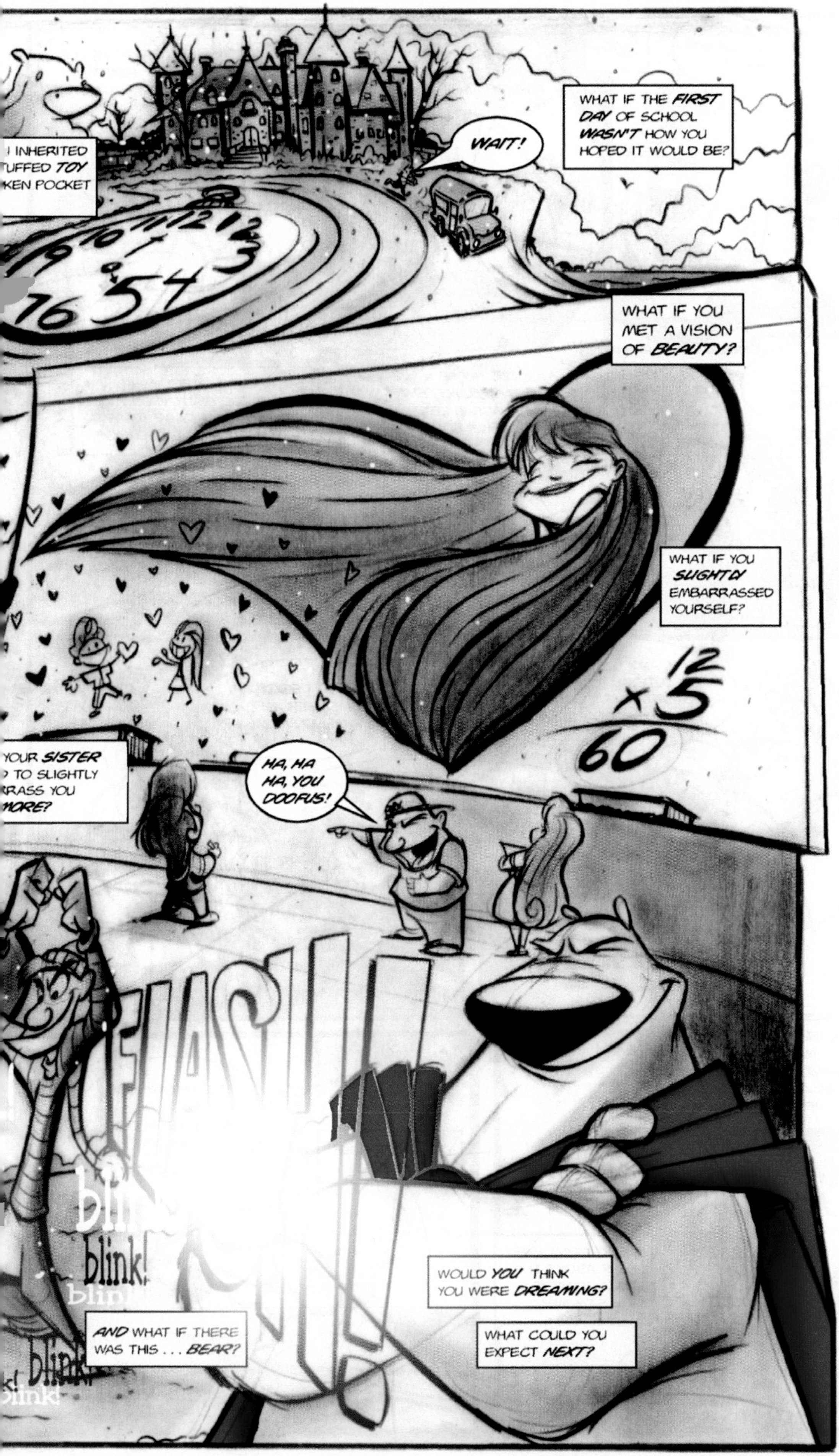

I INHERITED
TUFFED TOY
KEN POCKET
WAIT!
WHAT IF THE FIRST DAY OF SCHOOL WASN'T HOW YOU HOPED IT WOULD BE?
WHAT IF YOU MET A VISION OF BEAUTY?
WHAT IF YOU SLIGHTLY EMBARRASSED YOURSELF?
12 x 5 60
YOUR SISTER
TO SLIGHTLY
RASS YOU
MORE?
HA, HA HA, YOU DOOFUS!
blink!
blink!
AND WHAT IF THERE WAS THIS . . . BEAR?
WOULD YOU THINK YOU WERE DREAMING?
WHAT COULD YOU EXPECT NEXT?

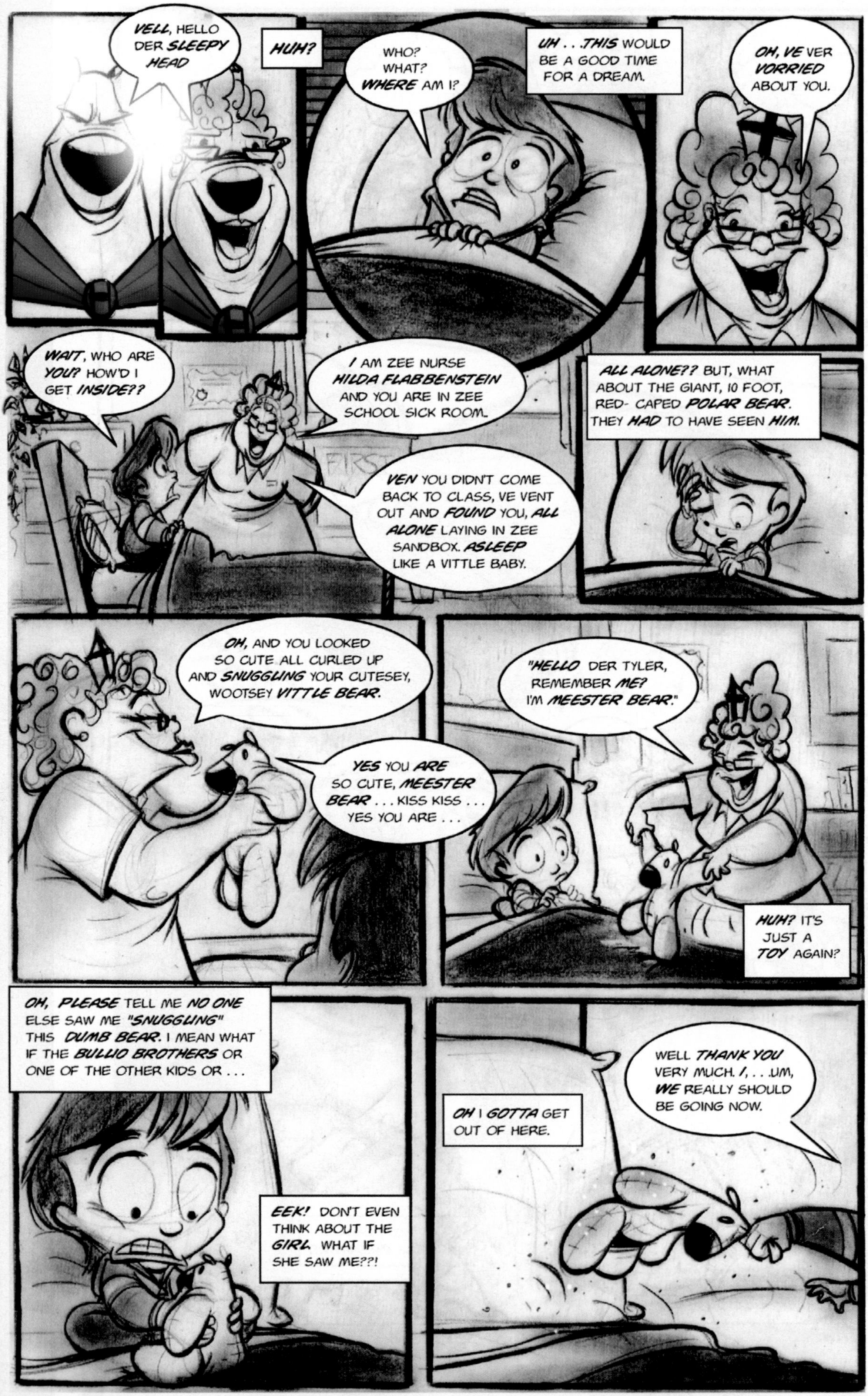
VELL, HELLO DER SLEEPY HEAD
HUH?
WHO? WHAT? WHERE AM I?
UH . . .THIS WOULD BE A GOOD TIME FOR A DREAM.
OH, VE VER VORRIED ABOUT YOU.
WAIT, WHO ARE YOU? HOW'D I GET INSIDE??
I AM ZEE NURSE HILDA FLABBENSTEIN AND YOU ARE IN ZEE SCHOOL SICK ROOM.
VEN YOU DIDN'T COME BACK TO CLASS, VE VENT OUT AND FOUND YOU, ALL ALONE LAYING IN ZEE SANDBOX. ASLEEP LIKE A VITTLE BABY.
ALL ALONE?? BUT, WHAT ABOUT THE GIANT, 10 FOOT, RED- CAPED POLAR BEAR. THEY HAD TO HAVE SEEN HIM.
OH, AND YOU LOOKED SO CUTE ALL CURLED UP AND SNUGGLING YOUR CUTESEY, WOOTSEY VITTLE BEAR.
YES YOU ARE SO CUTE, MEESTER BEAR . . . KISS KISS . . . YES YOU ARE . . .
"HELLO DER TYLER, REMEMBER ME? I'M MEESTER BEAR."
HUH? IT'S JUST A TOY AGAIN?
OH, PLEASE TELL ME NO ONE ELSE SAW ME "SNUGGLING" THIS DUMB BEAR. I MEAN WHAT IF THE BULLIO BROTHERS OR ONE OF THE OTHER KIDS OR . . .
EEK! DON'T EVEN THINK ABOUT THE GIRL. WHAT IF SHE SAW ME??!
OH I GOTTA GET OUT OF HERE.
WELL THANK YOU VERY MUCH. I, . . .UM, WE REALLY SHOULD BE GOING NOW.

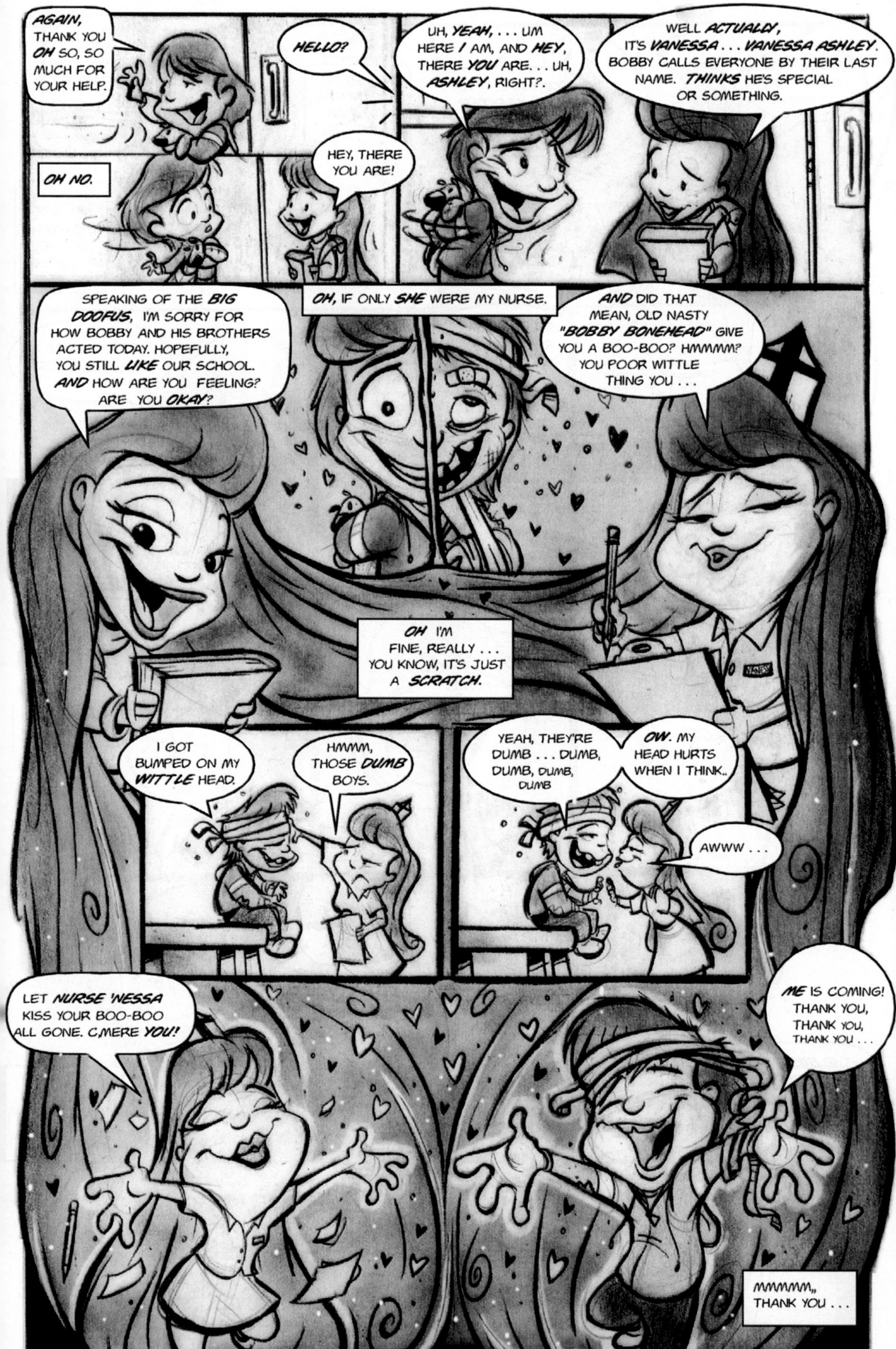
AGAIN, THANK YOU OH SO, SO MUCH FOR YOUR HELP.
HELLO?
UH, YEAH, . . . UM HERE I AM, AND HEY, THERE YOU ARE. . . UH, ASHLEY, RIGHT?.
WELL ACTUALLY, IT'S VANESSA . . . VANESSA ASHLEY. BOBBY CALLS EVERYONE BY THEIR LAST NAME. THINKS HE'S SPECIAL OR SOMETHING.
OH NO.
HEY, THERE YOU ARE!
SPEAKING OF THE BIG DOOFUS, I'M SORRY FOR HOW BOBBY AND HIS BROTHERS ACTED TODAY. HOPEFULLY, YOU STILL LIKE OUR SCHOOL. AND HOW ARE YOU FEELING? ARE YOU OKAY?
OH, IF ONLY SHE WERE MY NURSE.
AND DID THAT MEAN, OLD NASTY "BOBBY BONEHEAD" GIVE YOU A BOO-BOO? HMMMM? YOU POOR WITTLE THING YOU . . .
OH I'M FINE, REALLY . . . YOU KNOW, IT'S JUST A SCRATCH.
I GOT BUMPED ON MY WITTLE HEAD.
HMMM, THOSE DUMB BOYS.
YEAH, THEY'RE DUMB . . . DUMB, DUMB, DUMB, DUMB
OW. MY HEAD HURTS WHEN I THINK..
AWWW . . .
LET NURSE 'NESSA KISS YOUR BOO-BOO ALL GONE. C,MERE YOU!
ME IS COMING! THANK YOU, THANK YOU, THANK YOU . . .
MMMMM,, THANK YOU . . .

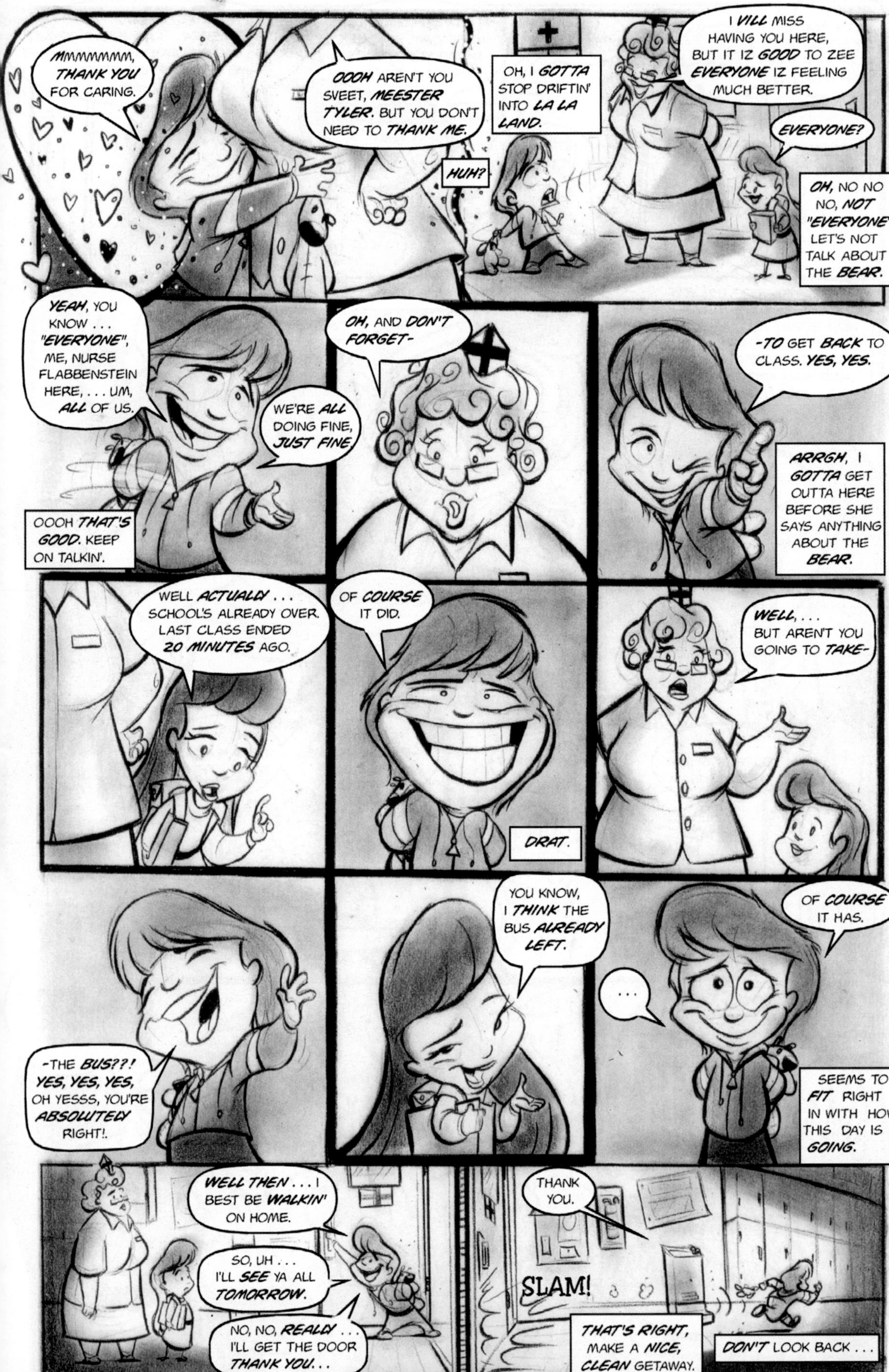
MMMMMMM, THANK YOU FOR CARING.
OOOH AREN'T YOU SVEET, MEESTER TYLER. BUT YOU DON'T NEED TO THANK ME.
HUH?
OH, I GOTTA STOP DRIFTIN' INTO LA LA LAND.
I VILL MISS HAVING YOU HERE, BUT IT IZ GOOD TO ZEE EVERYONE IZ FEELING MUCH BETTER.
EVERYONE?
OH, NO NO NO, NOT "EVERYONE" LET'S NOT TALK ABOUT THE BEAR.
YEAH, YOU KNOW . . . "EVERYONE", ME, NURSE FLABBENSTEIN HERE, . . . UM, ALL OF US.
WE'RE ALL DOING FINE, JUST FINE.
OOOH THAT'S GOOD. KEEP ON TALKIN'.
OH, AND DON'T FORGET-
-TO GET BACK TO CLASS. YES, YES.
ARRGH, I GOTTA GET OUTTA HERE BEFORE SHE SAYS ANYTHING ABOUT THE BEAR.
WELL ACTUALLY . . . SCHOOL'S ALREADY OVER. LAST CLASS ENDED 20 MINUTES AGO.
OF COURSE IT DID.
DRAT.
WELL, . . . BUT AREN'T YOU GOING TO TAKE-
-THE BUS??! YES, YES, YES, OH YESSS, YOU'RE ABSOLUTELY RIGHT!.
YOU KNOW, I THINK THE BUS ALREADY LEFT.
OF COURSE IT HAS.
. . .
SEEMS TO FIT RIGHT IN WITH HOW THIS DAY IS GOING.
WELL THEN . . . I BEST BE WALKIN' ON HOME.
SO, UH . . . I'LL SEE YA ALL TOMORROW.
NO, NO, REALLY . . . I'LL GET THE DOOR THANK YOU . . .
THANK YOU.
SLAM!
THAT'S RIGHT, MAKE A NICE, CLEAN GETAWAY.
DON'T LOOK BACK . . .

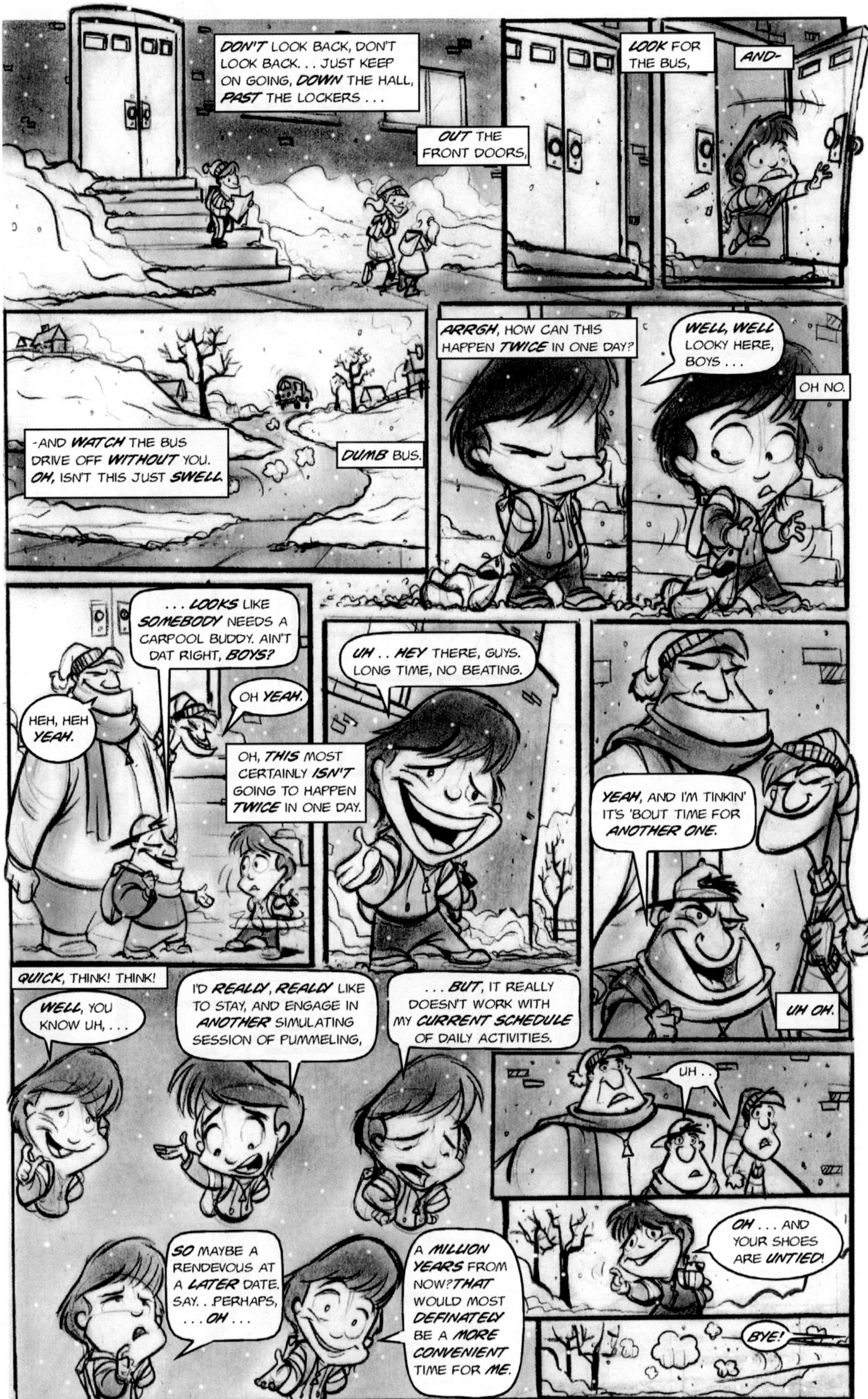
DON'T LOOK BACK, DON'T LOOK BACK. . . JUST KEEP ON GOING, DOWN THE HALL, PAST THE LOCKERS . . .
OUT THE FRONT DOORS,
LOOK FOR THE BUS,
AND-
-AND WATCH THE BUS DRIVE OFF WITHOUT YOU. OH, ISN'T THIS JUST SWELL.
DUMB BUS.
ARRGH, HOW CAN THIS HAPPEN TWICE IN ONE DAY?
WELL, WELL LOOKY HERE, BOYS . . .
OH NO.
. . . LOOKS LIKE SOMEBODY NEEDS A CARPOOL BUDDY. AIN'T DAT RIGHT, BOYS?
HEH, HEH YEAH.
OH YEAH.
OH, THIS MOST CERTAINLY ISN'T GOING TO HAPPEN TWICE IN ONE DAY.
UH . . HEY THERE, GUYS. LONG TIME, NO BEATING.
YEAH, AND I'M TINKIN' IT'S 'BOUT TIME FOR ANOTHER ONE.
UH OH.
QUICK, THINK! THINK!
WELL, YOU KNOW UH, . . .
I'D REALLY, REALLY LIKE TO STAY, AND ENGAGE IN ANOTHER SIMULATING SESSION OF PUMMELING,
. . . BUT, IT REALLY DOESN'T WORK WITH MY CURRENT SCHEDULE OF DAILY ACTIVITIES.
UH . .
SO MAYBE A RENDEVOUS AT A LATER DATE. SAY. . PERHAPS, . . . OH . . .
A MILLION YEARS FROM NOW?THAT WOULD MOST DEFINATELY BE A MORE CONVENIENT TIME FOR ME.
OH . . . AND YOUR SHOES ARE UNTIED!
BYE!

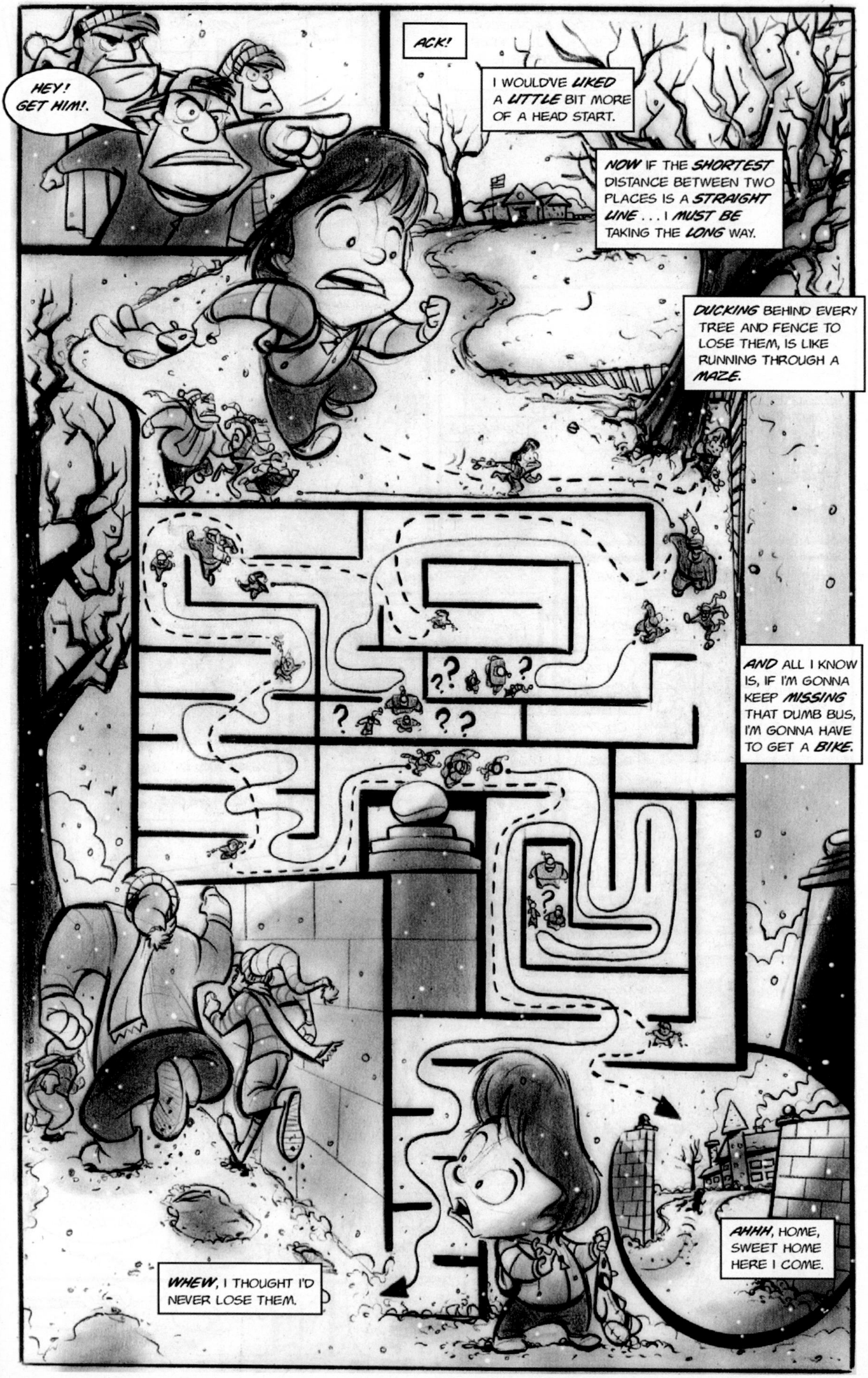
HEY! GET HIM!.
ACK!
I WOULD'VE LIKED A LITTLE BIT MORE OF A HEAD START.
NOW IF THE SHORTEST DISTANCE BETWEEN TWO PLACES IS A STRAIGHT LINE . . . I MUST BE TAKING THE LONG WAY.
DUCKING BEHIND EVERY TREE AND FENCE TO LOSE THEM, IS LIKE RUNNING THROUGH A MAZE.
AND ALL I KNOW IS, IF I'M GONNA KEEP MISSING THAT DUMB BUS, I'M GONNA HAVE TO GET A BIKE.
WHEW, I THOUGHT I'D NEVER LOSE THEM.
AHHH, HOME, SWEET HOME HERE I COME.

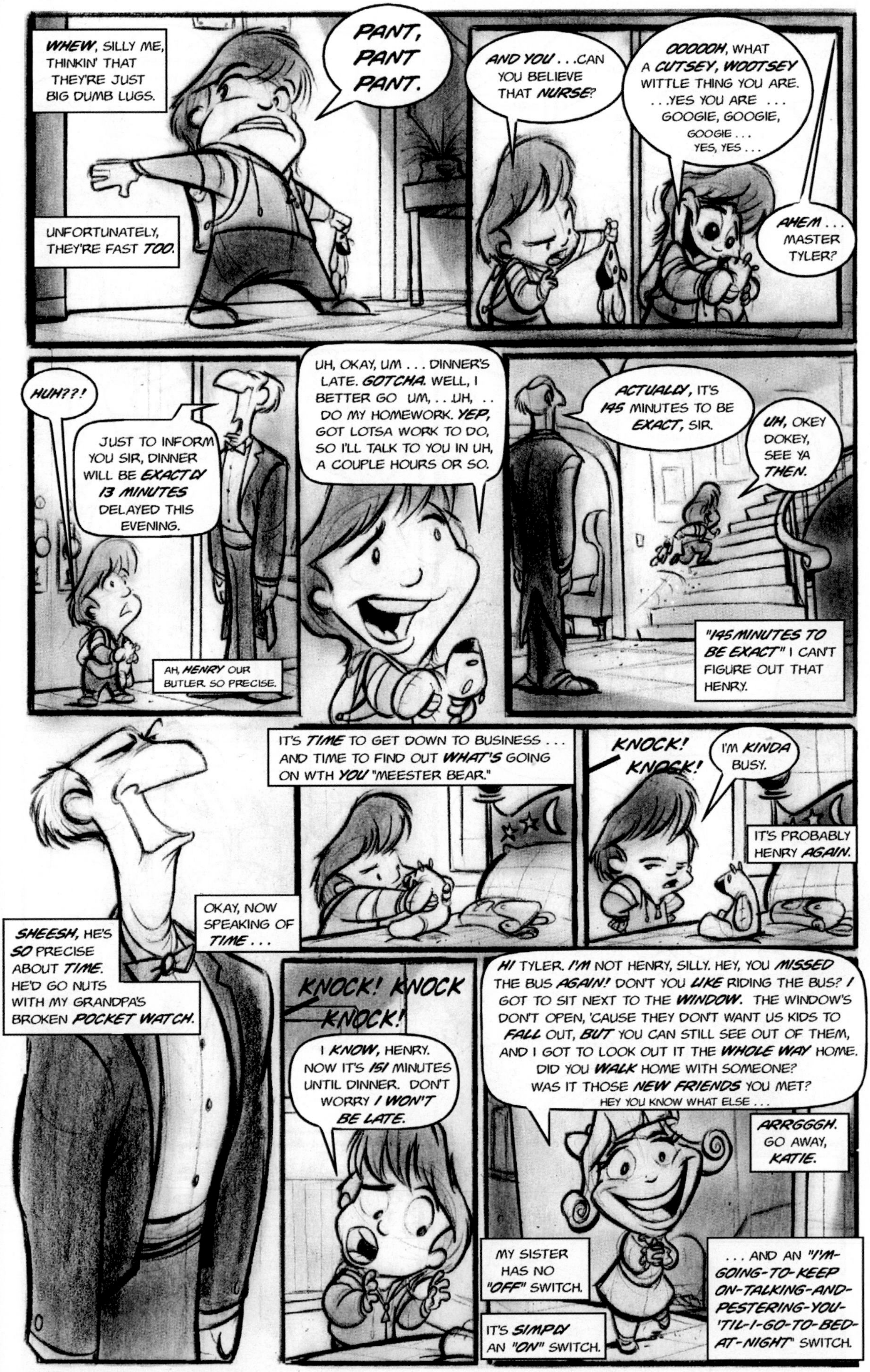
WHEW, SILLY ME, THINKIN' THAT THEY'RE JUST BIG DUMB LUGS.
PANT, PANT PANT.
UNFORTUNATELY, THEY'RE FAST TOO.
AND YOU . . .CAN YOU BELIEVE THAT NURSE?
OOOOOOH, WHAT A CUTSEY, WOOTSEY WITTLE THING YOU ARE. . . .YES YOU ARE . . . GOOGIE, GOOGIE, GOOGIE . . . YES, YES . . .
AHEM . . . MASTER TYLER?
HUH??!
JUST TO INFORM YOU SIR, DINNER WILL BE EXACTLY 13 MINUTES DELAYED THIS EVENING.
AH, HENRY OUR BUTLER SO PRECISE.
UH, OKAY, UM . . . DINNER'S LATE. GOTCHA. WELL, I BETTER GO UM, . . .UH, . . DO MY HOMEWORK. YEP, GOT LOTSA WORK TO DO, SO I'LL TALK TO YOU IN UH, A COUPLE HOURS OR SO.
ACTUALLY, IT'S 145 MINUTES TO BE EXACT, SIR.
UH, OKEY DOKEY, SEE YA THEN.
"145 MINUTES TO BE EXACT" I CAN'T FIGURE OUT THAT HENRY.
SHEESH, HE'S SO PRECISE ABOUT TIME. HE'D GO NUTS WITH MY GRANDPA'S BROKEN POCKET WATCH.
OKAY, NOW SPEAKING OF TIME . . .
IT'S TIME TO GET DOWN TO BUSINESS . . . AND TIME TO FIND OUT WHAT'S GOING ON WTH YOU "MEESTER BEAR."
KNOCK! KNOCK!
I'M KINDA BUSY.
IT'S PROBABLY HENRY AGAIN.
KNOCK! KNOCK KNOCK!
I KNOW, HENRY. NOW IT'S 151 MINUTES UNTIL DINNER. DON'T WORRY I WON'T BE LATE.
HI TYLER. I'M NOT HENRY, SILLY. HEY, YOU MISSED THE BUS AGAIN! DON'T YOU LIKE RIDING THE BUS? I GOT TO SIT NEXT TO THE WINDOW. THE WINDOW'S DON'T OPEN, 'CAUSE THEY DON'T WANT US KIDS TO FALL OUT, BUT YOU CAN STILL SEE OUT OF THEM, AND I GOT TO LOOK OUT IT THE WHOLE WAY HOME. DID YOU WALK HOME WITH SOMEONE? WAS IT THOSE NEW FRIENDS YOU MET? HEY YOU KNOW WHAT ELSE . . .
ARRGGGH. GO AWAY, KATIE.
MY SISTER HAS NO "OFF" SWITCH.
IT'S SIMPLY AN "ON" SWITCH.
. . . AND AN "I'M-GOING-TO-KEEP ON-TALKING-AND-PESTERING-YOU-'TIL-I-GO-TO-BED-AT-NIGHT" SWITCH.

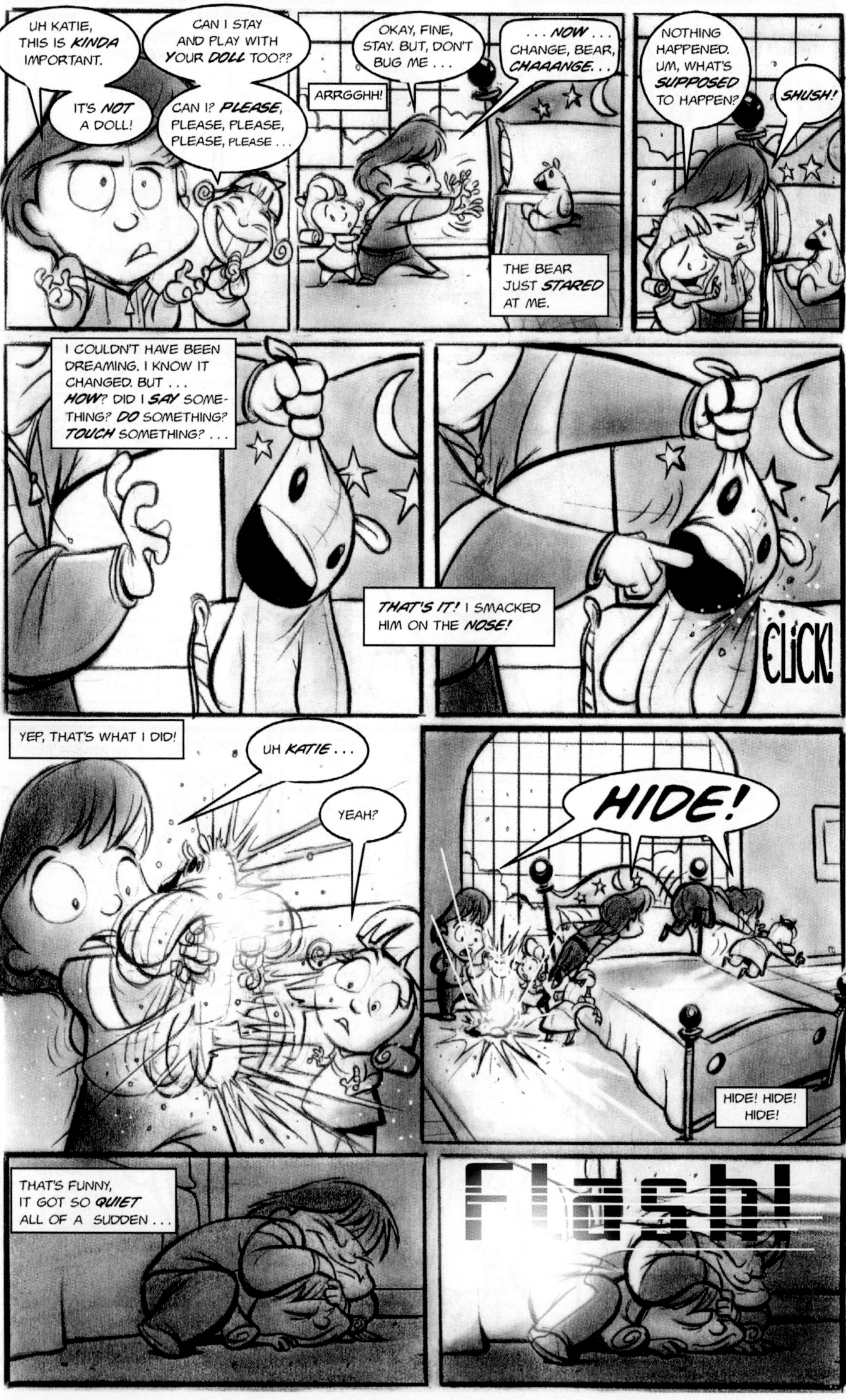
UH KATIE, THIS IS KINDA IMPORTANT.
CAN I STAY AND PLAY WITH YOUR DOLL TOO??
IT'S NOT A DOLL!
CAN I? PLEASE, PLEASE, PLEASE, PLEASE, PLEASE . . .
ARRGGHH!
OKAY, FINE, STAY. BUT, DON'T BUG ME . . .
. . . NOW . . . CHANGE, BEAR, CHAAAANGE. . .
THE BEAR JUST STARED AT ME.
NOTHING HAPPENED. UM, WHAT'S SUPPOSED TO HAPPEN?
SHUSH!
I COULDN'T HAVE BEEN DREAMING. I KNOW IT CHANGED. BUT . . . HOW? DID I SAY SOMETHING? DO SOMETHING? TOUCH SOMETHING? . . .
THAT'S IT! I SMACKED HIM ON THE NOSE!
CLICK!
YEP, THAT'S WHAT I DID!
UH KATIE . . .
YEAH?
HIDE!
HIDE! HIDE! HIDE!
THAT'S FUNNY, IT GOT SO QUIET ALL OF A SUDDEN . . .
Flash!

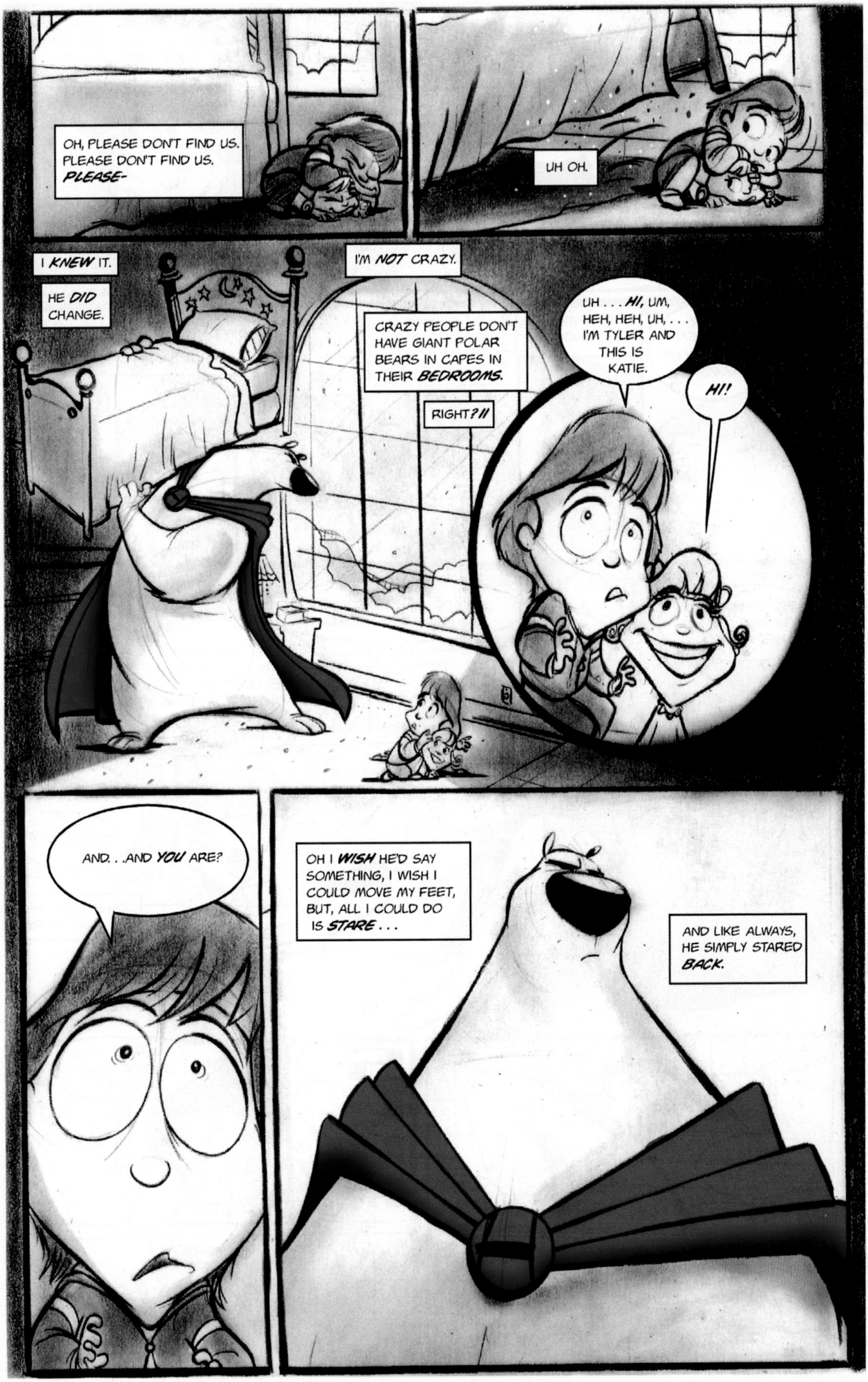
OH, PLEASE DON'T FIND US. PLEASE DON'T FIND US. PLEASE-
UH OH.
I KNEW IT.
HE DID CHANGE.
I'M NOT CRAZY.
CRAZY PEOPLE DON'T HAVE GIANT POLAR BEARS IN CAPES IN THEIR BEDROOMS.
RIGHT?!!
UH . . . HI, UM, HEH, HEH, UH, . . . I'M TYLER AND THIS IS KATIE.
HI!
AND. . .AND YOU ARE?
OH I WISH HE'D SAY SOMETHING, I WISH I COULD MOVE MY FEET, BUT, ALL I COULD DO IS STARE . . .
AND LIKE ALWAYS, HE SIMPLY STARED BACK.

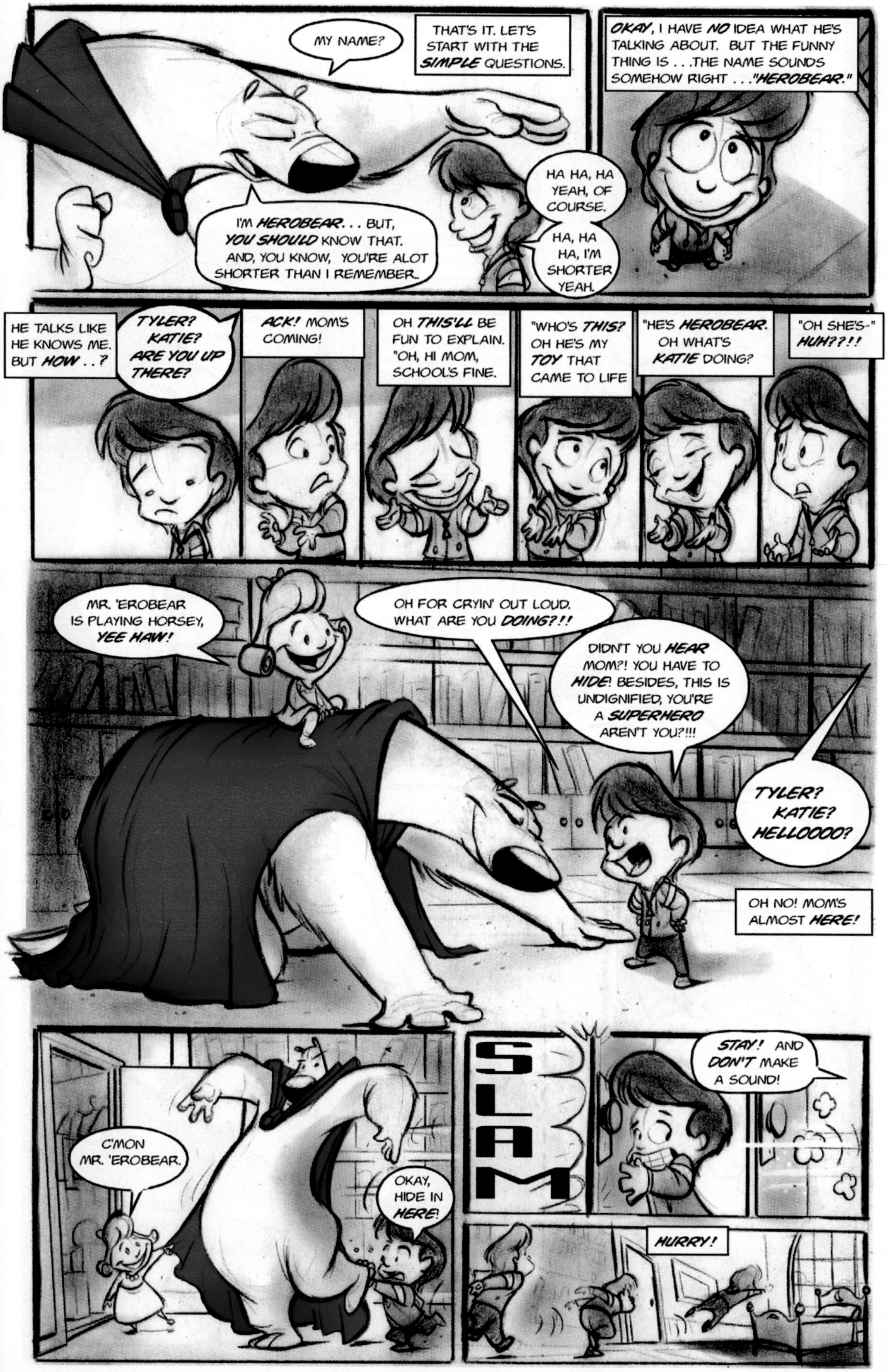
MY NAME?
THAT'S IT. LET'S START WITH THE SIMPLE QUESTIONS.
I'M HEROBEAR... BUT, YOU SHOULD KNOW THAT. AND, YOU KNOW, YOU'RE ALOT SHORTER THAN I REMEMBER.
HA HA, HA YEAH, OF COURSE.
HA, HA HA, I'M SHORTER YEAH.
OKAY, I HAVE NO IDEA WHAT HE'S TALKING ABOUT. BUT THE FUNNY THING IS . . .THE NAME SOUNDS SOMEHOW RIGHT . . ."HEROBEAR."
HE TALKS LIKE HE KNOWS ME. BUT HOW . . ?
TYLER? KATIE? ARE YOU UP THERE?
ACK! MOM'S COMING!
OH THIS'LL BE FUN TO EXPLAIN. "OH, HI MOM, SCHOOL'S FINE.
"WHO'S THIS? OH HE'S MY TOY THAT CAME TO LIFE
"HE'S HEROBEAR. OH WHAT'S KATIE DOING?
"OH SHE'S-" HUH??!!
MR. 'EROBEAR IS PLAYING HORSEY, YEE HAW!
OH FOR CRYIN' OUT LOUD. WHAT ARE YOU DOING?!!
DIDN'T YOU HEAR MOM?! YOU HAVE TO HIDE! BESIDES, THIS IS UNDIGNIFIED, YOU'RE A SUPERHERO AREN'T YOU?!!!
TYLER? KATIE? HELLOOOO?
OH NO! MOM'S ALMOST HERE!
C'MON MR. 'EROBEAR.
OKAY, HIDE IN HERE!
SLAM
STAY! AND DON'T MAKE A SOUND!
HURRY!

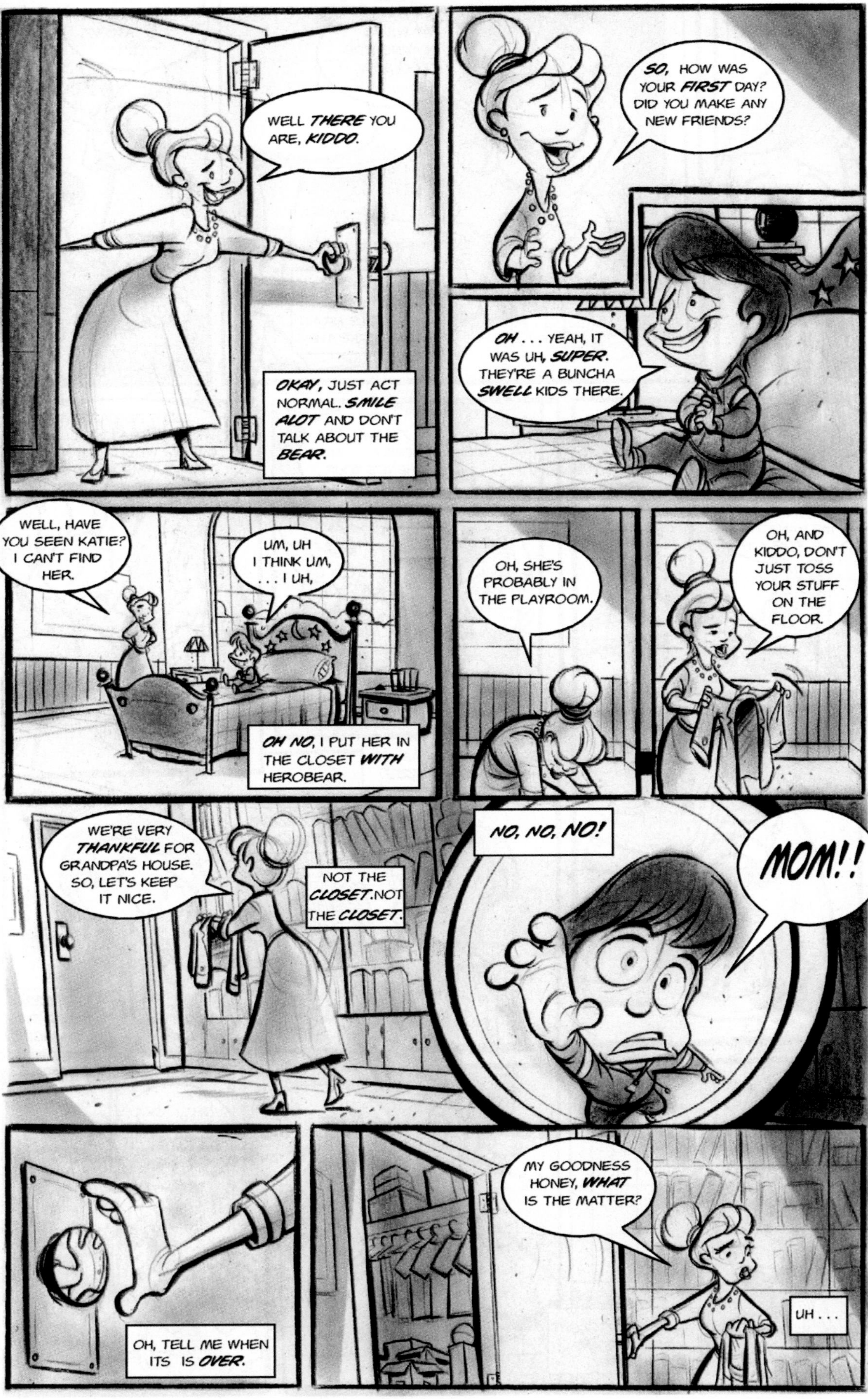
WELL THERE YOU ARE, KIDDO.
OKAY, JUST ACT NORMAL. SMILE ALOT AND DON'T TALK ABOUT THE BEAR.
SO, HOW WAS YOUR FIRST DAY? DID YOU MAKE ANY NEW FRIENDS?
OH . . . YEAH, IT WAS UH, SUPER. THEY'RE A BUNCHA SWELL KIDS THERE.
WELL, HAVE YOU SEEN KATIE? I CAN'T FIND HER.
UM, UH I THINK UM, . . . I UH,
OH NO, I PUT HER IN THE CLOSET WITH HEROBEAR.
OH, SHE'S PROBABLY IN THE PLAYROOM.
OH, AND KIDDO, DON'T JUST TOSS YOUR STUFF ON THE FLOOR.
WE'RE VERY THANKFUL FOR GRANDPA'S HOUSE. SO, LET'S KEEP IT NICE.
NOT THE CLOSET. NOT THE CLOSET.
NO, NO, NO!
MOM!!
OH, TELL ME WHEN ITS IS OVER.
MY GOODNESS HONEY, WHAT IS THE MATTER?
UH . . .

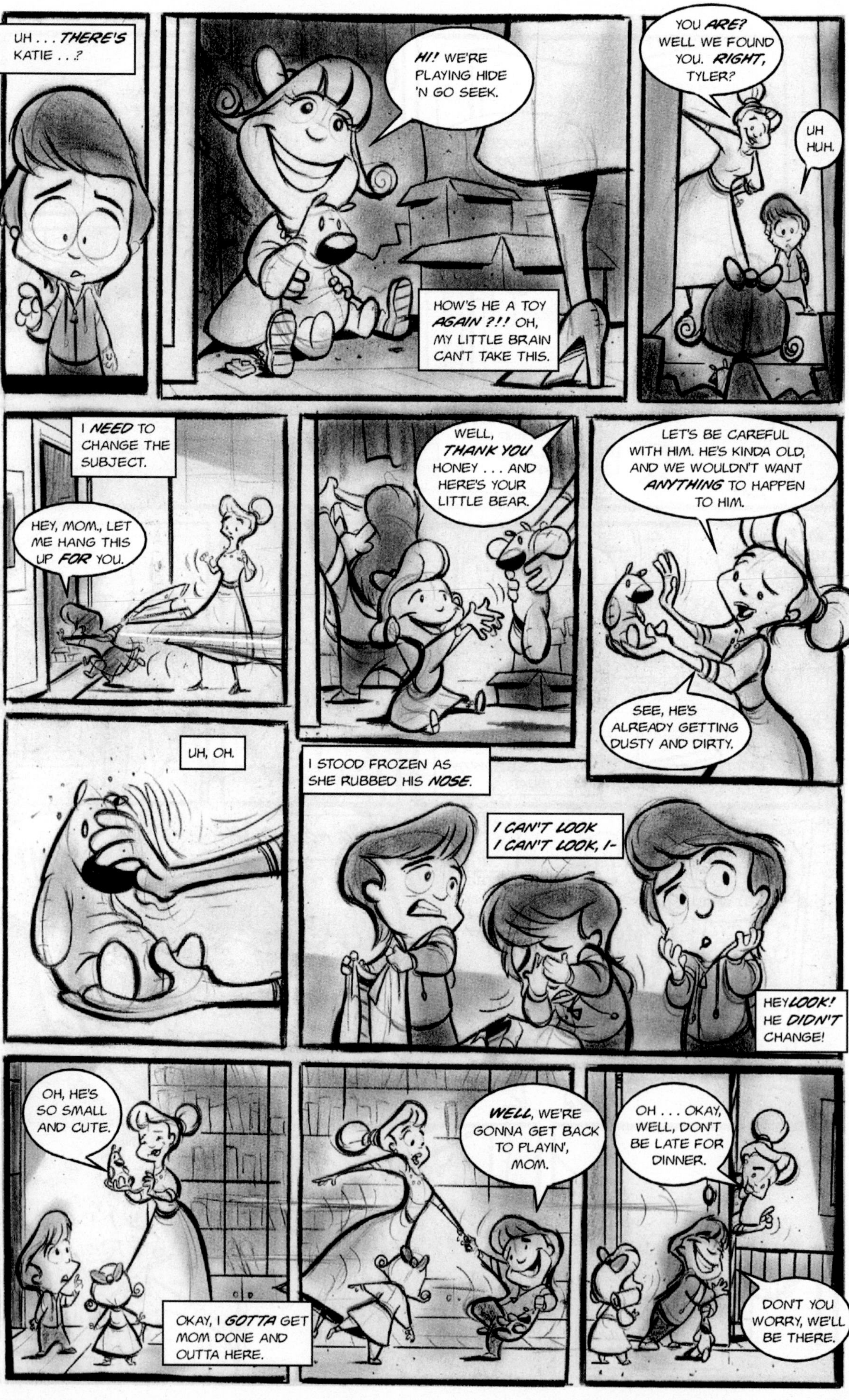
UH . . . THERE'S KATIE . . ?
HI! WE'RE PLAYING HIDE 'N GO SEEK.
HOW'S HE A TOY AGAIN ?!! OH, MY LITTLE BRAIN CAN'T TAKE THIS.
YOU ARE? WELL WE FOUND YOU. RIGHT, TYLER?
UH HUH.
I NEED TO CHANGE THE SUBJECT.
HEY, MOM., LET ME HANG THIS UP FOR YOU.
WELL, THANK YOU HONEY . . . AND HERE'S YOUR LITTLE BEAR.
LET'S BE CAREFUL WITH HIM. HE'S KINDA OLD, AND WE WOULDN'T WANT ANYTHING TO HAPPEN TO HIM.
SEE, HE'S ALREADY GETTING DUSTY AND DIRTY.
UH, OH.
I STOOD FROZEN AS SHE RUBBED HIS NOSE.
I CAN'T LOOK I CAN'T LOOK, I-
HEY LOOK! HE DIDN'T CHANGE!
OH, HE'S SO SMALL AND CUTE.
OKAY, I GOTTA GET MOM DONE AND OUTTA HERE.
WELL, WE'RE GONNA GET BACK TO PLAYIN', MOM.
OH . . . OKAY, WELL, DON'T BE LATE FOR DINNER.
DON'T YOU WORRY, WE'LL BE THERE.

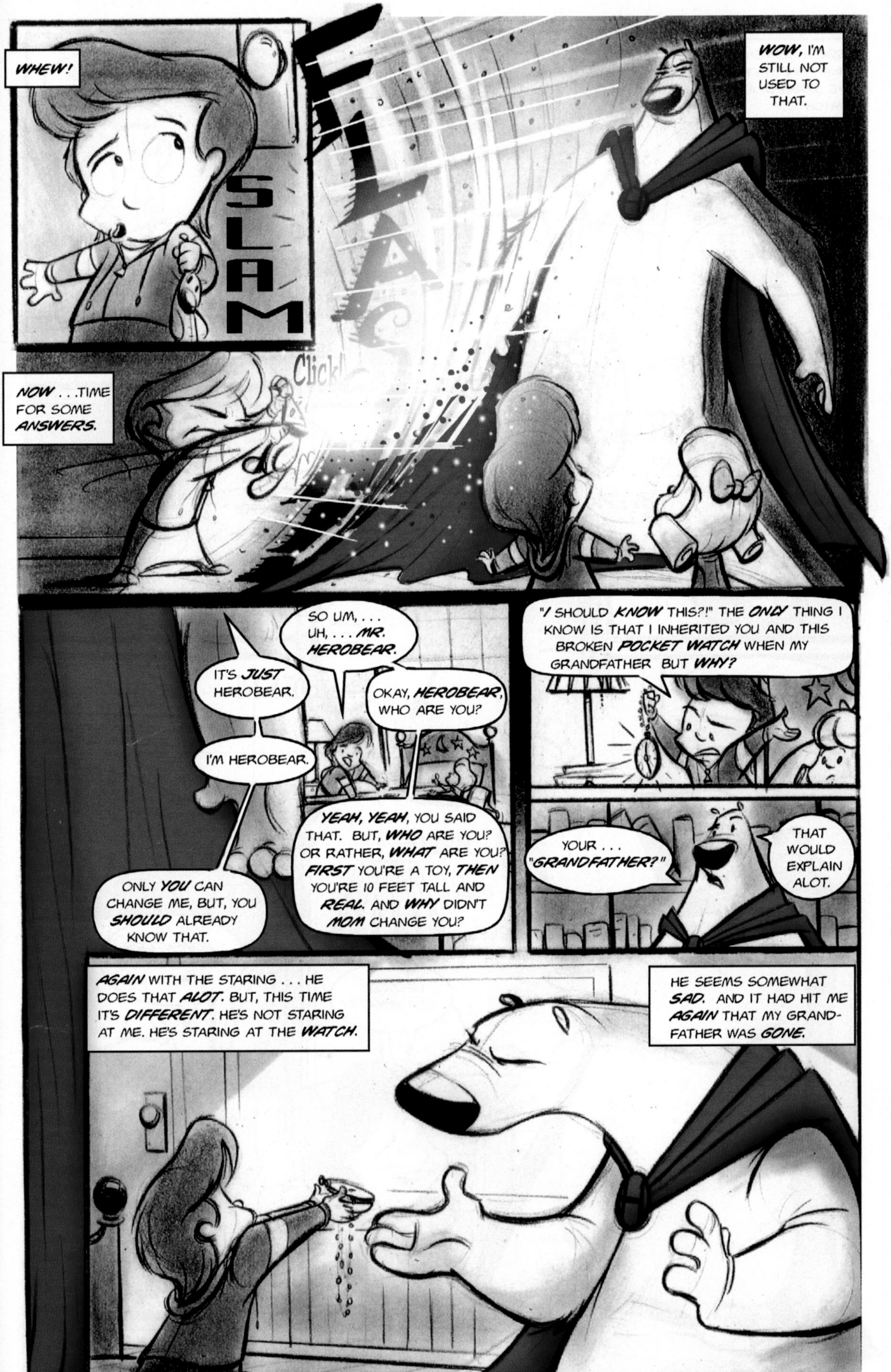
WHEW!
SLAM
WOW, I'M STILL NOT USED TO THAT.
NOW . . .TIME FOR SOME ANSWERS.
Click!
SO UM, . . . UH, . . . MR. HEROBEAR.
IT'S JUST HEROBEAR.
OKAY, HEROBEAR, WHO ARE YOU?
I'M HEROBEAR.
YEAH, YEAH, YOU SAID THAT. BUT, WHO ARE YOU? OR RATHER, WHAT ARE YOU? FIRST YOU'RE A TOY, THEN YOU'RE 10 FEET TALL AND REAL. AND WHY DIDN'T MOM CHANGE YOU?
ONLY YOU CAN CHANGE ME, BUT, YOU SHOULD ALREADY KNOW THAT.
"I SHOULD KNOW THIS?!" THE ONLY THING I KNOW IS THAT I INHERITED YOU AND THIS BROKEN POCKET WATCH WHEN MY GRANDFATHER BUT WHY?
YOUR . . . "GRANDFATHER?"
THAT WOULD EXPLAIN ALOT.
AGAIN WITH THE STARING . . . HE DOES THAT ALOT. BUT, THIS TIME IT'S DIFFERENT. HE'S NOT STARING AT ME. HE'S STARING AT THE WATCH.
HE SEEMS SOMEWHAT SAD. AND IT HAD HIT ME AGAIN THAT MY GRAND-FATHER WAS GONE.

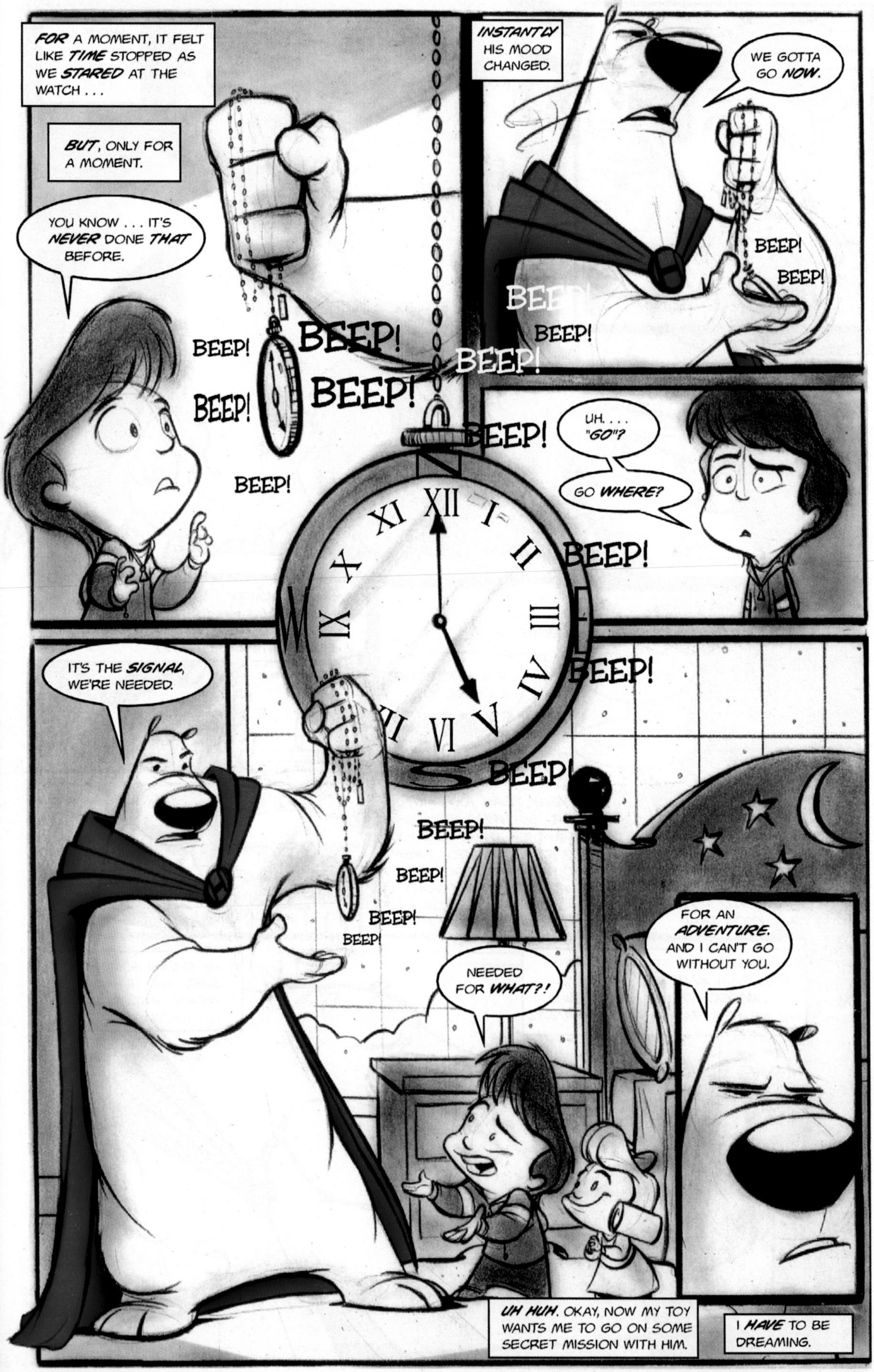
FOR A MOMENT, IT FELT LIKE TIME STOPPED AS WE STARED AT THE WATCH . . .
BUT, ONLY FOR A MOMENT.
YOU KNOW . . . IT'S NEVER DONE THAT BEFORE.
BEEP!
BEEP!
BEEP!
BEEP!
BEEP!
INSTANTLY HIS MOOD CHANGED.
WE GOTTA GO NOW.
BEEP!
BEEP!
BEEP!
BEEP!
BEEP!
UH. . . . "GO"?
GO WHERE?
BEEP!
BEEP!
BEEP!
BEEP!
IT'S THE SIGNAL, WE'RE NEEDED.
BEEP!
BEEP!
BEEP!
BEEP!
NEEDED FOR WHAT?!
FOR AN ADVENTURE. AND I CAN'T GO WITHOUT YOU.
UH HUH. OKAY, NOW MY TOY WANTS ME TO GO ON SOME SECRET MISSION WITH HIM.
I HAVE TO BE DREAMING.

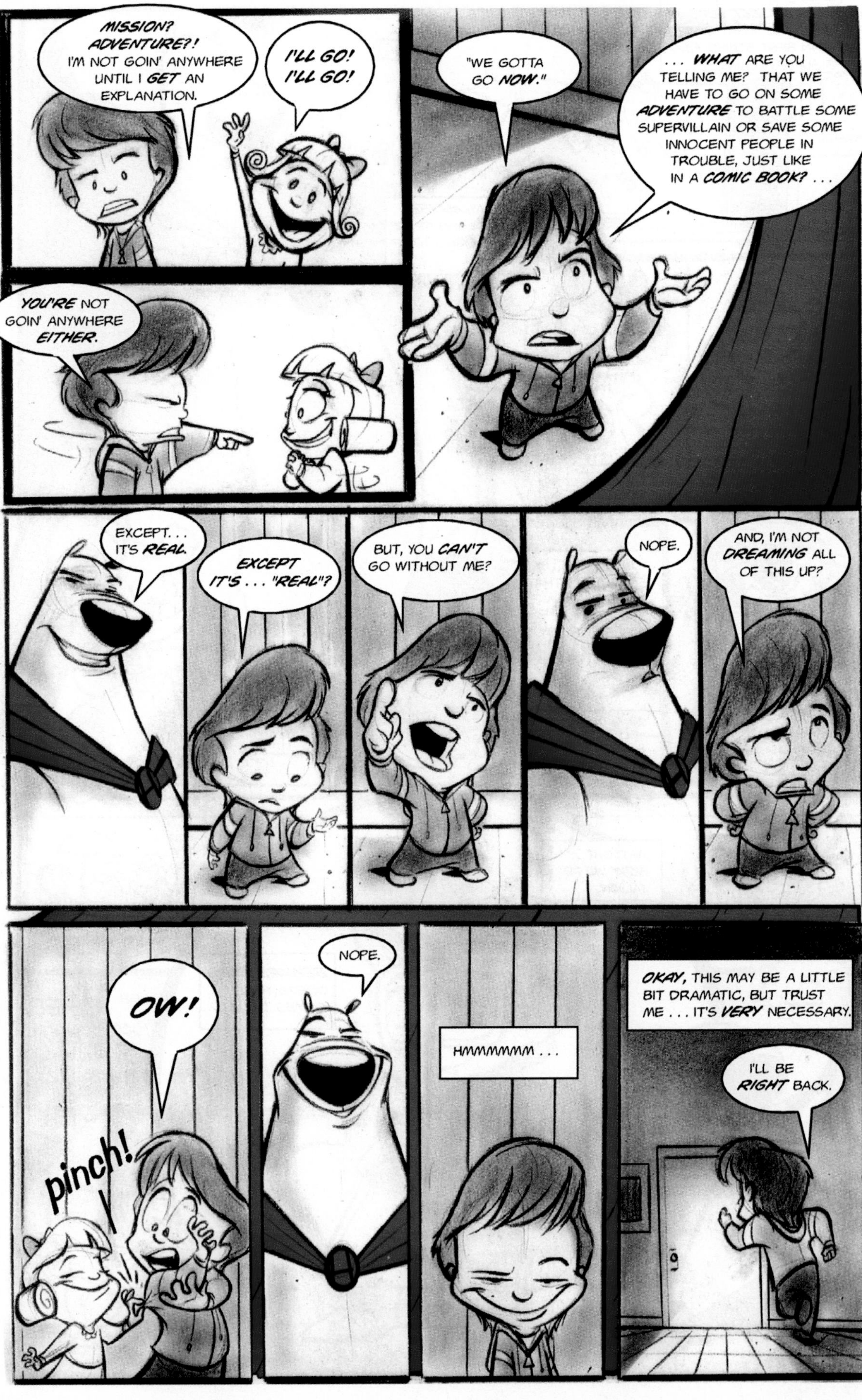

MISSION? ADVENTURE?! I'M NOT GOIN' ANYWHERE UNTIL I GET AN EXPLANATION.
I'LL GO! I'LL GO!
YOU'RE NOT GOIN' ANYWHERE EITHER.
"WE GOTTA GO NOW."
. . . WHAT ARE YOU TELLING ME? THAT WE HAVE TO GO ON SOME ADVENTURE TO BATTLE SOME SUPERVILLAIN OR SAVE SOME INNOCENT PEOPLE IN TROUBLE, JUST LIKE IN A COMIC BOOK? . . .
EXCEPT. . . IT'S REAL.
EXCEPT IT'S . . . "REAL"?
BUT, YOU CAN'T GO WITHOUT ME?
NOPE.
AND, I'M NOT DREAMING ALL OF THIS UP?
OW!
pinch!
NOPE.
HMMMMMM . . .
OKAY, THIS MAY BE A LITTLE BIT DRAMATIC, BUT TRUST ME . . . IT'S VERY NECESSARY.
I'LL BE RIGHT BACK.

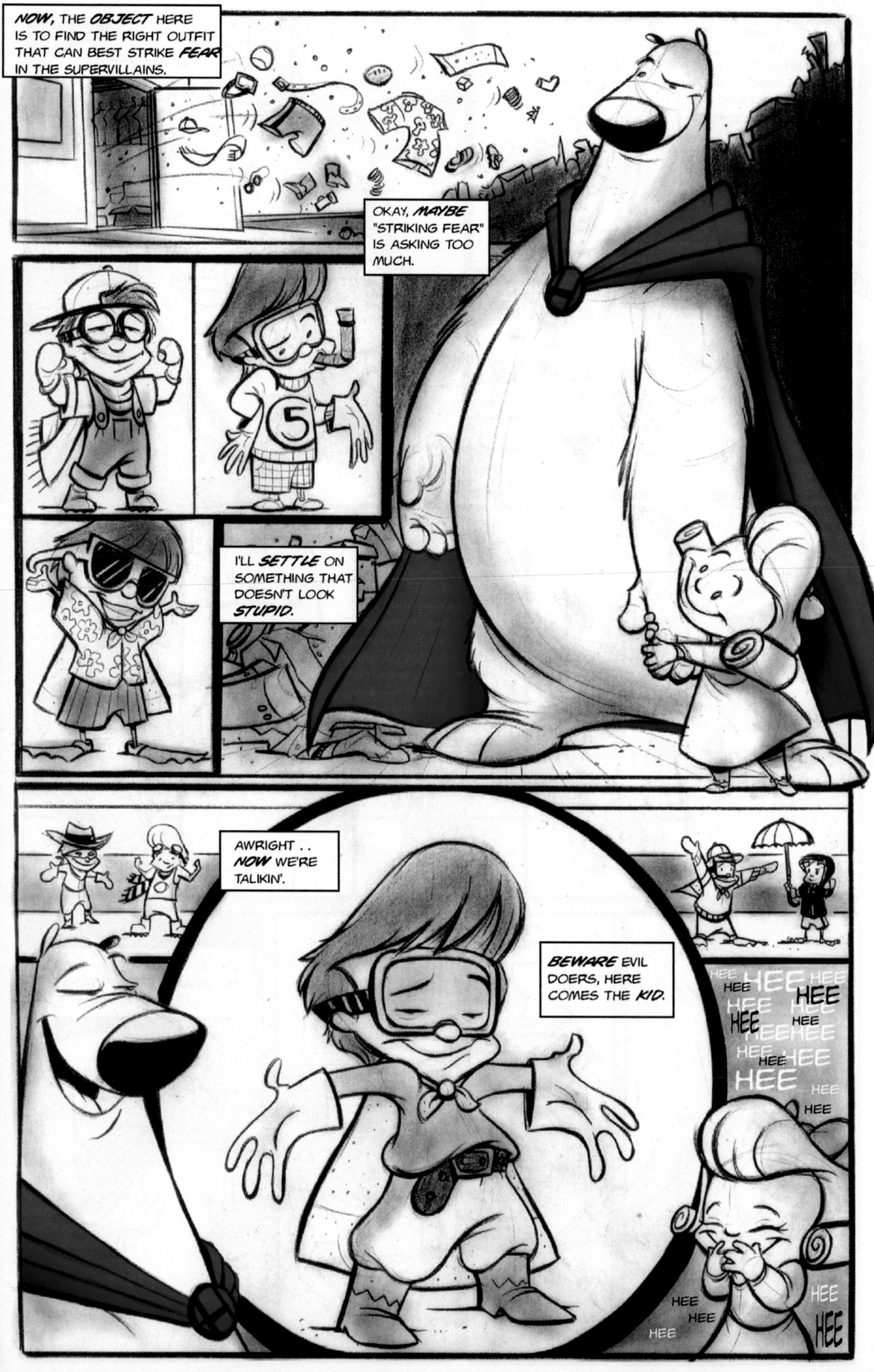

NOW, THE OBJECT HERE IS TO FIND THE RIGHT OUTFIT THAT CAN BEST STRIKE FEAR IN THE SUPERVILLAINS.
OKAY, MAYBE "STRIKING FEAR" IS ASKING TOO MUCH.
I'LL SETTLE ON SOMETHING THAT DOESN'T LOOK STUPID.
AWRIGHT . . NOW WE'RE TALIKIN'.
BEWARE EVIL DOERS, HERE COMES THE KID.
HEE HEE HEE HEE HEE HEE HEE HEE HEE HEE HEE HEE HEE HEE HEE HEE
HEE HEE HEE HEE HEE

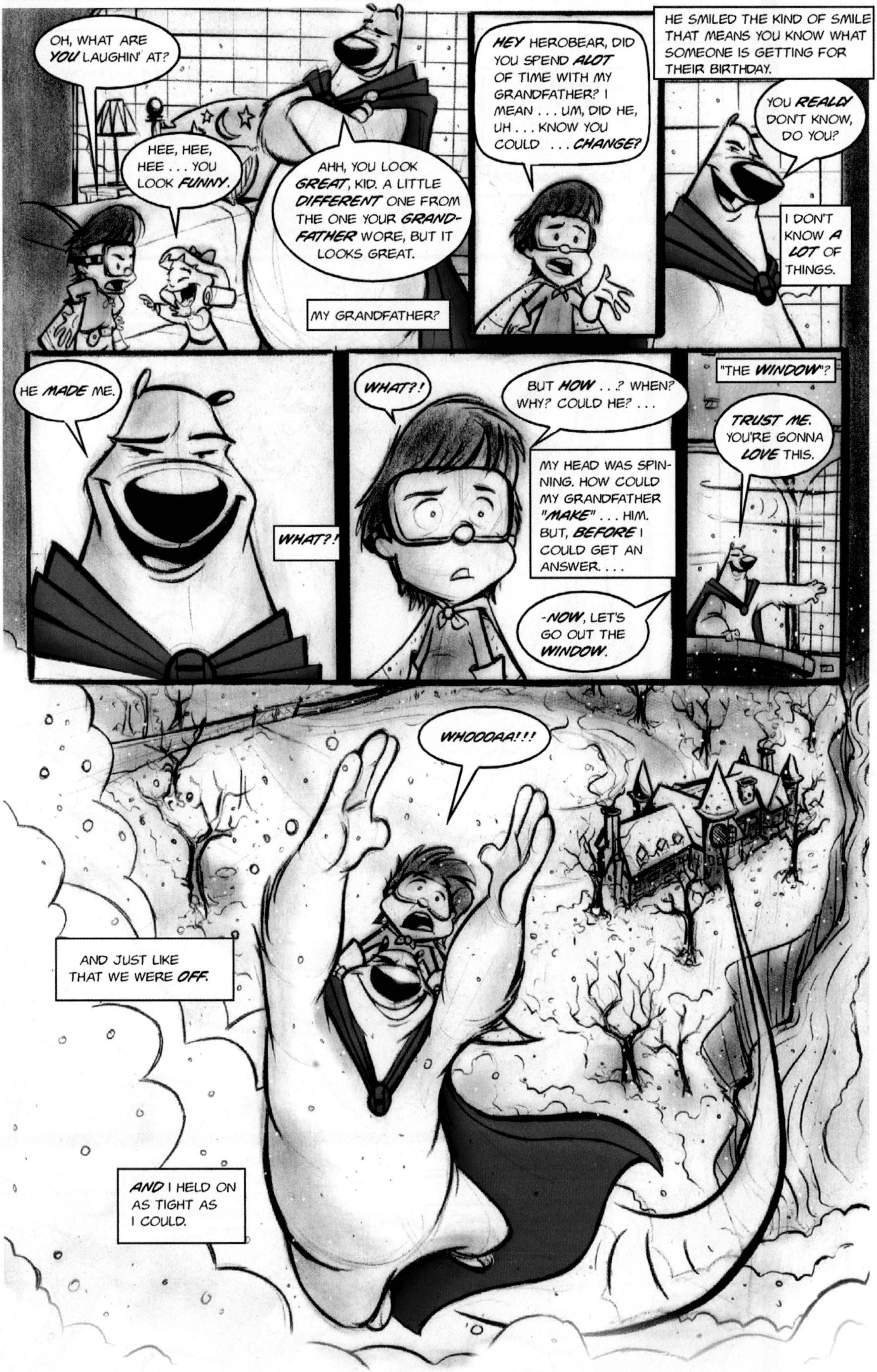
OH, WHAT ARE YOU LAUGHIN' AT?
HEE, HEE, HEE . . . YOU LOOK FUNNY.
AHH, YOU LOOK GREAT, KID. A LITTLE DIFFERENT ONE FROM THE ONE YOUR GRANDFATHER WORE, BUT IT LOOKS GREAT.
MY GRANDFATHER?
HEY HEROBEAR, DID YOU SPEND ALOT OF TIME WITH MY GRANDFATHER? I MEAN . . . UM, DID HE, UH . . . KNOW YOU COULD . . . CHANGE?
HE SMILED THE KIND OF SMILE THAT MEANS YOU KNOW WHAT SOMEONE IS GETTING FOR THEIR BIRTHDAY.
YOU REALLY DON'T KNOW, DO YOU?
I DON'T KNOW A LOT OF THINGS.
HE MADE ME.
WHAT?!
WHAT?!
BUT HOW . . .? WHEN? WHY? COULD HE? . . .
MY HEAD WAS SPINNING. HOW COULD MY GRANDFATHER "MAKE" . . . HIM. BUT, BEFORE I COULD GET AN ANSWER. . . .
-NOW, LET'S GO OUT THE WINDOW.
"THE WINDOW"?
TRUST ME. YOU'RE GONNA LOVE THIS.
WHOOOOAA!!!
AND JUST LIKE THAT WE WERE OFF.
AND I HELD ON AS TIGHT AS I COULD.

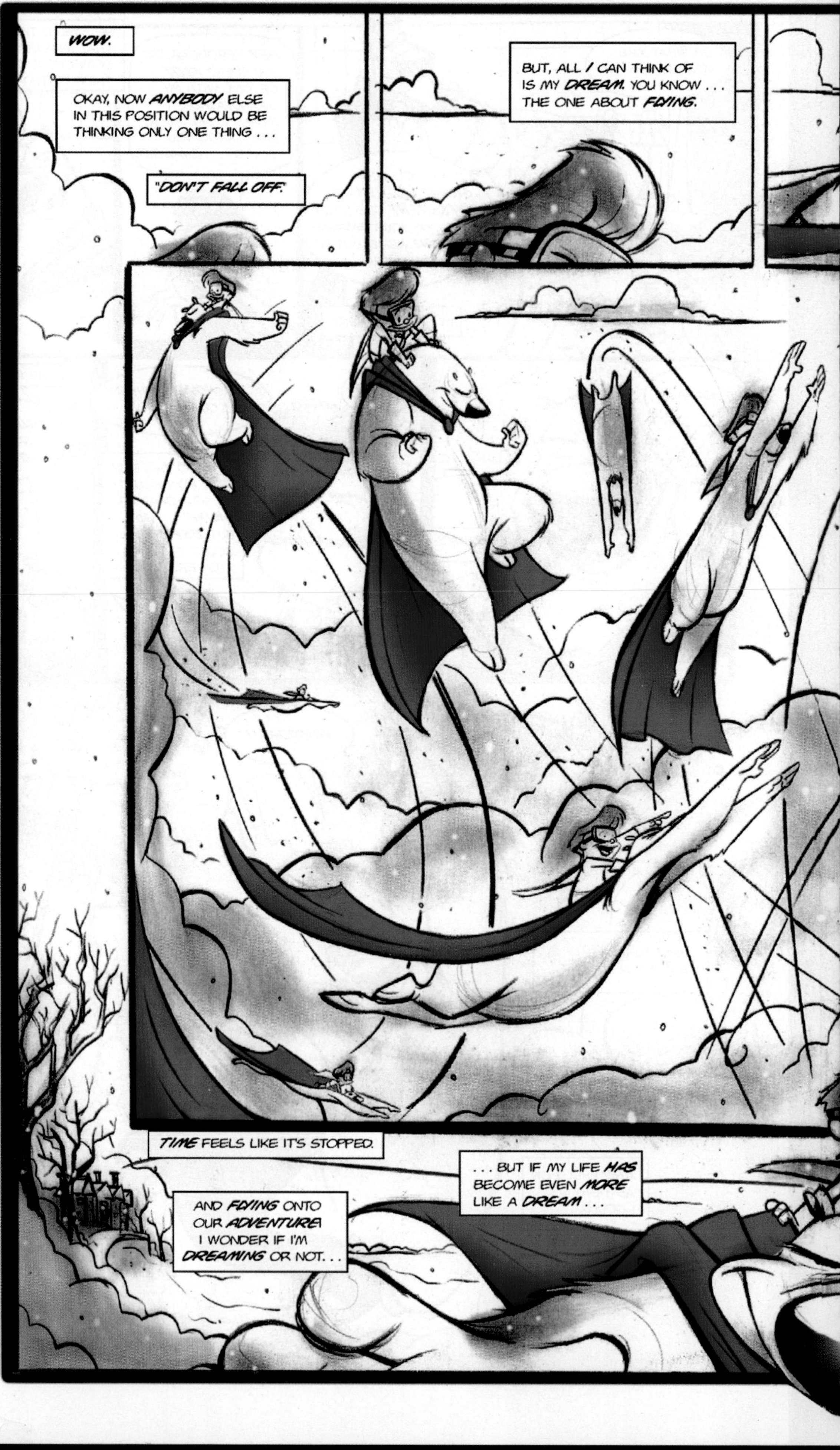
WOW.
OKAY, NOW ANYBODY ELSE IN THIS POSITION WOULD BE THINKING ONLY ONE THING . . .
"DON'T FALL OFF."
BUT, ALL I CAN THINK OF IS MY DREAM. YOU KNOW . . . THE ONE ABOUT FLYING.
TIME FEELS LIKE IT'S STOPPED.
AND FLYING ONTO OUR ADVENTURE! I WONDER IF I'M DREAMING OR NOT. . .
. . . BUT IF MY LIFE HAS BECOME EVEN MORE LIKE A DREAM . . .

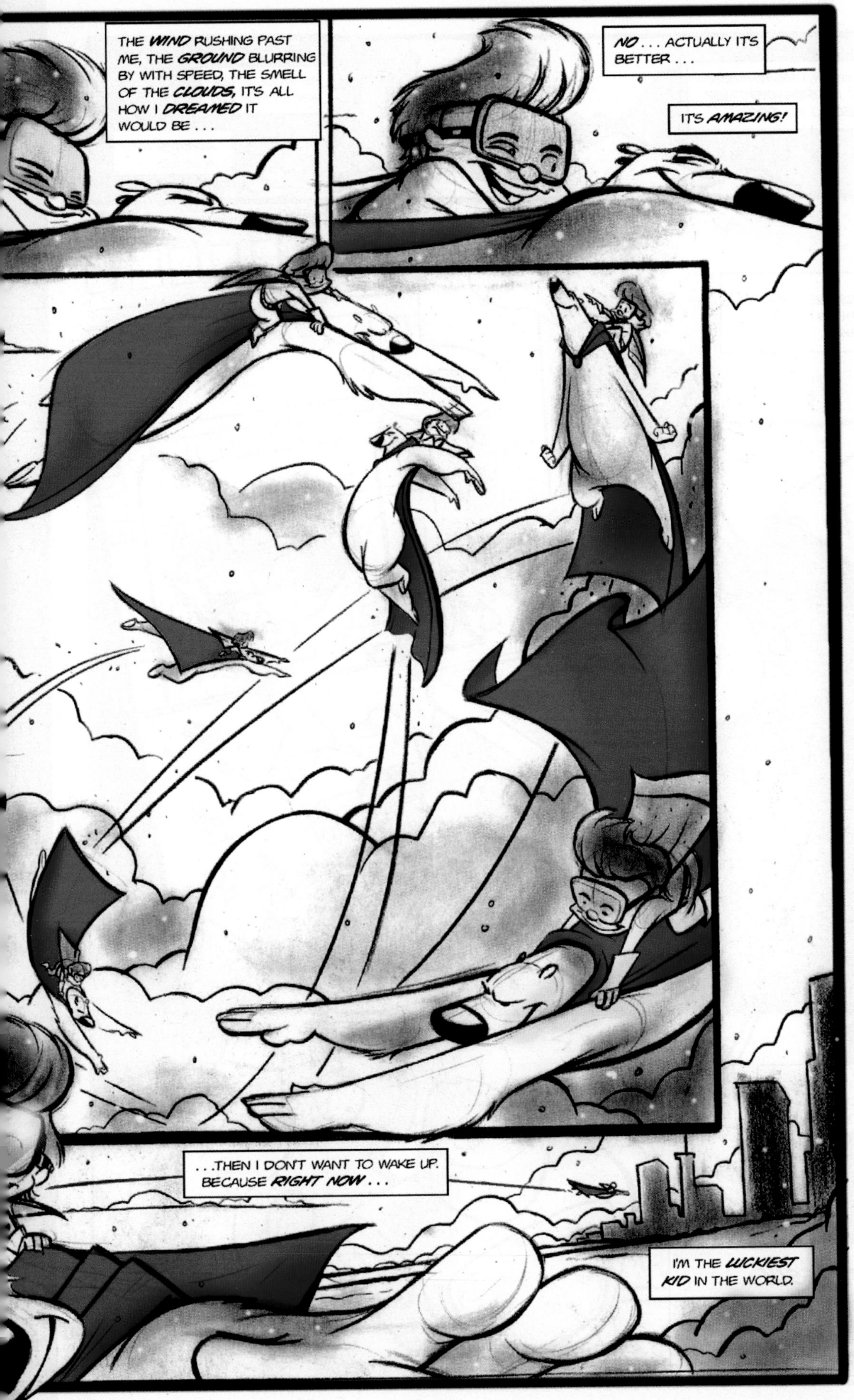
THE WIND RUSHING PAST ME, THE GROUND BLURRING BY WITH SPEED, THE SMELL OF THE CLOUDS, IT'S ALL HOW I DREAMED IT WOULD BE . . .
NO . . . ACTUALLY IT'S BETTER . . .
IT'S AMAZING!
. . .THEN I DON'T WANT TO WAKE UP. BECAUSE RIGHT NOW . . .
I'M THE LUCKIEST KID IN THE WORLD.

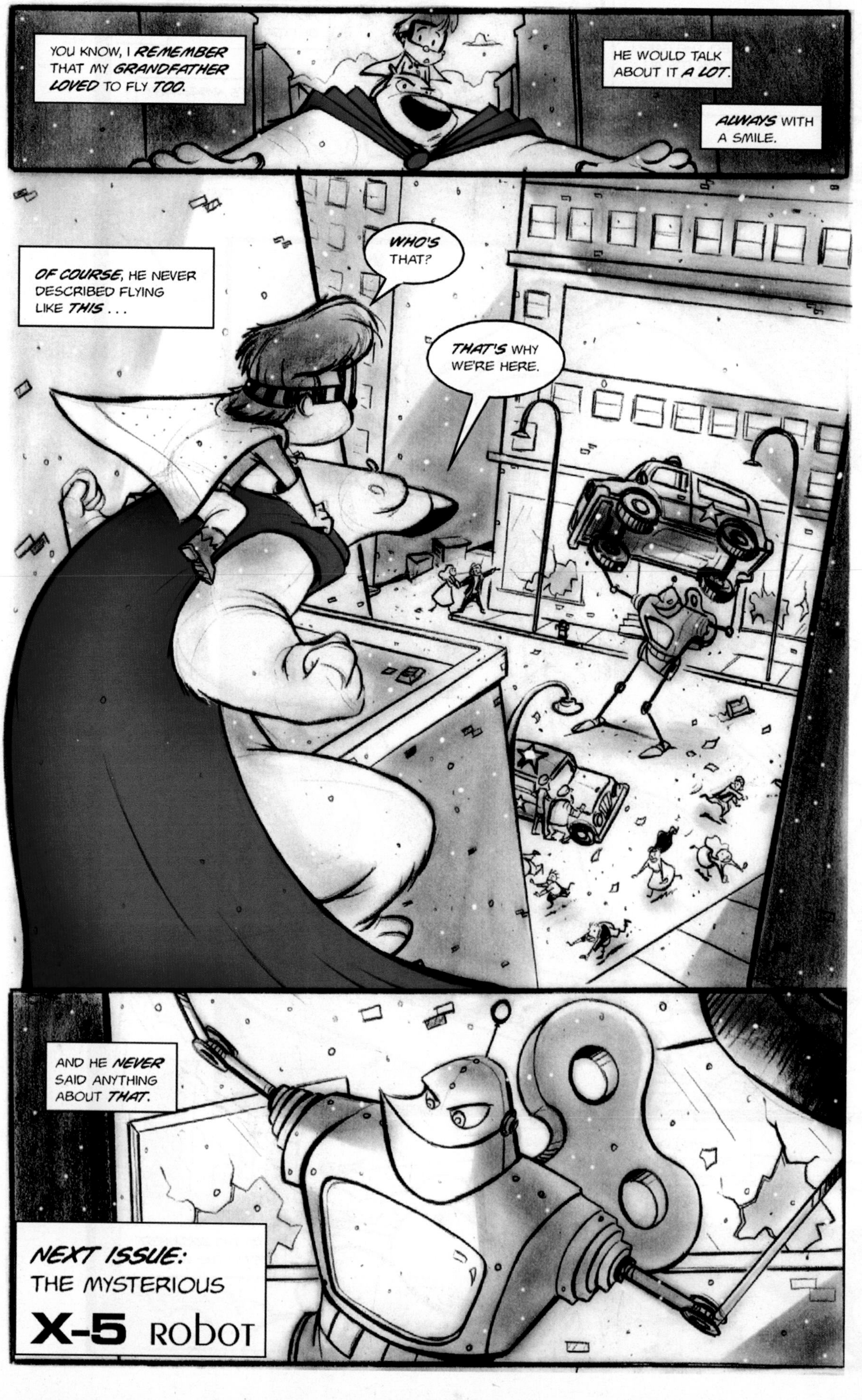
YOU KNOW, I REMEMBER THAT MY GRANDFATHER LOVED TO FLY TOO.
HE WOULD TALK ABOUT IT A LOT.
ALWAYS WITH A SMILE.
OF COURSE, HE NEVER DESCRIBED FLYING LIKE THIS . . .
WHO'S THAT?
THAT'S WHY WE'RE HERE.
AND HE NEVER SAID ANYTHING ABOUT THAT.
NEXT ISSUE: THE MYSTERIOUS X-5 ROBOT

obear and the kid is that perfect combination of great art and
story that fans are looking for. An absolute must!"
RARA(OWNER OF ATLANTIS FANTASYWORLD IN SANTA CRUZ, CA.)

"HeroBear and the kid is is one of those truly rare finds the
you of that exhilarating time in your life when you were a ch
your imagination was bigger than the whole world. A brillian
combination of kinetic animation-like artwork mixed with a k
storytelling. A real gem."
J.SCOTT CAMPBELL (aRTIST AND CREATOR OF DANGER GIRL)

nkel's strengths as an artist are equally matched by his taler
writer. Herobear is easy enough to follow for kids, smart eno
the mature comic fan, yet action-packed enough for the
ditionalists- all due to Kunkel's greatest strength ... characteriz
SEIJAS (WIZARD MAGAZINE, STAFF WRITER)

"Mike Kunkel's Herobear and the kid is one of tho
that you can't help but enjoy ... it's an engaging ble
comics you read as a kid AND the adventures tha
dream up after. Wonderfully drawn with a fun stor
no surprise that this is a book that everyone is talki
MIKE BRENNAN(CREATOR OF ELECTRIC GIRL)

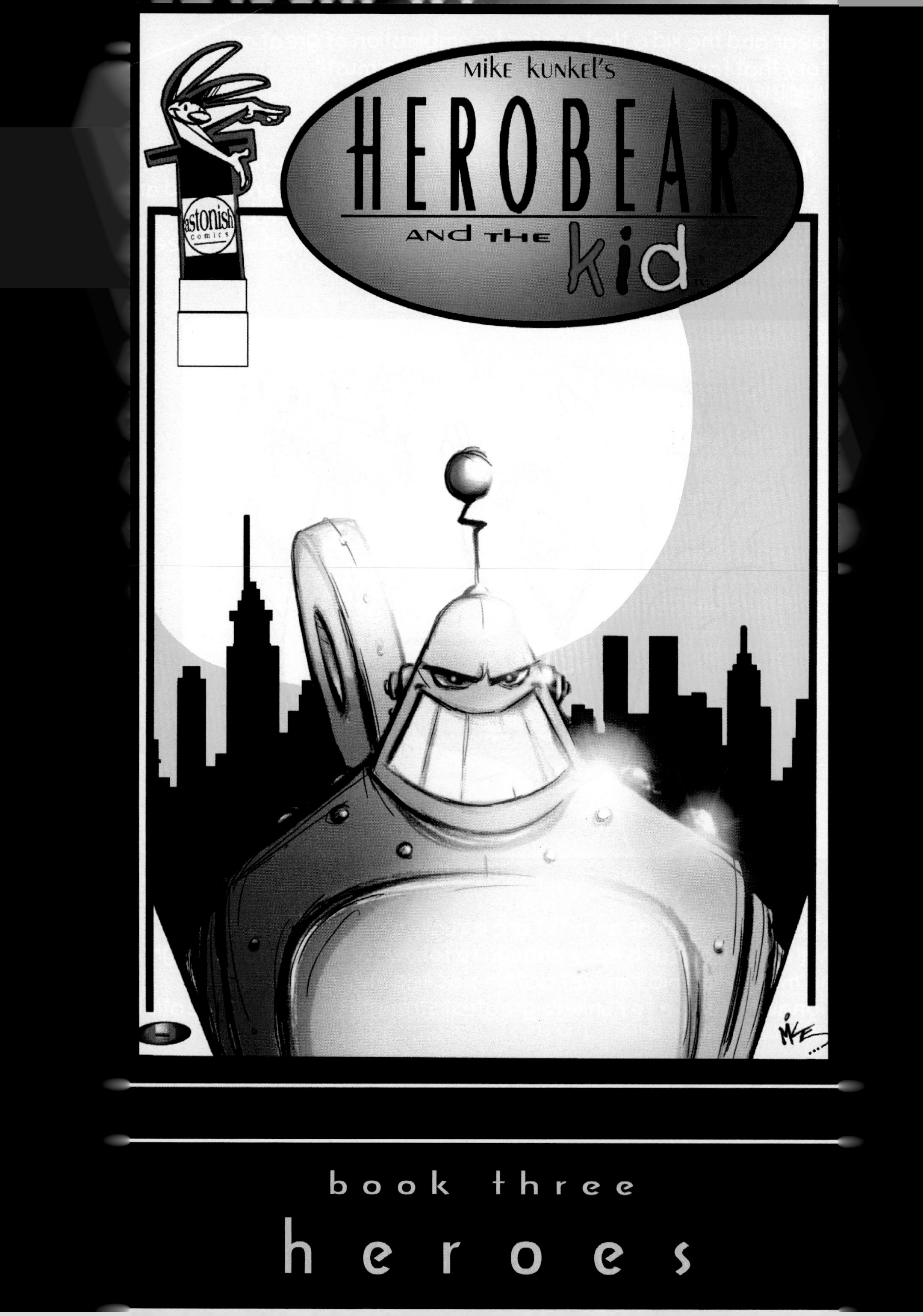
MIKE KUNKEL'S
HEROBEAR
AND THE kid
astonish comics

book three

heroes

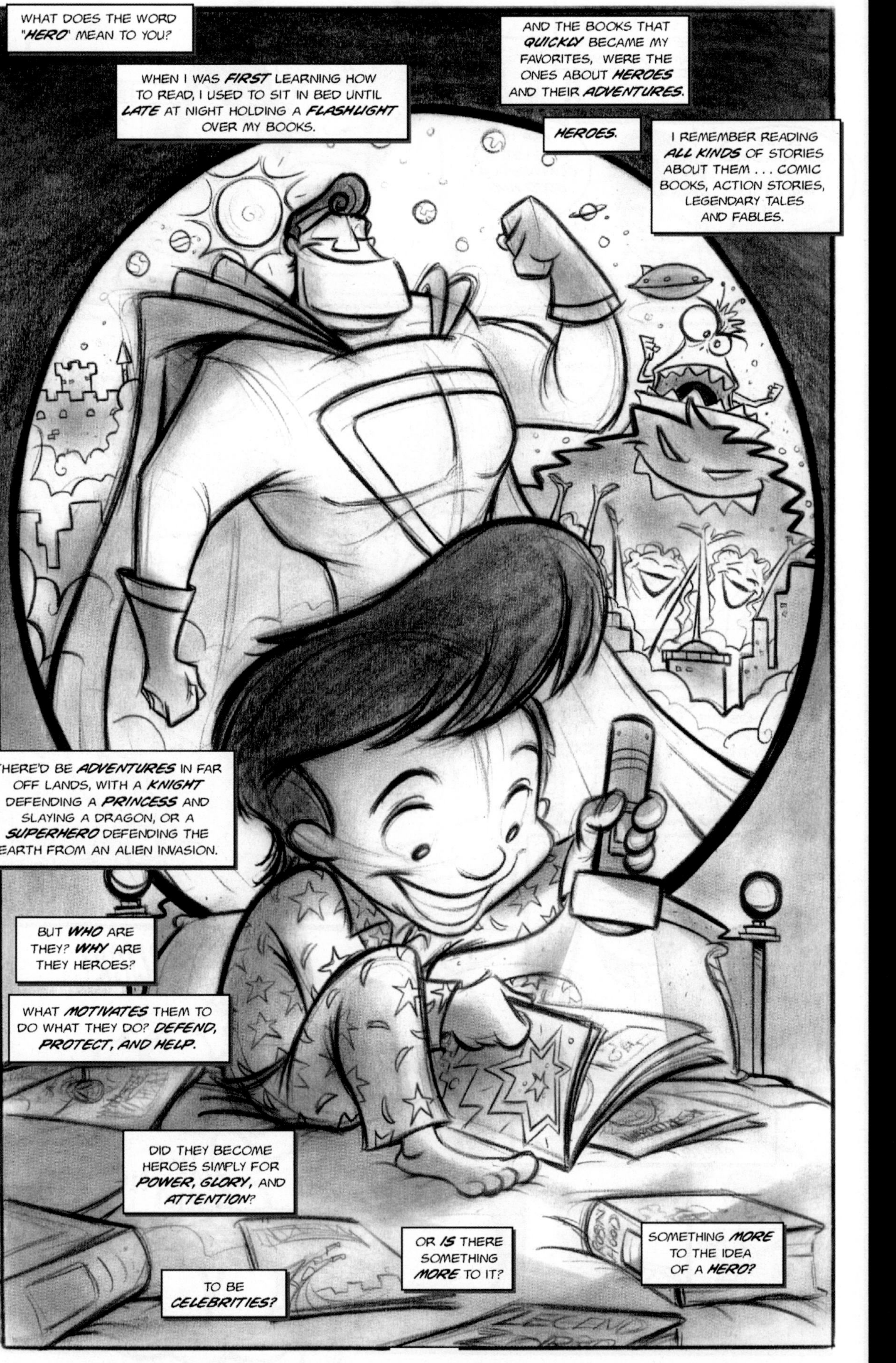
WHAT DOES THE WORD "HERO" MEAN TO YOU?
WHEN I WAS FIRST LEARNING HOW TO READ, I USED TO SIT IN BED UNTIL LATE AT NIGHT HOLDING A FLASHLIGHT OVER MY BOOKS.
AND THE BOOKS THAT QUICKLY BECAME MY FAVORITES, WERE THE ONES ABOUT HEROES AND THEIR ADVENTURES.
HEROES.
I REMEMBER READING ALL KINDS OF STORIES ABOUT THEM . . . COMIC BOOKS, ACTION STORIES, LEGENDARY TALES AND FABLES.
THERE'D BE ADVENTURES IN FAR OFF LANDS, WITH A KNIGHT DEFENDING A PRINCESS AND SLAYING A DRAGON, OR A SUPERHERO DEFENDING THE EARTH FROM AN ALIEN INVASION.
BUT WHO ARE THEY? WHY ARE THEY HEROES?
WHAT MOTIVATES THEM TO DO WHAT THEY DO? DEFEND, PROTECT, AND HELP.
DID THEY BECOME HEROES SIMPLY FOR POWER, GLORY, AND ATTENTION?
TO BE CELEBRITIES?
OR IS THERE SOMETHING MORE TO IT?
SOMETHING MORE TO THE IDEA OF A HERO?

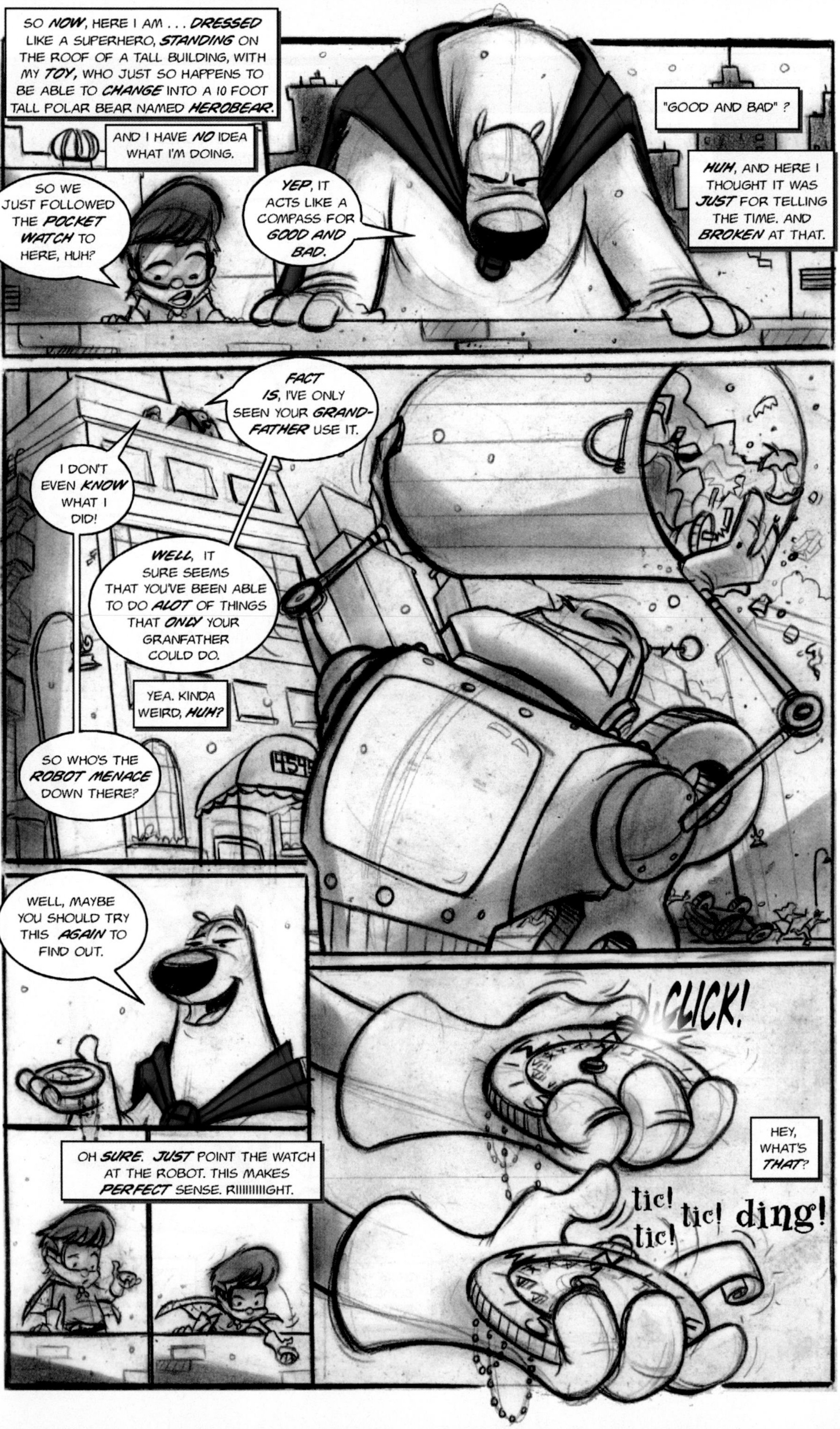

SO NOW, HERE I AM . . . DRESSED LIKE A SUPERHERO, STANDING ON THE ROOF OF A TALL BUILDING, WITH MY TOY, WHO JUST SO HAPPENS TO BE ABLE TO CHANGE INTO A 10 FOOT TALL POLAR BEAR NAMED HEROBEAR.
AND I HAVE NO IDEA WHAT I'M DOING.
SO WE JUST FOLLOWED THE POCKET WATCH TO HERE, HUH?
YEP, IT ACTS LIKE A COMPASS FOR GOOD AND BAD.
"GOOD AND BAD" ?
HUH, AND HERE I THOUGHT IT WAS JUST FOR TELLING THE TIME. AND BROKEN AT THAT.
FACT IS, I'VE ONLY SEEN YOUR GRAND-FATHER USE IT.
I DON'T EVEN KNOW WHAT I DID!
WELL, IT SURE SEEMS THAT YOU'VE BEEN ABLE TO DO ALOT OF THINGS THAT ONLY YOUR GRANFATHER COULD DO.
YEA. KINDA WEIRD, HUH?
SO WHO'S THE ROBOT MENACE DOWN THERE?
WELL, MAYBE YOU SHOULD TRY THIS AGAIN TO FIND OUT.
CLICK!
OH SURE. JUST POINT THE WATCH AT THE ROBOT. THIS MAKES PERFECT SENSE. RIIIIIIIIGHT.
HEY, WHAT'S THAT?
tic! tic! tic! ding!

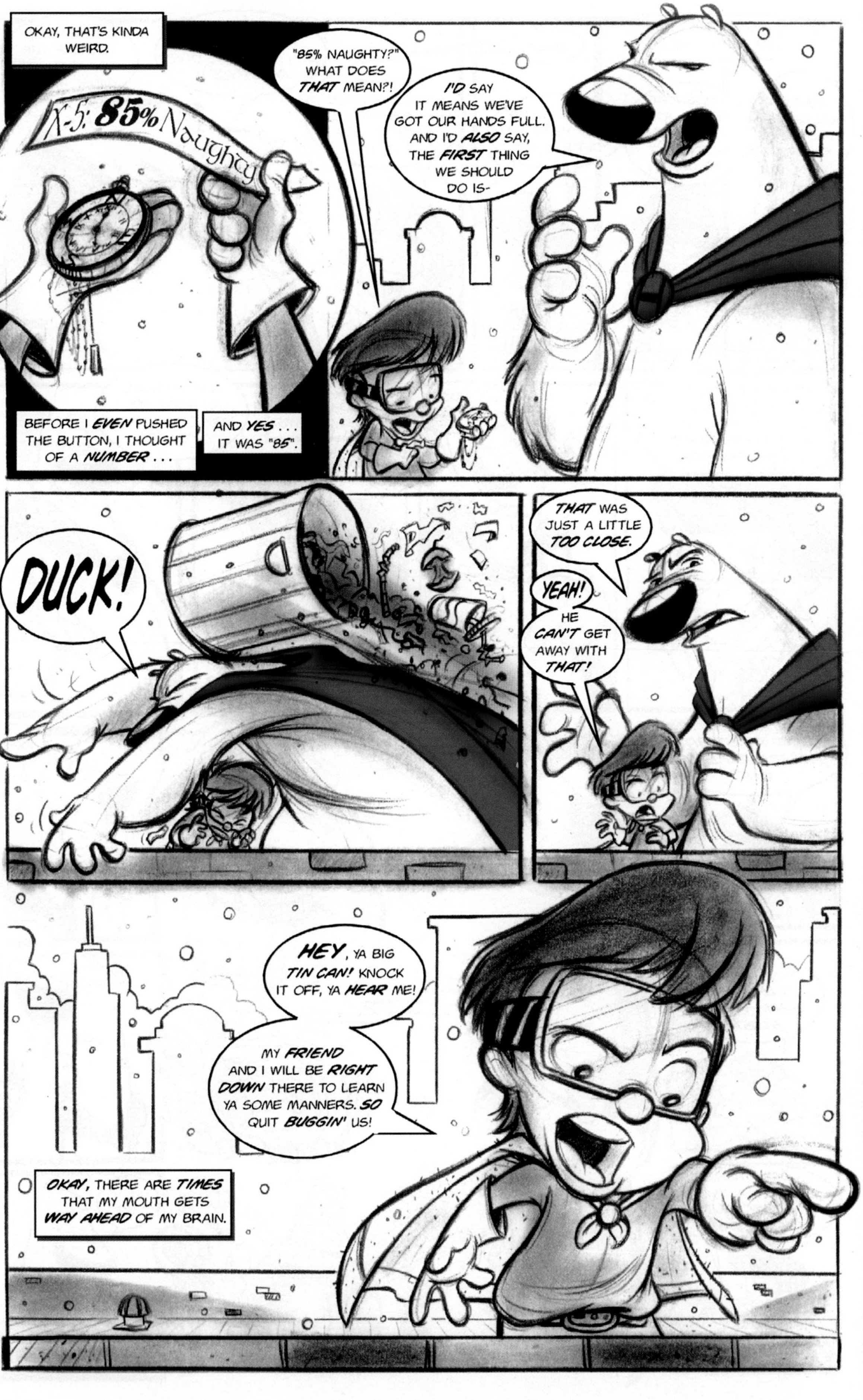
OKAY, THAT'S KINDA WEIRD.
X-5: 85% Naughty
BEFORE I EVEN PUSHED THE BUTTON, I THOUGHT OF A NUMBER . . .
AND YES . . . IT WAS "85".
"85% NAUGHTY?" WHAT DOES THAT MEAN?!
I'D SAY IT MEANS WE'VE GOT OUR HANDS FULL. AND I'D ALSO SAY, THE FIRST THING WE SHOULD DO IS-
DUCK!
THAT WAS JUST A LITTLE TOO CLOSE.
YEAH! HE CAN'T GET AWAY WITH THAT!
HEY, YA BIG TIN CAN! KNOCK IT OFF, YA HEAR ME!
MY FRIEND AND I WILL BE RIGHT DOWN THERE TO LEARN YA SOME MANNERS. SO QUIT BUGGIN' US!
OKAY, THERE ARE TIMES THAT MY MOUTH GETS WAY AHEAD OF MY BRAIN.

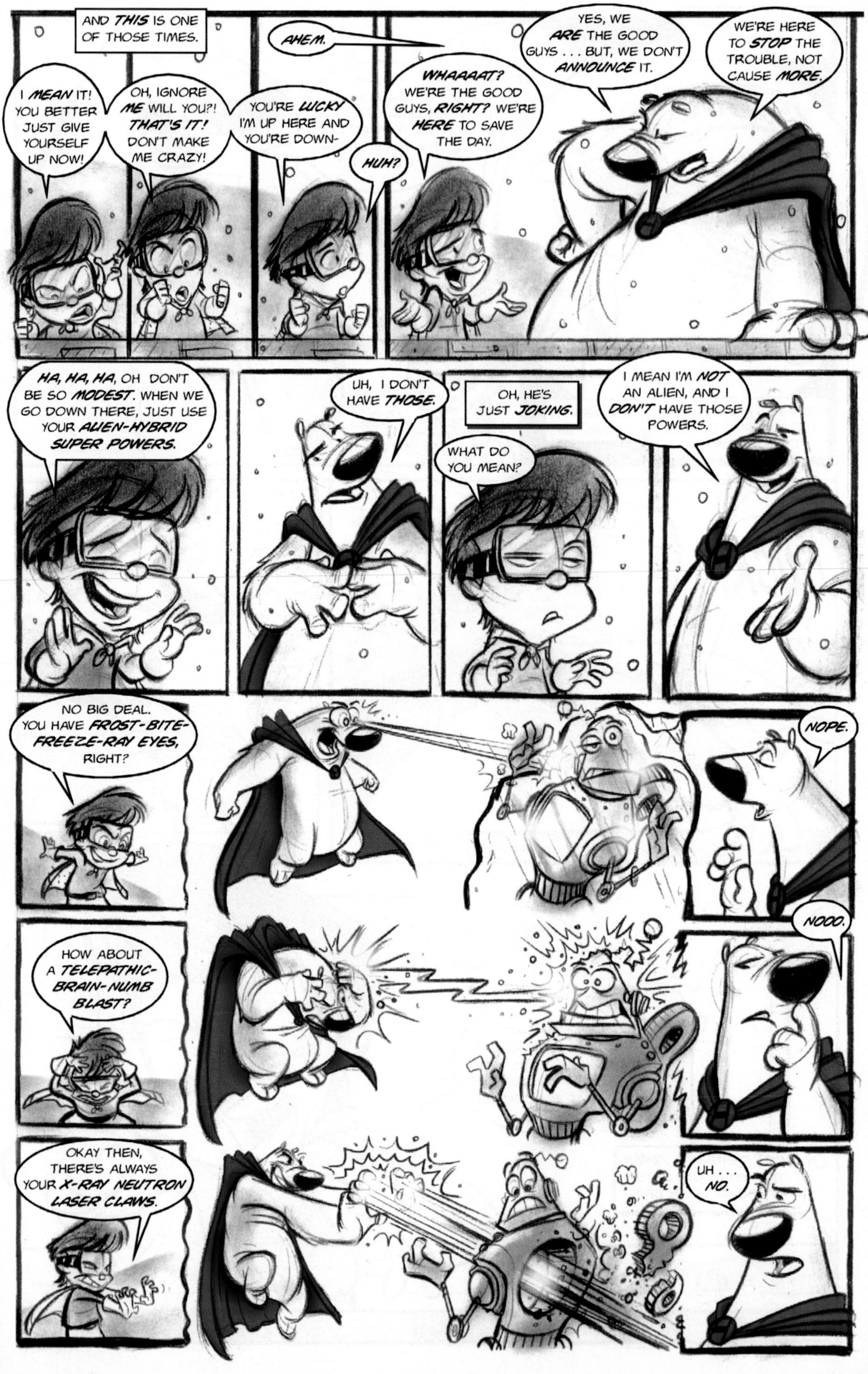

AND THIS IS ONE OF THOSE TIMES.
I MEAN IT! YOU BETTER JUST GIVE YOURSELF UP NOW!
OH, IGNORE ME WILL YOU?! THAT'S IT! DON'T MAKE ME CRAZY!
AHEM.
YOU'RE LUCKY I'M UP HERE AND YOU'RE DOWN-
HUH?
WHAAAAT? WE'RE THE GOOD GUYS, RIGHT? WE'RE HERE TO SAVE THE DAY.
YES, WE ARE THE GOOD GUYS . . . BUT, WE DON'T ANNOUNCE IT.
WE'RE HERE TO STOP THE TROUBLE, NOT CAUSE MORE.
HA, HA, HA, OH DON'T BE SO MODEST. WHEN WE GO DOWN THERE, JUST USE YOUR ALIEN-HYBRID SUPER POWERS.
UH, I DON'T HAVE THOSE.
OH, HE'S JUST JOKING.
WHAT DO YOU MEAN?
I MEAN I'M NOT AN ALIEN, AND I DON'T HAVE THOSE POWERS.
NO BIG DEAL. YOU HAVE FROST-BITE-FREEZE-RAY EYES, RIGHT?
NOPE.
HOW ABOUT A TELEPATHIC-BRAIN-NUMB BLAST?
NOOO.
OKAY THEN, THERE'S ALWAYS YOUR X-RAY NEUTRON LASER CLAWS.
UH . . . NO.

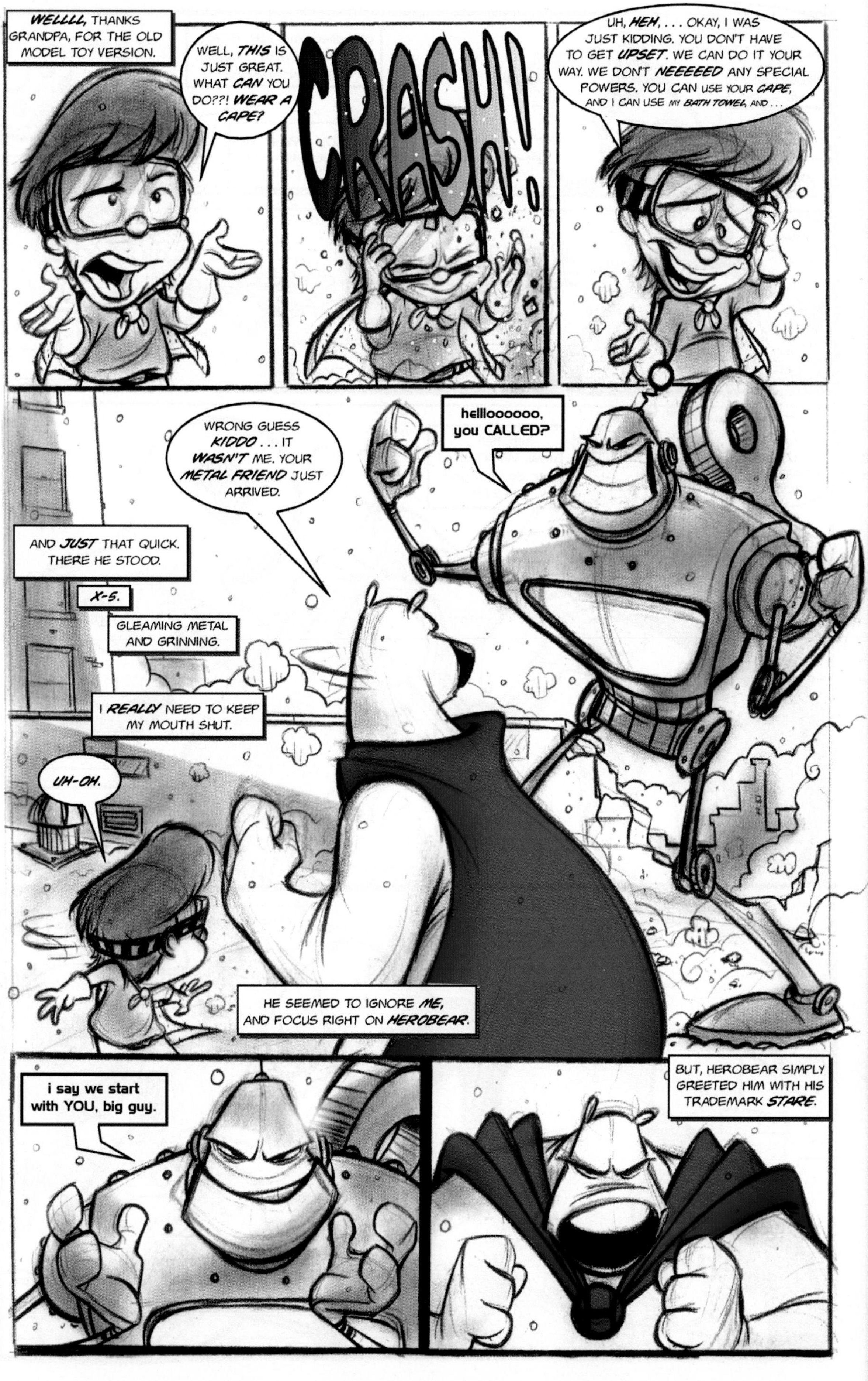
WELLLL, THANKS GRANDPA, FOR THE OLD MODEL TOY VERSION.
WELL, THIS IS JUST GREAT. WHAT CAN YOU DO??! WEAR A CAPE?
CRASH!!
UH, HEH, . . . OKAY, I WAS JUST KIDDING. YOU DON'T HAVE TO GET UPSET. WE CAN DO IT YOUR WAY. WE DON'T NEEEEED ANY SPECIAL POWERS. YOU CAN USE YOUR CAPE, AND I CAN USE MY BATH TOWEL, AND . . .
WRONG GUESS KIDDO . . . IT WASN'T ME. YOUR METAL FRIEND JUST ARRIVED.
hellloooooo, you CALLED?
AND JUST THAT QUICK. THERE HE STOOD.
X-5.
GLEAMING METAL AND GRINNING.
I REALLY NEED TO KEEP MY MOUTH SHUT.
UH-OH.
HE SEEMED TO IGNORE ME, AND FOCUS RIGHT ON HEROBEAR.
i say we start with YOU, big guy.
BUT, HEROBEAR SIMPLY GREETED HIM WITH HIS TRADEMARK STARE.

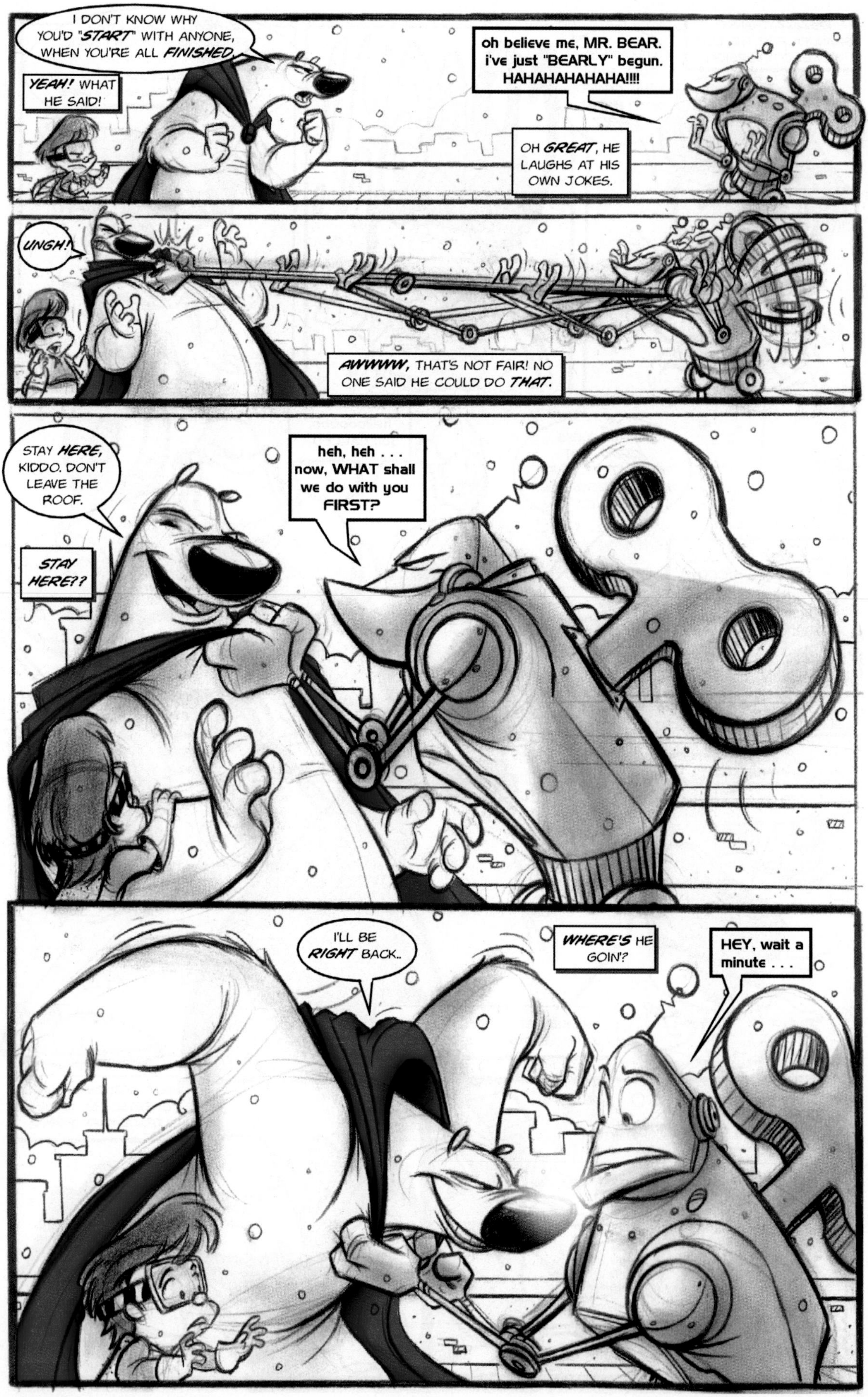
I DON'T KNOW WHY YOU'D "START" WITH ANYONE, WHEN YOU'RE ALL FINISHED.
YEAH! WHAT HE SAID!
oh believe me, MR. BEAR. i've just "BEARLY" begun. HAHAHAHAHAHA!!!!
OH GREAT, HE LAUGHS AT HIS OWN JOKES.
UNGH!
AWWWW, THAT'S NOT FAIR! NO ONE SAID HE COULD DO THAT.
STAY HERE, KIDDO. DON'T LEAVE THE ROOF.
heh, heh . . . now, WHAT shall we do with you FIRST?
STAY HERE??
I'LL BE RIGHT BACK..
WHERE'S HE GOIN'?
HEY, wait a minute . . .

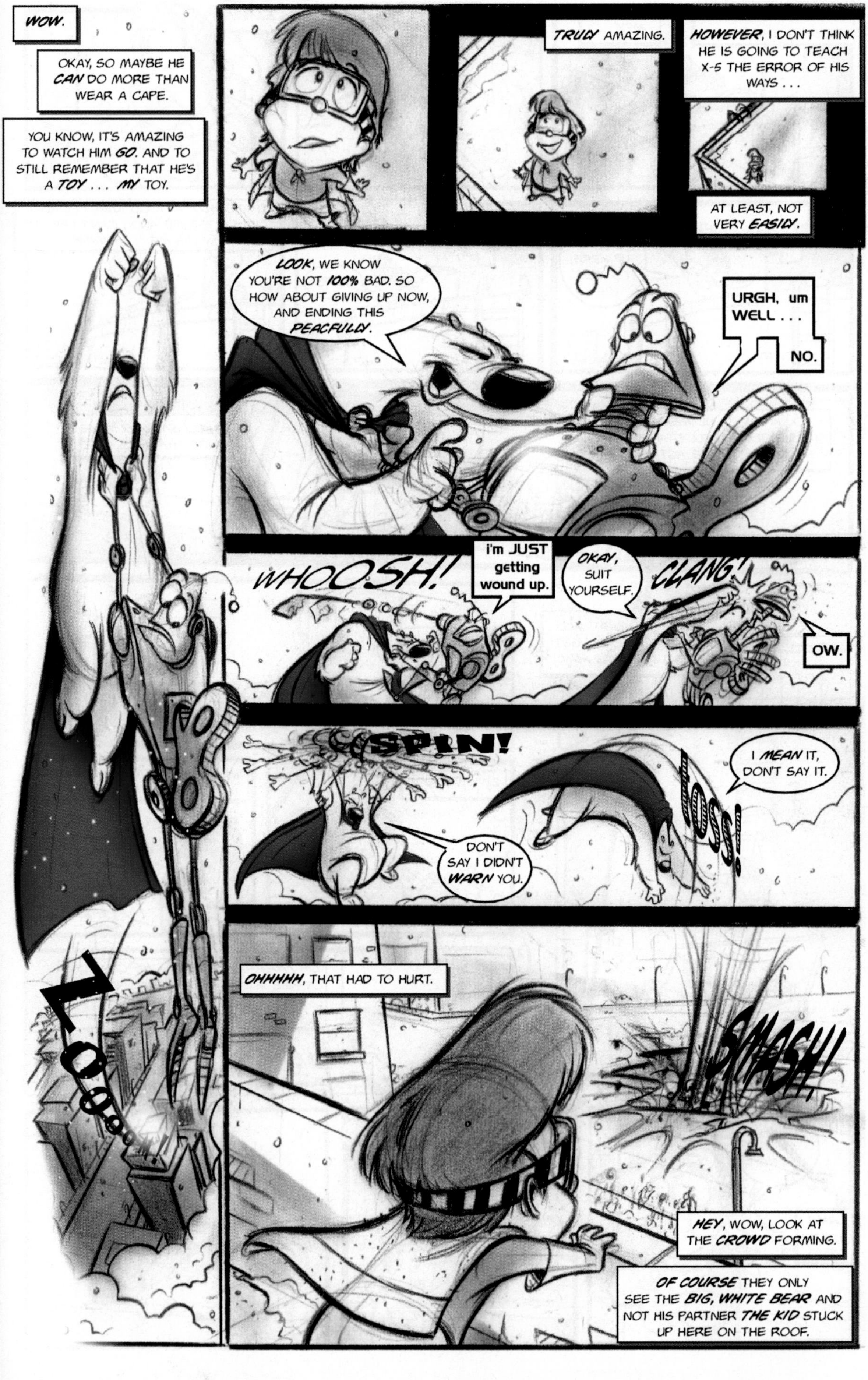
WOW.
OKAY, SO MAYBE HE CAN DO MORE THAN WEAR A CAPE.
YOU KNOW, IT'S AMAZING TO WATCH HIM GO. AND TO STILL REMEMBER THAT HE'S A TOY . . . MY TOY.
TRULY AMAZING.
HOWEVER, I DON'T THINK HE IS GOING TO TEACH X-5 THE ERROR OF HIS WAYS . . .
AT LEAST, NOT VERY EASILY.
LOOK, WE KNOW YOU'RE NOT 100% BAD. SO HOW ABOUT GIVING UP NOW, AND ENDING THIS PEACFULLY.
URGH, um WELL . . .
NO.
WHOOSH!
i'm JUST getting wound up.
OKAY, SUIT YOURSELF.
CLANG!
OW.
SPIN!
I MEAN IT, DON'T SAY IT.
DON'T SAY I DIDN'T WARN YOU.
OOPS!
ZOOOooom!
OHHHHH, THAT HAD TO HURT.
SMASH!
HEY, WOW, LOOK AT THE CROWD FORMING.
OF COURSE THEY ONLY SEE THE BIG, WHITE BEAR AND NOT HIS PARTNER THE KID STUCK UP HERE ON THE ROOF.

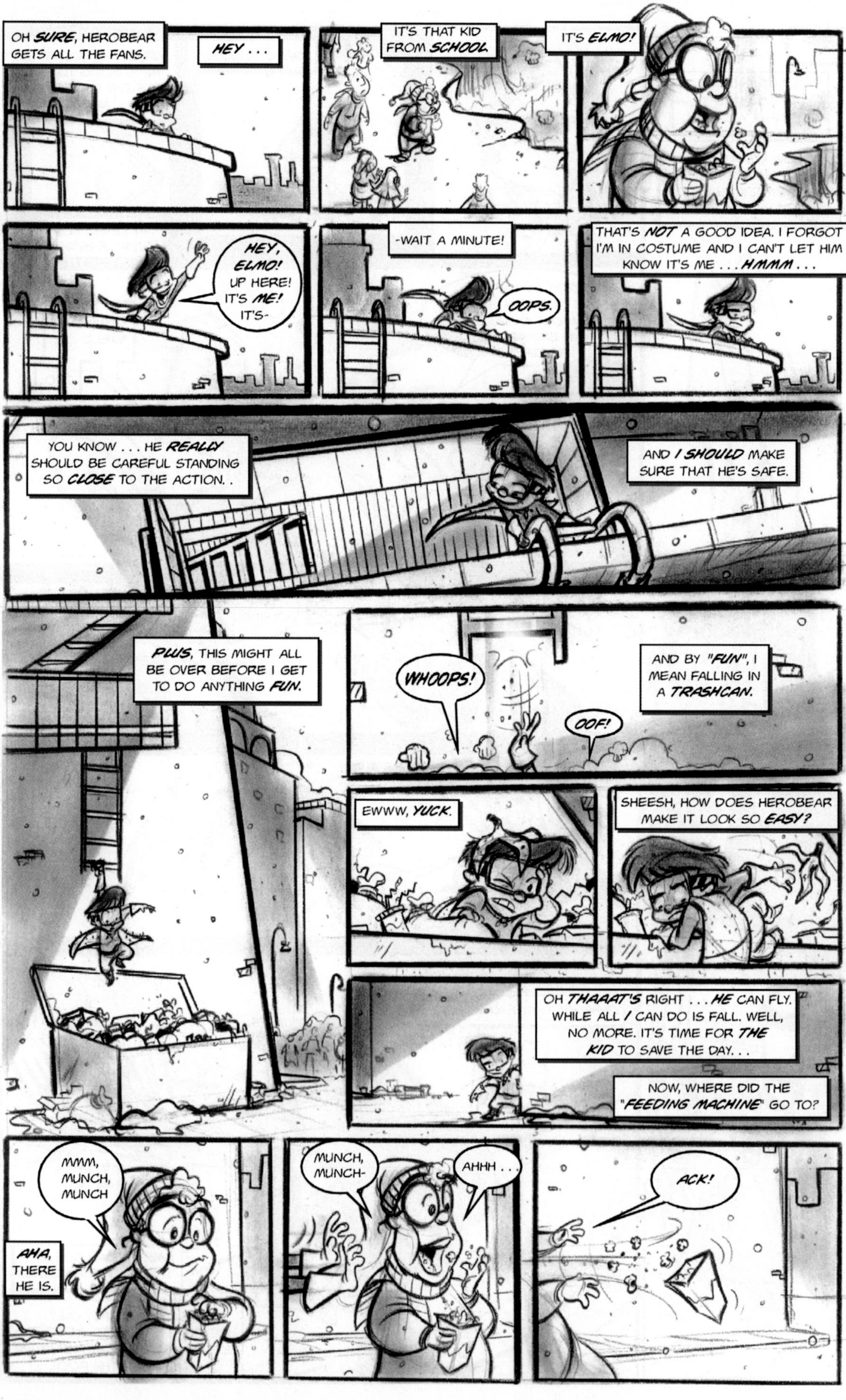
OH SURE, HEROBEAR GETS ALL THE FANS.
HEY . . .
IT'S THAT KID FROM SCHOOL.
IT'S ELMO!
HEY, ELMO! UP HERE! IT'S ME! IT'S-
-WAIT A MINUTE!
OOPS.
THAT'S NOT A GOOD IDEA. I FORGOT I'M IN COSTUME AND I CAN'T LET HIM KNOW IT'S ME . . . HMMM . . .
YOU KNOW . . . HE REALLY SHOULD BE CAREFUL STANDING SO CLOSE TO THE ACTION. .
AND I SHOULD MAKE SURE THAT HE'S SAFE.
PLUS, THIS MIGHT ALL BE OVER BEFORE I GET TO DO ANYTHING FUN.
WHOOPS!
AND BY "FUN", I MEAN FALLING IN A TRASHCAN.
OOF!
EWWW, YUCK.
SHEESH, HOW DOES HEROBEAR MAKE IT LOOK SO EASY?
OH THAAAT'S RIGHT . . . HE CAN FLY. WHILE ALL I CAN DO IS FALL. WELL, NO MORE. IT'S TIME FOR THE KID TO SAVE THE DAY. . .
NOW, WHERE DID THE "FEEDING MACHINE" GO TO?
MMM, MUNCH, MUNCH
AHA, THERE HE IS.
MUNCH, MUNCH-
AHHH . .
ACK!

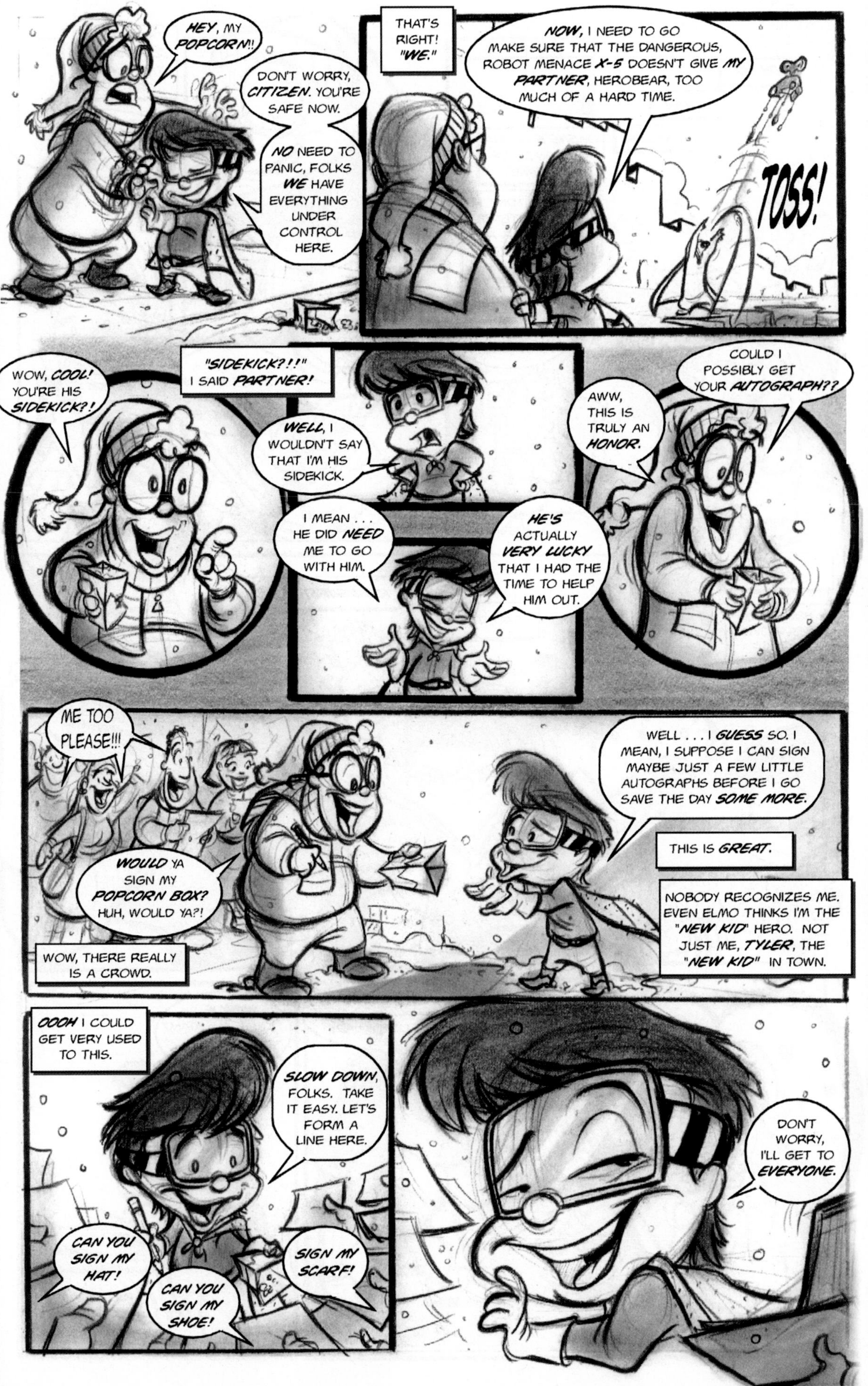
HEY, MY POPCORN!!
DON'T WORRY, CITIZEN. YOU'RE SAFE NOW.
NO NEED TO PANIC, FOLKS WE HAVE EVERYTHING UNDER CONTROL HERE.
THAT'S RIGHT! "WE."
NOW, I NEED TO GO MAKE SURE THAT THE DANGEROUS, ROBOT MENACE X-5 DOESN'T GIVE MY PARTNER, HEROBEAR, TOO MUCH OF A HARD TIME.
TOSS!
WOW, COOL! YOU'RE HIS SIDEKICK?!
"SIDEKICK?!!" I SAID PARTNER!
WELL, I WOULDN'T SAY THAT I'M HIS SIDEKICK.
I MEAN . . . HE DID NEED ME TO GO WITH HIM.
HE'S ACTUALLY VERY LUCKY THAT I HAD THE TIME TO HELP HIM OUT.
AWW, THIS IS TRULY AN HONOR.
COULD I POSSIBLY GET YOUR AUTOGRAPH??
ME TOO PLEASE!!!
WOULD YA SIGN MY POPCORN BOX? HUH, WOULD YA?!
WOW, THERE REALLY IS A CROWD.
WELL . . . I GUESS SO. I MEAN, I SUPPOSE I CAN SIGN MAYBE JUST A FEW LITTLE AUTOGRAPHS BEFORE I GO SAVE THE DAY SOME MORE.
THIS IS GREAT.
NOBODY RECOGNIZES ME. EVEN ELMO THINKS I'M THE "NEW KID" HERO. NOT JUST ME, TYLER, THE "NEW KID" IN TOWN.
OOOH I COULD GET VERY USED TO THIS.
SLOW DOWN, FOLKS. TAKE IT EASY. LET'S FORM A LINE HERE.
CAN YOU SIGN MY HAT!
CAN YOU SIGN MY SHOE!
SIGN MY SCARF!
DON'T WORRY, I'LL GET TO EVERYONE.

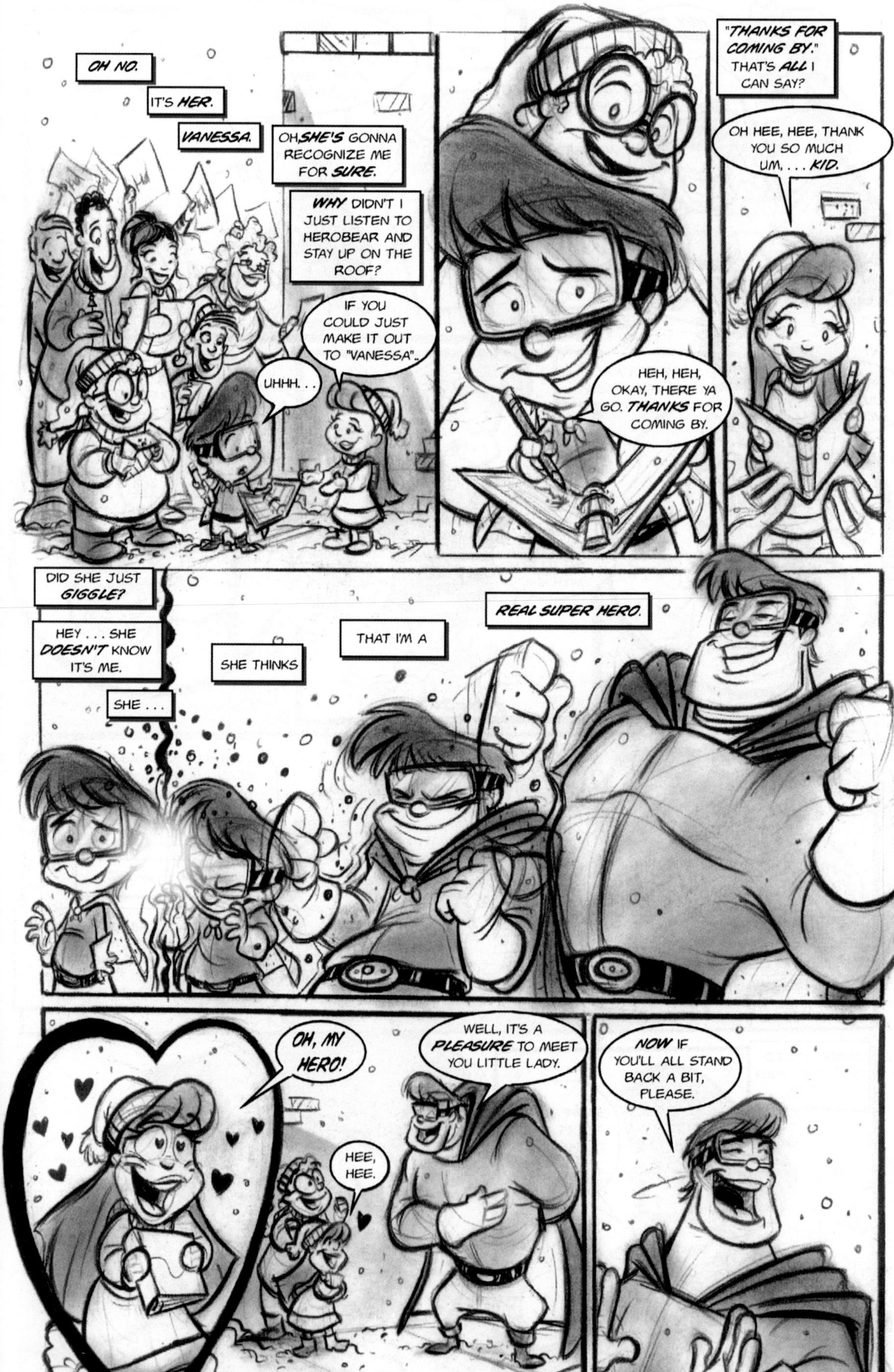
OH NO.
IT'S HER.
VANESSA.
OH, SHE'S GONNA RECOGNIZE ME FOR SURE.
WHY DIDN'T I JUST LISTEN TO HEROBEAR AND STAY UP ON THE ROOF?
IF YOU COULD JUST MAKE IT OUT TO "VANESSA".
UHHH. . .
HEH, HEH, OKAY, THERE YA GO. THANKS FOR COMING BY.
"THANKS FOR COMING BY." THAT'S ALL I CAN SAY?
OH HEE, HEE, THANK YOU SO MUCH UM, . . . KID.
DID SHE JUST GIGGLE?
HEY . . . SHE DOESN'T KNOW IT'S ME.
SHE . . .
SHE THINKS
THAT I'M A
REAL SUPER HERO.
OH, MY HERO!
HEE, HEE.
WELL, IT'S A PLEASURE TO MEET YOU LITTLE LADY.
NOW IF YOU'LL ALL STAND BACK A BIT, PLEASE.

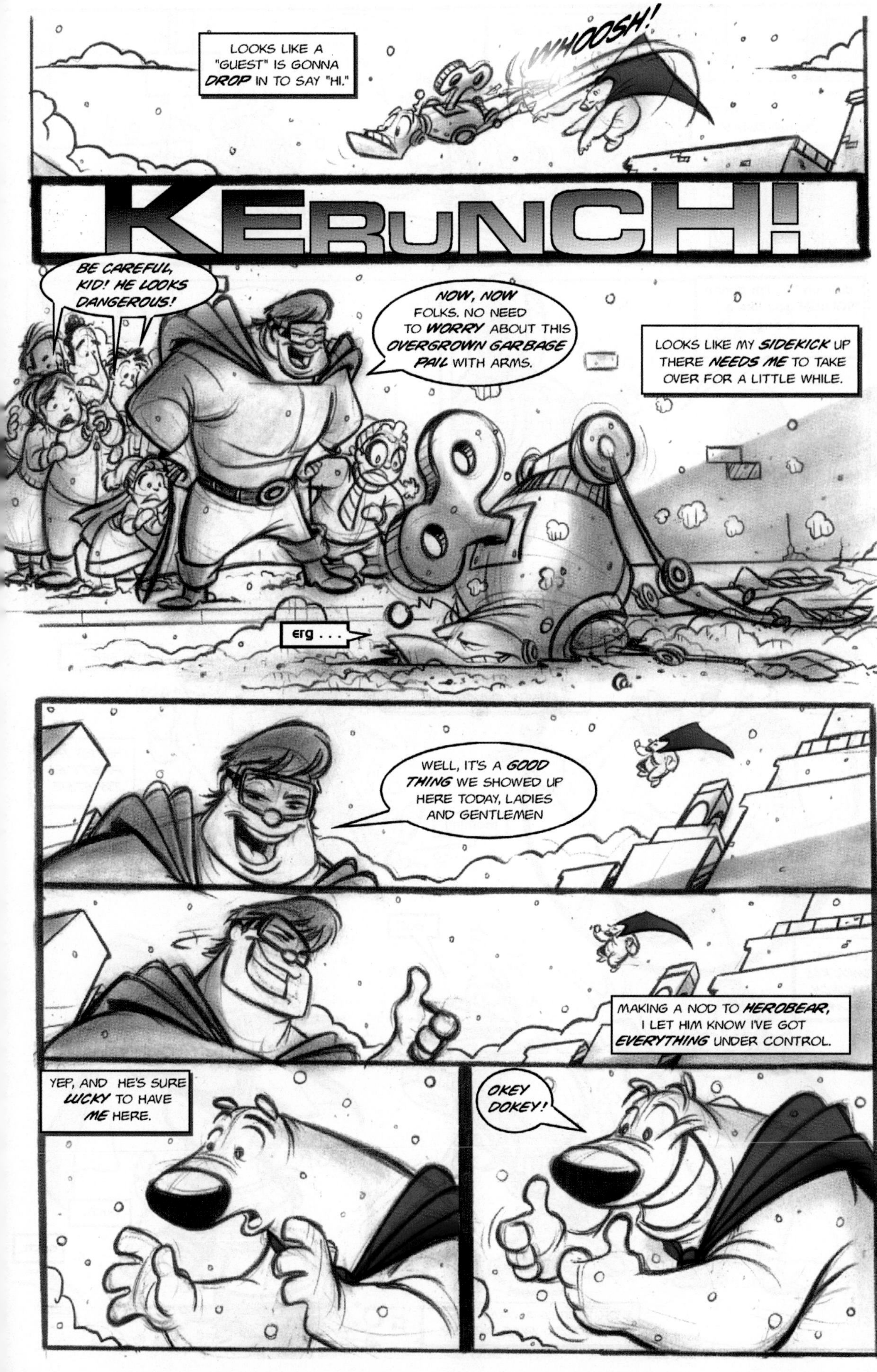

LOOKS LIKE A "GUEST" IS GONNA DROP IN TO SAY "HI."
WHOOSH!
KERUNCH!
BE CAREFUL, KID! HE LOOKS DANGEROUS!
NOW, NOW FOLKS. NO NEED TO WORRY ABOUT THIS OVERGROWN GARBAGE PAIL WITH ARMS.
LOOKS LIKE MY SIDEKICK UP THERE NEEDS ME TO TAKE OVER FOR A LITTLE WHILE.
erg . . .
WELL, IT'S A GOOD THING WE SHOWED UP HERE TODAY, LADIES AND GENTLEMEN
MAKING A NOD TO HEROBEAR, I LET HIM KNOW I'VE GOT EVERYTHING UNDER CONTROL.
YEP, AND HE'S SURE LUCKY TO HAVE ME HERE.
OKEY DOKEY!

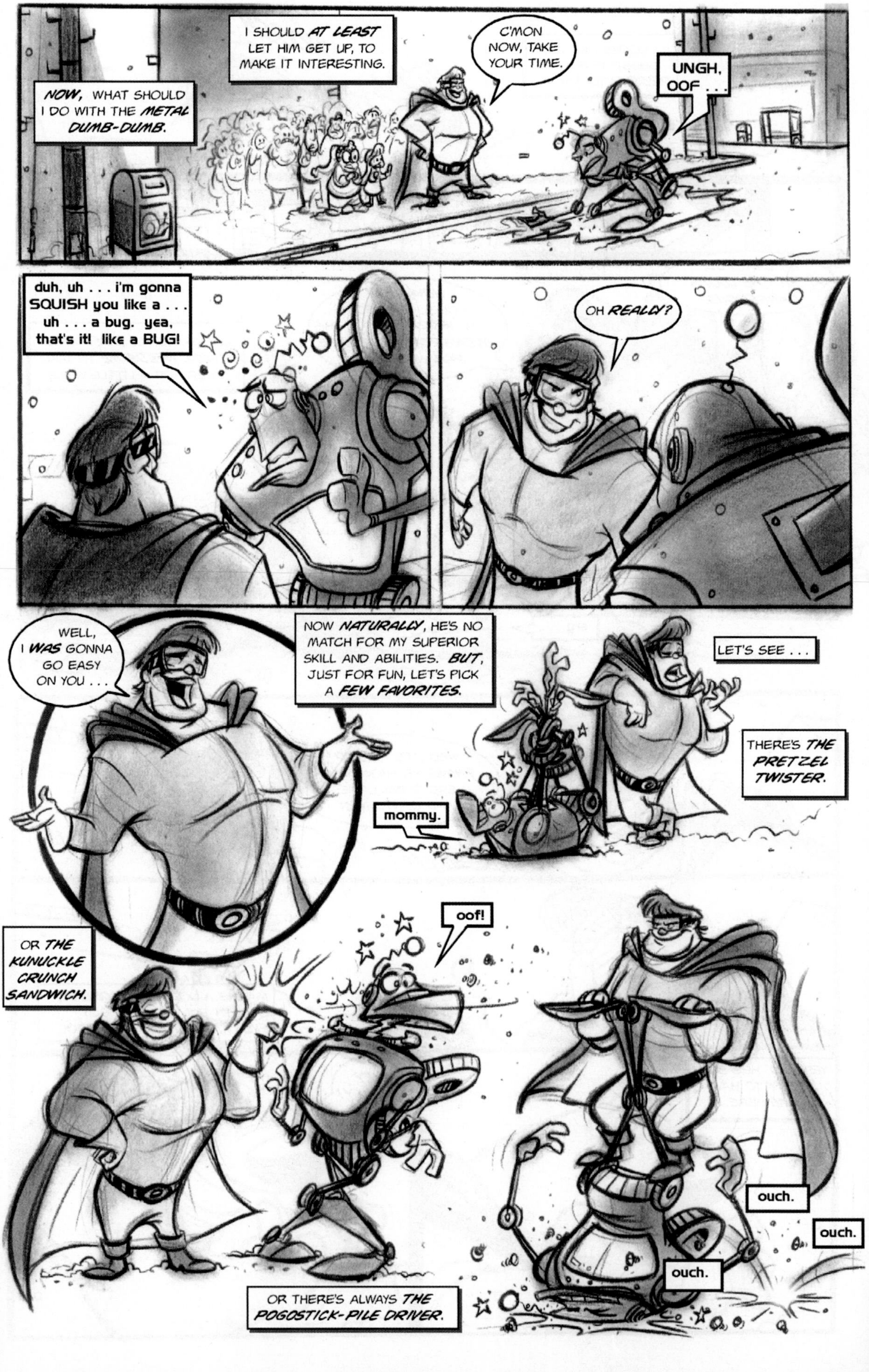
NOW, WHAT SHOULD I DO WITH THE METAL DUMB-DUMB.
I SHOULD AT LEAST LET HIM GET UP, TO MAKE IT INTERESTING.
C'MON NOW, TAKE YOUR TIME.
UNGH, OOF . . .
duh, uh . . . i'm gonna SQUISH you like a . . . uh . . . a bug. yea, that's it! like a BUG!
OH REALLY?
WELL, I WAS GONNA GO EASY ON YOU . . .
NOW NATURALLY, HE'S NO MATCH FOR MY SUPERIOR SKILL AND ABILITIES. BUT, JUST FOR FUN, LET'S PICK A FEW FAVORITES.
LET'S SEE . . .
THERE'S THE PRETZEL TWISTER.
mommy.
OR THE KUNUCKLE CRUNCH SANDWICH.
oof!
OR THERE'S ALWAYS THE POGOSTICK-PILE DRIVER.
ouch.
ouch.
ouch.

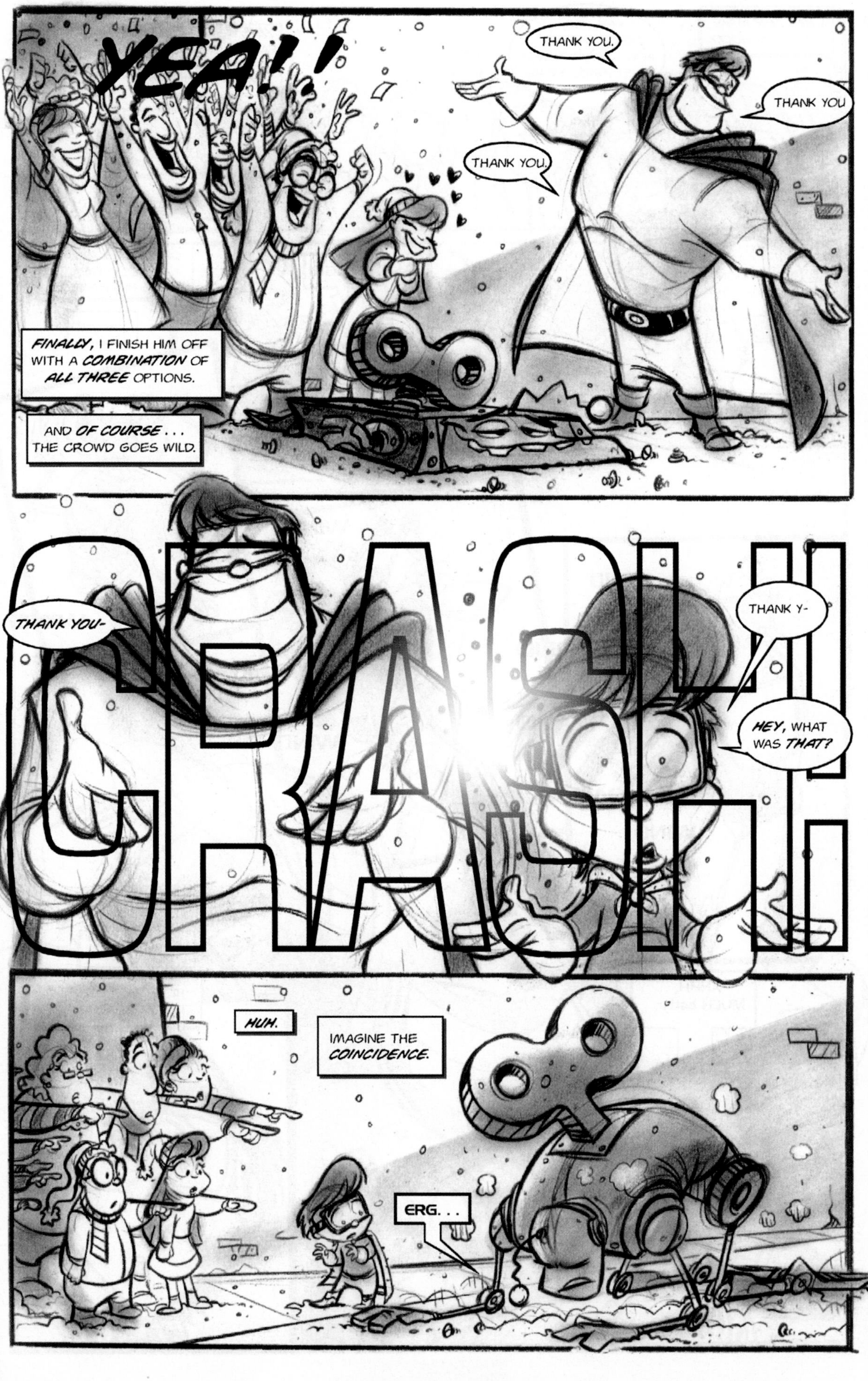
YEA!!!
THANK YOU.
THANK YOU
THANK YOU.
FINALLY, I FINISH HIM OFF WITH A COMBINATION OF ALL THREE OPTIONS.
AND OF COURSE . . . THE CROWD GOES WILD.
CRASH!!
THANK YOU-
THANK Y-
HEY, WHAT WAS THAT?
HUH.
IMAGINE THE COINCIDENCE.
ERG. . .

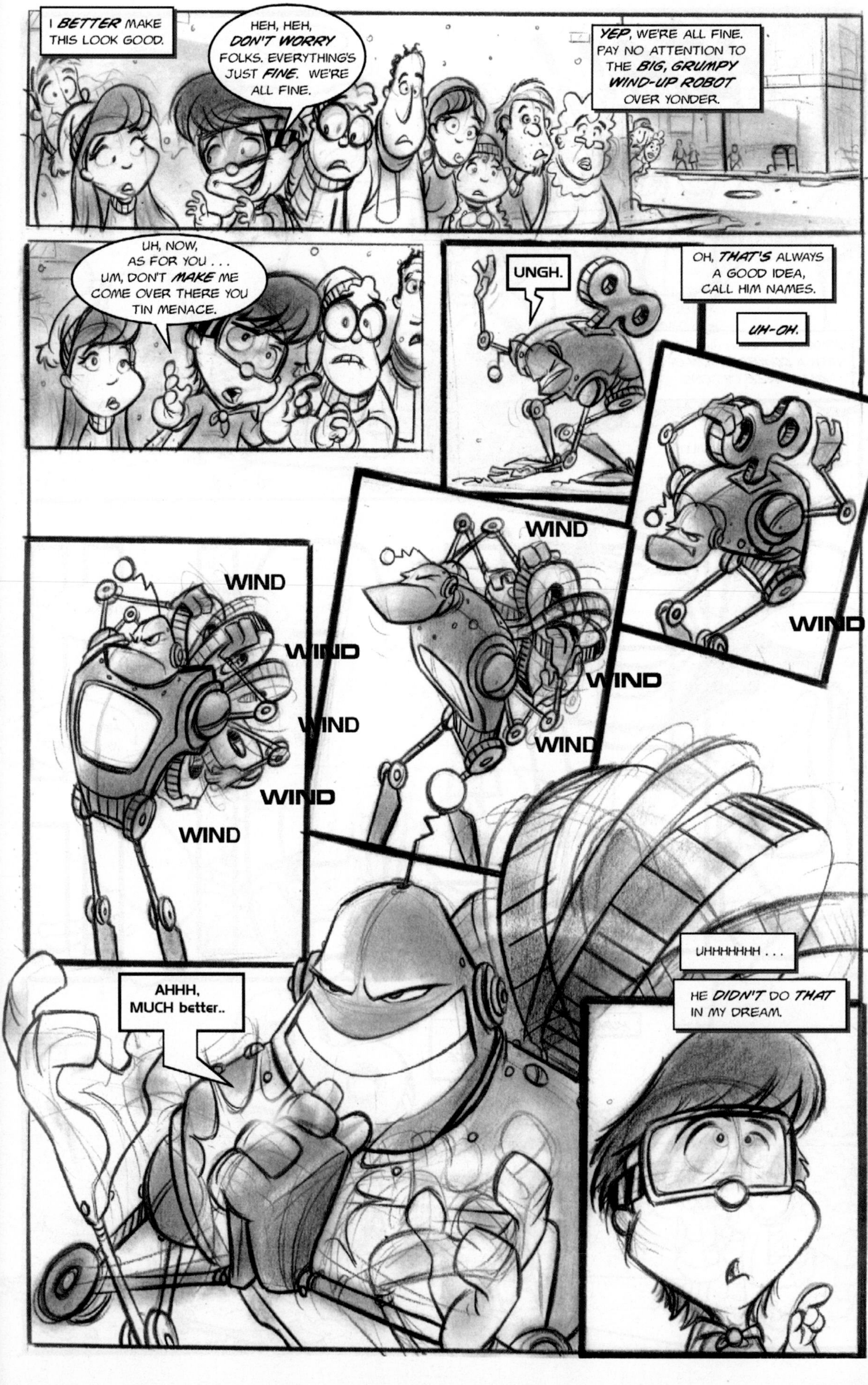

I BETTER MAKE THIS LOOK GOOD.
HEH, HEH, DON'T WORRY FOLKS. EVERYTHING'S JUST FINE. WE'RE ALL FINE.
YEP, WE'RE ALL FINE. PAY NO ATTENTION TO THE BIG, GRUMPY WIND-UP ROBOT OVER YONDER.
UH, NOW, AS FOR YOU . . . UM, DON'T MAKE ME COME OVER THERE YOU TIN MENACE.
UNGH.
OH, THAT'S ALWAYS A GOOD IDEA, CALL HIM NAMES.
UH-OH.
WIND
WIND
WIND
WIND
WIND
WIND
WIND
WIND
WIND
AHHH, MUCH better..
UHHHHHHH . . .
HE DIDN'T DO THAT IN MY DREAM.

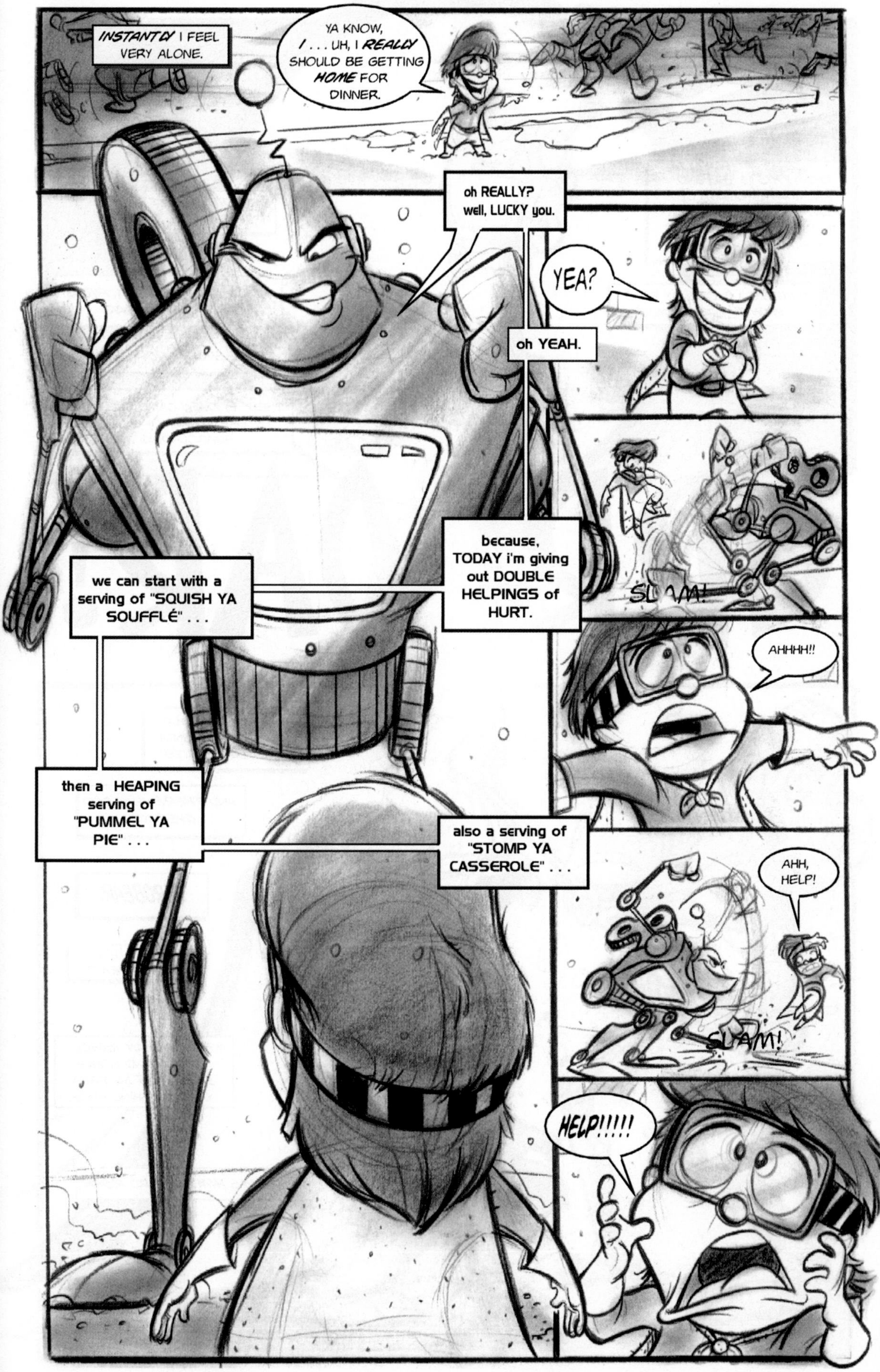
INSTANTLY I FEEL VERY ALONE.
YA KNOW, I . . . UH, I REALLY SHOULD BE GETTING HOME FOR DINNER.
oh REALLY? well, LUCKY you.
YEA?
oh YEAH.
because, TODAY i'm giving out DOUBLE HELPINGS of HURT.
SLAM!
we can start with a serving of "SQUISH YA SOUFFLÉ" . . .
AHHHH!!
then a HEAPING serving of "PUMMEL YA PIE" . . .
also a serving of "STOMP YA CASSEROLE" . . .
AHH, HELP!
SLAM!
HELP!!!!!

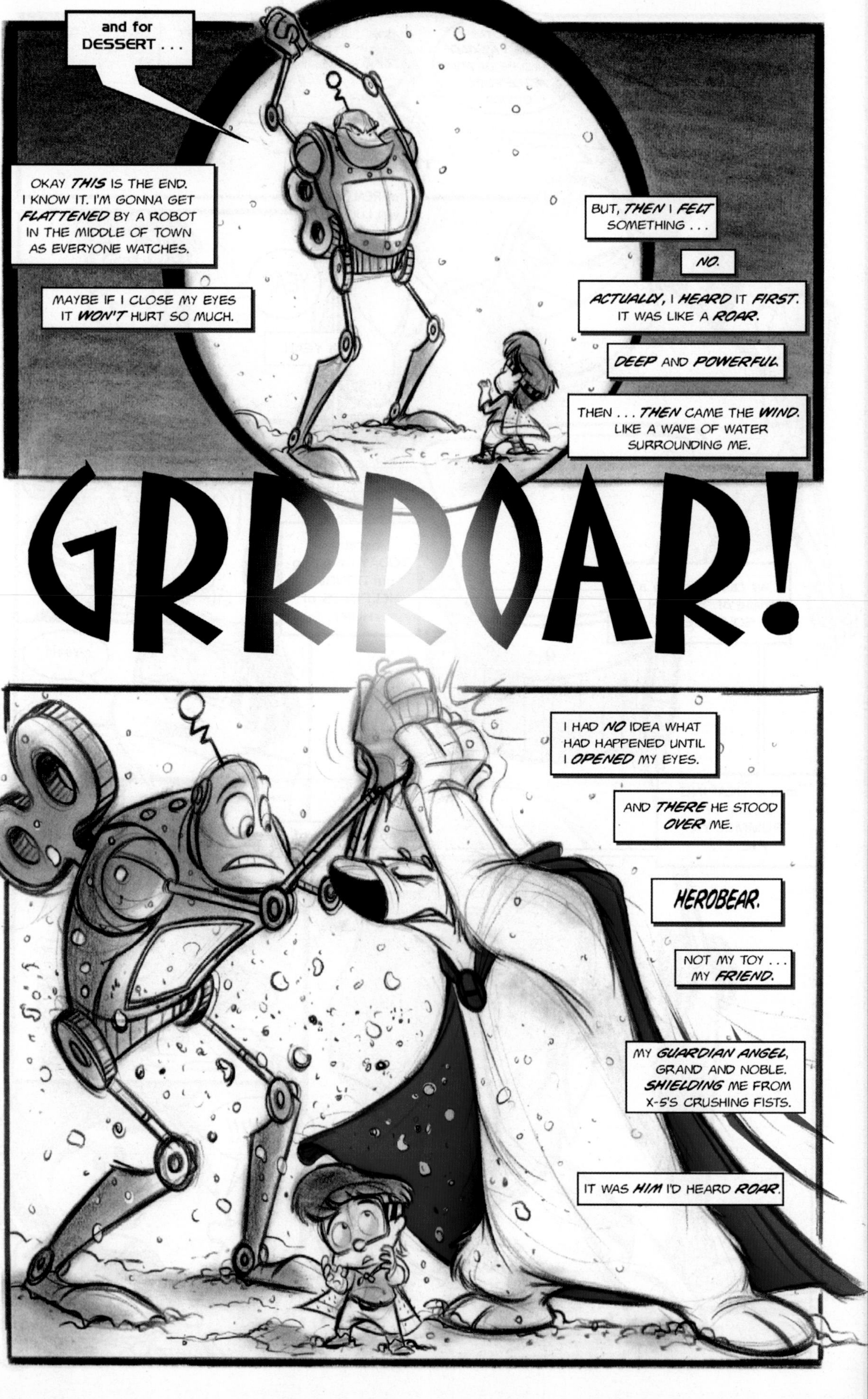

and for DESSERT . . .
OKAY THIS IS THE END. I KNOW IT. I'M GONNA GET FLATTENED BY A ROBOT IN THE MIDDLE OF TOWN AS EVERYONE WATCHES.
MAYBE IF I CLOSE MY EYES IT WON'T HURT SO MUCH.
BUT, THEN I FELT SOMETHING . . .
NO.
ACTUALLY, I HEARD IT FIRST. IT WAS LIKE A ROAR.
DEEP AND POWERFUL.
THEN . . . THEN CAME THE WIND. LIKE A WAVE OF WATER SURROUNDING ME.
GRRROAR!
I HAD NO IDEA WHAT HAD HAPPENED UNTIL I OPENED MY EYES.
AND THERE HE STOOD OVER ME.
HEROBEAR.
NOT MY TOY . . . MY FRIEND.
MY GUARDIAN ANGEL, GRAND AND NOBLE. SHIELDING ME FROM X-5'S CRUSHING FISTS.
IT WAS HIM I'D HEARD ROAR.

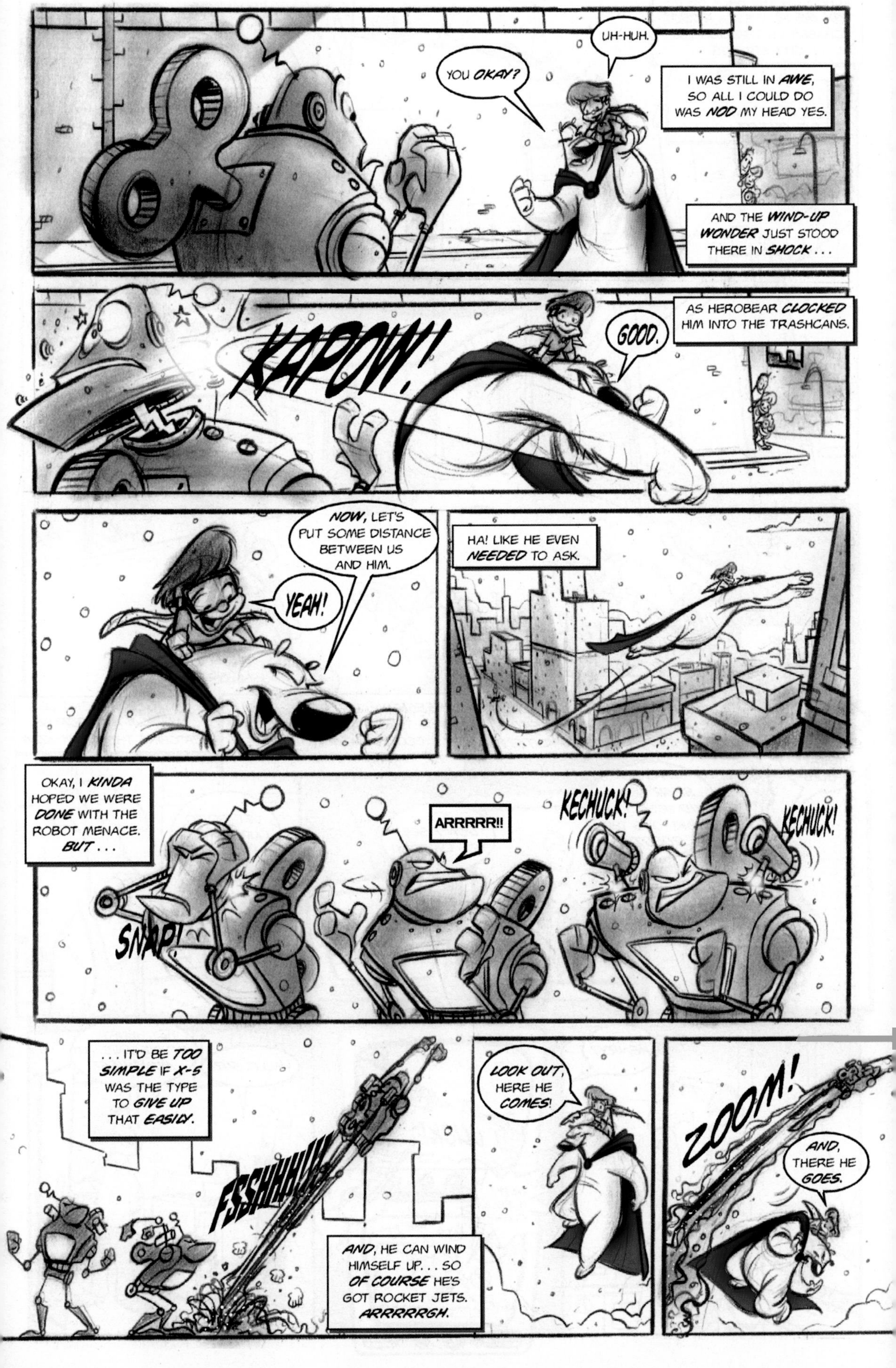

YOU OKAY?
UH-HUH.
I WAS STILL IN AWE, SO ALL I COULD DO WAS NOD MY HEAD YES.
AND THE WIND-UP WONDER JUST STOOD THERE IN SHOCK . . .
AS HEROBEAR CLOCKED HIM INTO THE TRASHCANS.
KAPOW!
GOOD.
NOW, LET'S PUT SOME DISTANCE BETWEEN US AND HIM.
YEAH!
HA! LIKE HE EVEN NEEDED TO ASK.
OKAY, I KINDA HOPED WE WERE DONE WITH THE ROBOT MENACE. BUT . . .
SNAP!
ARRRRR!!
KECHUCK!
KECHUCK!
. . . IT'D BE TOO SIMPLE IF X-5 WAS THE TYPE TO GIVE UP THAT EASILY.
FSSHHHH!!
AND, HE CAN WIND HIMSELF UP. . . SO OF COURSE HE'S GOT ROCKET JETS. ARRRRRGH.
LOOK OUT, HERE HE COMES!
ZOOM!
AND, THERE HE GOES.

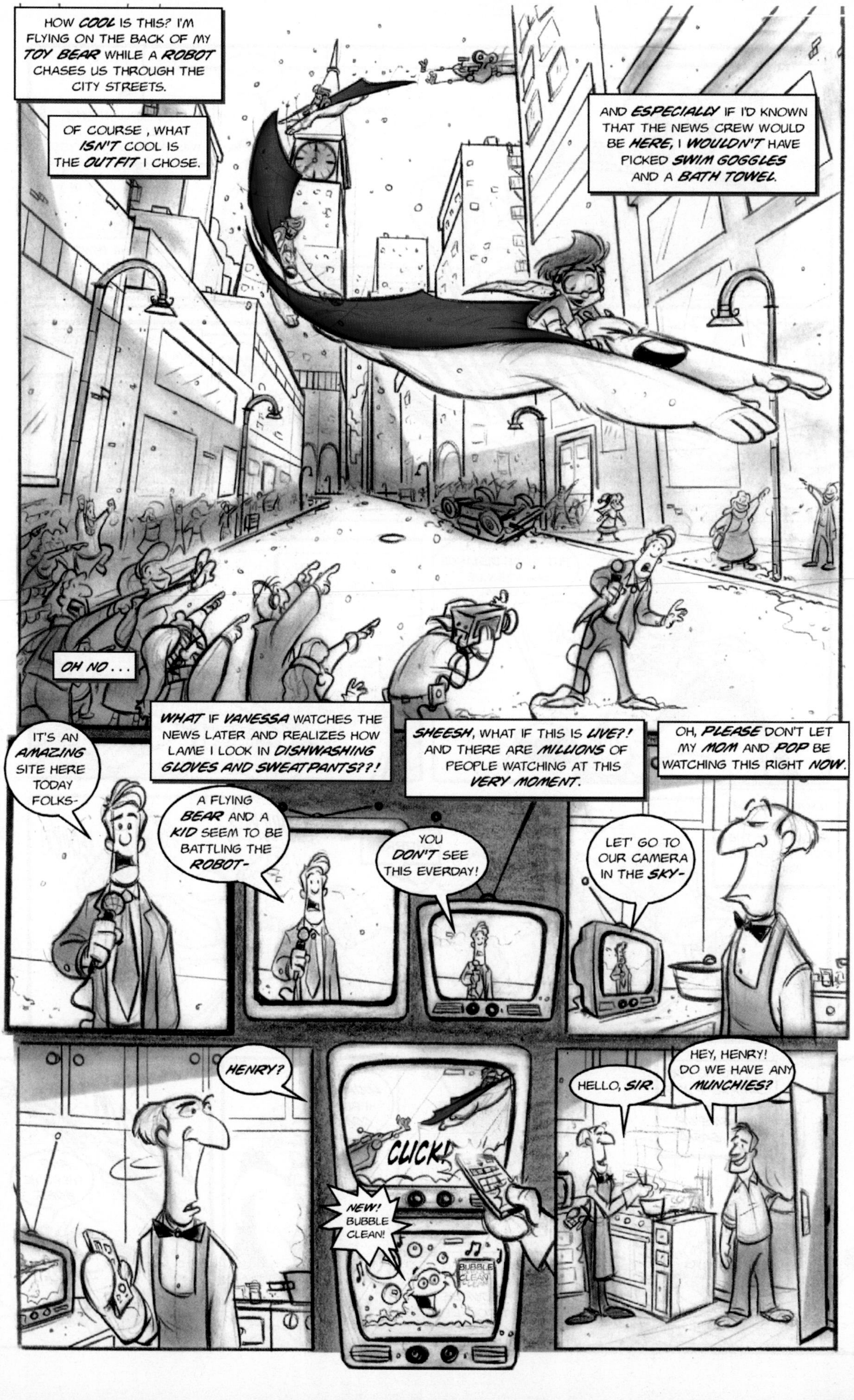
HOW COOL IS THIS? I'M FLYING ON THE BACK OF MY TOY BEAR WHILE A ROBOT CHASES US THROUGH THE CITY STREETS.
OF COURSE, WHAT ISN'T COOL IS THE OUTFIT I CHOSE.
AND ESPECIALLY IF I'D KNOWN THAT THE NEWS CREW WOULD BE HERE, I WOULDN'T HAVE PICKED SWIM GOGGLES AND A BATH TOWEL.
OH NO...
WHAT IF VANESSA WATCHES THE NEWS LATER AND REALIZES HOW LAME I LOOK IN DISHWASHING GLOVES AND SWEATPANTS??!
IT'S AN AMAZING SITE HERE TODAY FOLKS-
SHEESH, WHAT IF THIS IS LIVE?! AND THERE ARE MILLIONS OF PEOPLE WATCHING AT THIS VERY MOMENT.
A FLYING BEAR AND A KID SEEM TO BE BATTLING THE ROBOT-
YOU DON'T SEE THIS EVERDAY!
OH, PLEASE DON'T LET MY MOM AND POP BE WATCHING THIS RIGHT NOW.
LET' GO TO OUR CAMERA IN THE SKY-
HENRY?
CLICK!
NEW! BUBBLE CLEAN!
BUBBLE CLEAN
HELLO, SIR.
HEY, HENRY! DO WE HAVE ANY MUNCHIES?

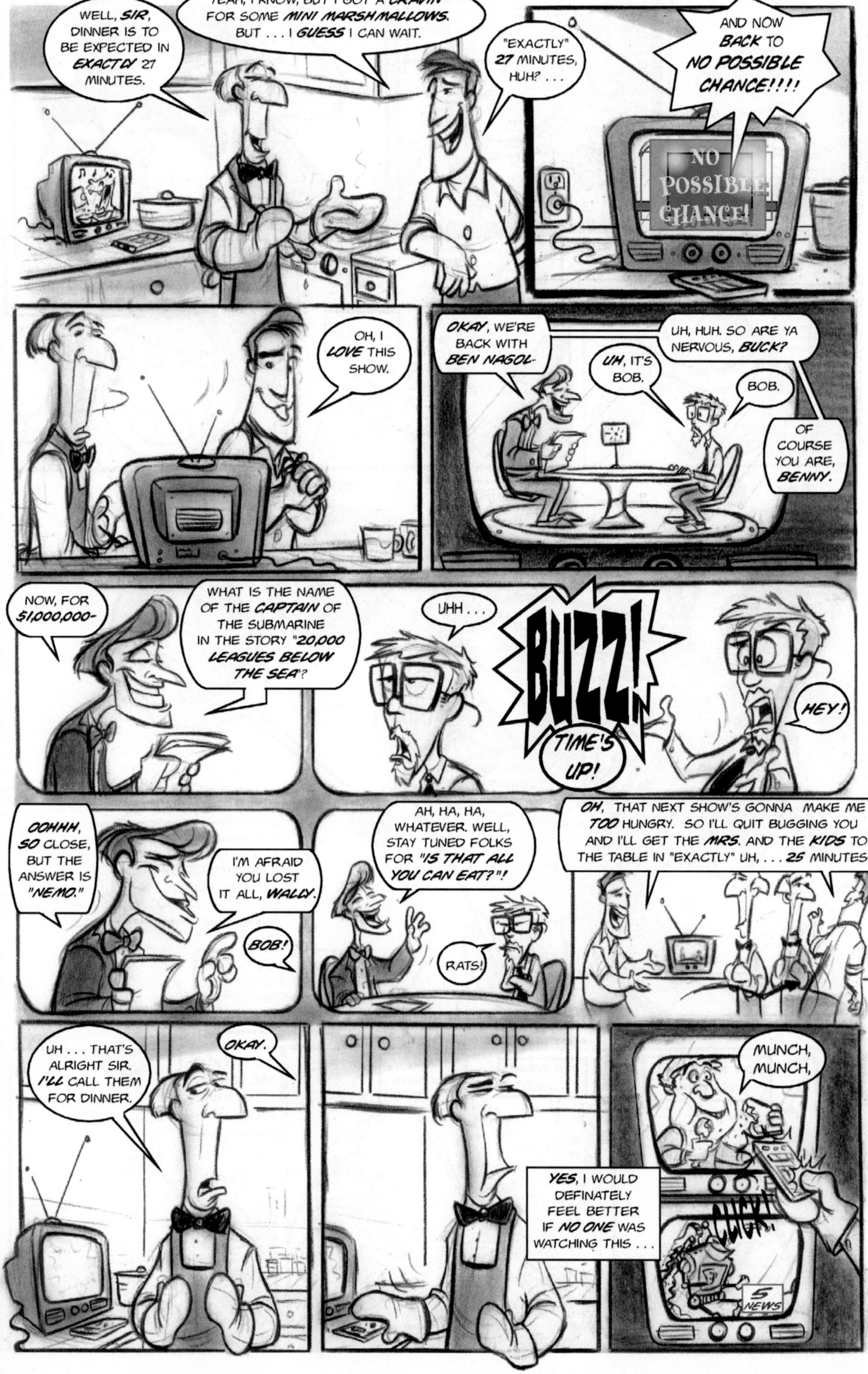
WELL, SIR, DINNER IS TO BE EXPECTED IN EXACTLY 27 MINUTES.
YEAH, I KNOW, BUT I GOT A CRAVIN' FOR SOME MINI MARSHMALLOWS. BUT . . . I GUESS I CAN WAIT.
"EXACTLY" 27 MINUTES, HUH? . . .
AND NOW BACK TO NO POSSIBLE CHANCE!!!!
NO POSSIBLE CHANCE!
OH, I LOVE THIS SHOW.
OKAY, WE'RE BACK WITH BEN NAGOL-
UH, HUH. SO ARE YA NERVOUS, BUCK?
UH, IT'S BOB.
BOB.
OF COURSE YOU ARE, BENNY.
NOW, FOR $1,000,000-
WHAT IS THE NAME OF THE CAPTAIN OF THE SUBMARINE IN THE STORY "20,000 LEAGUES BELOW THE SEA"?
UHH . . .
BUZZ!
TIME'S UP!
HEY!
OOHHH, SO CLOSE, BUT THE ANSWER IS "NEMO."
I'M AFRAID YOU LOST IT ALL, WALLY.
BOB!
AH, HA, HA, WHATEVER. WELL, STAY TUNED FOLKS FOR "IS THAT ALL YOU CAN EAT?"!
RATS!
OH, THAT NEXT SHOW'S GONNA MAKE ME TOO HUNGRY. SO I'LL QUIT BUGGING YOU AND I'LL GET THE MRS. AND THE KIDS TO THE TABLE IN "EXACTLY" UH, . . . 25 MINUTES.
UH . . . THAT'S ALRIGHT SIR. I'LL CALL THEM FOR DINNER.
OKAY.
YES, I WOULD DEFINATELY FEEL BETTER IF NO ONE WAS WATCHING THIS . . .
MUNCH, MUNCH,
CLICK!
5 NEWS

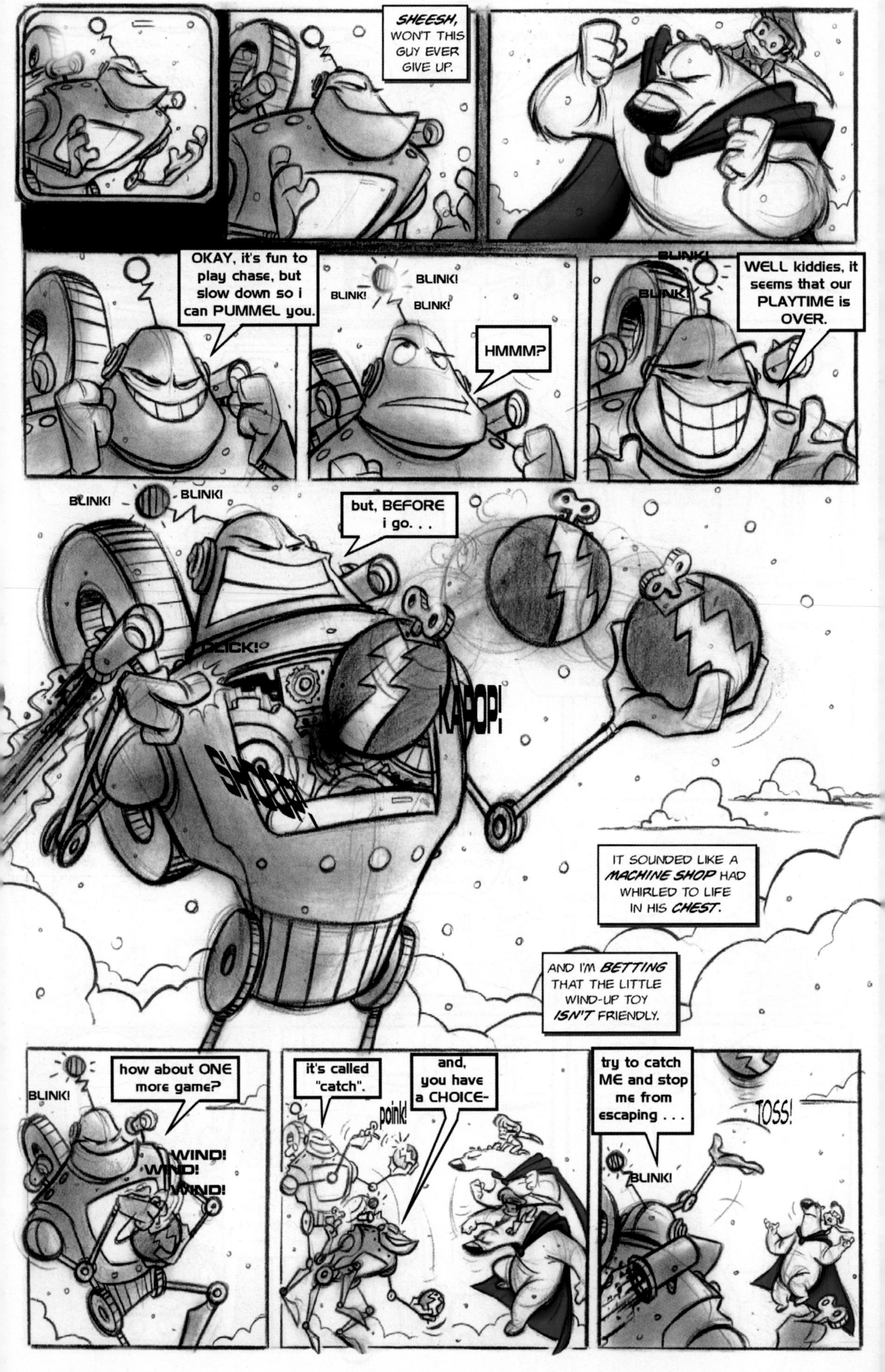

SHEESH, WON'T THIS GUY EVER GIVE UP.
OKAY, it's fun to play chase, but slow down so i can PUMMEL you.
BLINK!
BLINK!
BLINK!
HMMM?
BLINK!
BLINK!
WELL kiddies, it seems that our PLAYTIME is OVER.
BLINK!
BLINK!
but, BEFORE i go. . .
CLICK!
KAPOP!
SHOOM!
IT SOUNDED LIKE A MACHINE SHOP HAD WHIRLED TO LIFE IN HIS CHEST.
AND I'M BETTING THAT THE LITTLE WIND-UP TOY ISN'T FRIENDLY.
BLINK!
how about ONE more game?
WIND!
WIND!
WIND!
it's called "catch".
and, you have a CHOICE-
poink!
try to catch ME and stop me from escaping . . .
TOSS!
BLINK!

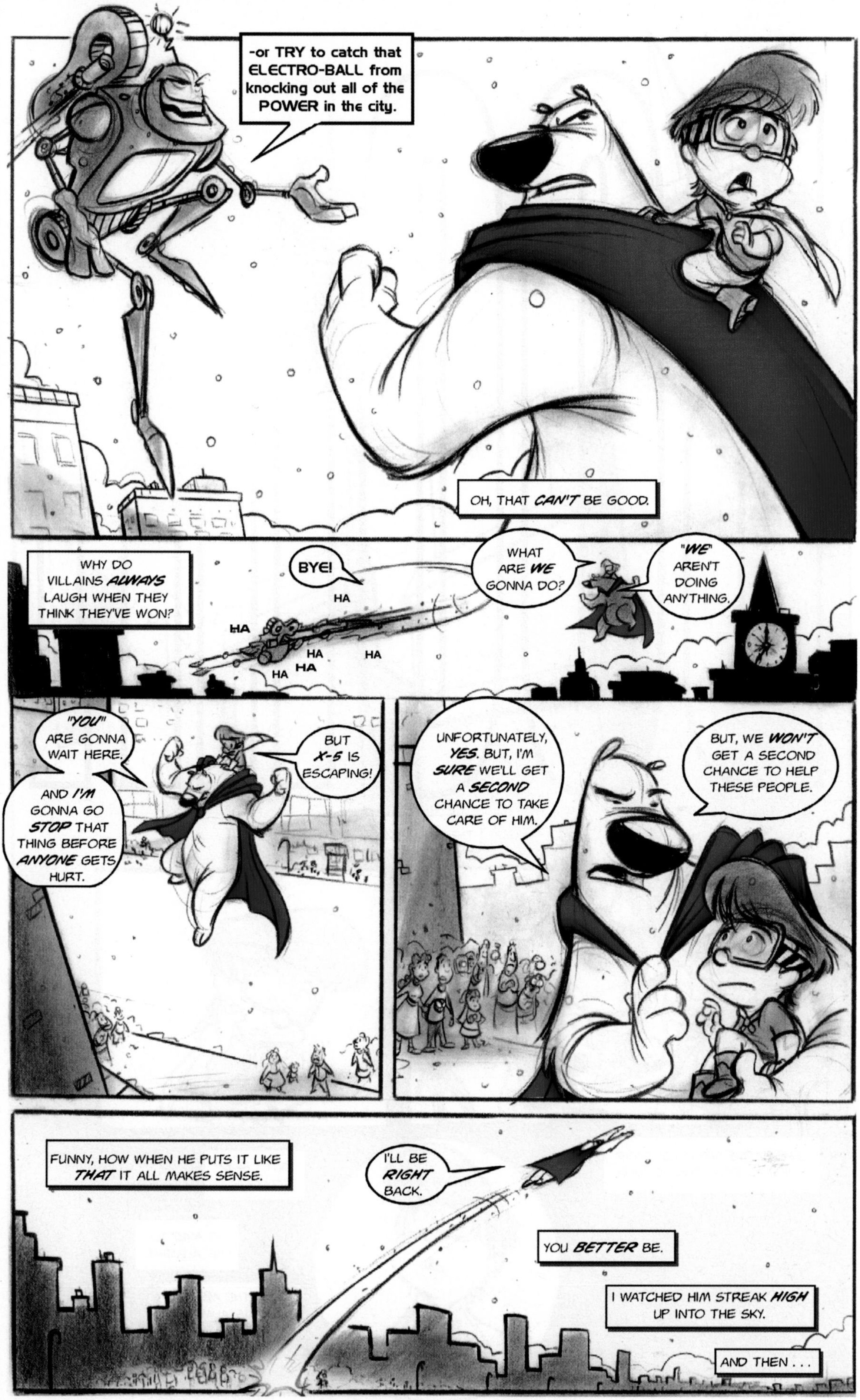
-or TRY to catch that ELECTRO-BALL from knocking out all of the POWER in the city.
OH, THAT CAN'T BE GOOD.
WHY DO VILLAINS ALWAYS LAUGH WHEN THEY THINK THEY'VE WON?
BYE!
HA
HA
HA
HA
HA
HA
WHAT ARE WE GONNA DO?
"WE" AREN'T DOING ANYTHING.
"YOU" ARE GONNA WAIT HERE.
AND I'M GONNA GO STOP THAT THING BEFORE ANYONE GETS HURT.
BUT X-5 IS ESCAPING!
UNFORTUNATELY, YES. BUT, I'M SURE WE'LL GET A SECOND CHANCE TO TAKE CARE OF HIM.
BUT, WE WON'T GET A SECOND CHANCE TO HELP THESE PEOPLE.
FUNNY, HOW WHEN HE PUTS IT LIKE THAT IT ALL MAKES SENSE.
I'LL BE RIGHT BACK.
YOU BETTER BE.
I WATCHED HIM STREAK HIGH UP INTO THE SKY.
AND THEN . . .

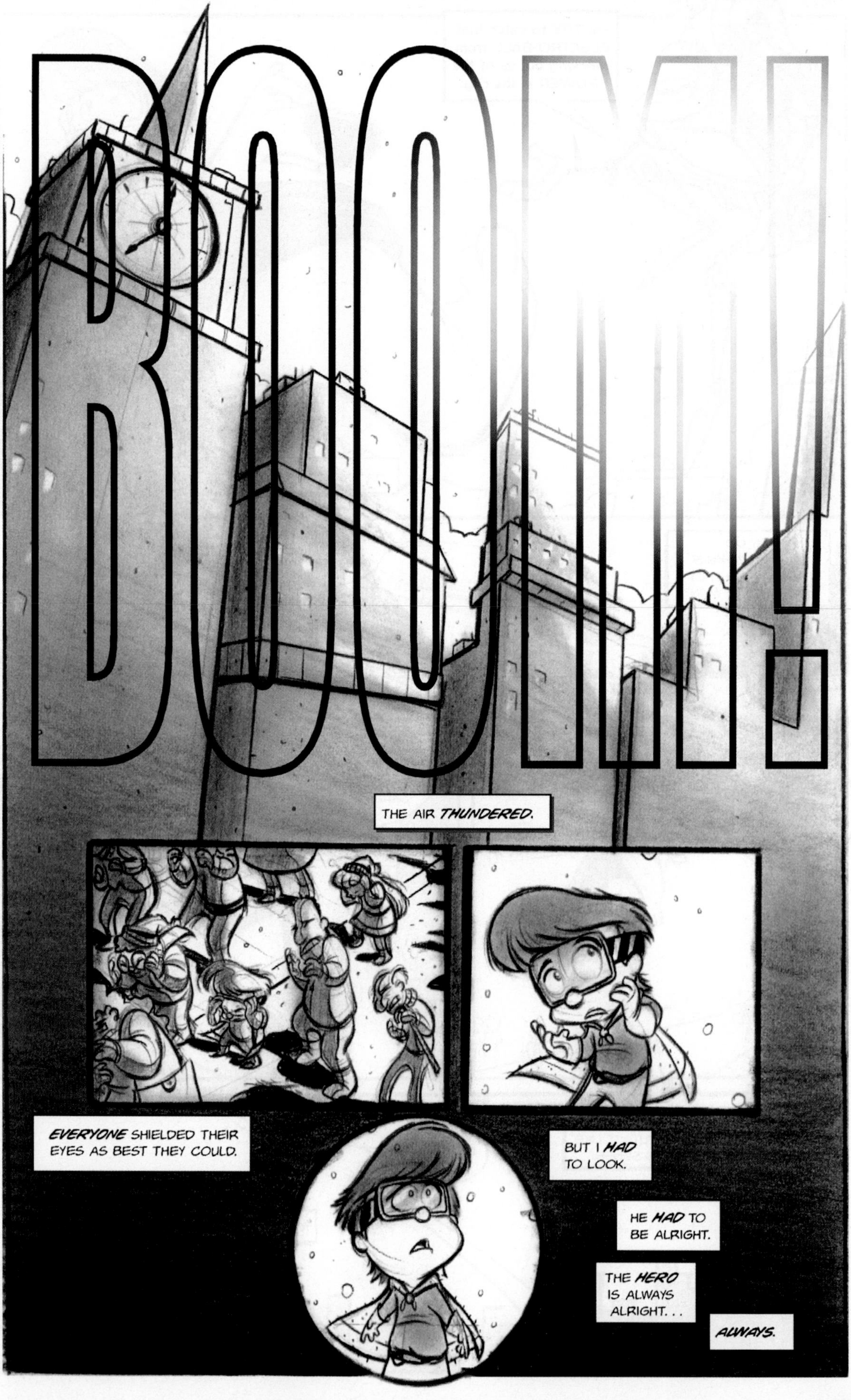
BOOM!
THE AIR THUNDERED.
EVERYONE SHIELDED THEIR EYES AS BEST THEY COULD.
BUT I HAD TO LOOK.
HE HAD TO BE ALRIGHT.
THE HERO IS ALWAYS ALRIGHT. . .
ALWAYS.

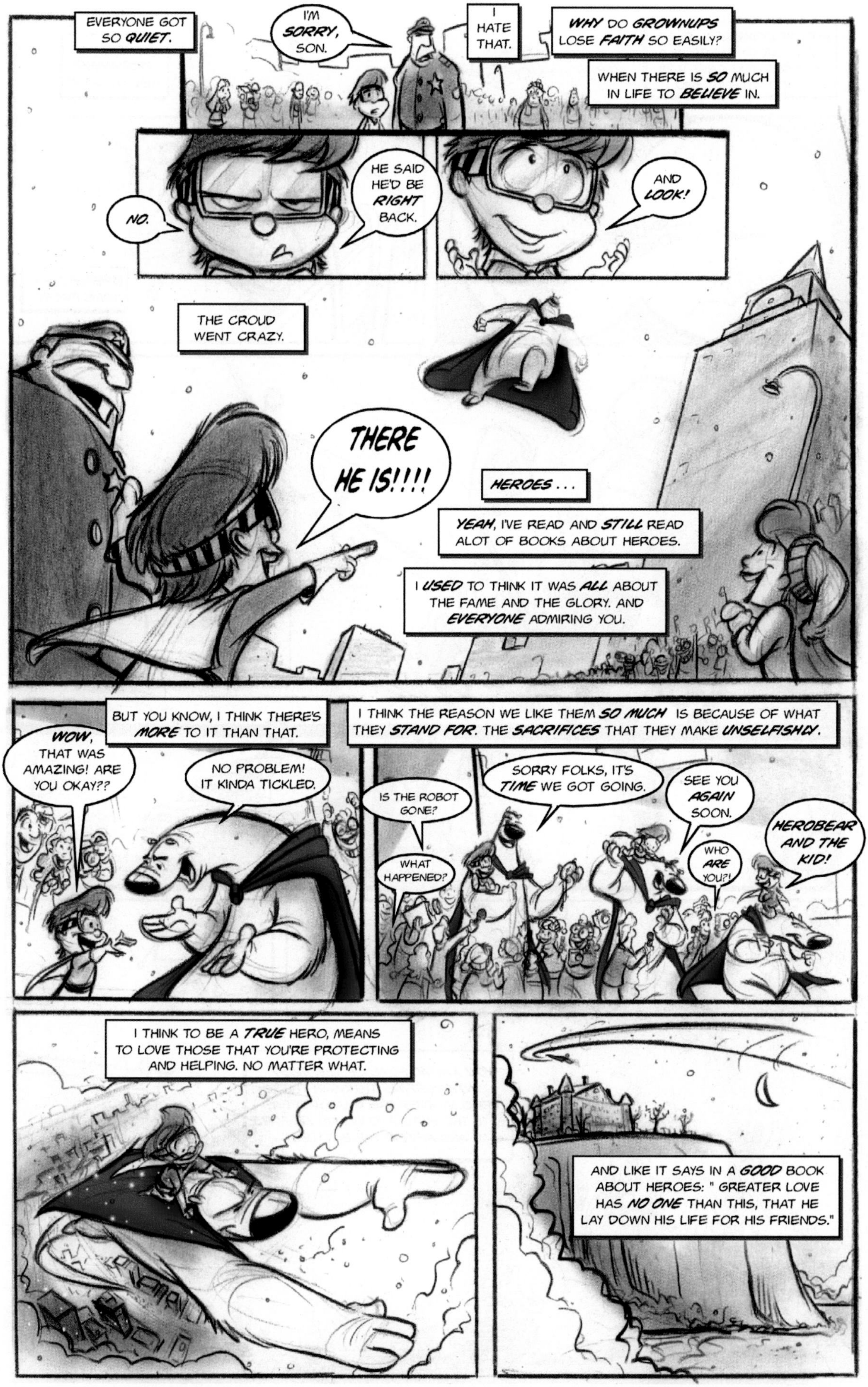
EVERYONE GOT SO QUIET.
I'M SORRY, SON.
I HATE THAT.
WHY DO GROWNUPS LOSE FAITH SO EASILY?
WHEN THERE IS SO MUCH IN LIFE TO BELIEVE IN.
NO.
HE SAID HE'D BE RIGHT BACK.
AND LOOK!
THE CROUD WENT CRAZY.
THERE HE IS!!!!
HEROES...
YEAH, I'VE READ AND STILL READ ALOT OF BOOKS ABOUT HEROES.
I USED TO THINK IT WAS ALL ABOUT THE FAME AND THE GLORY. AND EVERYONE ADMIRING YOU.
BUT YOU KNOW, I THINK THERE'S MORE TO IT THAN THAT.
WOW, THAT WAS AMAZING! ARE YOU OKAY??
NO PROBLEM! IT KINDA TICKLED.
I THINK THE REASON WE LIKE THEM SO MUCH IS BECAUSE OF WHAT THEY STAND FOR. THE SACRIFICES THAT THEY MAKE UNSELFISHLY.
IS THE ROBOT GONE?
WHAT HAPPENED?
SORRY FOLKS, IT'S TIME WE GOT GOING.
SEE YOU AGAIN SOON.
WHO ARE YOU?!
HEROBEAR AND THE KID!
I THINK TO BE A TRUE HERO, MEANS TO LOVE THOSE THAT YOU'RE PROTECTING AND HELPING. NO MATTER WHAT.
AND LIKE IT SAYS IN A GOOD BOOK ABOUT HEROES: " GREATER LOVE HAS NO ONE THAN THIS, THAT HE LAY DOWN HIS LIFE FOR HIS FRIENDS."

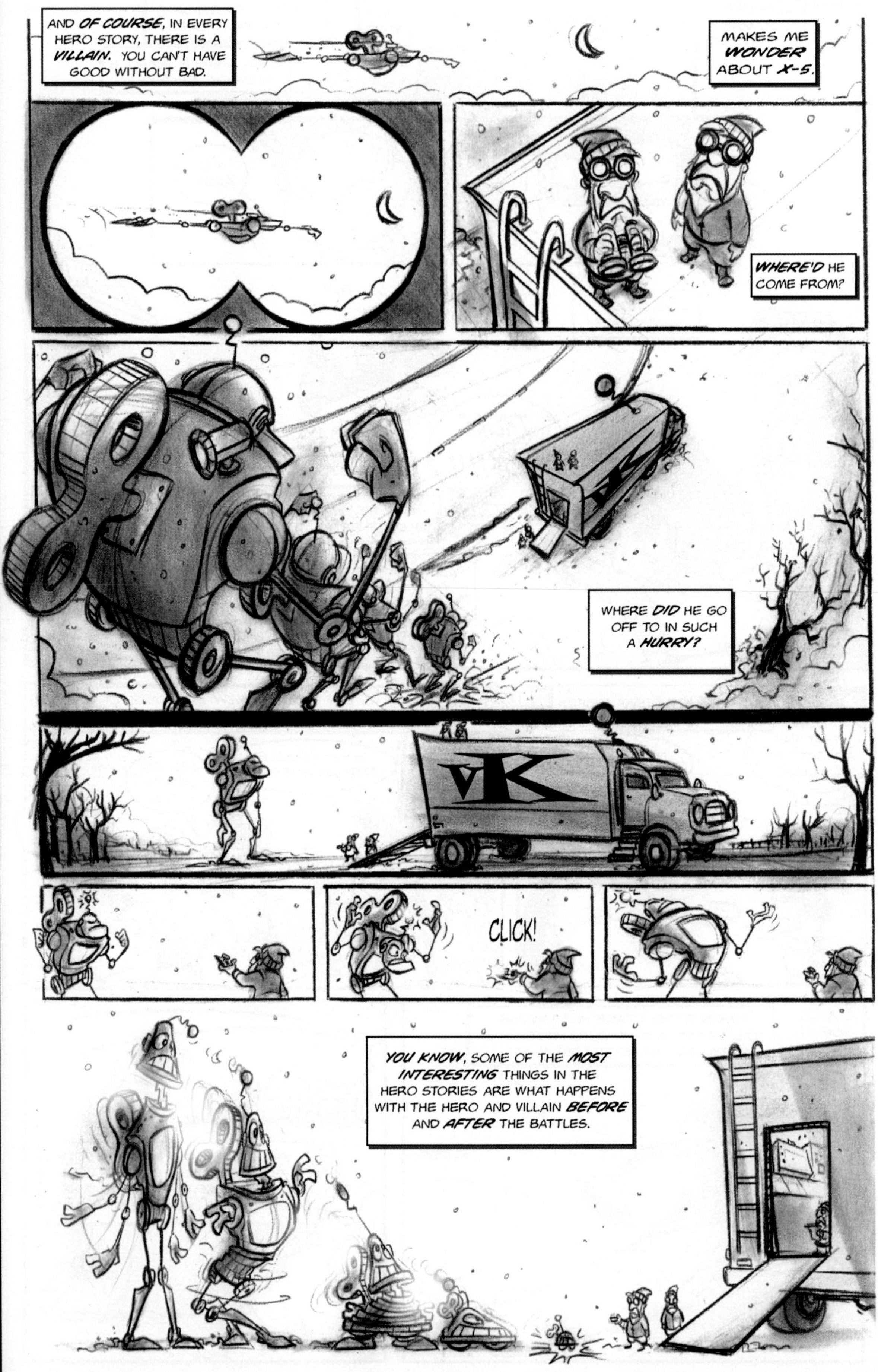
AND OF COURSE, IN EVERY HERO STORY, THERE IS A VILLAIN. YOU CAN'T HAVE GOOD WITHOUT BAD.
MAKES ME WONDER ABOUT X-5.
WHERE'D HE COME FROM?
WHERE DID HE GO OFF TO IN SUCH A HURRY?
VK
CLICK!
YOU KNOW, SOME OF THE MOST INTERESTING THINGS IN THE HERO STORIES ARE WHAT HAPPENS WITH THE HERO AND VILLAIN BEFORE AND AFTER THE BATTLES.

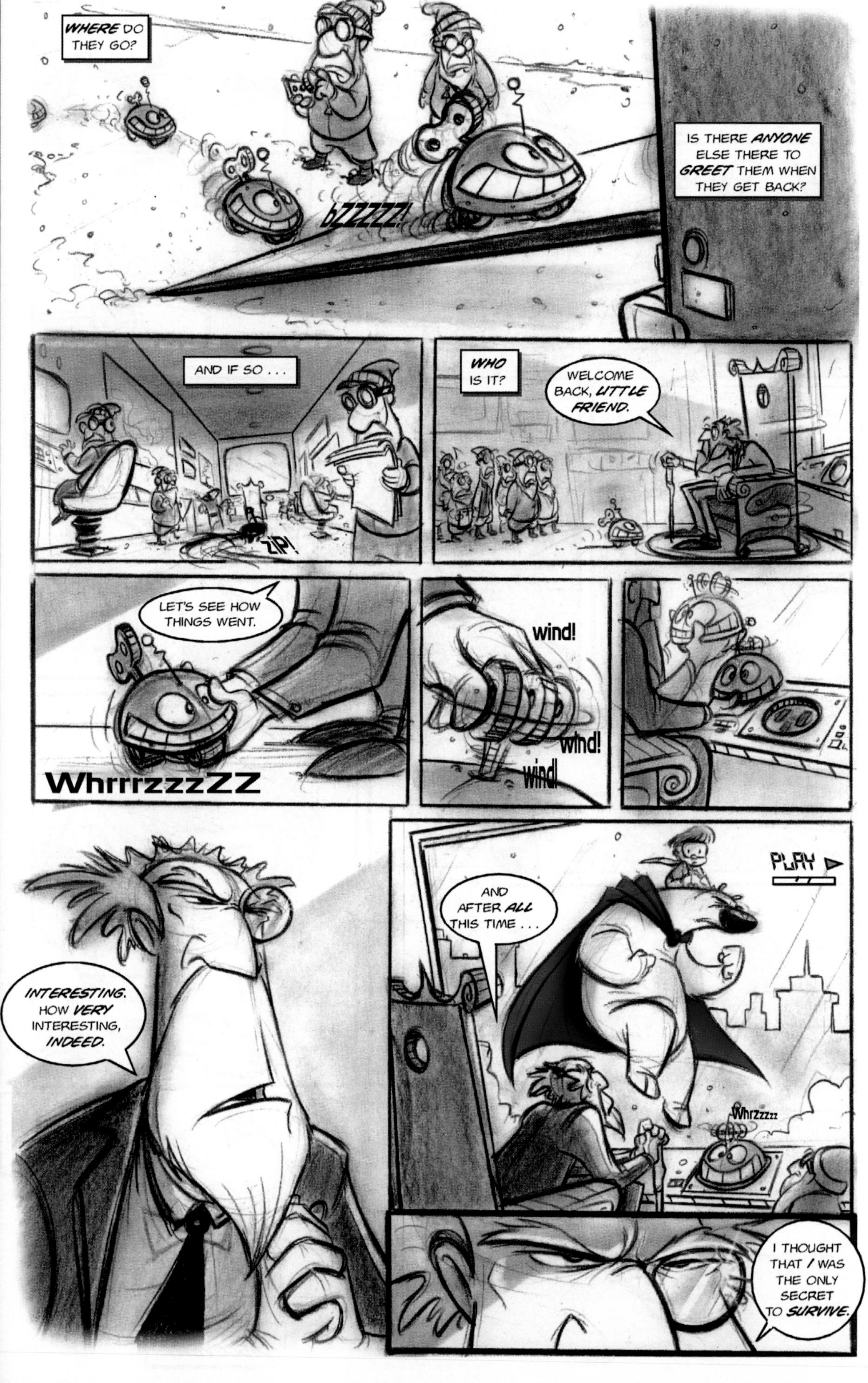
WHERE DO THEY GO?
bZZZZZ!
IS THERE ANYONE ELSE THERE TO GREET THEM WHEN THEY GET BACK?
AND IF SO . . .
ZIP!
WHO IS IT?
WELCOME BACK, LITTLE FRIEND.
LET'S SEE HOW THINGS WENT.
WhrrrzzzZZ
wind!
wind!
wind!
INTERESTING. HOW VERY INTERESTING, INDEED.
PLAY
AND AFTER ALL THIS TIME . . .
WhrZzzzz
I THOUGHT THAT I WAS THE ONLY SECRET TO SURVIVE.

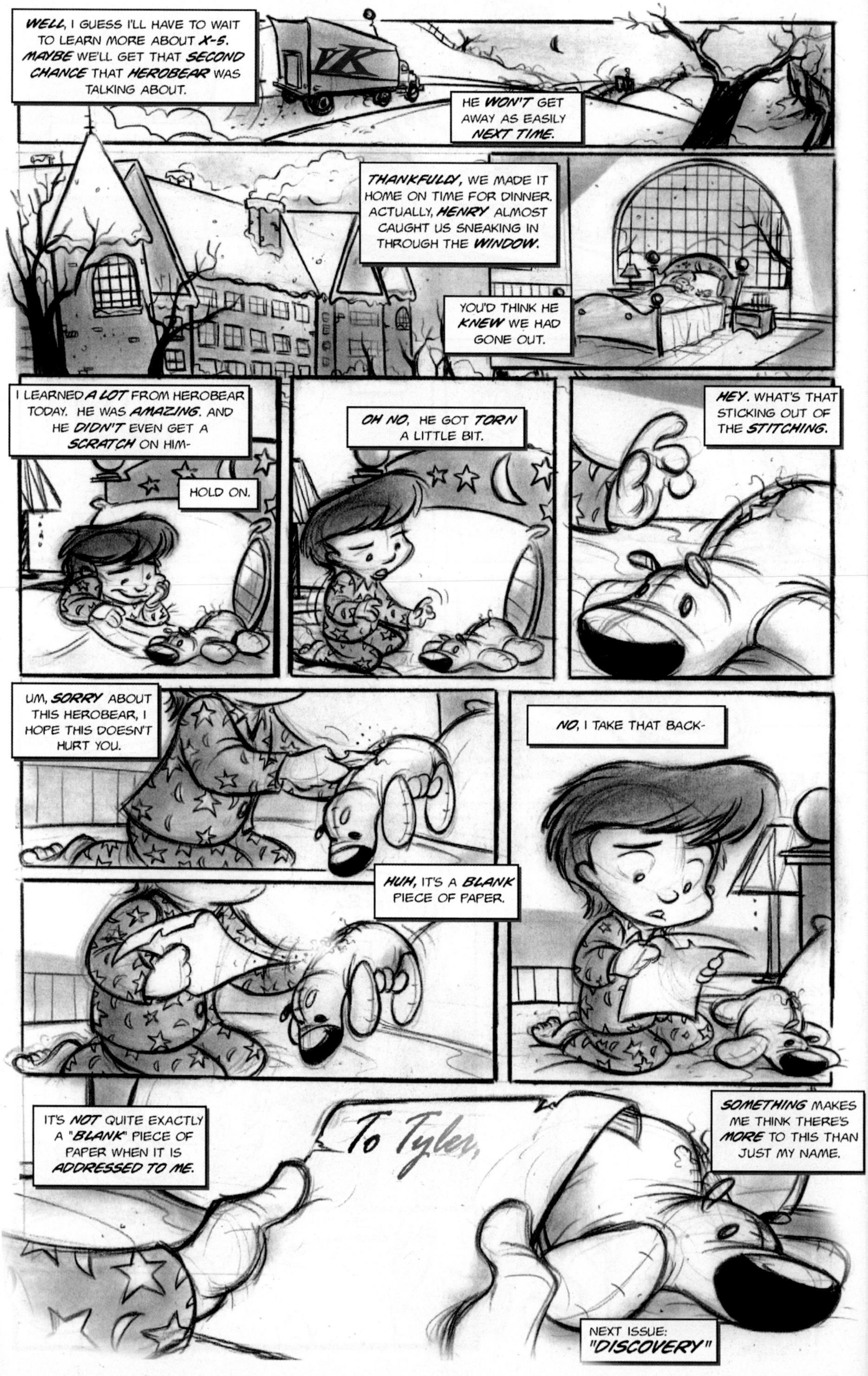

WELL, I GUESS I'LL HAVE TO WAIT TO LEARN MORE ABOUT X-5. MAYBE WE'LL GET THAT SECOND CHANCE THAT HEROBEAR WAS TALKING ABOUT.
HE WON'T GET AWAY AS EASILY NEXT TIME.
THANKFULLY, WE MADE IT HOME ON TIME FOR DINNER. ACTUALLY, HENRY ALMOST CAUGHT US SNEAKING IN THROUGH THE WINDOW.
YOU'D THINK HE KNEW WE HAD GONE OUT.
I LEARNED A LOT FROM HEROBEAR TODAY. HE WAS AMAZING. AND HE DIDN'T EVEN GET A SCRATCH ON HIM-
HOLD ON.
OH NO, HE GOT TORN A LITTLE BIT.
HEY. WHAT'S THAT STICKING OUT OF THE STITCHING.
UM, SORRY ABOUT THIS HEROBEAR, I HOPE THIS DOESN'T HURT YOU.
HUH, IT'S A BLANK PIECE OF PAPER.
NO, I TAKE THAT BACK-
IT'S NOT QUITE EXACTLY A "BLANK" PIECE OF PAPER WHEN IT IS ADDRESSED TO ME.
To Tyler,
SOMETHING MAKES ME THINK THERE'S MORE TO THIS THAN JUST MY NAME.
NEXT ISSUE: "DISCOVERY"

"**Wow**. It's very rare for a totally unknown artist to appear our of nowhere with a book as accomplished as this. Mike Kunkel has a totally realized beautiful style, and his storytelling and pacing are superb."
Comics International(www.comics-international.com)

"Mike Kunkel has brought to the page a story of wonderful innocence and sincere heroism that works on so many levels that it simply cannot be denied. It's so dang cute you just wanna reach inside the pages and hug everybody. Mark my words, Herobear and The Kid is one of those stories destined for the love of children all over the world, most of whom haven't even been born yet."
Christian Gossett (creator and artist of The Red Star)

"Kunkel's art style is a lot of the charm for me. He chose to print directly from his uninked pencils, and the end result is breathtaking. It feels spontaneous and young and exciting ...just like the protagonist and the rest of the story itself. I can't imagine Herobear and the Kid being drawn any other way."
Greg Mcelhatton (www.iCOMICS.COM)

"Kunkel's experience in animation shines through every page- not only in the style of the renderings, but in the pacing and action sequences. In short, a treasure. A treat."
R.C.Harvey (The Comics Journal and www.RCHARVEY.com)

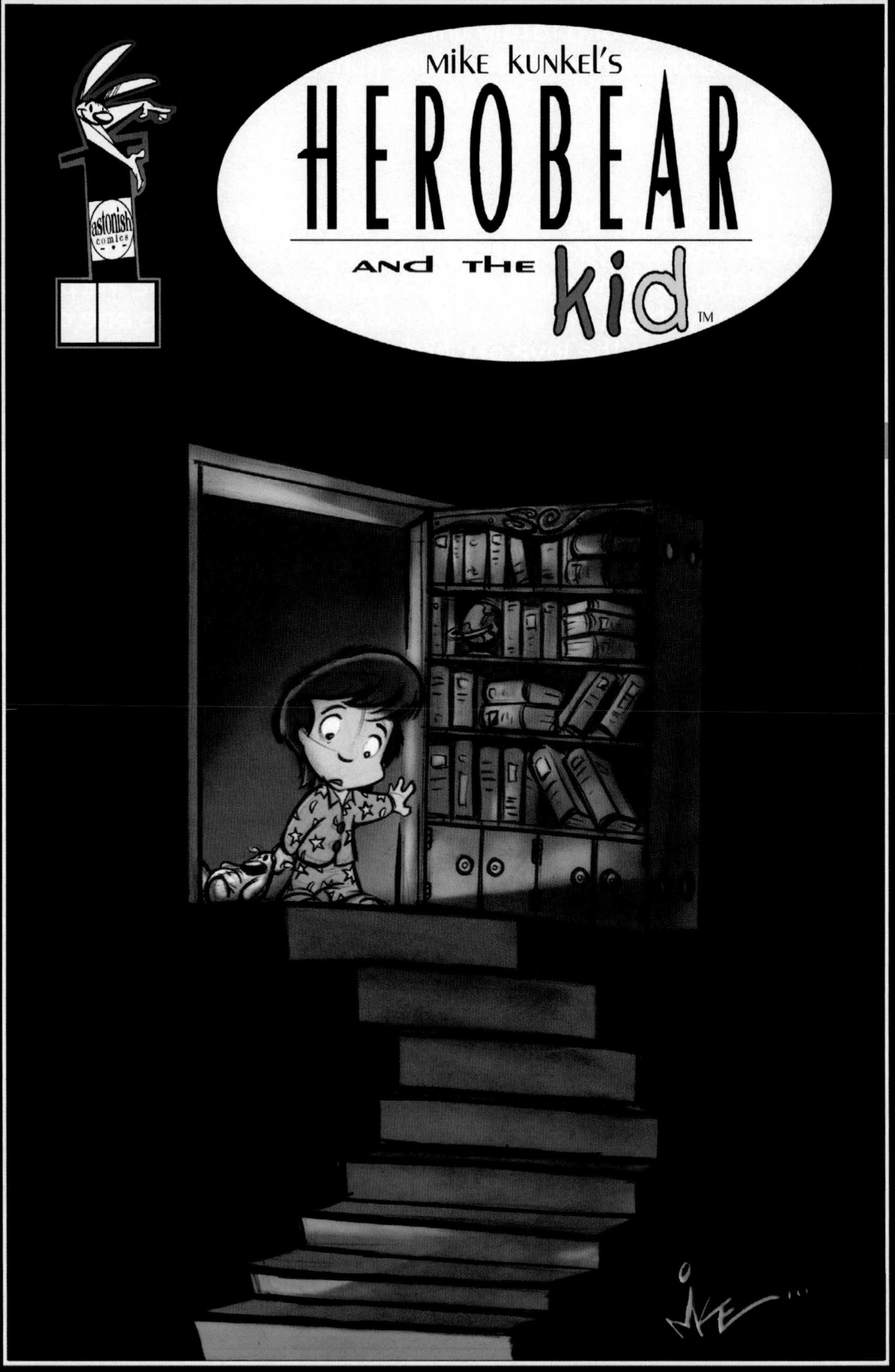
MIKE KUNKEL'S
HEROBEAR
AND THE kid
TM
astonish comics

book four

discovery

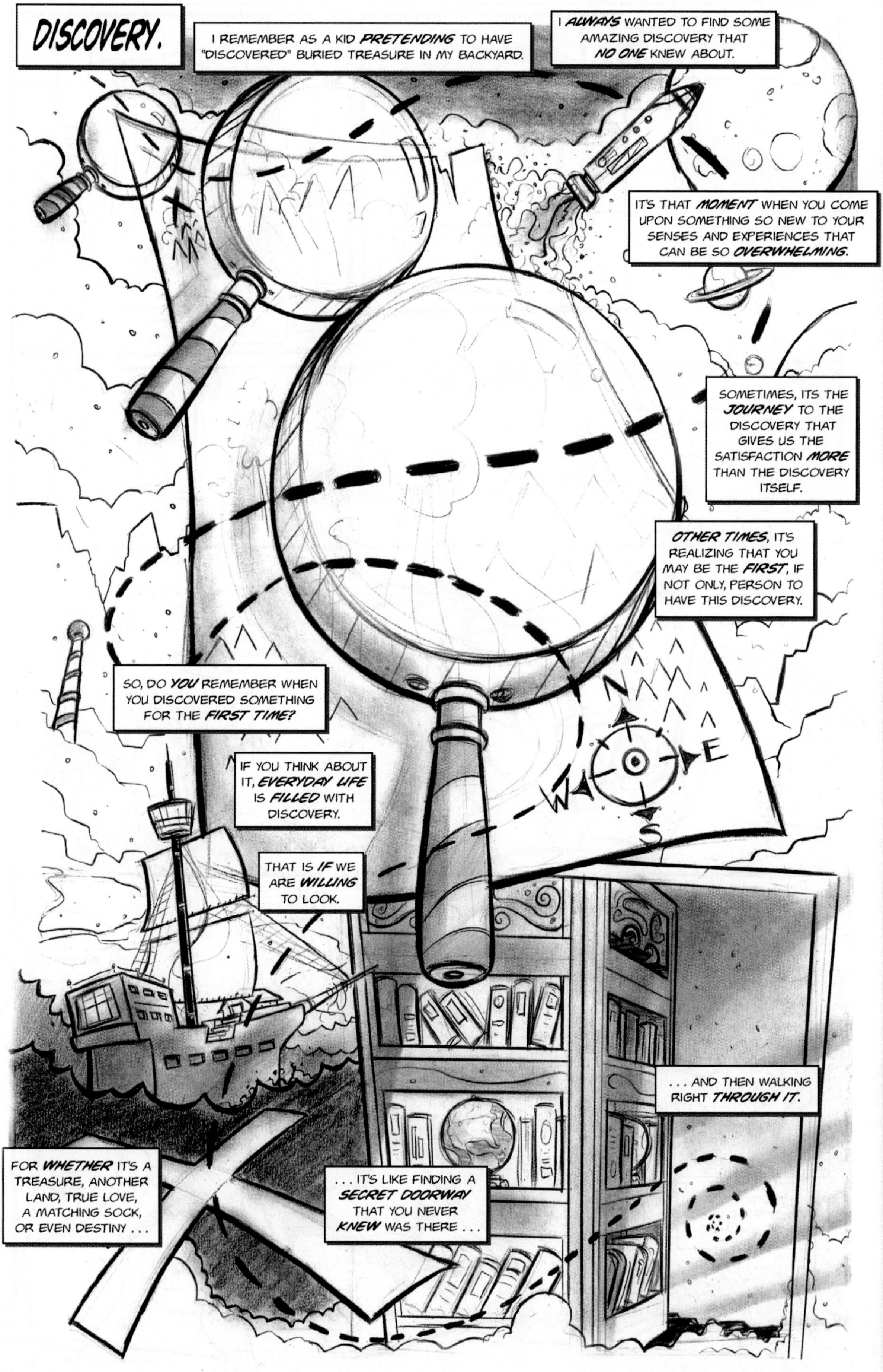
DISCOVERY.
I REMEMBER AS A KID PRETENDING TO HAVE "DISCOVERED" BURIED TREASURE IN MY BACKYARD.
I ALWAYS WANTED TO FIND SOME AMAZING DISCOVERY THAT NO ONE KNEW ABOUT.
IT'S THAT MOMENT WHEN YOU COME UPON SOMETHING SO NEW TO YOUR SENSES AND EXPERIENCES THAT CAN BE SO OVERWHELMING.
SOMETIMES, ITS THE JOURNEY TO THE DISCOVERY THAT GIVES US THE SATISFACTION MORE THAN THE DISCOVERY ITSELF.
OTHER TIMES, IT'S REALIZING THAT YOU MAY BE THE FIRST, IF NOT ONLY, PERSON TO HAVE THIS DISCOVERY.
SO, DO YOU REMEMBER WHEN YOU DISCOVERED SOMETHING FOR THE FIRST TIME?
IF YOU THINK ABOUT IT, EVERYDAY LIFE IS FILLED WITH DISCOVERY.
THAT IS IF WE ARE WILLING TO LOOK.
N
E
W
S
FOR WHETHER IT'S A TREASURE, ANOTHER LAND, TRUE LOVE, A MATCHING SOCK, OR EVEN DESTINY . . .
. . . IT'S LIKE FINDING A SECRET DOORWAY THAT YOU NEVER KNEW WAS THERE . . .
. . . AND THEN WALKING RIGHT THROUGH IT.

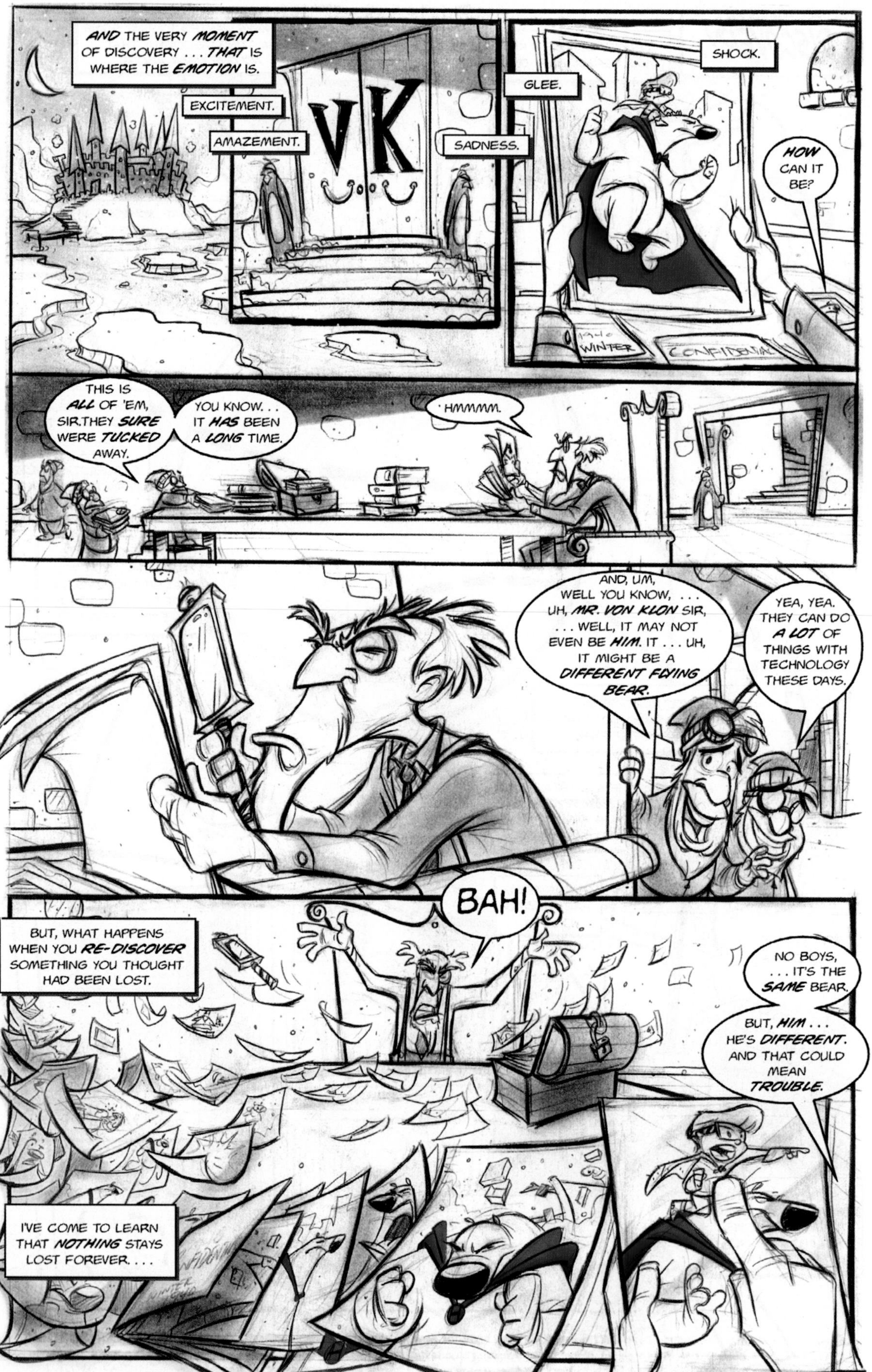
AND THE VERY MOMENT OF DISCOVERY . . . THAT IS WHERE THE EMOTION IS.
EXCITEMENT.
AMAZEMENT.
GLEE.
SADNESS.
SHOCK.
HOW CAN IT BE?
THIS IS ALL OF 'EM, SIR. THEY SURE WERE TUCKED AWAY.
YOU KNOW. . . IT HAS BEEN A LONG TIME.
HMMMM.
AND, UM, WELL YOU KNOW, . . . UH, MR. VON KLON SIR, . . . WELL, IT MAY NOT EVEN BE HIM. IT . . . UH, IT MIGHT BE A DIFFERENT FLYING BEAR.
YEA, YEA. THEY CAN DO A LOT OF THINGS WITH TECHNOLOGY THESE DAYS.
BAH!
BUT, WHAT HAPPENS WHEN YOU RE-DISCOVER SOMETHING YOU THOUGHT HAD BEEN LOST.
NO BOYS, . . . IT'S THE SAME BEAR.
BUT, HIM . . . HE'S DIFFERENT. AND THAT COULD MEAN TROUBLE.
I'VE COME TO LEARN THAT NOTHING STAYS LOST FOREVER . . .

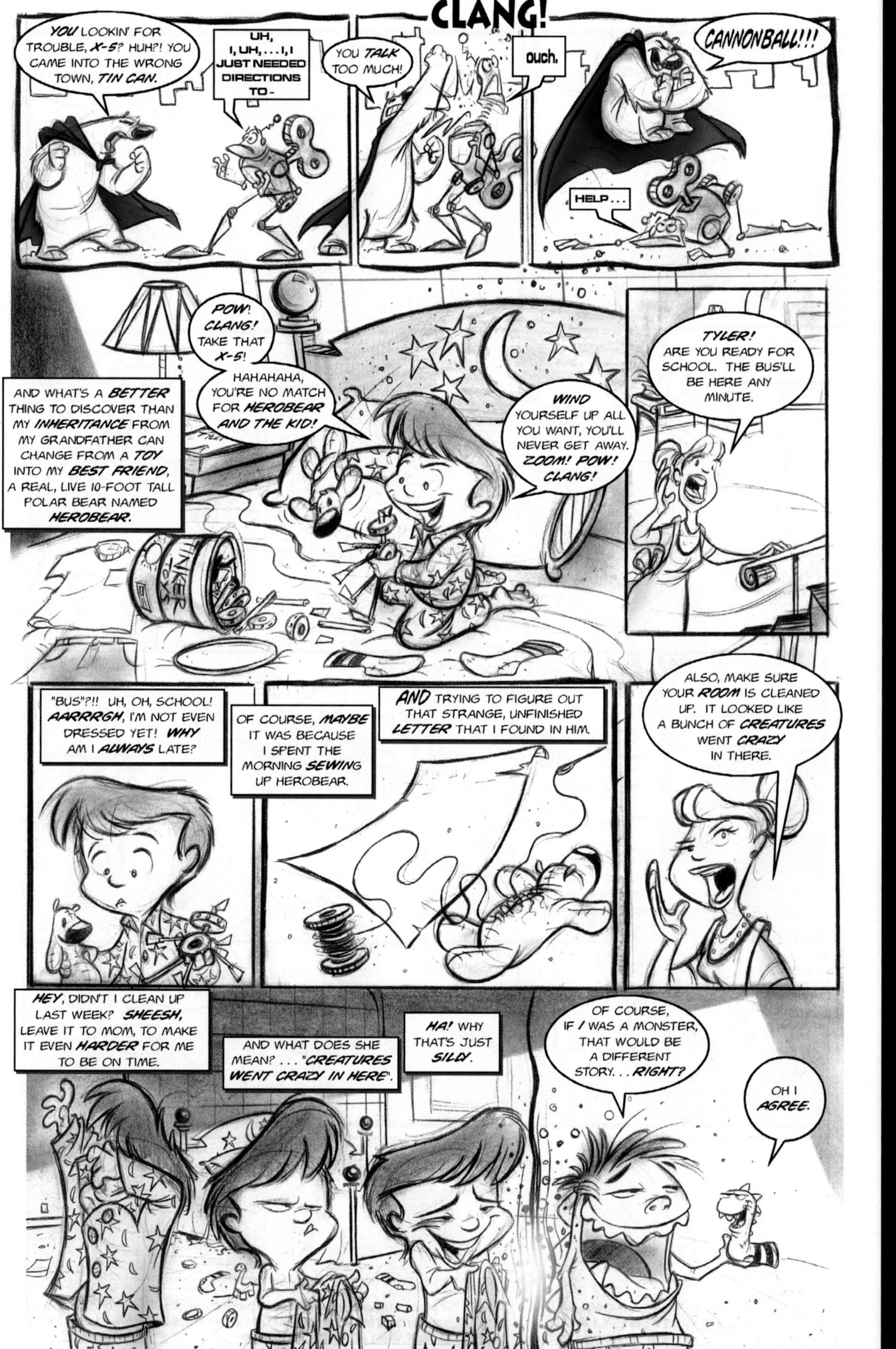

CLANG!
YOU LOOKIN' FOR TROUBLE, X-5? HUH?! YOU CAME INTO THE WRONG TOWN, TIN CAN.
UH, I, UH, . . . I, I JUST NEEDED DIRECTIONS TO-
YOU TALK TOO MUCH!
ouch.
CANNONBALL!!!
HELP . . .
POW! CLANG! TAKE THAT X-5!
HAHAHAHA, YOU'RE NO MATCH FOR HEROBEAR AND THE KID!
AND WHAT'S A BETTER THING TO DISCOVER THAN MY INHERITANCE FROM MY GRANDFATHER CAN CHANGE FROM A TOY INTO MY BEST FRIEND, A REAL, LIVE 10-FOOT TALL POLAR BEAR NAMED HEROBEAR.
WIND YOURSELF UP ALL YOU WANT, YOU'LL NEVER GET AWAY. ZOOM! POW! CLANG!
TINKER TOYS
TYLER! ARE YOU READY FOR SCHOOL. THE BUS'LL BE HERE ANY MINUTE.
"BUS"?!! UH, OH, SCHOOL! AARRRGH, I'M NOT EVEN DRESSED YET! WHY AM I ALWAYS LATE?
OF COURSE, MAYBE IT WAS BECAUSE I SPENT THE MORNING SEWING UP HEROBEAR.
AND TRYING TO FIGURE OUT THAT STRANGE, UNFINISHED LETTER THAT I FOUND IN HIM.
ALSO, MAKE SURE YOUR ROOM IS CLEANED UP. IT LOOKED LIKE A BUNCH OF CREATURES WENT CRAZY IN THERE.
HEY, DIDN'T I CLEAN UP LAST WEEK? SHEESH, LEAVE IT TO MOM, TO MAKE IT EVEN HARDER FOR ME TO BE ON TIME.
AND WHAT DOES SHE MEAN? . . . "CREATURES WENT CRAZY IN HERE".
HA! WHY THAT'S JUST SILLY.
OF COURSE, IF I WAS A MONSTER, THAT WOULD BE A DIFFERENT STORY. . . RIGHT?
OH I AGREE.

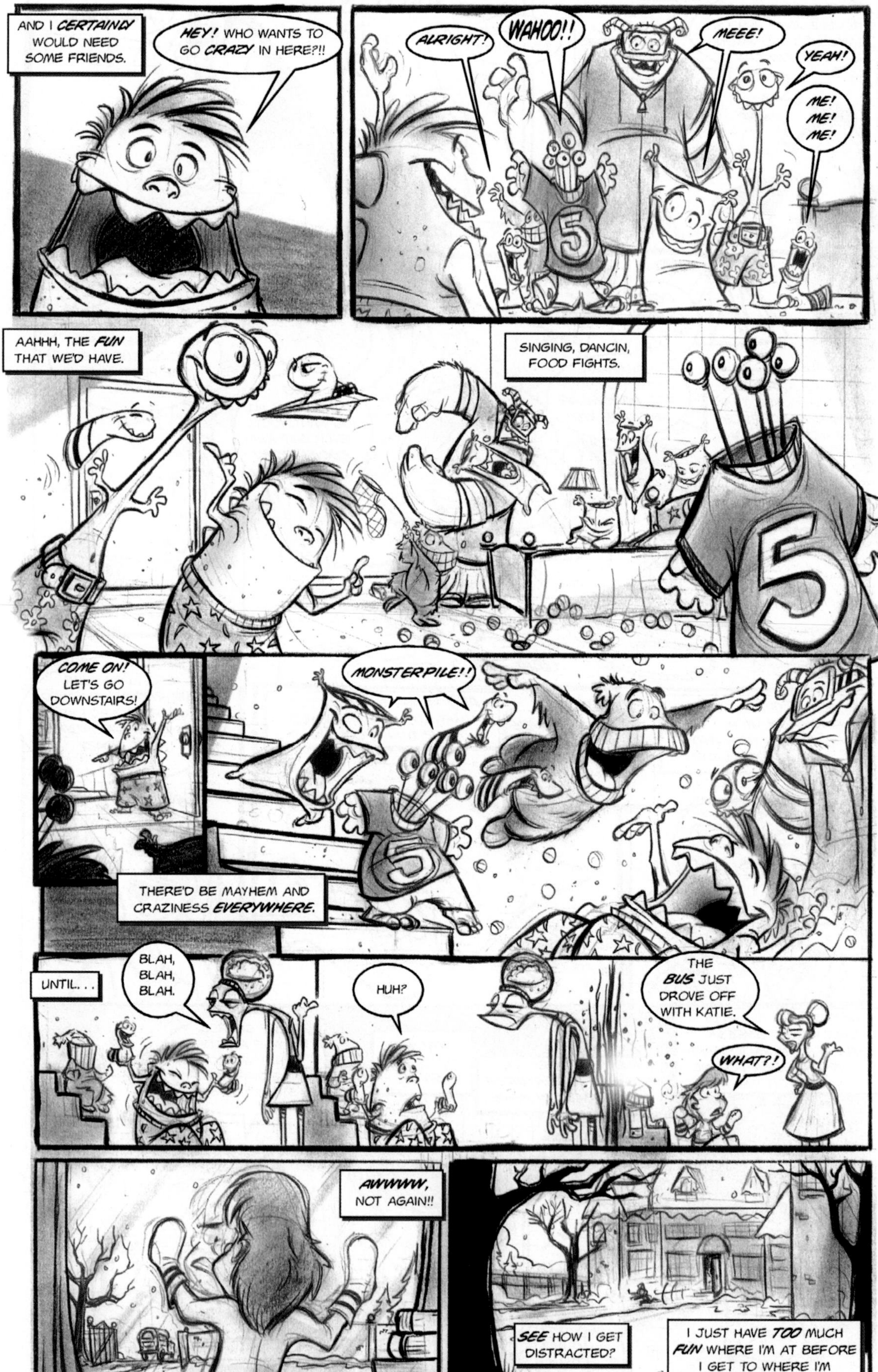

AND I CERTAINLY WOULD NEED SOME FRIENDS.
HEY! WHO WANTS TO GO CRAZY IN HERE?!!
ALRIGHT!
WAHOO!!
MEEE!
YEAH!
ME! ME! ME!
AAHHH, THE FUN THAT WE'D HAVE.
SINGING, DANCIN, FOOD FIGHTS.
COME ON! LET'S GO DOWNSTAIRS!
MONSTERPILE!!
THERE'D BE MAYHEM AND CRAZINESS EVERYWHERE.
UNTIL. . .
BLAH, BLAH, BLAH.
HUH?
THE BUS JUST DROVE OFF WITH KATIE.
WHAT?!
AWWWW, NOT AGAIN!!
SEE HOW I GET DISTRACTED?
I JUST HAVE TOO MUCH FUN WHERE I'M AT BEFORE I GET TO WHERE I'M SUPPOSED TO BE GOING.

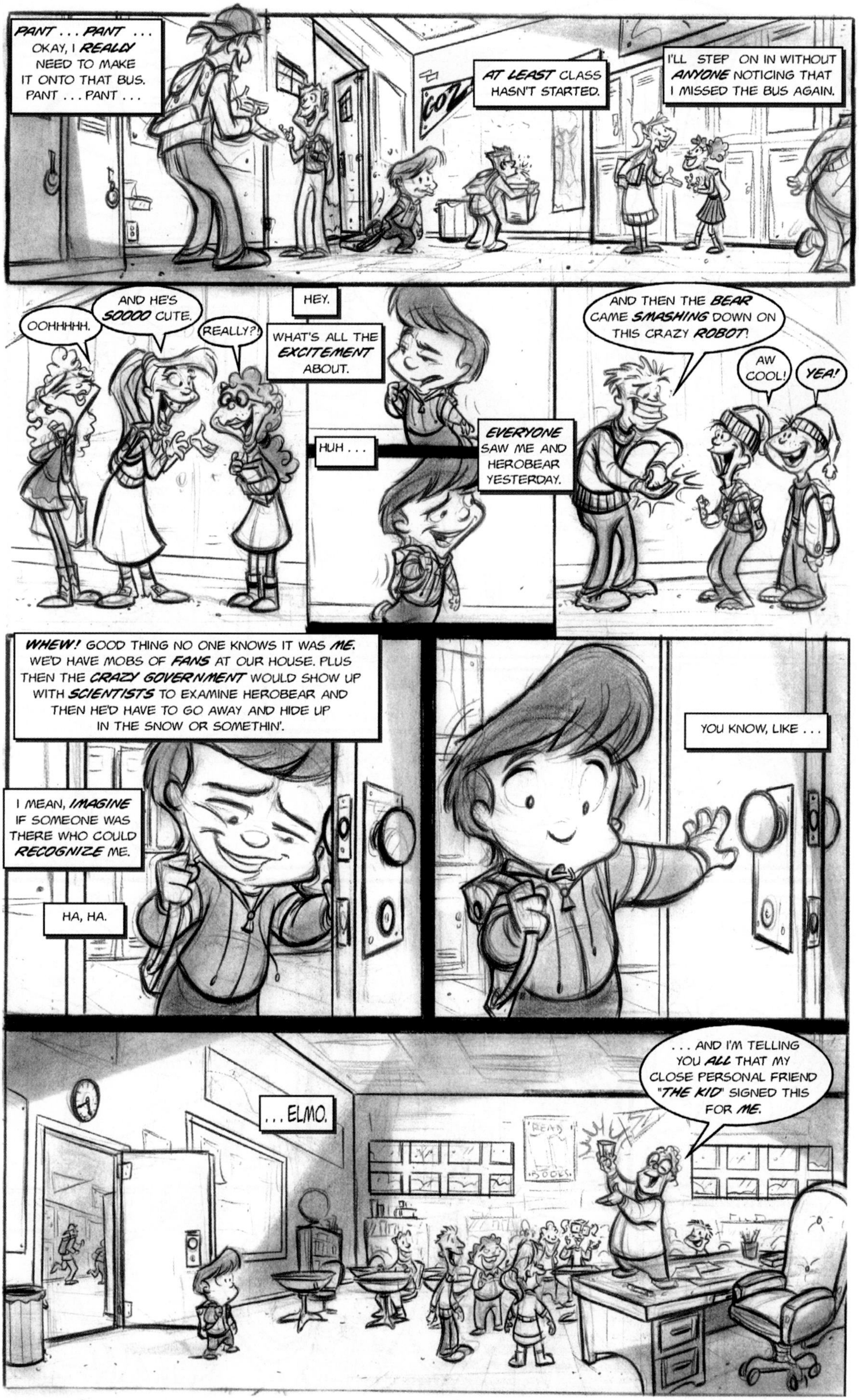

PANT . . . PANT . . . OKAY, I REALLY NEED TO MAKE IT ONTO THAT BUS. PANT . . . PANT . . .
AT LEAST CLASS HASN'T STARTED.
I'LL STEP ON IN WITHOUT ANYONE NOTICING THAT I MISSED THE BUS AGAIN.
OOHHHHH.
AND HE'S SOOOO CUTE.
REALLY?!
HEY.
WHAT'S ALL THE EXCITEMENT ABOUT.
HUH . . .
EVERYONE SAW ME AND HEROBEAR YESTERDAY.
AND THEN THE BEAR CAME SMASHING DOWN ON THIS CRAZY ROBOT!
AW COOL!
YEA!
WHEW! GOOD THING NO ONE KNOWS IT WAS ME. WE'D HAVE MOBS OF FANS AT OUR HOUSE. PLUS THEN THE CRAZY GOVERNMENT WOULD SHOW UP WITH SCIENTISTS TO EXAMINE HEROBEAR AND THEN HE'D HAVE TO GO AWAY AND HIDE UP IN THE SNOW OR SOMETHIN'.
I MEAN, IMAGINE IF SOMEONE WAS THERE WHO COULD RECOGNIZE ME.
HA, HA.
YOU KNOW, LIKE . . .
. . . ELMO.
. . . AND I'M TELLING YOU ALL THAT MY CLOSE PERSONAL FRIEND "THE KID" SIGNED THIS FOR ME.
READ BOOKS

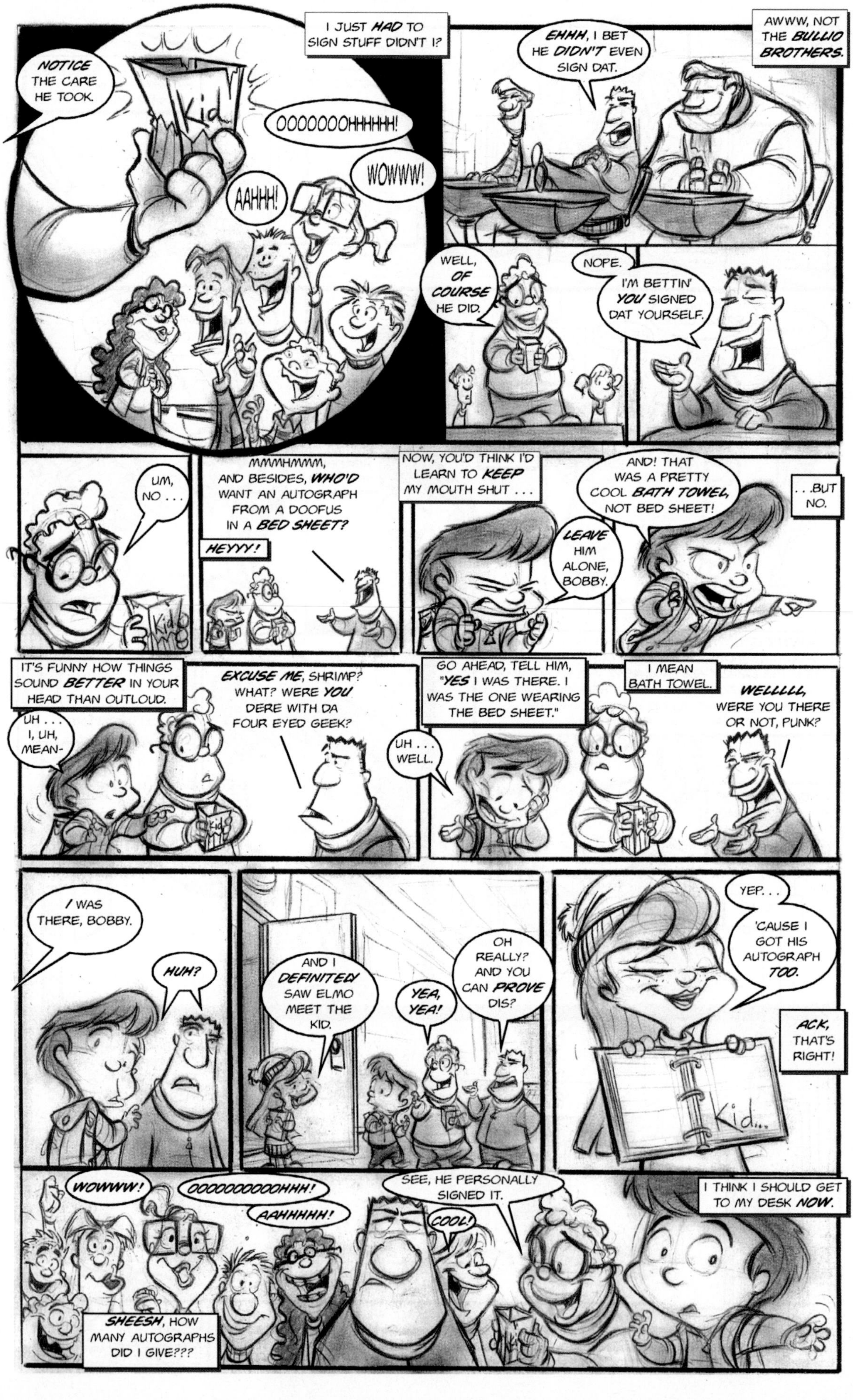
I JUST HAD TO SIGN STUFF DIDN'T I?
NOTICE THE CARE HE TOOK.
Kid
OOOOOOOHHHHHH!
WOWWW!
AAHHH!
AWWW, NOT THE BULLIO BROTHERS.
EHHH, I BET HE DIDN'T EVEN SIGN DAT.
WELL, OF COURSE HE DID.
NOPE.
I'M BETTIN' YOU SIGNED DAT YOURSELF.
UM, NO . . .
Kid
MMMHMMM, AND BESIDES, WHO'D WANT AN AUTOGRAPH FROM A DOOFUS IN A BED SHEET?
HEYYY!
NOW, YOU'D THINK I'D LEARN TO KEEP MY MOUTH SHUT . . .
LEAVE HIM ALONE, BOBBY.
AND! THAT WAS A PRETTY COOL BATH TOWEL, NOT BED SHEET!
. . .BUT NO.
IT'S FUNNY HOW THINGS SOUND BETTER IN YOUR HEAD THAN OUTLOUD.
UH . . . I, UH, MEAN-
EXCUSE ME, SHRIMP? WHAT? WERE YOU DERE WITH DA FOUR EYED GEEK?
GO AHEAD, TELL HIM, "YES I WAS THERE. I WAS THE ONE WEARING THE BED SHEET."
I MEAN BATH TOWEL.
UH . . . WELL.
WELLLLL, WERE YOU THERE OR NOT, PUNK?
I WAS THERE, BOBBY.
HUH?
AND I DEFINITELY SAW ELMO MEET THE KID.
YEA, YEA!
OH REALLY? AND YOU CAN PROVE DIS?
YEP. . .
'CAUSE I GOT HIS AUTOGRAPH TOO.
ACK, THAT'S RIGHT!
Kid...
WOWWW!
OOOOOOOOOOHHH!
AAHHHHH!
SEE, HE PERSONALLY SIGNED IT.
COOL!
I THINK I SHOULD GET TO MY DESK NOW.
SHEESH, HOW MANY AUTOGRAPHS DID I GIVE???

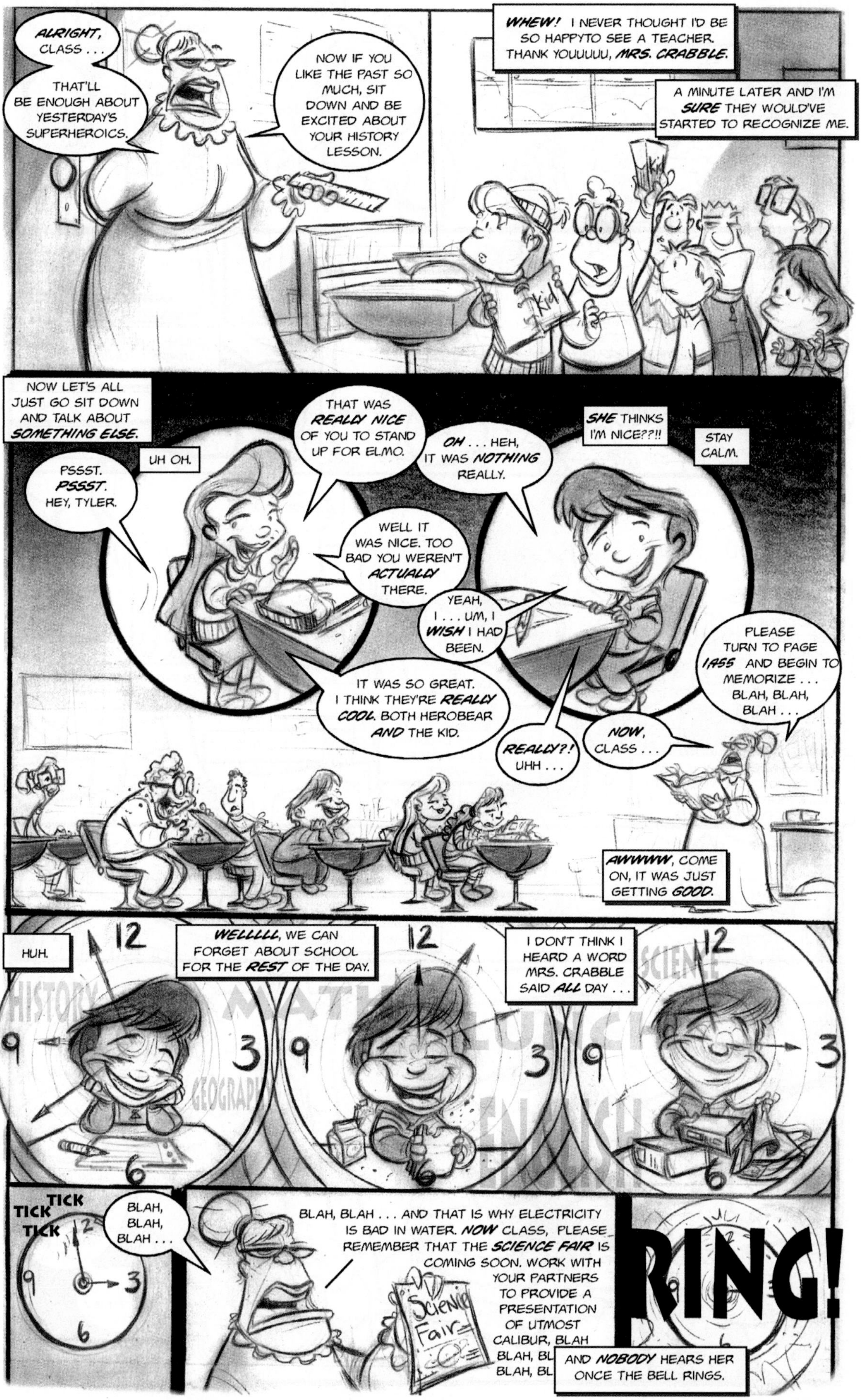
ALRIGHT, CLASS . . .
THAT'LL BE ENOUGH ABOUT YESTERDAY'S SUPERHEROICS.
NOW IF YOU LIKE THE PAST SO MUCH, SIT DOWN AND BE EXCITED ABOUT YOUR HISTORY LESSON.
WHEW! I NEVER THOUGHT I'D BE SO HAPPYTO SEE A TEACHER. THANK YOUUUUU, MRS. CRABBLE.
A MINUTE LATER AND I'M SURE THEY WOULD'VE STARTED TO RECOGNIZE ME.
NOW LET'S ALL JUST GO SIT DOWN AND TALK ABOUT SOMETHING ELSE.
PSSST. PSSST. HEY, TYLER.
UH OH.
THAT WAS REALLY NICE OF YOU TO STAND UP FOR ELMO.
OH . . . HEH, IT WAS NOTHING REALLY.
SHE THINKS I'M NICE??!!
STAY CALM.
WELL IT WAS NICE. TOO BAD YOU WEREN'T ACTUALLY THERE.
YEAH, I . . . UM, I WISH I HAD BEEN.
IT WAS SO GREAT. I THINK THEY'RE REALLY COOL. BOTH HEROBEAR AND THE KID.
REALLY?! UHH . . .
NOW, CLASS . . .
PLEASE TURN TO PAGE 1455 AND BEGIN TO MEMORIZE . . . BLAH, BLAH, BLAH . . .
AWWWW, COME ON, IT WAS JUST GETTING GOOD.
HUH.
WELLLLL, WE CAN FORGET ABOUT SCHOOL FOR THE REST OF THE DAY.
I DON'T THINK I HEARD A WORD MRS. CRABBLE SAID ALL DAY . . .
HISTORY
MATH
GEOGRAPHY
LUNCH
SCIENCE
ENGLISH
TICK TICK TICK
BLAH, BLAH, BLAH . . .
BLAH, BLAH . . . AND THAT IS WHY ELECTRICITY IS BAD IN WATER. NOW CLASS, PLEASE REMEMBER THAT THE SCIENCE FAIR IS COMING SOON. WORK WITH YOUR PARTNERS TO PROVIDE A PRESENTATION OF UTMOST CALIBUR, BLAH BLAH, BL BLAH, BL
Science Fair
RING!
AND NOBODY HEARS HER ONCE THE BELL RINGS.

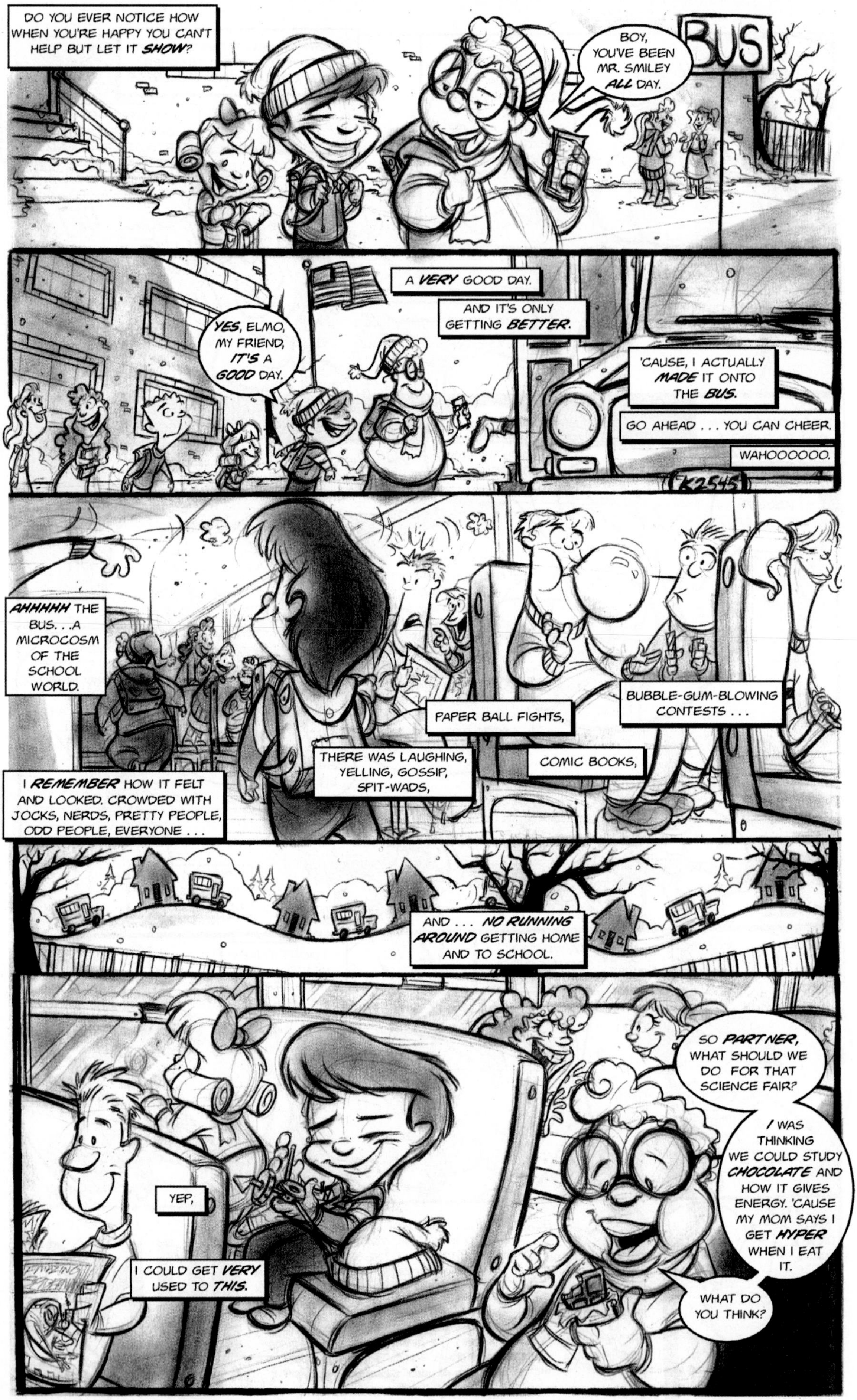

DO YOU EVER NOTICE HOW WHEN YOU'RE HAPPY YOU CAN'T HELP BUT LET IT SHOW?
BUS
BOY, YOU'VE BEEN MR. SMILEY ALL DAY.
A VERY GOOD DAY.
AND IT'S ONLY GETTING BETTER.
YES, ELMO, MY FRIEND, IT'S A GOOD DAY.
'CAUSE, I ACTUALLY MADE IT ONTO THE BUS.
GO AHEAD . . . YOU CAN CHEER.
WAHOOOOOO.
K2545
AHHHHH THE BUS. . .A MICROCOSM OF THE SCHOOL WORLD.
I REMEMBER HOW IT FELT AND LOOKED. CROWDED WITH JOCKS, NERDS, PRETTY PEOPLE, ODD PEOPLE, EVERYONE . . .
THERE WAS LAUGHING, YELLING, GOSSIP, SPIT-WADS,
PAPER BALL FIGHTS,
COMIC BOOKS,
BUBBLE-GUM-BLOWING CONTESTS . . .
AND . . . NO RUNNING AROUND GETTING HOME AND TO SCHOOL.
YEP,
I COULD GET VERY USED TO THIS.
SO PARTNER, WHAT SHOULD WE DO FOR THAT SCIENCE FAIR?
I WAS THINKING WE COULD STUDY CHOCOLATE AND HOW IT GIVES ENERGY. 'CAUSE MY MOM SAYS I GET HYPER WHEN I EAT IT.
WHAT DO YOU THINK?

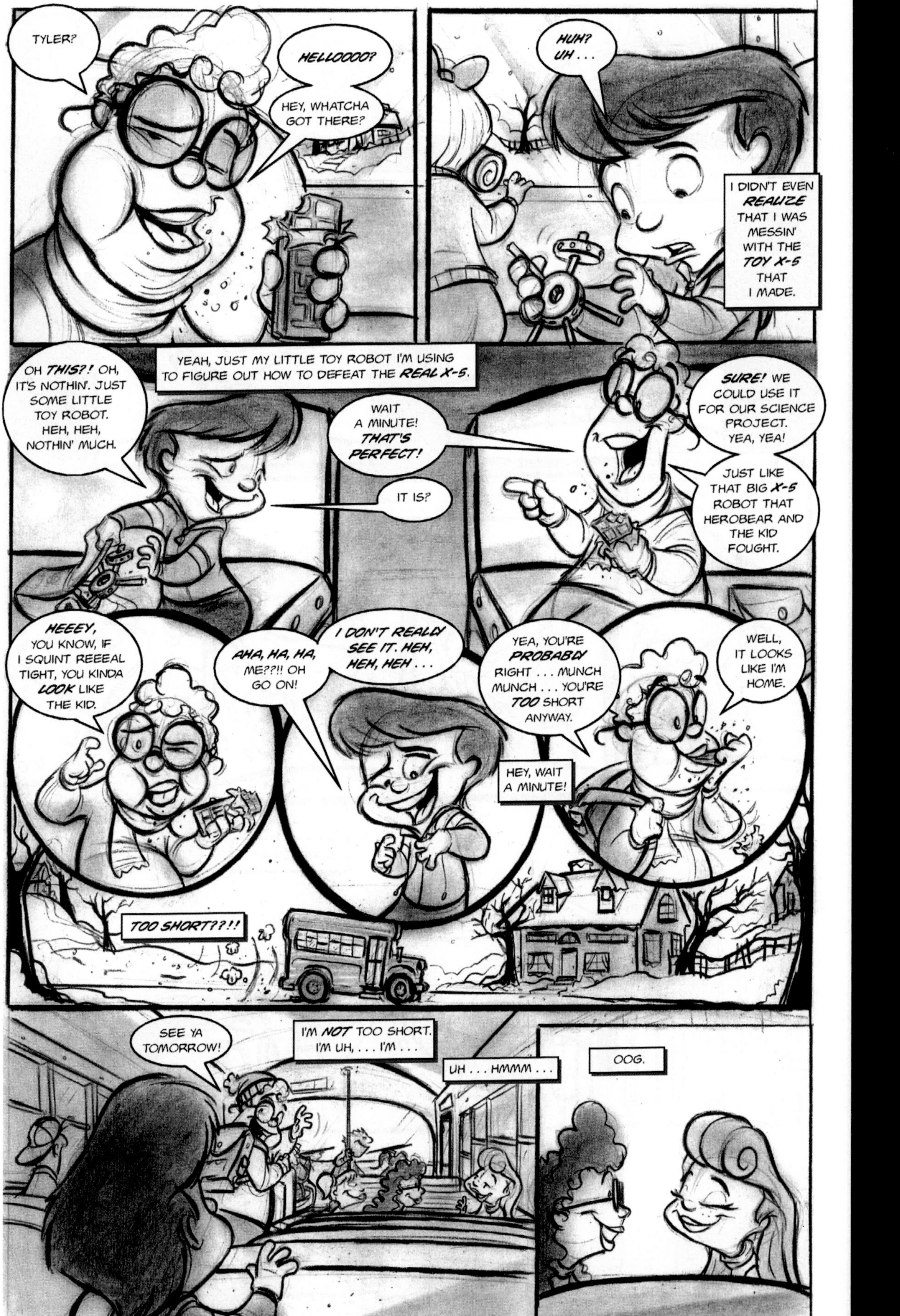

TYLER?
HELLOOOO?
HEY, WHATCHA GOT THERE?
HUH? UH . . .
I DIDN'T EVEN REALIZE THAT I WAS MESSIN' WITH THE TOY X-5 THAT I MADE.
YEAH, JUST MY LITTLE TOY ROBOT I'M USING TO FIGURE OUT HOW TO DEFEAT THE REAL X-5.
OH THIS?! OH, IT'S NOTHIN'. JUST SOME LITTLE TOY ROBOT. HEH, HEH, NOTHIN' MUCH.
WAIT A MINUTE! THAT'S PERFECT!
IT IS?
SURE! WE COULD USE IT FOR OUR SCIENCE PROJECT. YEA, YEA!
JUST LIKE THAT BIG X-5 ROBOT THAT HEROBEAR AND THE KID FOUGHT.
HEEEY, YOU KNOW, IF I SQUINT REEEAL TIGHT, YOU KINDA LOOK LIKE THE KID.
AHA, HA, HA, ME??!! OH GO ON!
I DON'T REALLY SEE IT. HEH, HEH, HEH . . .
YEA, YOU'RE PROBABLY RIGHT . . . MUNCH MUNCH . . . YOU'RE TOO SHORT ANYWAY.
WELL, IT LOOKS LIKE I'M HOME.
HEY, WAIT A MINUTE!
TOO SHORT??!!
SEE YA TOMORROW!
I'M NOT TOO SHORT. I'M UH, . . . I'M . . .
UH . . . HMMM . . .
OOG.

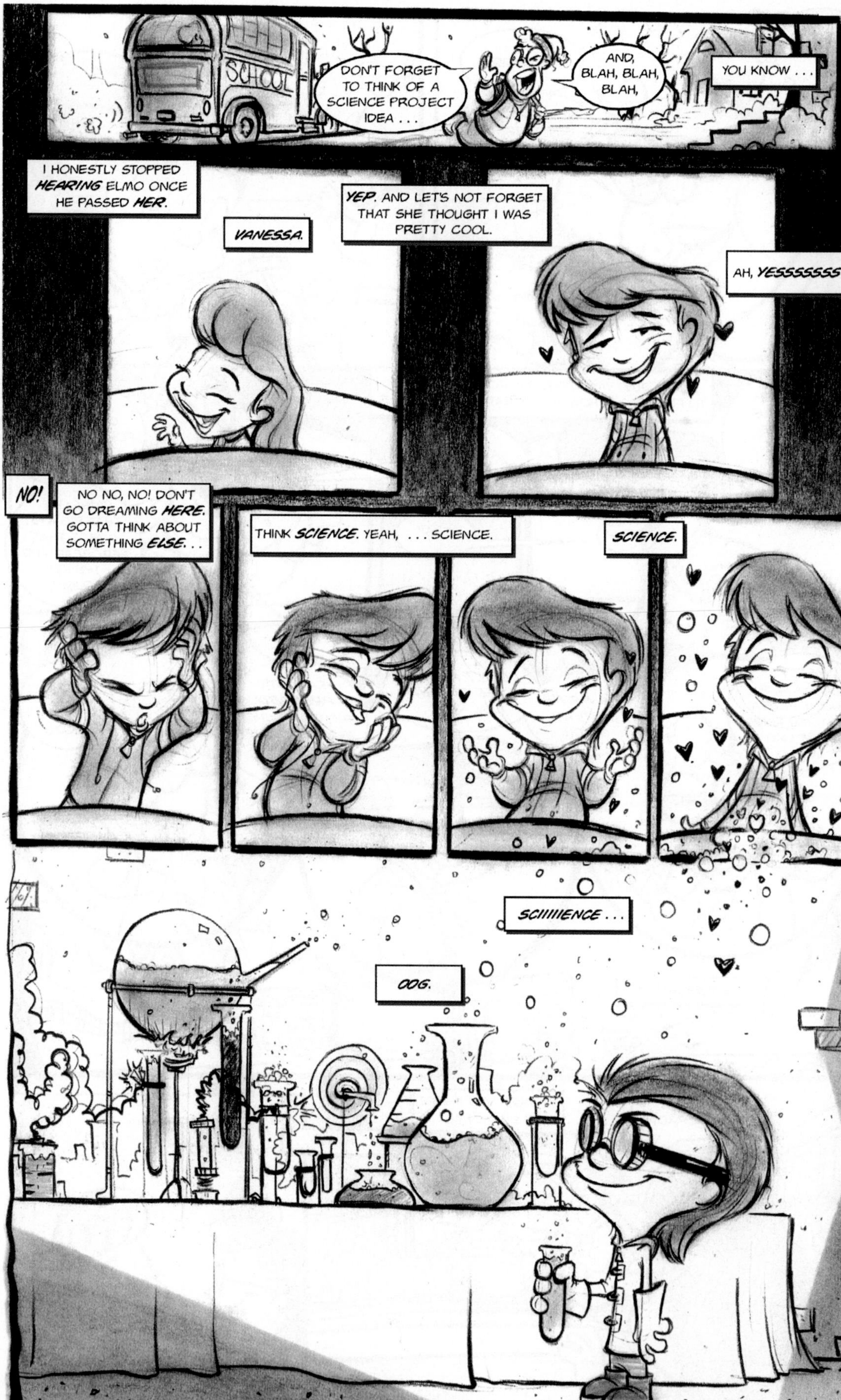

SCHOOL
DON'T FORGET TO THINK OF A SCIENCE PROJECT IDEA . . .
AND, BLAH, BLAH, BLAH,
YOU KNOW . . .
I HONESTLY STOPPED HEARING ELMO ONCE HE PASSED HER.
VANESSA.
YEP. AND LET'S NOT FORGET THAT SHE THOUGHT I WAS PRETTY COOL.
AH, YESSSSSSS . . .
NO!
NO NO, NO! DON'T GO DREAMING HERE. GOTTA THINK ABOUT SOMETHING ELSE. . .
THINK SCIENCE. YEAH, . . . SCIENCE.
SCIENCE.
SCIIIIIENCE . . .
OOG.

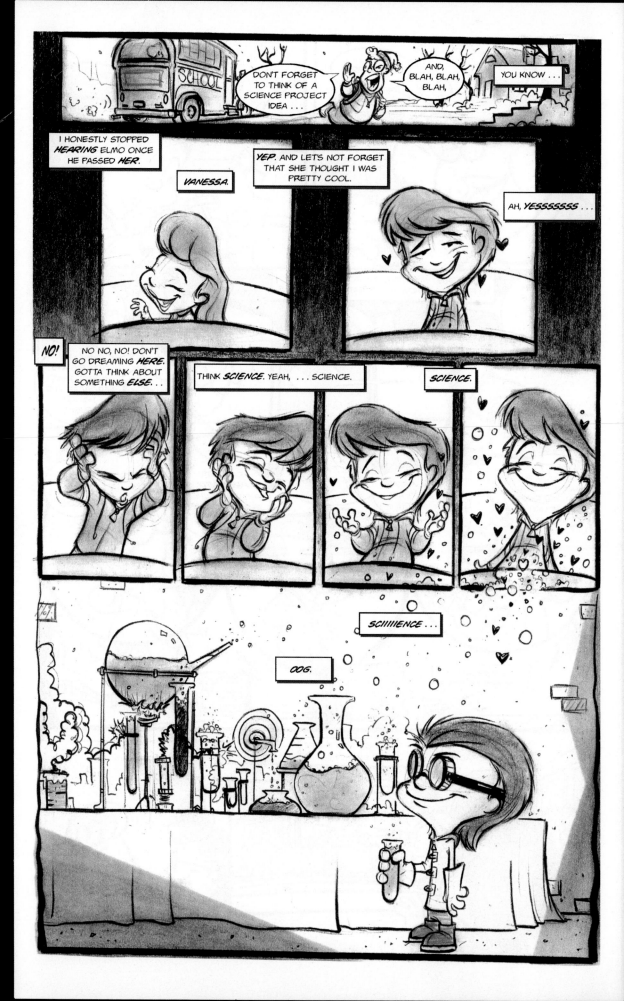

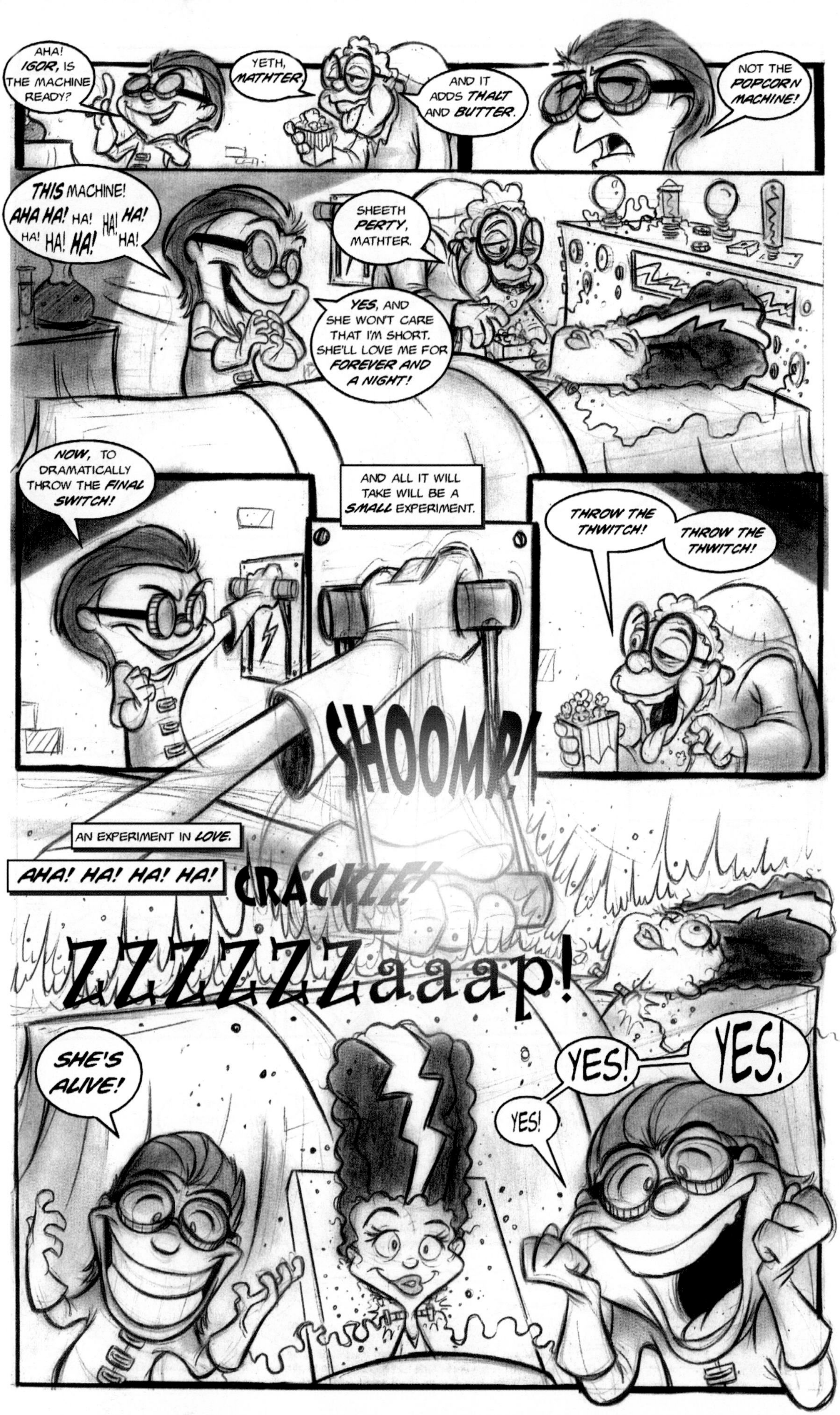
AHA! IGOR, IS THE MACHINE READY?
YETH, MATHTER.
AND IT ADDS THALT AND BUTTER.
NOT THE POPCORN MACHINE!
THIS MACHINE! AHA HA! HA! HA! HA! HA! HA! HA! HA!
SHEETH PERTY, MATHTER.
YES, AND SHE WON'T CARE THAT I'M SHORT. SHE'LL LOVE ME FOR FOREVER AND A NIGHT!
NOW, TO DRAMATICALLY THROW THE FINAL SWITCH!
AND ALL IT WILL TAKE WILL BE A SMALL EXPERIMENT.
THROW THE THWITCH!
THROW THE THWITCH!
SHOOMR!
AN EXPERIMENT IN LOVE.
AHA! HA! HA! HA!
CRACKLE!
ZZZZZZaaaap!
SHE'S ALIVE!
YES!
YES!
YES!

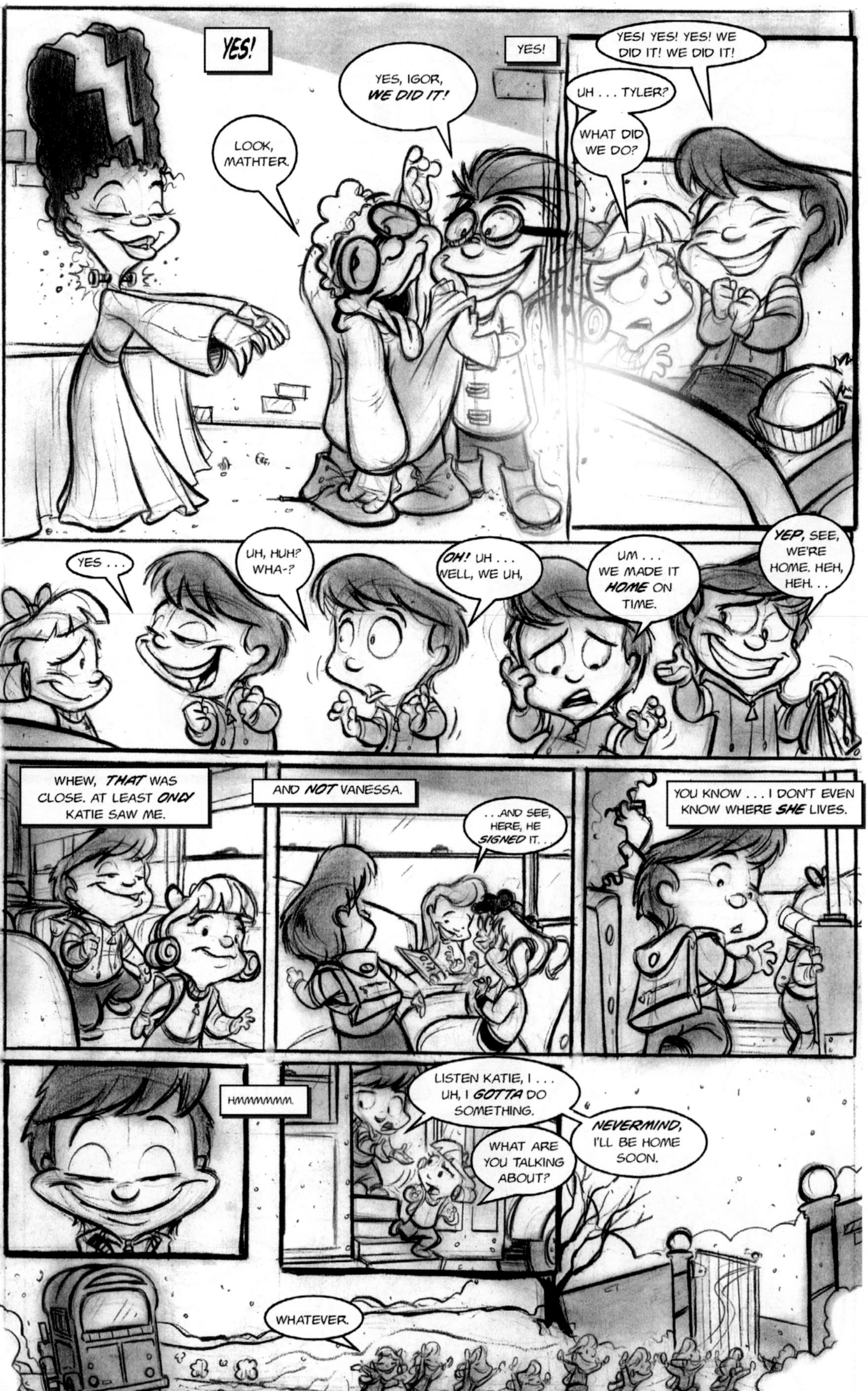
YES!
LOOK, MATHTER.
YES, IGOR, WE DID IT!
YES!
YES! YES! YES! WE DID IT! WE DID IT!
UH . . . TYLER?
WHAT DID WE DO?
YES . . .
UH, HUH? WHA-?
OH! UH . . . WELL, WE UH,
UM . . . WE MADE IT HOME ON TIME.
YEP, SEE, WE'RE HOME. HEH, HEH. . .
WHEW, THAT WAS CLOSE. AT LEAST ONLY KATIE SAW ME.
AND NOT VANESSA.
. . .AND SEE, HERE, HE SIGNED IT. . .
YOU KNOW . . . I DON'T EVEN KNOW WHERE SHE LIVES.
HMMMMMM.
LISTEN KATIE, I . . . UH, I GOTTA DO SOMETHING.
WHAT ARE YOU TALKING ABOUT?
NEVERMIND, I'LL BE HOME SOON.
WHATEVER.

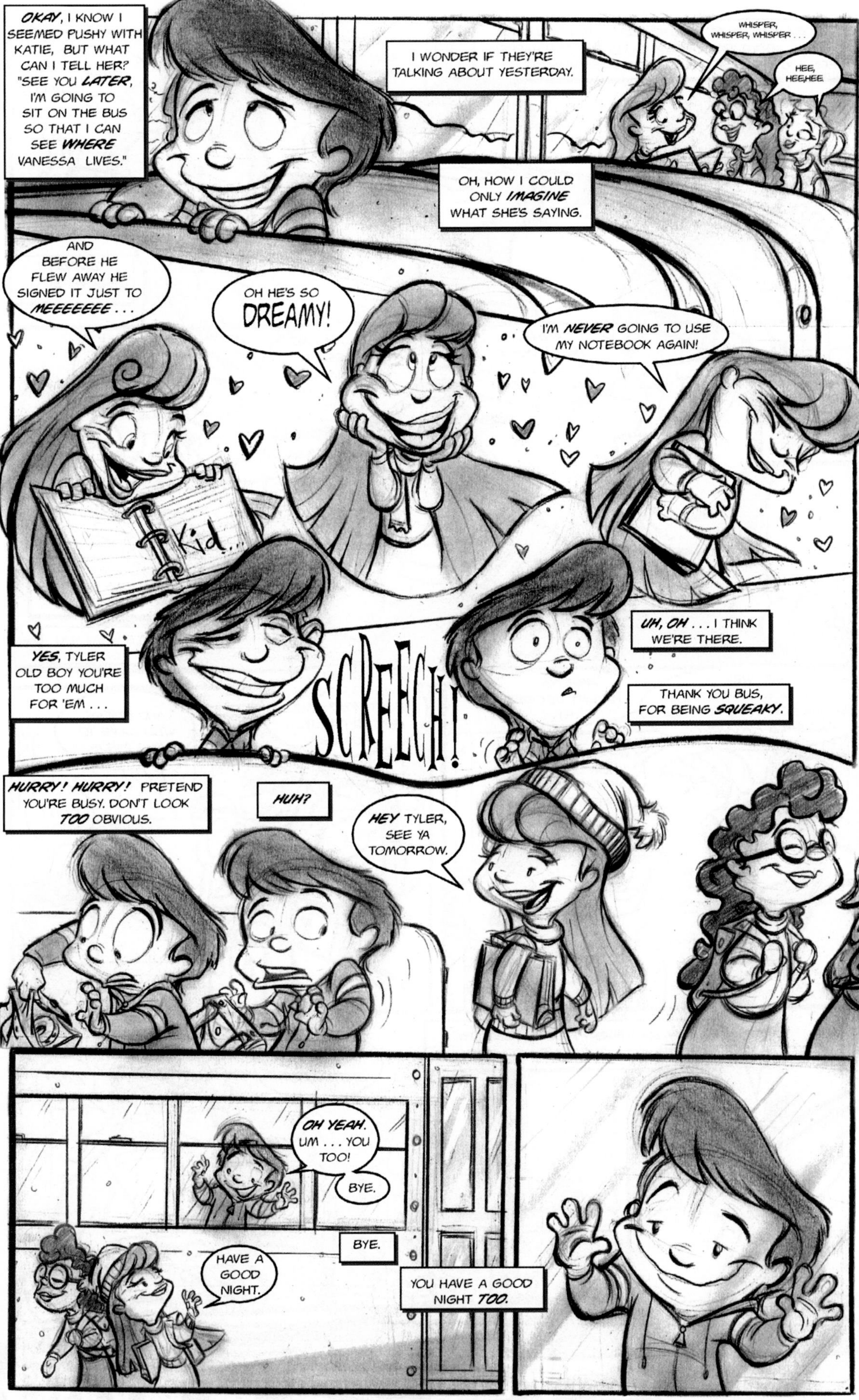
OKAY, I KNOW I SEEMED PUSHY WITH KATIE, BUT WHAT CAN I TELL HER? "SEE YOU LATER, I'M GOING TO SIT ON THE BUS SO THAT I CAN SEE WHERE VANESSA LIVES."
I WONDER IF THEY'RE TALKING ABOUT YESTERDAY.
WHISPER, WHISPER, WHISPER . . .
HEE, HEE,HEE
OH, HOW I COULD ONLY IMAGINE WHAT SHE'S SAYING.
AND BEFORE HE FLEW AWAY HE SIGNED IT JUST TO MEEEEEEE . . .
OH HE'S SO DREAMY!
I'M NEVER GOING TO USE MY NOTEBOOK AGAIN!
Kid...
YES, TYLER OLD BOY YOU'RE TOO MUCH FOR 'EM . . .
SCREECH!
UH, OH . . . I THINK WE'RE THERE.
THANK YOU BUS, FOR BEING SQUEAKY.
HURRY! HURRY! PRETEND YOU'RE BUSY. DON'T LOOK TOO OBVIOUS.
HUH?
HEY TYLER, SEE YA TOMORROW.
OH YEAH. UM . . . YOU TOO!
BYE.
BYE.
HAVE A GOOD NIGHT.
YOU HAVE A GOOD NIGHT TOO.

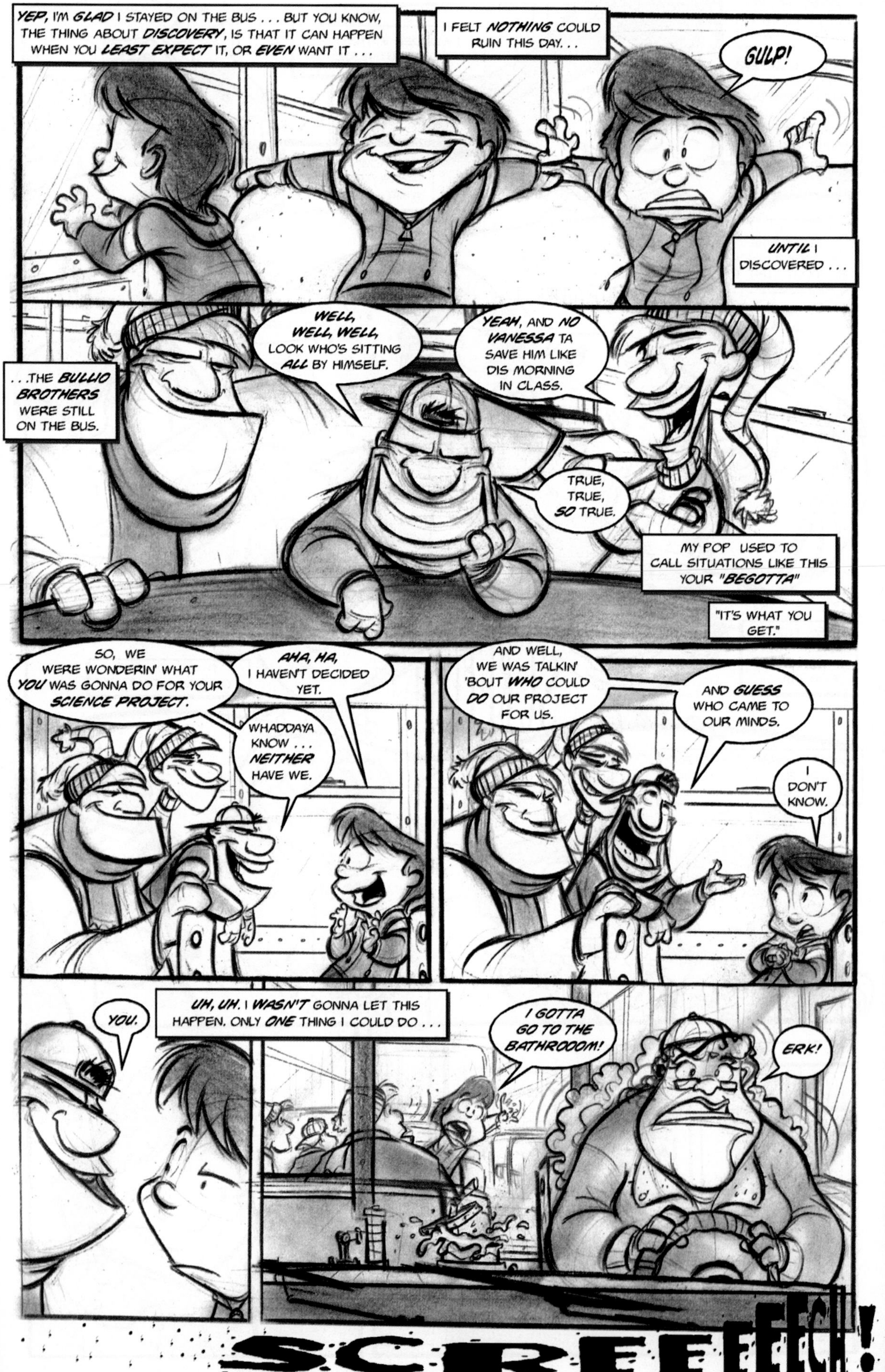

YEP, I'M GLAD I STAYED ON THE BUS . . . BUT YOU KNOW, THE THING ABOUT DISCOVERY, IS THAT IT CAN HAPPEN WHEN YOU LEAST EXPECT IT, OR EVEN WANT IT . . .
I FELT NOTHING COULD RUIN THIS DAY. . .
GULP!
UNTIL I DISCOVERED . . .
. . .THE BULLIO BROTHERS WERE STILL ON THE BUS.
WELL, WELL, WELL, LOOK WHO'S SITTING ALL BY HIMSELF.
YEAH, AND NO VANESSA TA SAVE HIM LIKE DIS MORNING IN CLASS.
TRUE, TRUE, SO TRUE.
MY POP USED TO CALL SITUATIONS LIKE THIS YOUR "BEGOTTA"
"IT'S WHAT YOU GET."
SO, WE WERE WONDERIN' WHAT YOU WAS GONNA DO FOR YOUR SCIENCE PROJECT.
AHA, HA, I HAVEN'T DECIDED YET.
WHADDAYA KNOW . . . NEITHER HAVE WE.
AND WELL, WE WAS TALKIN' 'BOUT WHO COULD DO OUR PROJECT FOR US.
AND GUESS WHO CAME TO OUR MINDS.
I DON'T KNOW.
YOU.
UH, UH. I WASN'T GONNA LET THIS HAPPEN. ONLY ONE THING I COULD DO . . .
I GOTTA GO TO THE BATHROOOM!
ERK!
SCREEEEECH!

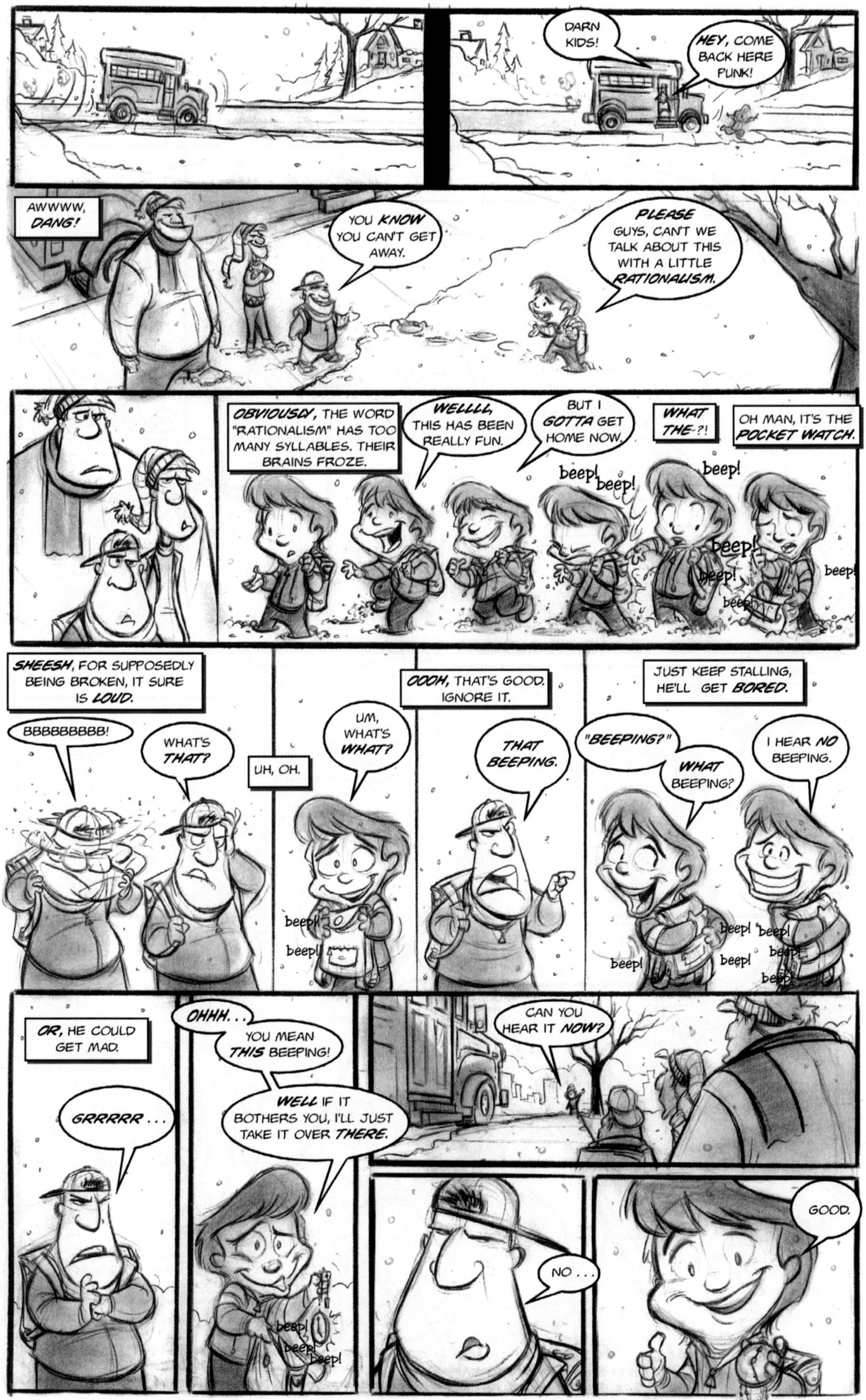
DARN KIDS!
HEY, COME BACK HERE PUNK!
AWWWW, DANG!
YOU KNOW YOU CAN'T GET AWAY.
PLEASE GUYS, CAN'T WE TALK ABOUT THIS WITH A LITTLE RATIONALISM.
OBVIOUSLY, THE WORD "RATIONALISM" HAS TOO MANY SYLLABLES. THEIR BRAINS FROZE.
WELLLL, THIS HAS BEEN REALLY FUN.
BUT I GOTTA GET HOME NOW.
beep! beep!
WHAT THE-?!
beep!
OH MAN, IT'S THE POCKET WATCH.
beep! beep! beep! beep!
SHEESH, FOR SUPPOSEDLY BEING BROKEN, IT SURE IS LOUD.
BBBBBBBBB!
WHAT'S THAT?
UH, OH.
UM, WHAT'S WHAT?
beep! beep!
OOOH, THAT'S GOOD. IGNORE IT.
THAT BEEPING.
JUST KEEP STALLING, HE'LL GET BORED.
"BEEPING?"
WHAT BEEPING?
I HEAR NO BEEPING.
beep! beep! beep! beep! beep! beep!
OR, HE COULD GET MAD.
GRRRRR . . .
OHHH. . . YOU MEAN THIS BEEPING!
WELL IF IT BOTHERS YOU, I'LL JUST TAKE IT OVER THERE.
beep! beep! beep!
CAN YOU HEAR IT NOW?
NO . . .
GOOD.

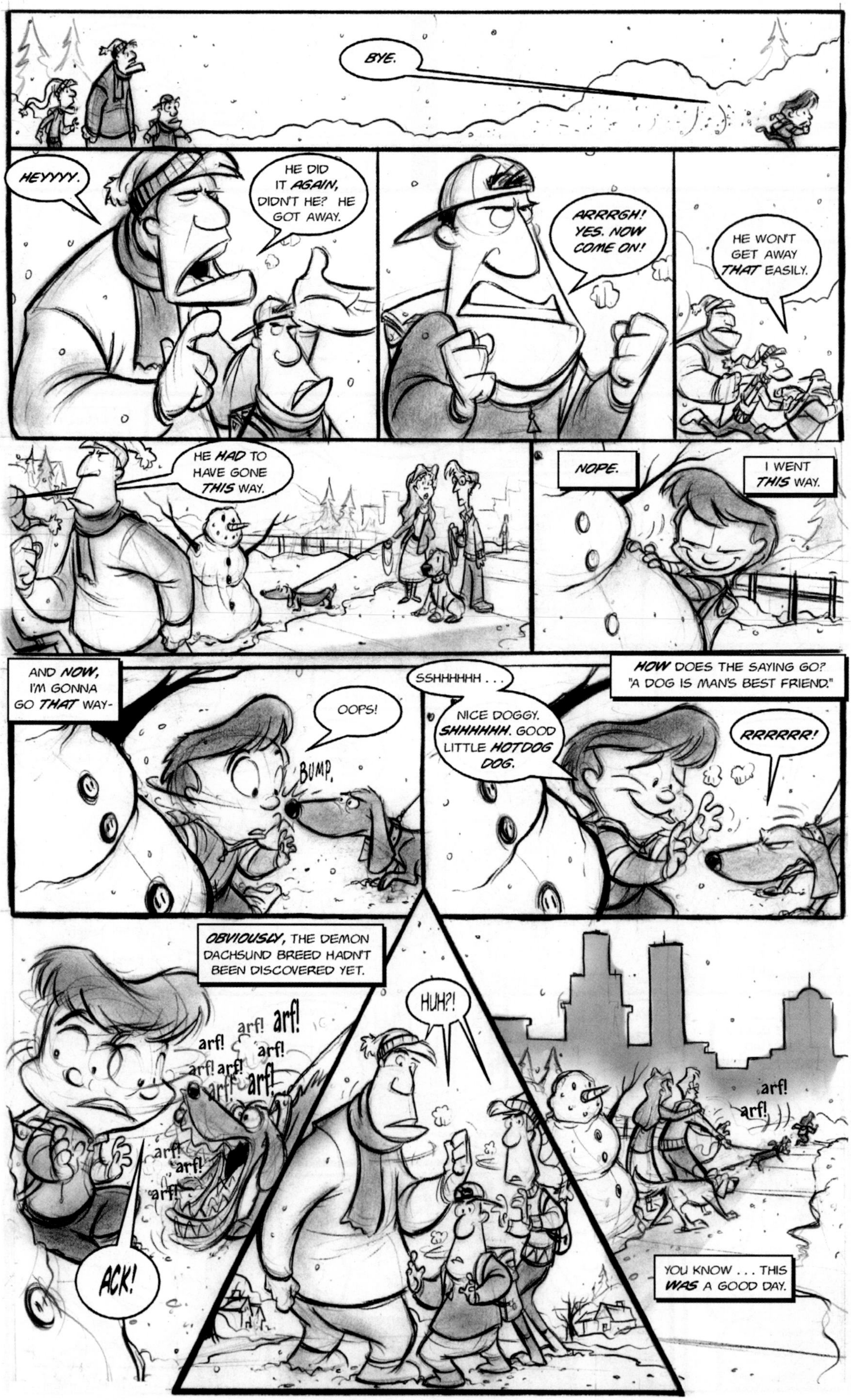
BYE.
HEYYYY.
HE DID IT AGAIN, DIDN'T HE? HE GOT AWAY.
ARRRGH! YES. NOW COME ON!
HE WON'T GET AWAY THAT EASILY.
HE HAD TO HAVE GONE THIS WAY.
NOPE.
I WENT THIS WAY.
AND NOW, I'M GONNA GO THAT WAY-
OOPS!
BUMP.
SSHHHHHH . . .
NICE DOGGY. SHHHHHH. GOOD LITTLE HOTDOG DOG.
HOW DOES THE SAYING GO? "A DOG IS MAN'S BEST FRIEND."
RRRRRR!
OBVIOUSLY, THE DEMON DACHSUND BREED HADN'T BEEN DISCOVERED YET.
arf! arf! arf! arf! arf! arf! arf!
arf! arf! arf!
ACK!
HUH?!
arf! arf!
YOU KNOW . . . THIS WAS A GOOD DAY.

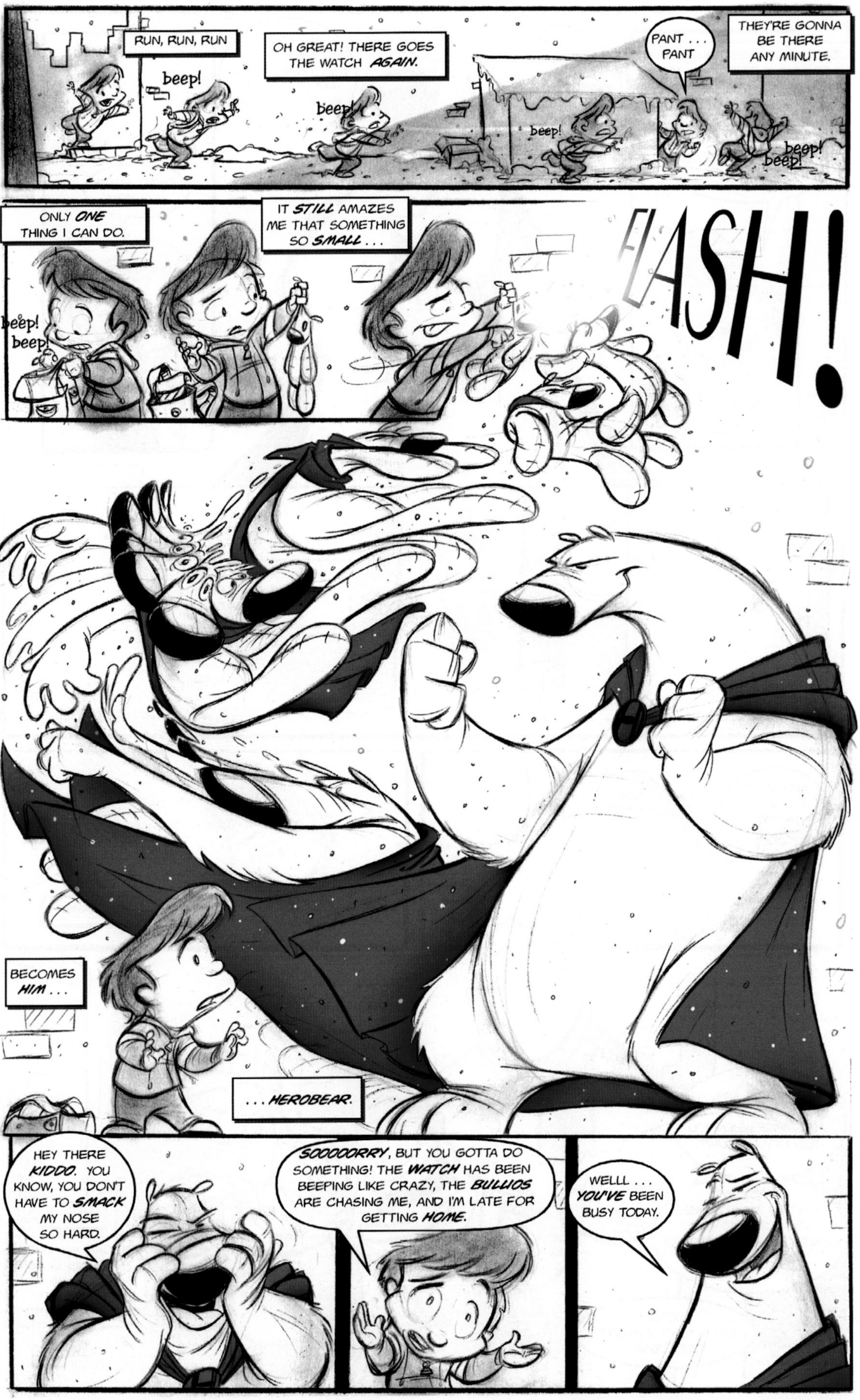
RUN, RUN, RUN
beep!
OH GREAT! THERE GOES THE WATCH AGAIN.
beep!
beep!
PANT . . . PANT
THEY'RE GONNA BE THERE ANY MINUTE.
beep!
beep!
ONLY ONE THING I CAN DO.
beep!
beep!
IT STILL AMAZES ME THAT SOMETHING SO SMALL . . .
FLASH!
BECOMES HIM . . .
. . . HEROBEAR.
HEY THERE KIDDO. YOU KNOW, YOU DON'T HAVE TO SMACK MY NOSE SO HARD.
SOOOOORRY, BUT YOU GOTTA DO SOMETHING! THE WATCH HAS BEEN BEEPING LIKE CRAZY, THE BULLIOS ARE CHASING ME, AND I'M LATE FOR GETTING HOME.
WELLL . . . YOU'VE BEEN BUSY TODAY.

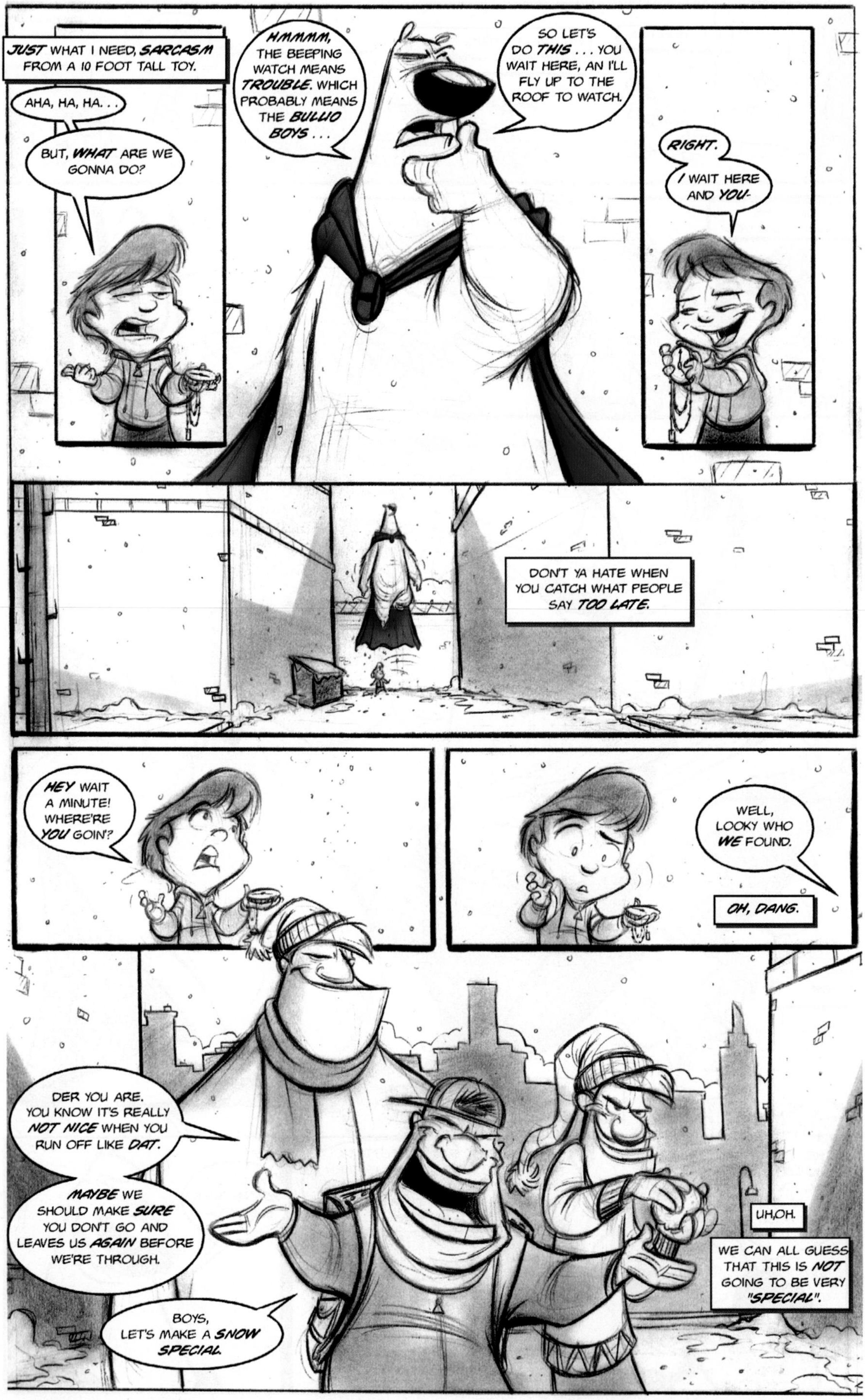

JUST WHAT I NEED, SARCASM FROM A 10 FOOT TALL TOY.
AHA, HA, HA. . .
BUT, WHAT ARE WE GONNA DO?
HMMMM, THE BEEPING WATCH MEANS TROUBLE. WHICH PROBABLY MEANS THE BULLIO BOYS . . .
SO LET'S DO THIS . . . YOU WAIT HERE, AN I'LL FLY UP TO THE ROOF TO WATCH.
RIGHT.
I WAIT HERE AND YOU-
DON'T YA HATE WHEN YOU CATCH WHAT PEOPLE SAY TOO LATE.
HEY WAIT A MINUTE! WHERE'RE YOU GOIN'?
WELL, LOOKY WHO WE FOUND.
OH, DANG.
DER YOU ARE. YOU KNOW IT'S REALLY NOT NICE WHEN YOU RUN OFF LIKE DAT.
MAYBE WE SHOULD MAKE SURE YOU DON'T GO AND LEAVES US AGAIN BEFORE WE'RE THROUGH.
BOYS, LET'S MAKE A SNOW SPECIAL.
UH,OH.
WE CAN ALL GUESS THAT THIS IS NOT GOING TO BE VERY "SPECIAL".

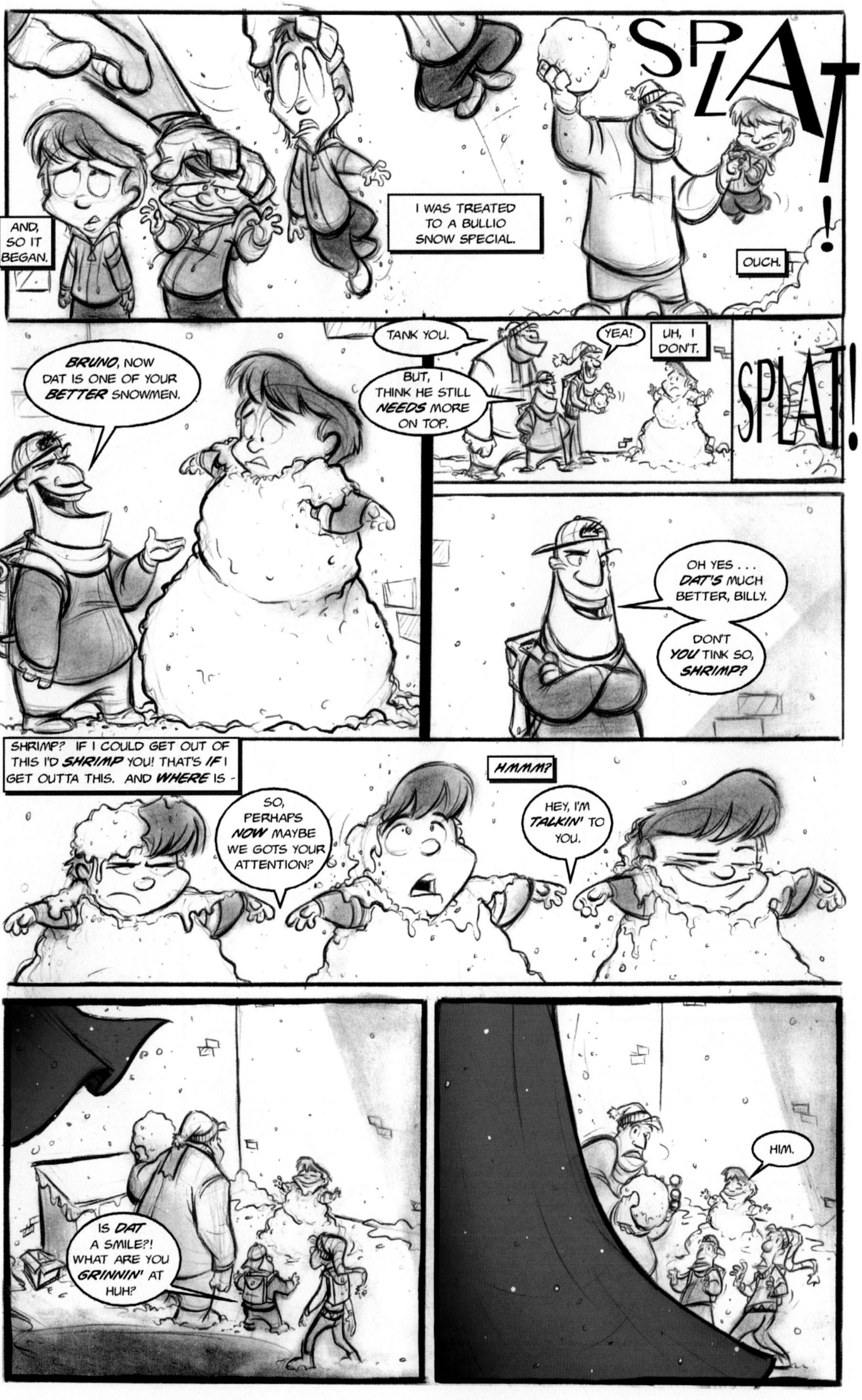
AND, SO IT BEGAN.
I WAS TREATED TO A BULLIO SNOW SPECIAL.
SPLAT!
OUCH.
BRUNO, NOW DAT IS ONE OF YOUR BETTER SNOWMEN.
TANK YOU.
BUT, I THINK HE STILL NEEDS MORE ON TOP.
YEA!
UH, I DON'T.
SPLAT!
OH YES . . . DAT'S MUCH BETTER, BILLY.
DON'T YOU TINK SO, SHRIMP?
SHRIMP? IF I COULD GET OUT OF THIS I'D SHRIMP YOU! THAT'S IF I GET OUTTA THIS. AND WHERE IS -
SO, PERHAPS NOW MAYBE WE GOTS YOUR ATTENTION?
HMMM?
HEY, I'M TALKIN' TO YOU.
IS DAT A SMILE?! WHAT ARE YOU GRINNIN' AT HUH?
HIM.

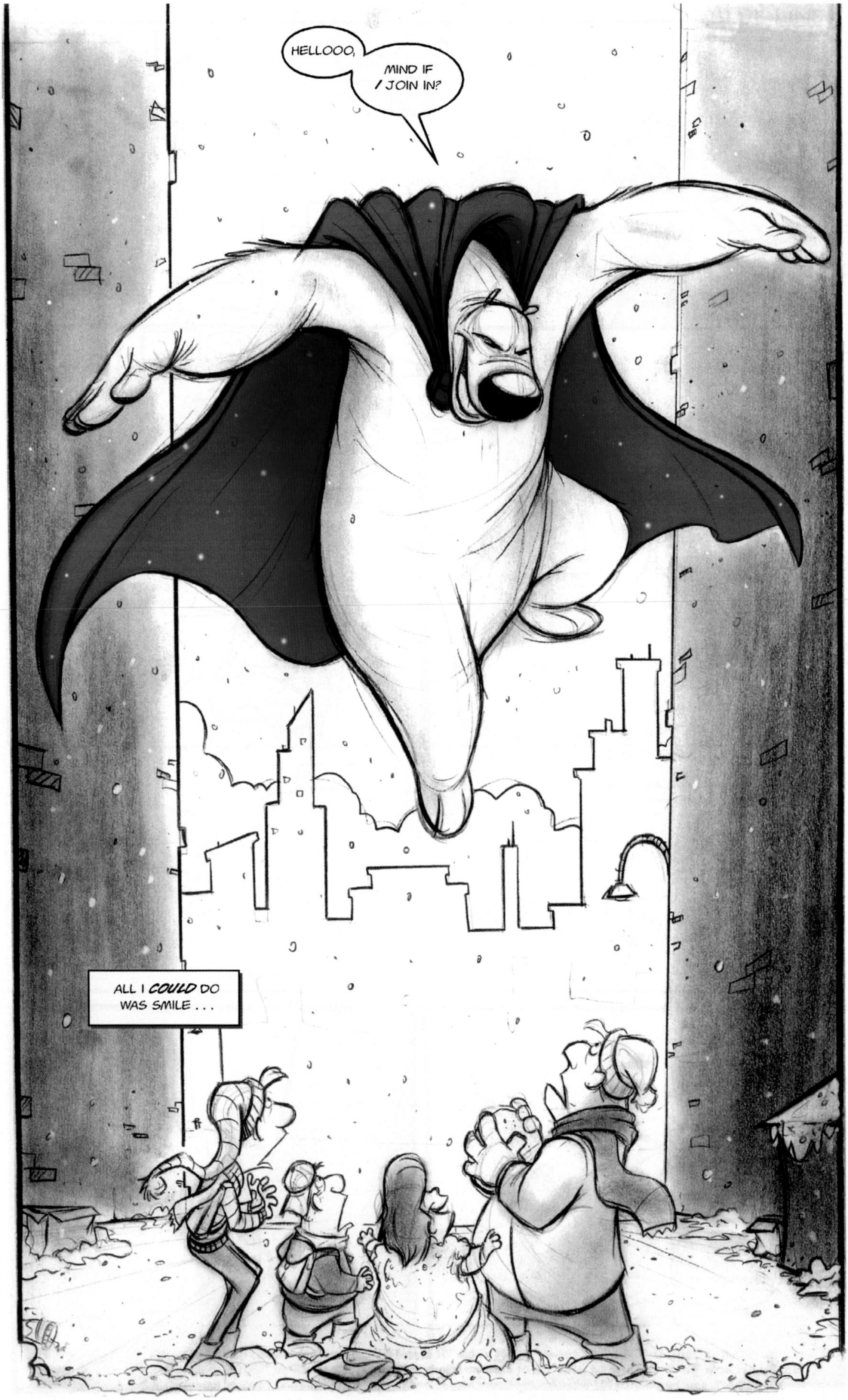
HELLOOO,
MIND IF I JOIN IN?
ALL I *COULD* DO WAS SMILE . . .

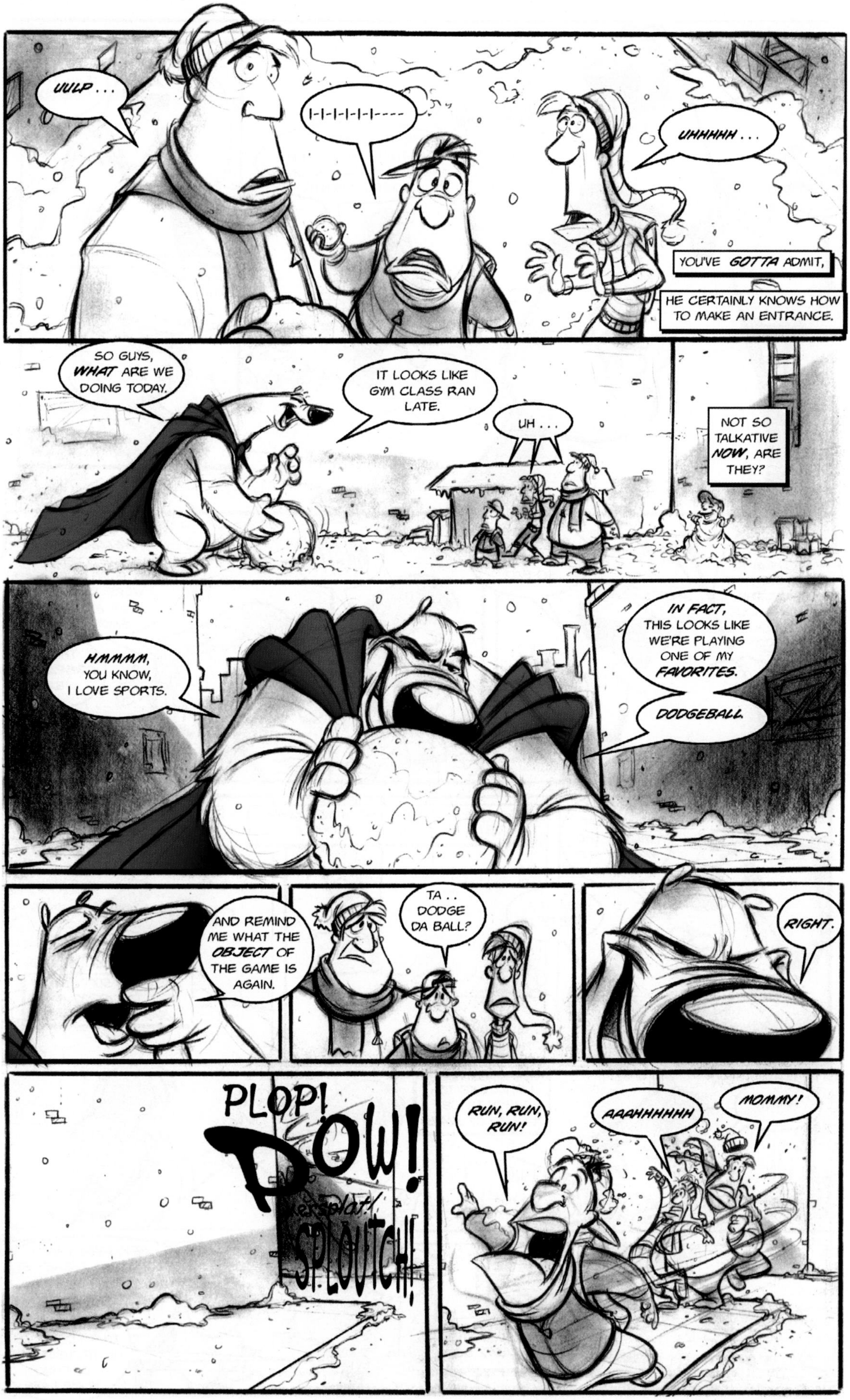
UULP . . .
I-I-I-I-I-I-I----
UHHHHH . . .
YOU'VE GOTTA ADMIT,
HE CERTAINLY KNOWS HOW TO MAKE AN ENTRANCE.
SO GUYS, WHAT ARE WE DOING TODAY.
IT LOOKS LIKE GYM CLASS RAN LATE.
UH . . .
NOT SO TALKATIVE NOW, ARE THEY?
HMMMM, YOU KNOW, I LOVE SPORTS.
IN FACT, THIS LOOKS LIKE WE'RE PLAYING ONE OF MY FAVORITES.
DODGEBALL.
AND REMIND ME WHAT THE OBJECT OF THE GAME IS AGAIN.
TA . . DODGE DA BALL?
RIGHT.
PLOP!
POW!
splat!
SPLOUTCH!
RUN, RUN, RUN!
AAAHHHHHH
MOMMY!

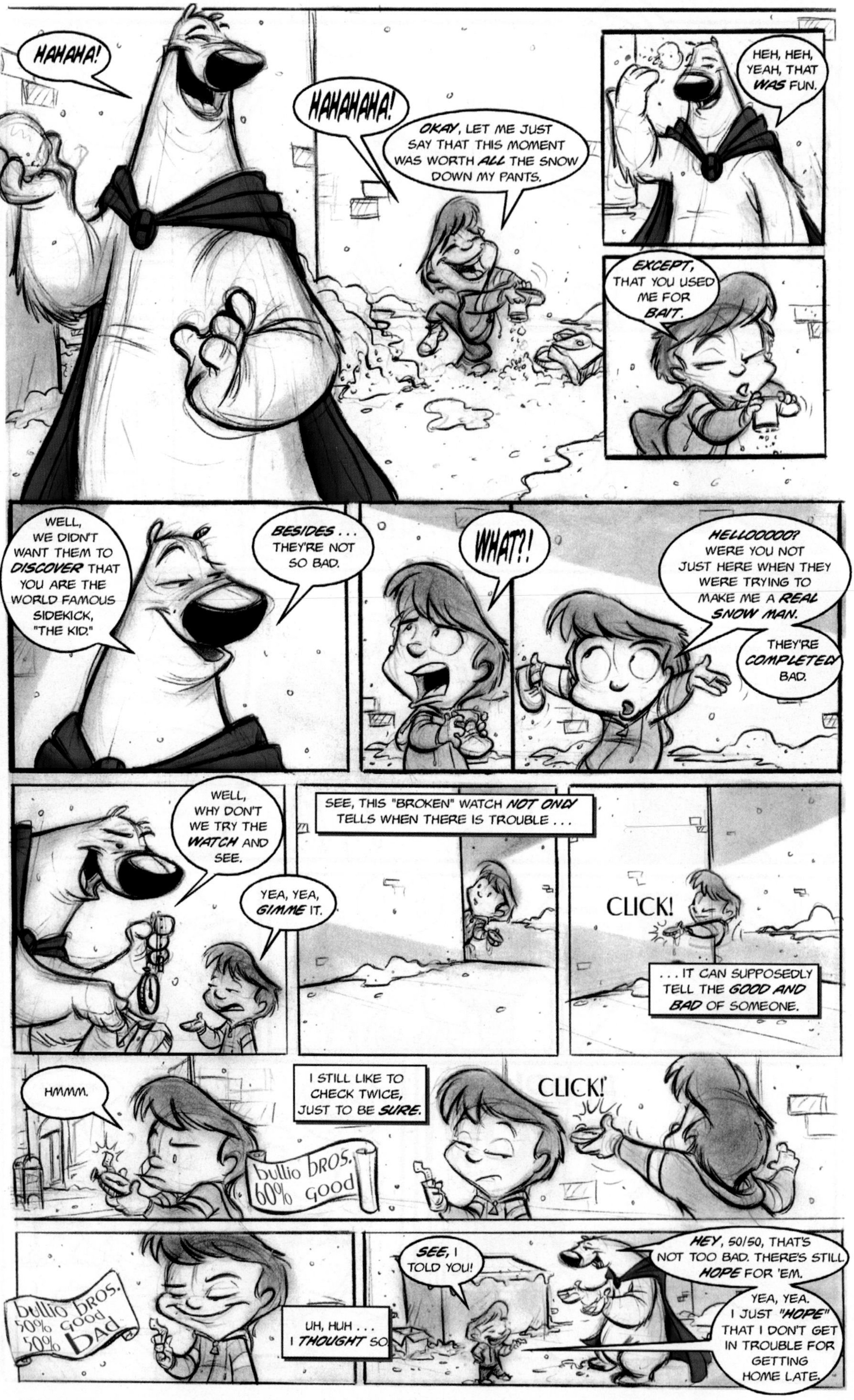
HAHAHA!
HAHAHAHA!
OKAY, LET ME JUST SAY THAT THIS MOMENT WAS WORTH ALL THE SNOW DOWN MY PANTS.
HEH, HEH, YEAH, THAT WAS FUN.
EXCEPT, THAT YOU USED ME FOR BAIT.
WELL, WE DIDN'T WANT THEM TO DISCOVER THAT YOU ARE THE WORLD FAMOUS SIDEKICK, "THE KID."
BESIDES . . . THEY'RE NOT SO BAD.
WHAT?!
HELLOOOOO? WERE YOU NOT JUST HERE WHEN THEY WERE TRYING TO MAKE ME A REAL SNOW MAN.
THEY'RE COMPLETELY BAD.
WELL, WHY DON'T WE TRY THE WATCH AND SEE.
YEA, YEA, GIMME IT.
SEE, THIS "BROKEN" WATCH NOT ONLY TELLS WHEN THERE IS TROUBLE . . .
CLICK!
. . . IT CAN SUPPOSEDLY TELL THE GOOD AND BAD OF SOMEONE.
HMMM.
bullio BROS. 60% Good
I STILL LIKE TO CHECK TWICE, JUST TO BE SURE.
CLICK!
bullio bros. 50% Good 50% bad
UH, HUH . . . I THOUGHT SO
SEE, I TOLD YOU!
HEY, 50/50, THAT'S NOT TOO BAD. THERE'S STILL HOPE FOR 'EM.
YEA, YEA. I JUST "HOPE" THAT I DON'T GET IN TROUBLE FOR GETTING HOME LATE.

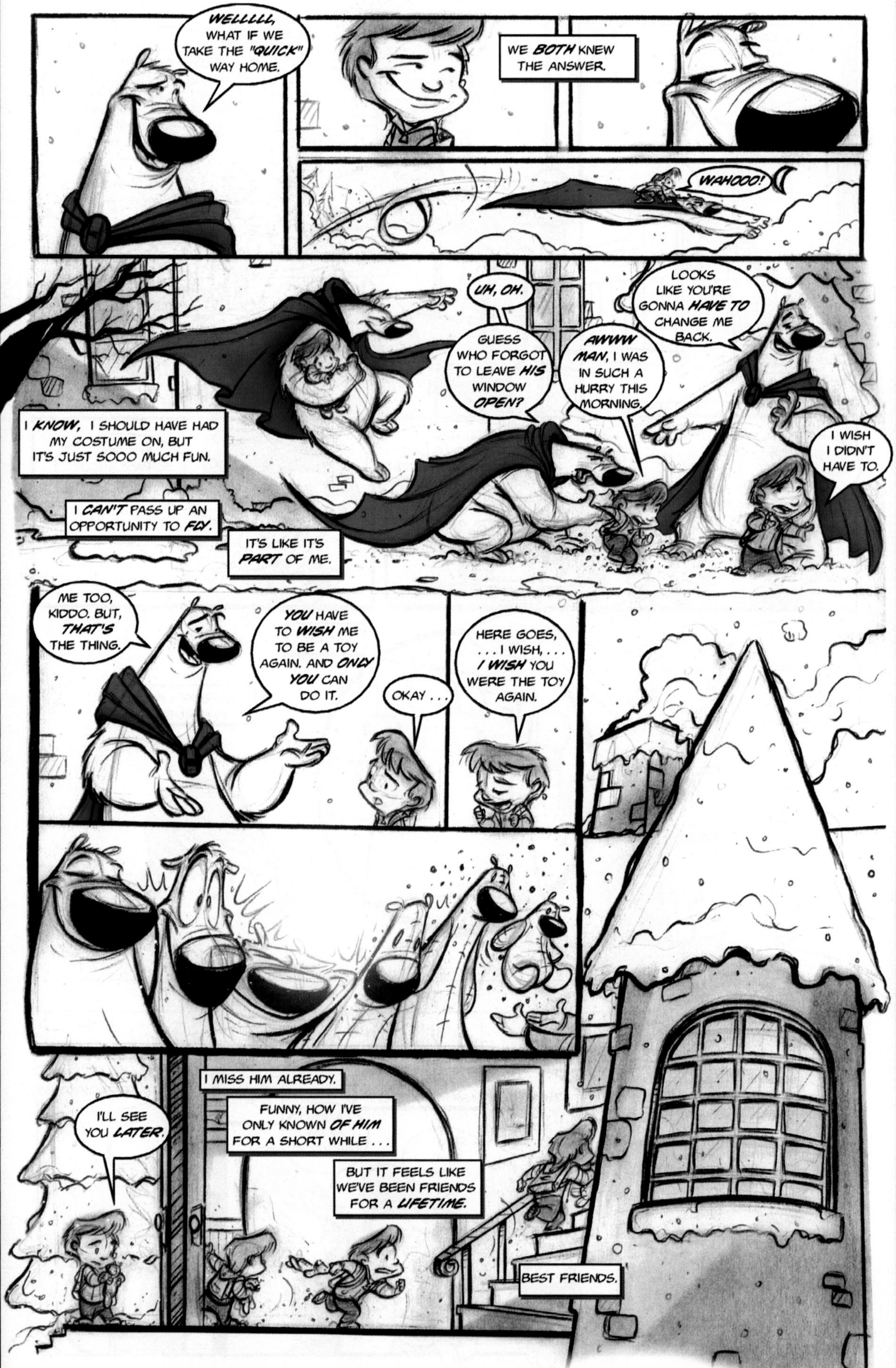
WELLLLL, WHAT IF WE TAKE THE "QUICK" WAY HOME.
WE BOTH KNEW THE ANSWER.
WAHOOO!
UH, OH.
GUESS WHO FORGOT TO LEAVE HIS WINDOW OPEN?
AWWW MAN, I WAS IN SUCH A HURRY THIS MORNING.
LOOKS LIKE YOU'RE GONNA HAVE TO CHANGE ME BACK.
I WISH I DIDN'T HAVE TO.
I KNOW, I SHOULD HAVE HAD MY COSTUME ON, BUT IT'S JUST SOOO MUCH FUN.
I CAN'T PASS UP AN OPPORTUNITY TO FLY.
IT'S LIKE IT'S PART OF ME.
ME TOO, KIDDO. BUT, THAT'S THE THING.
YOU HAVE TO WISH ME TO BE A TOY AGAIN. AND ONLY YOU CAN DO IT.
OKAY . . .
HERE GOES, . . . I WISH, . . . I WISH YOU WERE THE TOY AGAIN.
I'LL SEE YOU LATER.
I MISS HIM ALREADY.
FUNNY, HOW I'VE ONLY KNOWN OF HIM FOR A SHORT WHILE . . .
BUT IT FEELS LIKE WE'VE BEEN FRIENDS FOR A LIFETIME.
BEST FRIENDS.

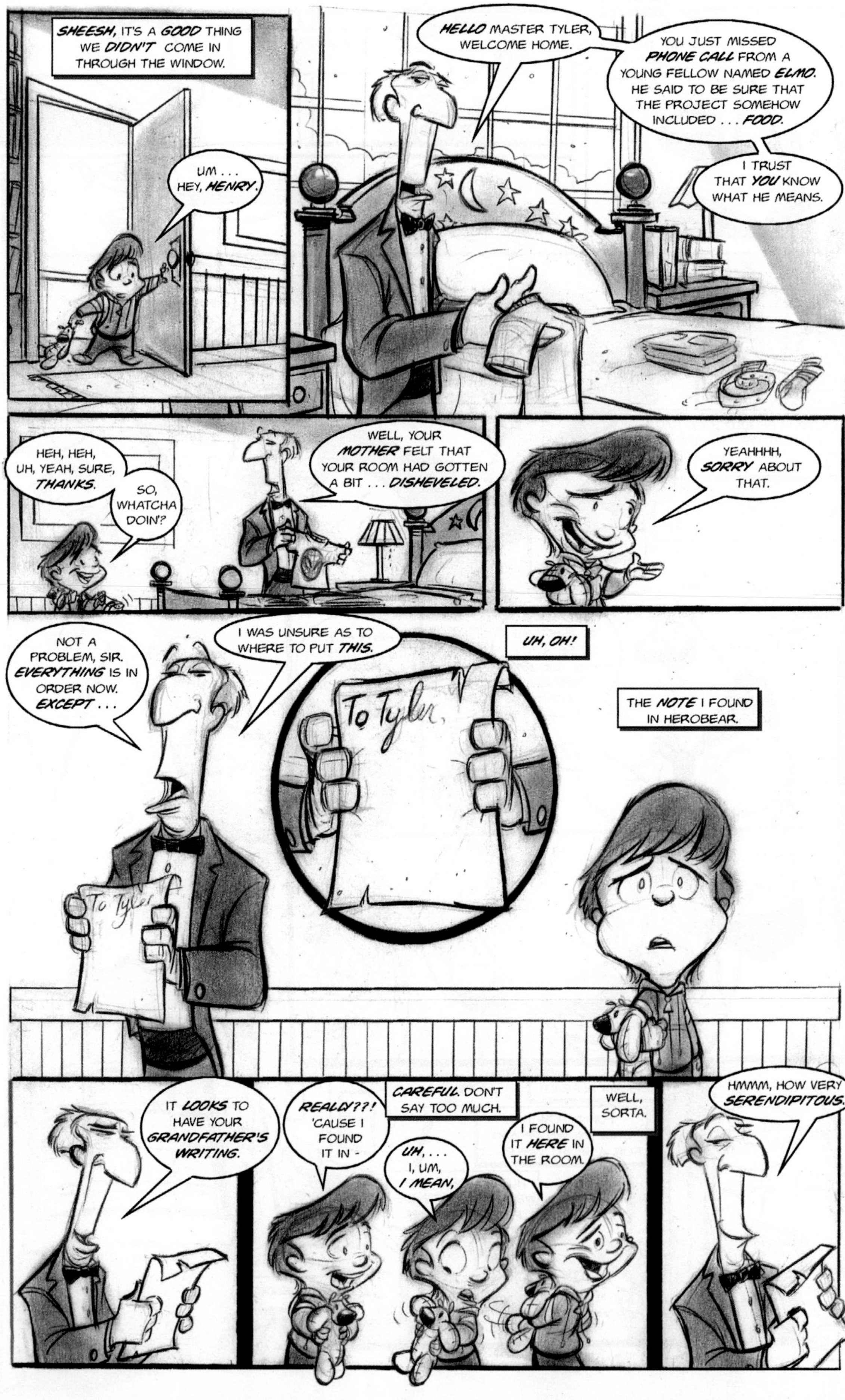

SHEESH, IT'S A GOOD THING WE DIDN'T COME IN THROUGH THE WINDOW.
UM . . . HEY, HENRY.
HELLO MASTER TYLER, WELCOME HOME.
YOU JUST MISSED PHONE CALL FROM A YOUNG FELLOW NAMED ELMO. HE SAID TO BE SURE THAT THE PROJECT SOMEHOW INCLUDED . . . FOOD.
I TRUST THAT YOU KNOW WHAT HE MEANS.
HEH, HEH, UH, YEAH, SURE, THANKS.
SO, WHATCHA DOIN'?
WELL, YOUR MOTHER FELT THAT YOUR ROOM HAD GOTTEN A BIT . . . DISHEVELED.
YEAHHHH, SORRY ABOUT THAT.
NOT A PROBLEM, SIR. EVERYTHING IS IN ORDER NOW. EXCEPT . . .
I WAS UNSURE AS TO WHERE TO PUT THIS.
To Tyler
UH, OH!
THE NOTE I FOUND IN HEROBEAR.
IT LOOKS TO HAVE YOUR GRANDFATHER'S WRITING.
REALLY??! 'CAUSE I FOUND IT IN -
CAREFUL. DON'T SAY TOO MUCH.
UH, . . . I, UM, I MEAN,
WELL, SORTA.
I FOUND IT HERE IN THE ROOM.
HMMM, HOW VERY SERENDIPITOUS.

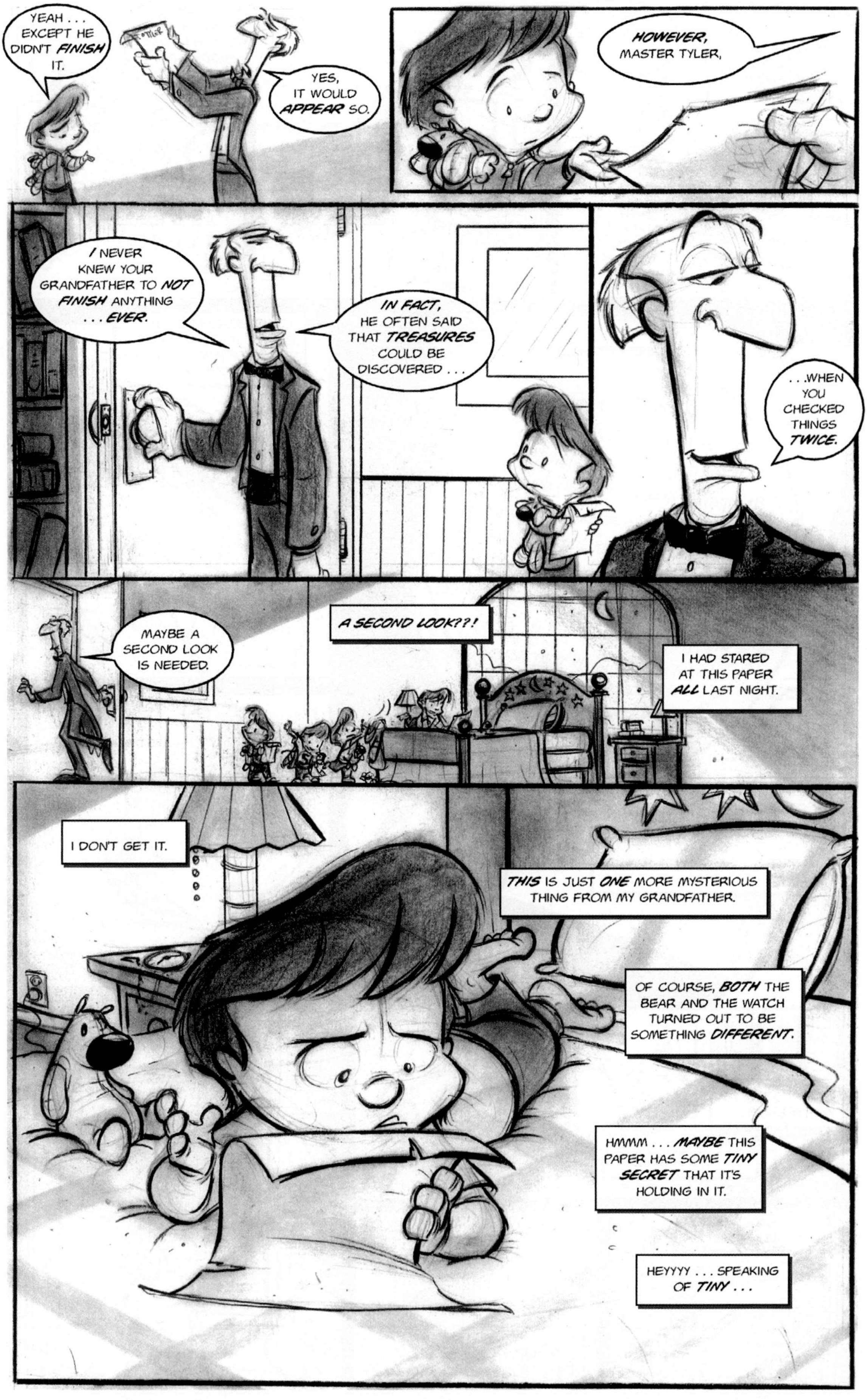
YEAH . . . EXCEPT HE DIDN'T FINISH IT.
YES, IT WOULD APPEAR SO.
HOWEVER, MASTER TYLER,
I NEVER KNEW YOUR GRANDFATHER TO NOT FINISH ANYTHING . . . EVER.
IN FACT, HE OFTEN SAID THAT TREASURES COULD BE DISCOVERED . . .
. . .WHEN YOU CHECKED THINGS TWICE.
MAYBE A SECOND LOOK IS NEEDED.
A SECOND LOOK??!
I HAD STARED AT THIS PAPER ALL LAST NIGHT.
I DON'T GET IT.
THIS IS JUST ONE MORE MYSTERIOUS THING FROM MY GRANDFATHER.
OF COURSE, BOTH THE BEAR AND THE WATCH TURNED OUT TO BE SOMETHING DIFFERENT.
HMMM . . . MAYBE THIS PAPER HAS SOME TINY SECRET THAT IT'S HOLDING IN IT.
HEYYYY . . . SPEAKING OF TINY . . .

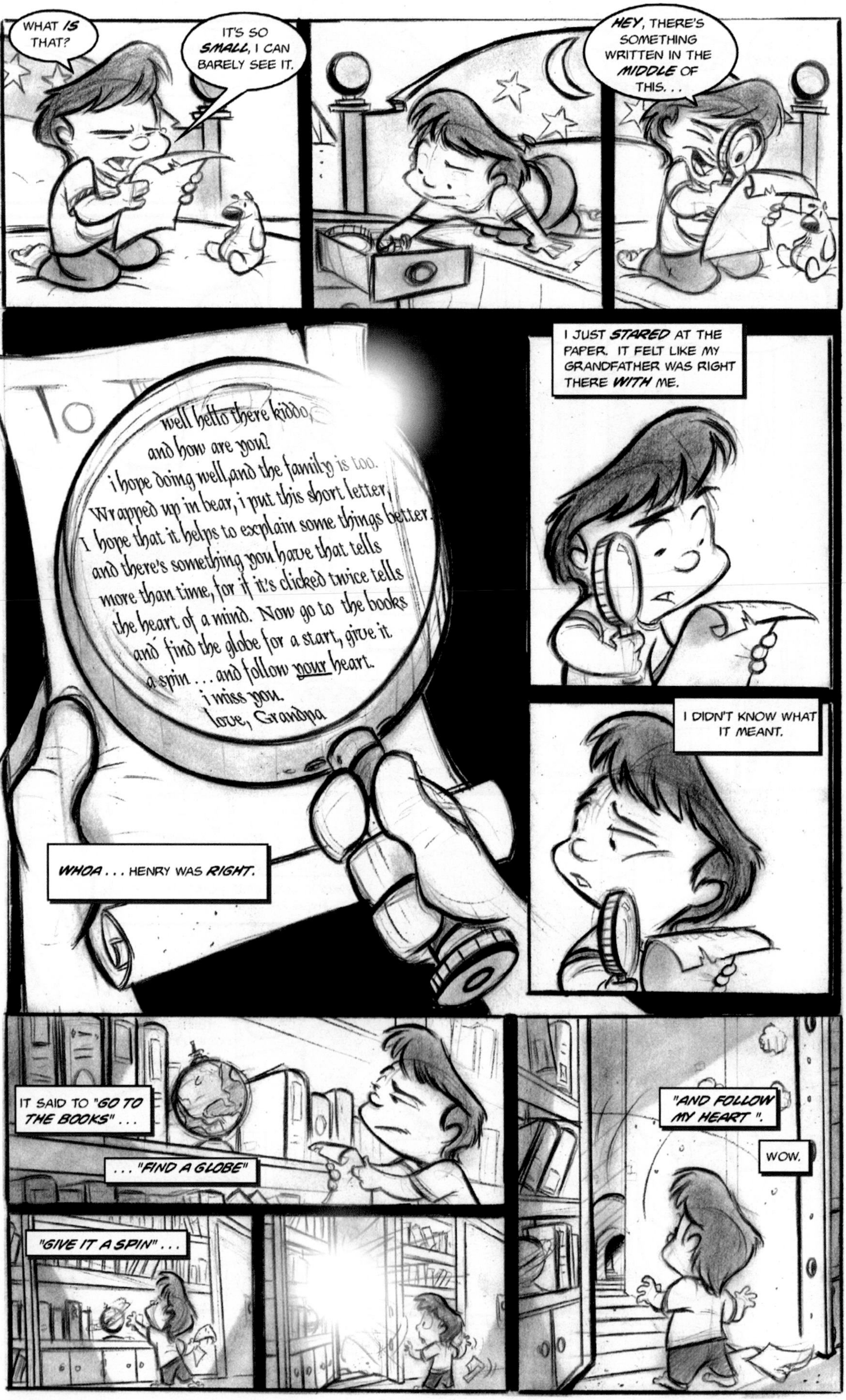
WHAT *IS* THAT?
IT'S SO *SMALL*, I CAN BARELY SEE IT.
HEY, THERE'S SOMETHING WRITTEN IN THE *MIDDLE* OF THIS. . .
well hello there kiddo,
and how are you?
i hope doing well, and the family is too.
Wrapped up in bear, i put this short letter,
I hope that it helps to explain some things better.
and there's something you have that tells
more than time, for if it's clicked twice tells
the heart of a mind. Now go to the books
and find the globe for a start, give it
a spin . . . and follow your heart.
i miss you.
love, Grandpa
WHOA . . . HENRY WAS *RIGHT*.
I JUST *STARED* AT THE PAPER. IT FELT LIKE MY GRANDFATHER WAS RIGHT THERE *WITH* ME.
I DIDN'T KNOW WHAT IT MEANT.
IT SAID TO "*GO TO THE BOOKS*" . . .
. . . "*FIND A GLOBE*"
"*GIVE IT A SPIN*" . . .
"*AND FOLLOW MY HEART*".
WOW.

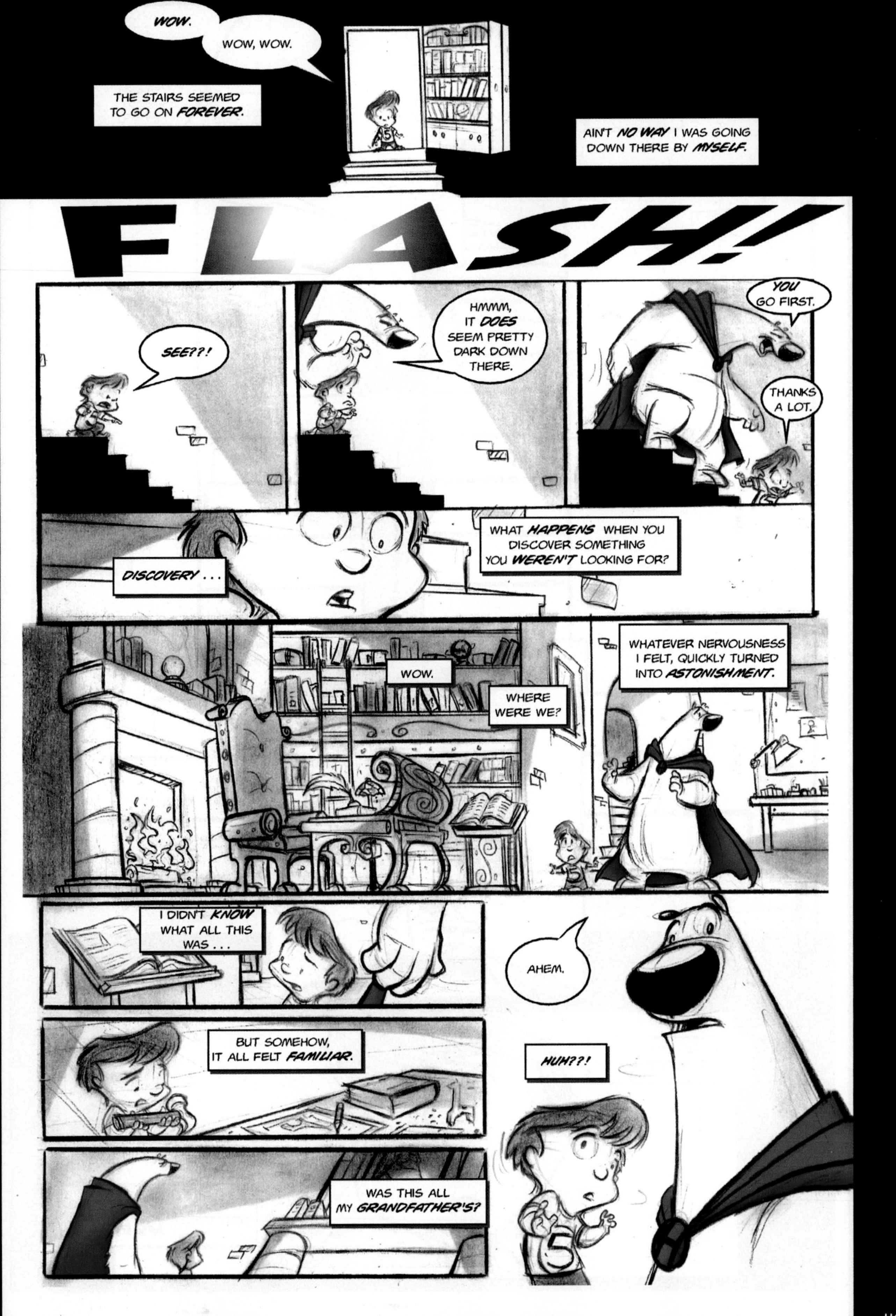
WOW.
WOW, WOW.
THE STAIRS SEEMED TO GO ON FOREVER.
AIN'T NO WAY I WAS GOING DOWN THERE BY MYSELF.
FLASH!
SEE??!
HMMM, IT DOES SEEM PRETTY DARK DOWN THERE.
YOU GO FIRST.
THANKS A LOT.
DISCOVERY . . .
WHAT HAPPENS WHEN YOU DISCOVER SOMETHING YOU WEREN'T LOOKING FOR?
WOW.
WHERE WERE WE?
WHATEVER NERVOUSNESS I FELT, QUICKLY TURNED INTO ASTONISHMENT.
I DIDN'T KNOW WHAT ALL THIS WAS . . .
AHEM.
BUT SOMEHOW, IT ALL FELT FAMILIAR.
HUH??!
WAS THIS ALL MY GRANDFATHER'S?

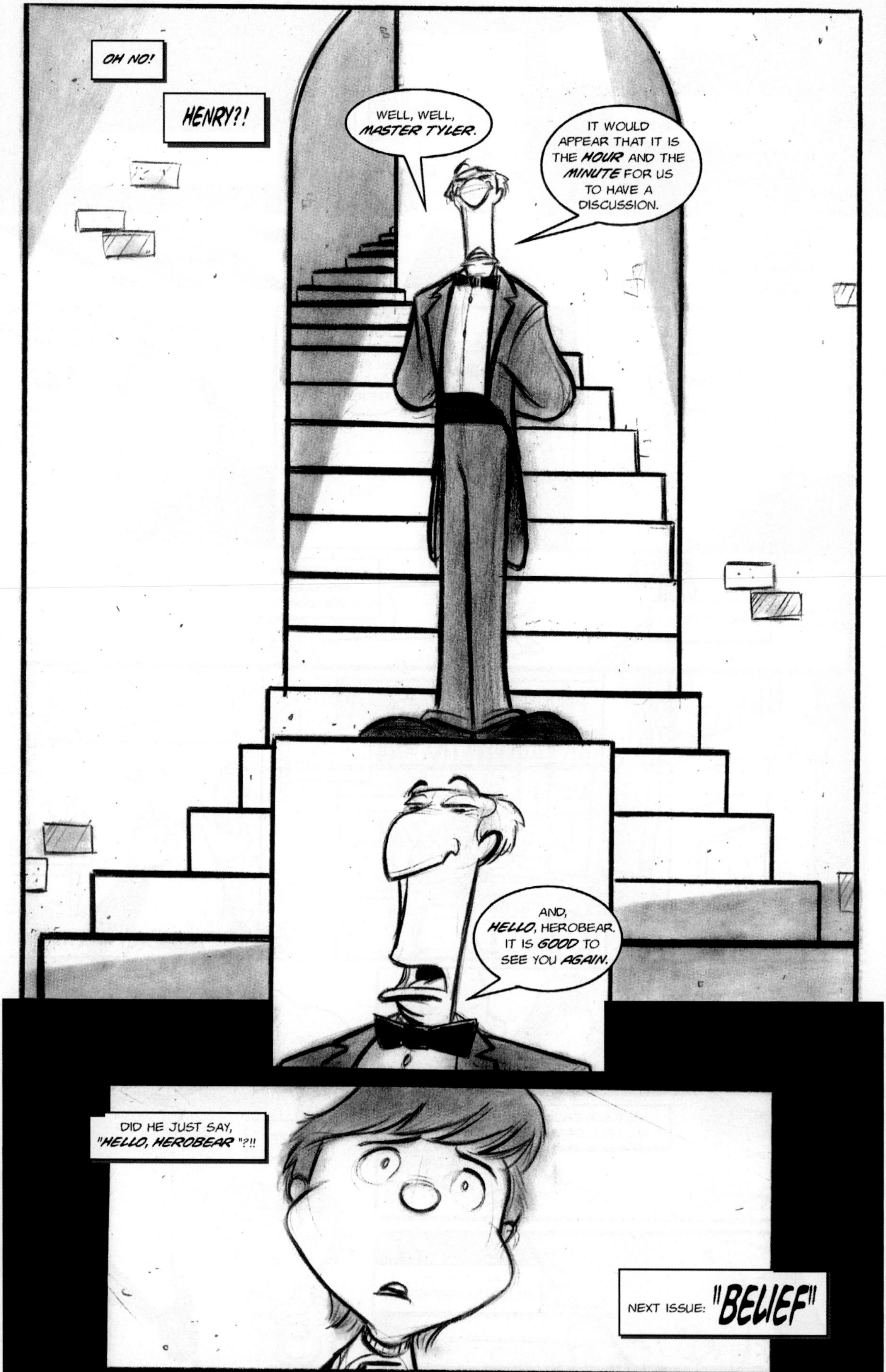
OH NO!
HENRY?!
WELL, WELL, MASTER TYLER.
IT WOULD APPEAR THAT IT IS THE HOUR AND THE MINUTE FOR US TO HAVE A DISCUSSION.
AND, HELLO, HEROBEAR. IT IS GOOD TO SEE YOU AGAIN.
DID HE JUST SAY, "HELLO, HEROBEAR"?!!
NEXT ISSUE: "BELIEF"

"The blend of charm and pathos that have been stitched into the fabric of Herobear and the kid will warm your heart like a toasty winter sweater, but warm or chilly, any day of the year is a good day to sit down with Mike Kunkel's inspired yarns!"
Scott Morse, (Creator of MAGIC PICKLE, SOULWIND, and art director of COW AND CHICKEN).

"With so many creators attempting to find that lost sense of wonder in comics, it's nice that someone like Kunkel comes along and shows us that the magic was there all all the time ... we were just looking in the wrong places. "
DIAMOND DIST. MAGAZINE (SMALL PRESS QUOTE)

"As a fellow creator, when I read other books it makes me want to be a better storyteller. When I read Herobear, it makes me want to be a better person. "
Courtney Huddleston (Artist and Creator of Decoy)

"Herobear is a visual hug. Warm cuddley, and reassuring to grown up children everywhere."
TERRY MOORE (WRITER AND CREATOR OF STRANGERS IN PARADISE)

"Mike Kunkel is going after the disillusioned audience of today--not with biting ironies and wittily sarcastic observations of modern life, but with a fantastical tale of wonder and magic that's geared toward winning over even the most jaded reader.
Jennifer M. Contino (www.Wizardworld.com)

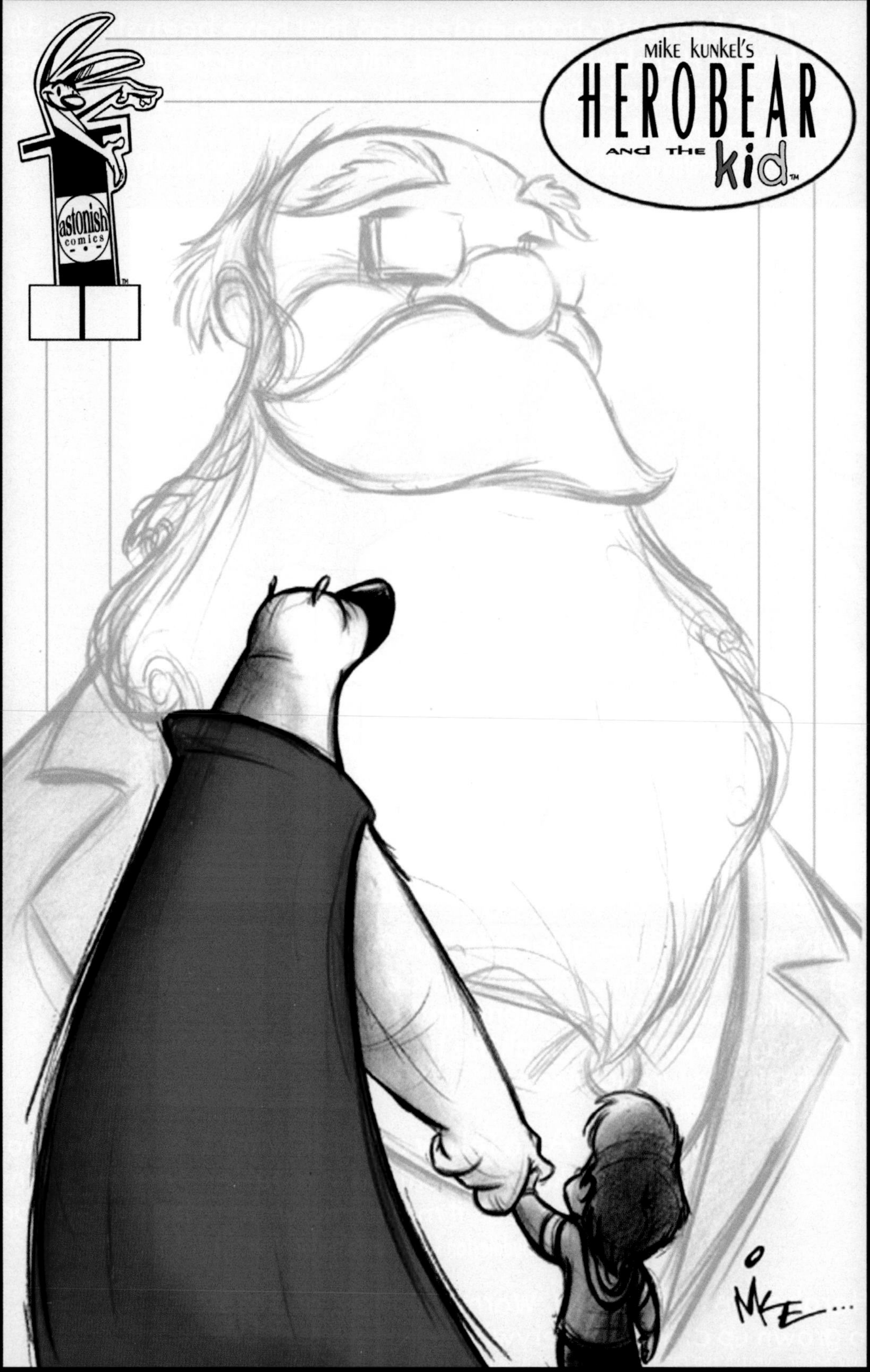
astonish comics
MIKE KUNKEL'S
HEROBEAR
AND THE kid
MIKE...

book five

belief

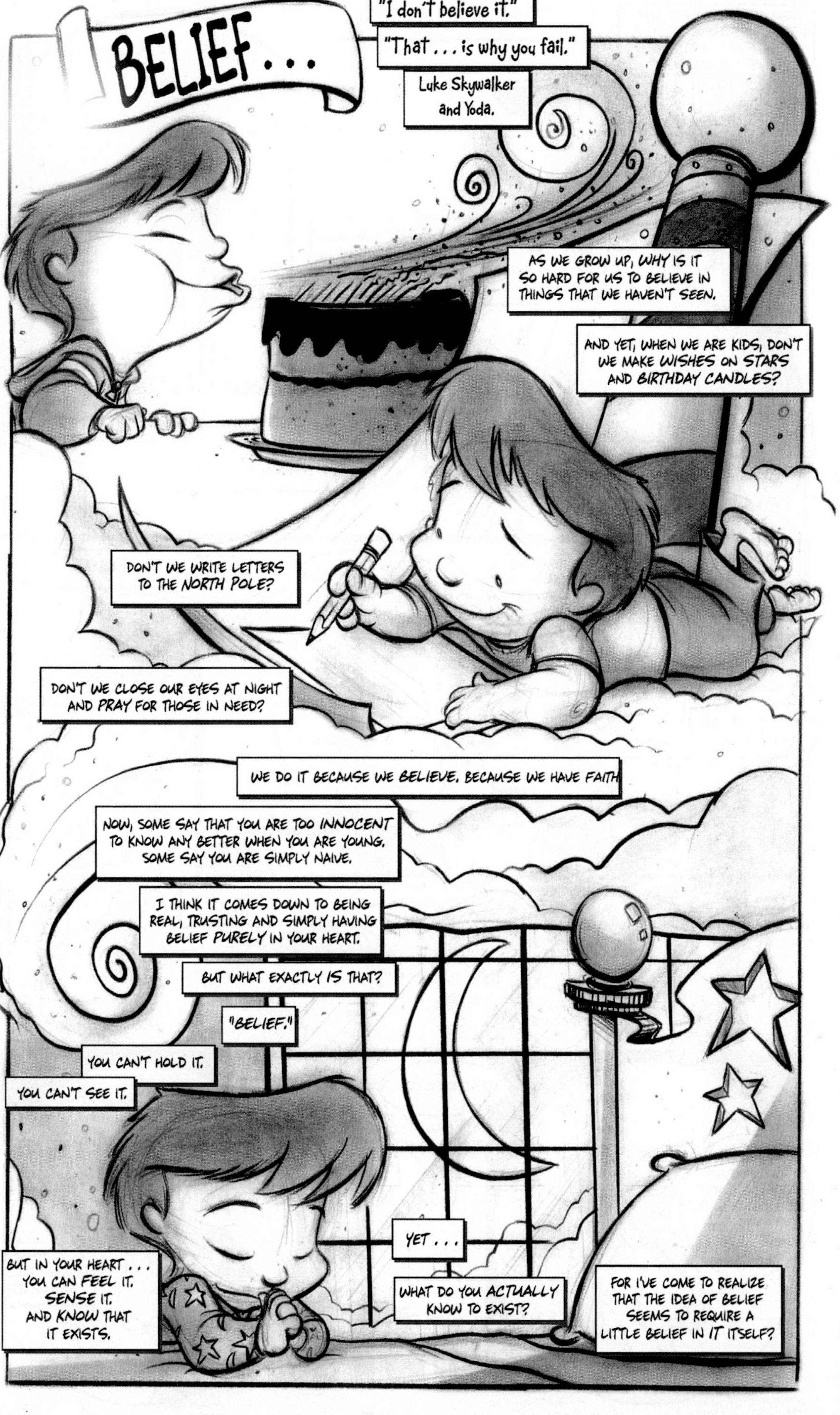
BELIEF . . .
"I don't believe it."
"That . . . is why you fail."
Luke Skywalker and Yoda.
AS WE GROW UP, WHY IS IT SO HARD FOR US TO BELIEVE IN THINGS THAT WE HAVEN'T SEEN.
AND YET, WHEN WE ARE KIDS, DON'T WE MAKE WISHES ON STARS AND BIRTHDAY CANDLES?
DON'T WE WRITE LETTERS TO THE NORTH POLE?
DON'T WE CLOSE OUR EYES AT NIGHT AND PRAY FOR THOSE IN NEED?
WE DO IT BECAUSE WE BELIEVE. BECAUSE WE HAVE FAITH
NOW, SOME SAY THAT YOU ARE TOO INNOCENT TO KNOW ANY BETTER WHEN YOU ARE YOUNG. SOME SAY YOU ARE SIMPLY NAIVE.
I THINK IT COMES DOWN TO BEING REAL, TRUSTING AND SIMPLY HAVING BELIEF PURELY IN YOUR HEART.
BUT WHAT EXACTLY IS THAT?
"BELIEF."
YOU CAN'T HOLD IT.
YOU CAN'T SEE IT.
BUT IN YOUR HEART . . . YOU CAN FEEL IT. SENSE IT. AND KNOW THAT IT EXISTS.
YET . . .
WHAT DO YOU ACTUALLY KNOW TO EXIST?
FOR I'VE COME TO REALIZE THAT THE IDEA OF BELIEF SEEMS TO REQUIRE A LITTLE BELIEF IN IT ITSELF?

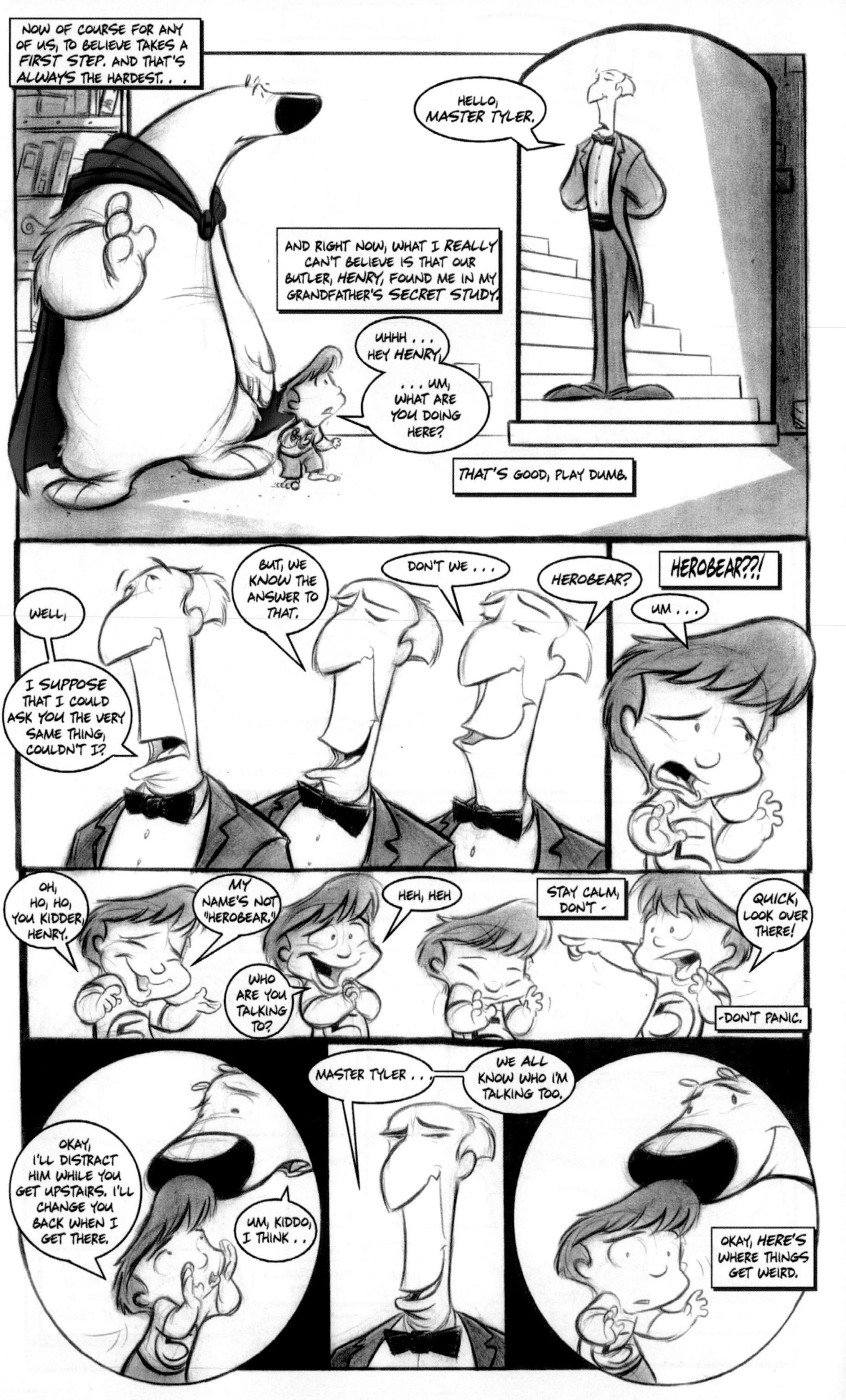

NOW OF COURSE FOR ANY OF US, TO BELIEVE TAKES A FIRST STEP. AND THAT'S ALWAYS THE HARDEST. . .
HELLO, MASTER TYLER.
AND RIGHT NOW, WHAT I REALLY CAN'T BELIEVE IS THAT OUR BUTLER, HENRY, FOUND ME IN MY GRANDFATHER'S SECRET STUDY.
UHHH . . . HEY HENRY,
. . . UM, WHAT ARE YOU DOING HERE?
THAT'S GOOD, PLAY DUMB.
WELL,
I SUPPOSE THAT I COULD ASK YOU THE VERY SAME THING, COULDN'T I?
BUT, WE KNOW THE ANSWER TO THAT.
DON'T WE . . .
HEROBEAR?
HEROBEAR??!
UM . . .
OH, HO, HO, YOU KIDDER, HENRY.
MY NAME'S NOT "HEROBEAR."
HEH, HEH
WHO ARE YOU TALKING TO?
STAY CALM, DON'T -
QUICK, LOOK OVER THERE!
-DON'T PANIC.
OKAY, I'LL DISTRACT HIM WHILE YOU GET UPSTAIRS. I'LL CHANGE YOU BACK WHEN I GET THERE.
UM, KIDDO, I THINK . .
MASTER TYLER . . .
WE ALL KNOW WHO I'M TALKING TOO.
OKAY, HERE'S WHERE THINGS GET WEIRD.

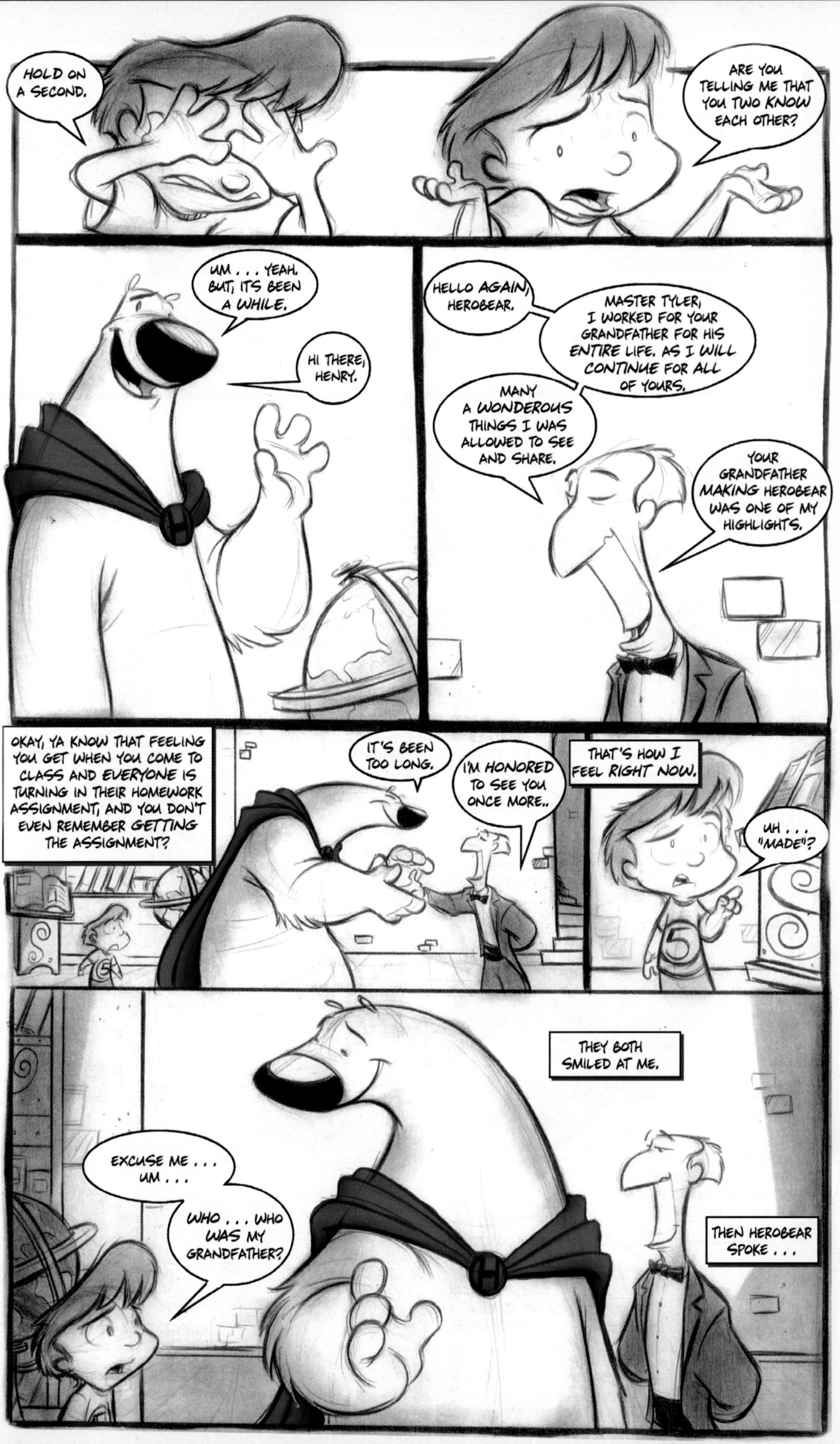
HOLD ON A SECOND.
ARE YOU TELLING ME THAT YOU TWO KNOW EACH OTHER?
UM . . . YEAH. BUT, ITS BEEN A WHILE.
HI THERE, HENRY.
HELLO AGAIN, HEROBEAR.
MASTER TYLER, I WORKED FOR YOUR GRANDFATHER FOR HIS ENTIRE LIFE. AS I WILL CONTINUE FOR ALL OF YOURS.
MANY A WONDEROUS THINGS I WAS ALLOWED TO SEE AND SHARE.
YOUR GRANDFATHER MAKING HEROBEAR WAS ONE OF MY HIGHLIGHTS.
OKAY, YA KNOW THAT FEELING YOU GET WHEN YOU COME TO CLASS AND EVERYONE IS TURNING IN THEIR HOMEWORK ASSIGNMENT, AND YOU DON'T EVEN REMEMBER GETTING THE ASSIGNMENT?
IT'S BEEN TOO LONG.
I'M HONORED TO SEE YOU ONCE MORE..
THAT'S HOW I FEEL RIGHT NOW.
UH . . . "MADE"?
THEY BOTH SMILED AT ME.
EXCUSE ME . . . UM . . .
WHO . . . WHO WAS MY GRANDFATHER?
THEN HEROBEAR SPOKE . . .

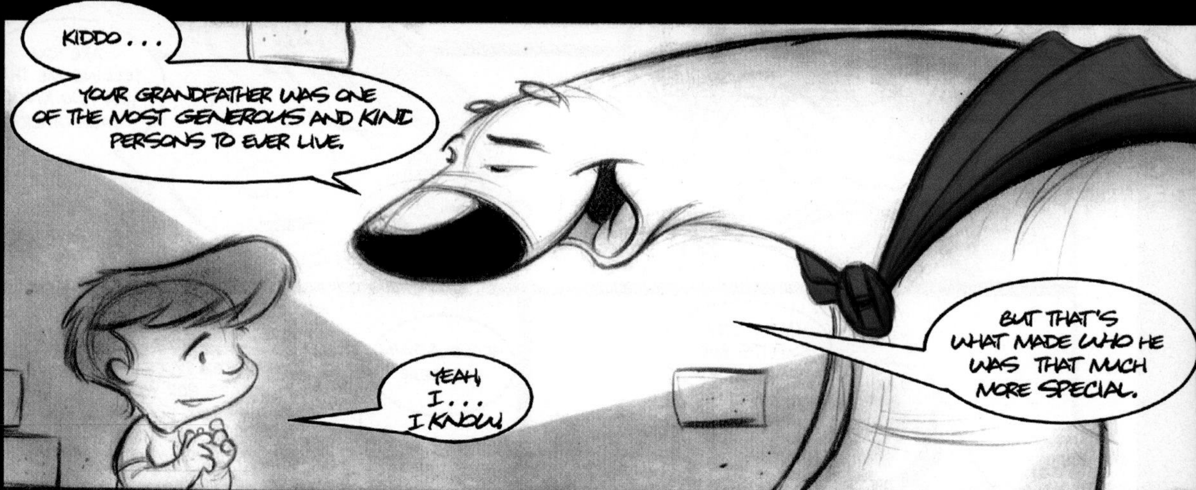
KIDDO . . .
YOUR GRANDFATHER WAS ONE OF THE MOST GENEROUS AND KIND PERSONS TO EVER LIVE.
YEAH, I . . . I KNOW.
BUT THAT'S WHAT MADE WHO HE WAS THAT MUCH MORE SPECIAL.

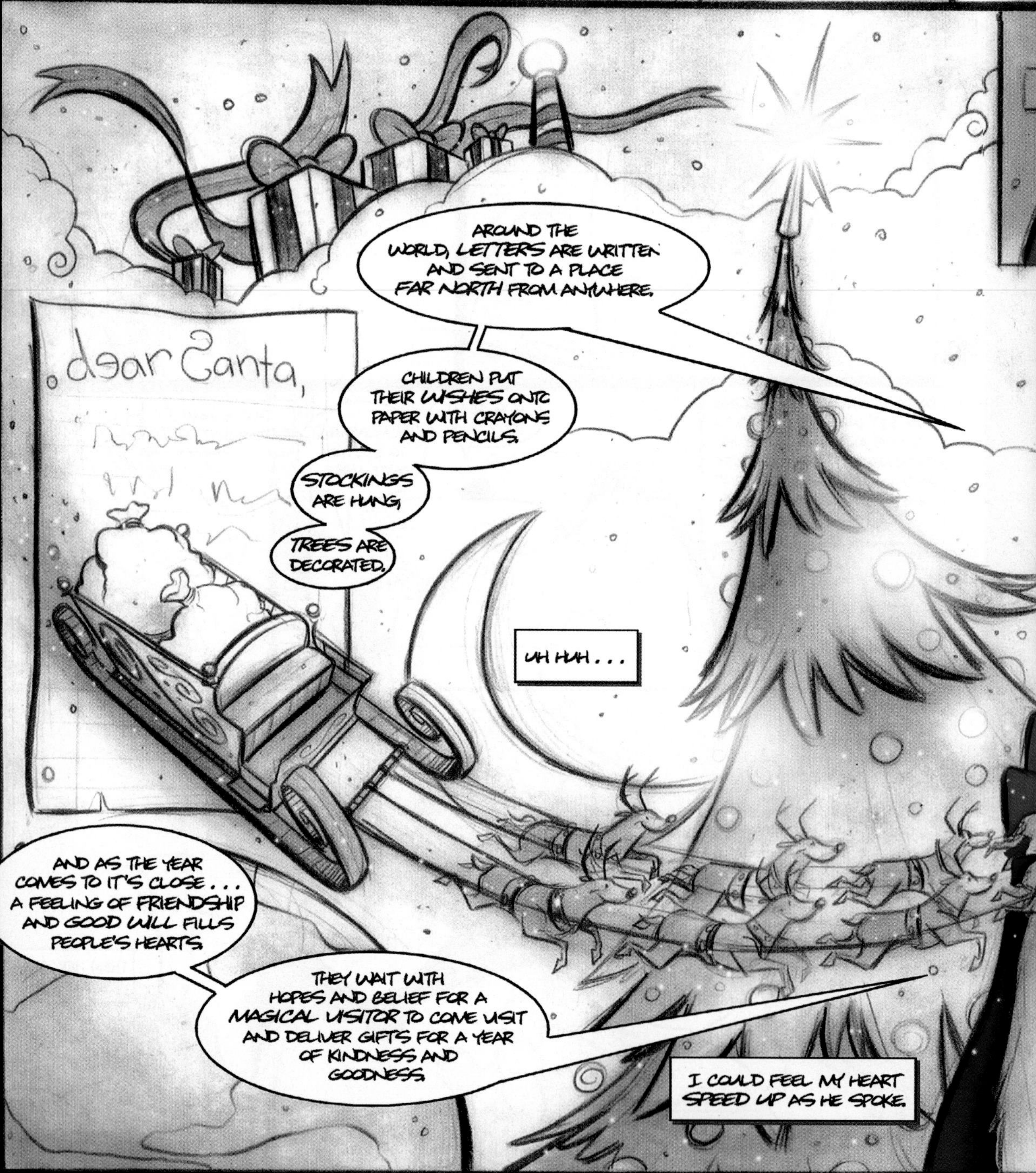
AROUND THE WORLD, LETTERS ARE WRITTEN AND SENT TO A PLACE FAR NORTH FROM ANYWHERE.
dear Santa,
CHILDREN PUT THEIR WISHES ONTO PAPER WITH CRAYONS AND PENCILS.
STOCKINGS ARE HUNG,
TREES ARE DECORATED.
UH HUH . . .
AND AS THE YEAR COMES TO IT'S CLOSE . . . A FEELING OF FRIENDSHIP AND GOOD WILL FILLS PEOPLE'S HEARTS.
THEY WAIT WITH HOPES AND BELIEF FOR A MAGICAL VISITOR TO COME VISIT AND DELIVER GIFTS FOR A YEAR OF KINDNESS AND GOODNESS.
I COULD FEEL MY HEART SPEED UP AS HE SPOKE.

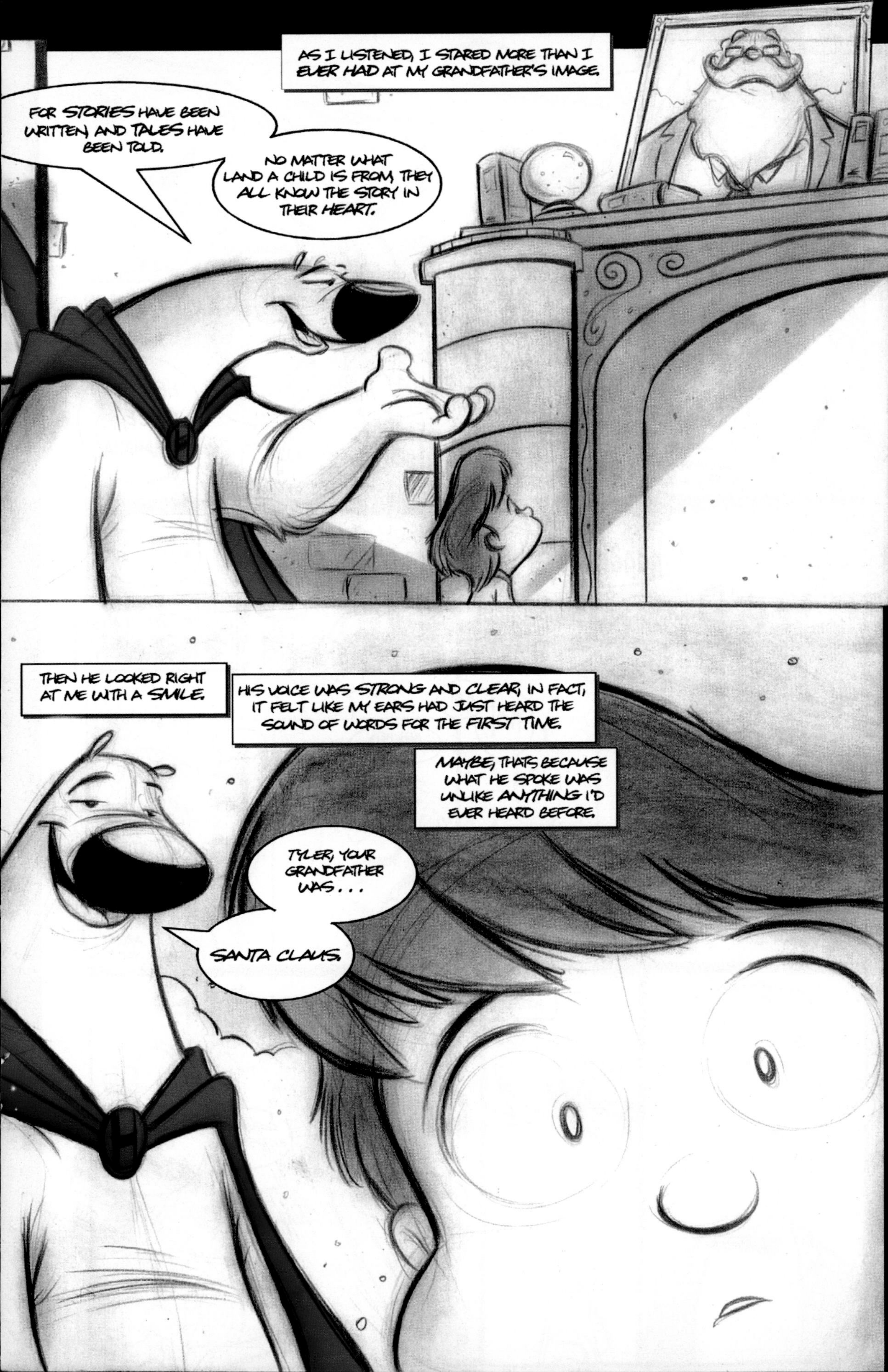
AS I LISTENED, I STARED MORE THAN I EVER HAD AT MY GRANDFATHER'S IMAGE.
FOR STORIES HAVE BEEN WRITTEN, AND TALES HAVE BEEN TOLD.
NO MATTER WHAT LAND A CHILD IS FROM, THEY ALL KNOW THE STORY IN THEIR HEART.
THEN HE LOOKED RIGHT AT ME WITH A SMILE.
HIS VOICE WAS STRONG AND CLEAR, IN FACT, IT FELT LIKE MY EARS HAD JUST HEARD THE SOUND OF WORDS FOR THE FIRST TIME.
MAYBE, THATS BECAUSE WHAT HE SPOKE WAS UNLIKE ANYTHING I'D EVER HEARD BEFORE.
TYLER, YOUR GRANDFATHER WAS . . .
SANTA CLAUS.

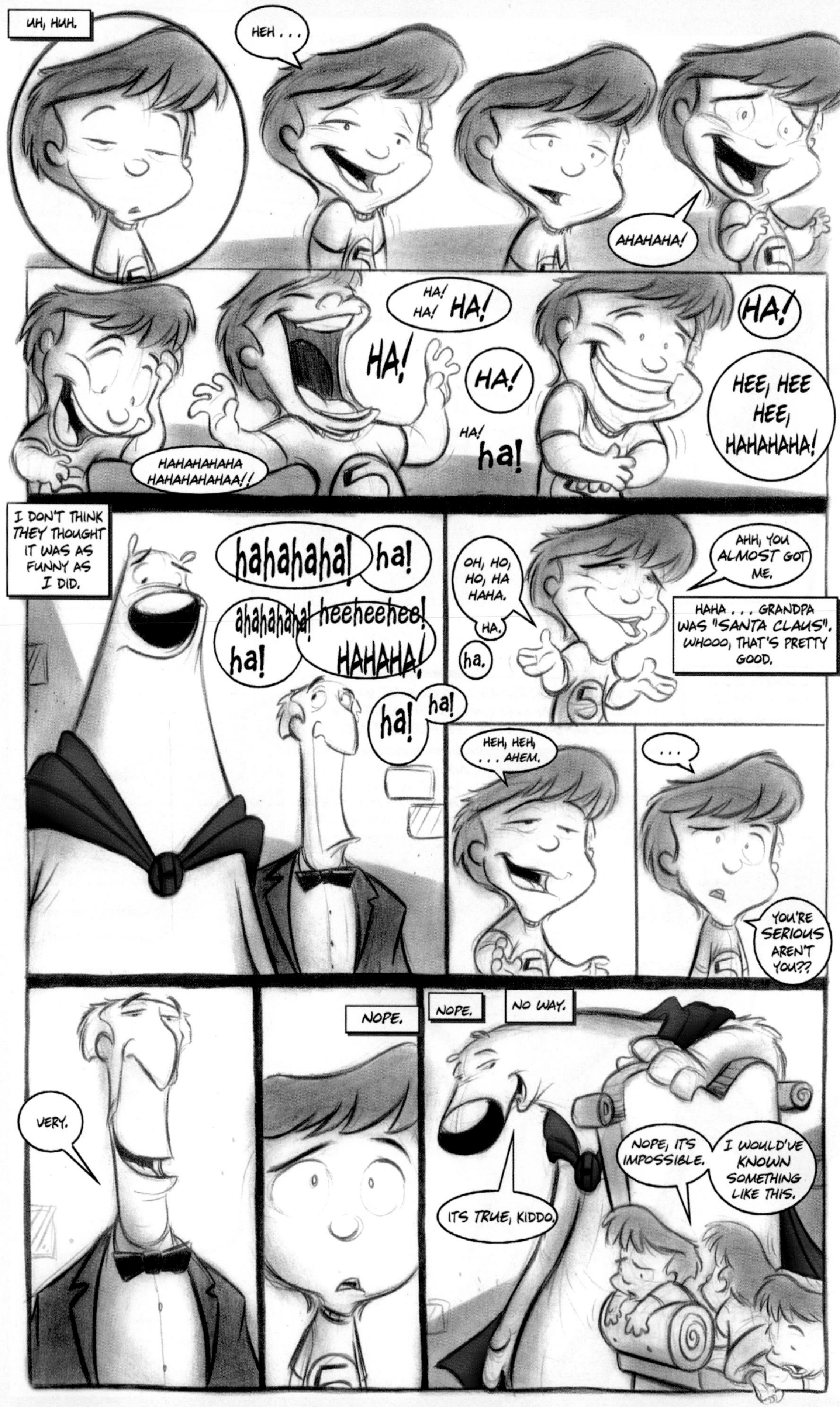

UH, HUH.
HEH . . .
AHAHAHA!
HAHAHAHAHA HAHAHAHAHAA!!
HA! HA! HA!
HA!
HA!
HA! ha!
HA!
HEE, HEE HEE, HAHAHAHA!
I DON'T THINK THEY THOUGHT IT WAS AS FUNNY AS I DID.
hahahaha! ha!
ahahahaha! heeheehee! ha! HAHAHA!
ha! ha!
OH, HO, HO, HA HAHA.
HA.
ha.
AHH, YOU ALMOST GOT ME.
HAHA . . . GRANDPA WAS "SANTA CLAUS". WHOOO, THAT'S PRETTY GOOD.
HEH, HEH, . . . AHEM.
. . .
YOU'RE SERIOUS AREN'T YOU??
VERY.
NOPE.
NOPE.
NO WAY.
ITS TRUE, KIDDO.
NOPE, ITS IMPOSSIBLE.
I WOULD'VE KNOWN SOMETHING LIKE THIS.

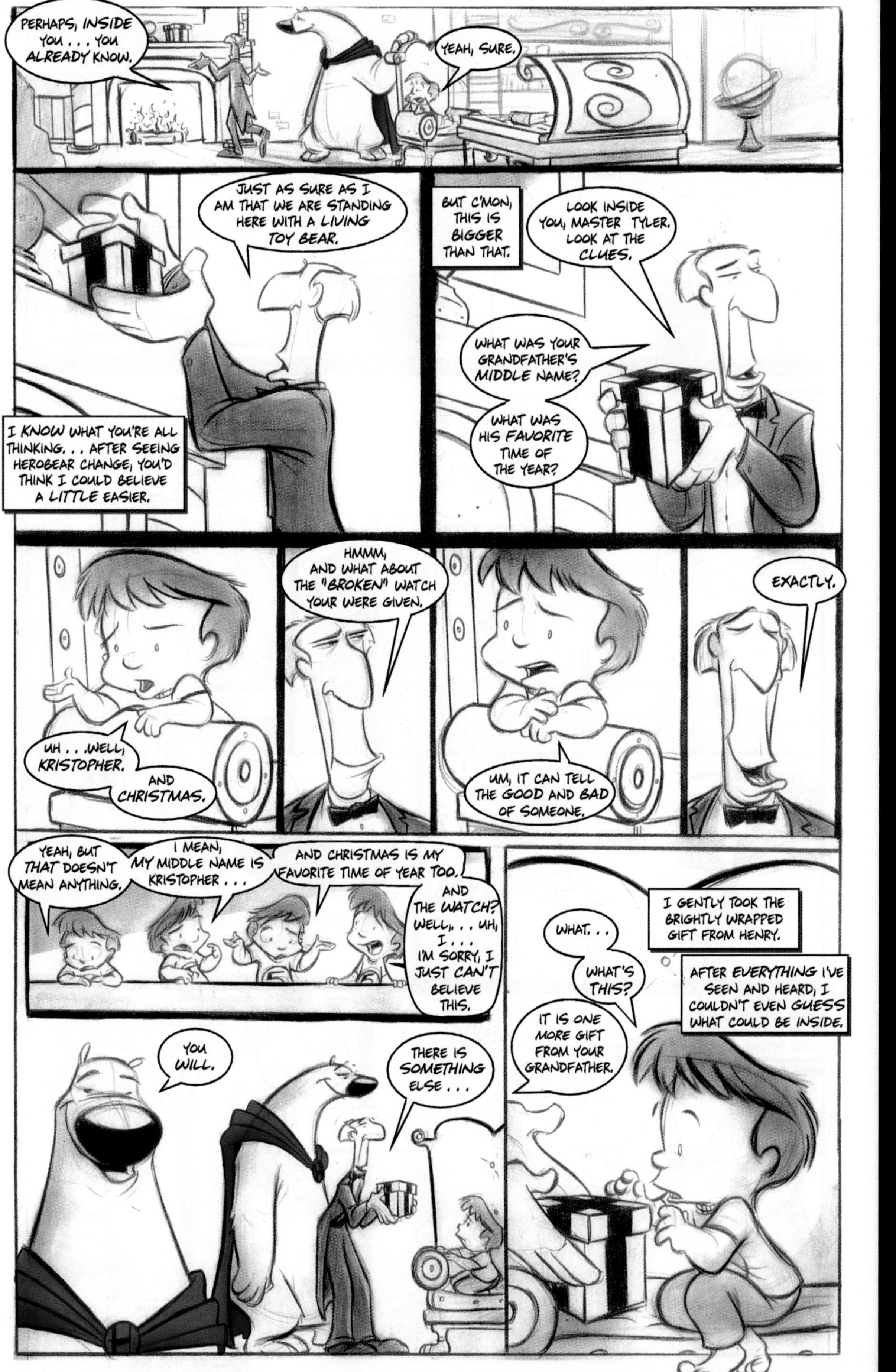
PERHAPS, INSIDE YOU . . . YOU ALREADY KNOW.
YEAH, SURE.
JUST AS SURE AS I AM THAT WE ARE STANDING HERE WITH A LIVING TOY BEAR.
I KNOW WHAT YOU'RE ALL THINKING. . . AFTER SEEING HEROBEAR CHANGE, YOU'D THINK I COULD BELIEVE A LITTLE EASIER.
BUT C'MON, THIS IS BIGGER THAN THAT.
LOOK INSIDE YOU, MASTER TYLER. LOOK AT THE CLUES.
WHAT WAS YOUR GRANDFATHER'S MIDDLE NAME?
WHAT WAS HIS FAVORITE TIME OF THE YEAR?
UH . . .WELL, KRISTOPHER.
AND CHRISTMAS.
HMMM, AND WHAT ABOUT THE "BROKEN" WATCH YOUR WERE GIVEN.
UM, IT CAN TELL THE GOOD AND BAD OF SOMEONE.
EXACTLY.
YEAH, BUT THAT DOESN'T MEAN ANYTHING.
I MEAN, MY MIDDLE NAME IS KRISTOPHER . . .
AND CHRISTMAS IS MY FAVORITE TIME OF YEAR TOO.
AND THE WATCH? WELL, . . UH, I . . . I'M SORRY, I JUST CAN'T BELIEVE THIS.
YOU WILL.
THERE IS SOMETHING ELSE . . .
I GENTLY TOOK THE BRIGHTLY WRAPPED GIFT FROM HENRY.
WHAT. . .
WHAT'S THIS?
AFTER EVERYTHING I'VE SEEN AND HEARD, I COULDN'T EVEN GUESS WHAT COULD BE INSIDE.
IT IS ONE MORE GIFT FROM YOUR GRANDFATHER.

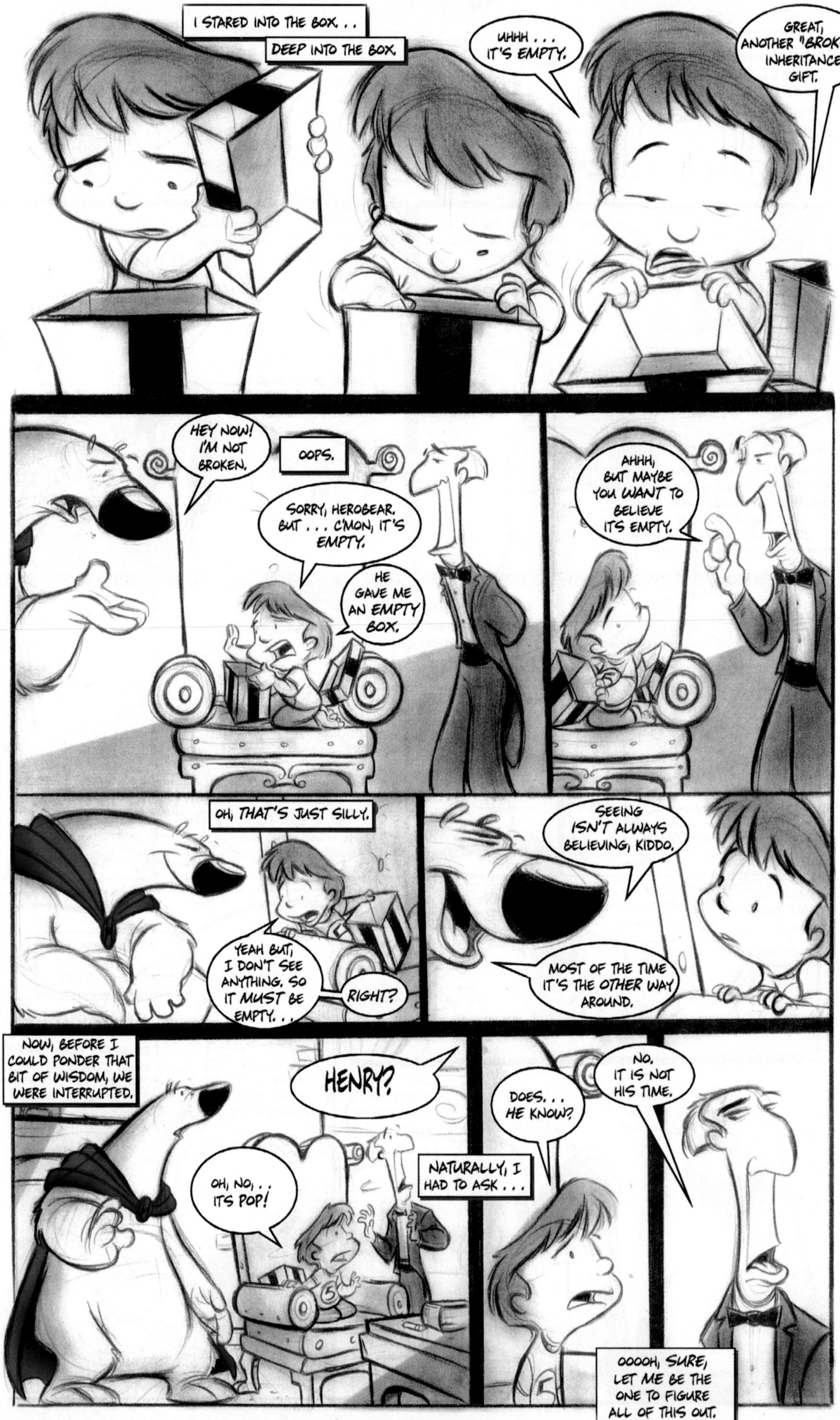
I STARED INTO THE BOX. . .
DEEP INTO THE BOX.
UHHH . . . IT'S EMPTY.
GREAT, ANOTHER "BROKEN" INHERITANCE GIFT.
HEY NOW! I'M NOT BROKEN.
OOPS.
SORRY, HEROBEAR. BUT . . . C'MON, IT'S EMPTY.
HE GAVE ME AN EMPTY BOX.
AHHH, BUT MAYBE YOU WANT TO BELIEVE ITS EMPTY.
OH, THAT'S JUST SILLY.
YEAH BUT, I DON'T SEE ANYTHING. SO IT MUST BE EMPTY. . .
RIGHT?
SEEING ISN'T ALWAYS BELIEVING, KIDDO.
MOST OF THE TIME IT'S THE OTHER WAY AROUND.
NOW, BEFORE I COULD PONDER THAT BIT OF WISDOM, WE WERE INTERRUPTED.
HENRY?
OH, NO. . . ITS POP!
NATURALLY, I HAD TO ASK . . .
DOES. . . HE KNOW?
NO. IT IS NOT HIS TIME.
OOOOH, SURE, LET ME BE THE ONE TO FIGURE ALL OF THIS OUT.

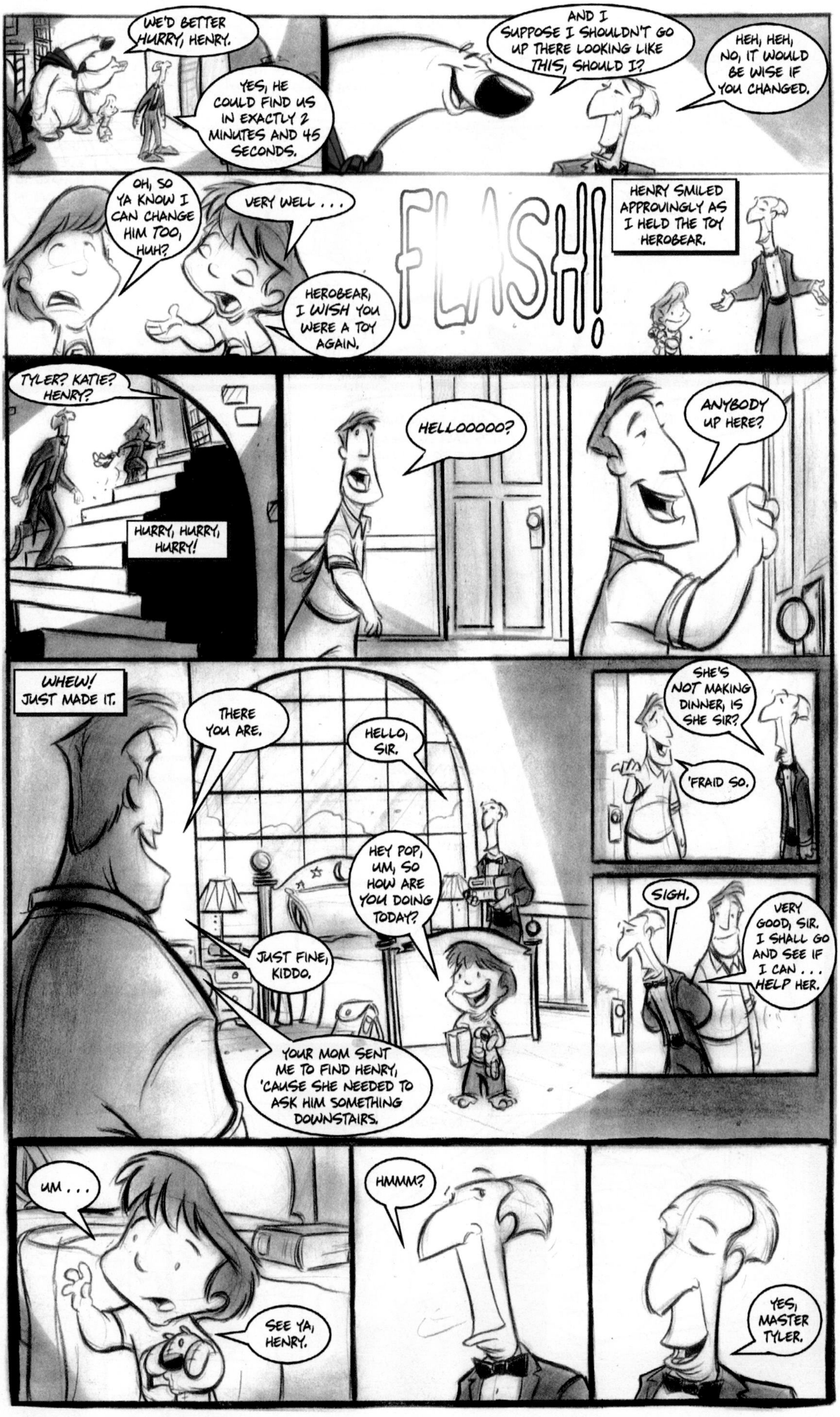

WE'D BETTER HURRY, HENRY.
YES, HE COULD FIND US IN EXACTLY 2 MINUTES AND 45 SECONDS.
AND I SUPPOSE I SHOULDN'T GO UP THERE LOOKING LIKE THIS, SHOULD I?
HEH, HEH, NO, IT WOULD BE WISE IF YOU CHANGED.
OH, SO YA KNOW I CAN CHANGE HIM TOO, HUH?
VERY WELL . . .
HEROBEAR, I WISH YOU WERE A TOY AGAIN.
FLASH!
HENRY SMILED APPROVINGLY AS I HELD THE TOY HEROBEAR.
TYLER? KATIE? HENRY?
HURRY, HURRY, HURRY!
HELLOOOOO?
ANYBODY UP HERE?
WHEW! JUST MADE IT.
THERE YOU ARE.
HELLO, SIR.
HEY POP, UM, SO HOW ARE YOU DOING TODAY?
JUST FINE, KIDDO.
YOUR MOM SENT ME TO FIND HENRY, 'CAUSE SHE NEEDED TO ASK HIM SOMETHING DOWNSTAIRS.
SHE'S NOT MAKING DINNER, IS SHE SIR?
'FRAID SO.
SIGH.
VERY GOOD, SIR. I SHALL GO AND SEE IF I CAN . . . HELP HER.
UM . . .
SEE YA, HENRY.
HMMM?
YES, MASTER TYLER.

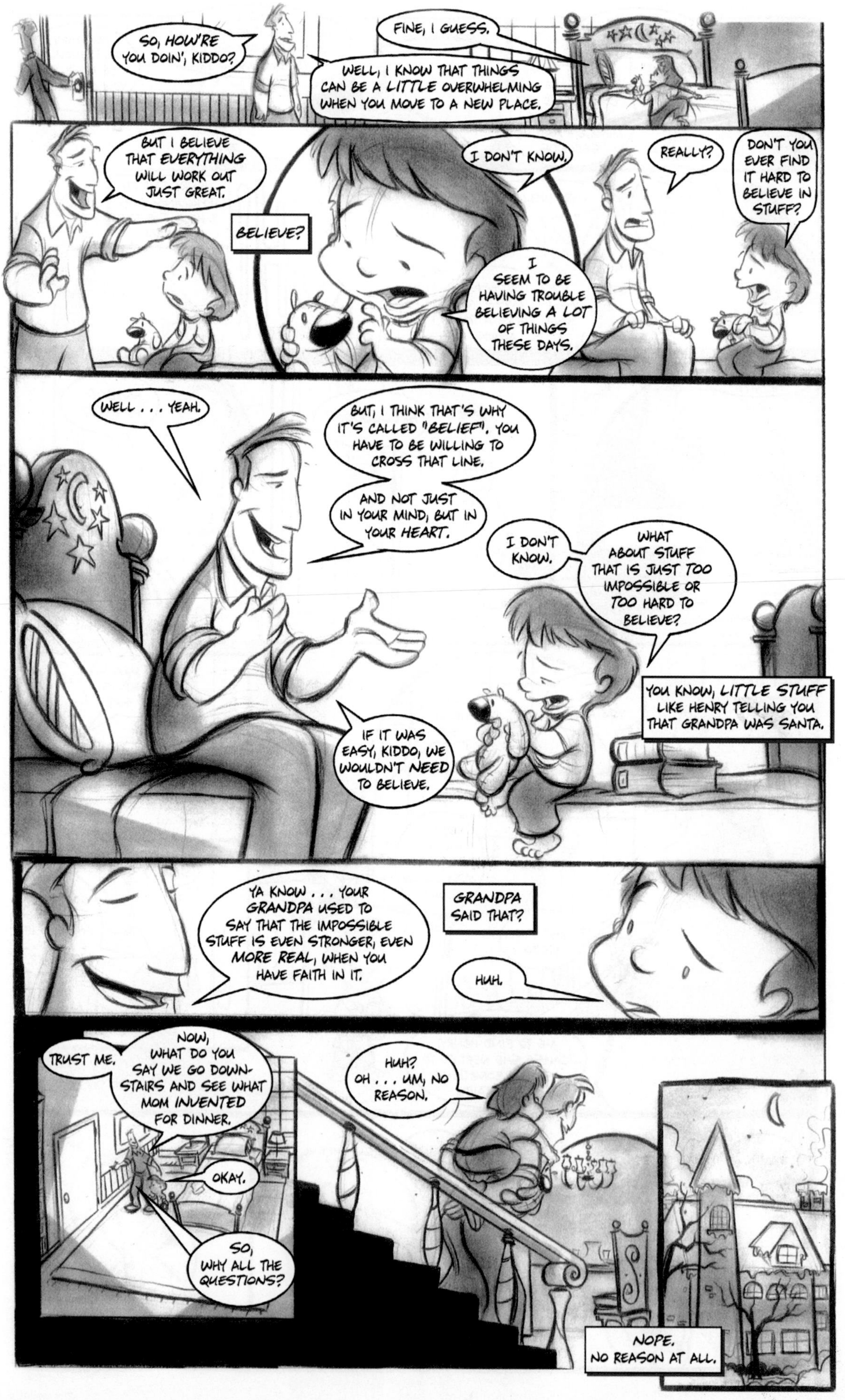

SO, HOW'RE YOU DOIN', KIDDO?
FINE, I GUESS.
WELL, I KNOW THAT THINGS CAN BE A LITTLE OVERWHELMING WHEN YOU MOVE TO A NEW PLACE.
BUT I BELIEVE THAT EVERYTHING WILL WORK OUT JUST GREAT.
BELIEVE?
I DON'T KNOW.
I SEEM TO BE HAVING TROUBLE BELIEVING A LOT OF THINGS THESE DAYS.
REALLY?
DON'T YOU EVER FIND IT HARD TO BELIEVE IN STUFF?
WELL . . . YEAH.
BUT, I THINK THAT'S WHY IT'S CALLED "BELIEF". YOU HAVE TO BE WILLING TO CROSS THAT LINE.
AND NOT JUST IN YOUR MIND, BUT IN YOUR HEART.
I DON'T KNOW.
WHAT ABOUT STUFF THAT IS JUST TOO IMPOSSIBLE OR TOO HARD TO BELIEVE?
YOU KNOW, LITTLE STUFF LIKE HENRY TELLING YOU THAT GRANDPA WAS SANTA.
IF IT WAS EASY, KIDDO, WE WOULDN'T NEED TO BELIEVE.
YA KNOW . . . YOUR GRANDPA USED TO SAY THAT THE IMPOSSIBLE STUFF IS EVEN STRONGER, EVEN MORE REAL, WHEN YOU HAVE FAITH IN IT.
GRANDPA SAID THAT?
HUH.
TRUST ME.
NOW, WHAT DO YOU SAY WE GO DOWN-STAIRS AND SEE WHAT MOM INVENTED FOR DINNER.
OKAY.
SO, WHY ALL THE QUESTIONS?
HUH? OH . . . UM, NO REASON.
NOPE. NO REASON AT ALL.

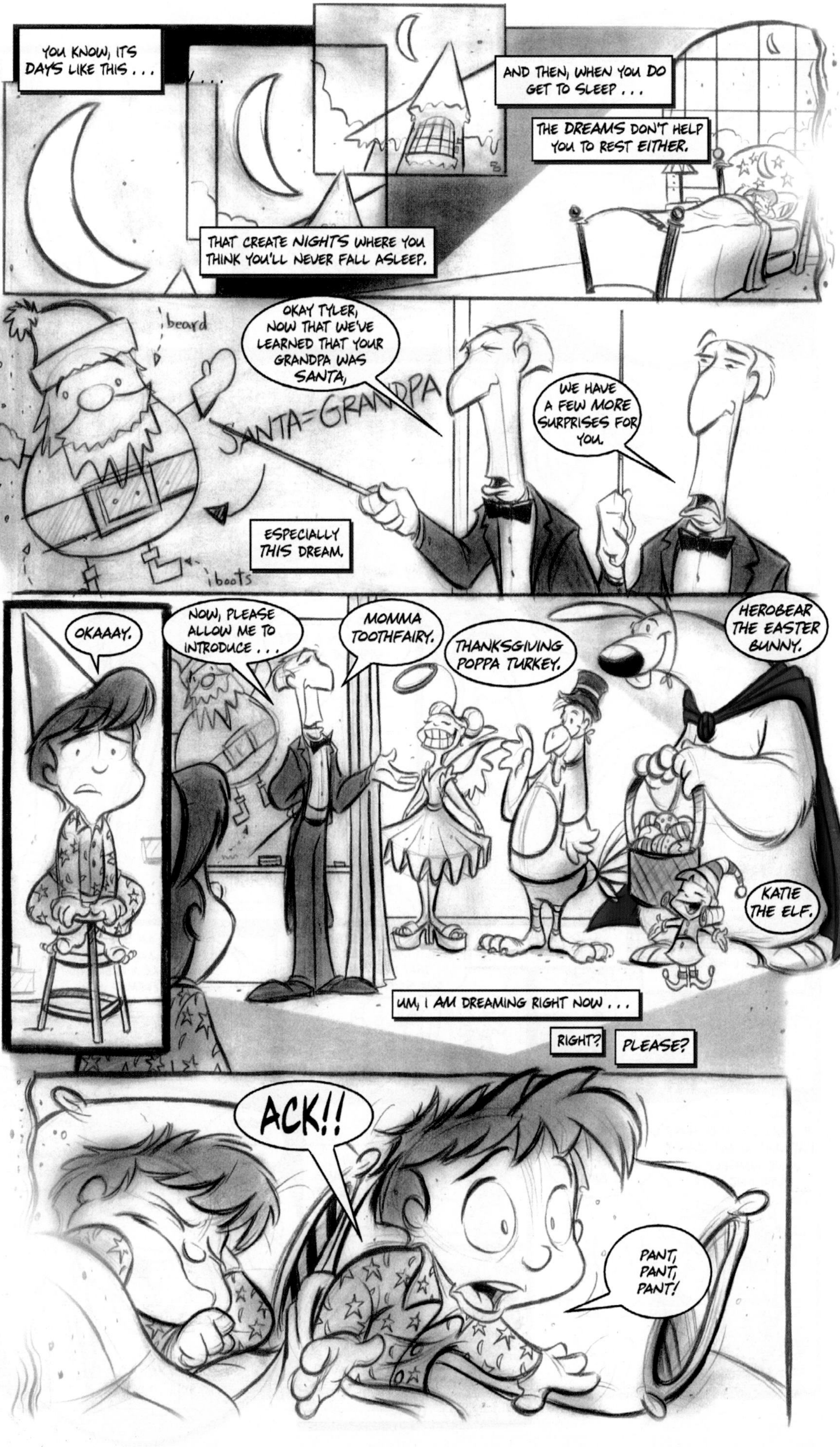
YOU KNOW, ITS DAYS LIKE THIS . . .
THAT CREATE NIGHTS WHERE YOU THINK YOU'LL NEVER FALL ASLEEP.
AND THEN, WHEN YOU DO GET TO SLEEP . . .
THE DREAMS DON'T HELP YOU TO REST EITHER.
beard
SANTA=GRANDPA
boots
OKAY TYLER, NOW THAT WE'VE LEARNED THAT YOUR GRANDPA WAS SANTA,
WE HAVE A FEW MORE SURPRISES FOR YOU.
ESPECIALLY THIS DREAM.
OKAAAY.
NOW, PLEASE ALLOW ME TO INTRODUCE . . .
MOMMA TOOTHFAIRY.
THANKSGIVING POPPA TURKEY.
HEROBEAR THE EASTER BUNNY.
KATIE THE ELF.
UM, I AM DREAMING RIGHT NOW . . .
RIGHT?
PLEASE?
ACK!!
PANT, PANT, PANT!

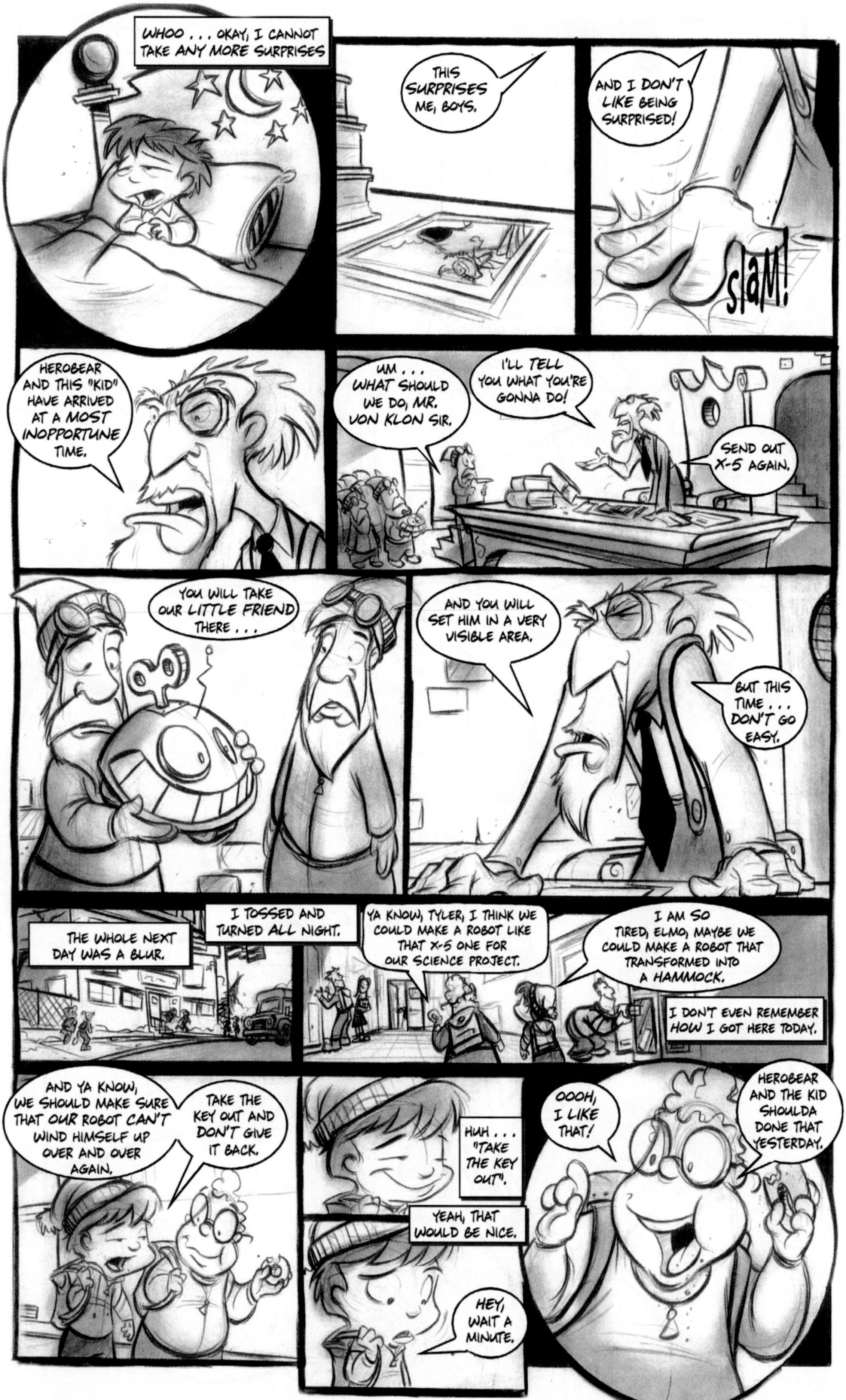

WHOO . . . OKAY, I CANNOT TAKE ANY MORE SURPRISES
THIS SURPRISES ME, BOYS.
AND I DON'T LIKE BEING SURPRISED!
SLAM!
HEROBEAR AND THIS "KID" HAVE ARRIVED AT A MOST INOPPORTUNE TIME.
UM . . . WHAT SHOULD WE DO, MR. VON KLON SIR.
I'LL TELL YOU WHAT YOU'RE GONNA DO!
SEND OUT X-5 AGAIN.
YOU WILL TAKE OUR LITTLE FRIEND THERE . . .
AND YOU WILL SET HIM IN A VERY VISIBLE AREA.
BUT THIS TIME . . . DON'T GO EASY.
THE WHOLE NEXT DAY WAS A BLUR.
I TOSSED AND TURNED ALL NIGHT.
YA KNOW, TYLER, I THINK WE COULD MAKE A ROBOT LIKE THAT X-5 ONE FOR OUR SCIENCE PROJECT.
I AM SO TIRED, ELMO, MAYBE WE COULD MAKE A ROBOT THAT TRANSFORMED INTO A HAMMOCK.
I DON'T EVEN REMEMBER HOW I GOT HERE TODAY.
AND YA KNOW, WE SHOULD MAKE SURE THAT OUR ROBOT CAN'T WIND HIMSELF UP OVER AND OVER AGAIN.
TAKE THE KEY OUT AND DON'T GIVE IT BACK.
HUH . . . "TAKE THE KEY OUT".
YEAH, THAT WOULD BE NICE.
HEY, WAIT A MINUTE.
OOOH, I LIKE THAT!
HEROBEAR AND THE KID SHOULDA DONE THAT YESTERDAY.

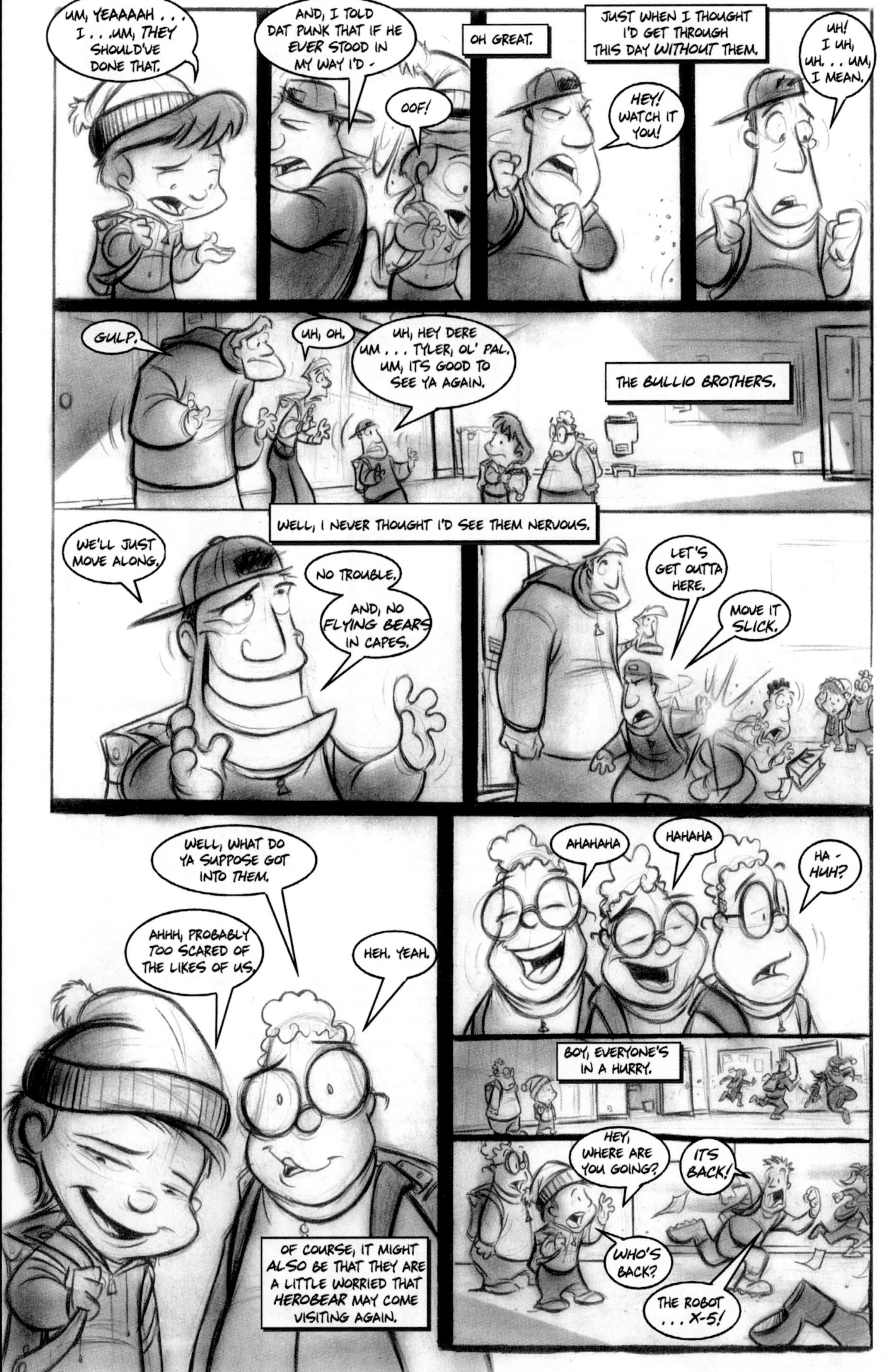

UM, YEAAAAH . . . I . . UM, THEY SHOULD'VE DONE THAT.
AND, I TOLD DAT PUNK THAT IF HE EVER STOOD IN MY WAY I'D -
OOF!
OH GREAT.
JUST WHEN I THOUGHT I'D GET THROUGH THIS DAY WITHOUT THEM.
HEY! WATCH IT YOU!
UH! I UH, UH. . . UM, I MEAN.
GULP.
UH, OH.
UH, HEY DERE UM . . . TYLER, OL' PAL. UM, ITS GOOD TO SEE YA AGAIN.
THE BULLIO BROTHERS.
WELL, I NEVER THOUGHT I'D SEE THEM NERVOUS.
WE'LL JUST MOVE ALONG.
NO TROUBLE.
AND, NO FLYING BEARS IN CAPES.
LET'S GET OUTTA HERE.
MOVE IT SLICK.
WELL, WHAT DO YA SUPPOSE GOT INTO THEM.
AHHH, PROBABLY TOO SCARED OF THE LIKES OF US.
HEH. YEAH.
OF COURSE, IT MIGHT ALSO BE THAT THEY ARE A LITTLE WORRIED THAT HEROBEAR MAY COME VISITING AGAIN.
AHAHAHA
HAHAHA
HA - HUH?
BOY, EVERYONE'S IN A HURRY.
HEY, WHERE ARE YOU GOING?
ITS BACK!
WHO'S BACK?
THE ROBOT . . . X-5!

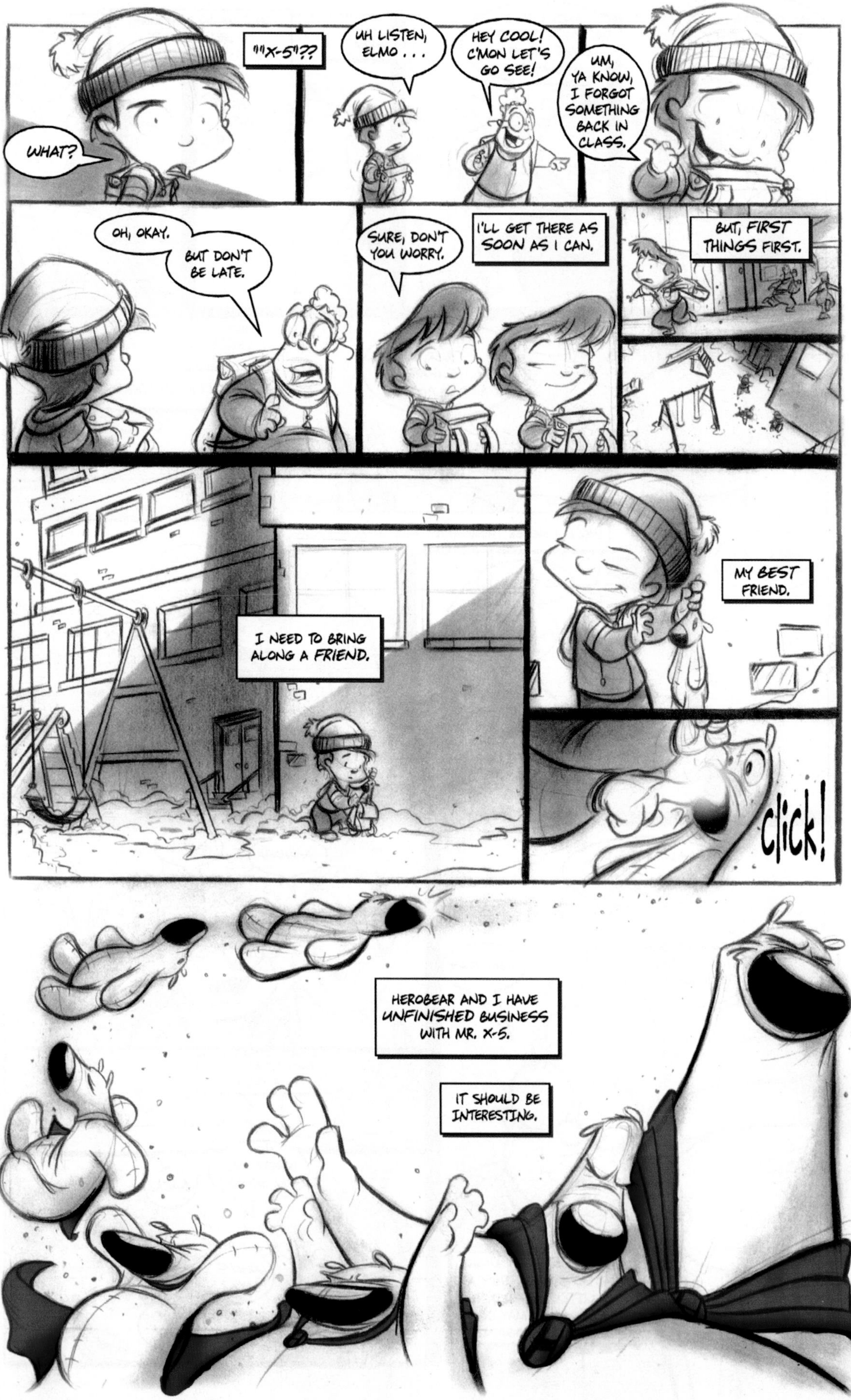
WHAT?
"X-5"??
UH LISTEN, ELMO . . .
HEY COOL! C'MON LET'S GO SEE!
UM, YA KNOW, I FORGOT SOMETHING BACK IN CLASS.
OH, OKAY.
BUT DON'T BE LATE.
SURE, DON'T YOU WORRY.
I'LL GET THERE AS SOON AS I CAN.
BUT, FIRST THINGS FIRST.
I NEED TO BRING ALONG A FRIEND.
MY BEST FRIEND.
click!
HEROBEAR AND I HAVE UNFINISHED BUSINESS WITH MR. X-5.
IT SHOULD BE INTERESTING.

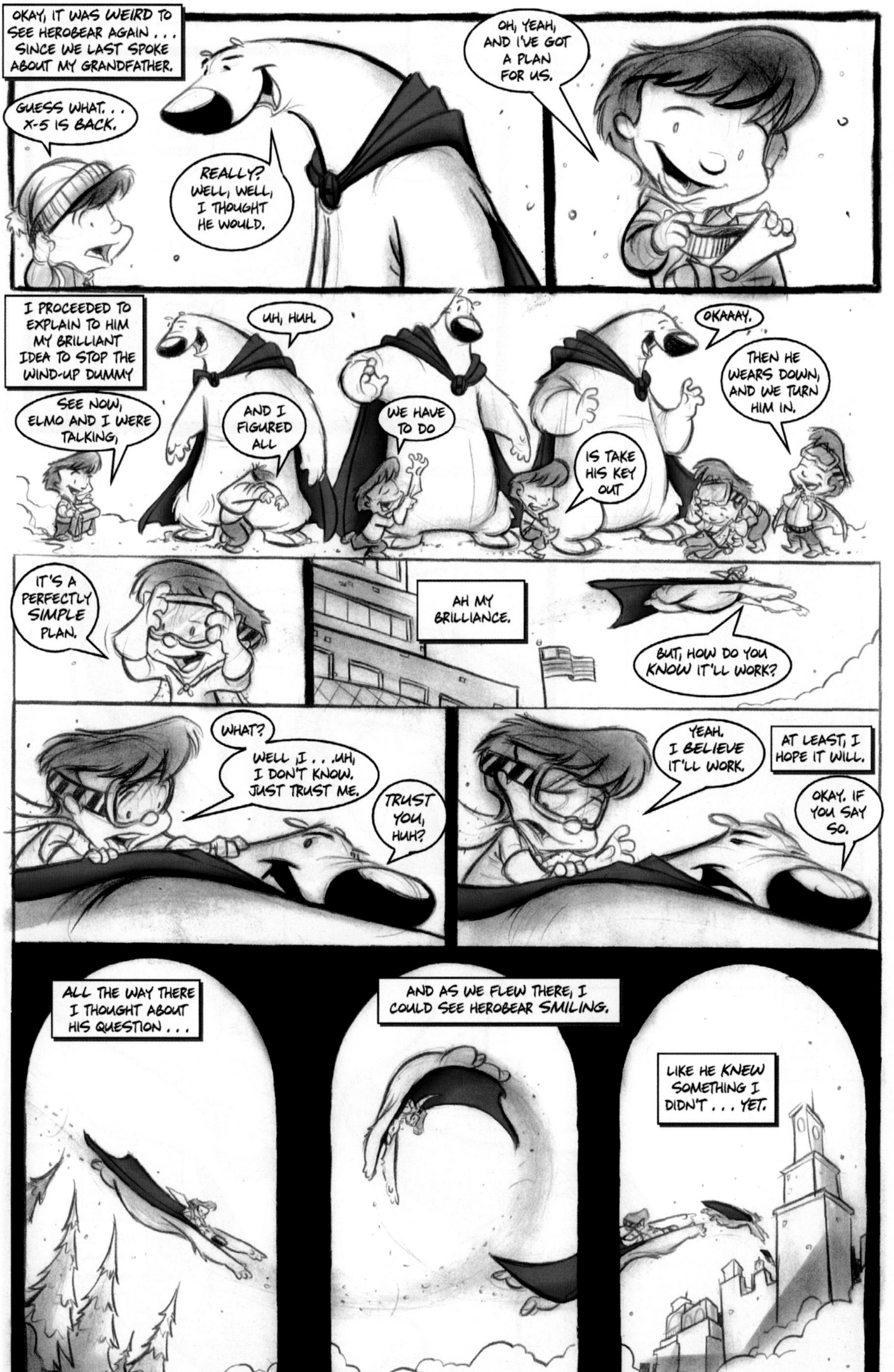
OKAY, IT WAS WEIRD TO SEE HEROBEAR AGAIN . . . SINCE WE LAST SPOKE ABOUT MY GRANDFATHER.
GUESS WHAT. . . X-5 IS BACK.
REALLY? WELL, WELL, I THOUGHT HE WOULD.
OH, YEAH, AND I'VE GOT A PLAN FOR US.
I PROCEEDED TO EXPLAIN TO HIM MY BRILLIANT IDEA TO STOP THE WIND-UP DUMMY
SEE NOW, ELMO AND I WERE TALKING,
UH, HUH.
AND I FIGURED ALL
WE HAVE TO DO
IS TAKE HIS KEY OUT
OKAAAY.
THEN HE WEARS DOWN, AND WE TURN HIM IN.
IT'S A PERFECTLY SIMPLE PLAN.
AH MY BRILLIANCE.
BUT, HOW DO YOU KNOW IT'LL WORK?
WHAT?
WELL, I . . . UH, I DON'T KNOW. JUST TRUST ME.
TRUST YOU, HUH?
YEAH. I BELIEVE IT'LL WORK.
AT LEAST, I HOPE IT WILL.
OKAY. IF YOU SAY SO.
ALL THE WAY THERE I THOUGHT ABOUT HIS QUESTION . . .
AND AS WE FLEW THERE, I COULD SEE HEROBEAR SMILING.
LIKE HE KNEW SOMETHING I DIDN'T . . . YET.

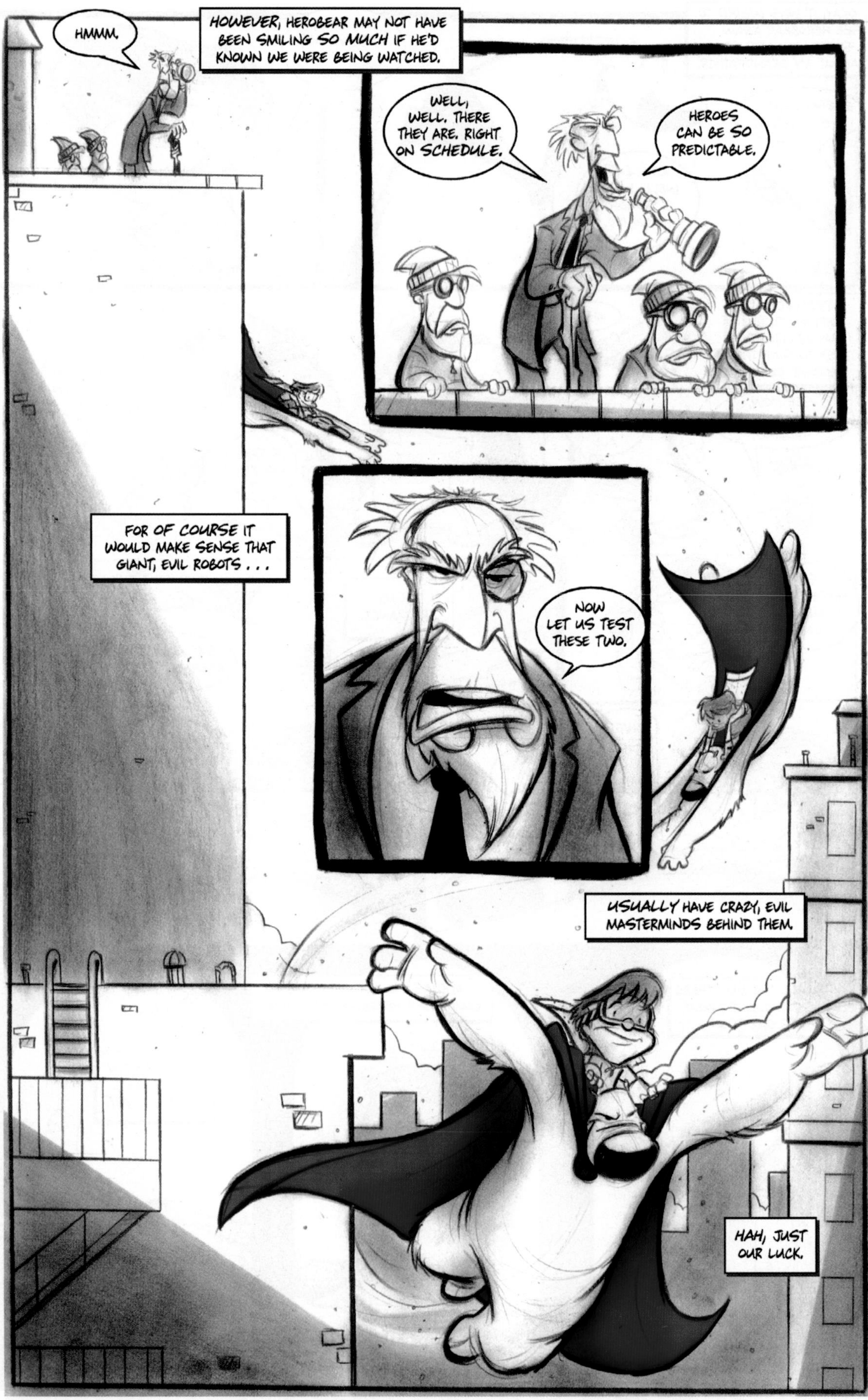
HMMM.
HOWEVER, HEROBEAR MAY NOT HAVE BEEN SMILING SO MUCH IF HE'D KNOWN WE WERE BEING WATCHED.
WELL, WELL. THERE THEY ARE. RIGHT ON SCHEDULE.
HEROES CAN BE SO PREDICTABLE.
FOR OF COURSE IT WOULD MAKE SENSE THAT GIANT, EVIL ROBOTS . . .
NOW LET US TEST THESE TWO.
USUALLY HAVE CRAZY, EVIL MASTERMINDS BEHIND THEM.
HAH, JUST OUR LUCK.

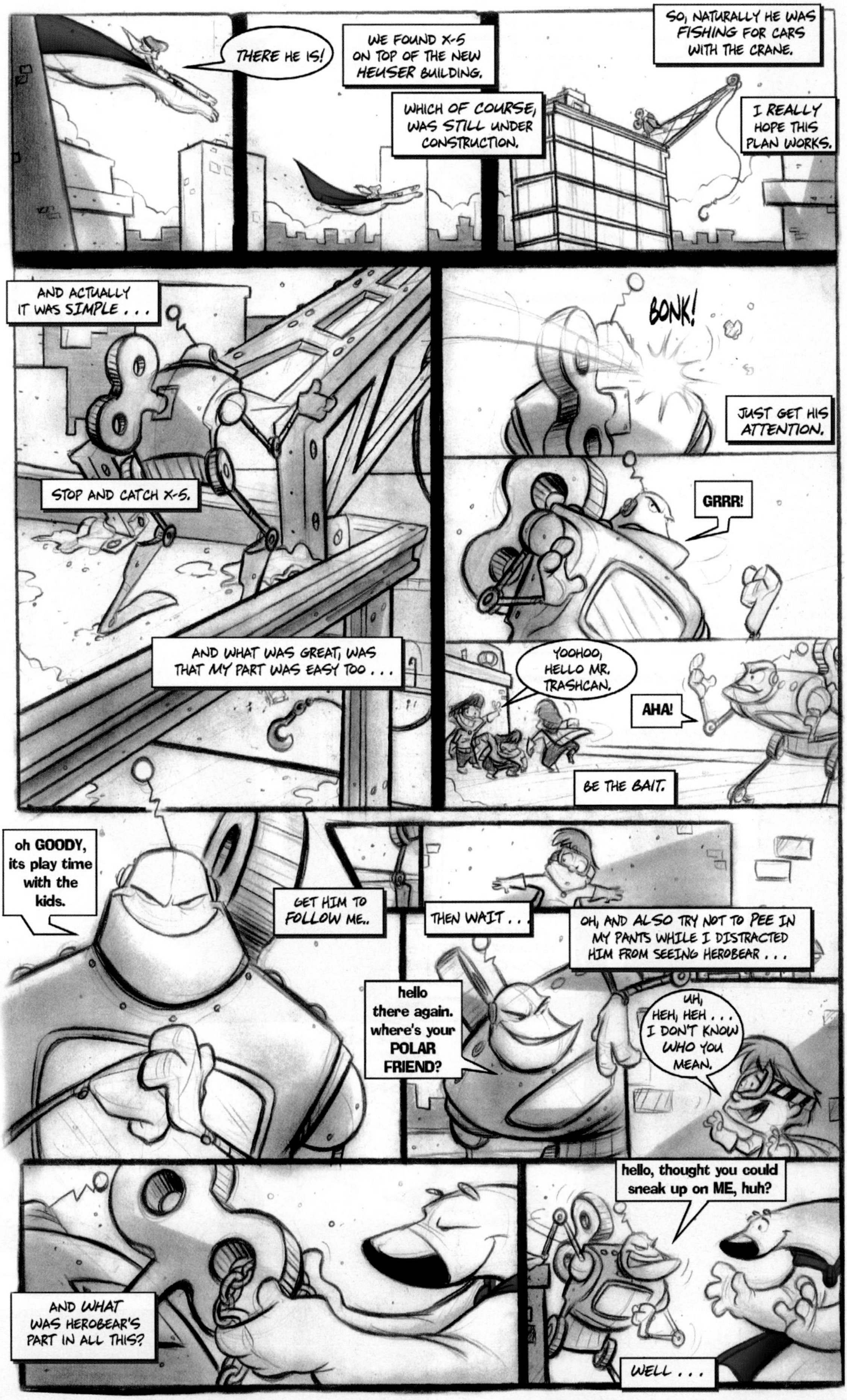
THERE HE IS!
WE FOUND X-5 ON TOP OF THE NEW HEUSER BUILDING.
WHICH OF COURSE, WAS STILL UNDER CONSTRUCTION.
SO, NATURALLY HE WAS FISHING FOR CARS WITH THE CRANE.
I REALLY HOPE THIS PLAN WORKS.
AND ACTUALLY IT WAS SIMPLE . . .
BONK!
JUST GET HIS ATTENTION.
STOP AND CATCH X-5.
GRRR!
AND WHAT WAS GREAT, WAS THAT MY PART WAS EASY TOO . . .
YOOHOO, HELLO MR. TRASHCAN.
AHA!
BE THE BAIT.
oh GOODY, its play time with the kids.
GET HIM TO FOLLOW ME..
THEN WAIT . . .
OH, AND ALSO TRY NOT TO PEE IN MY PANTS WHILE I DISTRACTED HIM FROM SEEING HEROBEAR . . .
hello there again. where's your POLAR FRIEND?
UH, HEH, HEH . . . I DON'T KNOW WHO YOU MEAN.
AND WHAT WAS HEROBEAR'S PART IN ALL THIS?
hello, thought you could sneak up on ME, huh?
WELL . . .

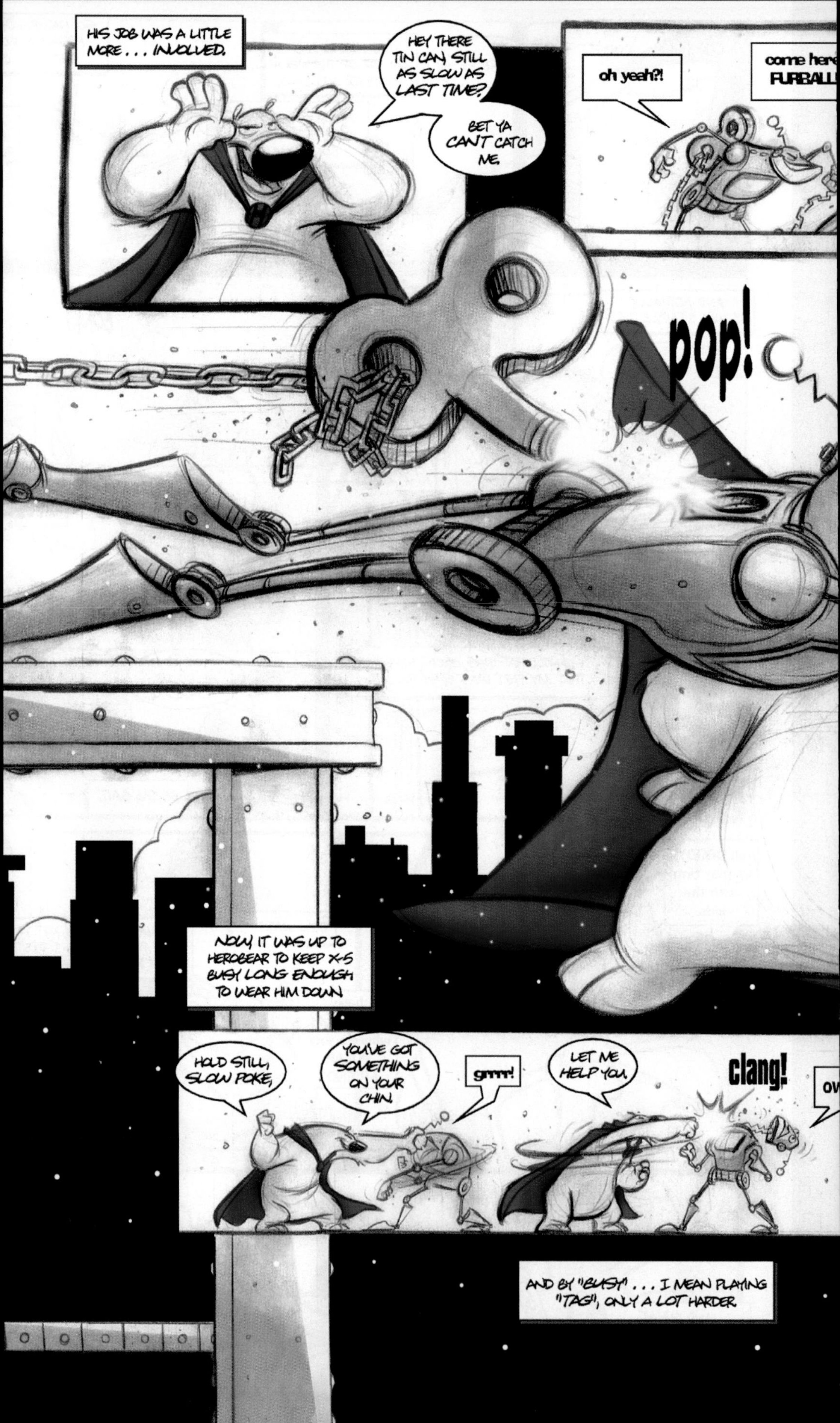
HIS JOB WAS A LITTLE MORE . . . INVOLVED.
HEY THERE TIN CAN, STILL AS SLOW AS LAST TIME?
BET YA CAN'T CATCH ME.
oh yeah?!
come here
FURBALL
pop!
NOW, IT WAS UP TO HEROBEAR TO KEEP X-5 BUSY LONG ENOUGH TO WEAR HIM DOWN.
HOLD STILL, SLOW POKE,
YOU'VE GOT SOMETHING ON YOUR CHIN.
grrrr!
LET ME HELP YOU.
clang!
ow
AND BY "BUSY" . . . I MEAN PLAYING "TAG", ONLY A LOT HARDER.

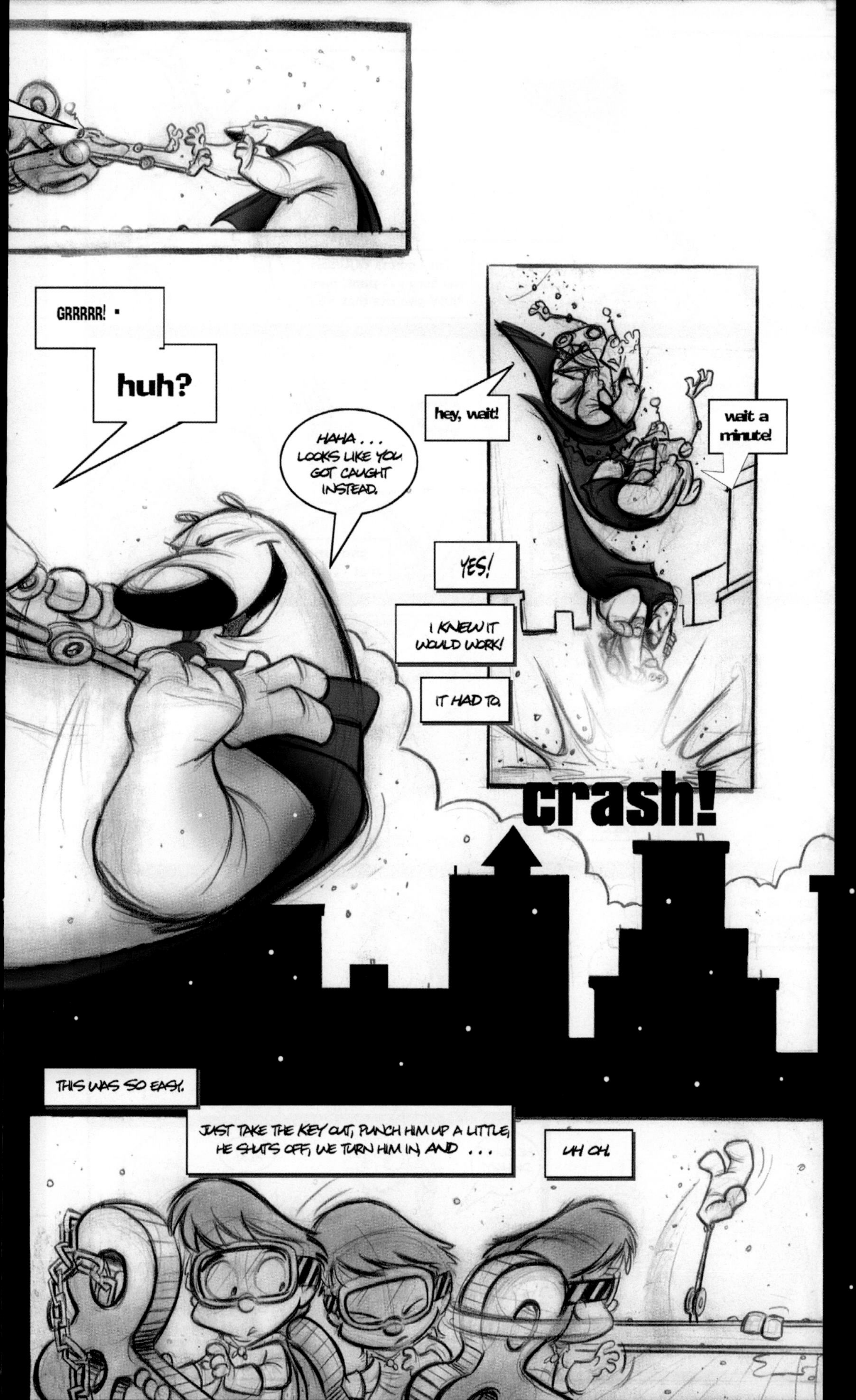
GRRRRR!
huh?
HAHA . . . LOOKS LIKE YOU GOT CAUGHT INSTEAD.
hey, wait!
wait a minute!
YES!
I KNEW IT WOULD WORK!
IT HAD TO.
crash!
THIS WAS SO EASY.
JUST TAKE THE KEY OUT, PUNCH HIM UP A LITTLE, HE SHUTS OFF, WE TURN HIM IN, AND . . .
UH OH.

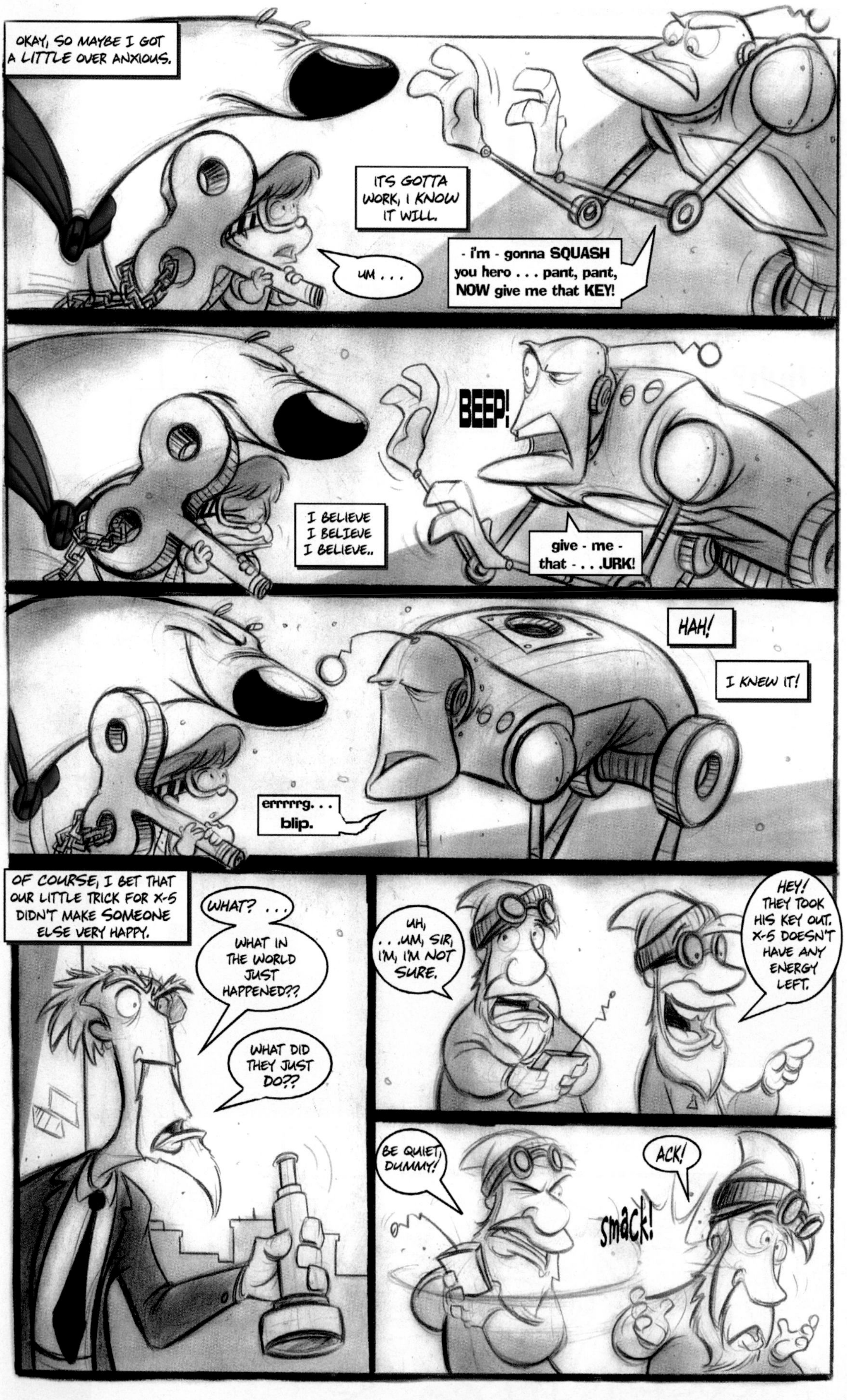

OKAY, SO MAYBE I GOT A LITTLE OVER ANXIOUS.
ITS GOTTA WORK, I KNOW IT WILL.
UM . . .
- i'm - gonna SQUASH you hero . . . pant, pant, NOW give me that KEY!
BEEP!
I BELIEVE I BELIEVE I BELIEVE..
give - me - that - . . .URK!
HAH!
I KNEW IT!
errrrrg. . . blip.
OF COURSE, I BET THAT OUR LITTLE TRICK FOR X-5 DIDN'T MAKE SOMEONE ELSE VERY HAPPY.
WHAT? . . .
WHAT IN THE WORLD JUST HAPPENED??
WHAT DID THEY JUST DO??
UH, . . .UM, SIR, I'M, I'M NOT SURE.
HEY! THEY TOOK HIS KEY OUT. X-5 DOESN'T HAVE ANY ENERGY LEFT.
BE QUIET, DUMMY!
ACK!
smack!

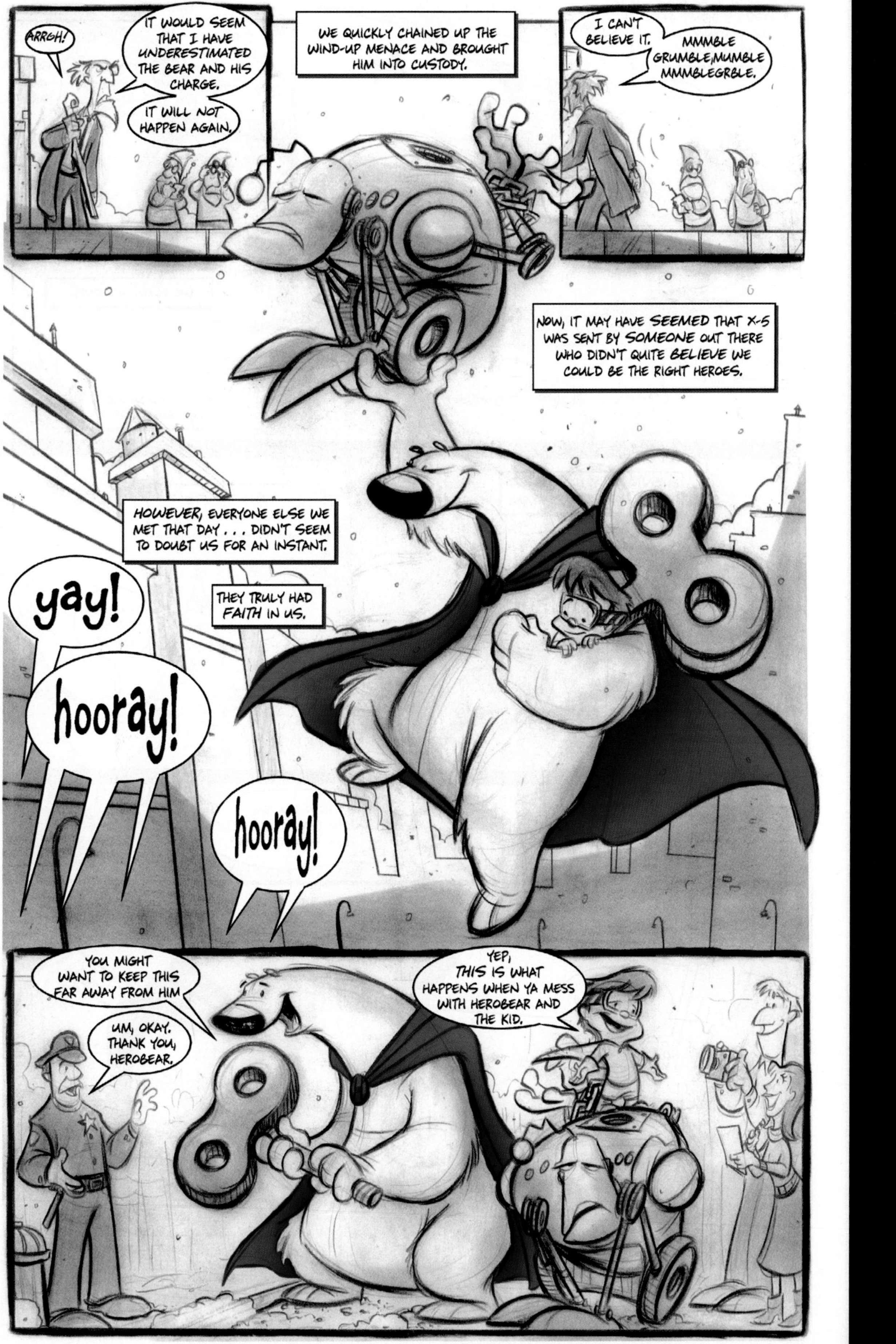
ARRGH!
IT WOULD SEEM THAT I HAVE UNDERESTIMATED THE BEAR AND HIS CHARGE.
IT WILL NOT HAPPEN AGAIN.
WE QUICKLY CHAINED UP THE WIND-UP MENACE AND BROUGHT HIM INTO CUSTODY.
I CAN'T BELIEVE IT.
MMMBLE GRUMBLE,MUMBLE MMMBLEGRBLE.
NOW, IT MAY HAVE SEEMED THAT X-5 WAS SENT BY SOMEONE OUT THERE WHO DIDN'T QUITE BELIEVE WE COULD BE THE RIGHT HEROES.
HOWEVER, EVERYONE ELSE WE MET THAT DAY . . . DIDN'T SEEM TO DOUBT US FOR AN INSTANT.
THEY TRULY HAD FAITH IN US.
yay!
hooray!
hooray!
YOU MIGHT WANT TO KEEP THIS FAR AWAY FROM HIM
UM, OKAY. THANK YOU, HEROBEAR.
YEP, THIS IS WHAT HAPPENS WHEN YA MESS WITH HEROBEAR AND THE KID.

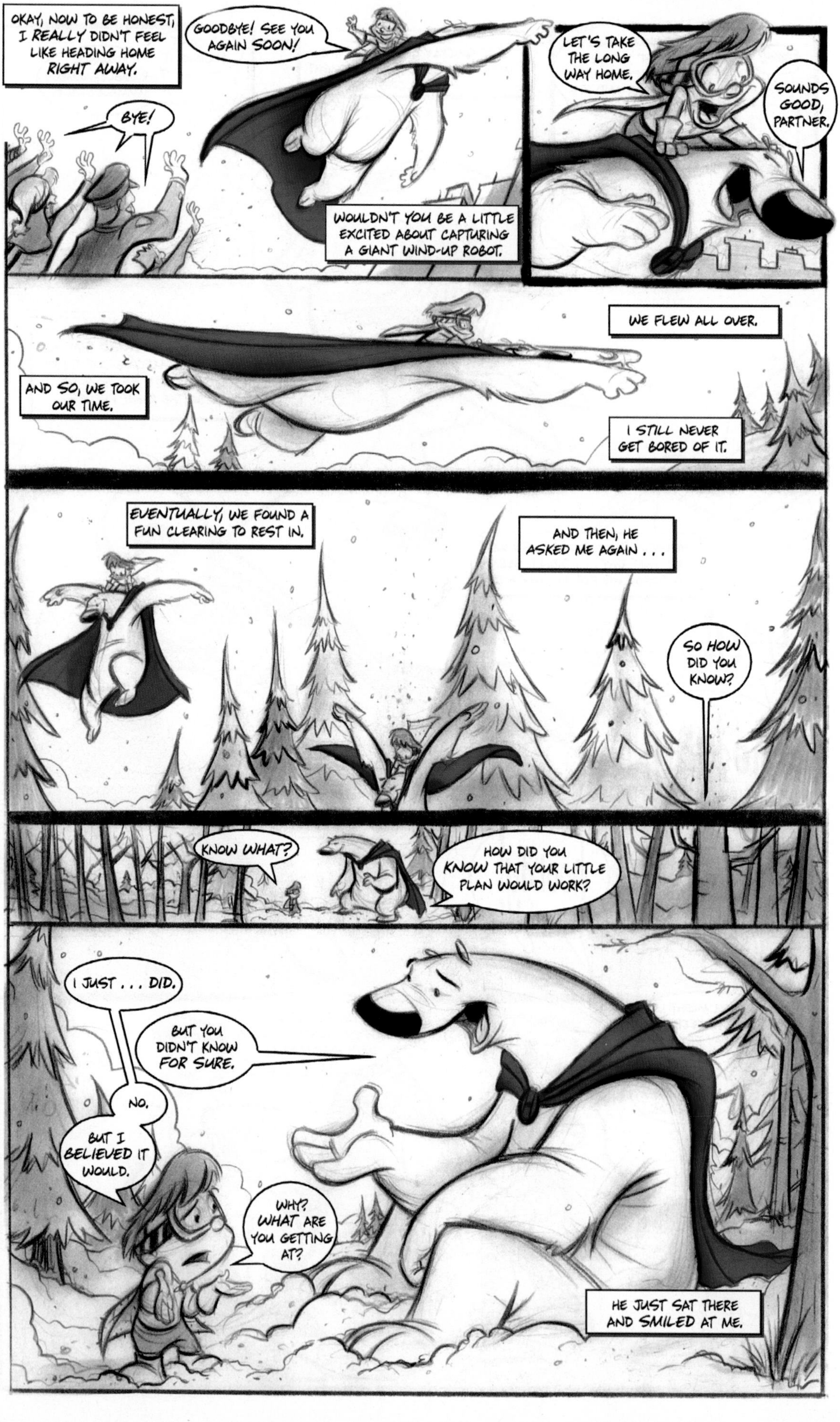
OKAY, NOW TO BE HONEST, I REALLY DIDN'T FEEL LIKE HEADING HOME RIGHT AWAY.
GOODBYE! SEE YOU AGAIN SOON!
BYE!
WOULDN'T YOU BE A LITTLE EXCITED ABOUT CAPTURING A GIANT WIND-UP ROBOT.
LET'S TAKE THE LONG WAY HOME.
SOUNDS GOOD, PARTNER.
WE FLEW ALL OVER.
AND SO, WE TOOK OUR TIME.
I STILL NEVER GET BORED OF IT.
EVENTUALLY, WE FOUND A FUN CLEARING TO REST IN.
AND THEN, HE ASKED ME AGAIN . . .
SO HOW DID YOU KNOW?
KNOW WHAT?
HOW DID YOU KNOW THAT YOUR LITTLE PLAN WOULD WORK?
I JUST . . . DID.
BUT YOU DIDN'T KNOW FOR SURE.
NO.
BUT I BELIEVED IT WOULD.
WHY? WHAT ARE YOU GETTING AT?
HE JUST SAT THERE AND SMILED AT ME.

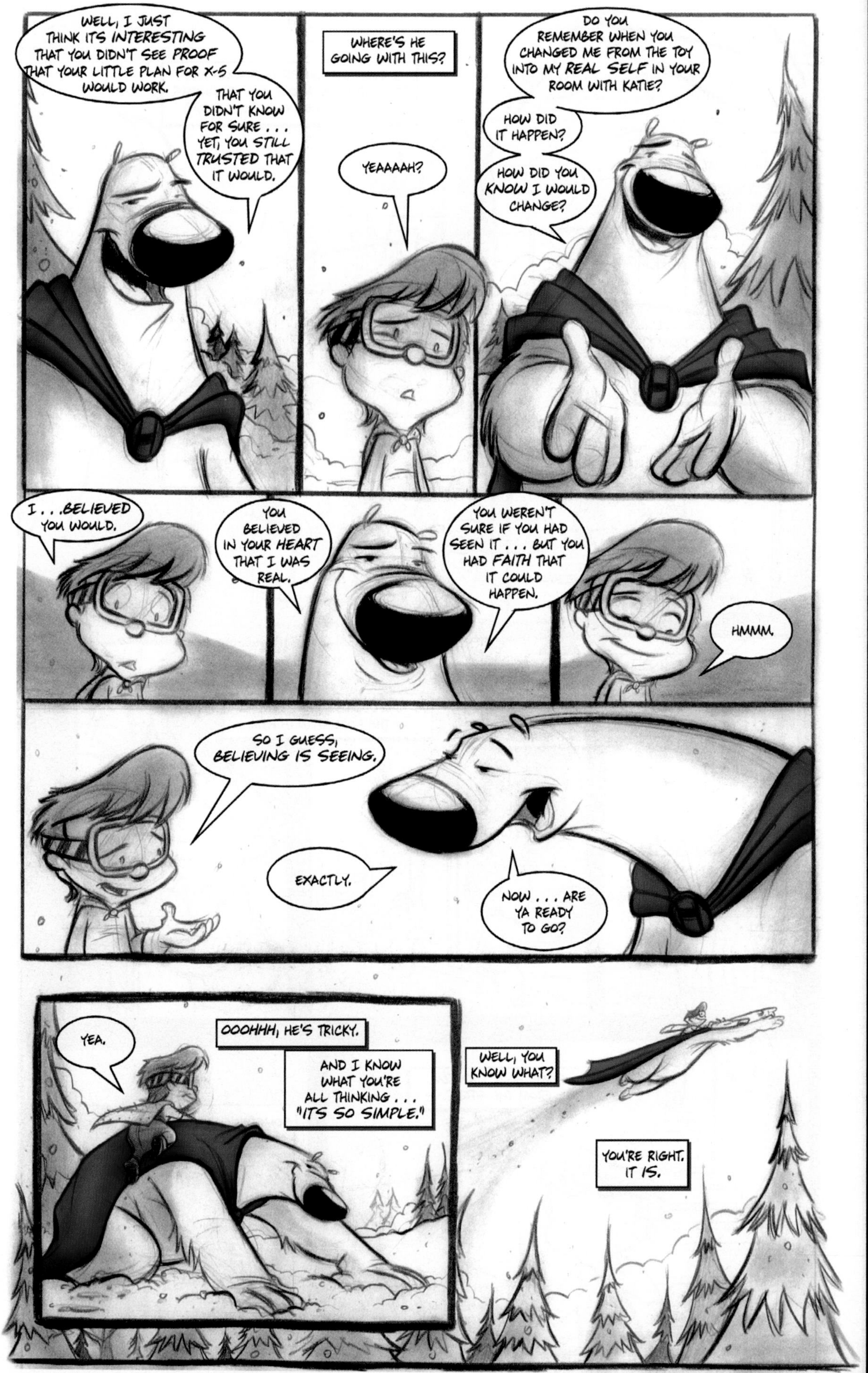
WELL, I JUST THINK ITS INTERESTING THAT YOU DIDN'T SEE PROOF THAT YOUR LITTLE PLAN FOR X-5 WOULD WORK.
THAT YOU DIDN'T KNOW FOR SURE . . . YET, YOU STILL TRUSTED THAT IT WOULD.
WHERE'S HE GOING WITH THIS?
YEAAAAH?
DO YOU REMEMBER WHEN YOU CHANGED ME FROM THE TOY INTO MY REAL SELF IN YOUR ROOM WITH KATIE?
HOW DID IT HAPPEN?
HOW DID YOU KNOW I WOULD CHANGE?
I . . .BELIEVED YOU WOULD.
YOU BELIEVED IN YOUR HEART THAT I WAS REAL.
YOU WEREN'T SURE IF YOU HAD SEEN IT . . . BUT YOU HAD FAITH THAT IT COULD HAPPEN.
HMMM.
SO I GUESS, BELIEVING IS SEEING.
EXACTLY.
NOW . . . ARE YA READY TO GO?
YEA.
OOOHHH, HE'S TRICKY.
AND I KNOW WHAT YOU'RE ALL THINKING . . . "ITS SO SIMPLE."
WELL, YOU KNOW WHAT?
YOU'RE RIGHT. IT IS.

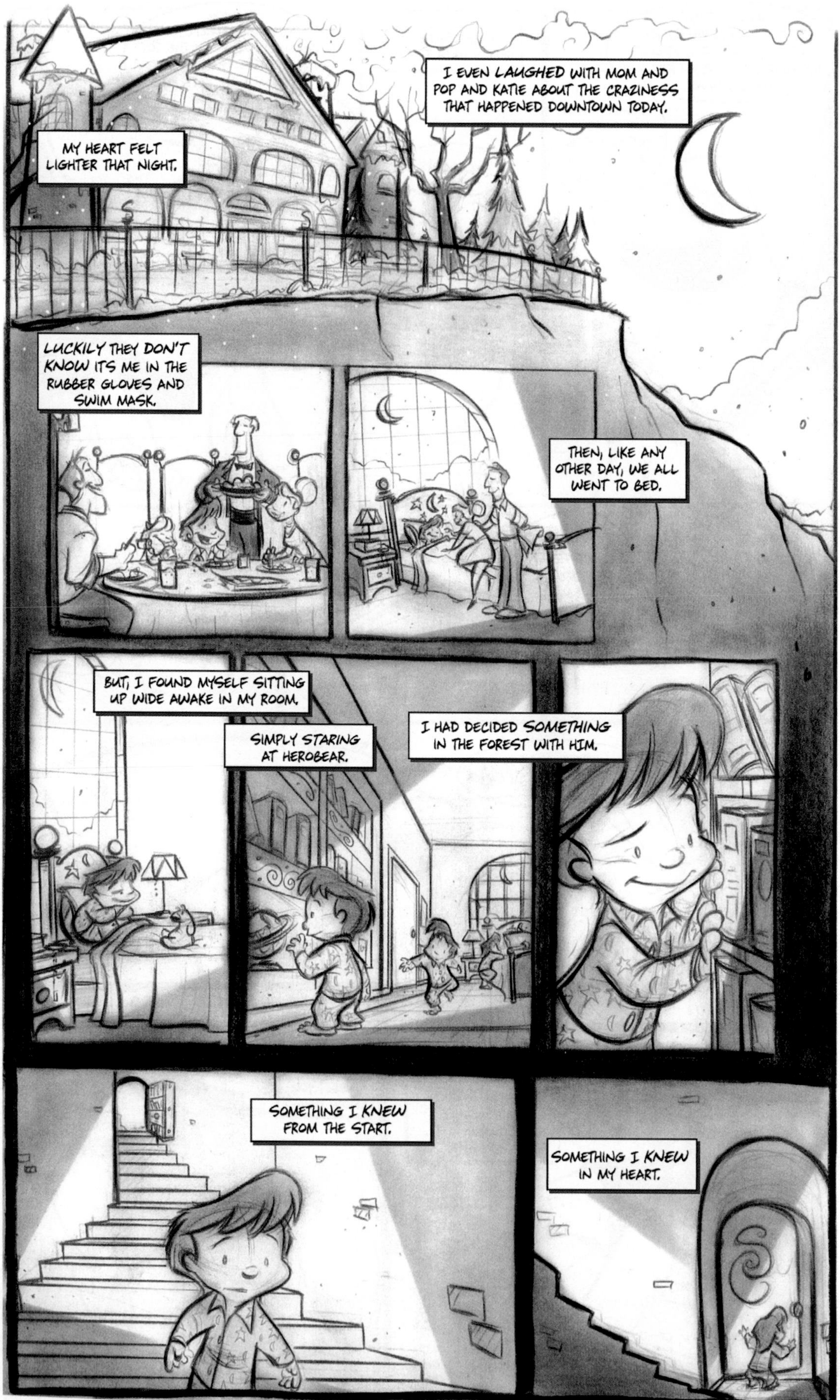
MY HEART FELT LIGHTER THAT NIGHT.
I EVEN LAUGHED WITH MOM AND POP AND KATIE ABOUT THE CRAZINESS THAT HAPPENED DOWNTOWN TODAY.
LUCKILY THEY DON'T KNOW ITS ME IN THE RUBBER GLOVES AND SWIM MASK.
THEN, LIKE ANY OTHER DAY, WE ALL WENT TO BED.
BUT, I FOUND MYSELF SITTING UP WIDE AWAKE IN MY ROOM.
SIMPLY STARING AT HEROBEAR.
I HAD DECIDED SOMETHING IN THE FOREST WITH HIM.
SOMETHING I KNEW FROM THE START.
SOMETHING I KNEW IN MY HEART.

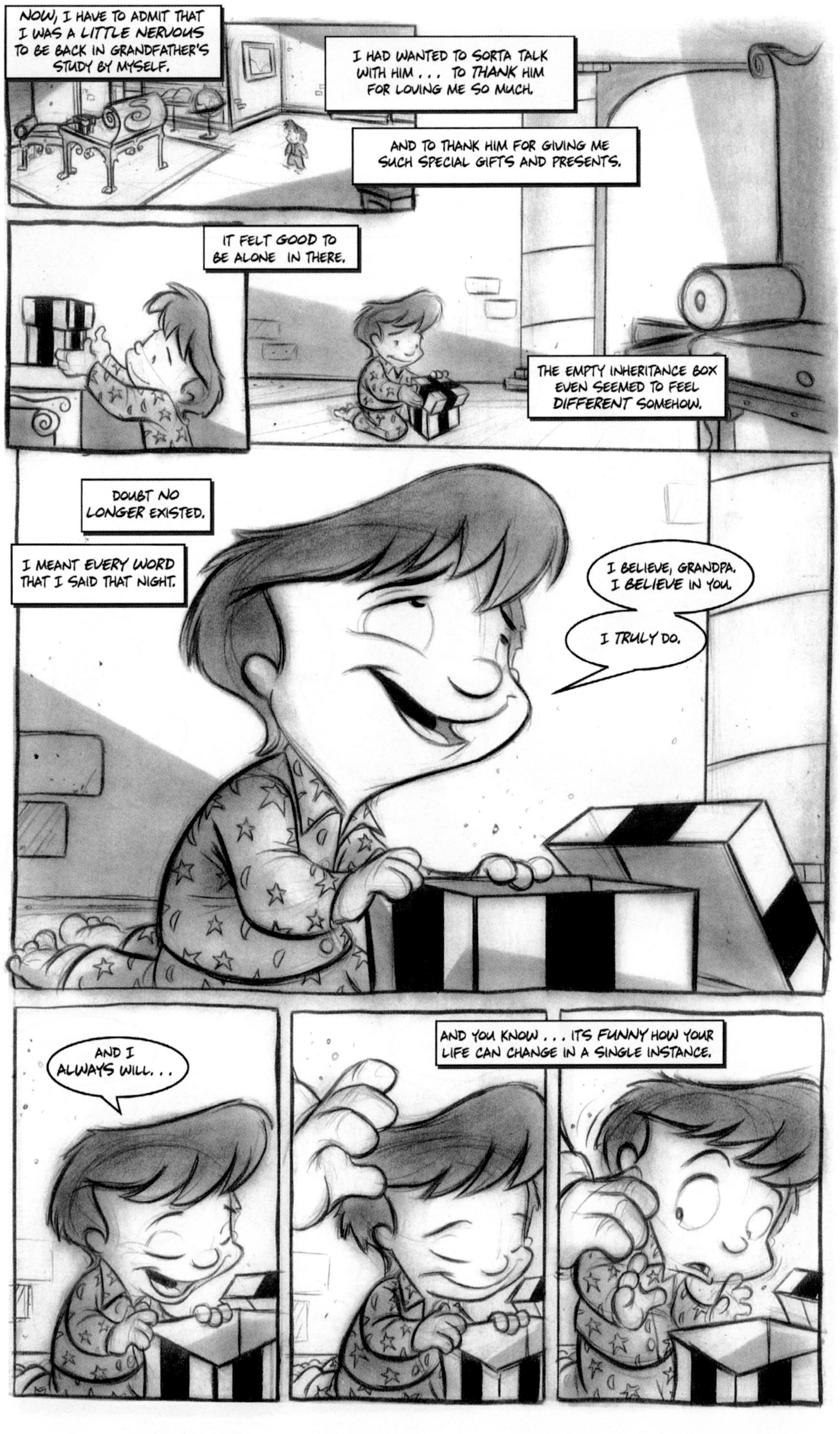

NOW, I HAVE TO ADMIT THAT I WAS A LITTLE NERVOUS TO BE BACK IN GRANDFATHER'S STUDY BY MYSELF.
I HAD WANTED TO SORTA TALK WITH HIM . . . TO THANK HIM FOR LOVING ME SO MUCH.
AND TO THANK HIM FOR GIVING ME SUCH SPECIAL GIFTS AND PRESENTS.
IT FELT GOOD TO BE ALONE IN THERE.
THE EMPTY INHERITANCE BOX EVEN SEEMED TO FEEL DIFFERENT SOMEHOW.
DOUBT NO LONGER EXISTED.
I MEANT EVERY WORD THAT I SAID THAT NIGHT.
I BELIEVE, GRANDPA. I BELIEVE IN YOU.
I TRULY DO.
AND I ALWAYS WILL. . .
AND YOU KNOW . . . ITS FUNNY HOW YOUR LIFE CAN CHANGE IN A SINGLE INSTANCE.

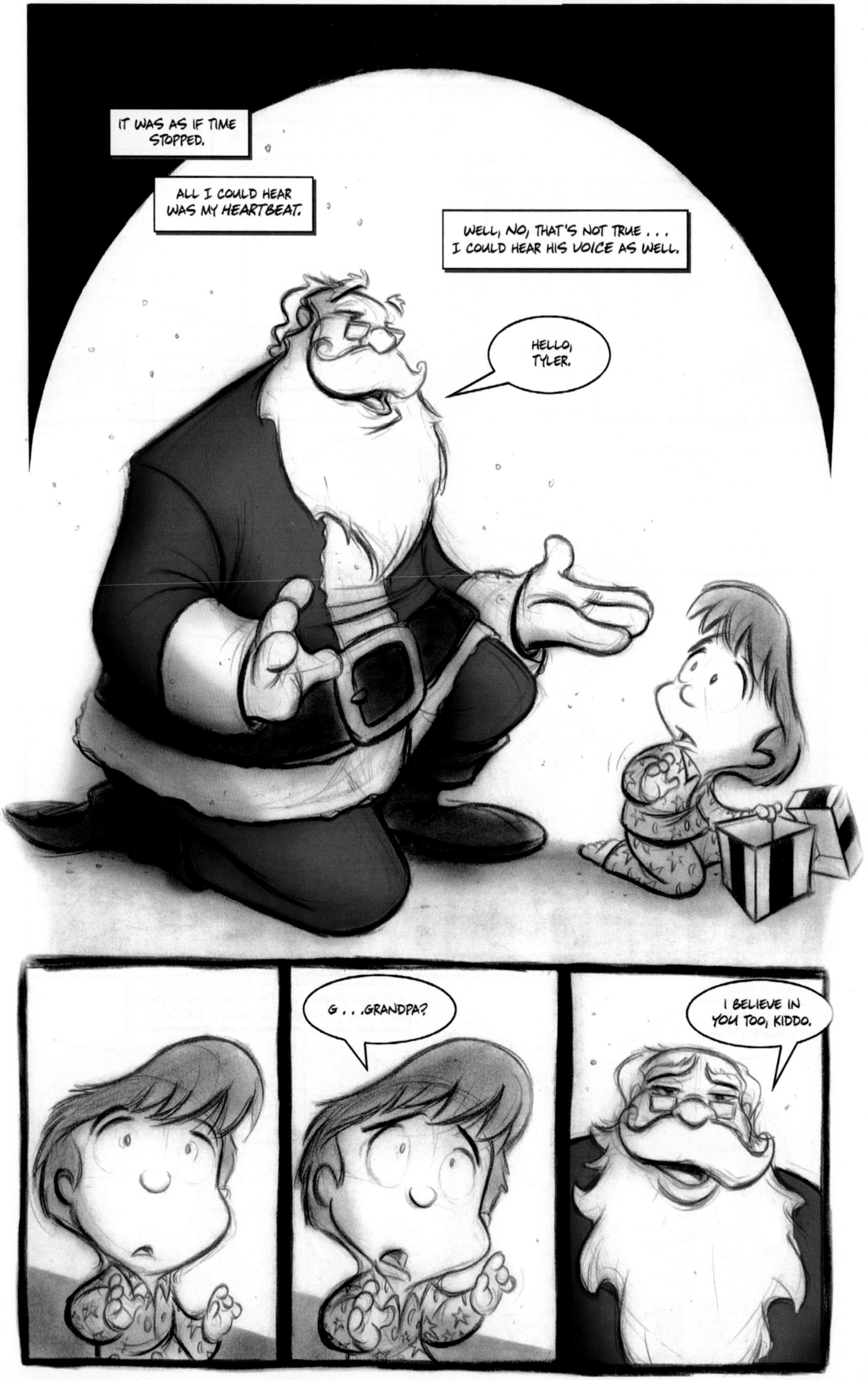
IT WAS AS IF TIME STOPPED.
ALL I COULD HEAR WAS MY HEARTBEAT.
WELL, NO, THAT'S NOT TRUE . . . I COULD HEAR HIS VOICE AS WELL.
HELLO, TYLER.
G . . .GRANDPA?
I BELIEVE IN YOU TOO, KIDDO.

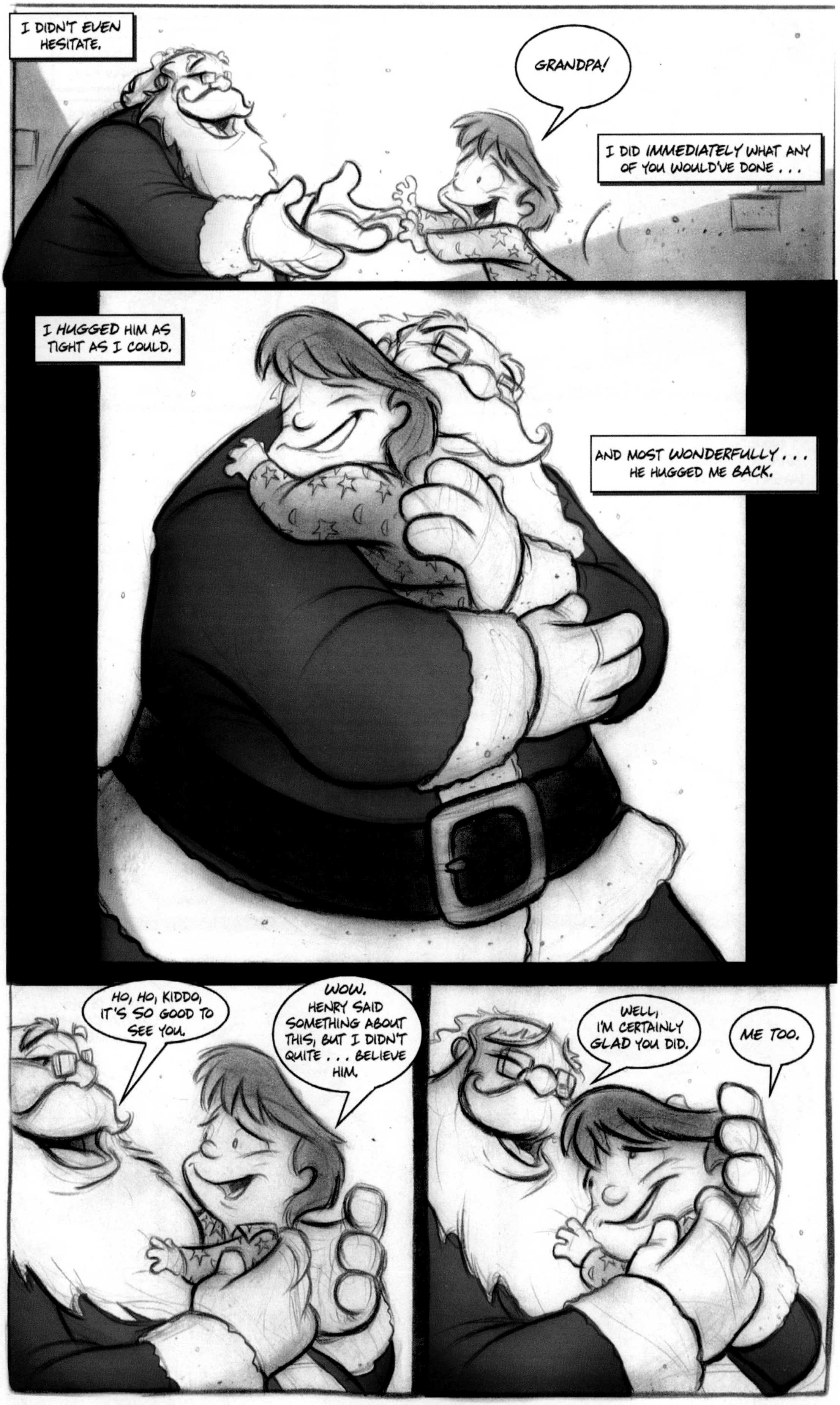
I DIDN'T EVEN HESITATE.
GRANDPA!
I DID IMMEDIATELY WHAT ANY OF YOU WOULD'VE DONE . . .
I HUGGED HIM AS TIGHT AS I COULD.
AND MOST WONDERFULLY . . . HE HUGGED ME BACK.
HO, HO, KIDDO, IT'S SO GOOD TO SEE YOU.
WOW. HENRY SAID SOMETHING ABOUT THIS, BUT I DIDN'T QUITE . . . BELIEVE HIM.
WELL, I'M CERTAINLY GLAD YOU DID.
ME TOO.

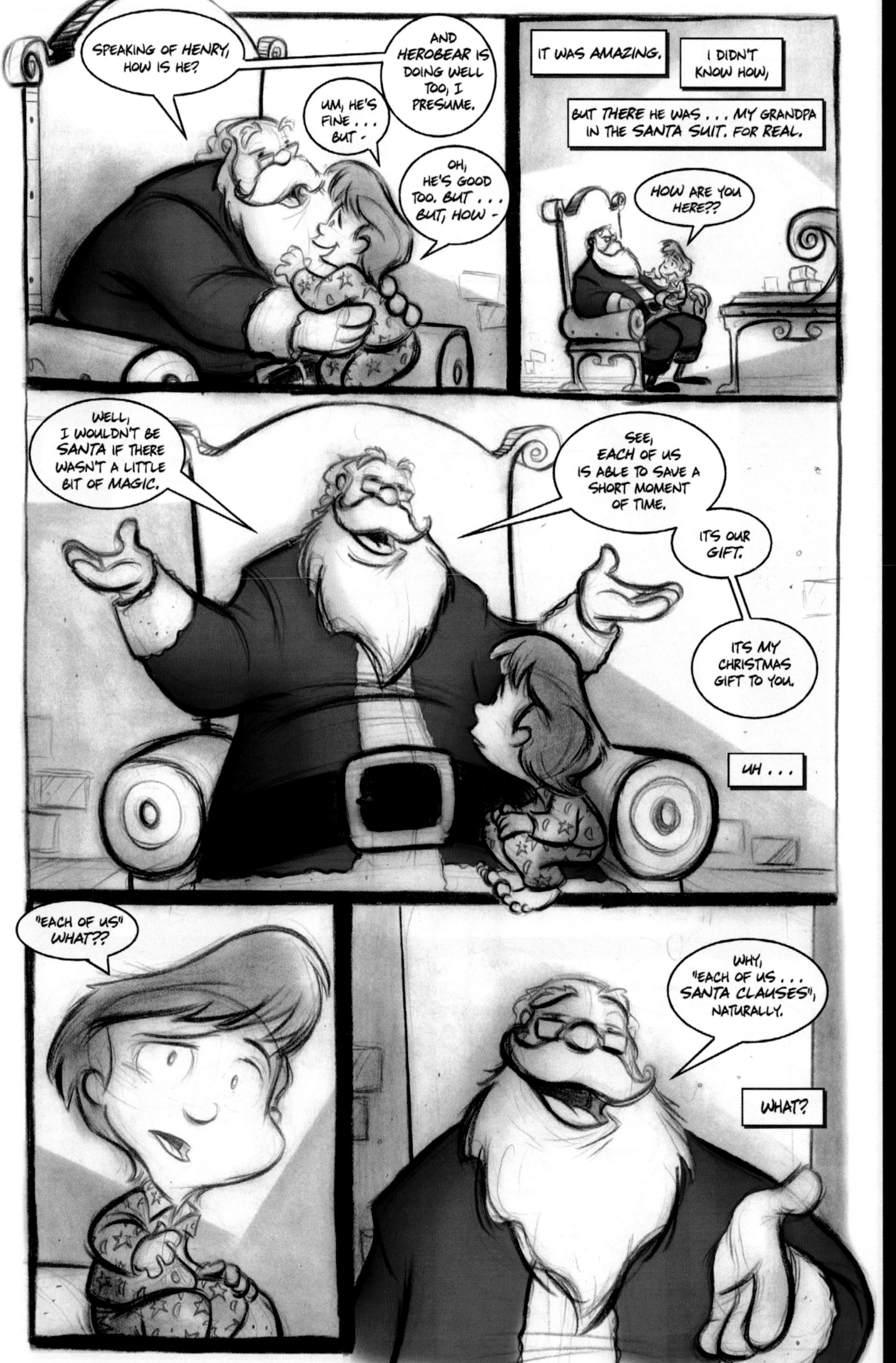
SPEAKING OF HENRY, HOW IS HE?
UM, HE'S FINE . . . BUT -
AND HEROBEAR IS DOING WELL TOO, I PRESUME.
OH, HE'S GOOD TOO. BUT . . . BUT, HOW -
IT WAS AMAZING.
I DIDN'T KNOW HOW,
BUT THERE HE WAS . . . MY GRANDPA IN THE SANTA SUIT. FOR REAL.
HOW ARE YOU HERE??
WELL, I WOULDN'T BE SANTA IF THERE WASN'T A LITTLE BIT OF MAGIC.
SEE, EACH OF US IS ABLE TO SAVE A SHORT MOMENT OF TIME.
ITS OUR GIFT.
ITS MY CHRISTMAS GIFT TO YOU.
UH . . .
"EACH OF US" WHAT??
WHY, "EACH OF US . . . SANTA CLAUSES", NATURALLY.
WHAT?

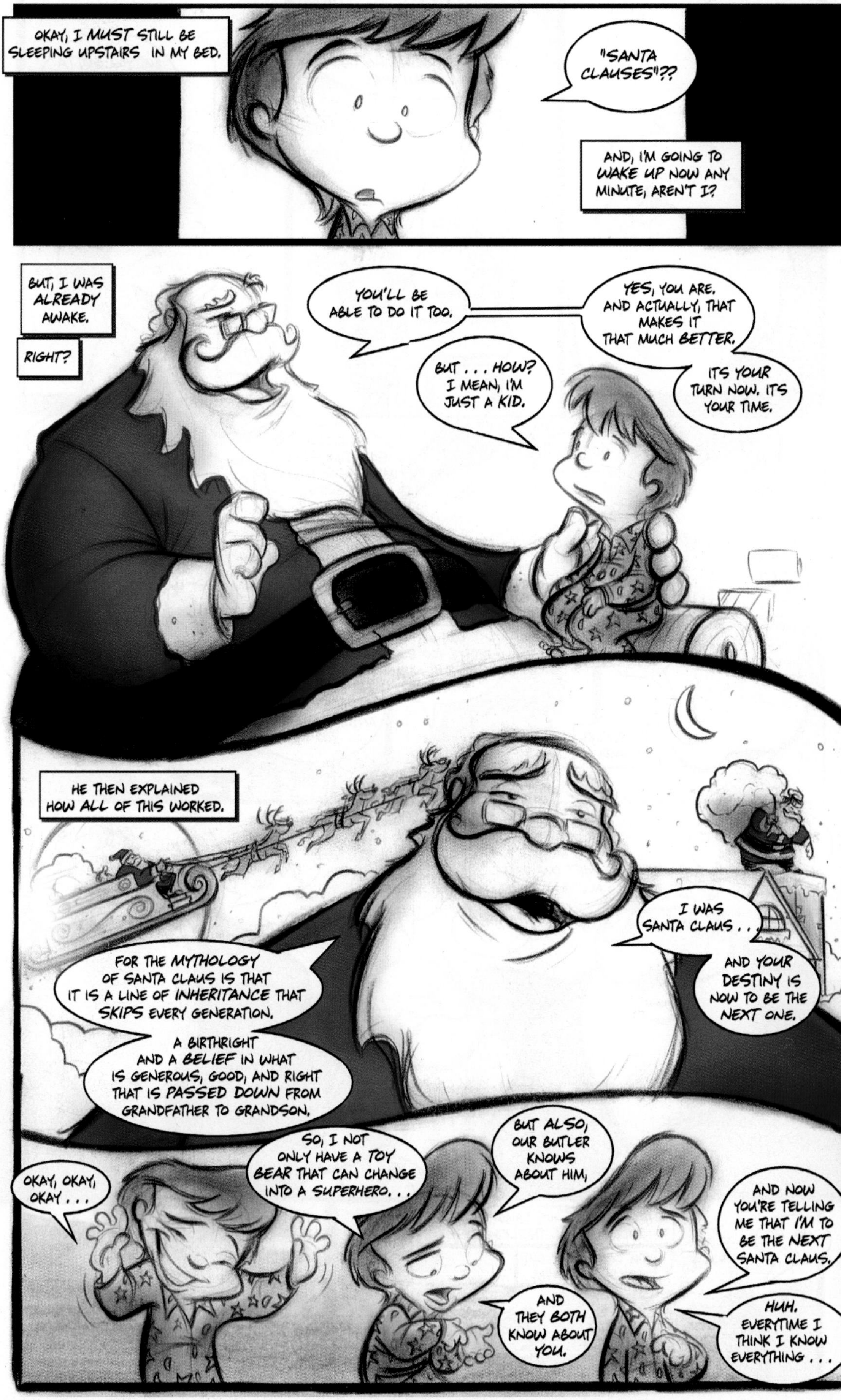
OKAY, I MUST STILL BE SLEEPING UPSTAIRS IN MY BED.
"SANTA CLAUSES"??
AND, I'M GOING TO WAKE UP NOW ANY MINUTE, AREN'T I?
BUT, I WAS ALREADY AWAKE.
RIGHT?
YOU'LL BE ABLE TO DO IT TOO.
YES, YOU ARE. AND ACTUALLY, THAT MAKES IT THAT MUCH BETTER.
BUT . . . HOW? I MEAN, I'M JUST A KID.
ITS YOUR TURN NOW. ITS YOUR TIME.
HE THEN EXPLAINED HOW ALL OF THIS WORKED.
I WAS SANTA CLAUS . . .
AND YOUR DESTINY IS NOW TO BE THE NEXT ONE.
FOR THE MYTHOLOGY OF SANTA CLAUS IS THAT IT IS A LINE OF INHERITANCE THAT SKIPS EVERY GENERATION.
A BIRTHRIGHT AND A BELIEF IN WHAT IS GENEROUS, GOOD, AND RIGHT THAT IS PASSED DOWN FROM GRANDFATHER TO GRANDSON.
OKAY, OKAY, OKAY . . .
SO, I NOT ONLY HAVE A TOY BEAR THAT CAN CHANGE INTO A SUPERHERO. . .
BUT ALSO, OUR BUTLER KNOWS ABOUT HIM,
AND THEY BOTH KNOW ABOUT YOU.
AND NOW YOU'RE TELLING ME THAT I'M TO BE THE NEXT SANTA CLAUS.
HUH. EVERYTIME I THINK I KNOW EVERYTHING . . .

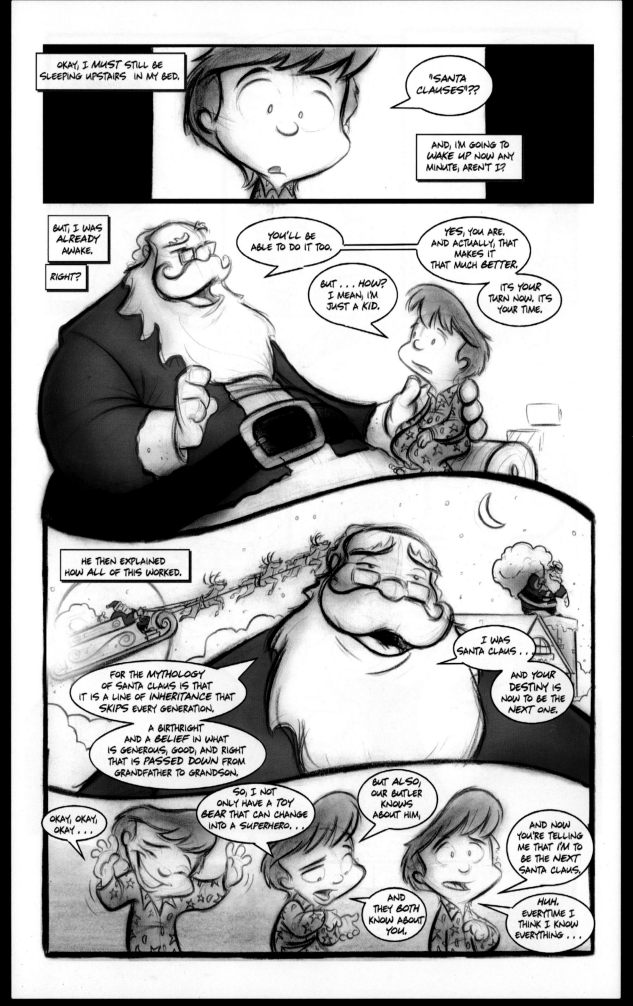

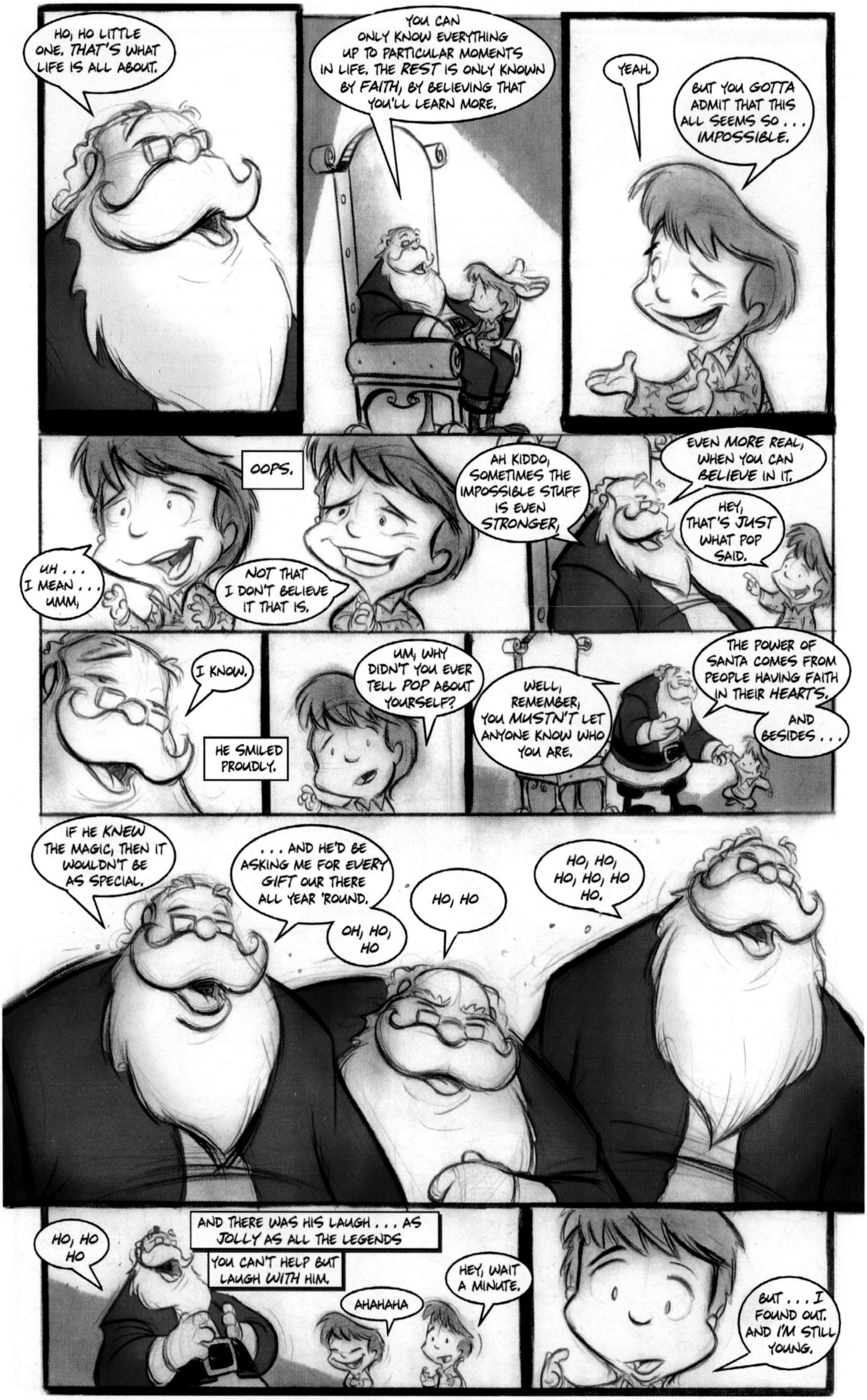
HO, HO LITTLE ONE. THAT'S WHAT LIFE IS ALL ABOUT.
YOU CAN ONLY KNOW EVERYTHING UP TO PARTICULAR MOMENTS IN LIFE. THE REST IS ONLY KNOWN BY FAITH, BY BELIEVING THAT YOU'LL LEARN MORE.
YEAH.
BUT YOU GOTTA ADMIT THAT THIS ALL SEEMS SO . . . IMPOSSIBLE.
UH . . . I MEAN . . . UMM,
OOPS.
NOT THAT I DON'T BELIEVE IT THAT IS.
AH KIDDO, SOMETIMES THE IMPOSSIBLE STUFF IS EVEN STRONGER,
EVEN MORE REAL, WHEN YOU CAN BELIEVE IN IT.
HEY, THAT'S JUST WHAT POP SAID.
I KNOW.
HE SMILED PROUDLY.
UM, WHY DIDN'T YOU EVER TELL POP ABOUT YOURSELF?
WELL, REMEMBER, YOU MUSTN'T LET ANYONE KNOW WHO YOU ARE.
THE POWER OF SANTA COMES FROM PEOPLE HAVING FAITH IN THEIR HEARTS.
AND BESIDES . . .
IF HE KNEW THE MAGIC, THEN IT WOULDN'T BE AS SPECIAL.
. . . AND HE'D BE ASKING ME FOR EVERY GIFT OUR THERE ALL YEAR 'ROUND.
OH, HO, HO
HO, HO
HO, HO, HO, HO, HO HO.
HO, HO HO
AND THERE WAS HIS LAUGH . . . AS JOLLY AS ALL THE LEGENDS
YOU CAN'T HELP BUT LAUGH WITH HIM.
AHAHAHA
HEY, WAIT A MINUTE.
BUT . . . I FOUND OUT. AND I'M STILL YOUNG.

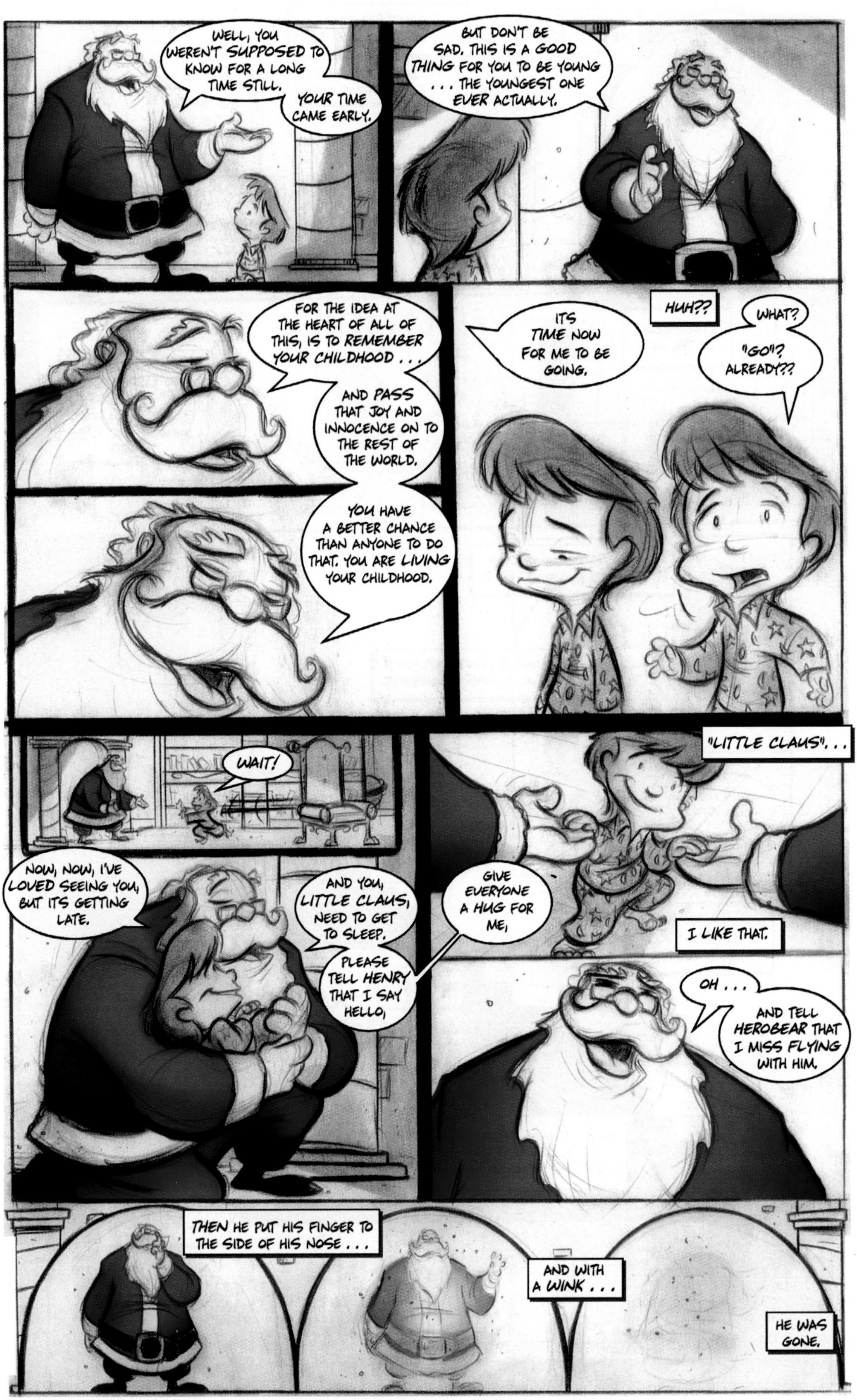

WELL, YOU WEREN'T SUPPOSED TO KNOW FOR A LONG TIME STILL.
YOUR TIME CAME EARLY.
BUT DON'T BE SAD. THIS IS A GOOD THING FOR YOU TO BE YOUNG . . . THE YOUNGEST ONE EVER ACTUALLY.
FOR THE IDEA AT THE HEART OF ALL OF THIS, IS TO REMEMBER YOUR CHILDHOOD . . .
AND PASS THAT JOY AND INNOCENCE ON TO THE REST OF THE WORLD.
YOU HAVE A BETTER CHANCE THAN ANYONE TO DO THAT. YOU ARE LIVING YOUR CHILDHOOD.
ITS TIME NOW FOR ME TO BE GOING.
HUH??
WHAT?
"GO"? ALREADY??
WAIT!
NOW, NOW, I'VE LOVED SEEING YOU, BUT ITS GETTING LATE.
AND YOU, LITTLE CLAUS, NEED TO GET TO SLEEP.
PLEASE TELL HENRY THAT I SAY HELLO,
GIVE EVERYONE A HUG FOR ME,
"LITTLE CLAUS" . . .
I LIKE THAT.
OH . . .
AND TELL HEROBEAR THAT I MISS FLYING WITH HIM.
THEN HE PUT HIS FINGER TO THE SIDE OF HIS NOSE . . .
AND WITH A WINK . . .
HE WAS GONE.

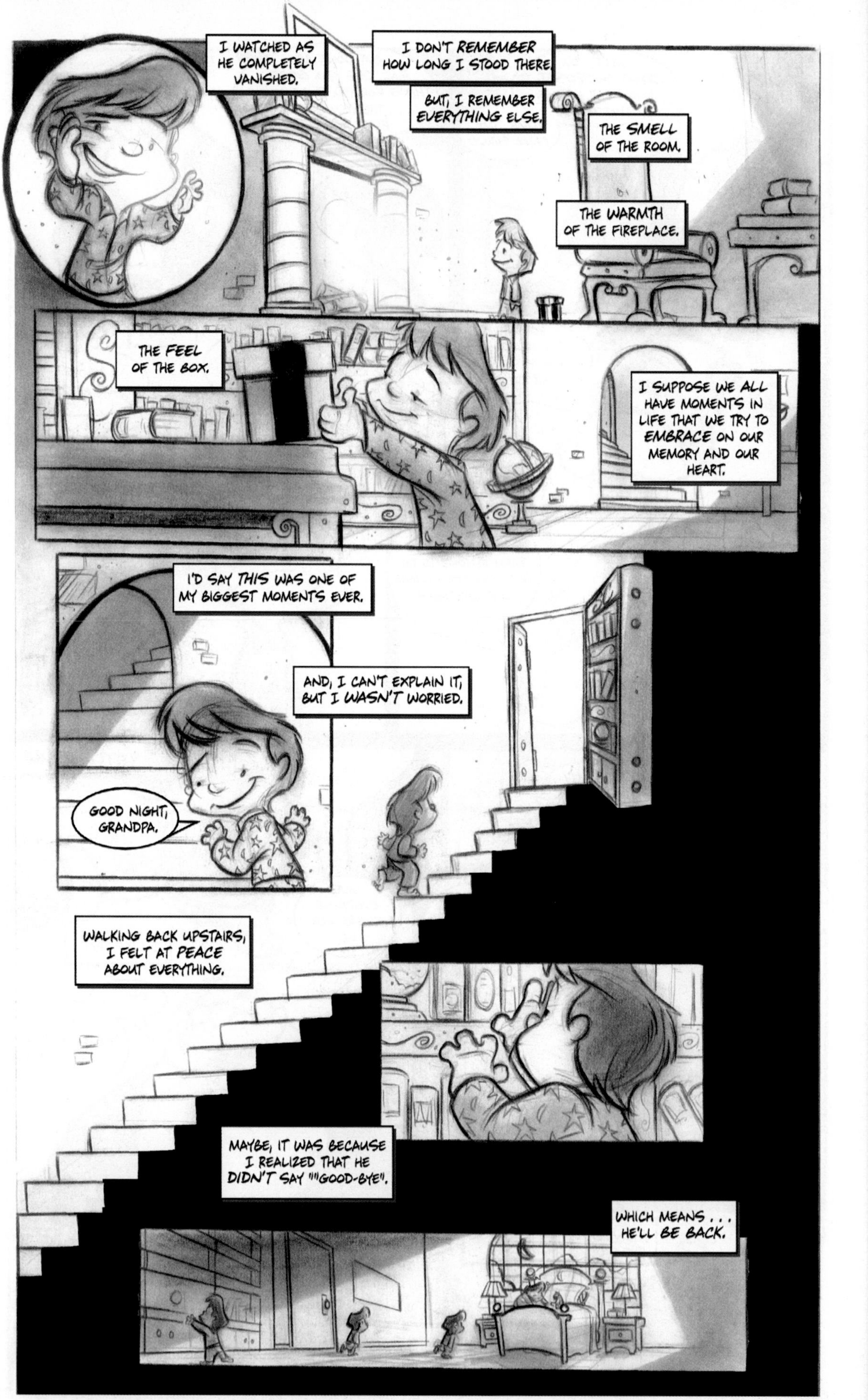
I WATCHED AS HE COMPLETELY VANISHED.
I DON'T REMEMBER HOW LONG I STOOD THERE.
BUT, I REMEMBER EVERYTHING ELSE.
THE SMELL OF THE ROOM.
THE WARMTH OF THE FIREPLACE.
THE FEEL OF THE BOX.
I SUPPOSE WE ALL HAVE MOMENTS IN LIFE THAT WE TRY TO EMBRACE ON OUR MEMORY AND OUR HEART.
I'D SAY THIS WAS ONE OF MY BIGGEST MOMENTS EVER.
AND, I CAN'T EXPLAIN IT, BUT I WASN'T WORRIED.
GOOD NIGHT, GRANDPA.
WALKING BACK UPSTAIRS, I FELT AT PEACE ABOUT EVERYTHING.
MAYBE, IT WAS BECAUSE I REALIZED THAT HE DIDN'T SAY "GOOD-BYE".
WHICH MEANS . . . HE'LL BE BACK.

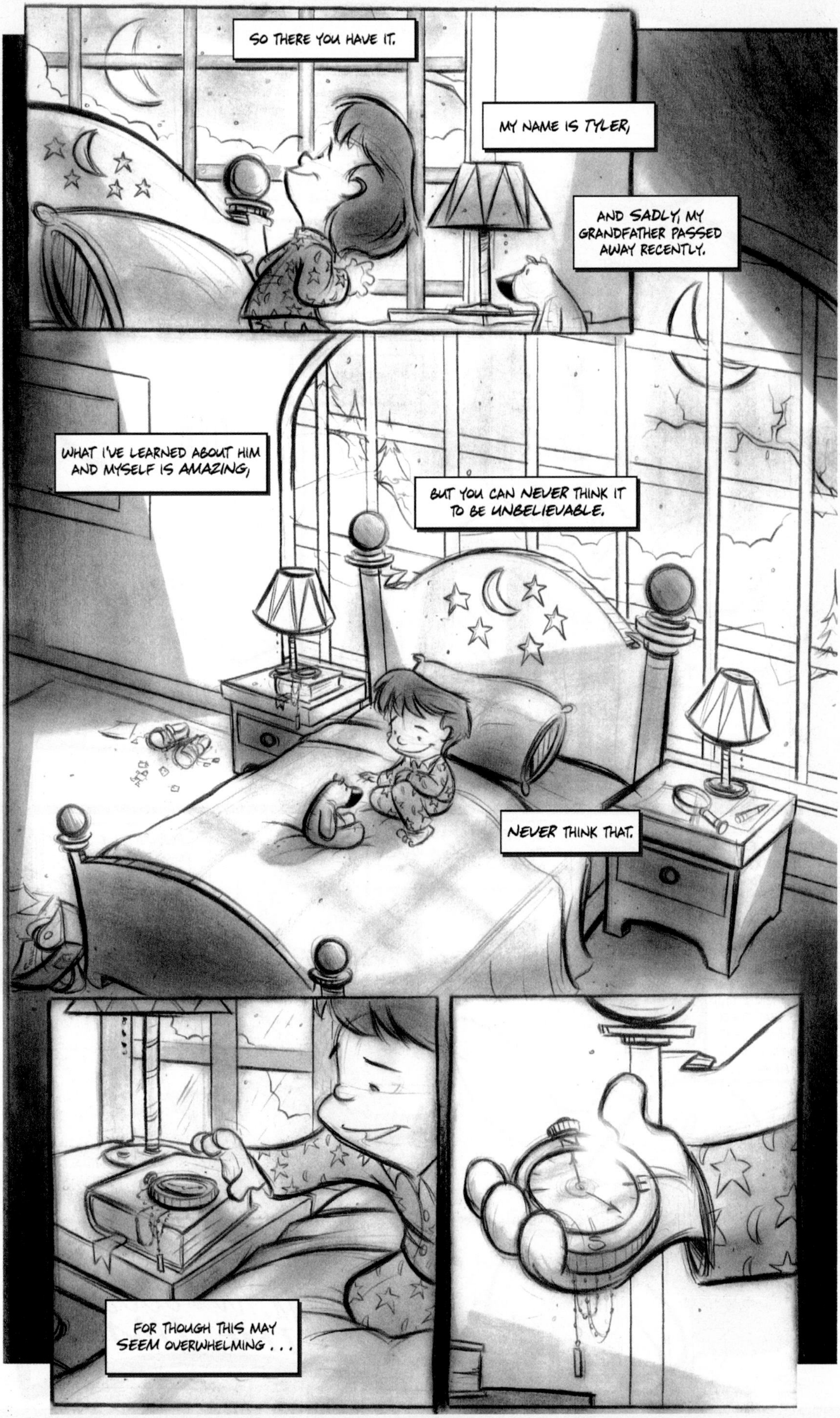
SO THERE YOU HAVE IT.
MY NAME IS TYLER,
AND SADLY, MY GRANDFATHER PASSED AWAY RECENTLY.
WHAT I'VE LEARNED ABOUT HIM AND MYSELF IS AMAZING,
BUT YOU CAN NEVER THINK IT TO BE UNBELIEVABLE.
NEVER THINK THAT.
FOR THOUGH THIS MAY SEEM OVERWHELMING . . .

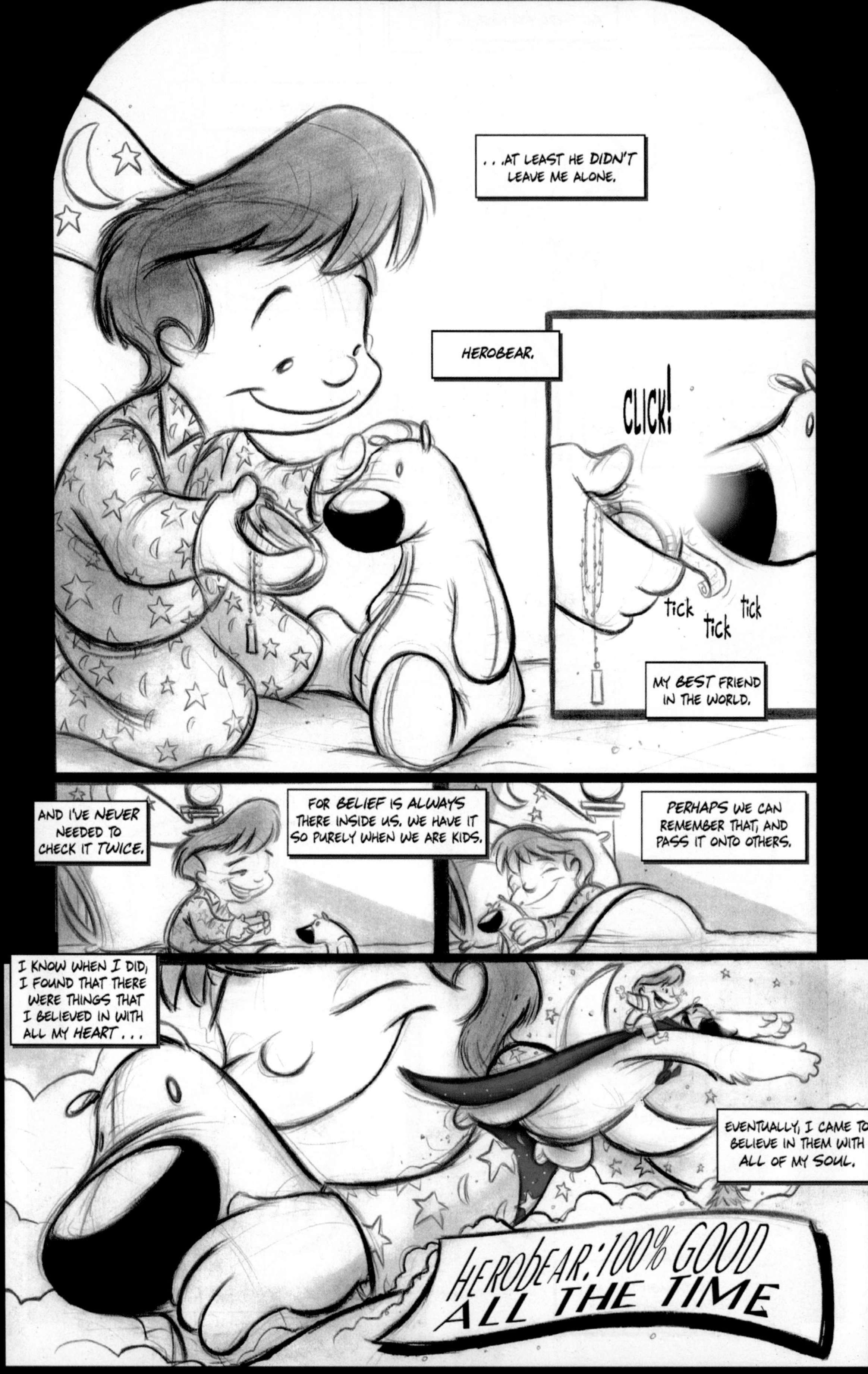
. . .AT LEAST HE DIDN'T LEAVE ME ALONE.
HEROBEAR.
CLICK!
tick
tick
tick
MY BEST FRIEND IN THE WORLD.
AND I'VE NEVER NEEDED TO CHECK IT TWICE.
FOR BELIEF IS ALWAYS THERE INSIDE US. WE HAVE IT SO PURELY WHEN WE ARE KIDS.
PERHAPS WE CAN REMEMBER THAT, AND PASS IT ONTO OTHERS.
I KNOW WHEN I DID, I FOUND THAT THERE WERE THINGS THAT I BELIEVED IN WITH ALL MY HEART . . .
EVENTUALLY, I CAME TO BELIEVE IN THEM WITH ALL OF MY SOUL.
HEROBEAR; 100% GOOD ALL THE TIME

THE END . . . OF CHAPTER ONE.

"AS I'm approaching middle-age, I've had a shift in my taste and attitude toward most comic books. I'm much more cynical and.... well, bored... with much of what's being done today. I feel as though I've lost much of that starry-eyed love I had for comics as a child. There's so much being done that gives me that "been there--seen that" kind of feeling.

But finding HEROBEAR AND THE KID has awakened old feelings of delight and excitement that I thought maybe I'd lost. From the first page-- the first GLANCE at Mike Kunkel's wonderful creation, I felt connected to his world. HEROBEAR has a charm all its own. Mike's writing, his artwork (oh, that beautiful ART of his...!) and the world he has created for Tyler and his giant cape-wearing polar bear buddy pulled me in immediately in a way that has only happened to me once or twice before since I became an adult and became a bit jaded about my chosen art form. It's a feeling I'm very happy to have back.

So thank you, Mike-- for HEROBEAR AND THE KID and for helping me find that child-like wonder for comics again."

Mike Wieringo(artist and Co-creator of Tellos, artist of Superman)

Mike Kunkel's Herobear and the Kid is definitely a "from-the-heart-feel-good" experience that made me feel like a kid all over again, and remember how great my childhood was.
Chuck Gordon (Producer of Field of Dreams, The Rocketeer, and October Sky)

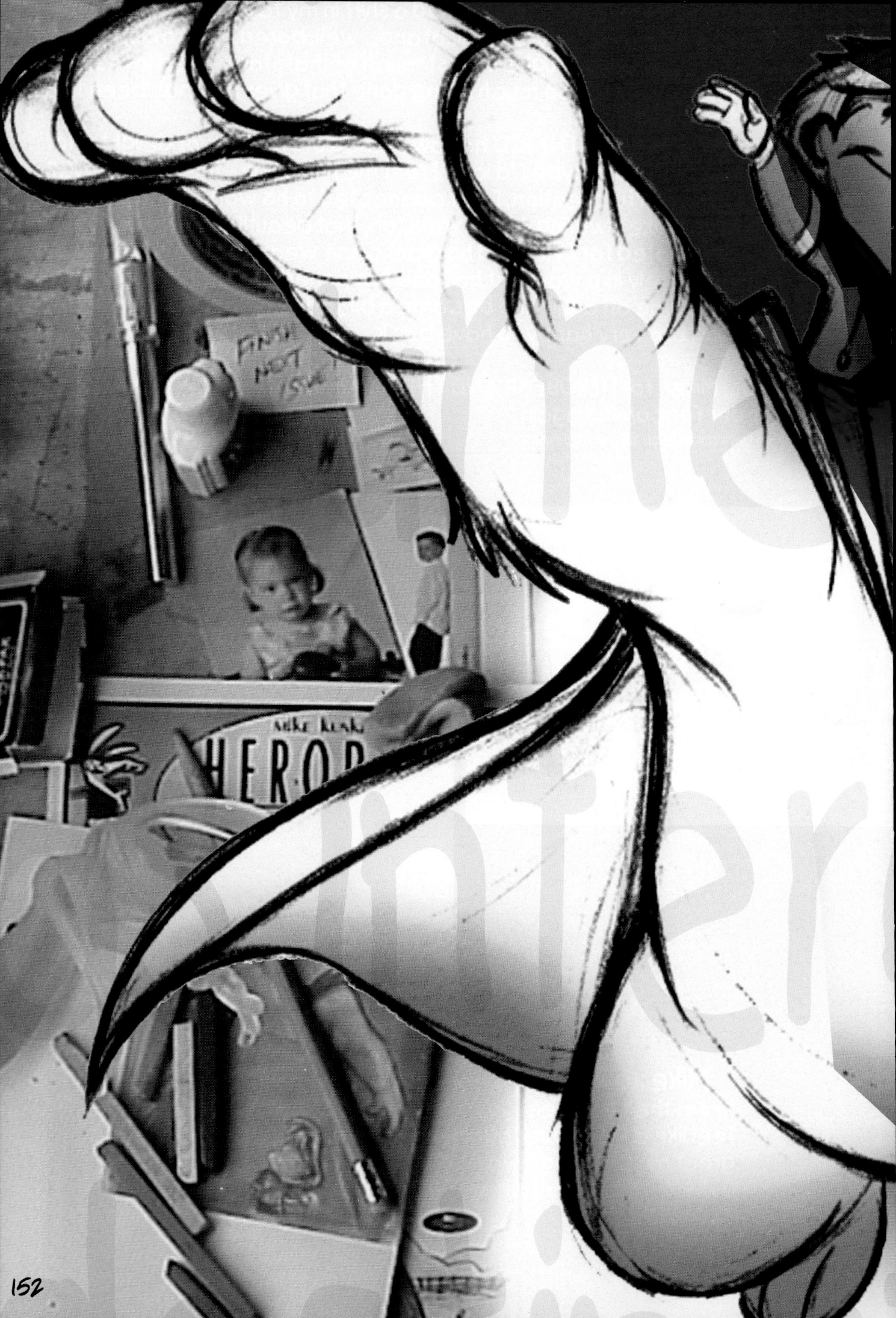
FINISH NEXT ISSUE!
HERO

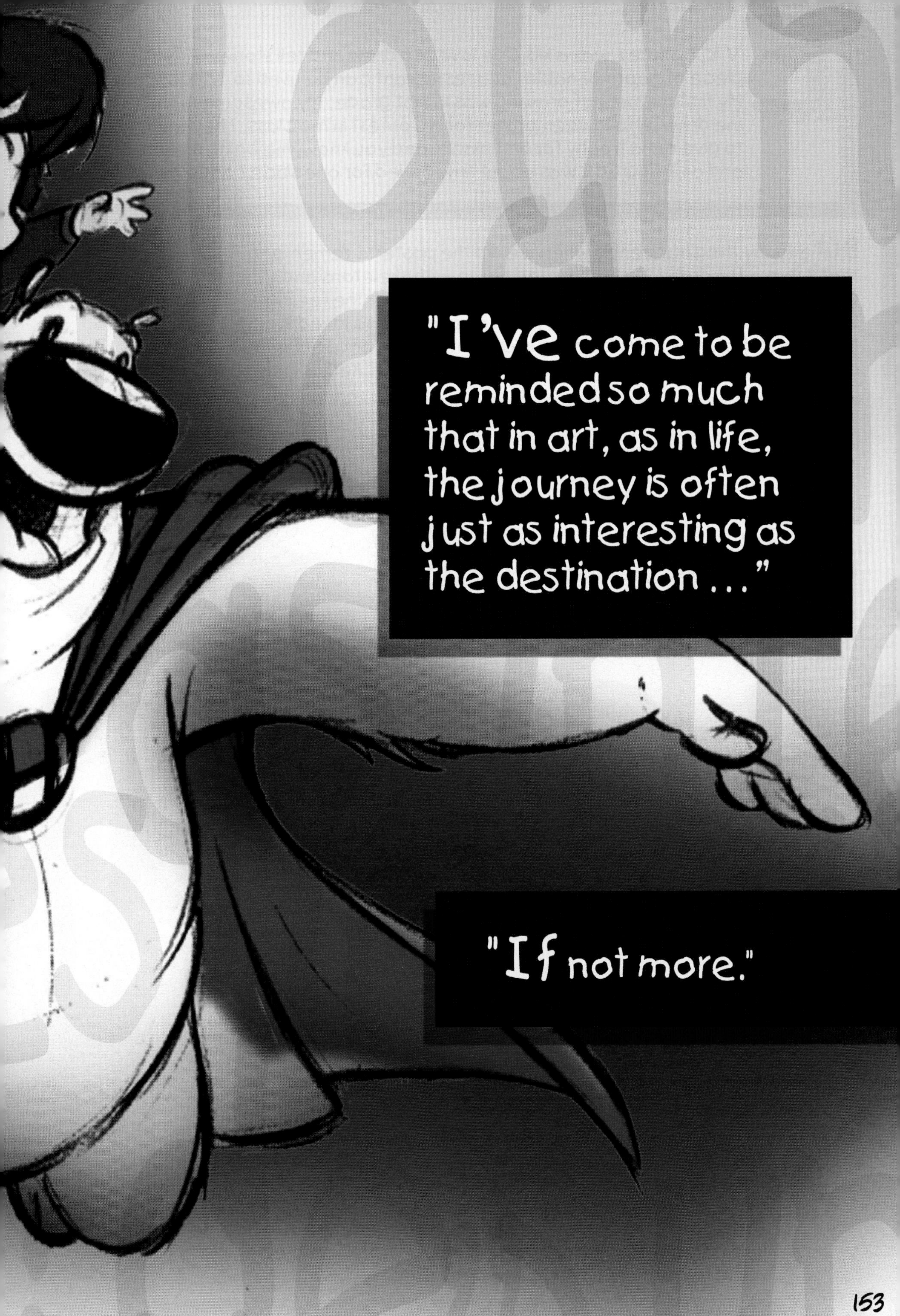

"I've come to be reminded so much that in art, as in life, the journey is often just as interesting as the destination ..."

"If not more."

Ever since I was a kid, I've loved to draw and tell stories. Any scrap piece of paper or napkin at a restaurant can be used to scribble on. My first memory of drawing was in first grade. My awesome mom helped me draw a Halloween poster for a contest in my class. They were going to give out a trophy for first place, and you know, me being 6 years old and all, I figured it was about time I tried for one since I hadn't won one yet.

But a funny thing happened when we did the poster. I remember that it was a fun drawing of a haunted house with skeletons and ghosts flying all over, but more than that, I remember the feeling I had drawing and creating a little world on paper. I so loved it. Now, I had drawn before. Coloring in coloring books and scribbling on typing paper. But this was different. Something clicked.

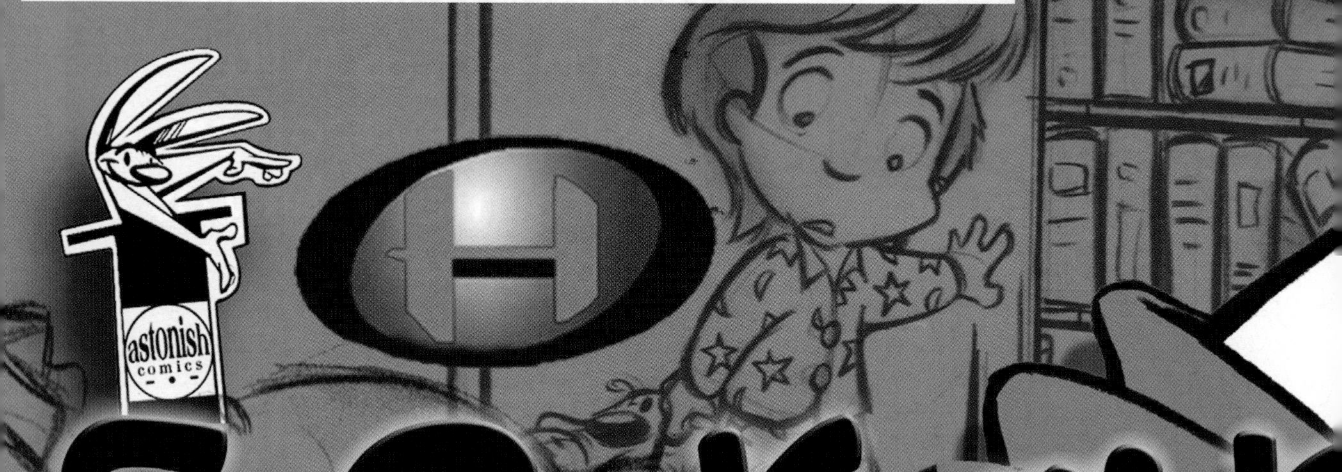
astonish
comics
scrap

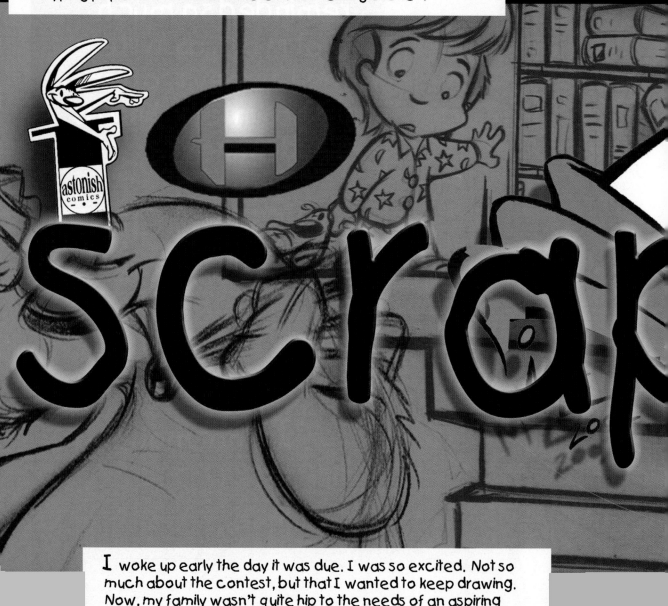

I woke up early the day it was due. I was so excited. Not so much about the contest, but that I wanted to keep drawing. Now, my family wasn't quite hip to the needs of an aspiring artist ...yet. Good art supplies were hard to find in the house. So, I found the only piece of drawing material I could find. Yep, you guessed it, my poster. Thankfully I started on the backside, which was blank. Notice I said, "started".

And, for some strange reason, I found myself drawing the football symbols off my bed sheets. I've always loved football, and logos for the Pittsburgh Steelers, the Miami Dolphins, the Atlanta Falcons, the San Diego Chargers and others all found their way onto the paper. And...when I ran out of room on the back, I turned over the poster to the front. Don't ask me why, I was in a fever. I had to create. Well needless to say, when my mom and dad got up that morning, they found a Halloween poster with skeletons, black cats, ghouls and the entire NFL haunting the house.

book

Now, of course, I didn't win the contest. It was an original image, but honestly, just too bizarre for first grade. However, I got more out of it than a simple little trophy ... I got the fever. I couldn't forget the feeling of needing to draw and create. And, I've never lost it.

What follows is a small sample of my inspirations that have resulted from my love for drawing and telling stories. I hope that you enjoy 'em as much as I've enjoyed creating 'em.

FLYING IN THE SWIMMING POOL.

I've been asked what kind of super power I would have if I could have any. Without a doubt I would have to say flying. No question. Of course, sticking to walls like a spider is certainly a very close second.

Now, when I was a kid, I would go and swim to the deep end of a swimming pool. I'd float out to the middle of it and hold my breath under the water. I'd then let out just enough air so that I would float right under the surface without touching the bottom or the sides of the pool. Then I would float around the water imagining I was flying like Superman.

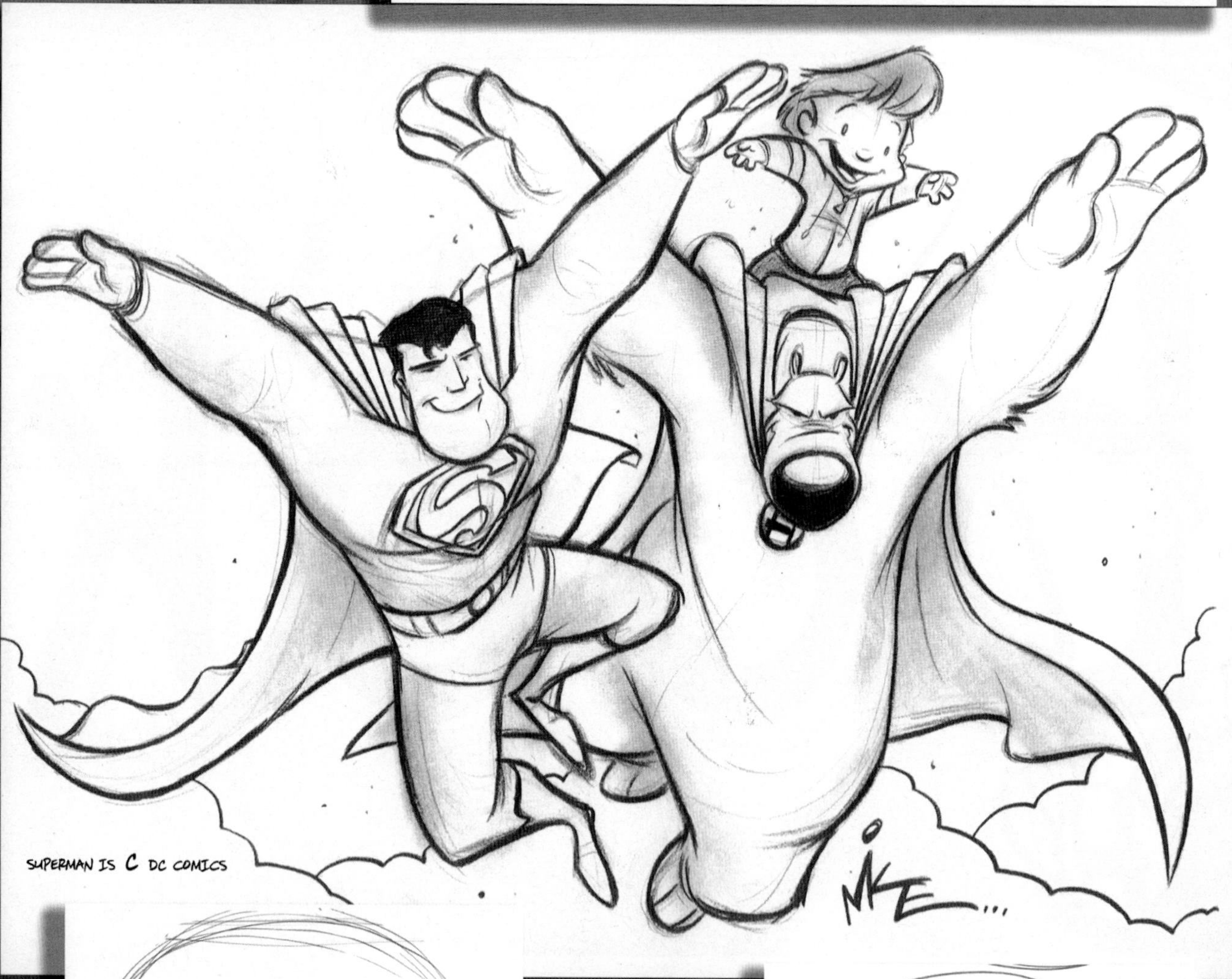
SUPERMAN IS C DC COMICS
MIKE...

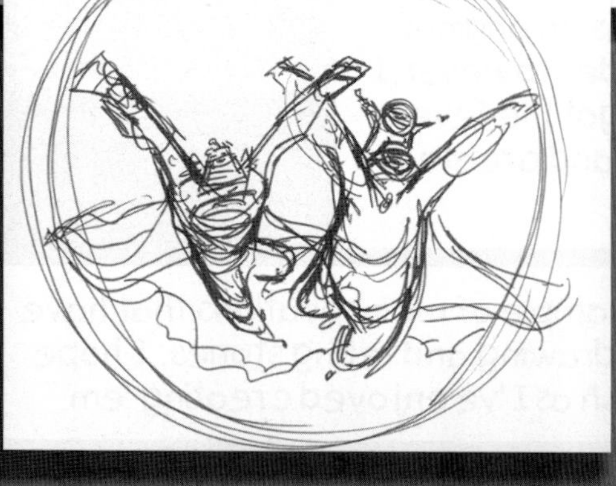

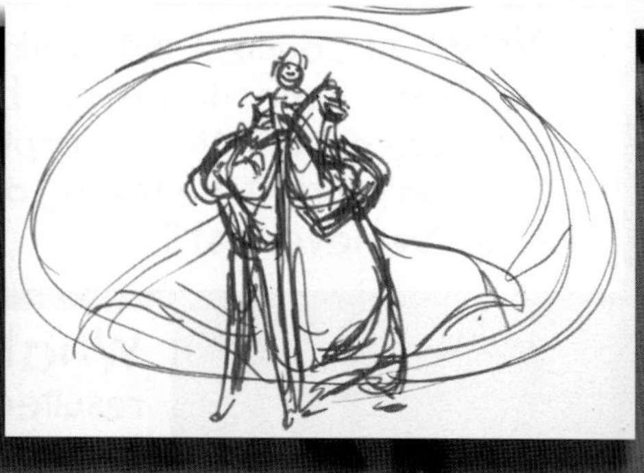

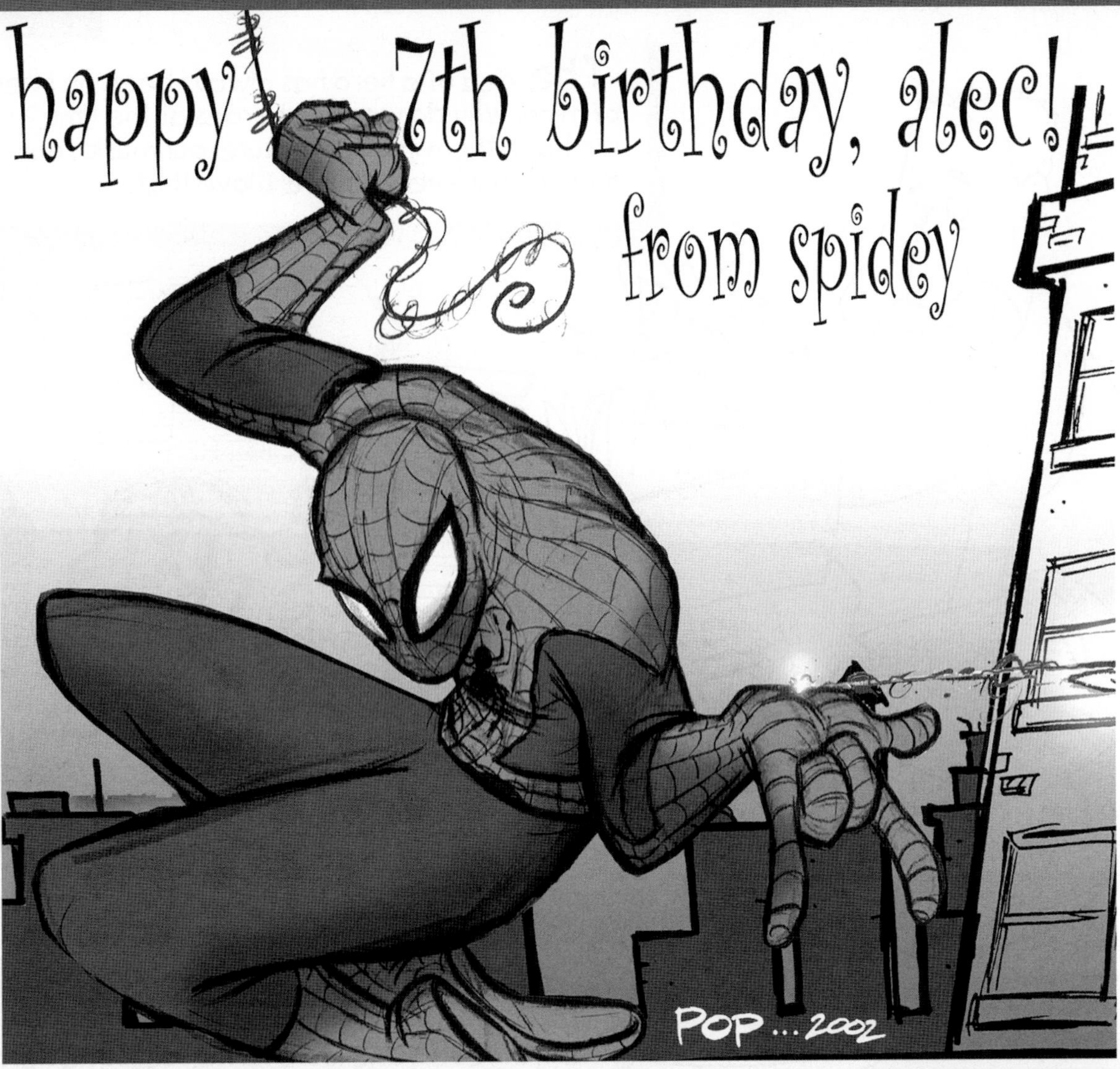
happy 7th birthday, alec!
from spidey
POP...2002

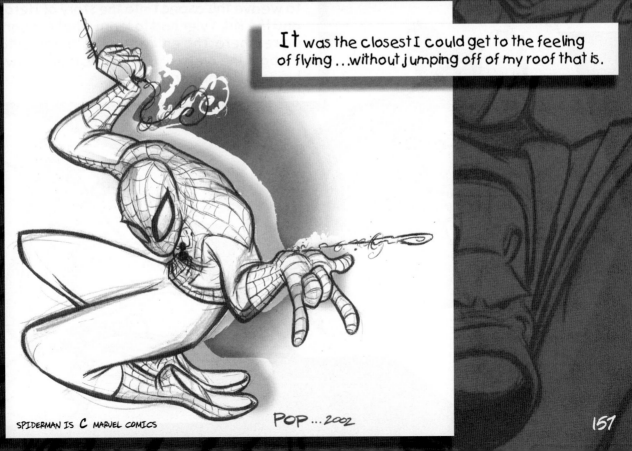

It was the closest I could get to the feeling of flying...without jumping off of my roof that is.

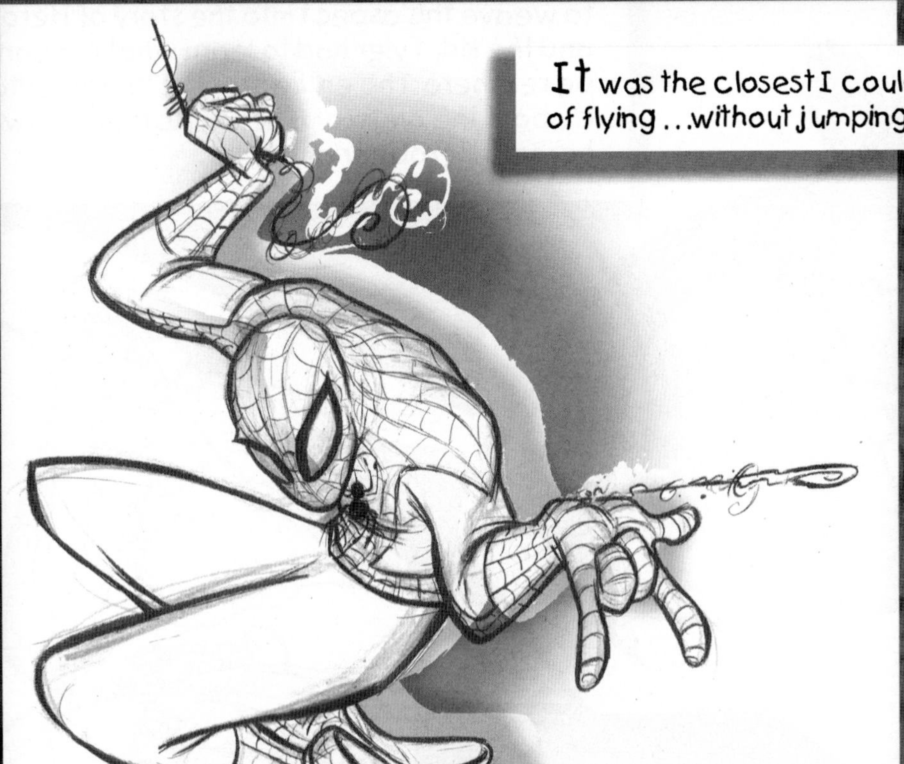
POP...2002

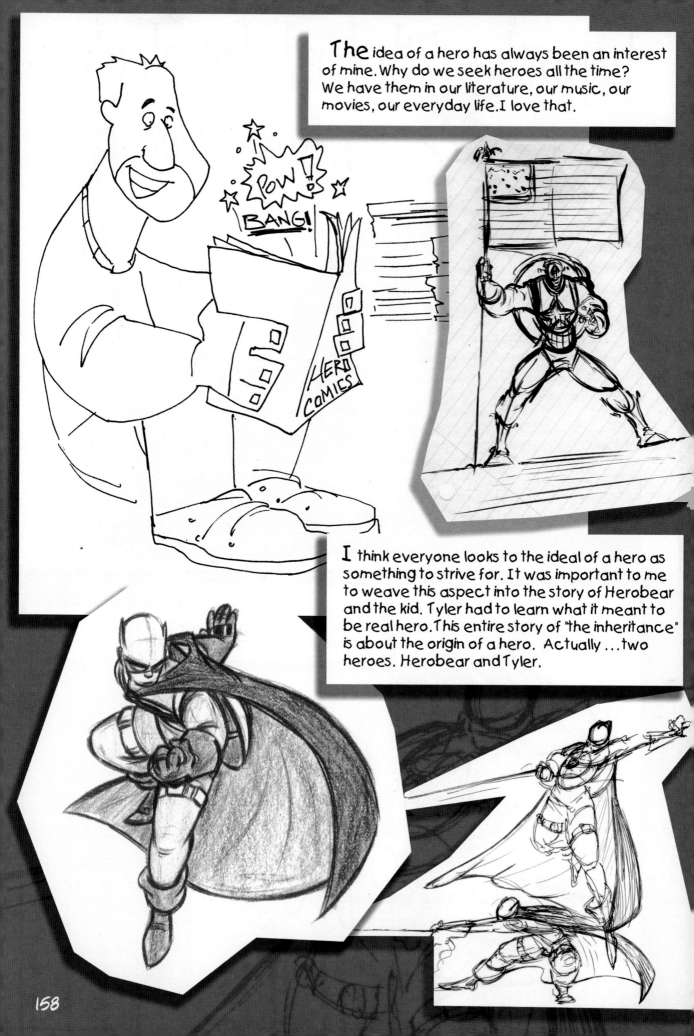

The idea of a hero has always been an interest of mine. Why do we seek heroes all the time? We have them in our literature, our music, our movies, our everyday life. I love that.

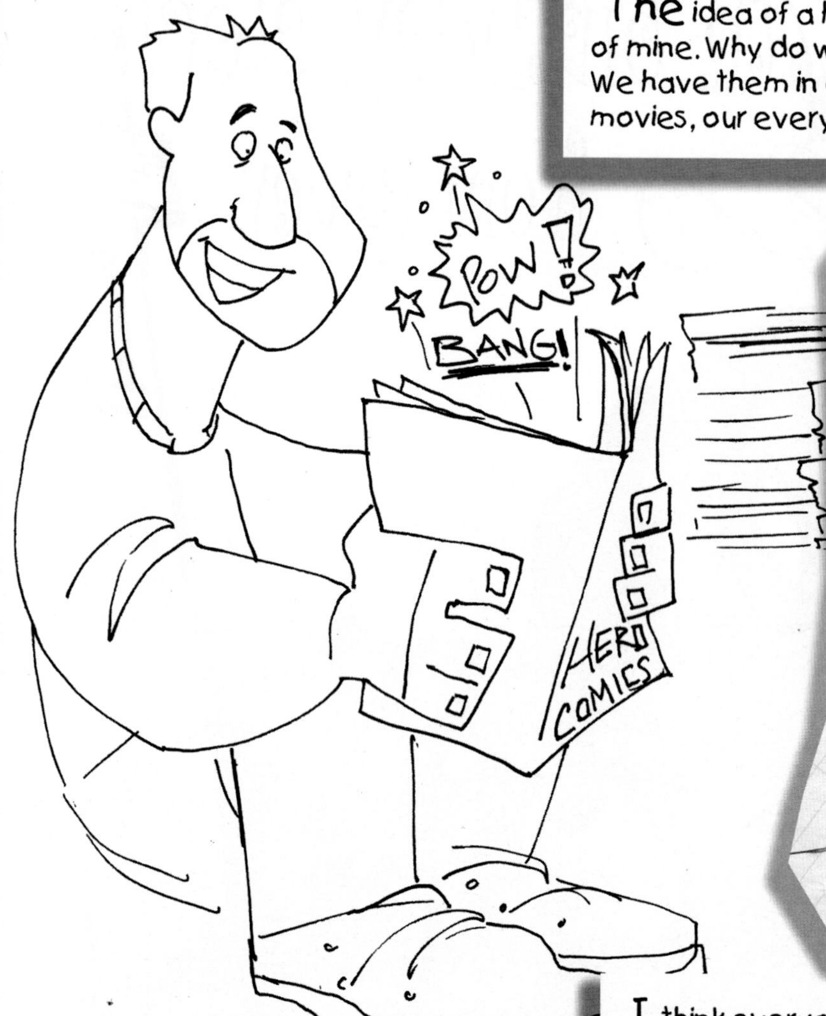
POW!!
BANG!
HERO COMICS

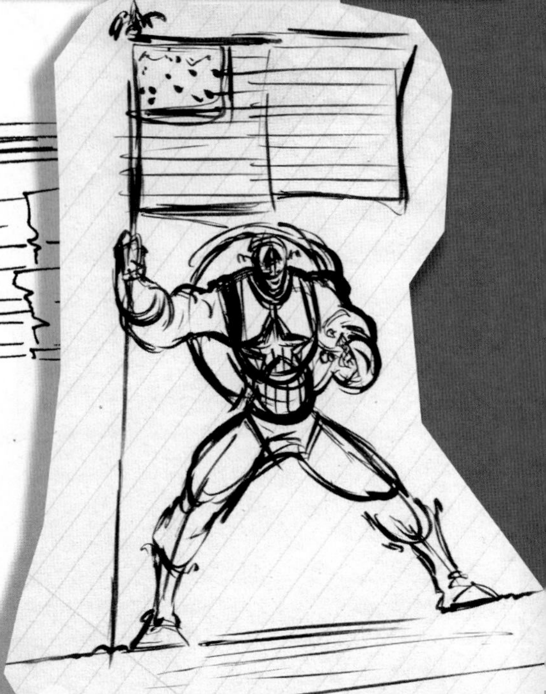

I think everyone looks to the ideal of a hero as something to strive for. It was important to me to weave this aspect into the story of Herobear and the kid. Tyler had to learn what it meant to be real hero. This entire story of "the inheritance" is about the origin of a hero. Actually . . . two heroes. Herobear and Tyler.

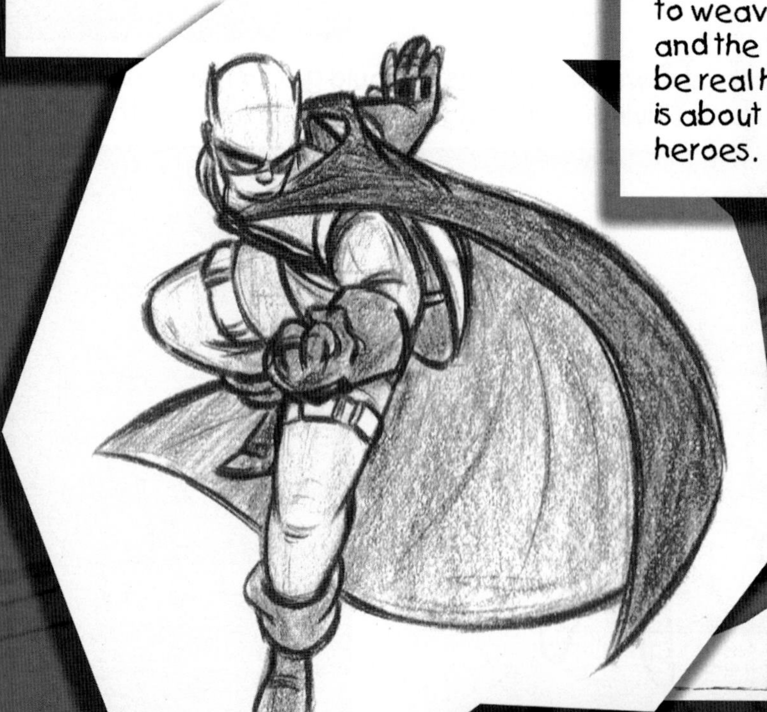

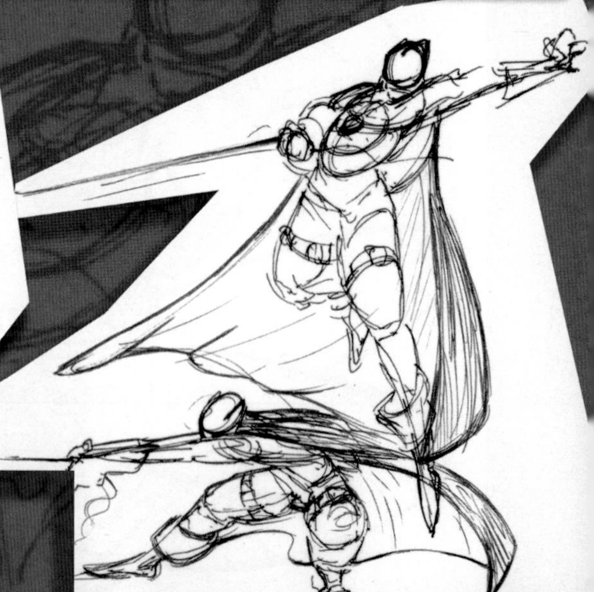

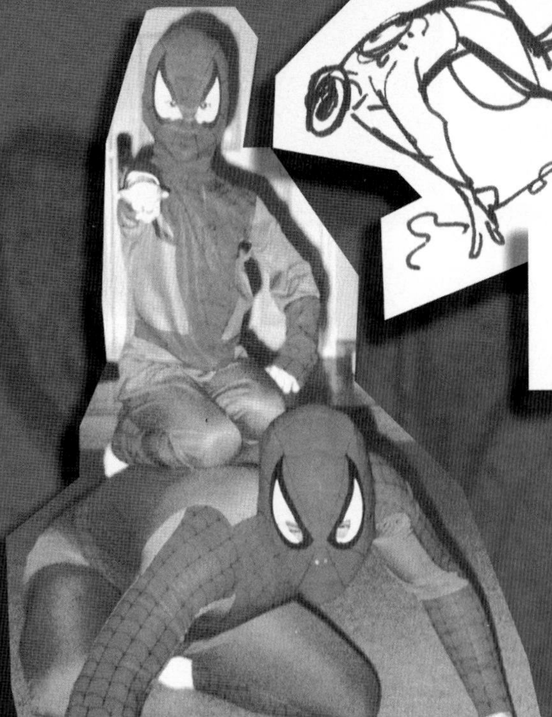

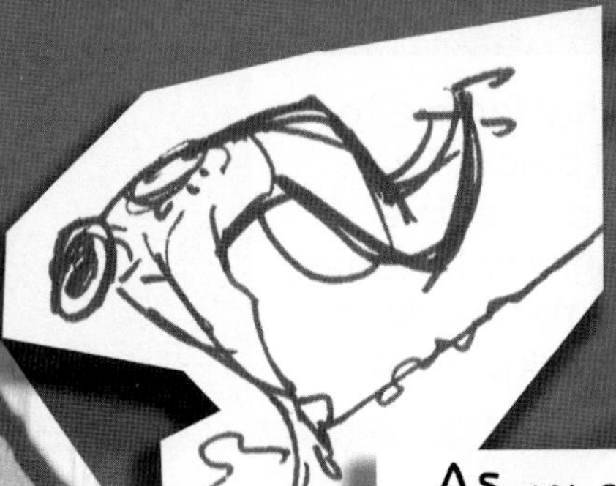

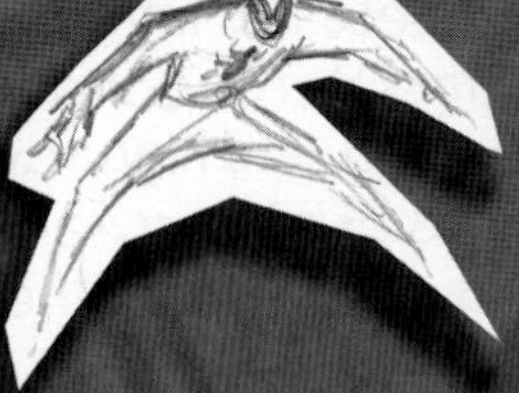

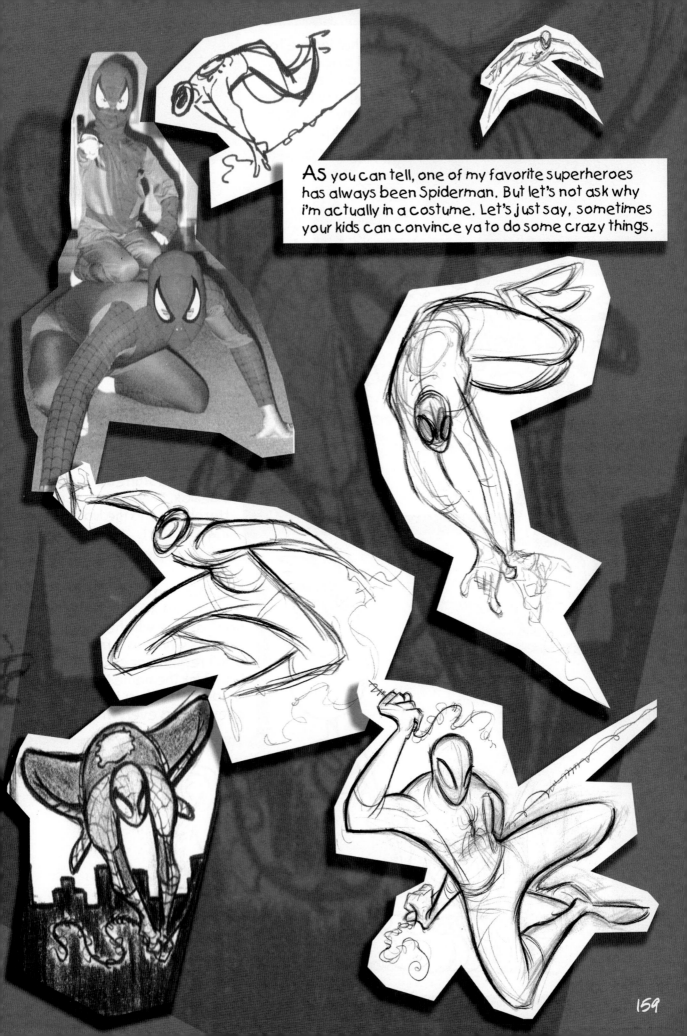

AS you can tell, one of my favorite superheroes
has always been Spiderman. But let's not ask why
i'm actually in a costume. Let's just say, sometimes
your kids can convince ya to do some crazy things.

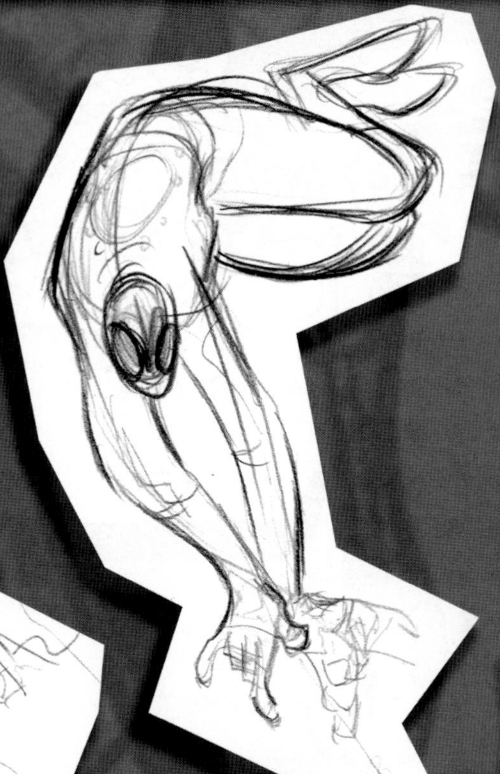

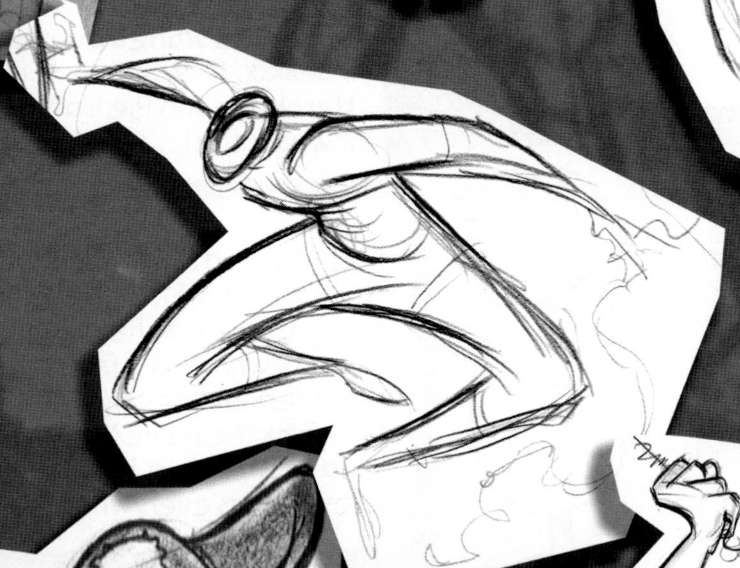

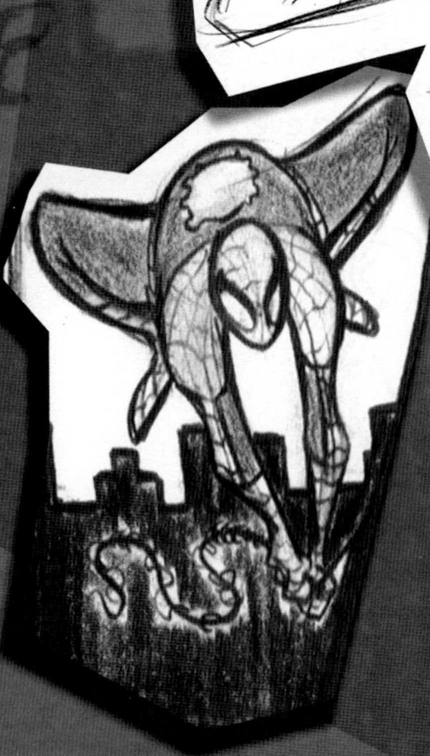

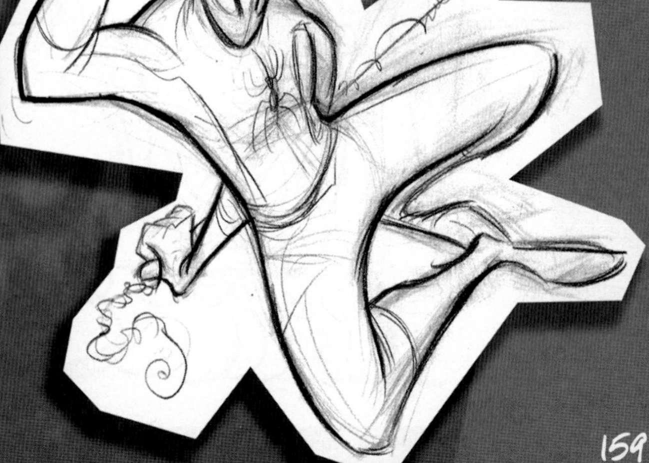

I guess this love for superheroes is what led me to creating Herobear and the kid in the first place. In junior high and high school I would draw all the time. All kinds of characters and stories. Though my teachers wouldn't admit it at the time, I think secretly they liked all my crazy drawings all over my homework papers.

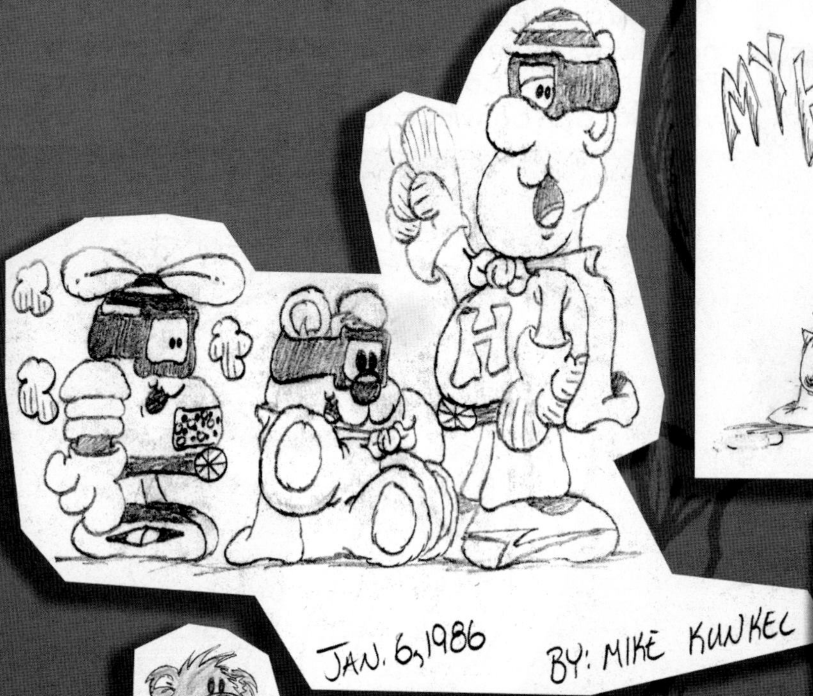
JAN. 6, 1986
BY: MIKE KUNKEL

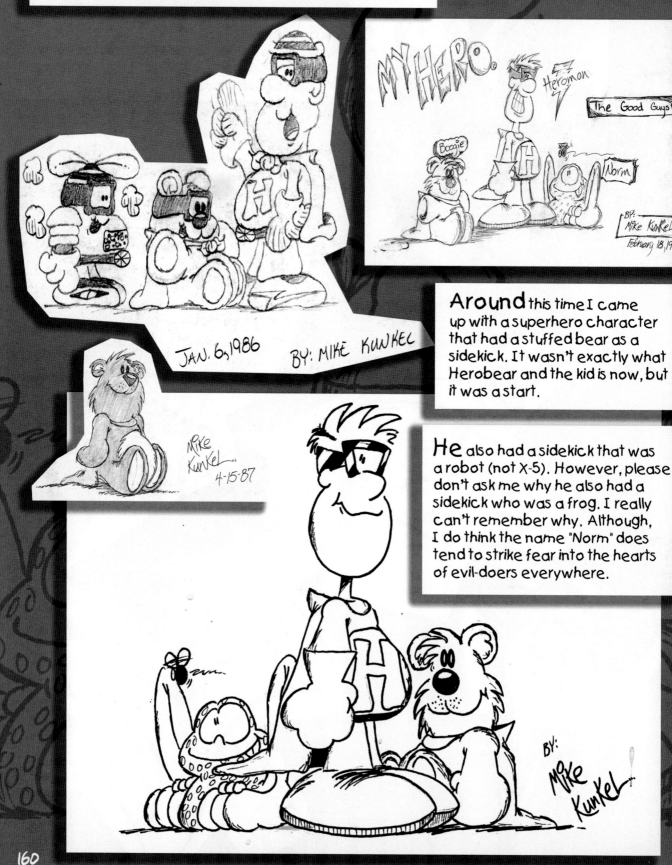

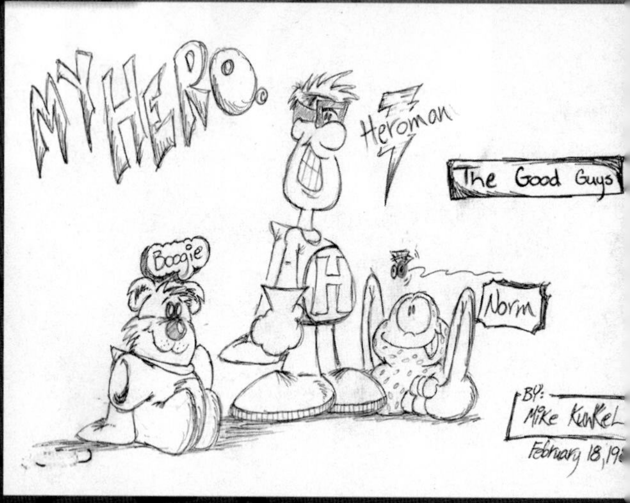
MY HERO.
Heroman
The Good Guys
Boogie
Norm
BY: Mike Kunkel
February 18,

Around this time I came up with a superhero character that had a stuffed bear as a sidekick. It wasn't exactly what Herobear and the kid is now, but it was a start.

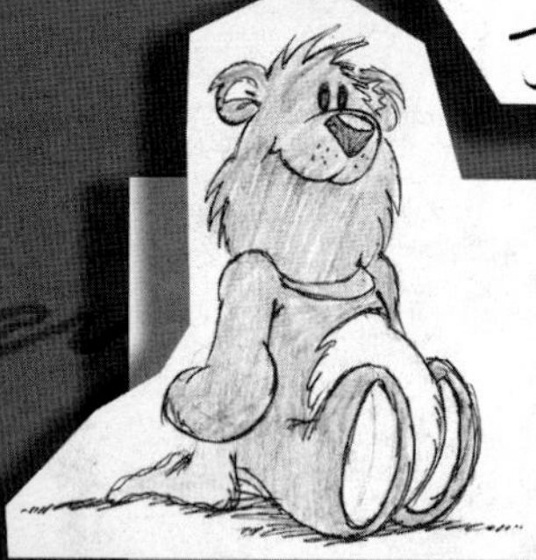
Mike Kunkel
4-15-87

He also had a sidekick that was a robot (not X-5). However, please don't ask me why he also had a sidekick who was a frog. I really can't remember why. Although, I do think the name "Norm" does tend to strike fear into the hearts of evil-doers everywhere.

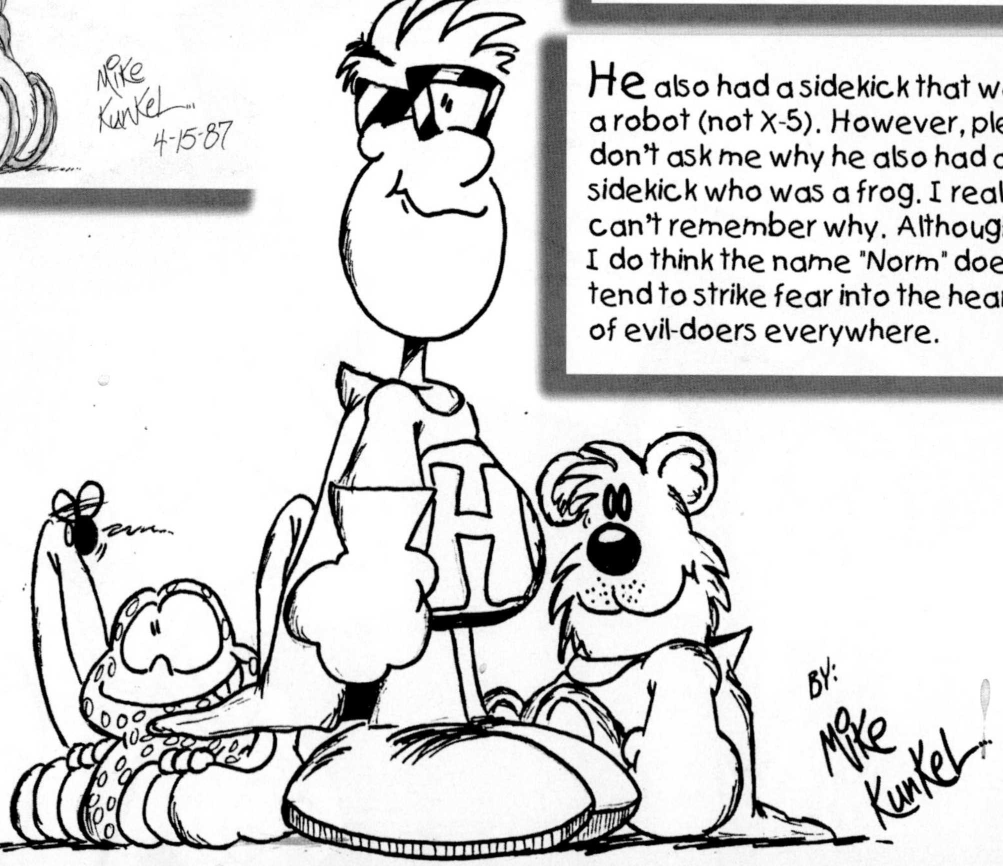
BY:
Mike Kunkel

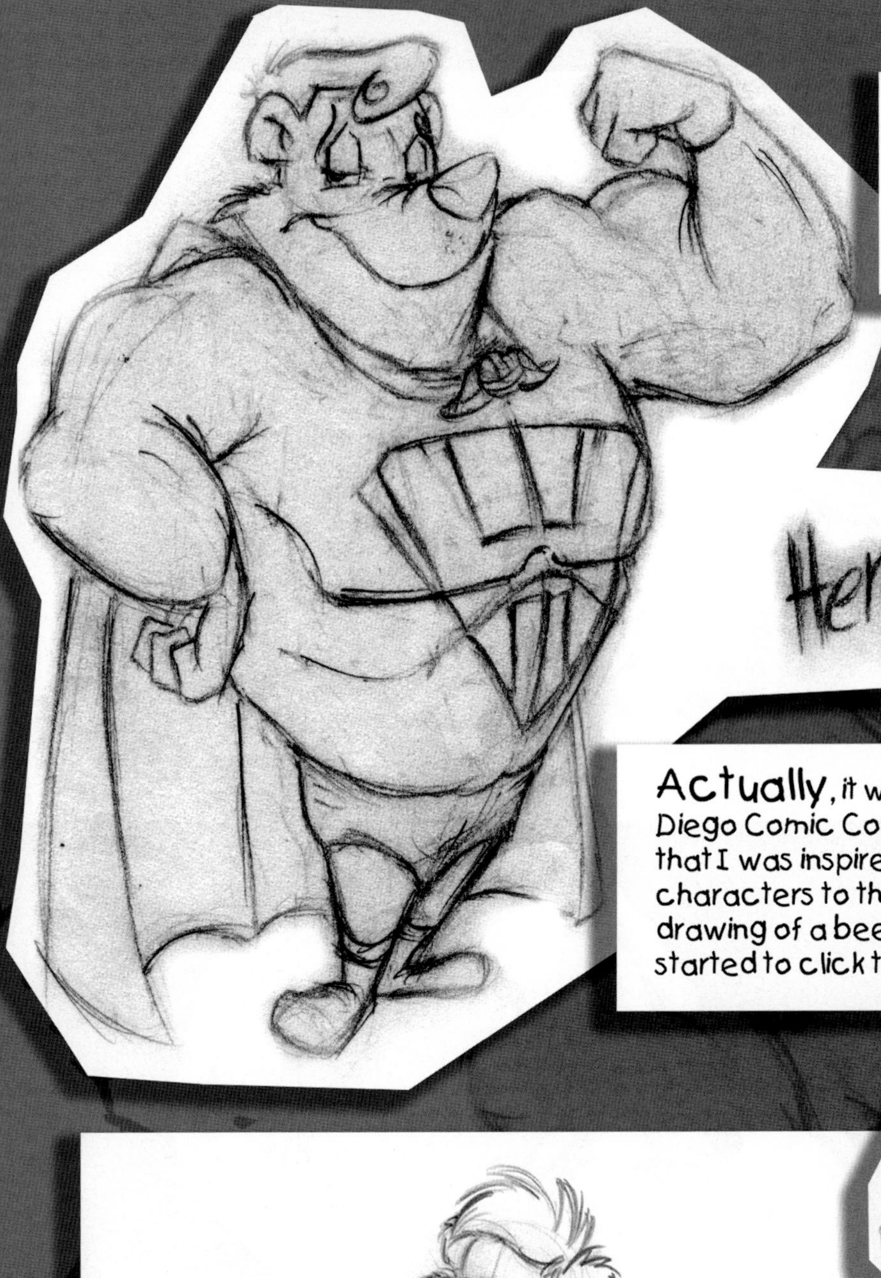

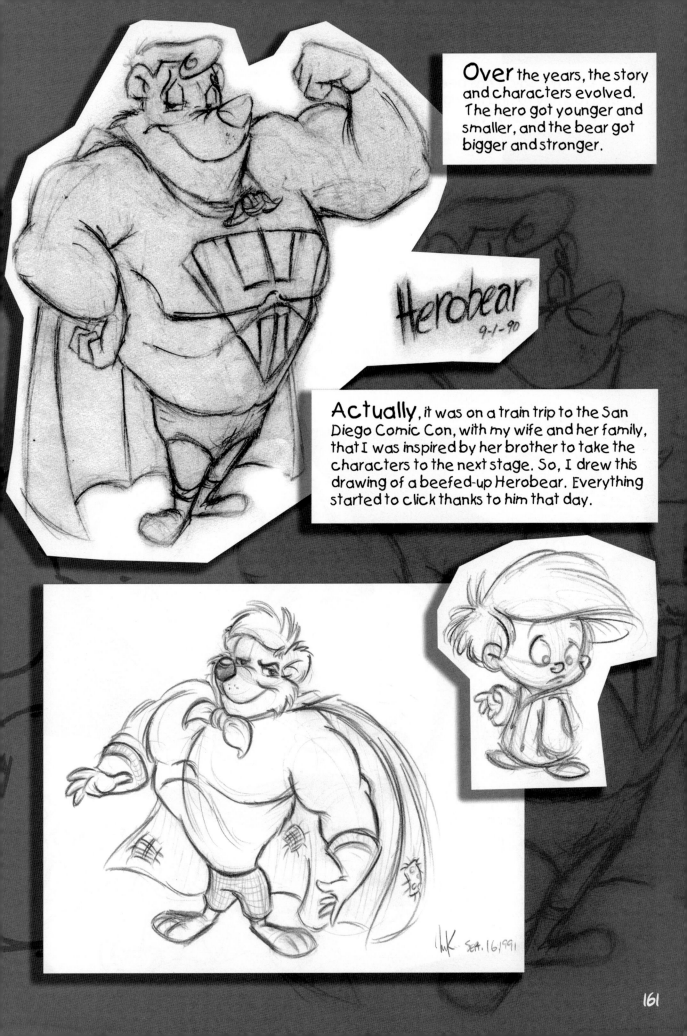

Over the years, the story and characters evolved. The hero got younger and smaller, and the bear got bigger and stronger.

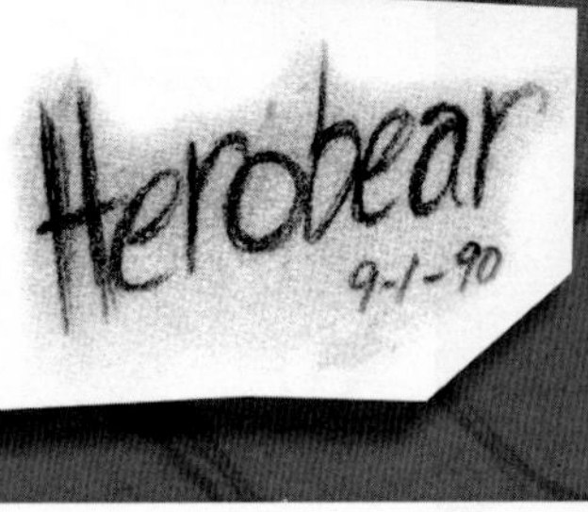
Herobear
9-1-90

Actually, it was on a train trip to the San Diego Comic Con, with my wife and her family, that I was inspired by her brother to take the characters to the next stage. So, I drew this drawing of a beefed-up Herobear. Everything started to click thanks to him that day.

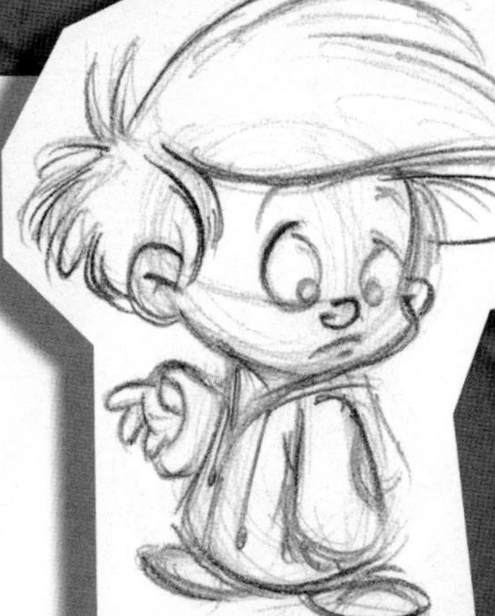

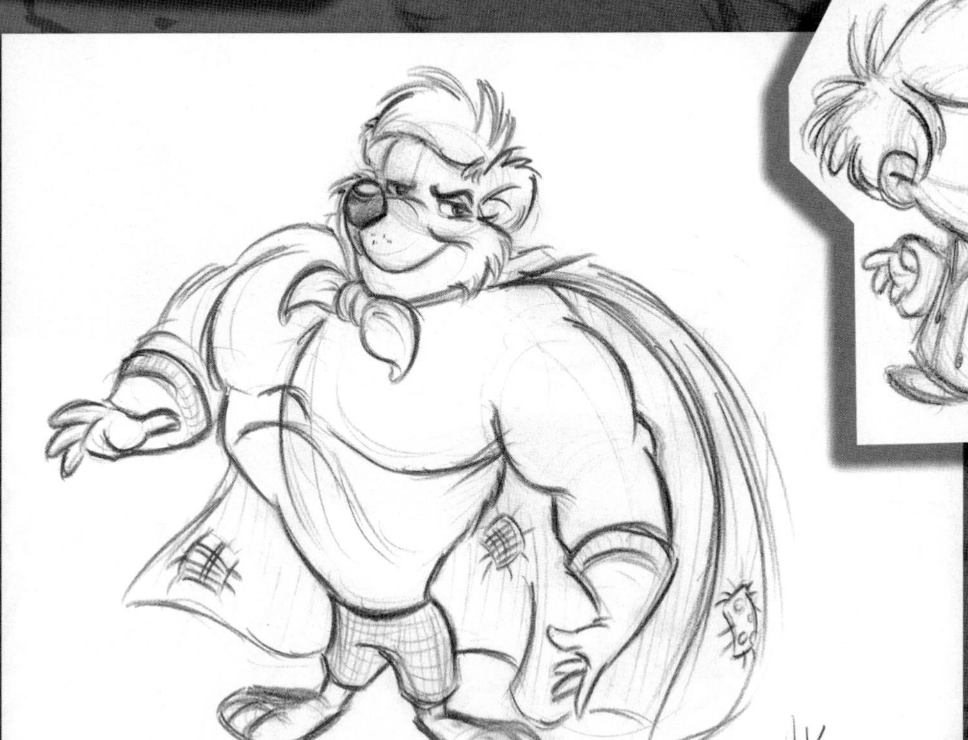
SEP. 16, 1991

Let me say, it has been a bit of a journey to find the right look for Herobear and Tyler.

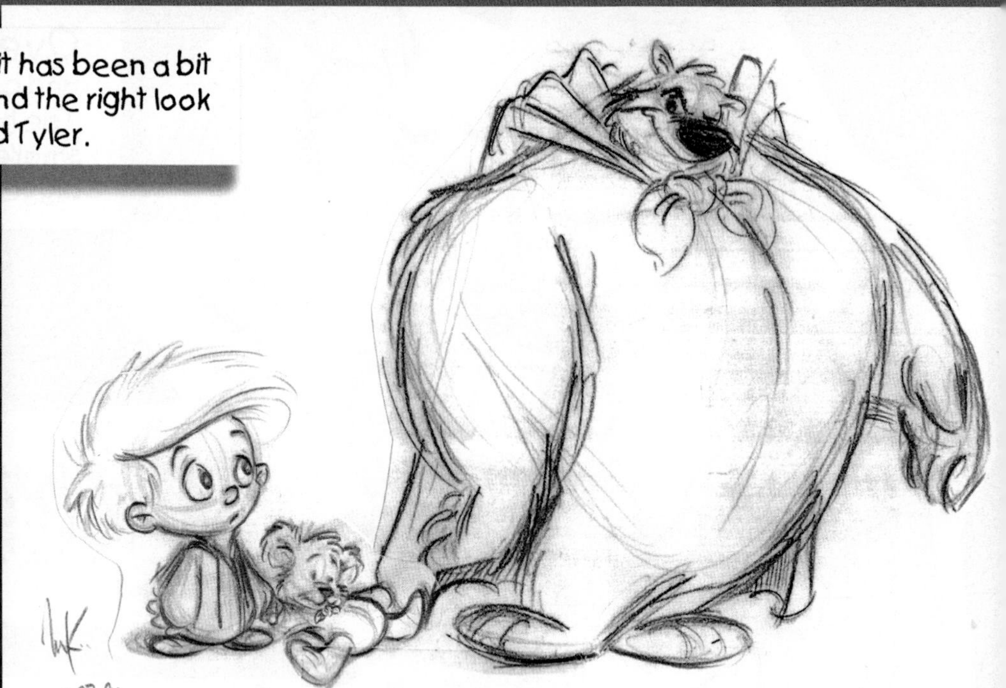
9-27-91

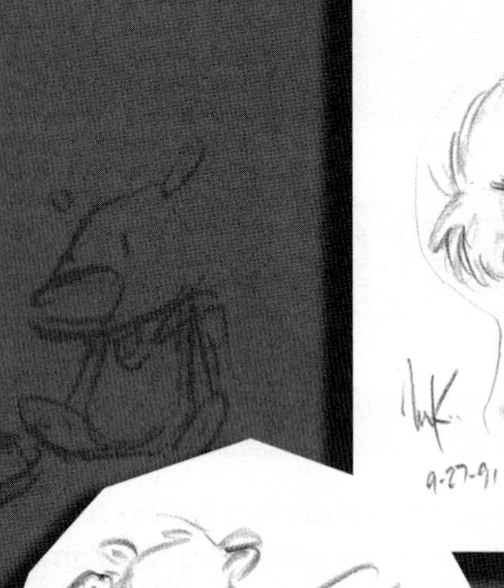

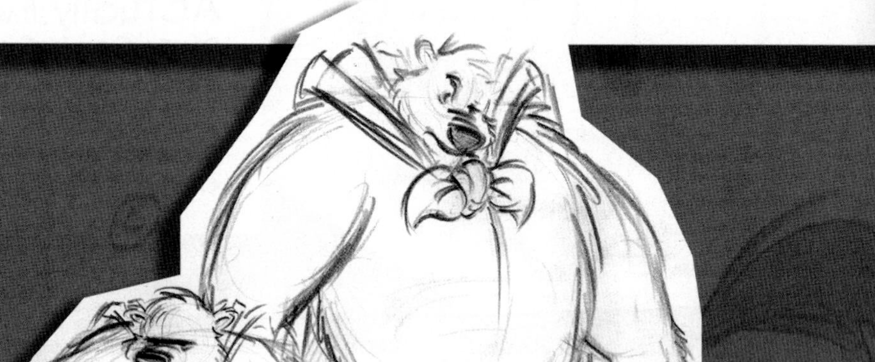
9-19-91

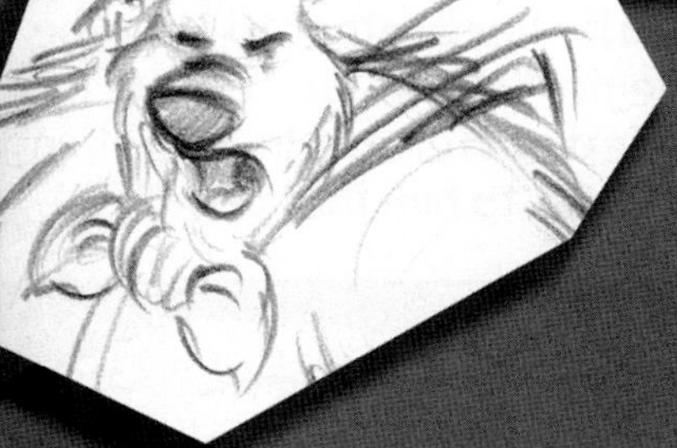

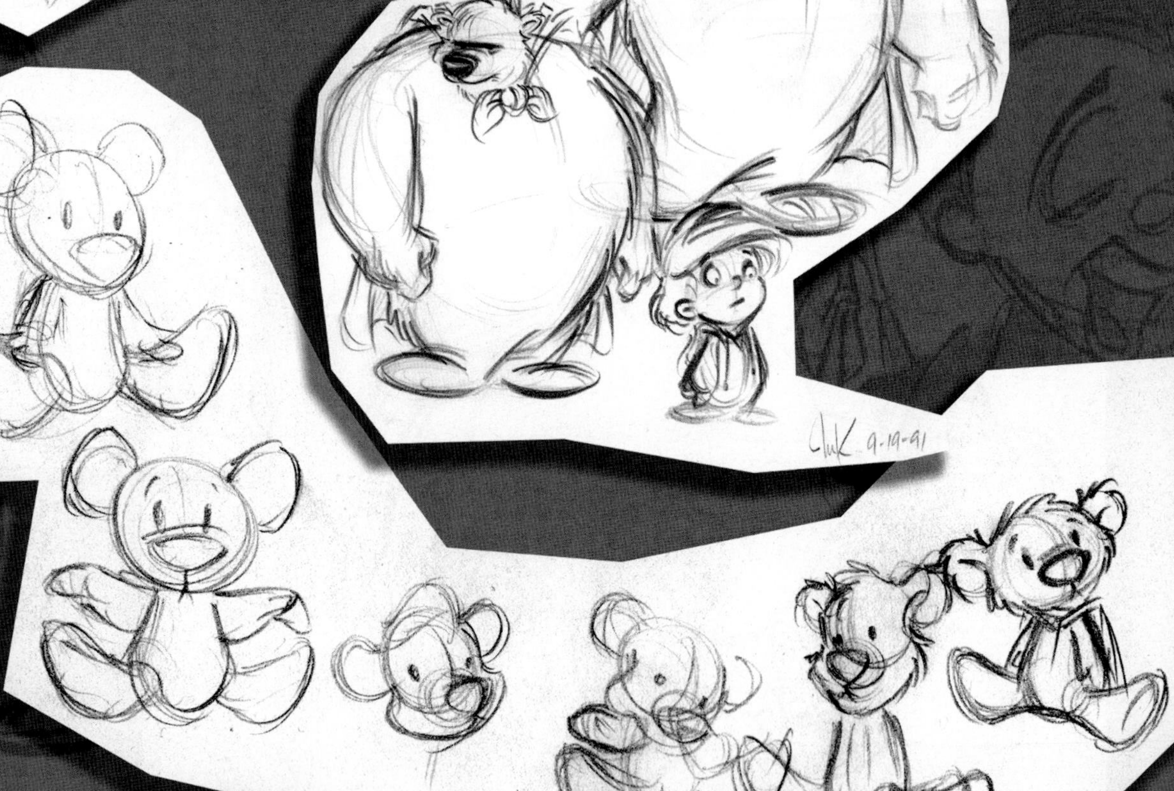

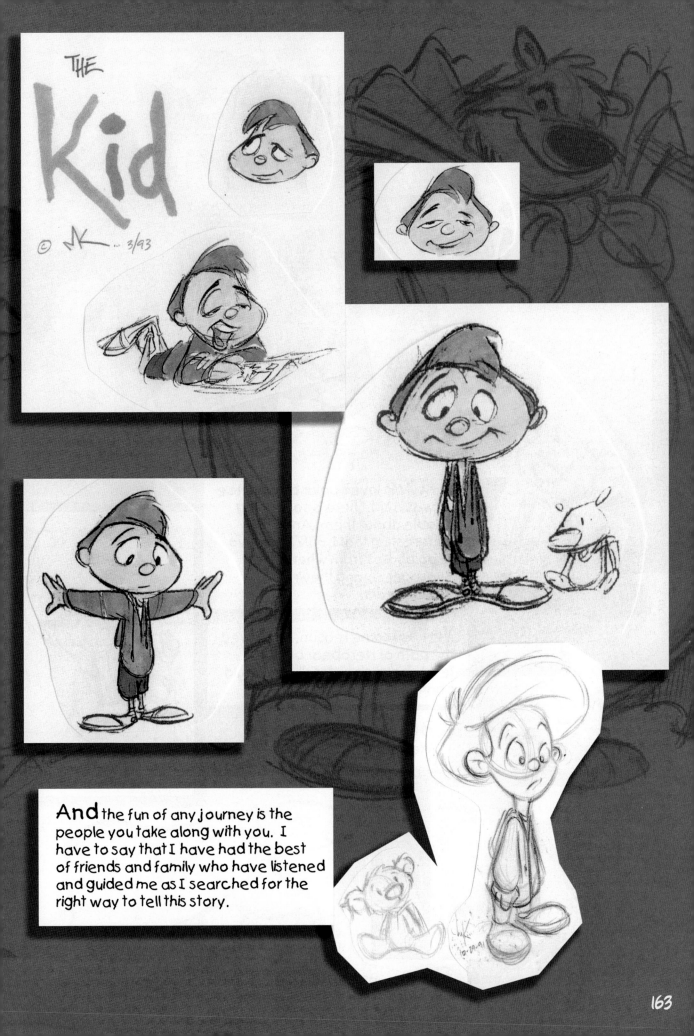

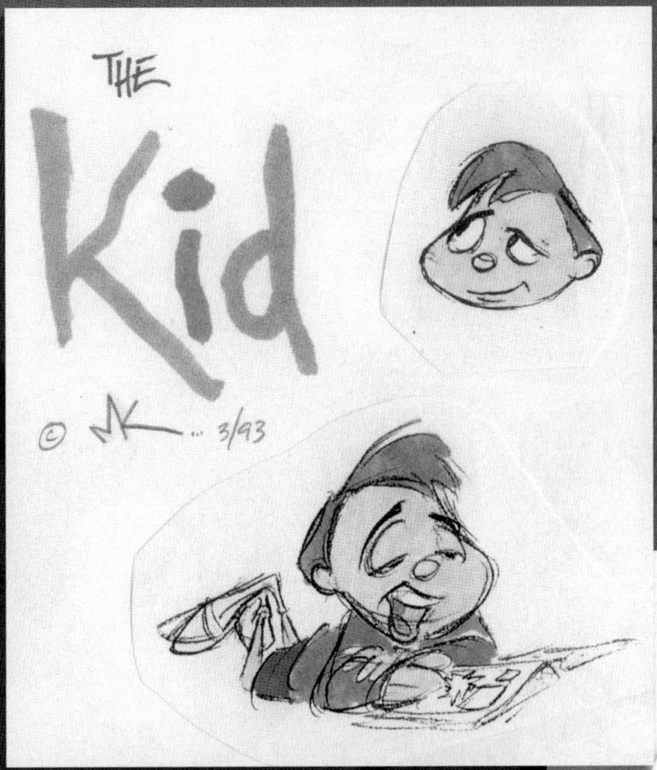
THE
Kid
© JK... 3/93

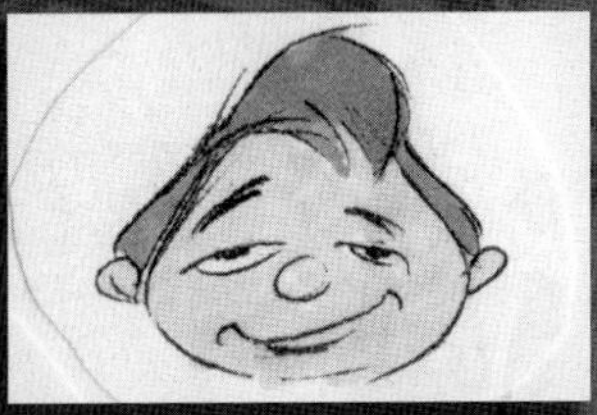

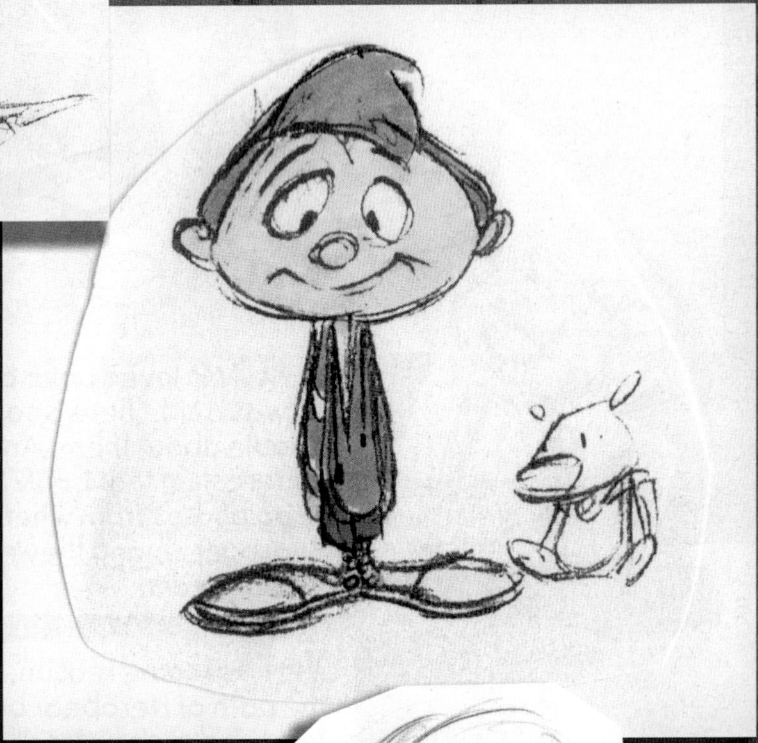

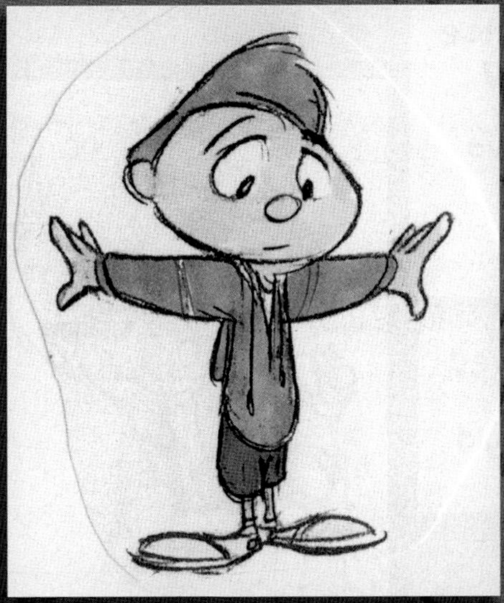

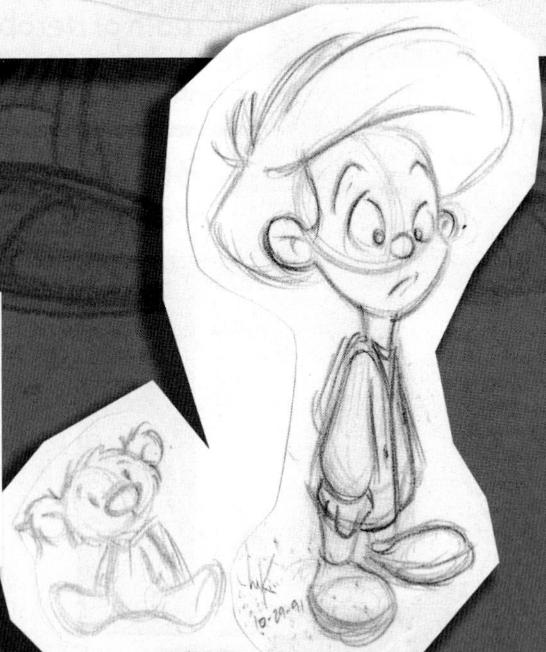

And the fun of any journey is the people you take along with you. I have to say that I have had the best of friends and family who have listened and guided me as I searched for the right way to tell this story.

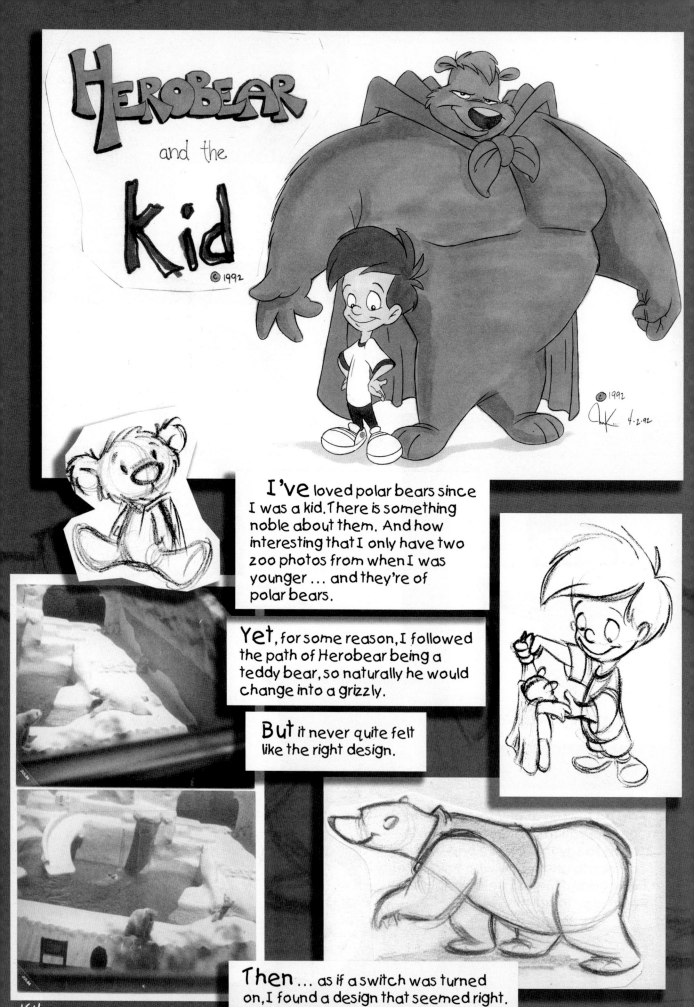

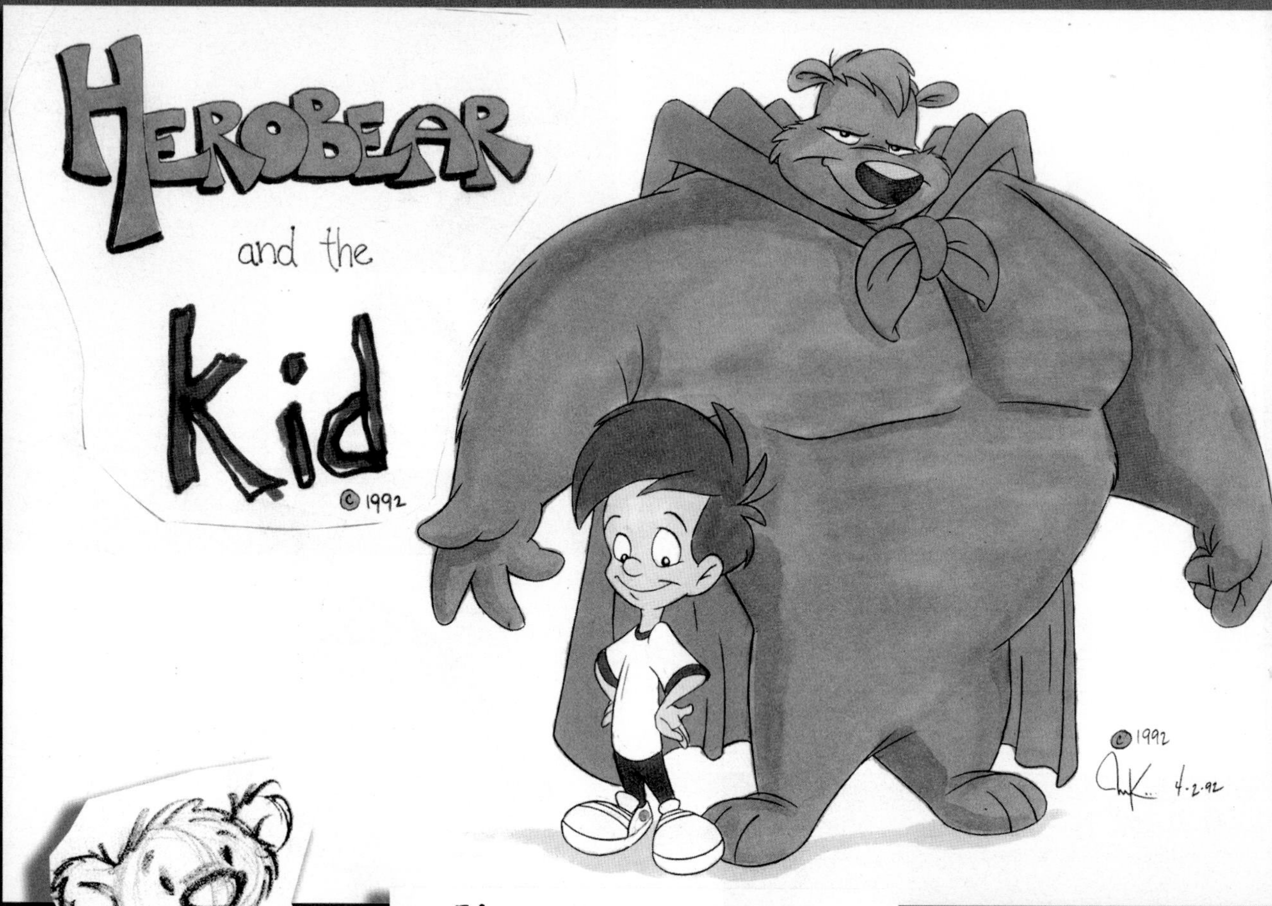
Herobear
and the
Kid
© 1992
© 1992
4-2-92

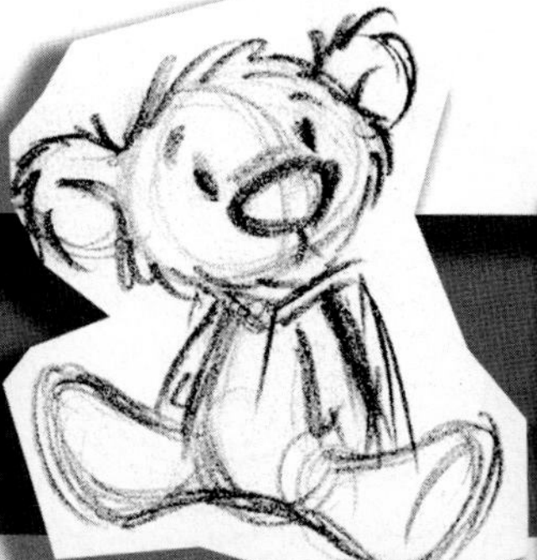

I've loved polar bears since I was a kid. There is something noble about them. And how interesting that I only have two zoo photos from when I was younger ... and they're of polar bears.

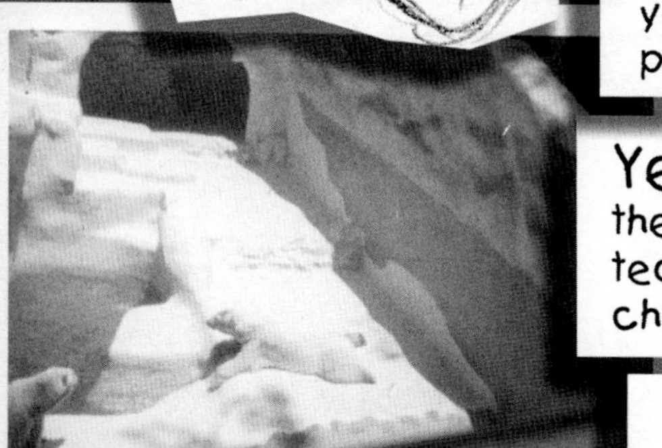

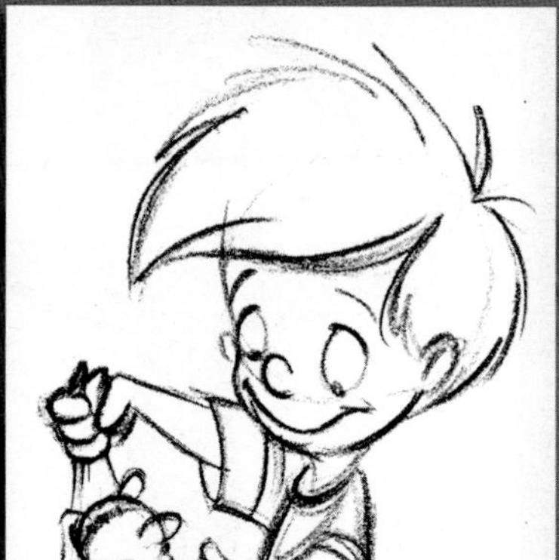

Yet, for some reason, I followed the path of Herobear being a teddy bear, so naturally he would change into a grizzly.

But it never quite felt like the right design.

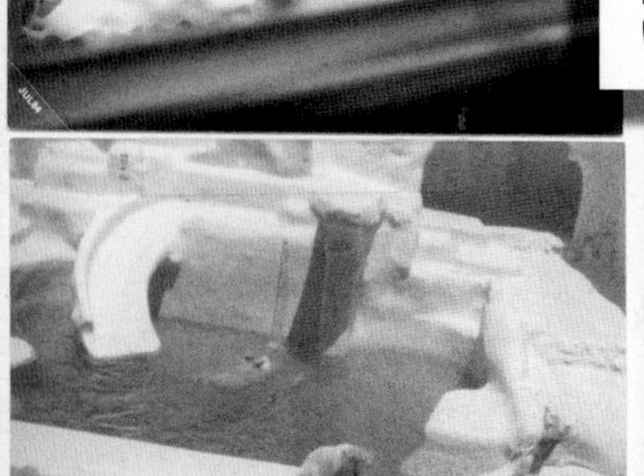

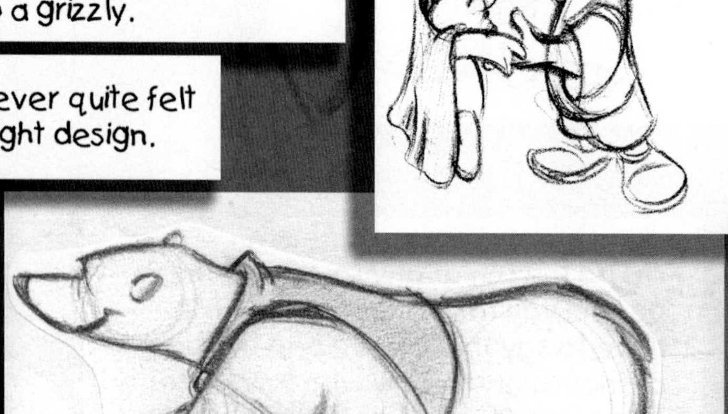

Then ... as if a switch was turned on, I found a design that seemed right.

I think it's interesting that the date between the marker images on these two pages is only about 3 weeks. Isn't art amazing? When you find the right design, it happens naturally.

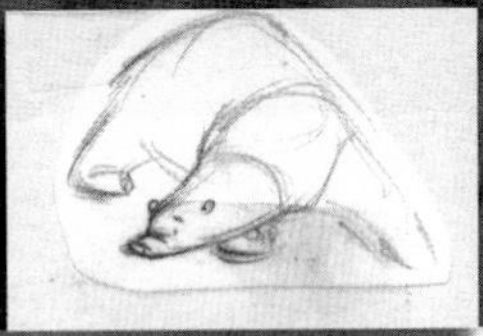

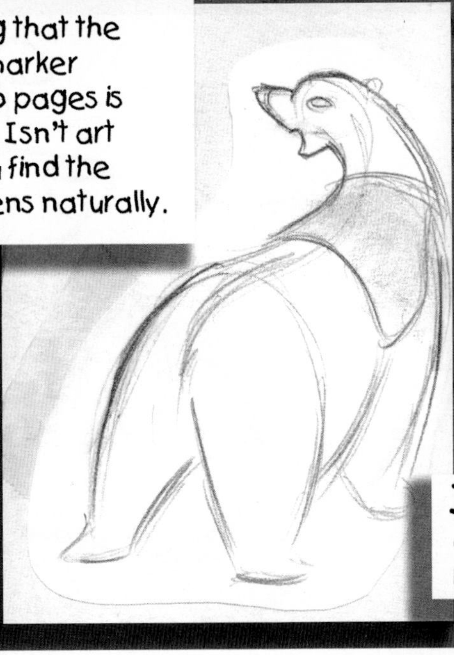

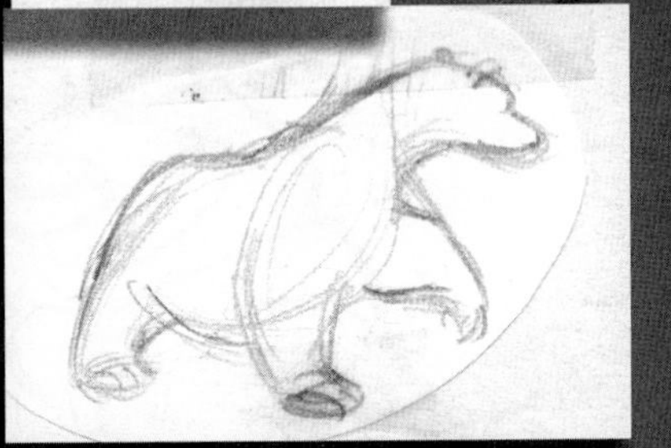

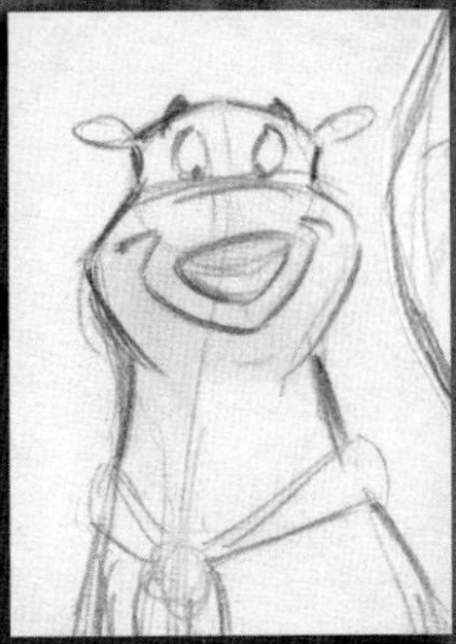

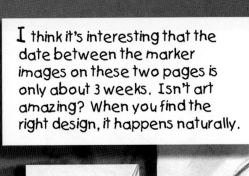

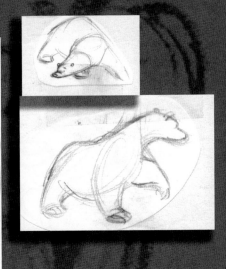

I guess you could say the same about everything in life. When it's right, it should happen naturally.

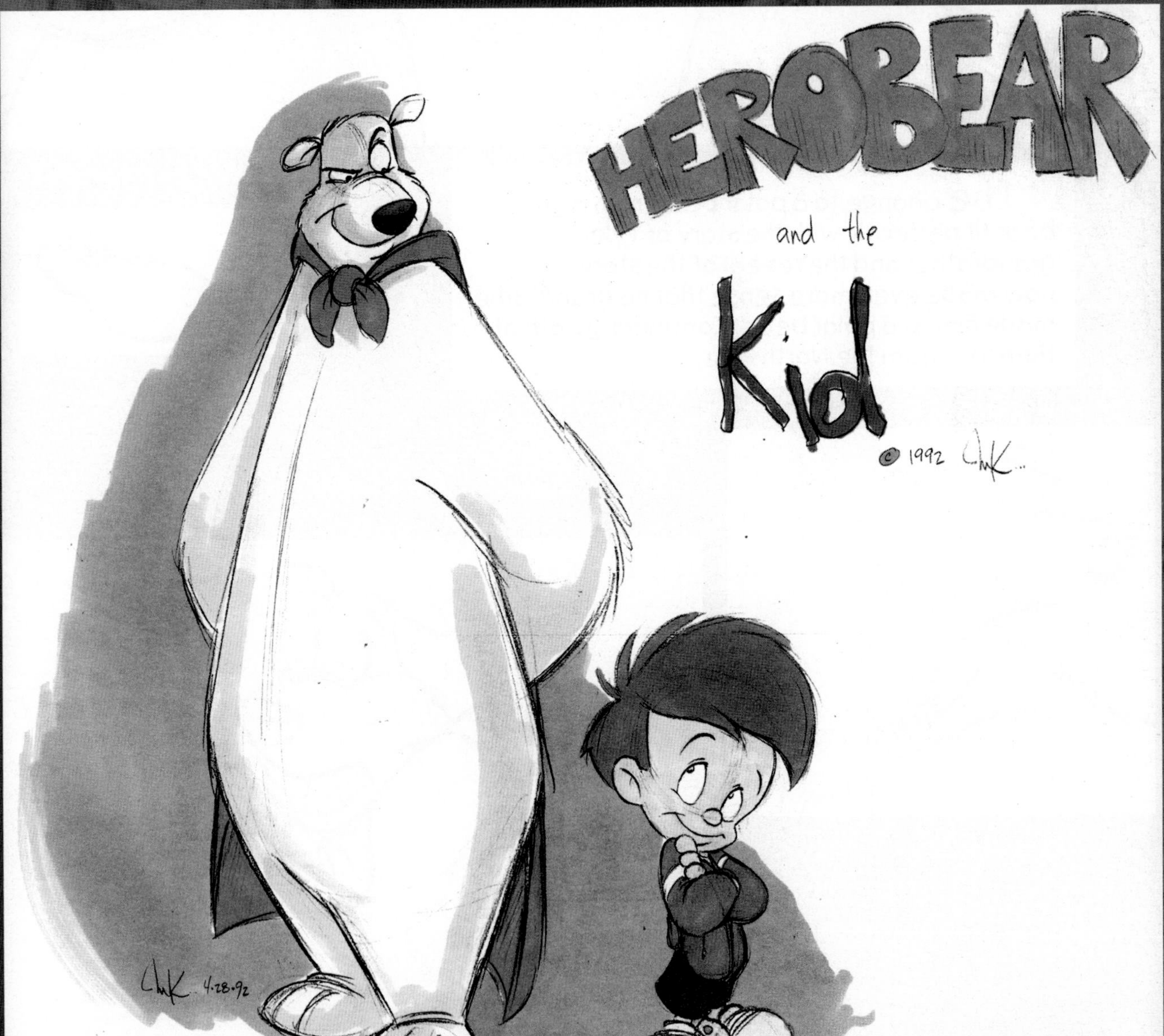

HEROBEAR
and the
Kid
© 1992

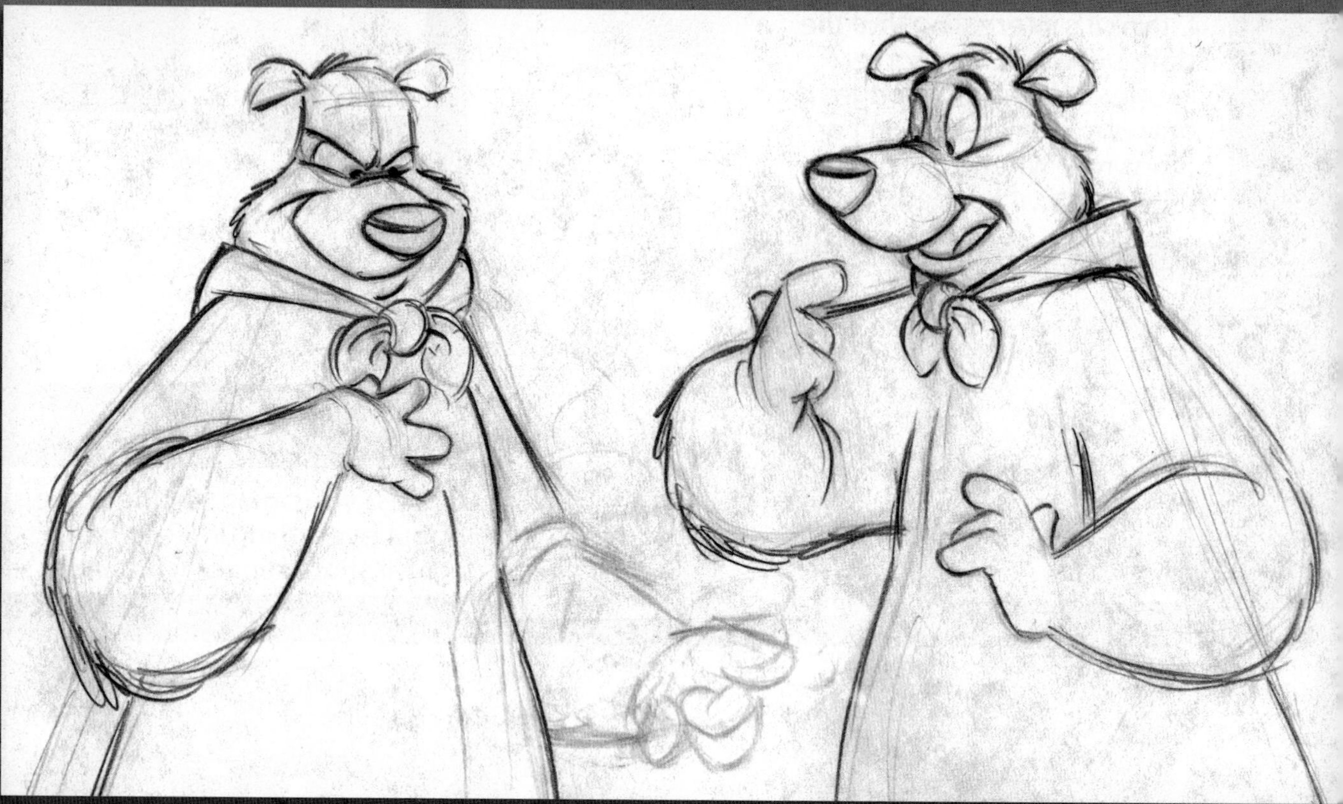

The change to a polar bear from a grizzly bear fit perfectly with the story of Tyler's grandfather and the reveal of the story. It now made even more sense that his grandfather made him as a polar bear. Considering both of them are from the North Pole.

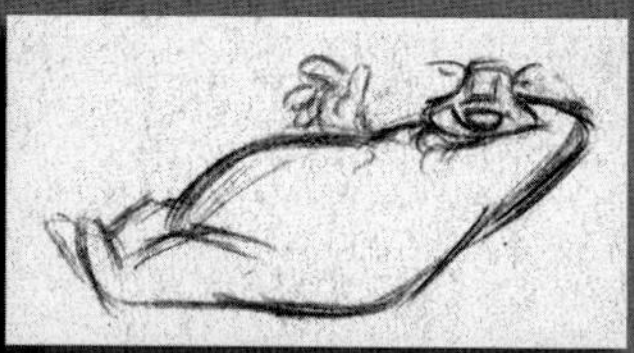

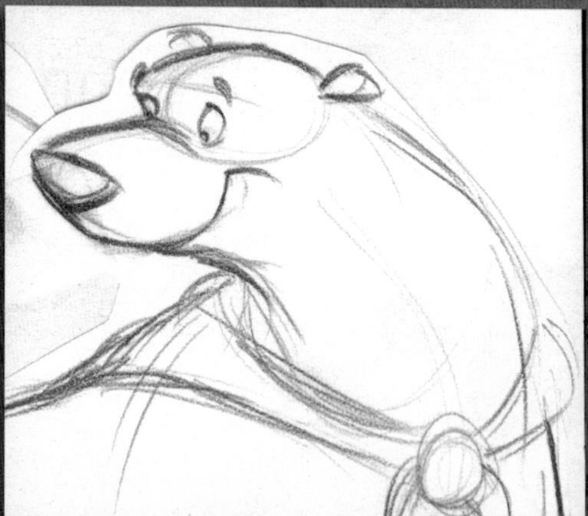

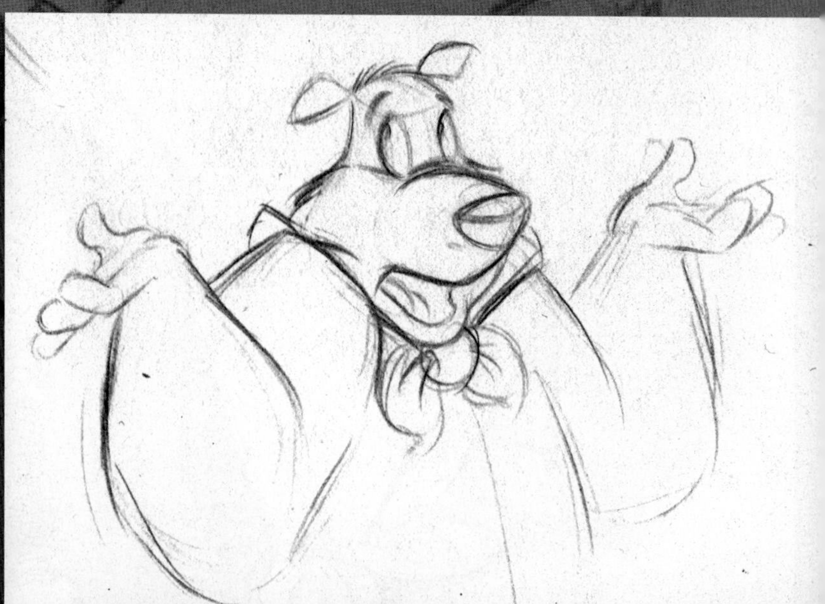

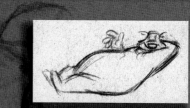

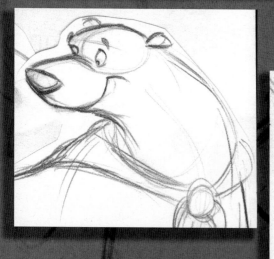

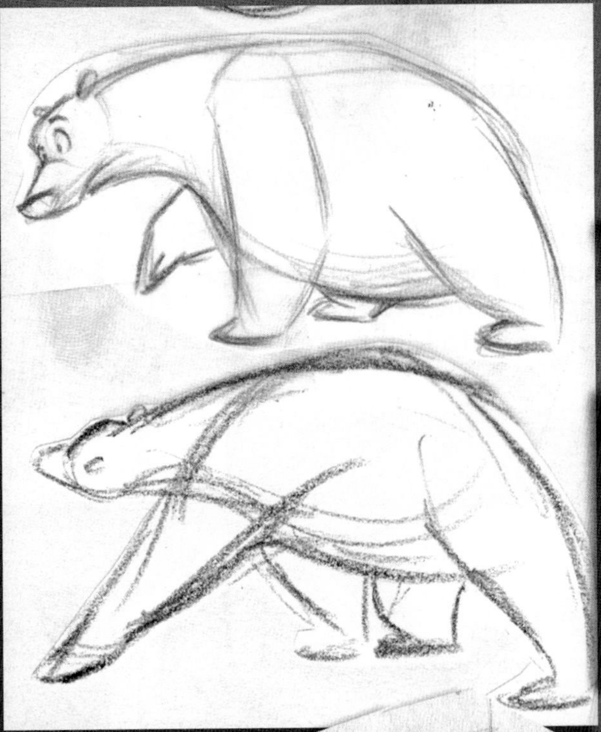

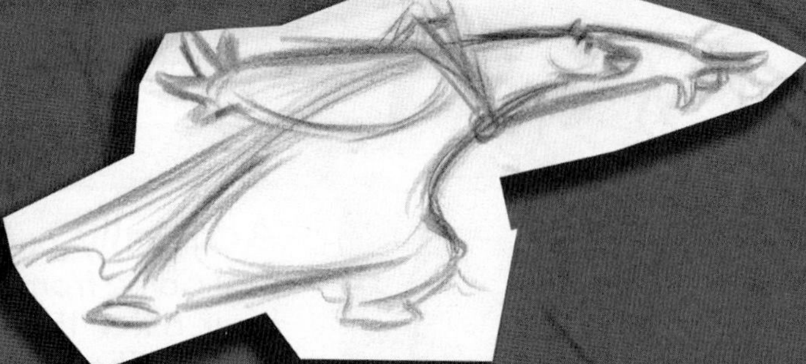

Now, the design for Herobear has really evolved and refined itself over time. Honestly, I really have had nothing to do with it. All I did was sit there occasionally and hold the pencil so that it could draw the shapes that it needed to be.

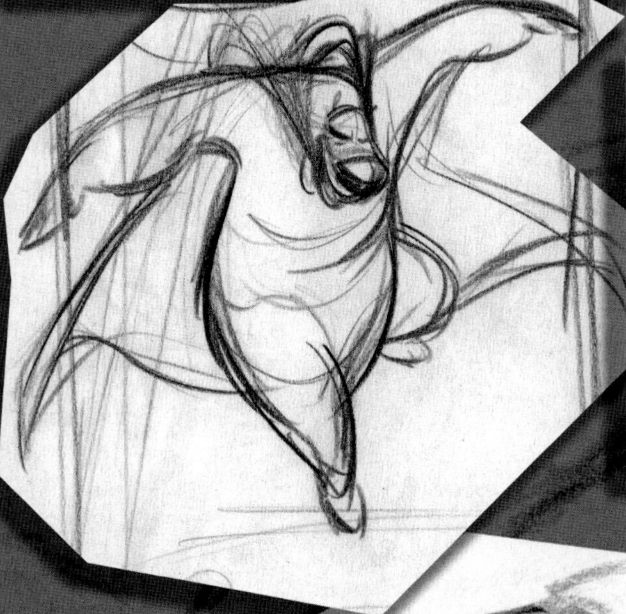

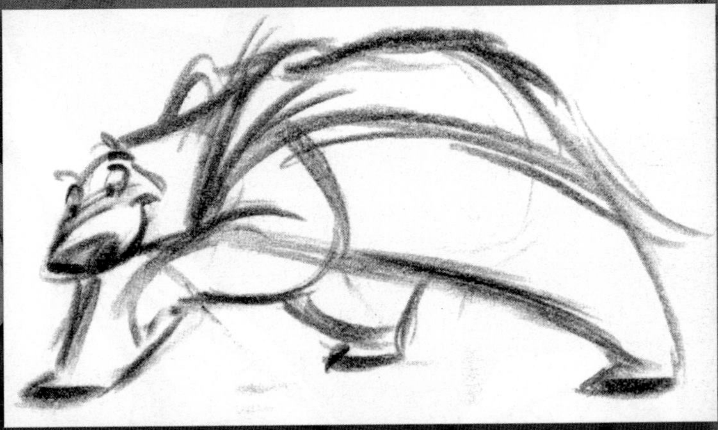

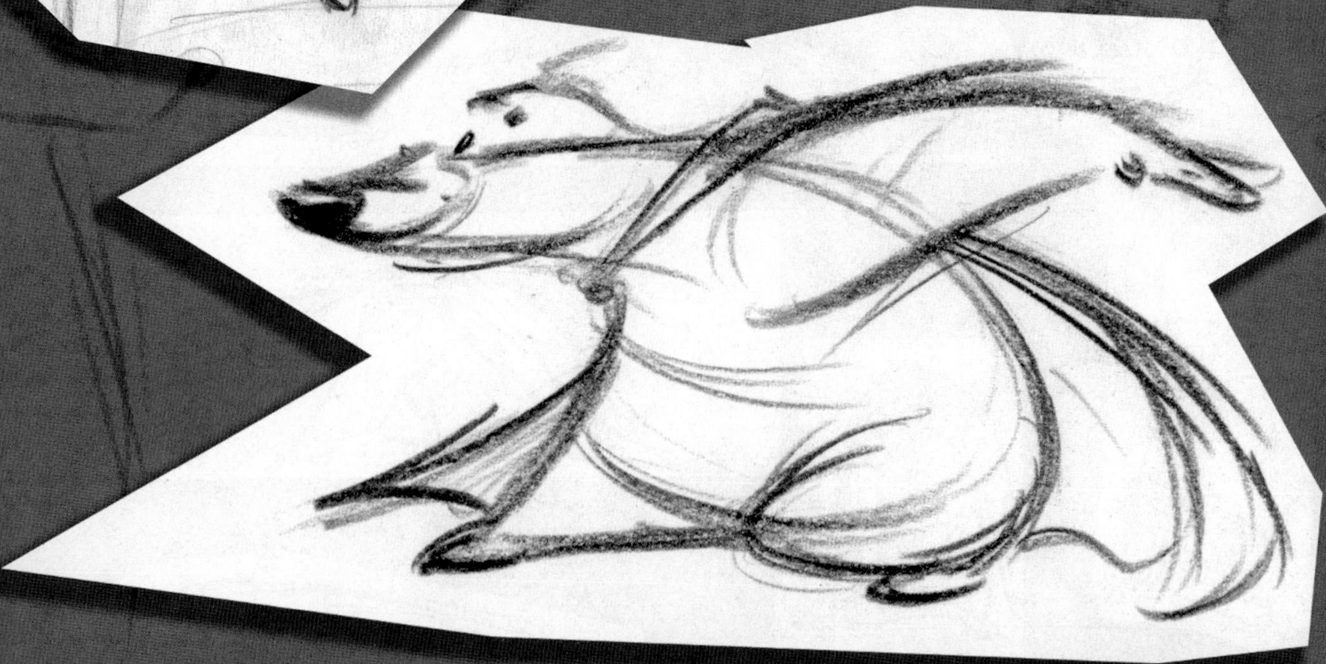

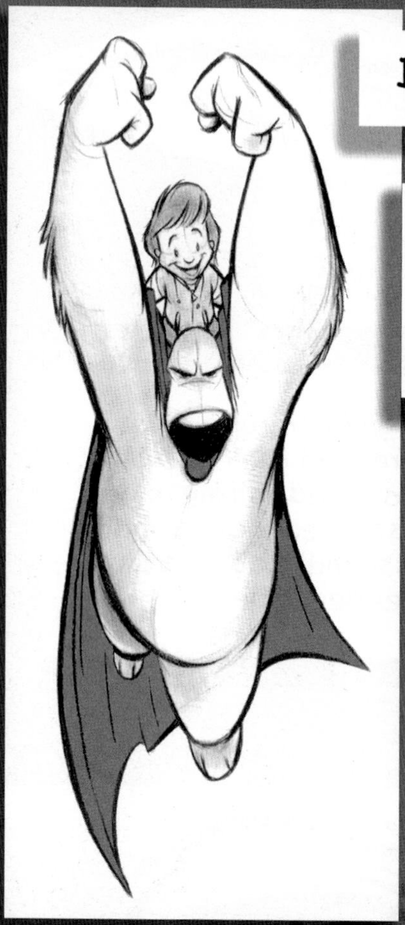

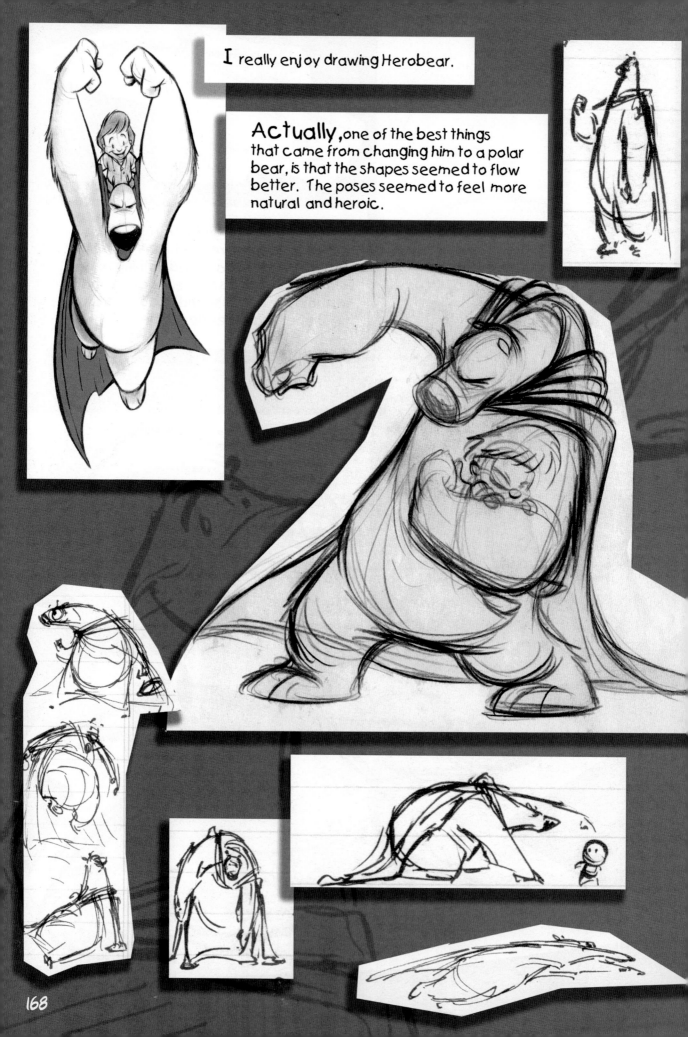

I really enjoy drawing Herobear.

Actually, one of the best things that came from changing him to a polar bear, is that the shapes seemed to flow better. The poses seemed to feel more natural and heroic.

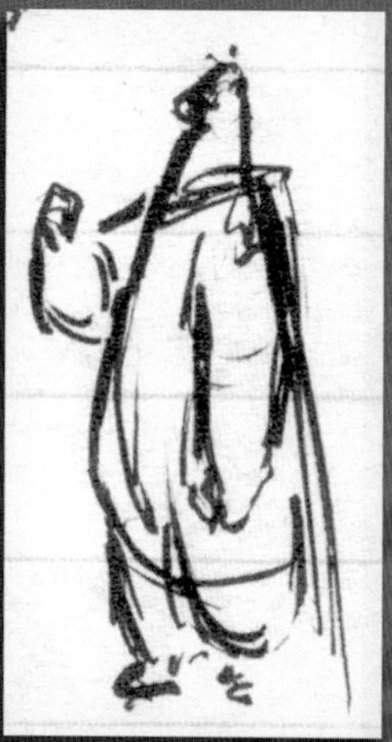

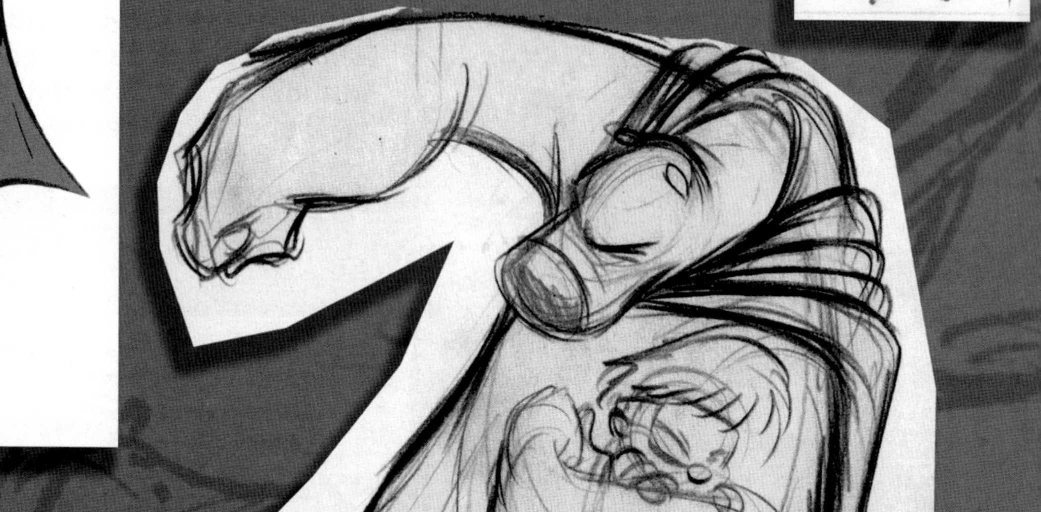

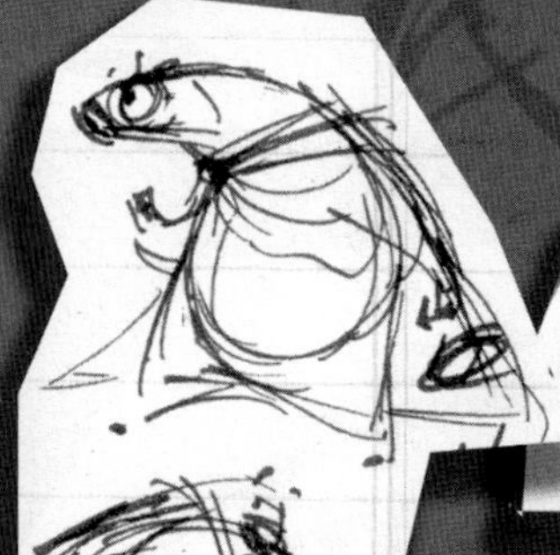

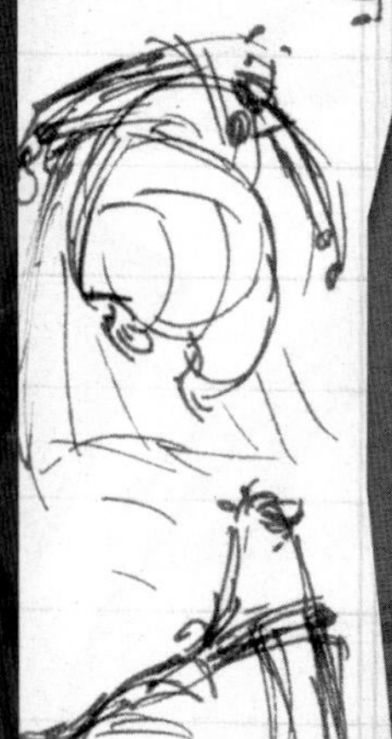

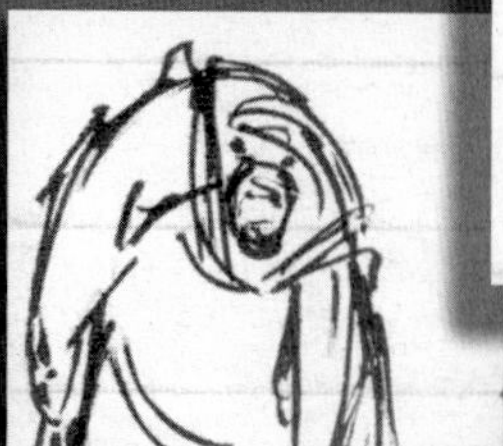

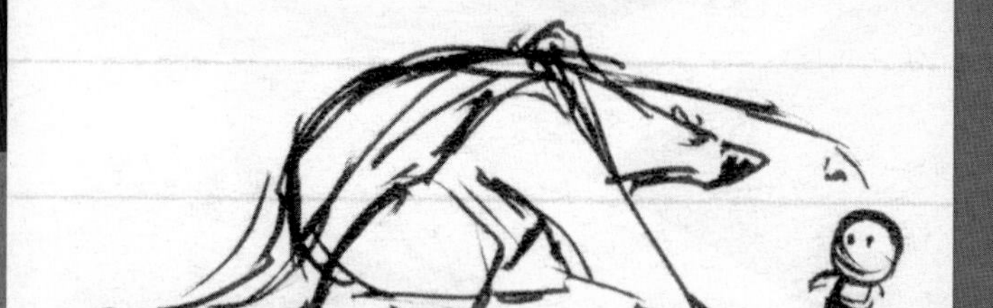

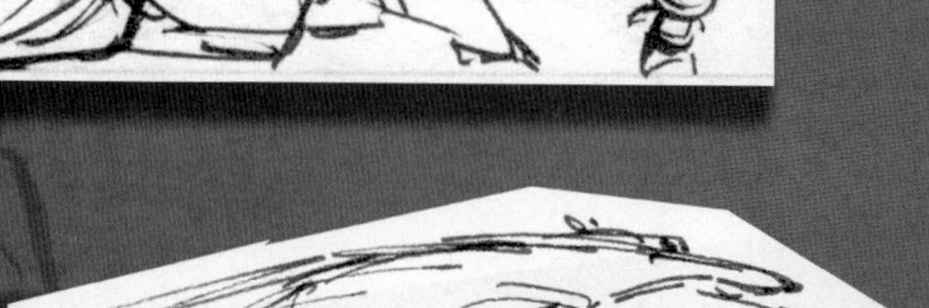

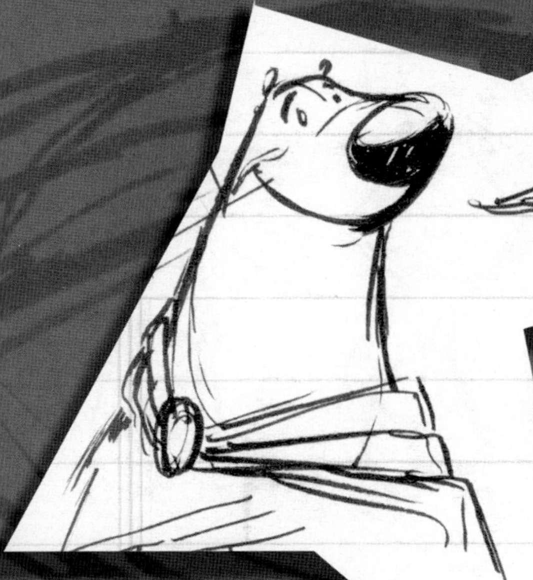

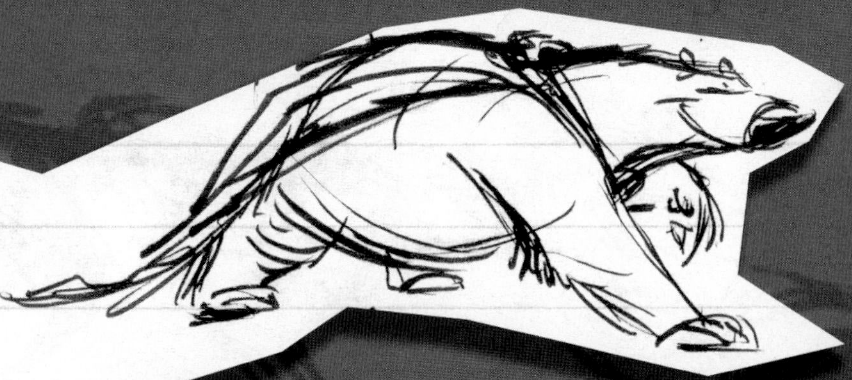

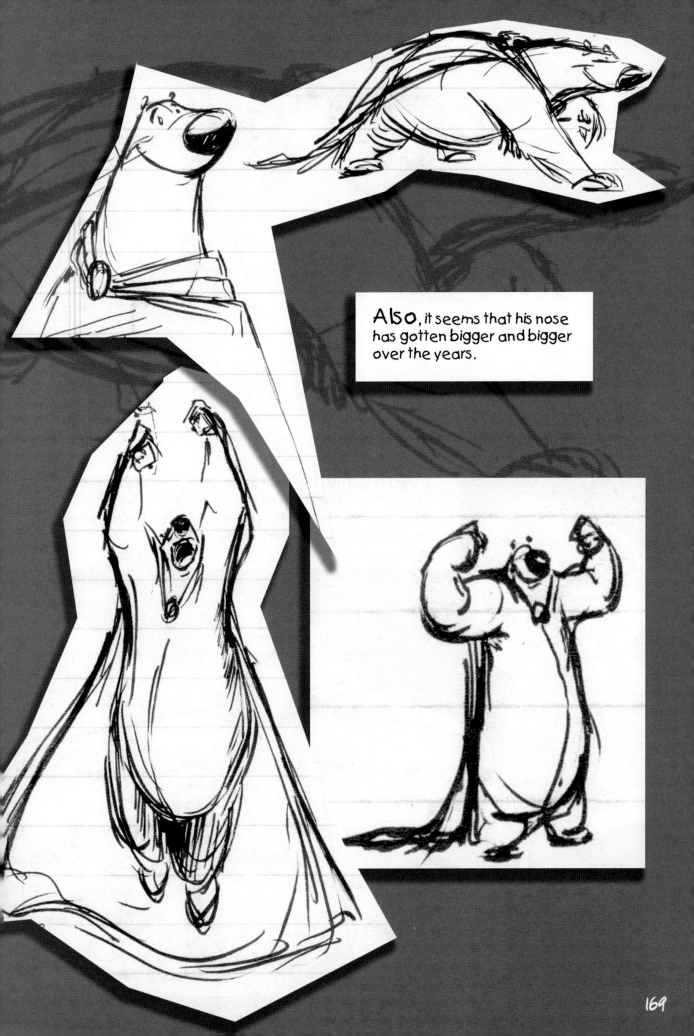

Also, it seems that his nose has gotten bigger and bigger over the years.

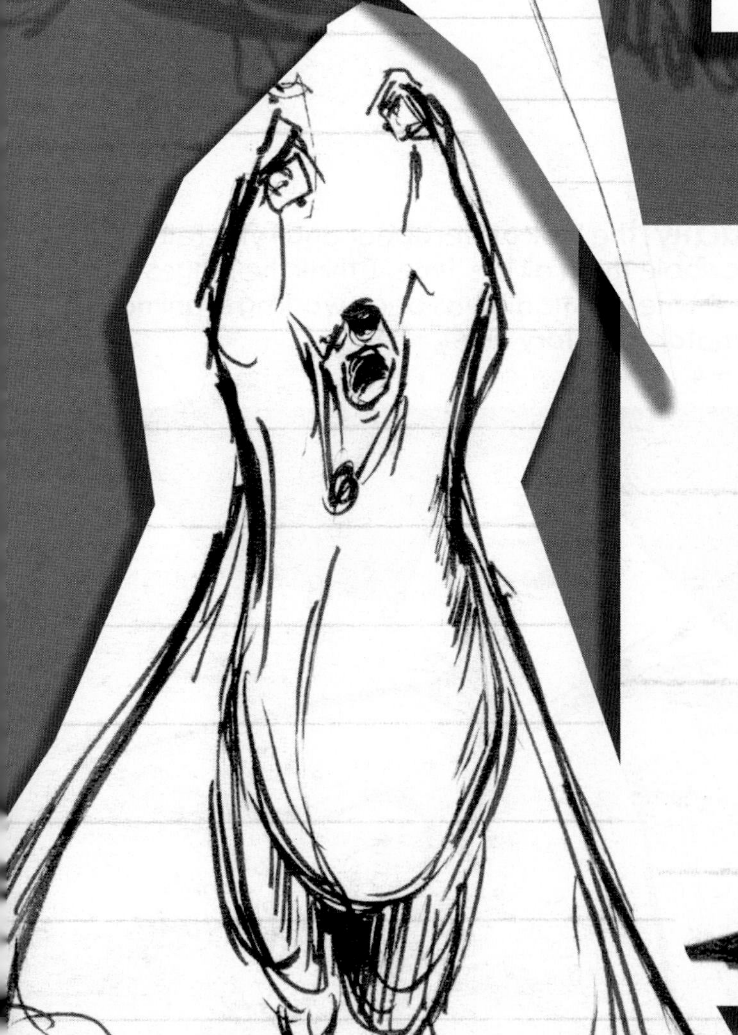

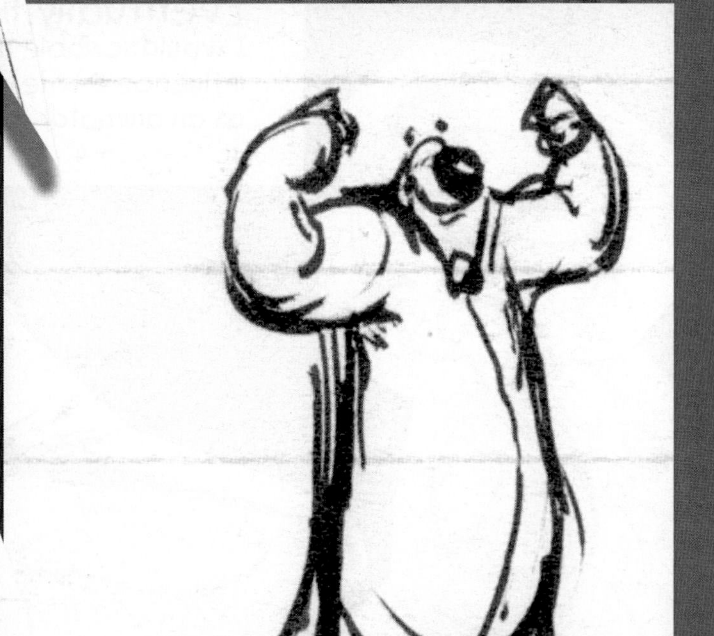

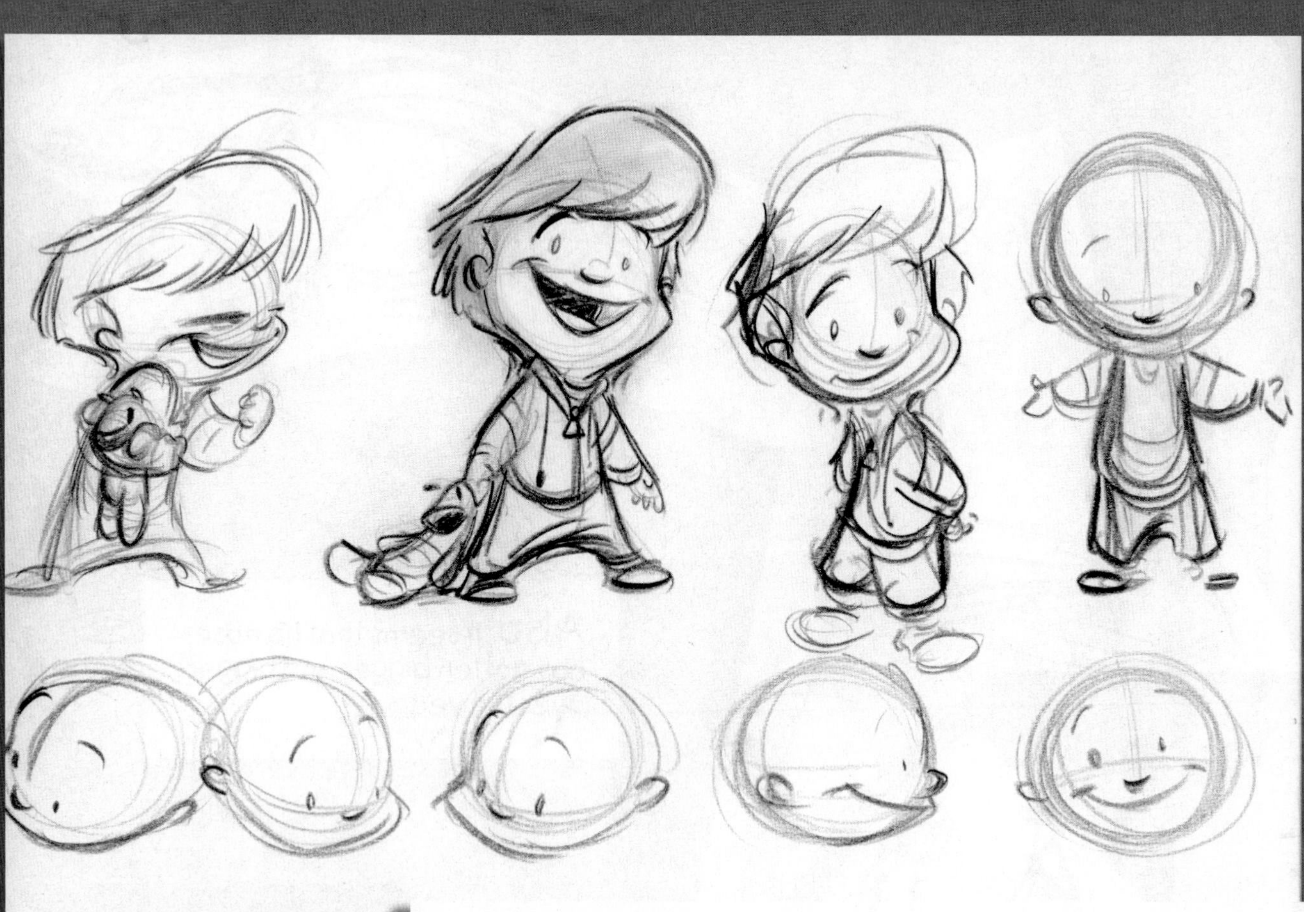

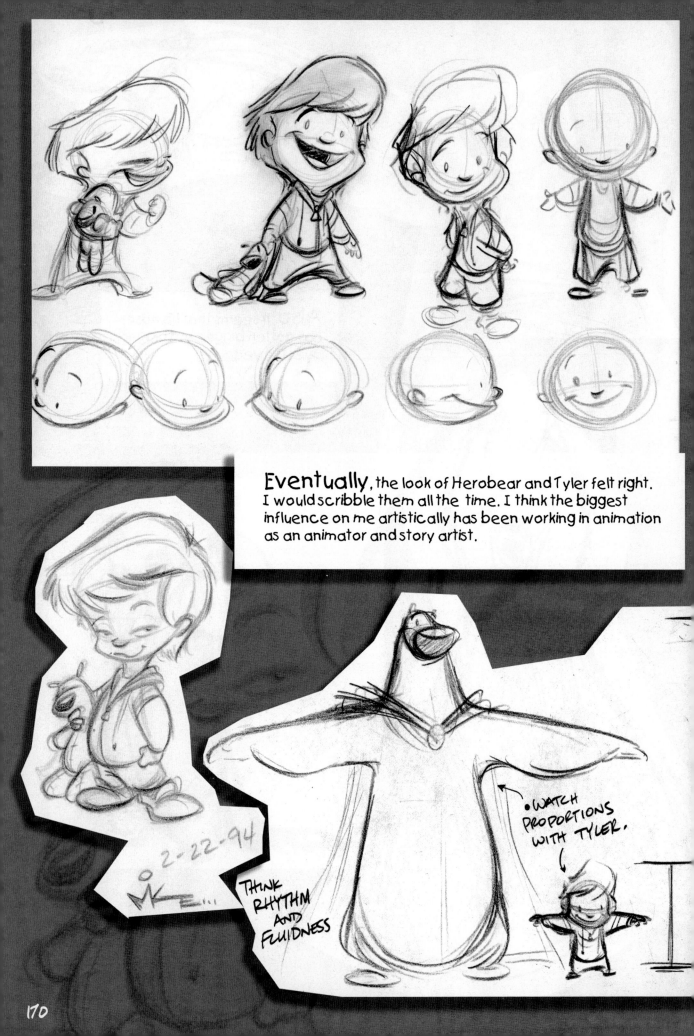

Eventually, the look of Herobear and Tyler felt right. I would scribble them all the time. I think the biggest influence on me artistically has been working in animation as an animator and story artist.

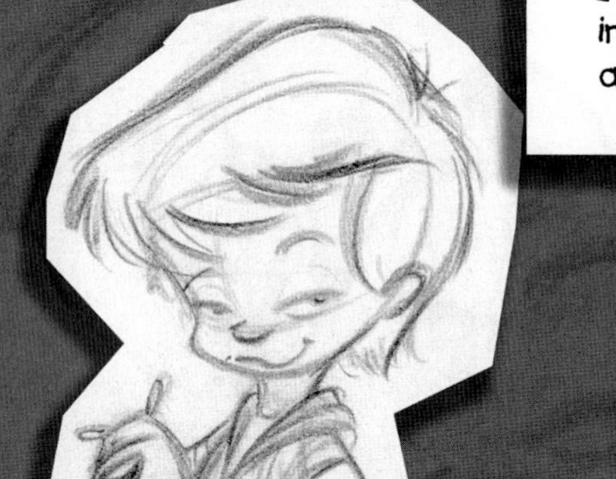
2-22-94

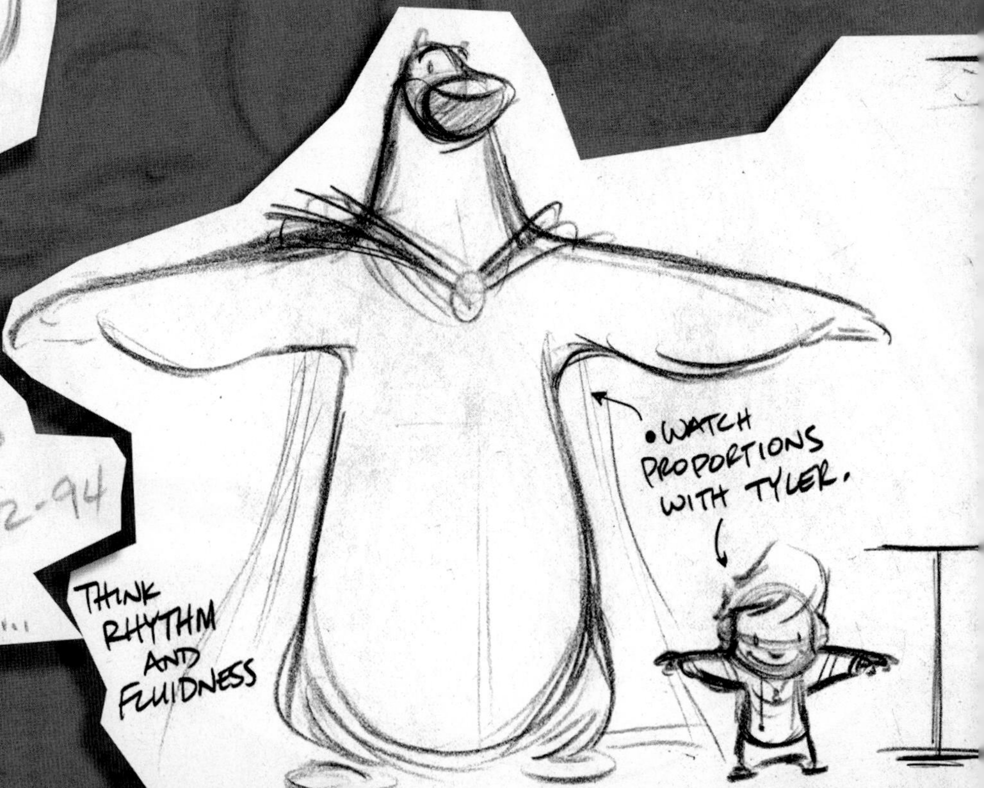
THINK RHYTHM AND FLUIDNESS
•WATCH PROPORTIONS WITH TYLER.

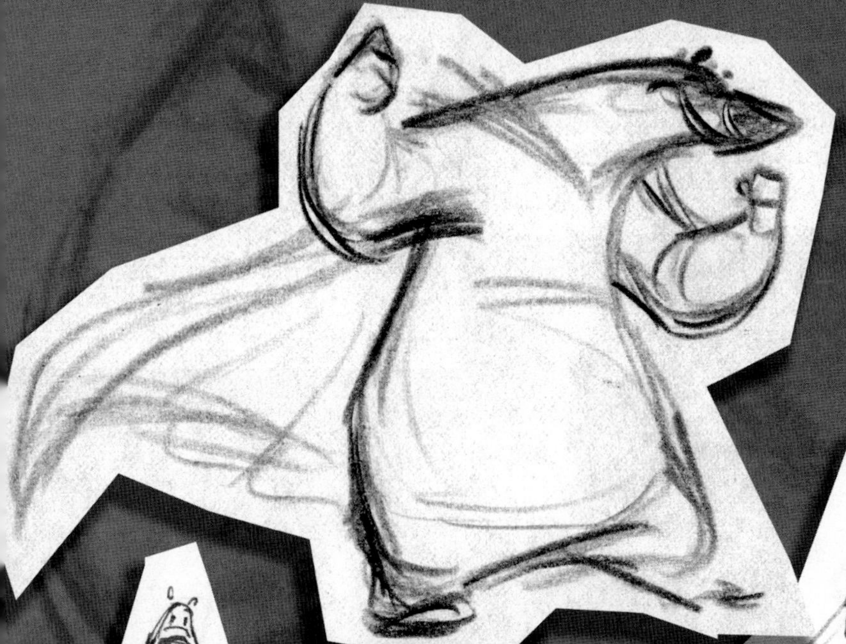

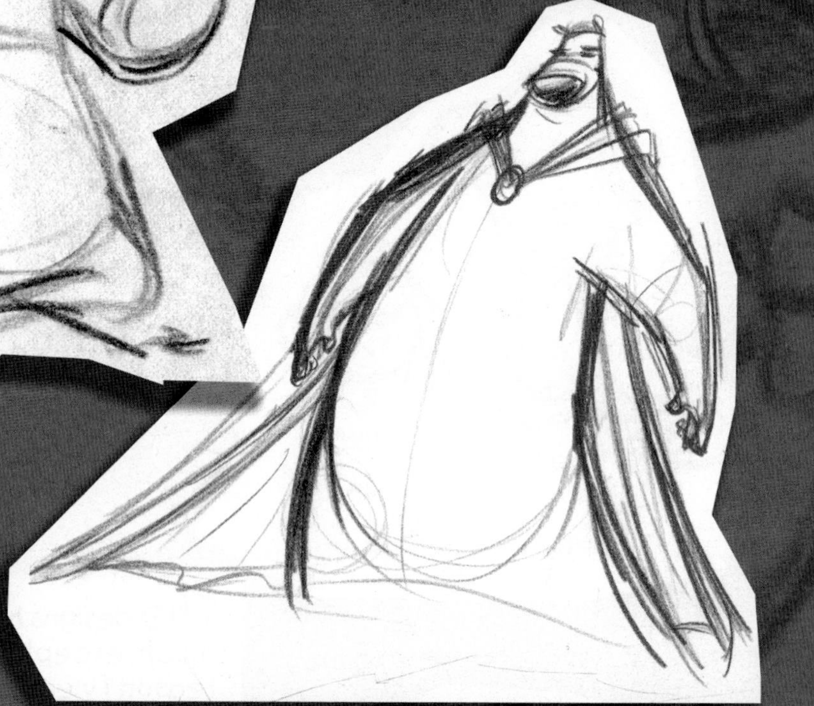

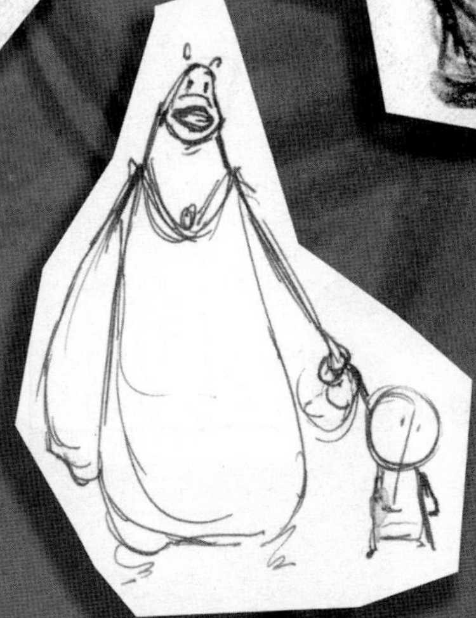

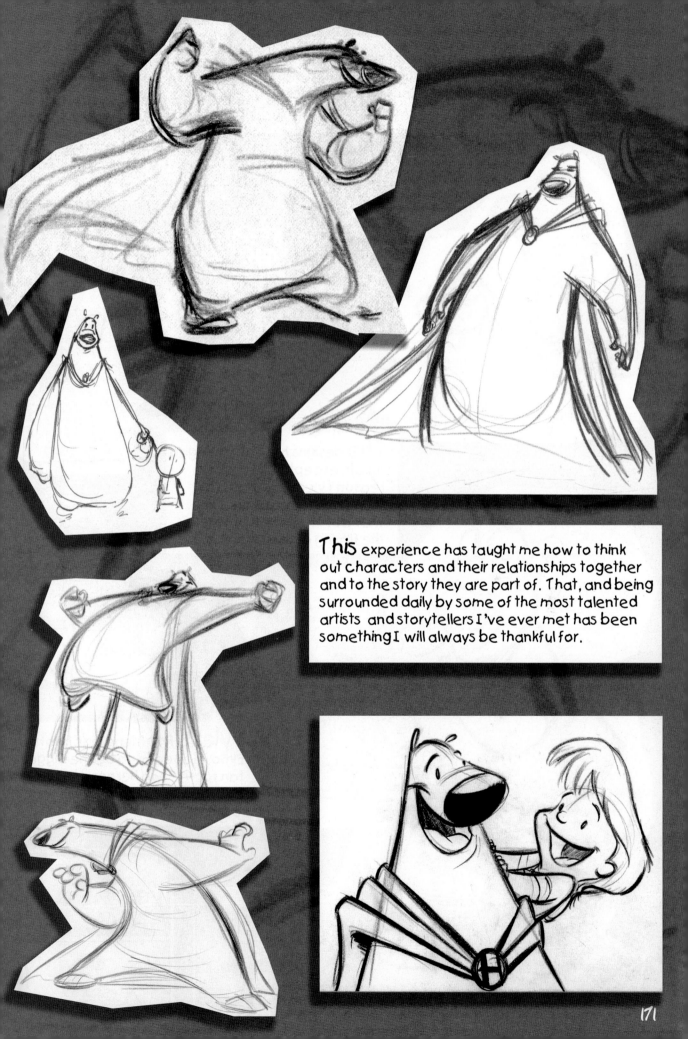

This experience has taught me how to think out characters and their relationships together and to the story they are part of. That, and being surrounded daily by some of the most talented artists and storytellers I've ever met has been something I will always be thankful for.

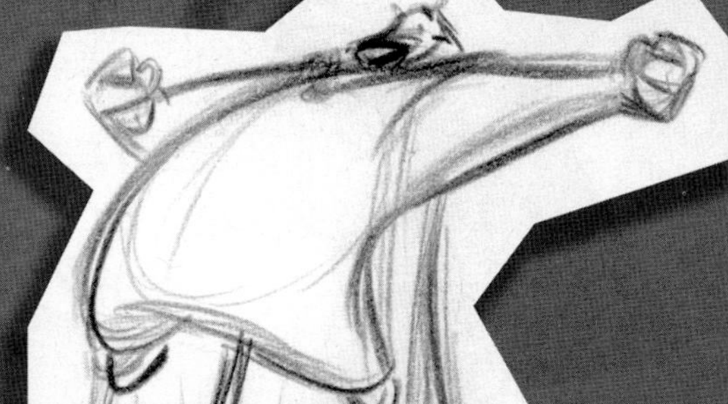

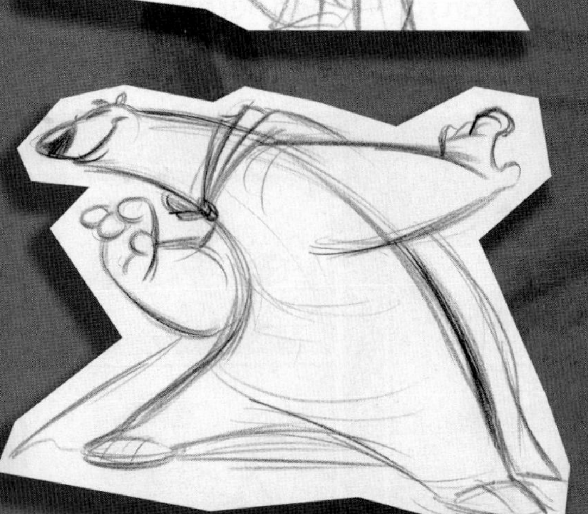

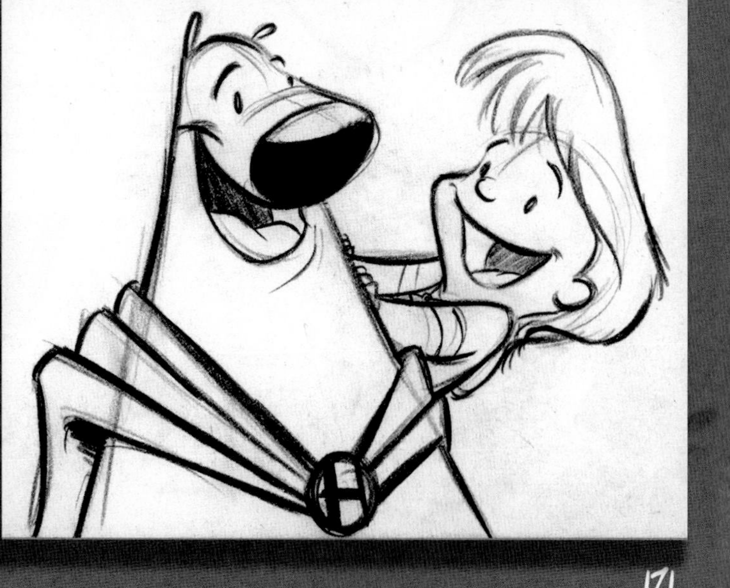

Now of course, once the designs for Herobear and Tyler began to work out, it was only a matter of time for the other characters to start to crawl out of the pencil onto paper and into the story.

His family has always been the same . . . a mom, a pop, and an annoying little sister. Pretty much my family when I was growing up. Except my sister wasn't too annoying . . . well, at least I should say that, since she may end up reading all of this.

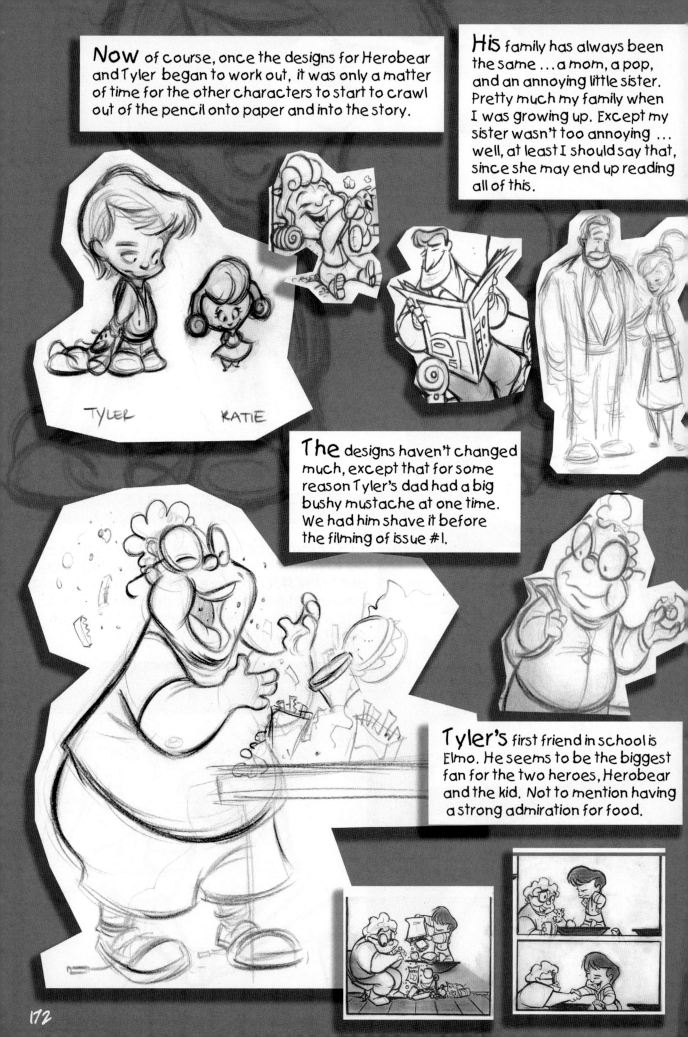

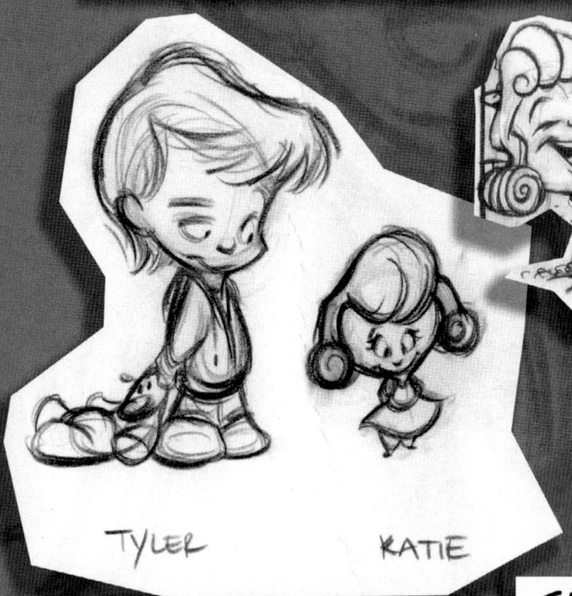
TYLER
KATIE

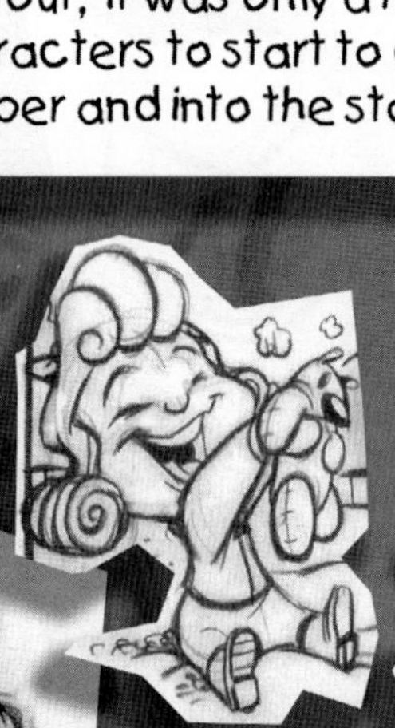

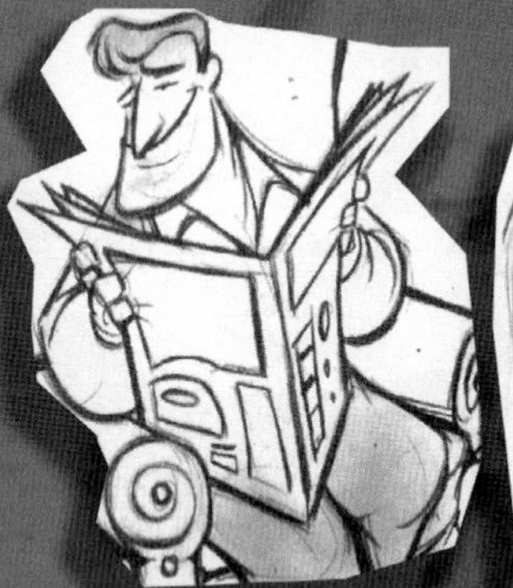

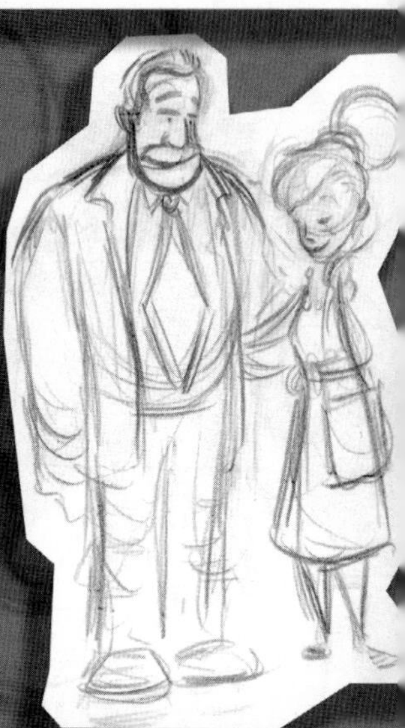

The designs haven't changed much, except that for some reason Tyler's dad had a big bushy mustache at one time. We had him shave it before the filming of issue #1.

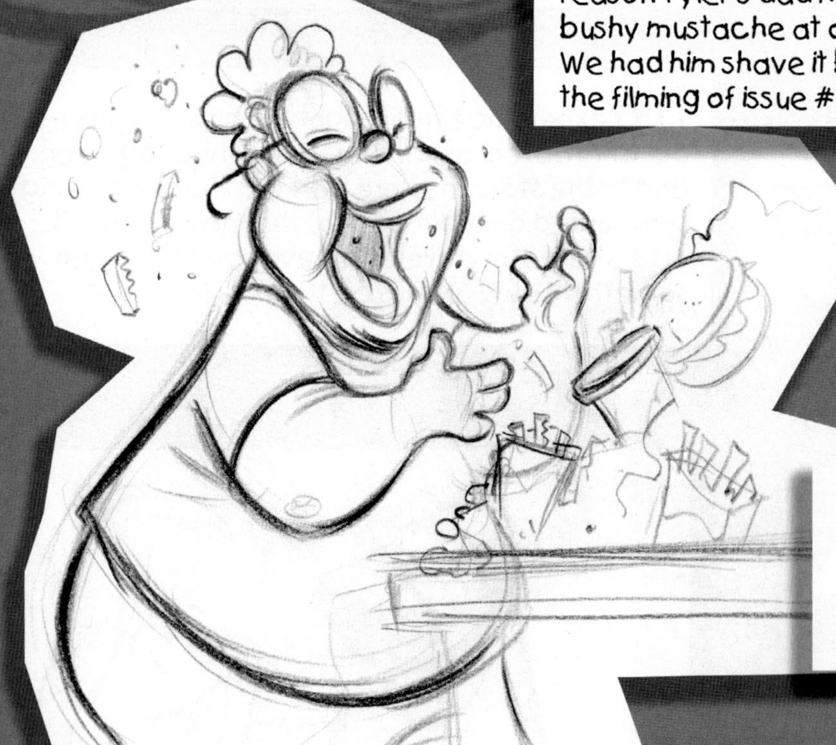

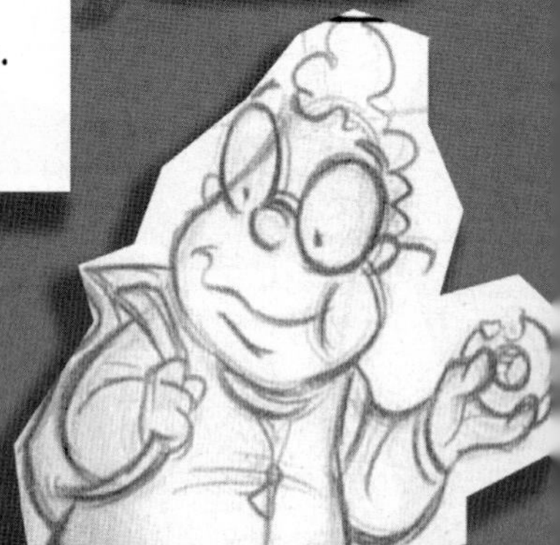

Tyler's first friend in school is Elmo. He seems to be the biggest fan for the two heroes, Herobear and the kid. Not to mention having a strong admiration for food.

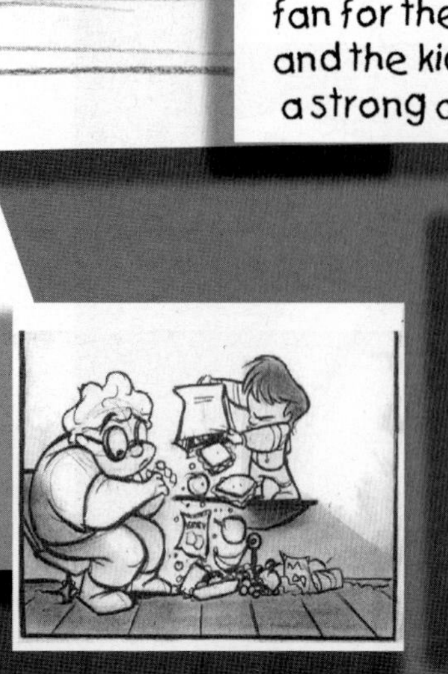

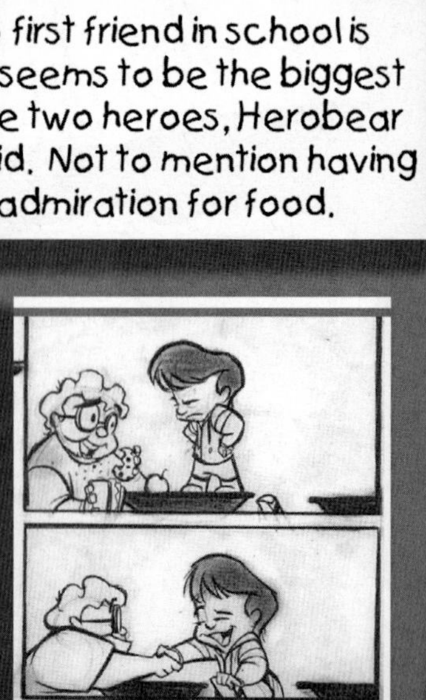

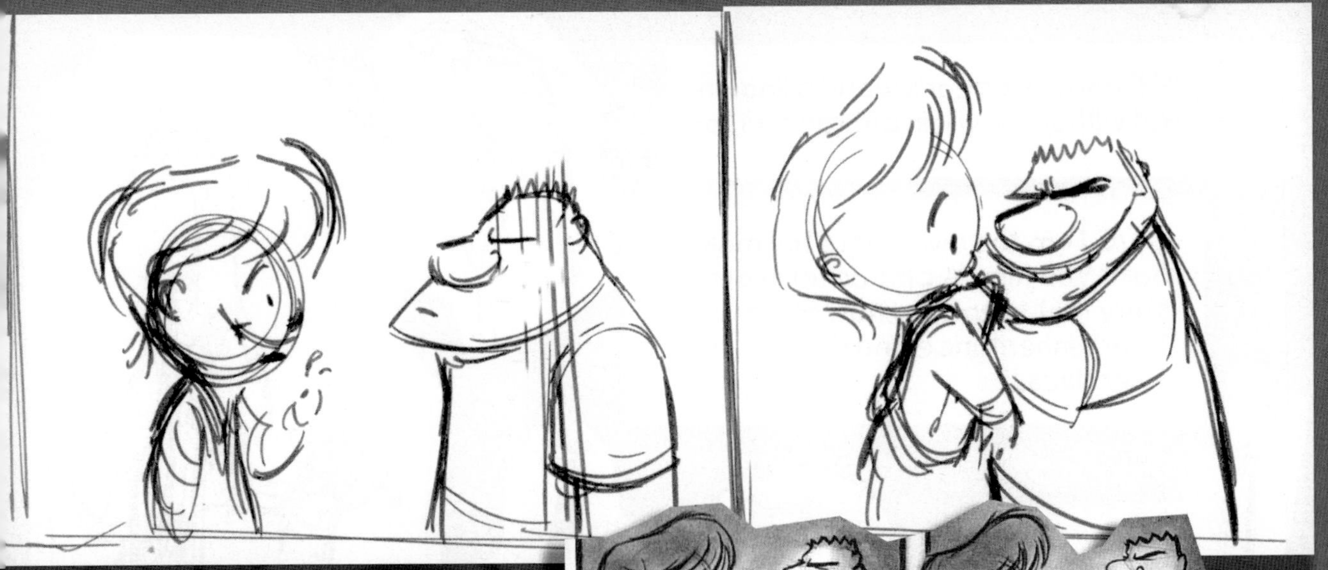

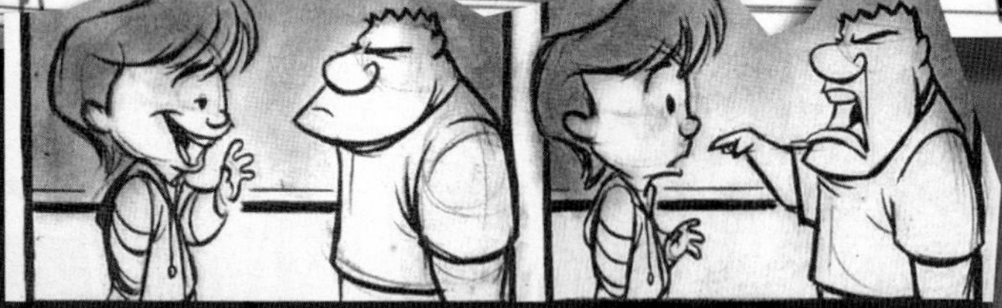

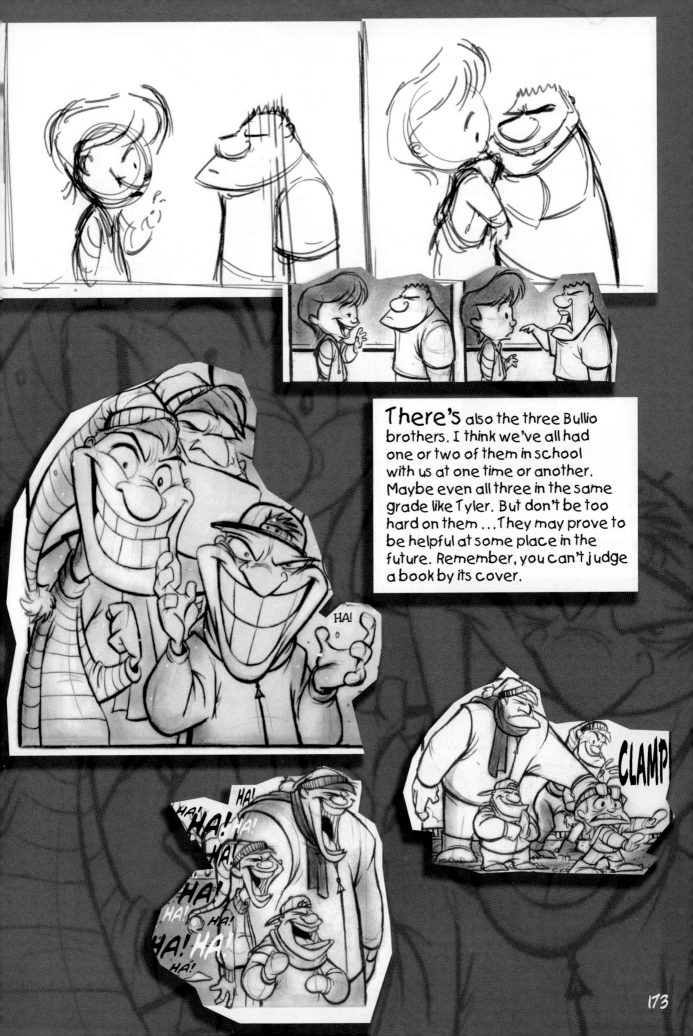

There's also the three Bullio brothers. I think we've all had one or two of them in school with us at one time or another. Maybe even all three in the same grade like Tyler. But don't be too hard on them ... They may prove to be helpful at some place in the future. Remember, you can't judge a book by its cover.

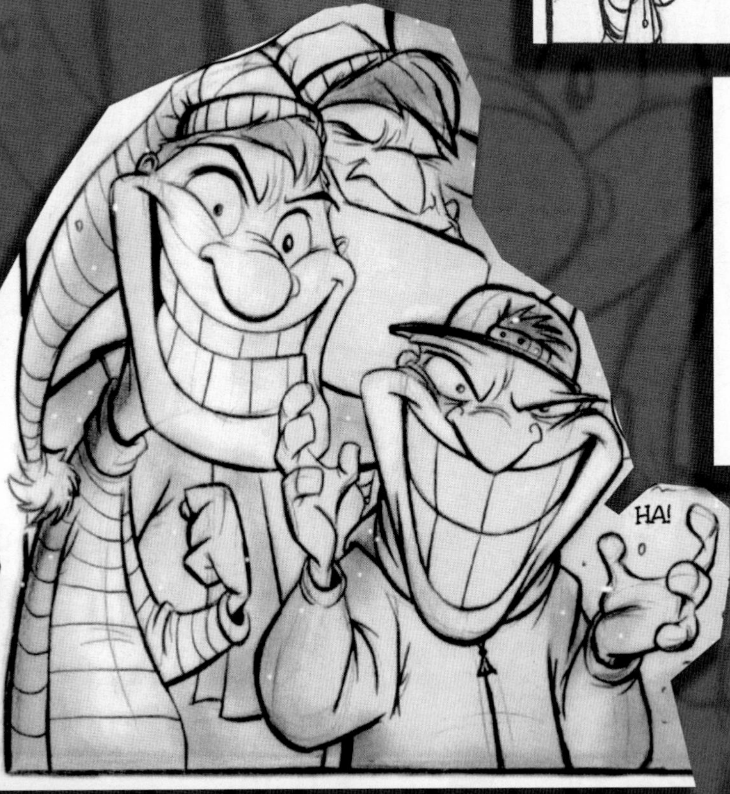
HA!

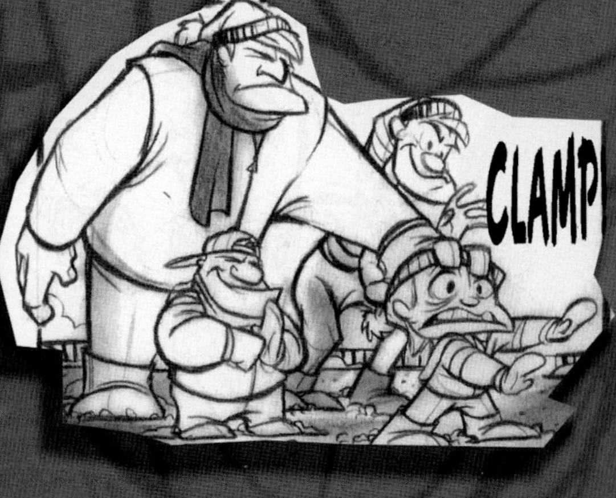
CLAMP!

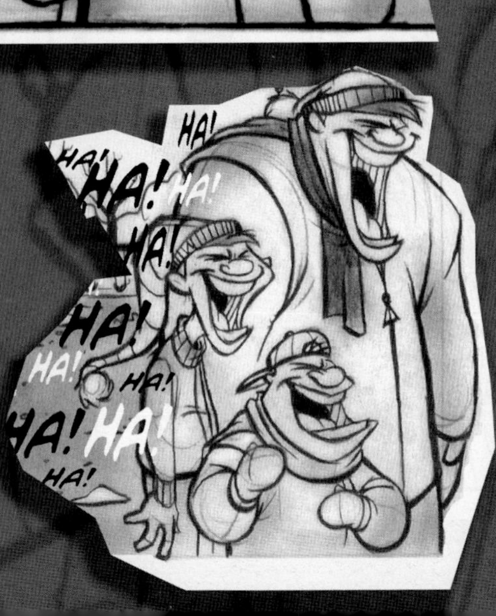
HA!
HA!
HA!
HA!
HA!
HA!
HA!
HA!
HA!
HA!
HA!

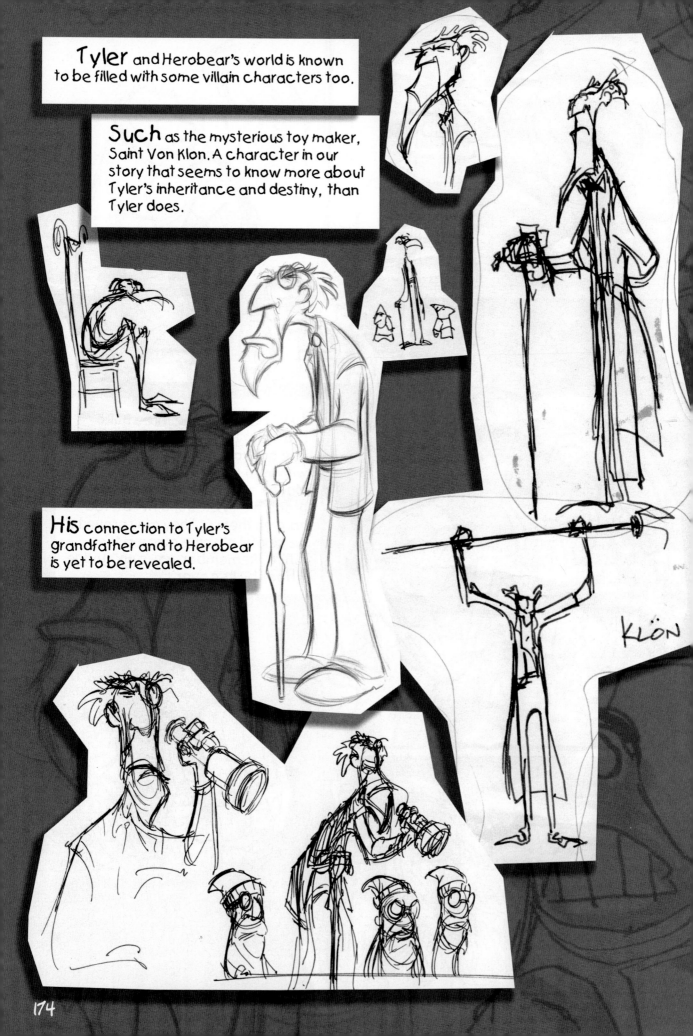

Tyler and Herobear's world is known to be filled with some villain characters too.

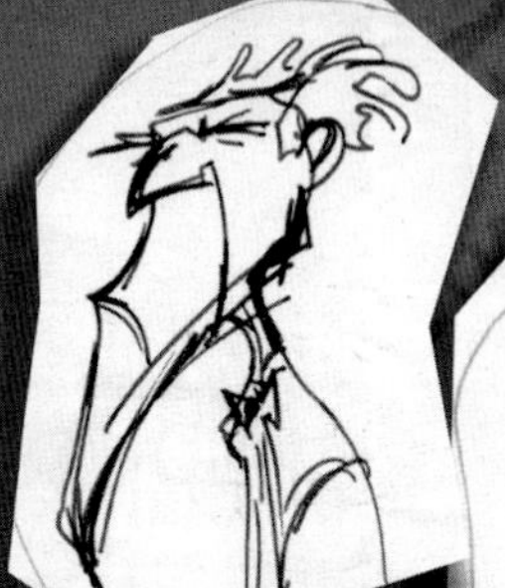

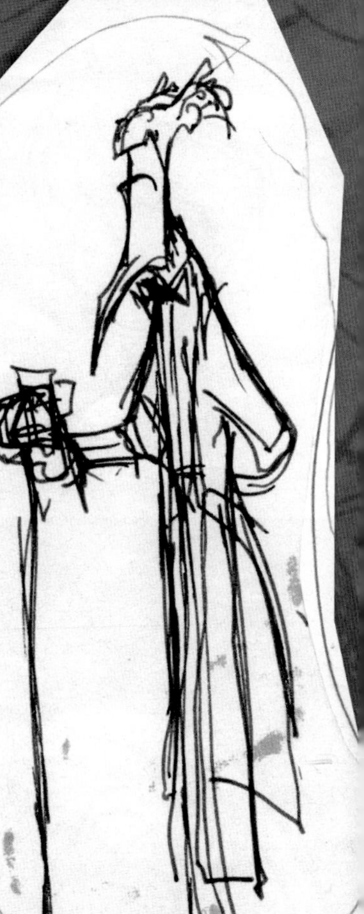
KLÖN

Such as the mysterious toy maker, Saint Von Klon. A character in our story that seems to know more about Tyler's inheritance and destiny, than Tyler does.

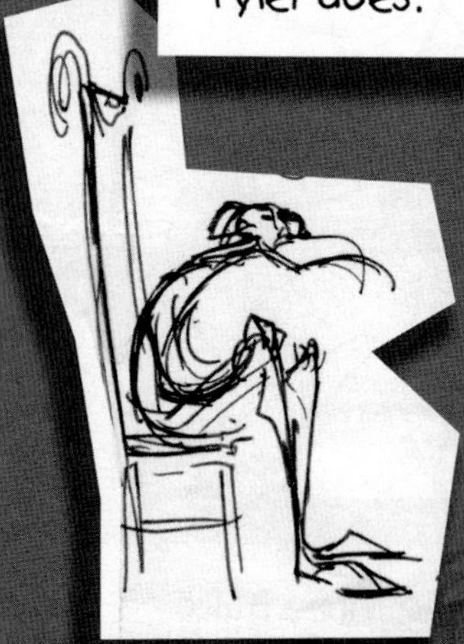

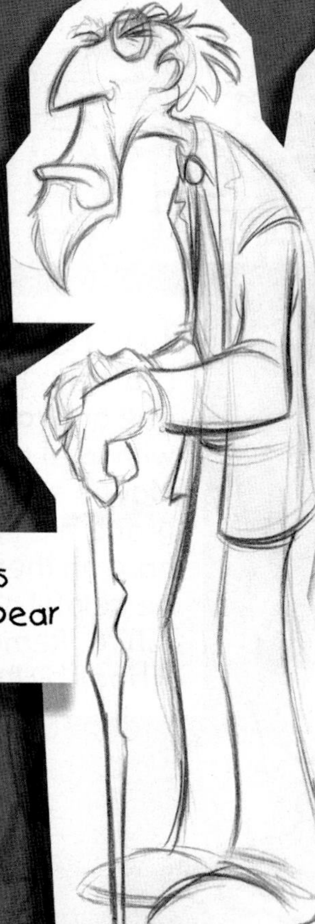

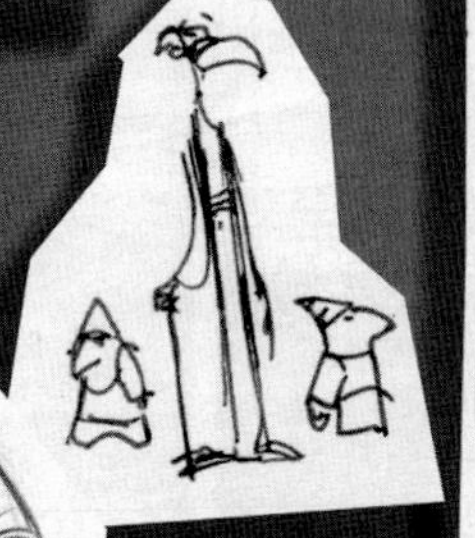

His connection to Tyler's grandfather and to Herobear is yet to be revealed.

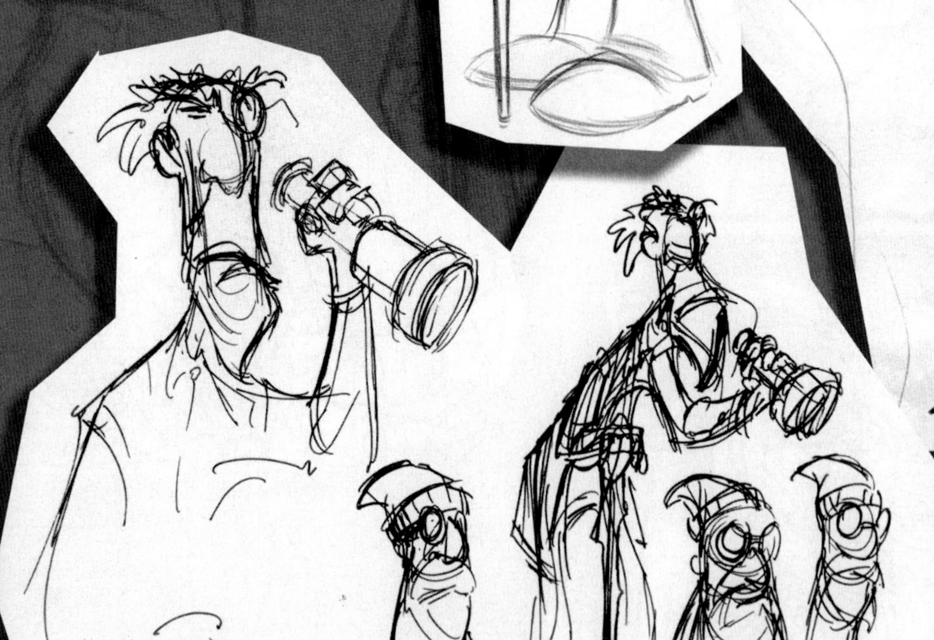

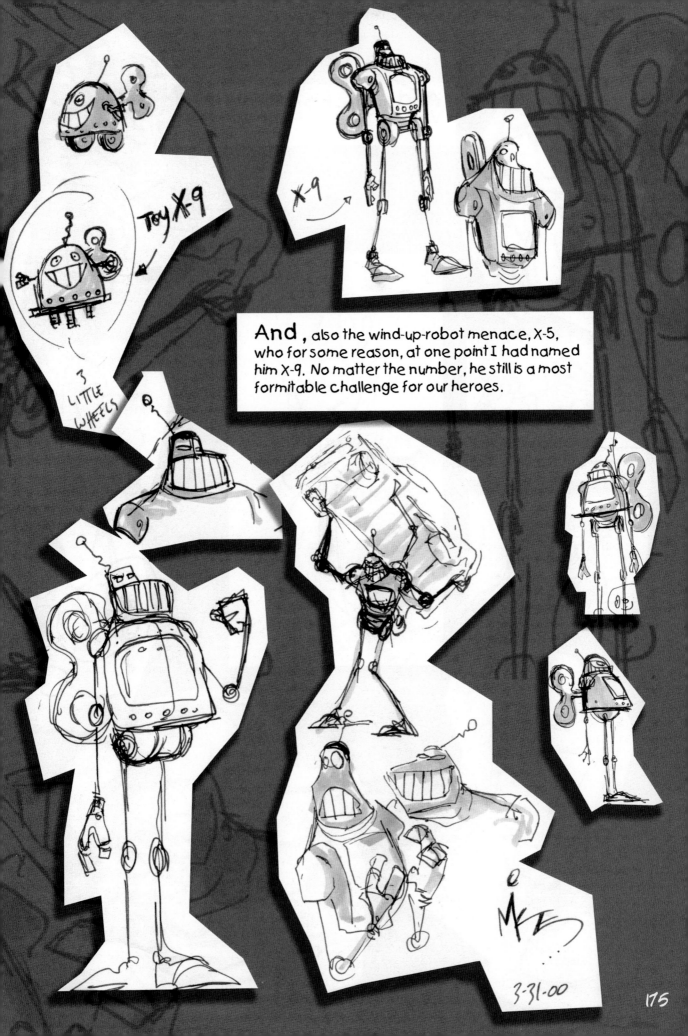

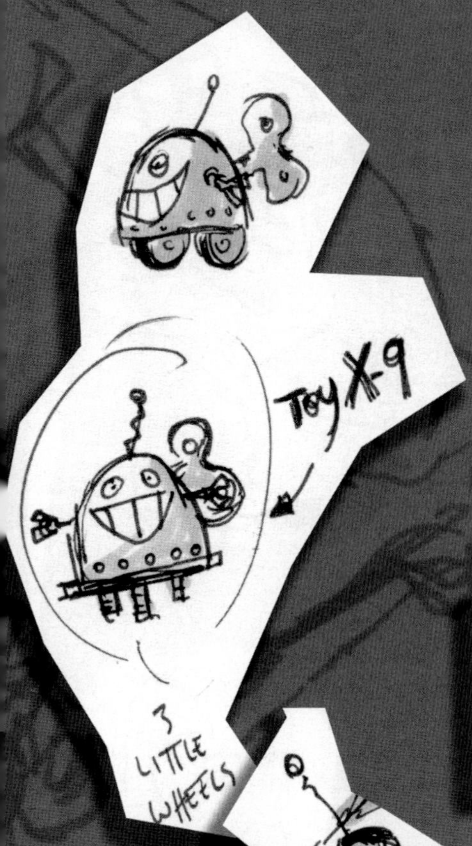
TOY X-9
3 LITTLE WHEELS

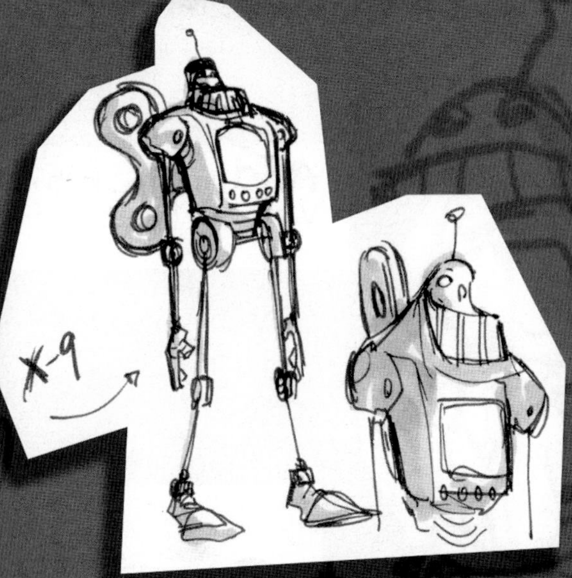
X-9

And, also the wind-up-robot menace, X-5, who for some reason, at one point I had named him X-9. No matter the number, he still is a most formitable challenge for our heroes.

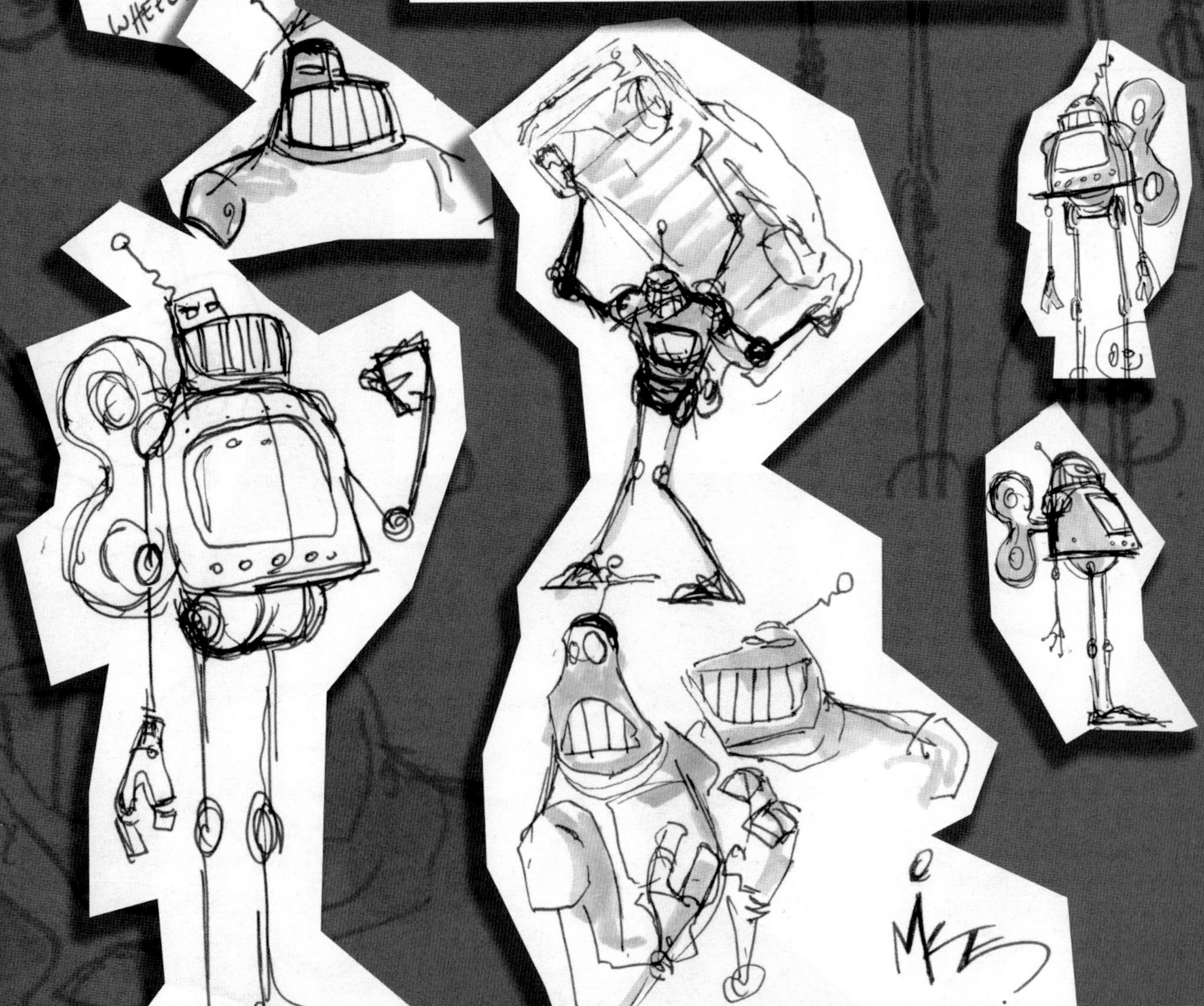
3-31-00

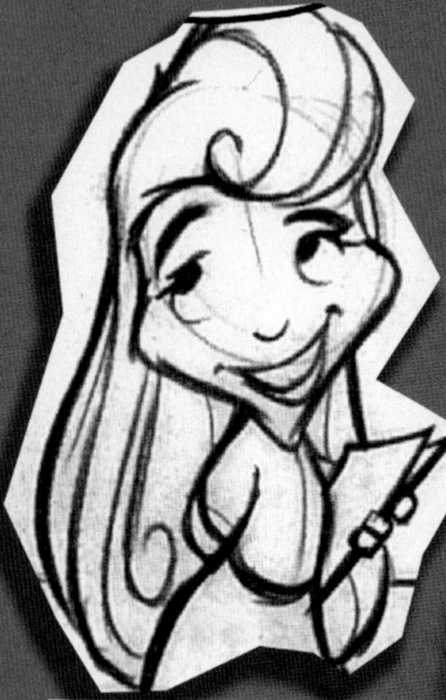

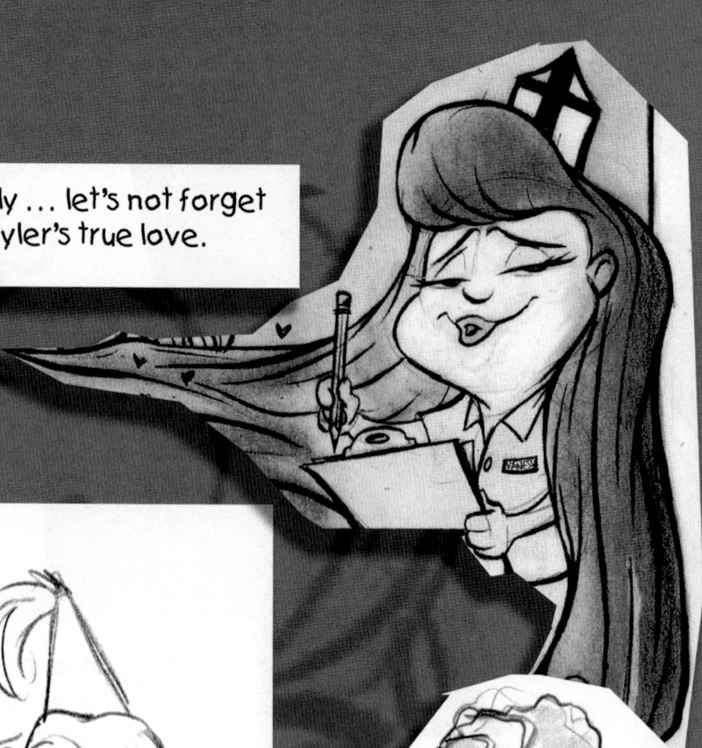

And finally . . . let's not forget Vanessa. Tyler's true love.

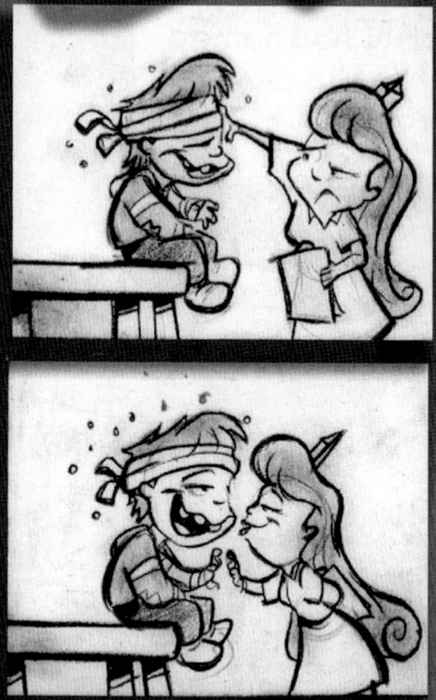

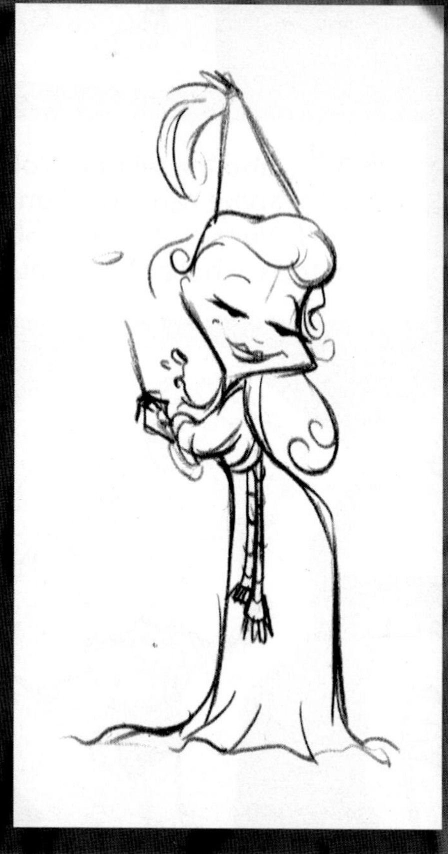

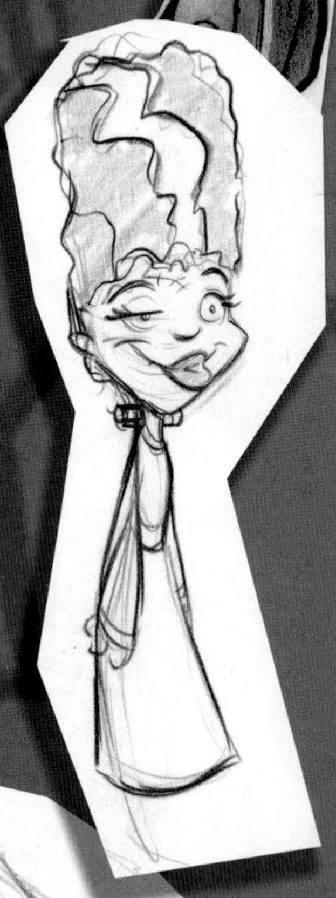

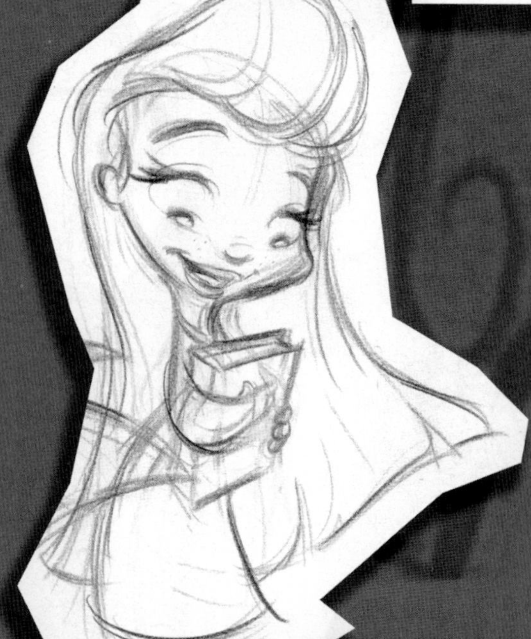

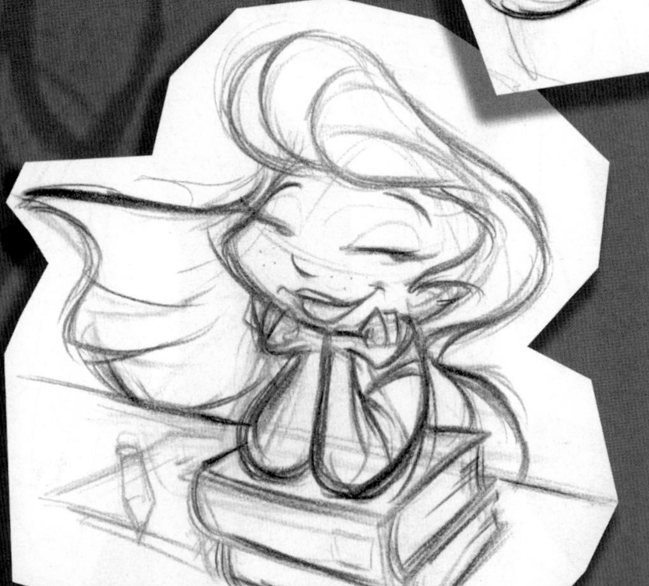

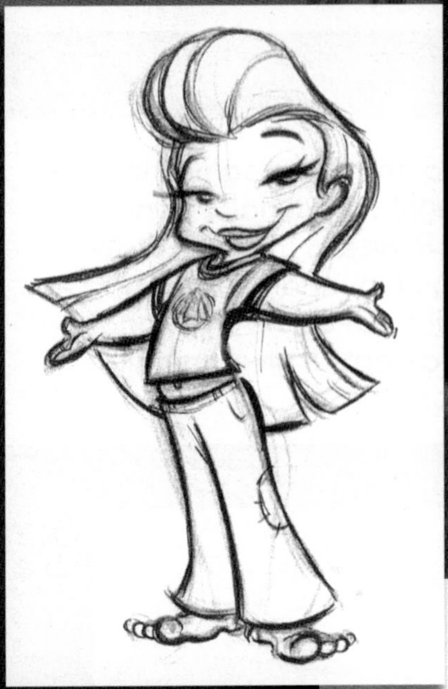
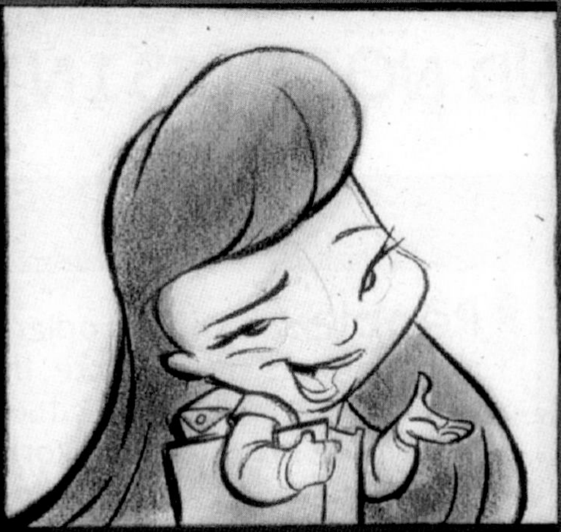
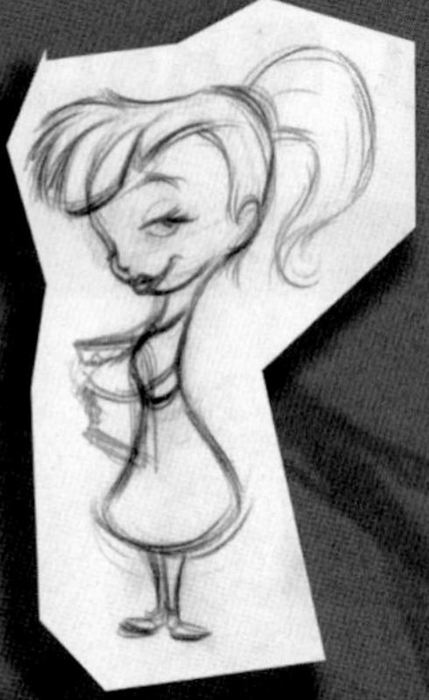

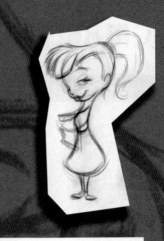

From day one, Tyler fell in love with the sweet Vanessa. And as expected, she usually is the cause of Tyler's crazy daydreams.

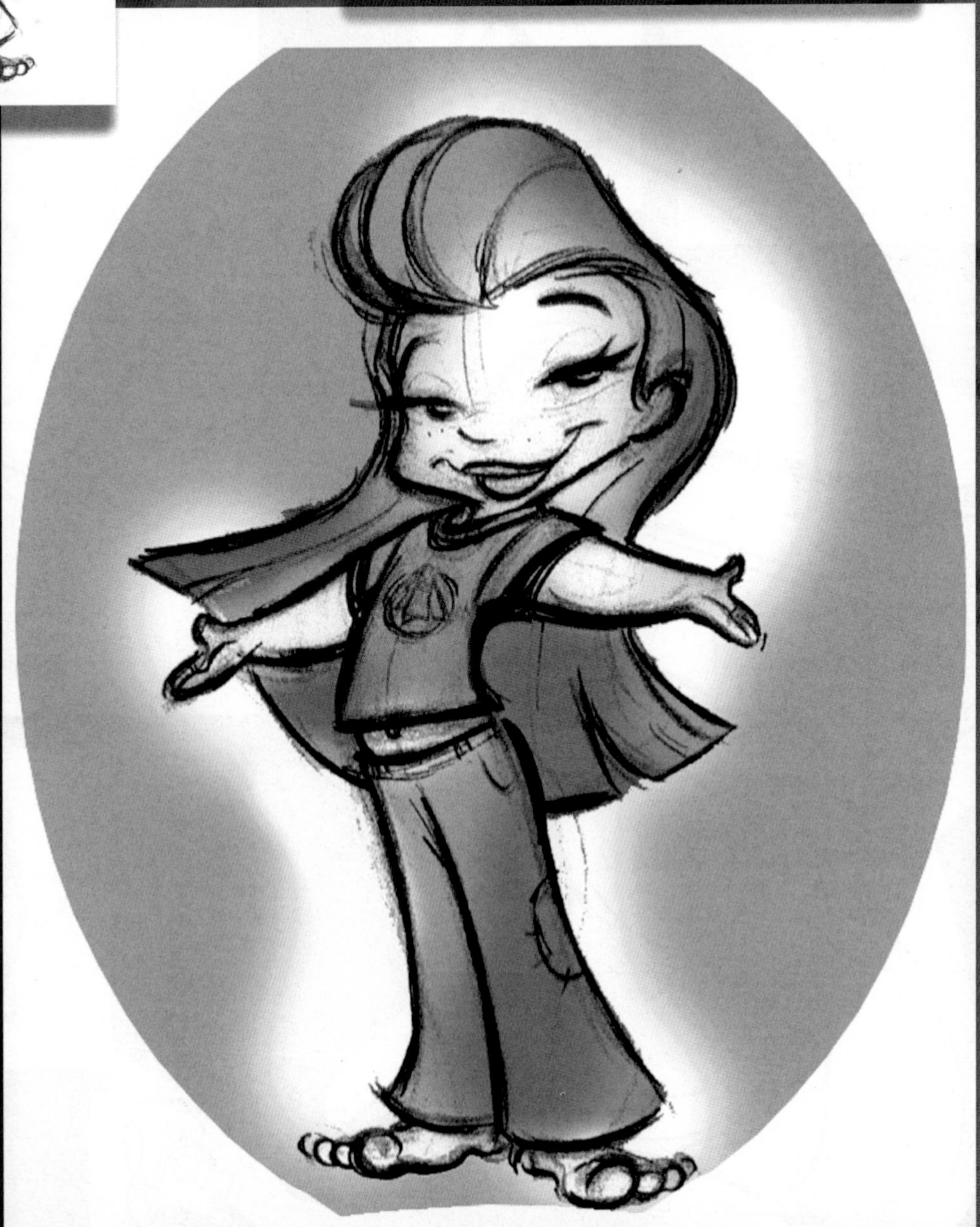

SCRIBBLES AND NOODLES IN THE MORNING.

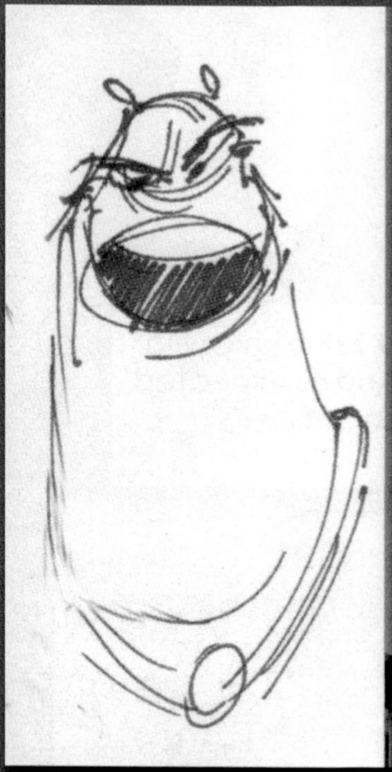

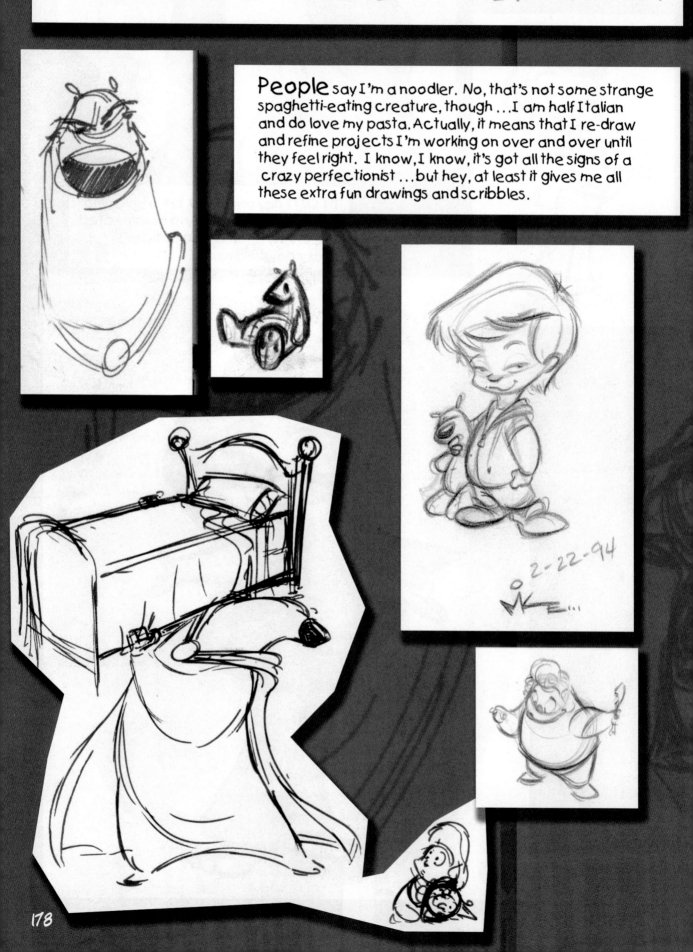

People say I'm a noodler. No, that's not some strange spaghetti-eating creature, though . . . I am half Italian and do love my pasta. Actually, it means that I re-draw and refine projects I'm working on over and over until they feel right. I know, I know, it's got all the signs of a crazy perfectionist . . . but hey, at least it gives me all these extra fun drawings and scribbles.

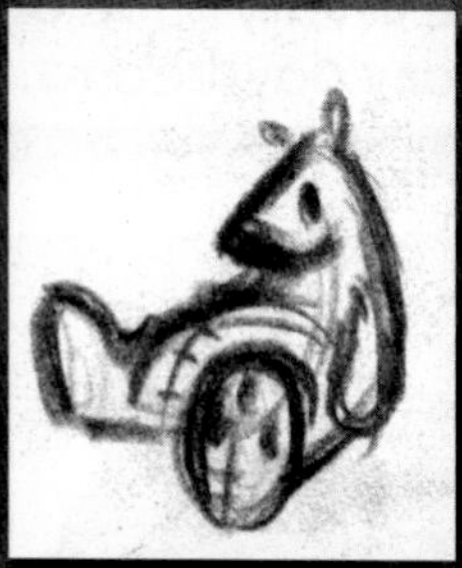

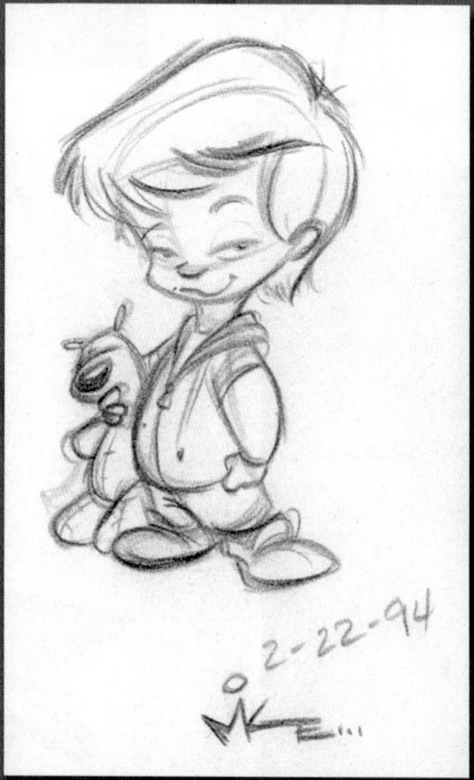
2-22-94

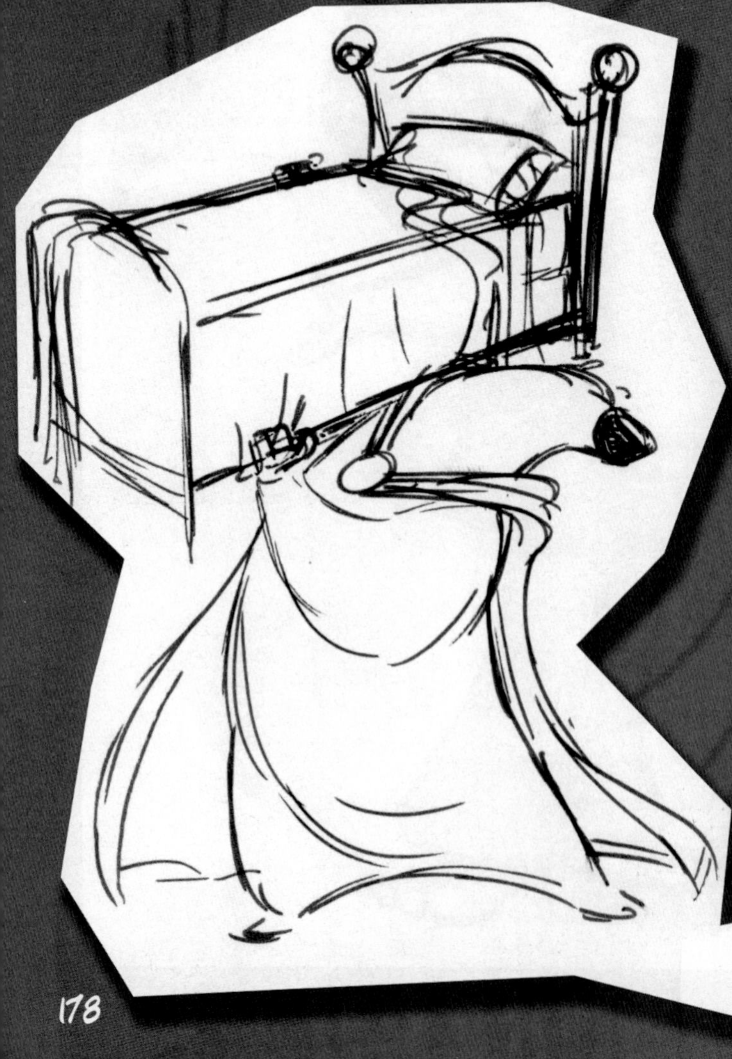

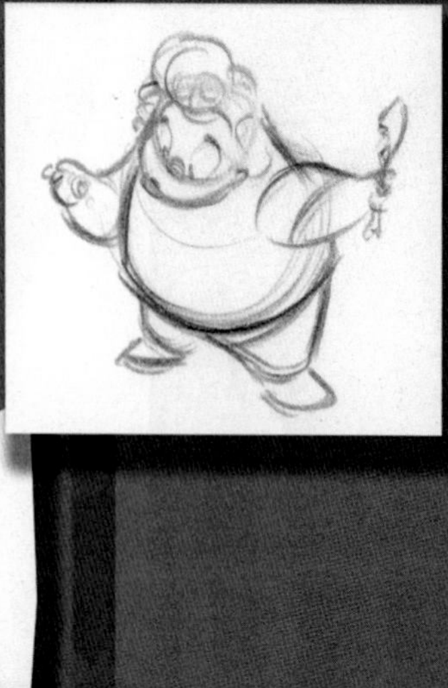

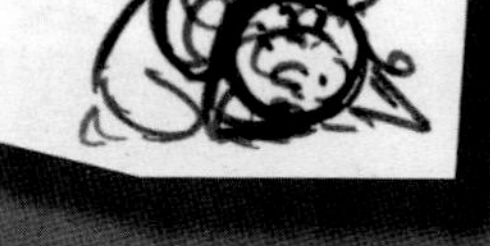

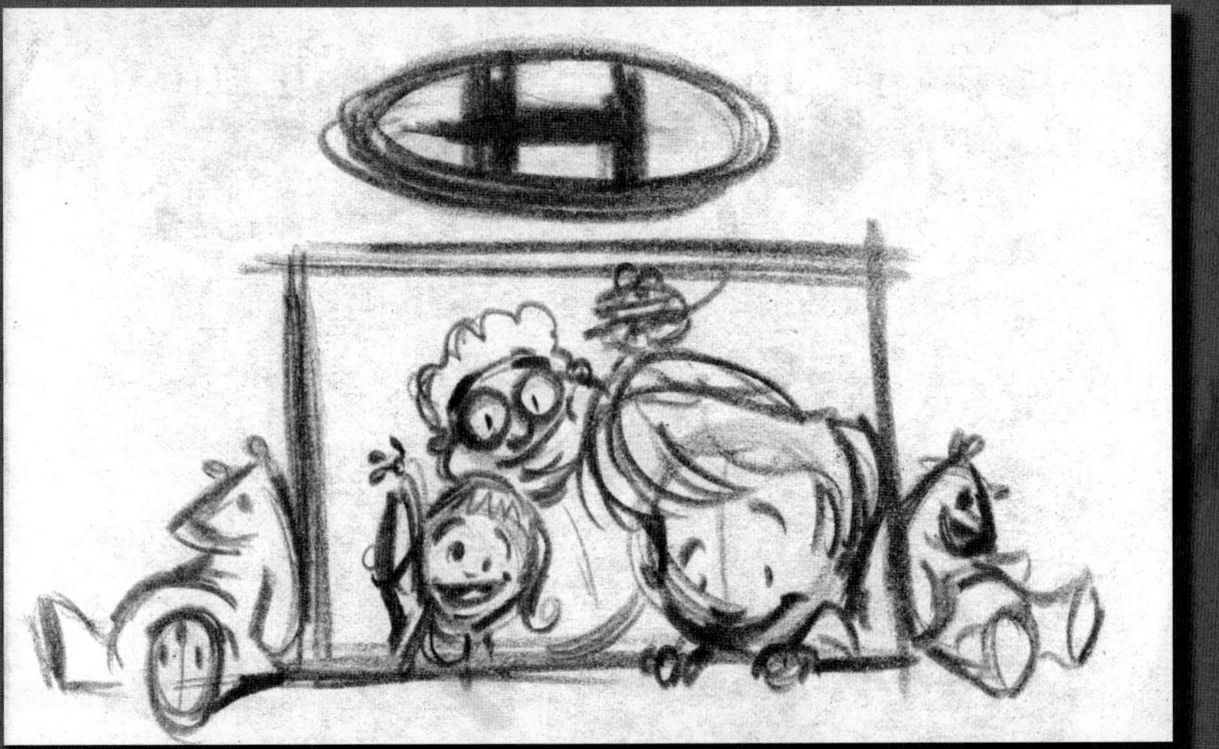

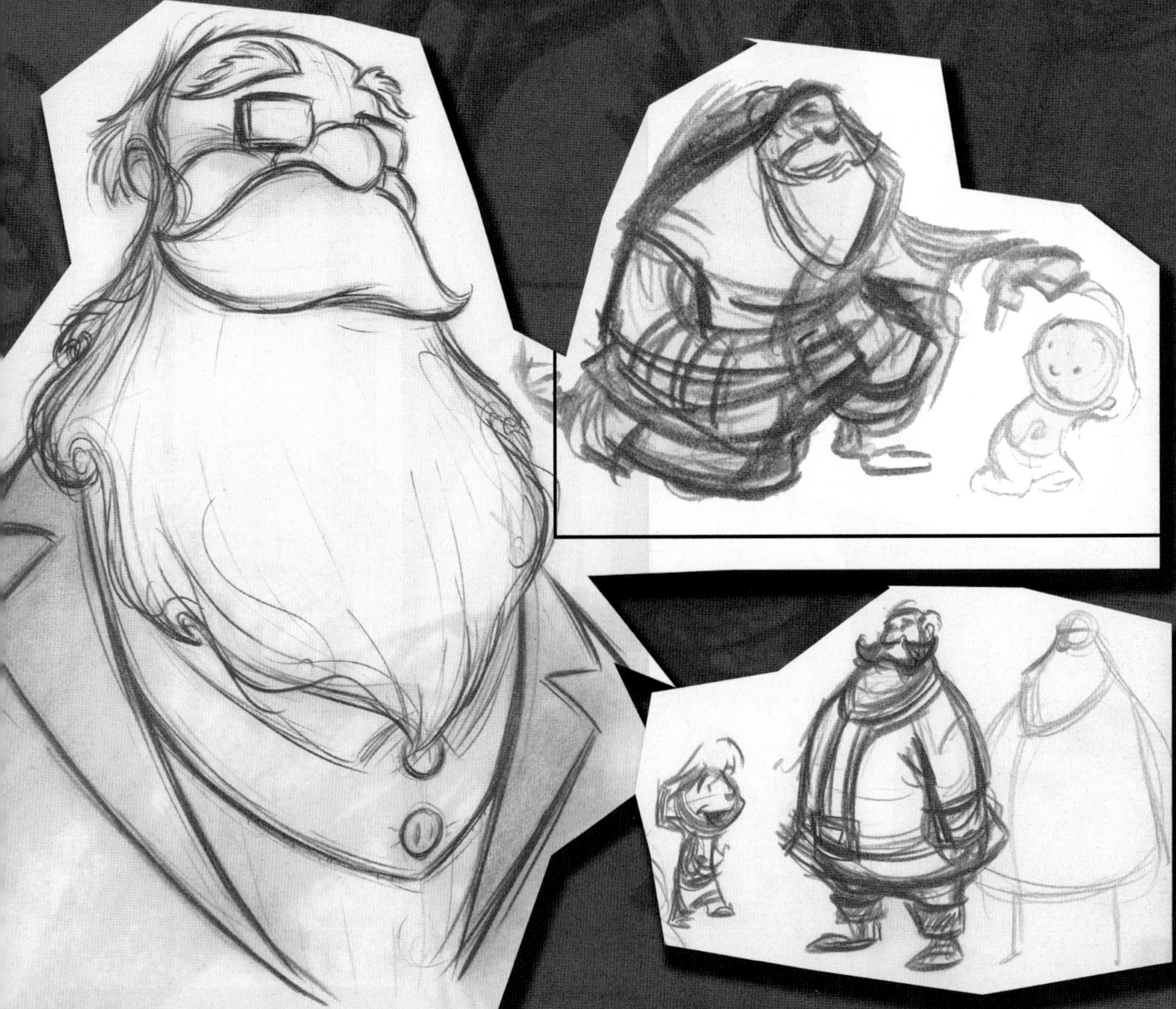

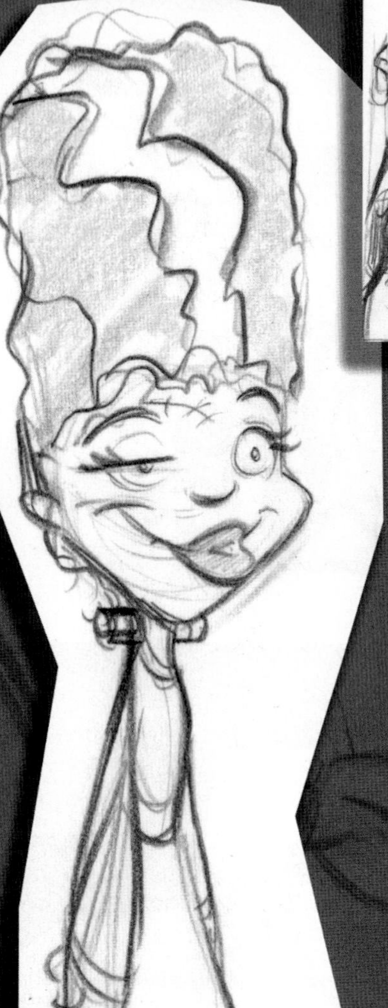

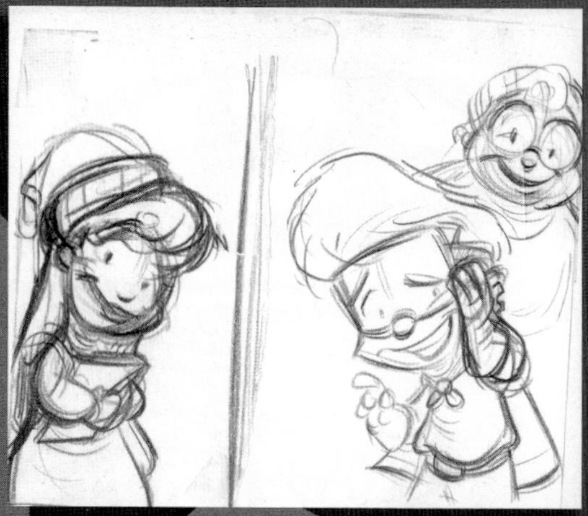

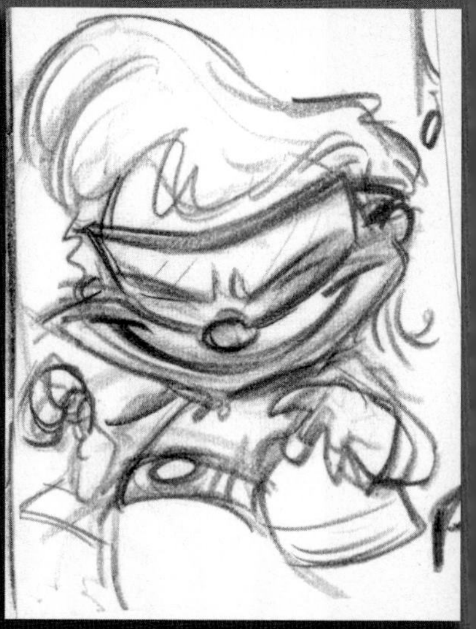

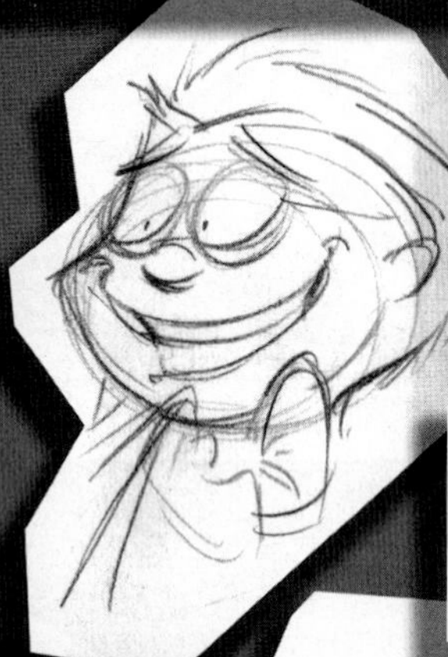

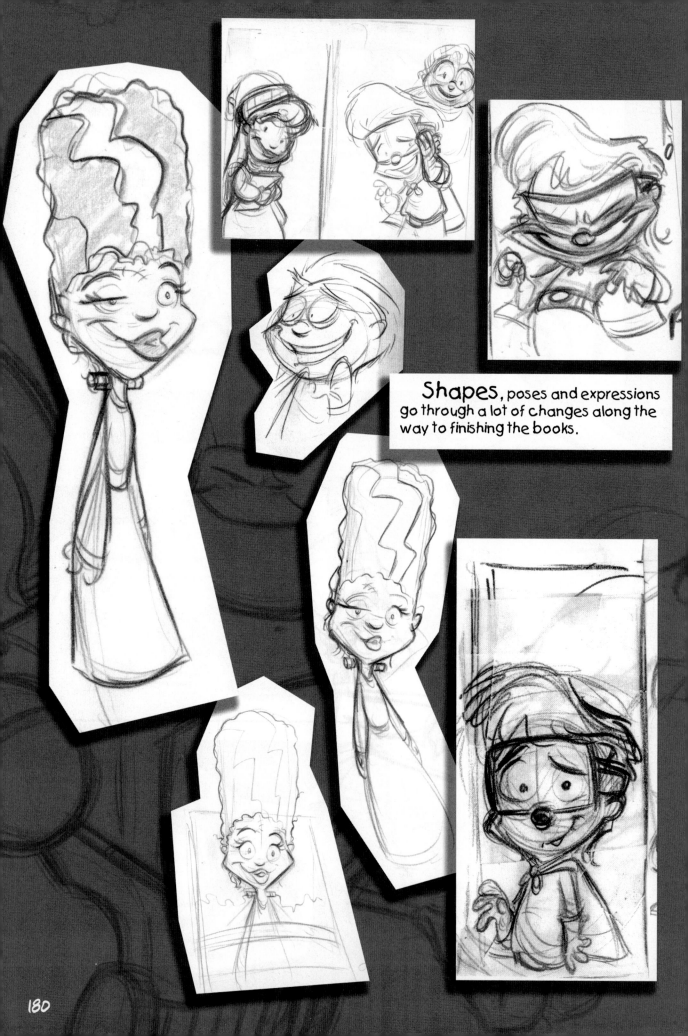

Shapes, poses and expressions go through a lot of changes along the way to finishing the books.

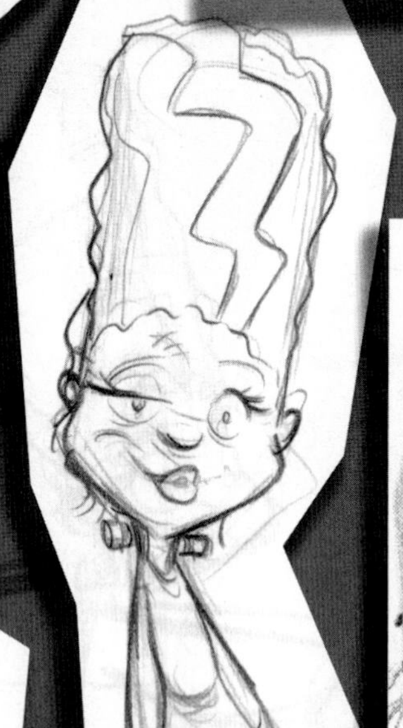

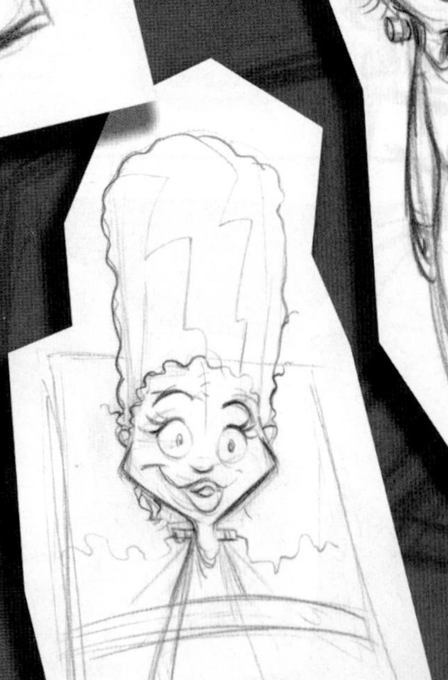

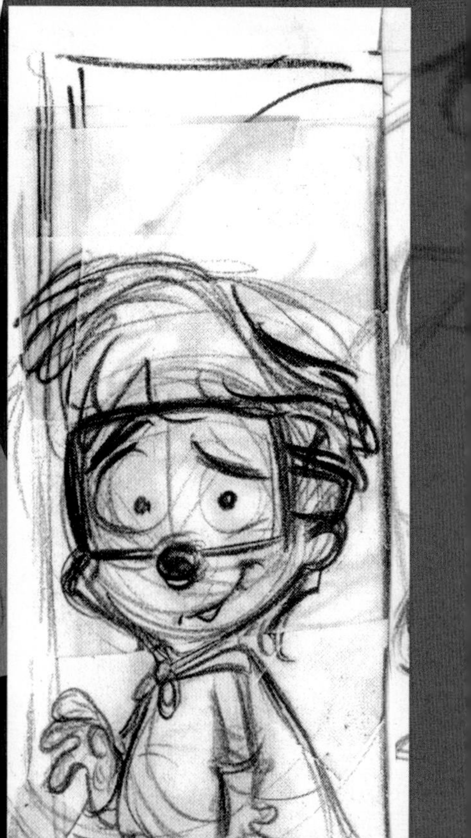

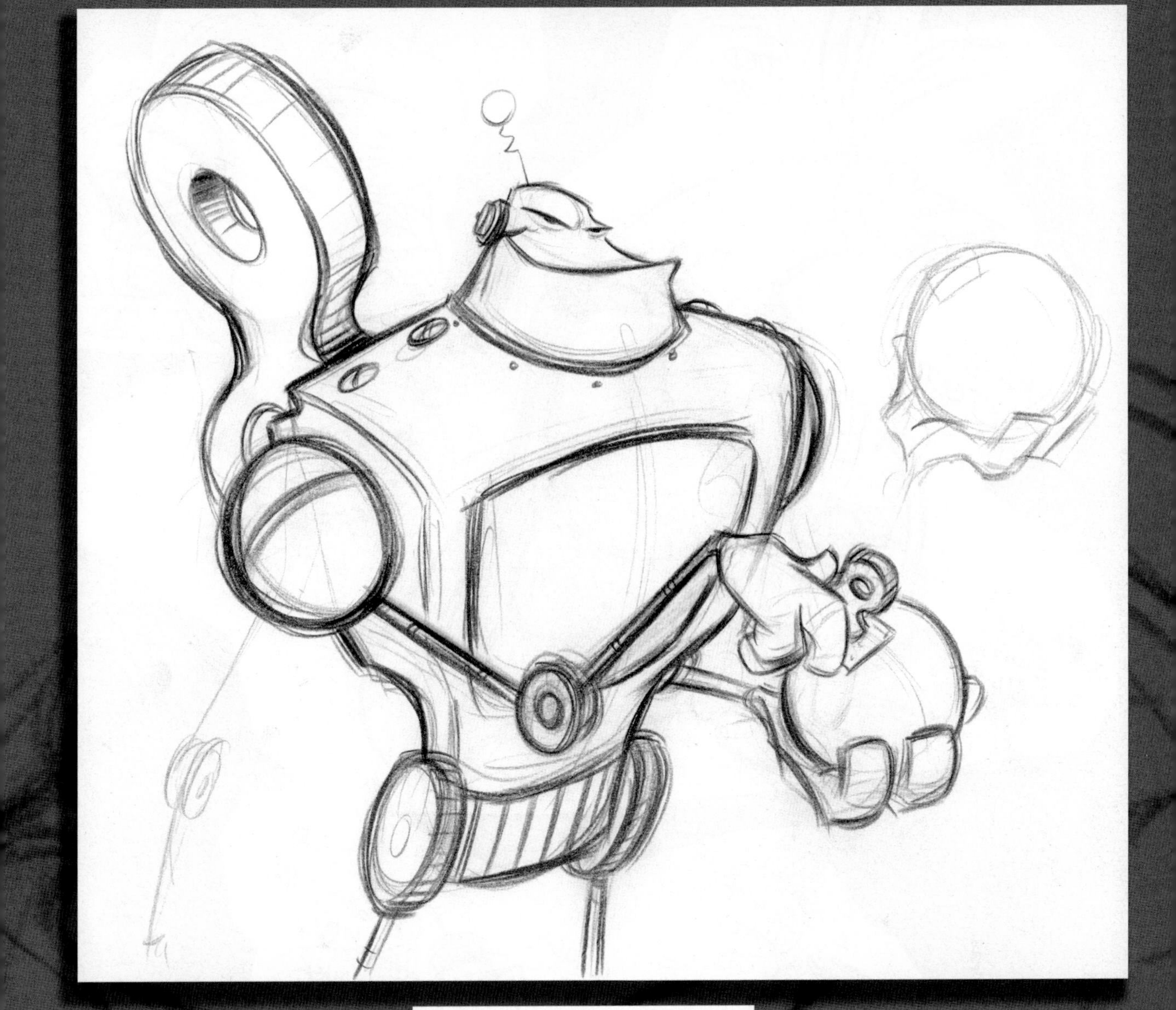

I'll usually redraw poses a few times to get the feel of the right emotion in the expressions.

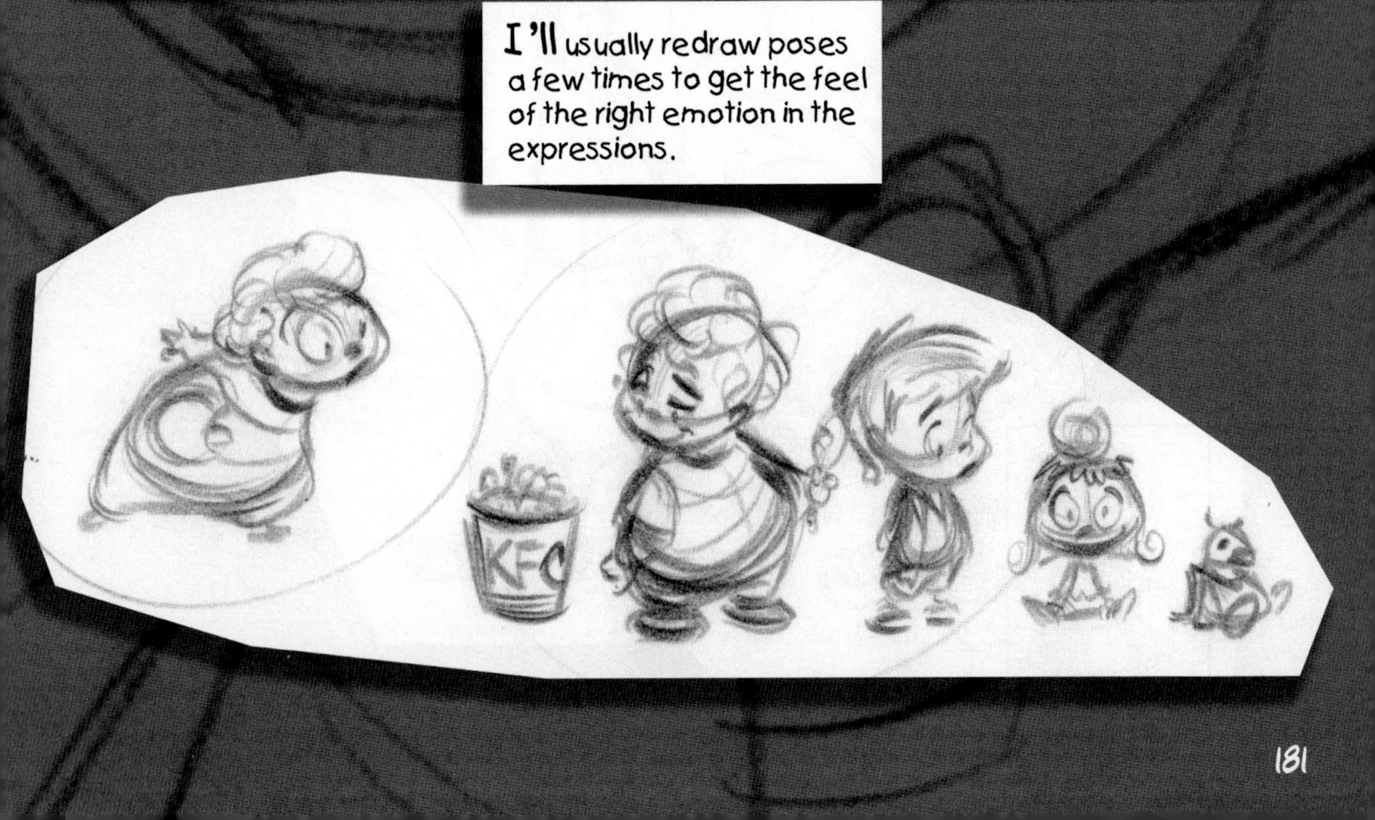
KFC

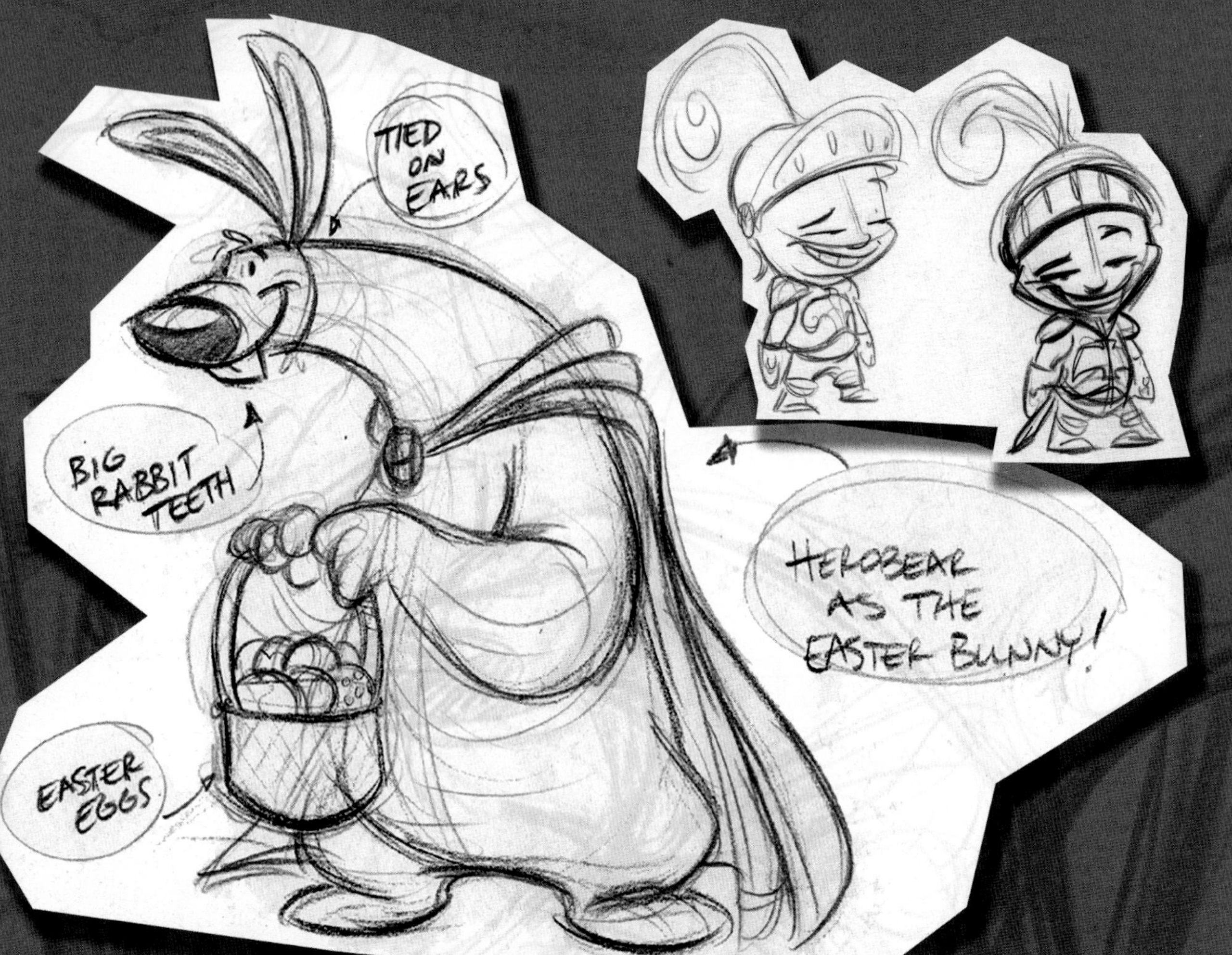
TIED ON EARS
BIG RABBIT TEETH
HEROBEAR AS THE EASTER BUNNY!
EASTER EGGS

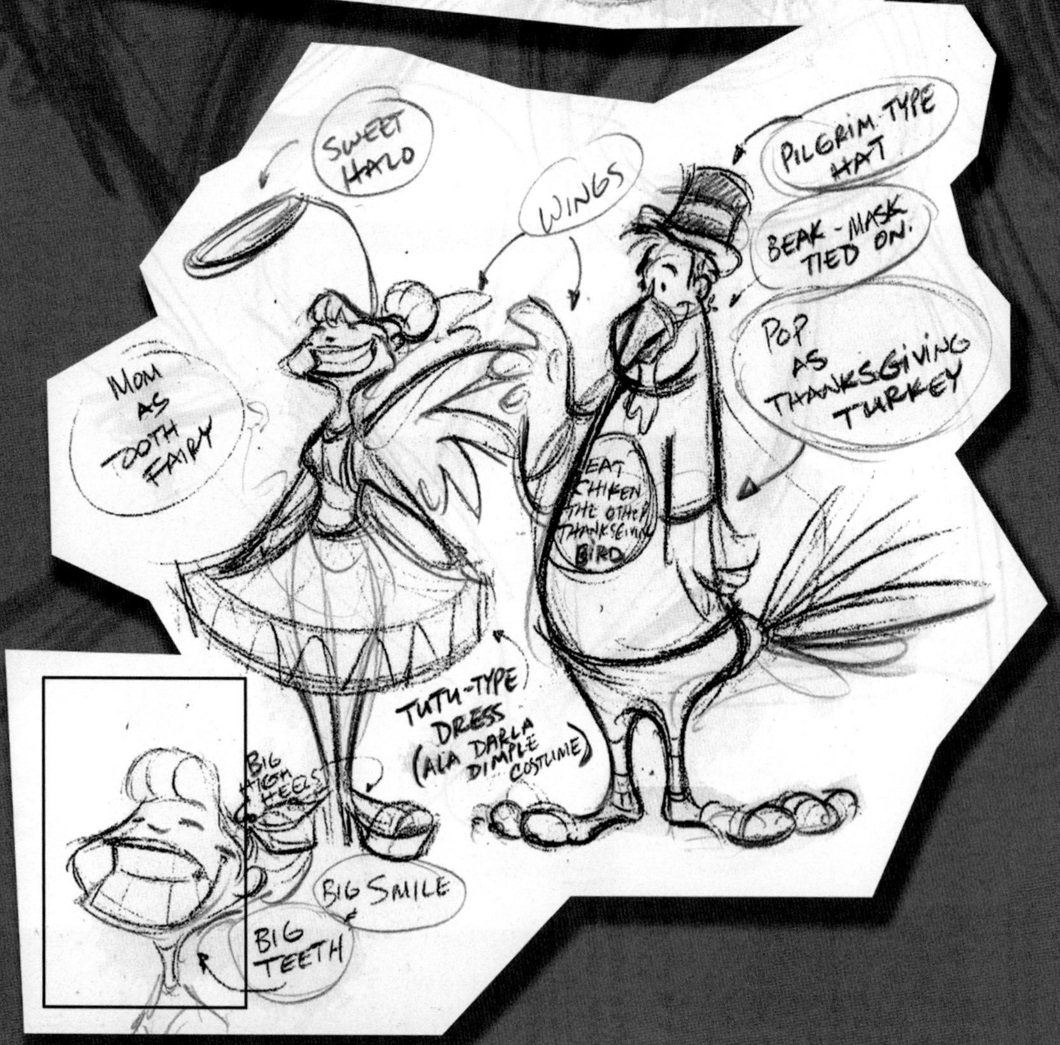
SWEET HALO
WINGS
PILGRIM-TYPE HAT
BEAK-MASK TIED ON.
MOM AS TOOTH FAIRY
POP AS THANKSGIVING TURKEY
EAT CHIKEN THE OTHER THANKSGIVING BIRD
TUTU-TYPE DRESS (ALA DARLA DIMPLE COSTUME)
BIG HIGH HEELS
BIG SMILE
BIG TEETH

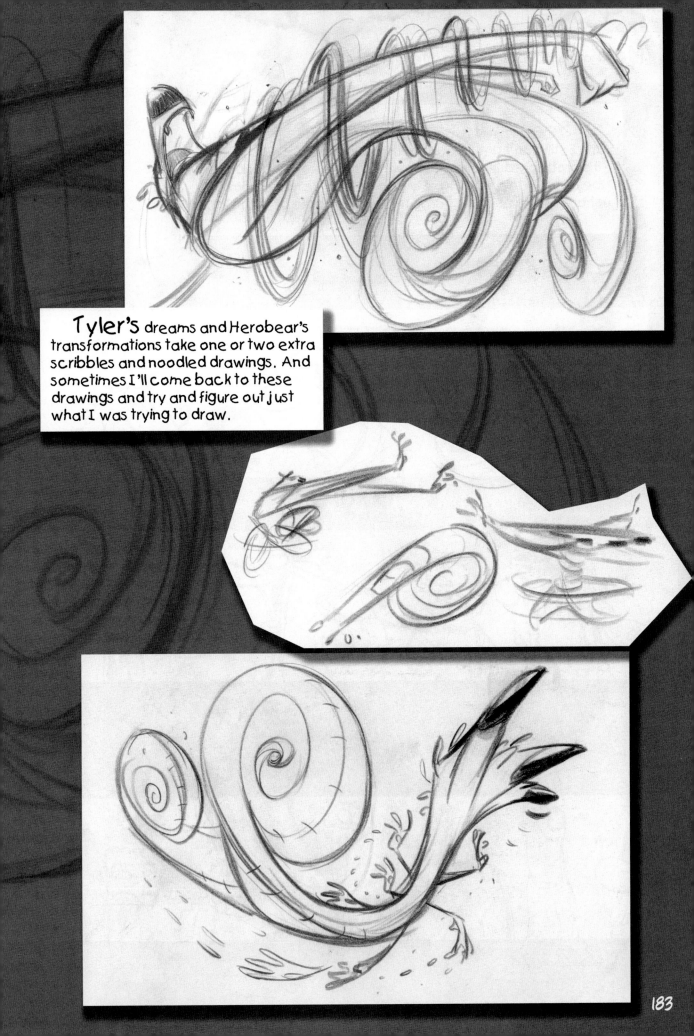

Tyler's dreams and Herobear's transformations take one or two extra scribbles and noodled drawings. And sometimes I'll come back to these drawings and try and figure out just what I was trying to draw.

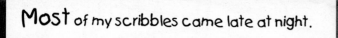

Most of my scribbles came late at night.

See, I'm not a morning person. No matter how hard I try, I still can't get up early with much ease. Of course, it's probably due to my discovering how creative you can be at 1:45 in the morning. I've come up with more of my share of stories and characters in the middle of the night.

I even keep my sketchbook near my bed to write down all the ideas that pop into my head after I've gone to sleep.

Never trust your brain to remember something. Write it down and put a sketch with it right away. You'll be surprised at what you come up with late at night.

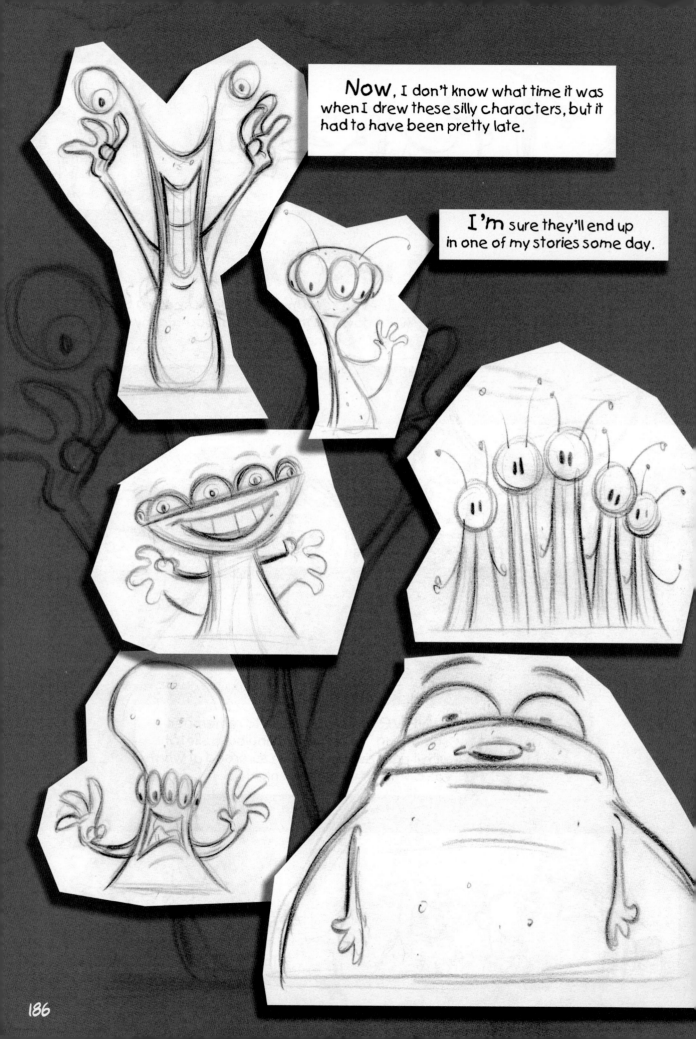

NOW, I don't know what time it was when I drew these silly characters, but it had to have been pretty late.

I'M sure they'll end up in one of my stories some day.

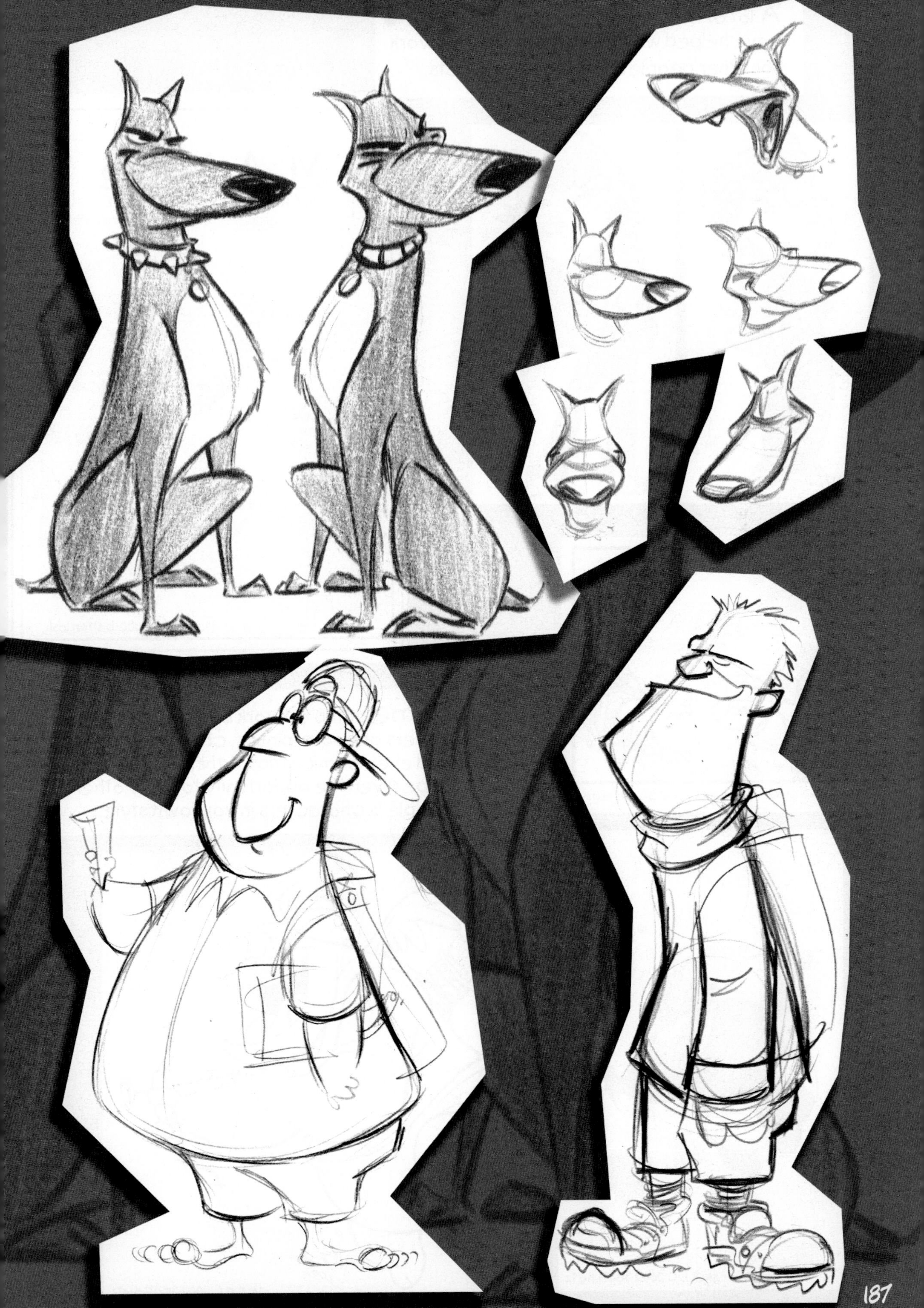

A lot of these late night scribble times have helped when i've been doing artwork for other people's books and projects.

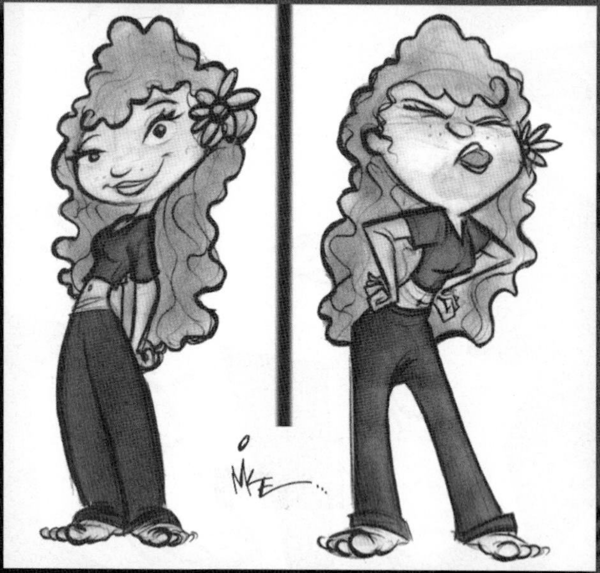

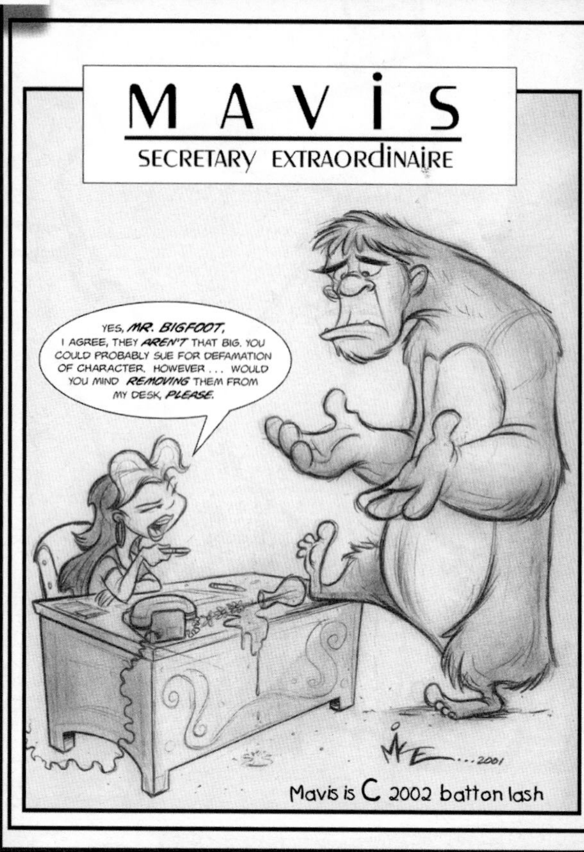
MAViS
SECRETARY EXTRAORdiNAiRE
YES, MR. BIGFOOT, I AGREE, THEY AREN'T THAT BIG. YOU COULD PROBABLY SUE FOR DEFAMATION OF CHARACTER. HOWEVER . . . WOULD YOU MIND REMOVING THEM FROM MY DESK, PLEASE.
Mavis is C 2002 batton lash

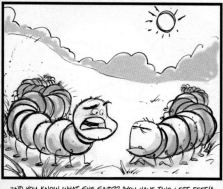

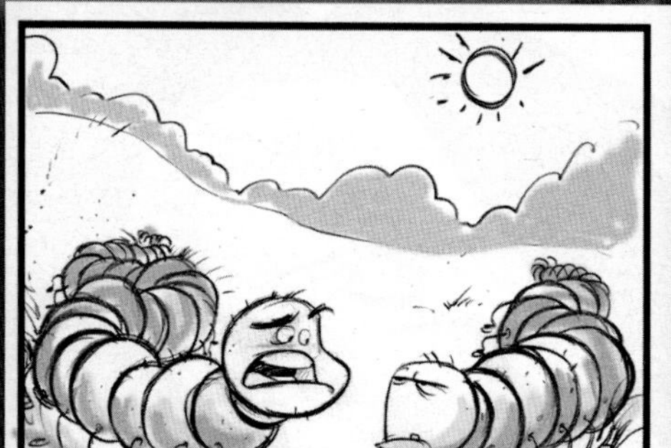
AND YOU KNOW WHAT SHE SAID?? "YOU HAVE TWO LEFT FEET!"

Some of this artwork is for websites, covers of books, pinups, character ideas, and even comic strips. I think it's really fun to be given the opportunity to draw other people 's characters in your own style.

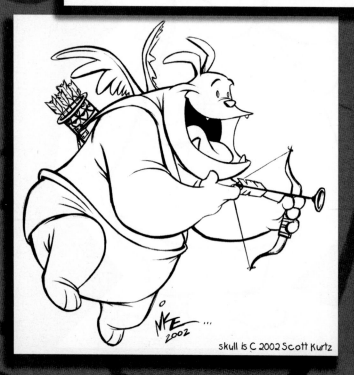

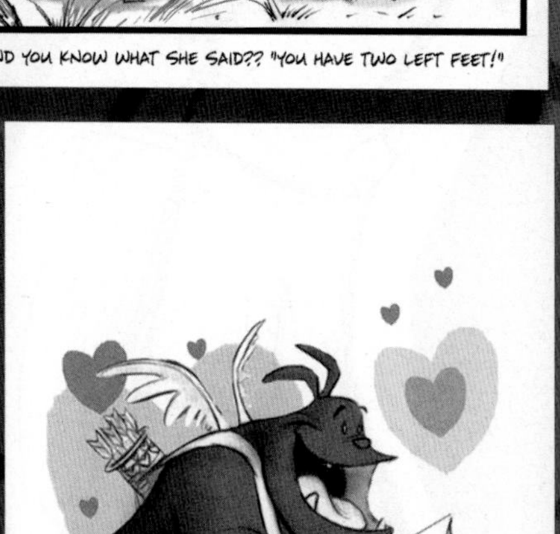
skull is C 2002 Scott Kurtz

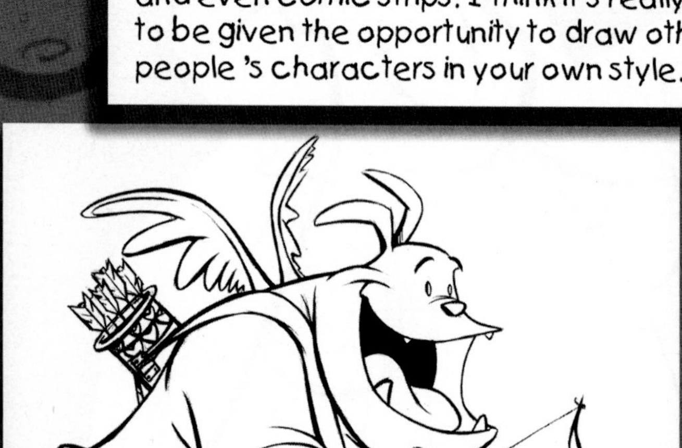
skull is C 2002 Scott Kurtz

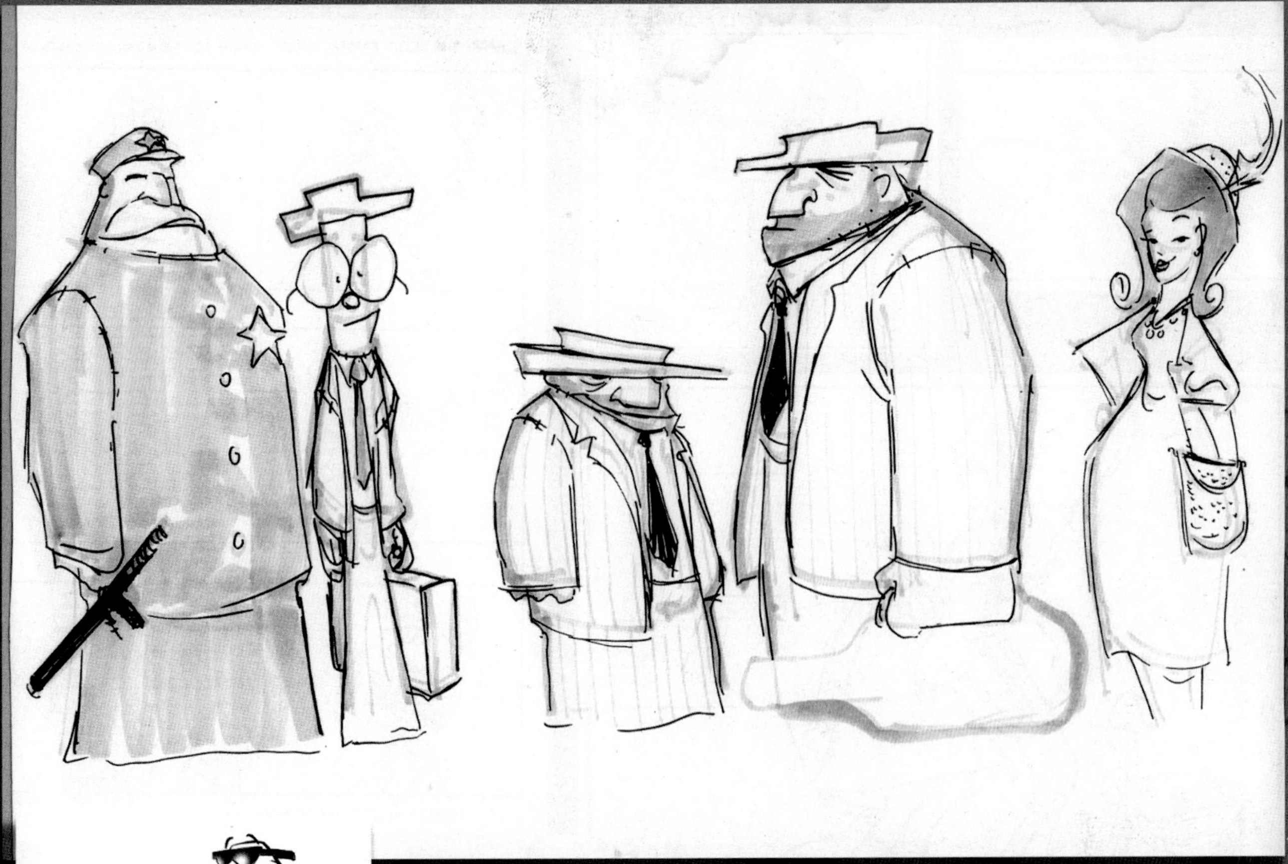

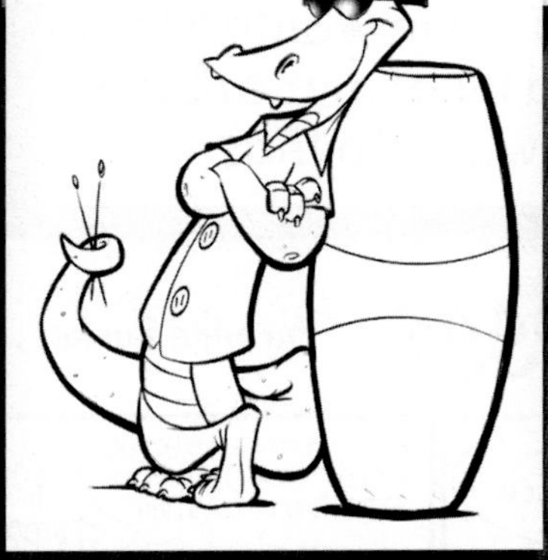

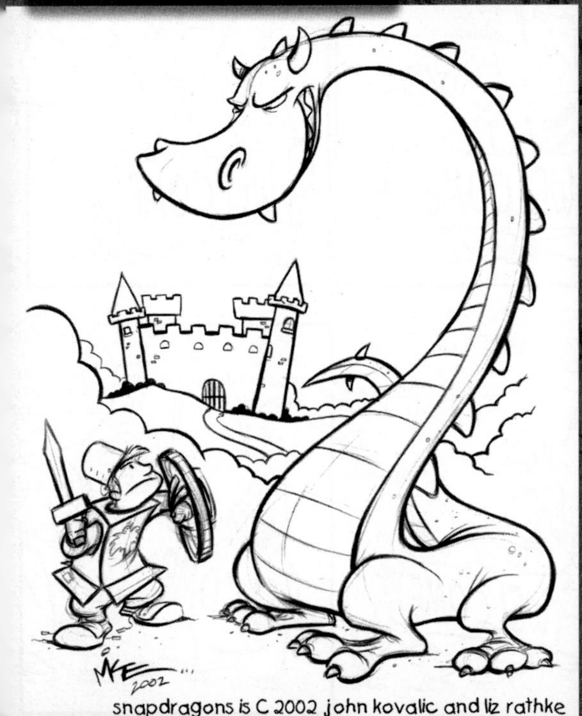
snapdragons is C 2002 john kovalic and liz rathke

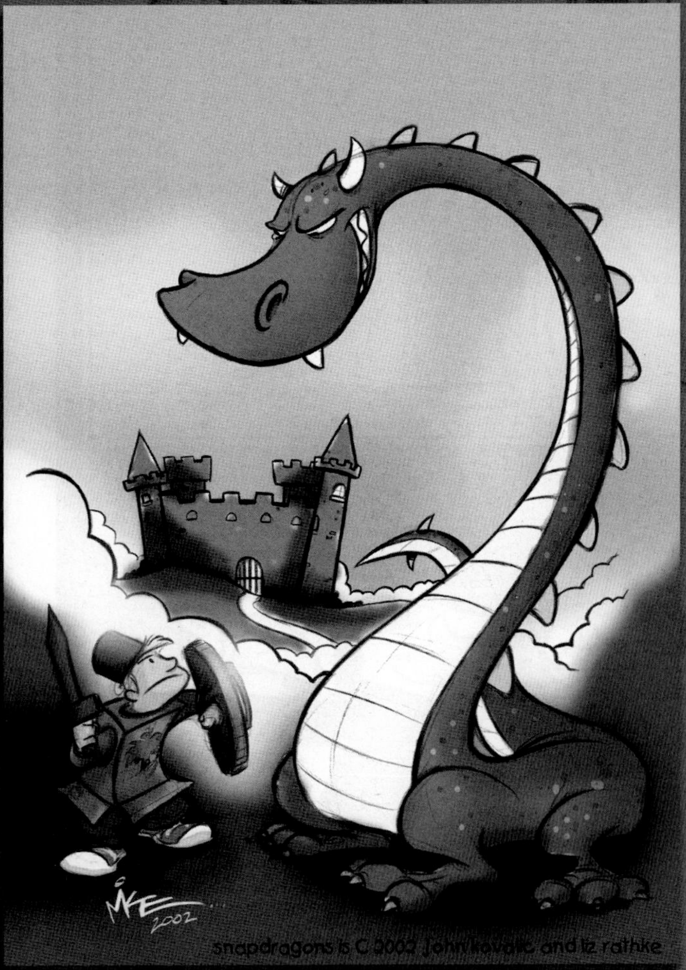
snapdragons is C 2002 john kovalic and liz rathke

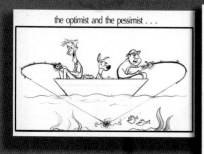

the optimist and the pessimist . . .

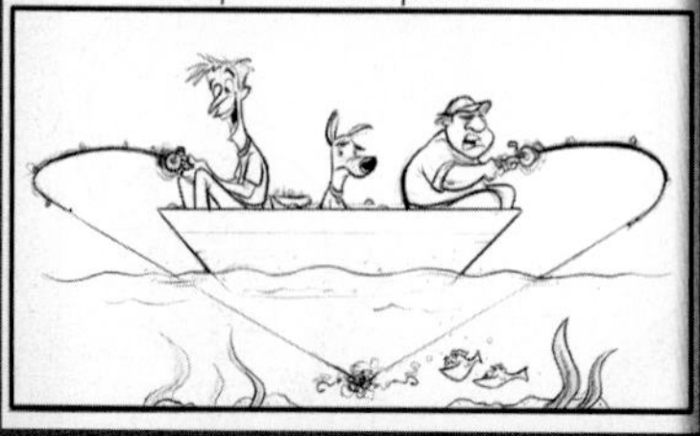

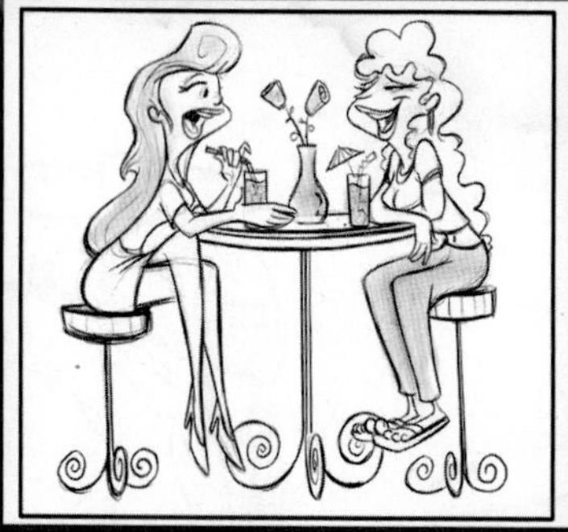

HARRY THE BLIND BARBER ROUGH POSES FOR NEW YORKER CARTOON

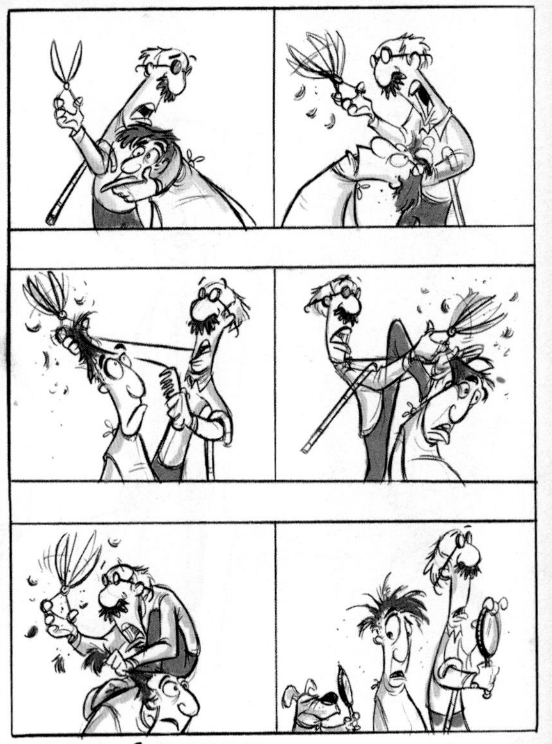

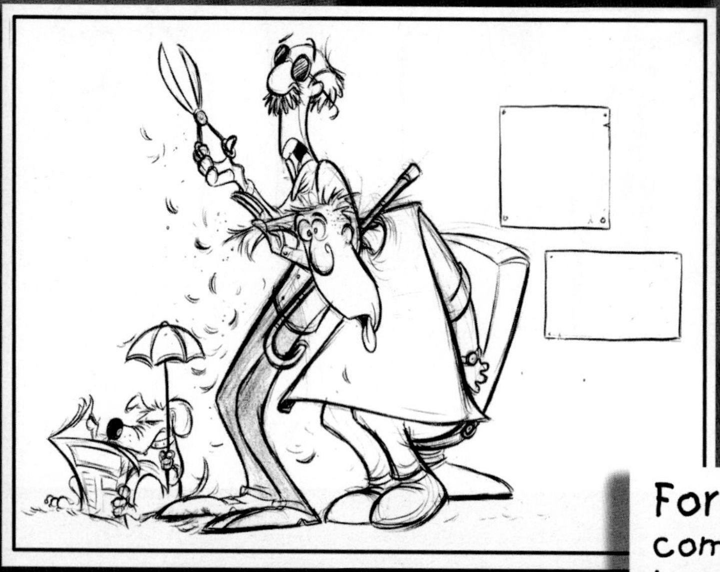

For a long time, I have wanted to do comic strips, so a lot of my scribbles have found their way into those.

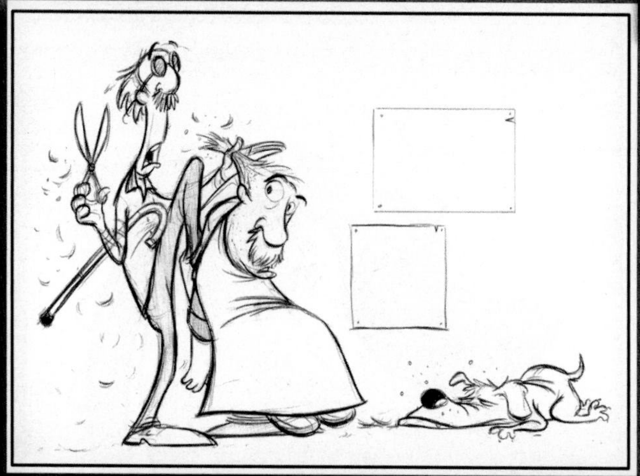

ham and eggs by mike kunkel . . .

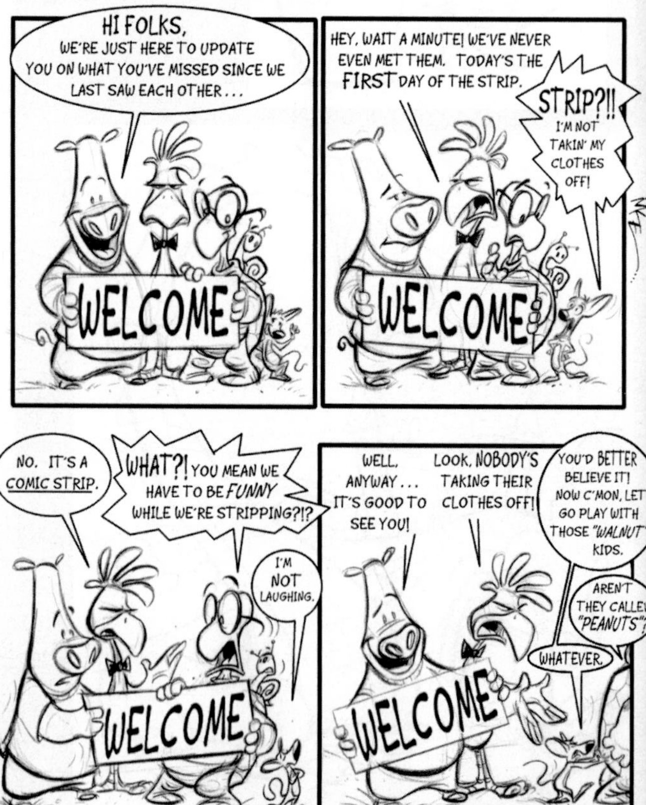
HI FOLKS, WE'RE JUST HERE TO UPDATE YOU ON WHAT YOU'VE MISSED SINCE WE LAST SAW EACH OTHER . . .
WELCOME
HEY, WAIT A MINUTE! WE'VE NEVER EVEN MET THEM. TODAY'S THE FIRST DAY OF THE STRIP.
STRIP?!! I'M NOT TAKIN' MY CLOTHES OFF!
WELCOME
NO. IT'S A COMIC STRIP.
WHAT?! YOU MEAN WE HAVE TO BE FUNNY WHILE WE'RE STRIPPING?!?
I'M NOT LAUGHING.
WELCOME
WELL, ANYWAY . . . IT'S GOOD TO SEE YOU!
LOOK, NOBODY'S TAKING THEIR CLOTHES OFF!
YOU'D BETTER BELIEVE IT! NOW C'MON, LET'S GO PLAY WITH THOSE "WALNUT" KIDS.
AREN'T THEY CALLED "PEANUTS"?
WHATEVER.
WELCOME

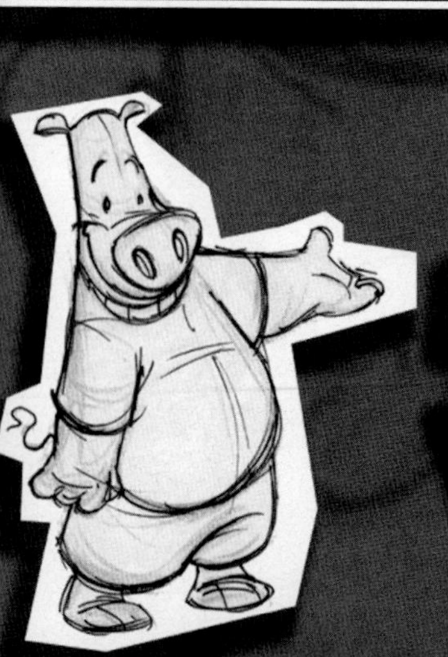

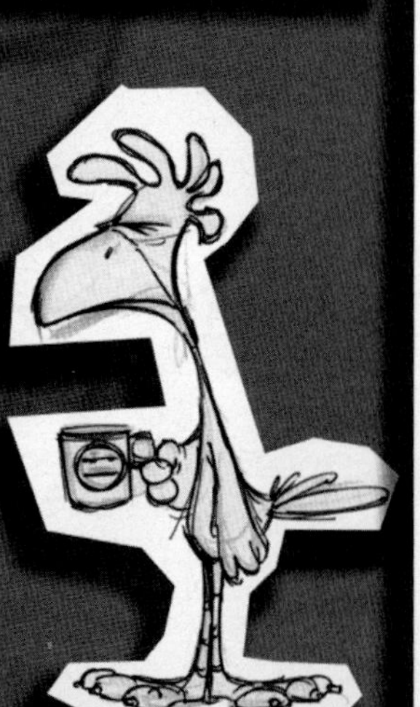

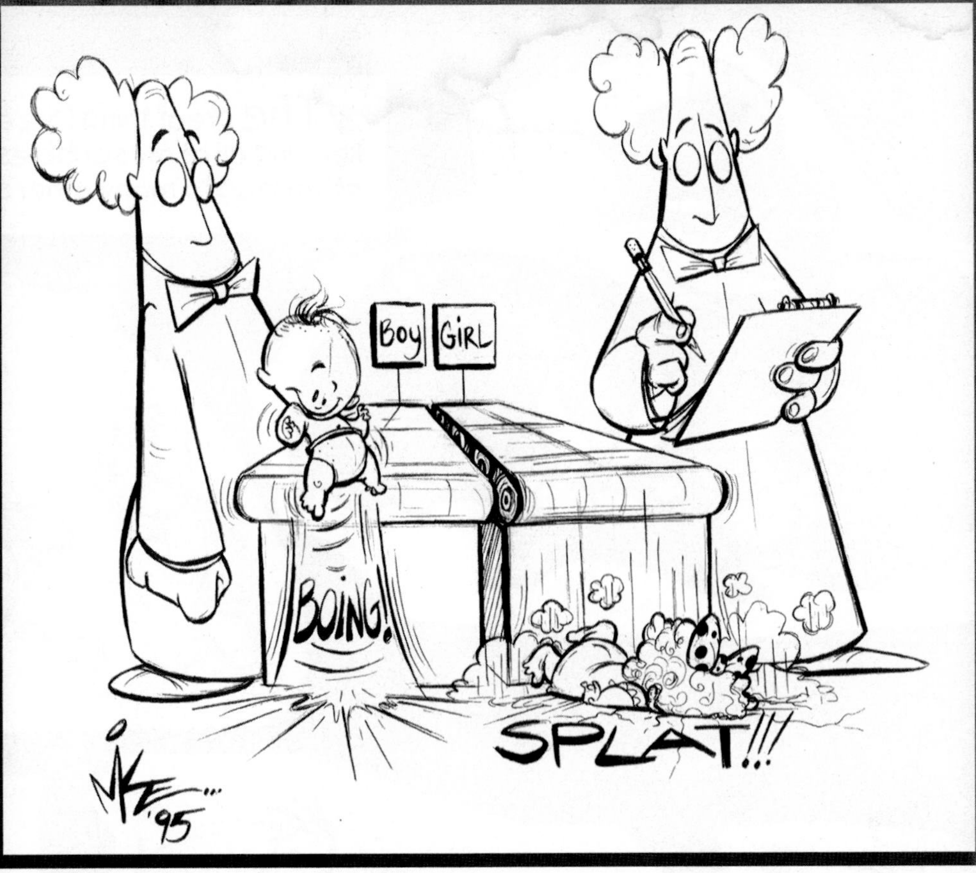
Boy
GIRL
BOING!
SPLAT!!!

A couple scribbles even ended up as birth announcements for my kids. First the "bouncing baby boy" theory was tested for our son, and then later a most special gift was brought by the stork in the form of our daughter.

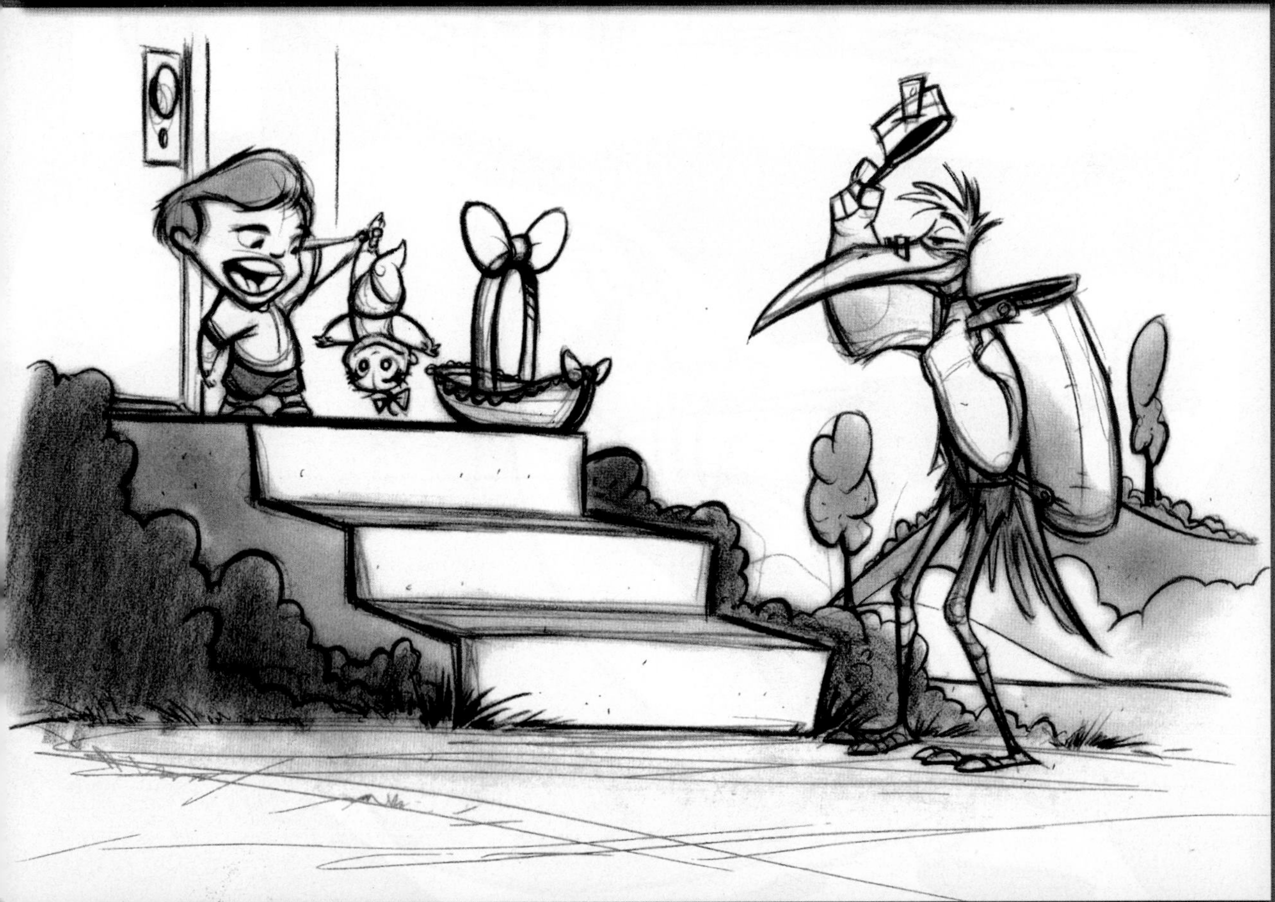

The great thing I've enjoyed about keeping all of my scribbles, is how they often lead to many other stories.

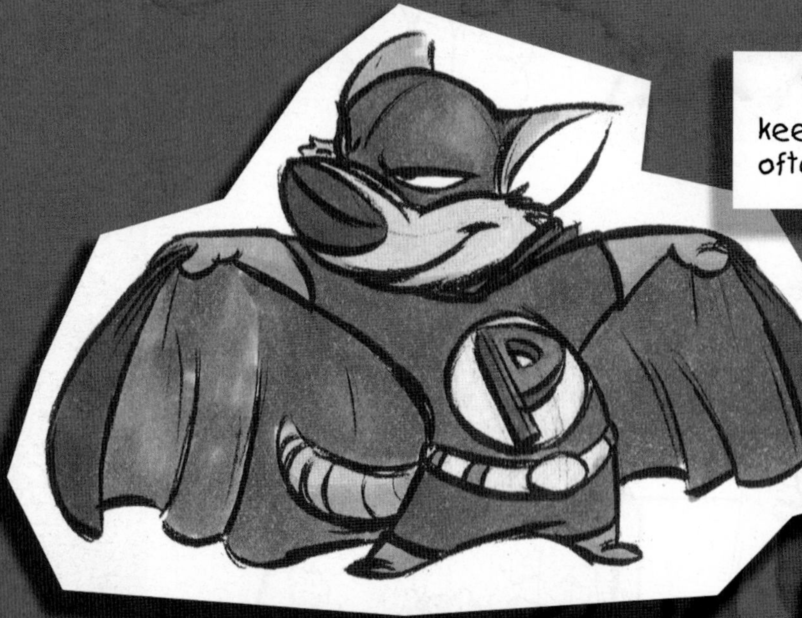

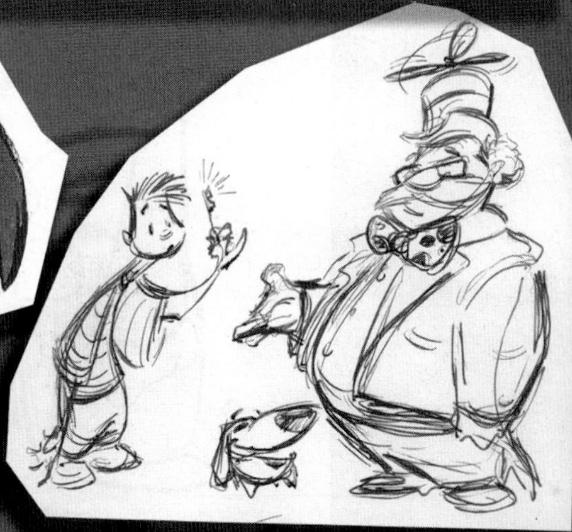

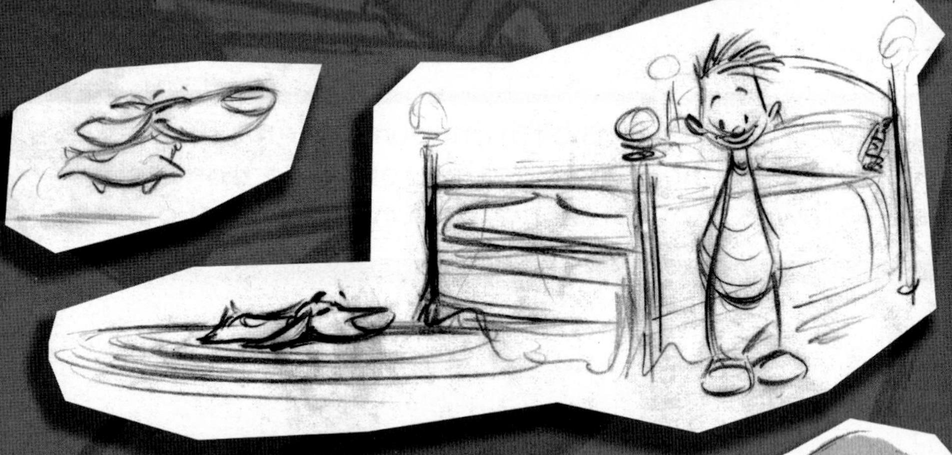

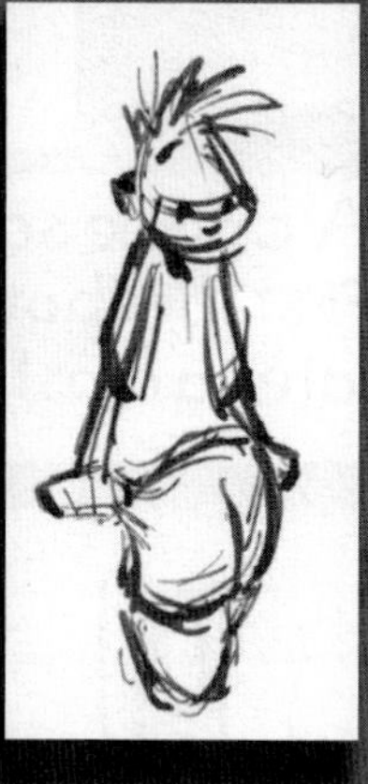

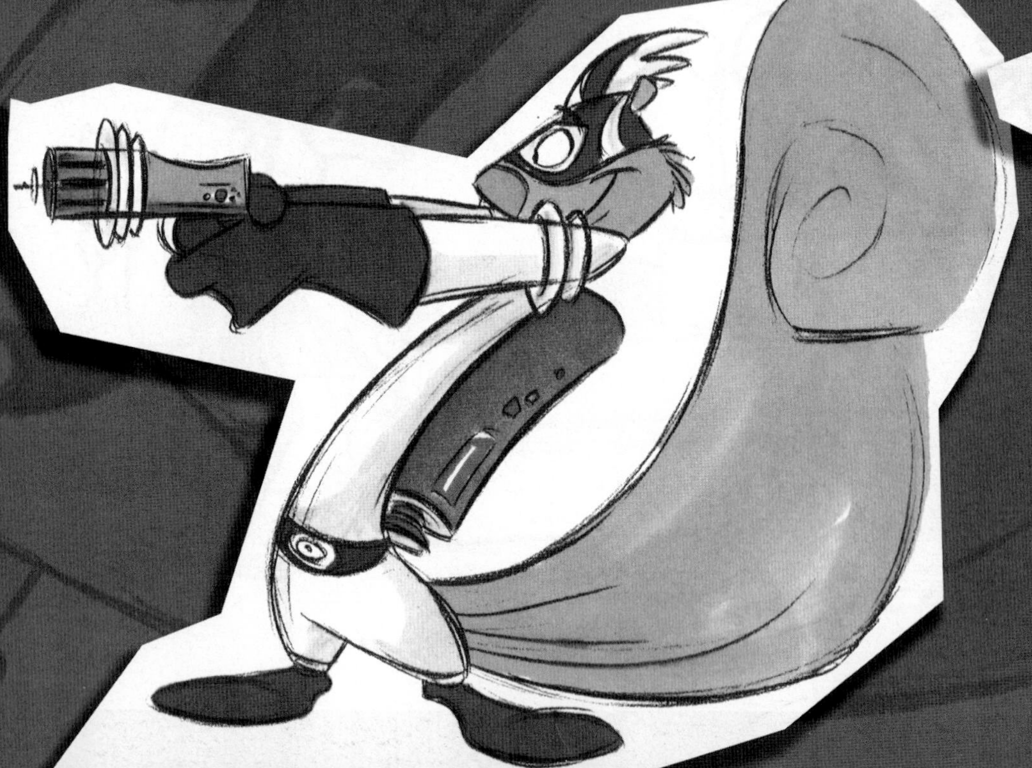

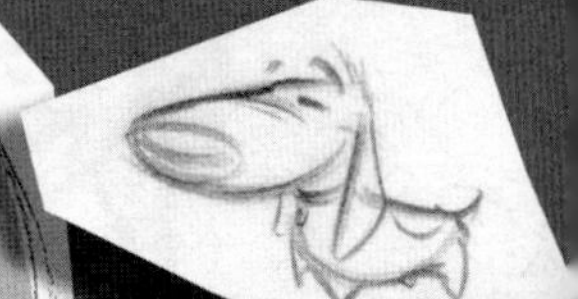

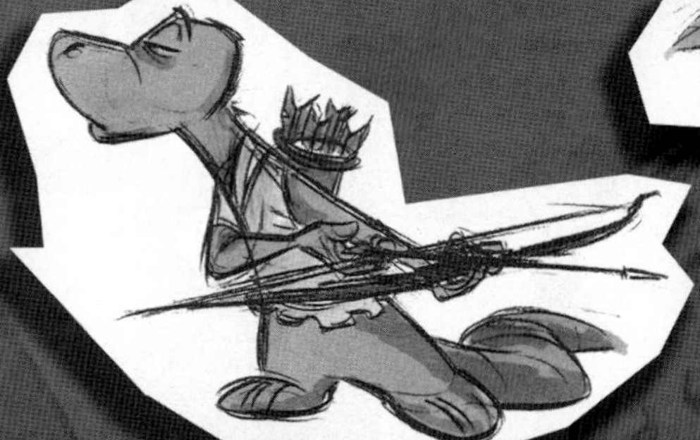

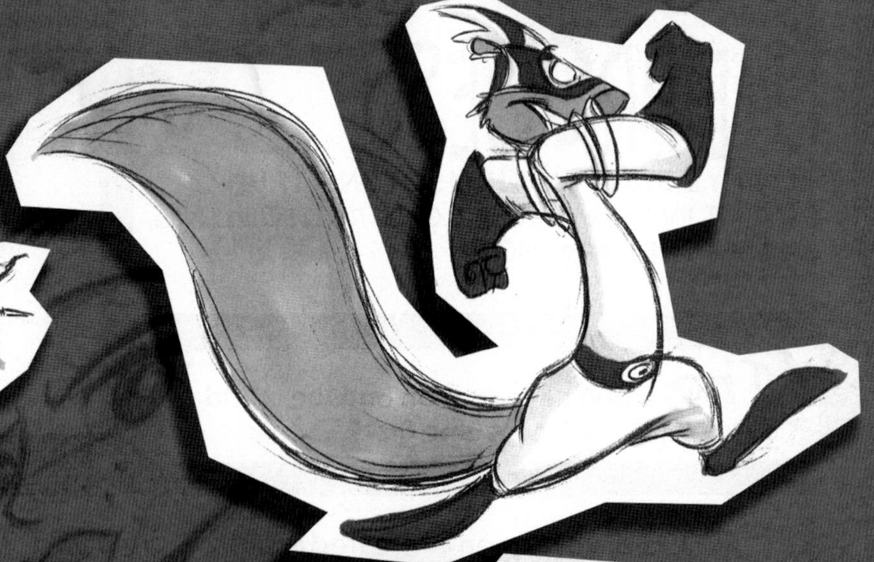

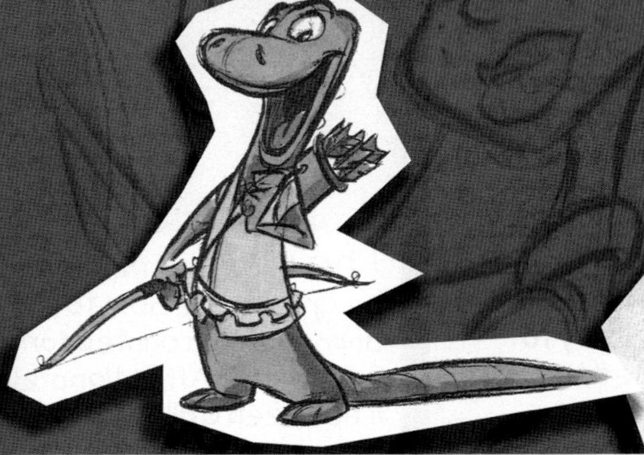

I look forward to the journey that each one of my scribbled characters will take on it's way to finding it's own story and place.

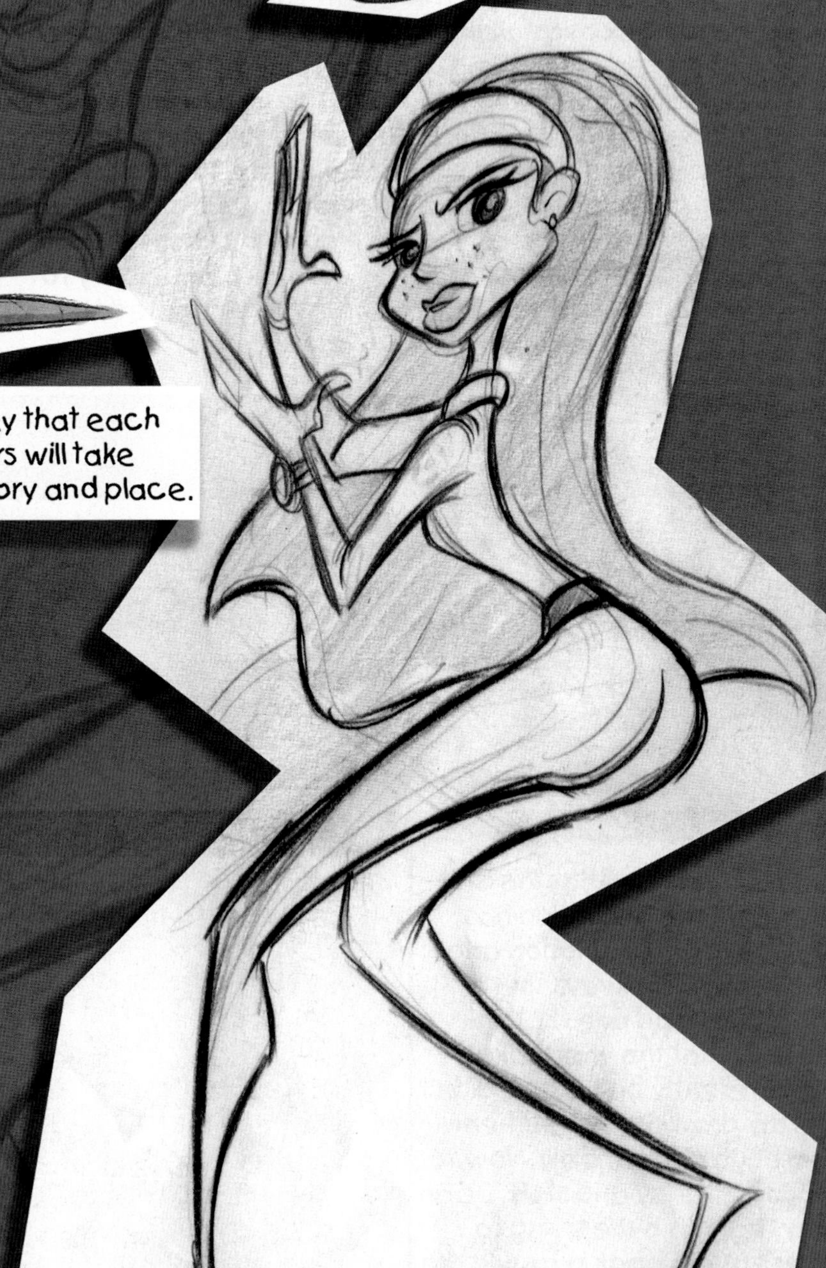

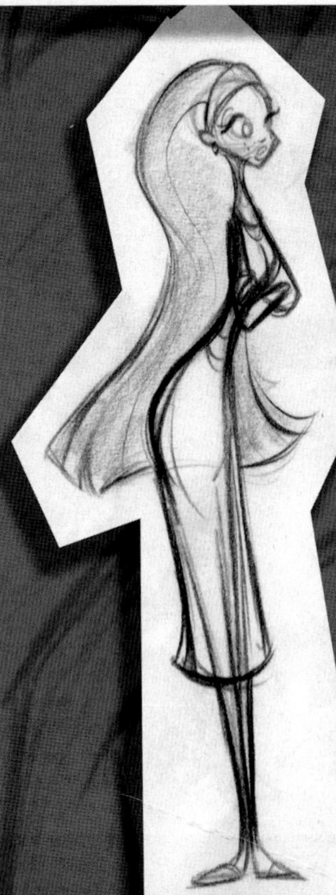

THE PROCESS

or "WHY DOES IT TAKE HIM SO LONG IF HE DOESN'T EVEN ERASE THE CONSTRUCTION LINES AND INK THE DRAWINGS?"

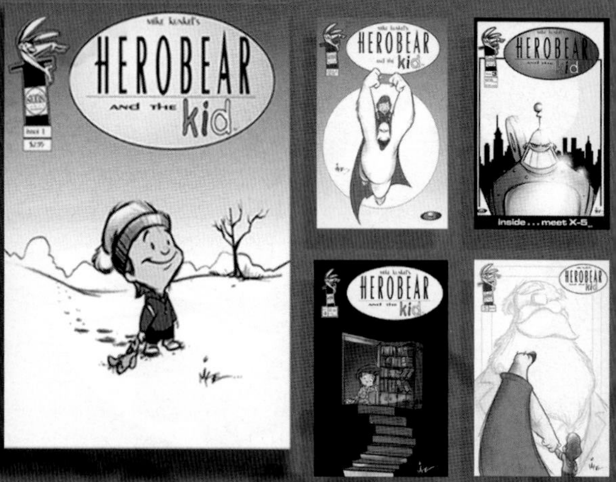

mike kunkel's
HEROBEAR
and the
kid
inside . . . meet X-5

The world of animation and the world of comics . . . which came first?

I've always been interested in both. I grew up reading comics all the time. And since 1990 i've been working in animation. If you can call getting to draw cartoons all day "working". It's too much fun. Now, what I love about animation is the ability to pull your audience into the world of the characters. And, the story telling opportunity of comics is so personal and close to your audience. The goal was to be able to combine both worlds. Showing characters emotions and ability to act out their dialogue was something I wanted to carry over into comics from animation.

The hope was that it would be great to be able to show animation in a printed form. So I tried it. Affectionately, it has been called a "printed pencil test" or more formally, "the Animation Way".

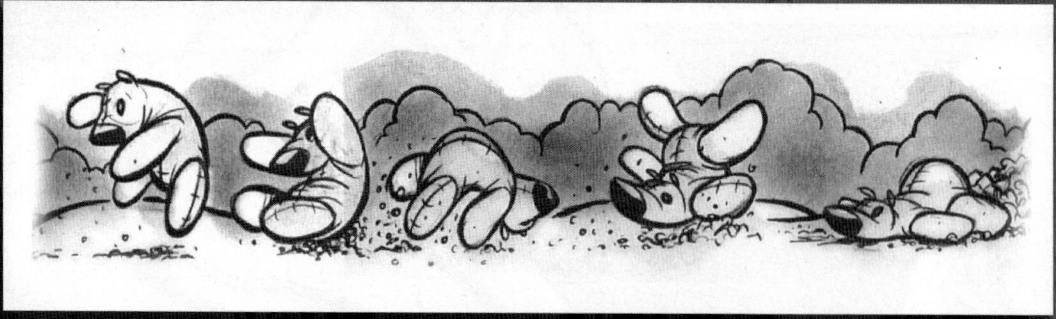

Okay, I know that this isn't the first time animation has been in comics. Motion and movement is always there so many good ones. I think though that this was looked at differently because I didn't ink my drawings. I left them all rough and scribbly. Now to sound all artsy and stuff, I can say that this is me trying to present the book in a style like an animator's rough drawings would look . . . but to be honest, it's also because I stink at inking.

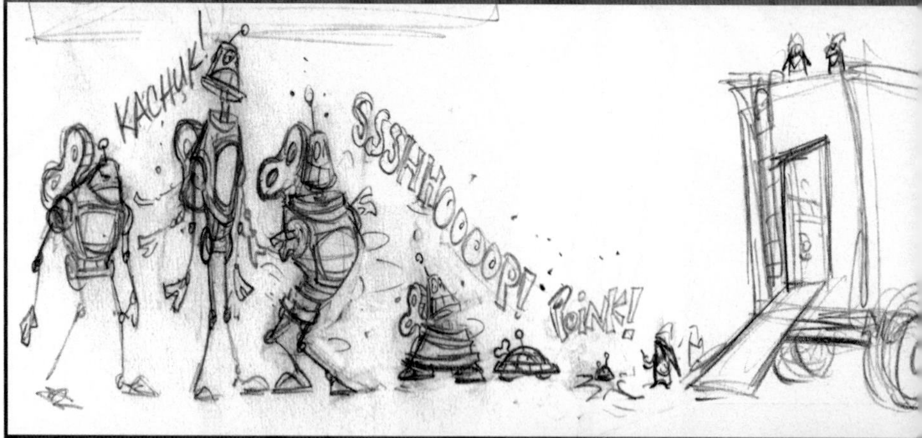

KACHUK!
SSSHHOOOOP!
POINK!

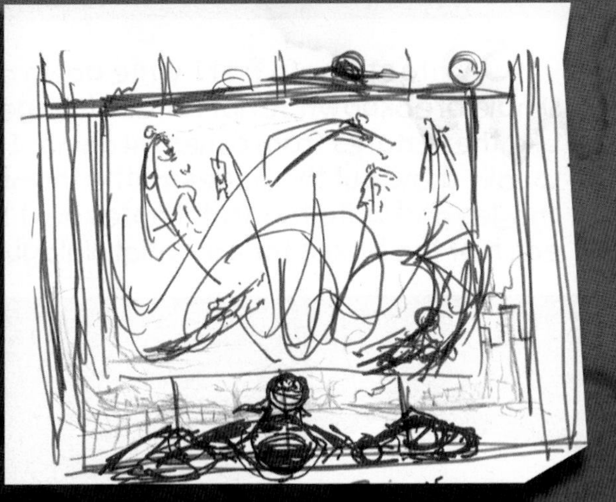

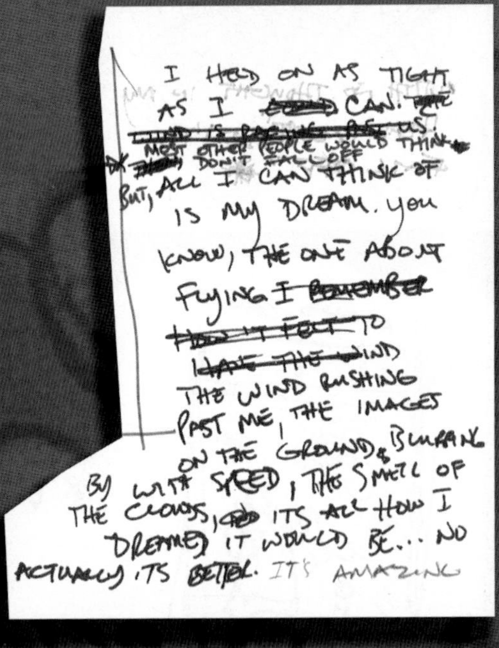
I HELD ON AS TIGHT
AS I CAN.
MOST OTHER PEOPLE WOULD THINK
DON'T FALL OFF
BUT, ALL I CAN THINK OF
IS MY DREAM. YOU
KNOW, THE ONE ABOUT
FLYING I
TO
THE WIND RUSHING
PAST ME, THE IMAGES
ON THE GROUND & BLURRING
BY WITH SPEED, THE SMELL OF
THE CLOUDS, ITS ALL HOW I
DREAMED IT WOULD BE... NO
ACTUALLY ITS BETTER. IT'S AMAZING

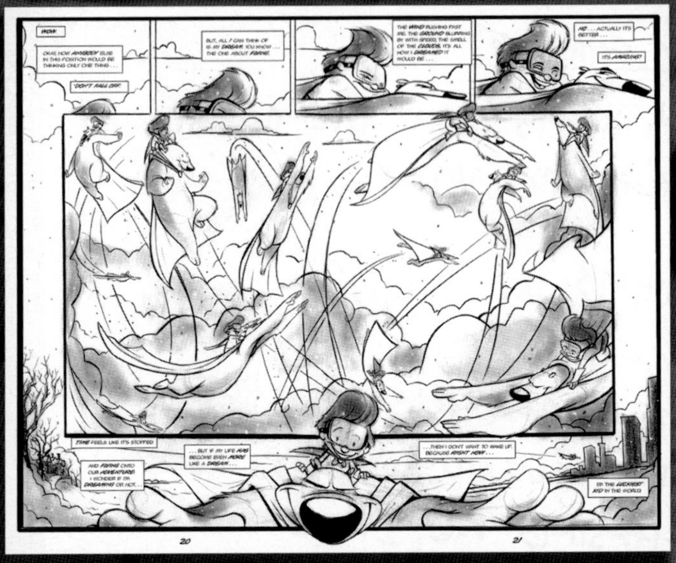

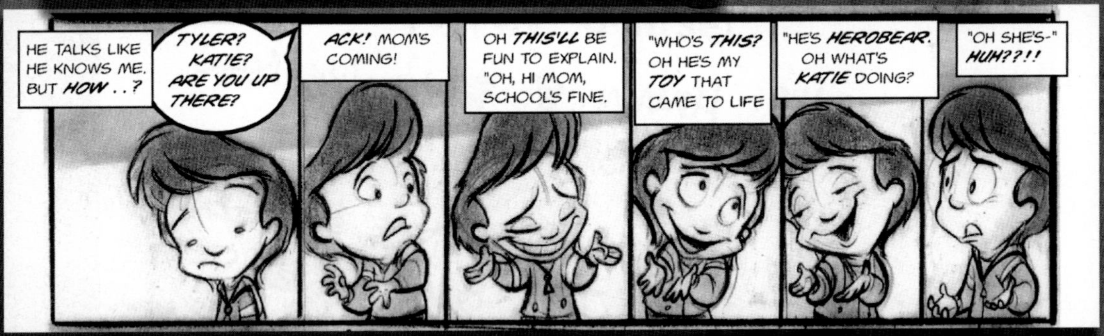
HE TALKS LIKE HE KNOWS ME. BUT HOW . . ?
TYLER? KATIE? ARE YOU UP THERE?
ACK! MOM'S COMING!
OH THIS'LL BE FUN TO EXPLAIN. "OH, HI MOM, SCHOOL'S FINE.
"WHO'S THIS? OH HE'S MY TOY THAT CAME TO LIFE
"HE'S HEROBEAR. OH WHAT'S KATIE DOING?
"OH SHE'S-" HUH??!!

The fun of combining animation with comics i've found, is in the acting and expressions. I love taking lines of dialogue and breaking them up into poses as if it were for a scene of animation. Of course this means way more drawings than are normal for a comic. See why the books are a "little" bit late sometimes?

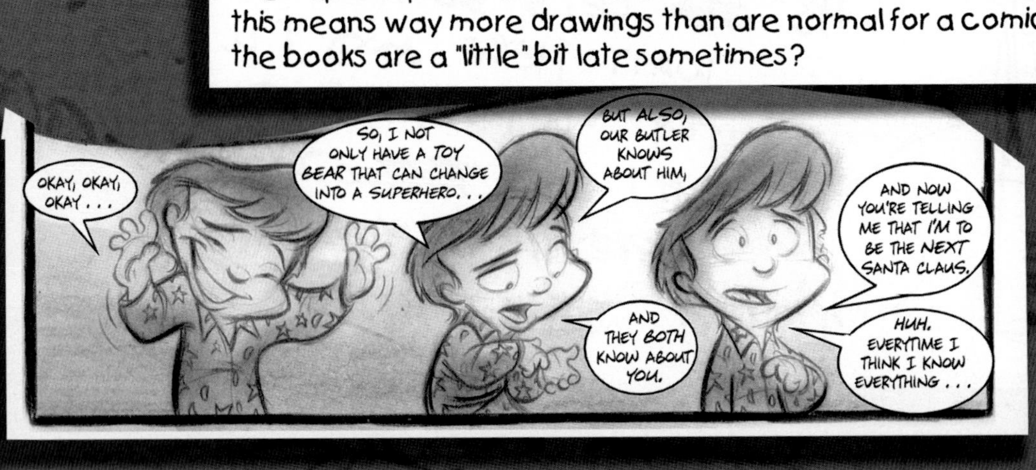
OKAY, OKAY, OKAY . . .
SO, I NOT ONLY HAVE A TOY BEAR THAT CAN CHANGE INTO A SUPERHERO . . .
BUT ALSO, OUR BUTLER KNOWS ABOUT HIM,
AND THEY BOTH KNOW ABOUT YOU.
AND NOW YOU'RE TELLING ME THAT I'M TO BE THE NEXT SANTA CLAUS.
HUH. EVERYTIME I THINK I KNOW EVERYTHING . . .

So to start off, first I write down a simple breakdown script for each page. Like these notes from issues #4 and 5, I'll usually draw out the pages in little thumbnail images and write the script notes next to each of the boxes for potential dialogue.

RUN AROUND CORNER

.TYLER CHANGES HB.

☆ WOW, THIS IS STILL THE COOLEST SIGHT TO WATCH.

HB: WHAT'S UP KIDDO?

T: THE WATCH HAS BEEN BEEPING, THE BULLIO BROTHERS ~~ARE~~ ~~NEED~~ CHASING ME, I'M LATE FOR GETTING HOME.

HB: HMMM. ~~&~~ ~~So~~ YOU'VE BEEN BUSY TODAY.

T: HAHA. WHAT ARE ~~WE~~ GONNA DO? THE BULLIO ~~BOYS~~ WILL BE ~~HERE~~ ~~TO~~ ANY MINUTE NOW.

HB: ~~OKA~~ LET'S DO THIS: YOU WAIT HERE AND I'LL FLY UP TO THE ROOF.

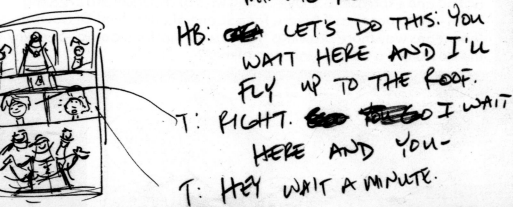

T: RIGHT. ~~SO~~ ~~YOU GO~~ I WAIT HERE AND YOU—

T: HEY WAIT A MINUTE.

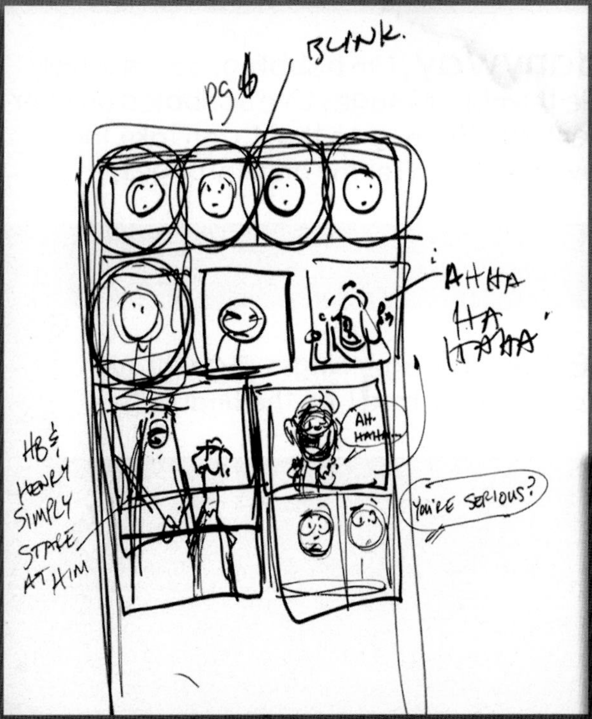
pg 6
BLINK.
AHHA HA HAHA
AH-HAHA
HB & HENRY SIMPLY STARE AT HIM
YOU'RE SERIOUS?

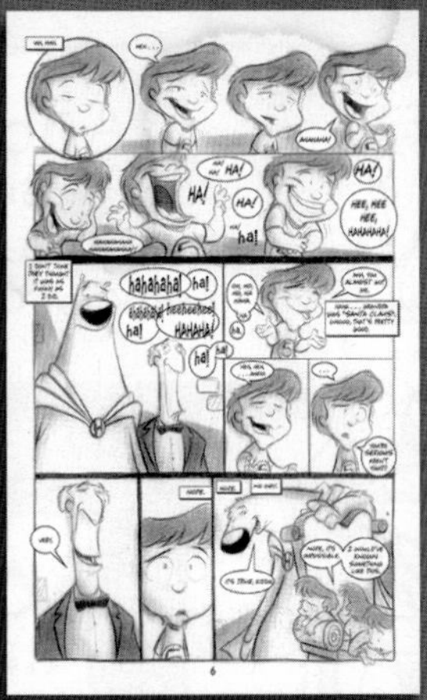

These drawings are very scribbly and really undecipherable to anyone but myself, but what they help me to do, is to work out the composition of each page. I'll then go and drive these images to my local Kinko's copy center to enlarge them to the right size for my original pages.

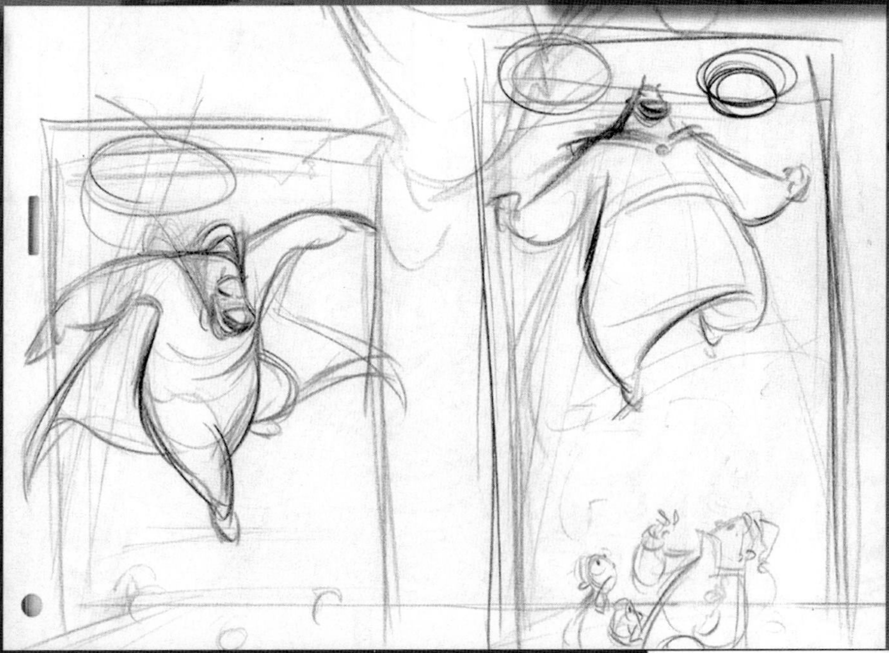

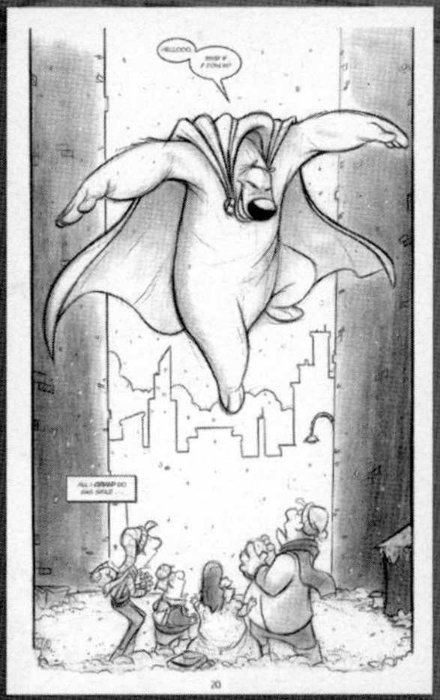

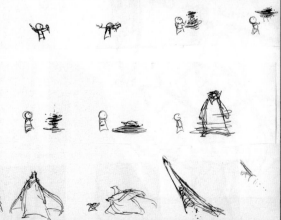

One side note here, I think the invention of Kinko's was a blessing and curse to all of us late night story creators. We all now know we can work really late and then drive over there and make copies and printouts and calendars at 5:45 in the morning. Evil, evil, evil, and heaven all rolled up in one. Because, now we have no excuse for not following our creative instincts to create stories at any time of the day.

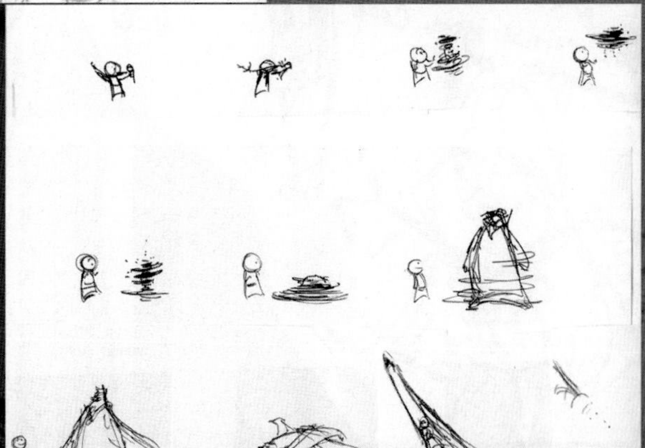

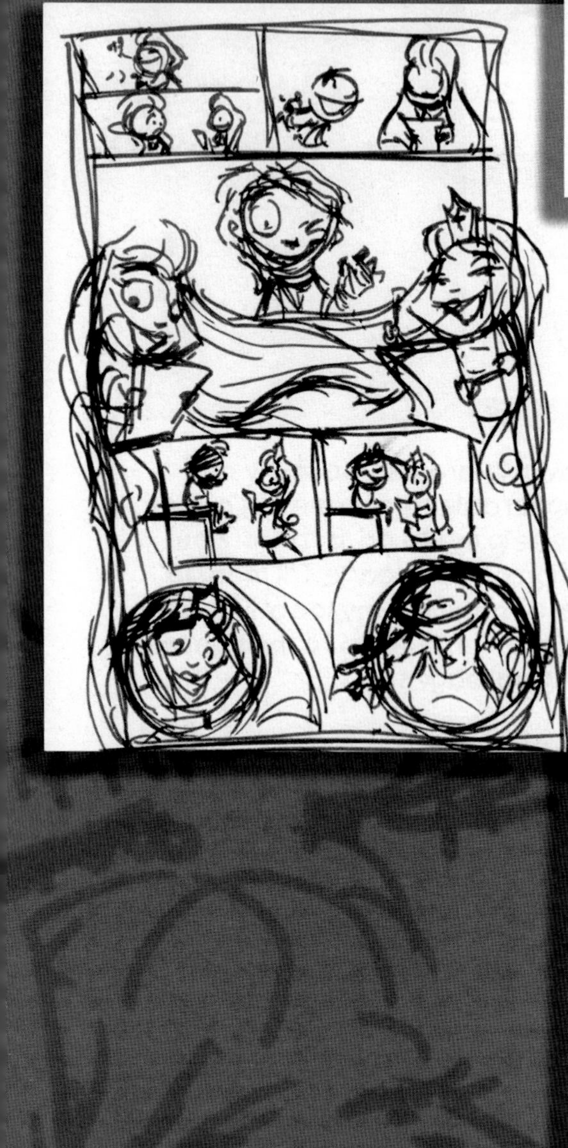

Aaaaaanyway, I'm babbling. So, I'll usually take those little thumbnail images I've scribbled on over to Kinko's. I'll enlarge them up so that I can take them home and draw over them for my original pages.

Often at this stage things will go through a few changes before I do the final page.

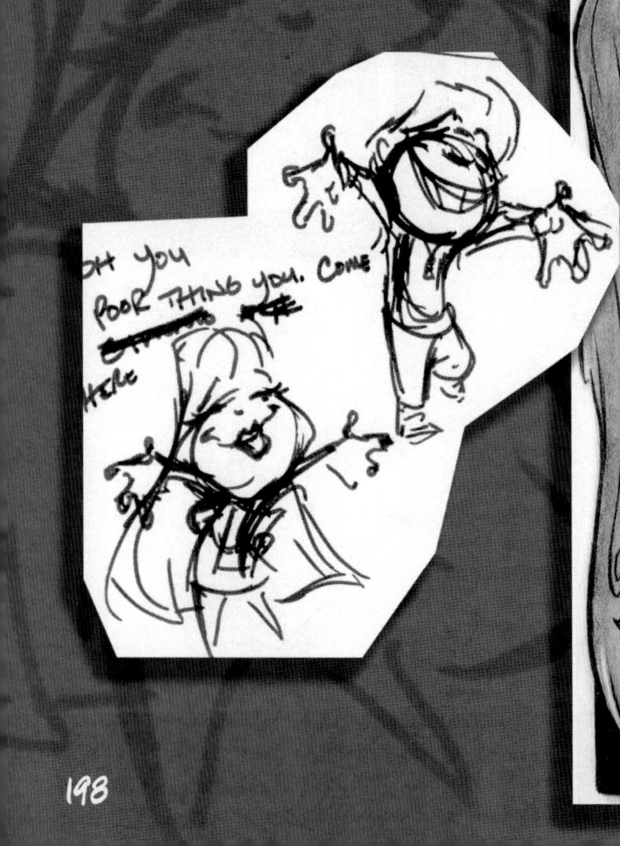

OH YOU
POOR THING YOU. COME
HERE

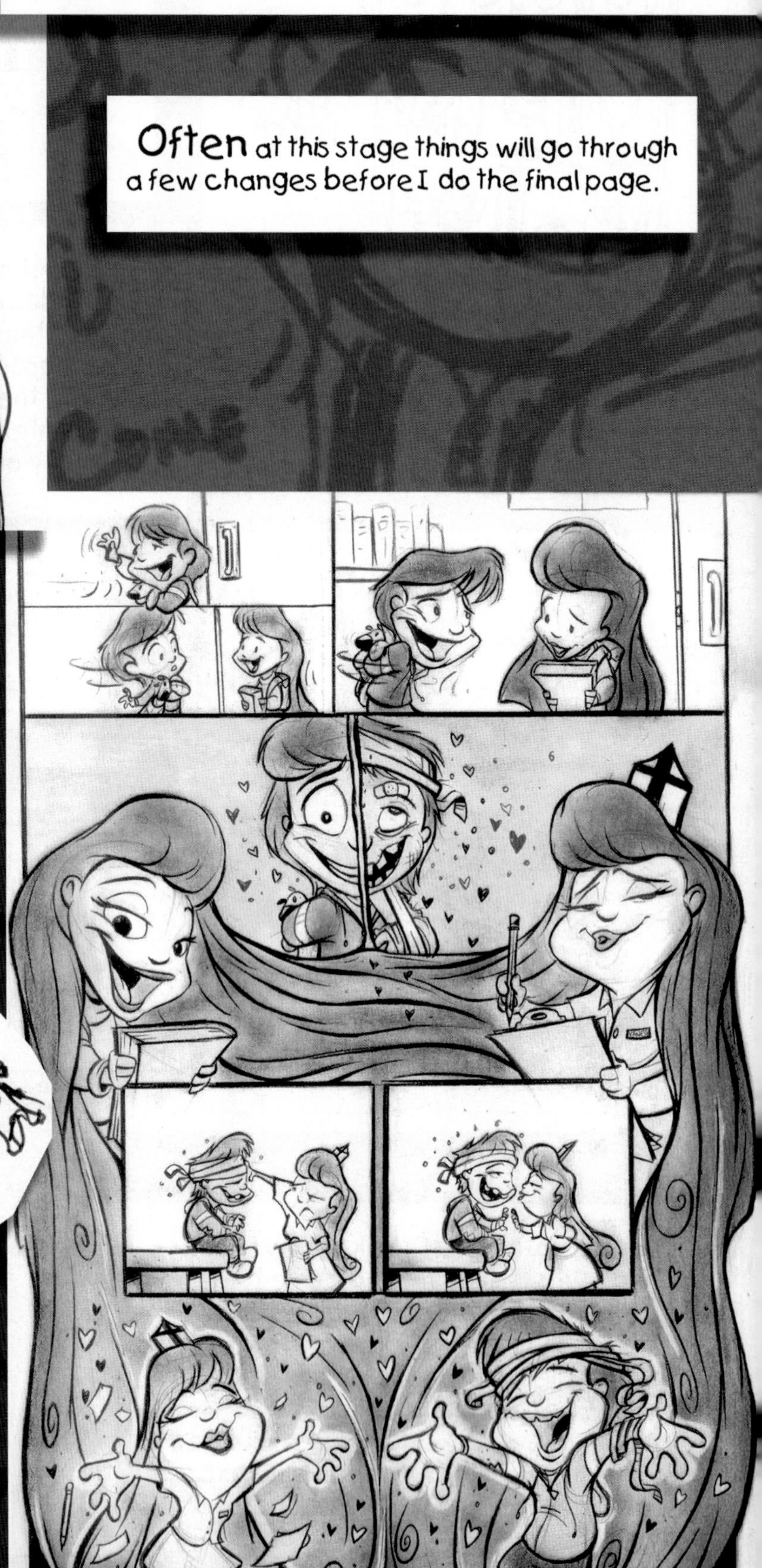

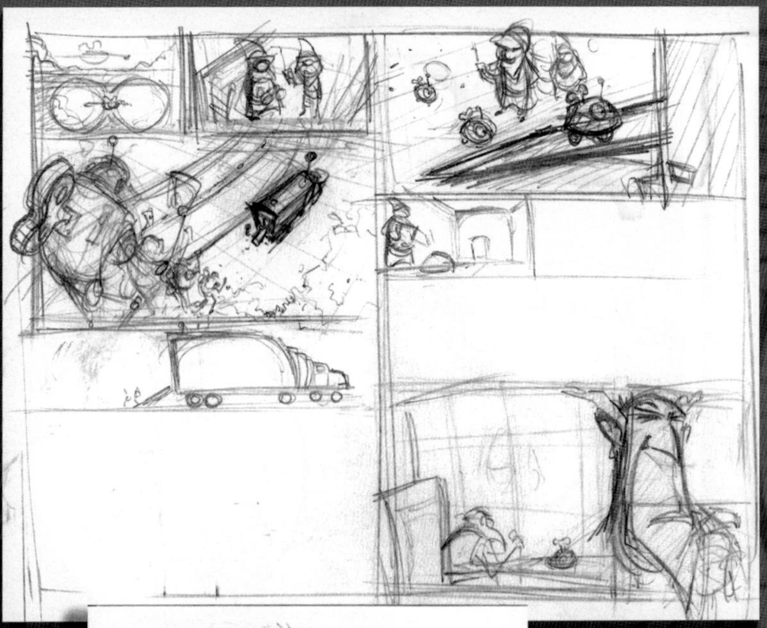

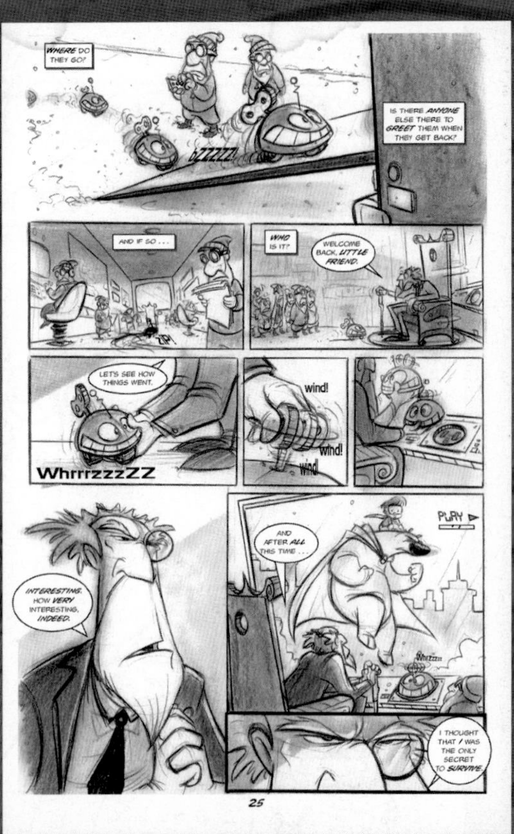

WHERE DO THEY GO?
IS THERE ANYONE ELSE THERE TO GREET THEM WHEN THEY GET BACK?
AND IF SO . . .
WHO IS IT?
WELCOME BACK, LITTLE FRIEND.
LET'S SEE HOW THINGS WENT.
WhrrrzzzZZ
wind!
wind!
wind!
INTERESTING. HOW VERY INTERESTING. INDEED.
AND AFTER ALL THIS TIME . . .
I THOUGHT THAT I WAS THE ONLY SECRET TO SURVIVE.
25

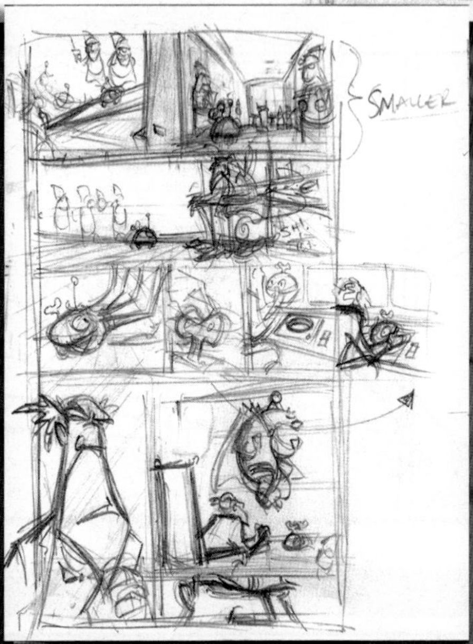

SMALLER

Sometimes, I can't make up my mind, so i'll even take ideas from a couple different thumbnail images, and then combine them to make the final pages.

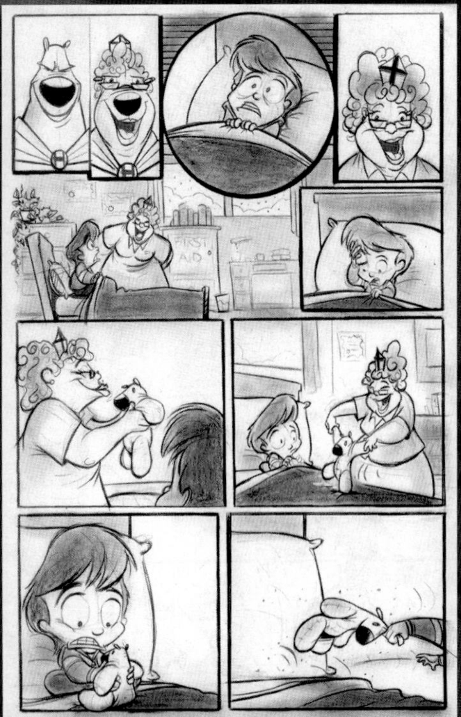

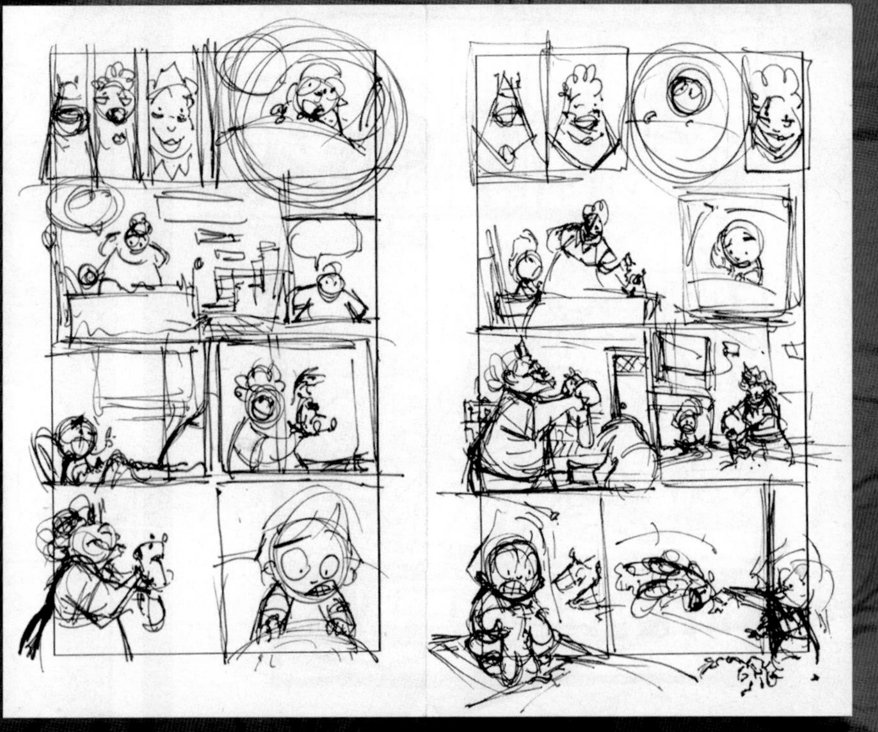

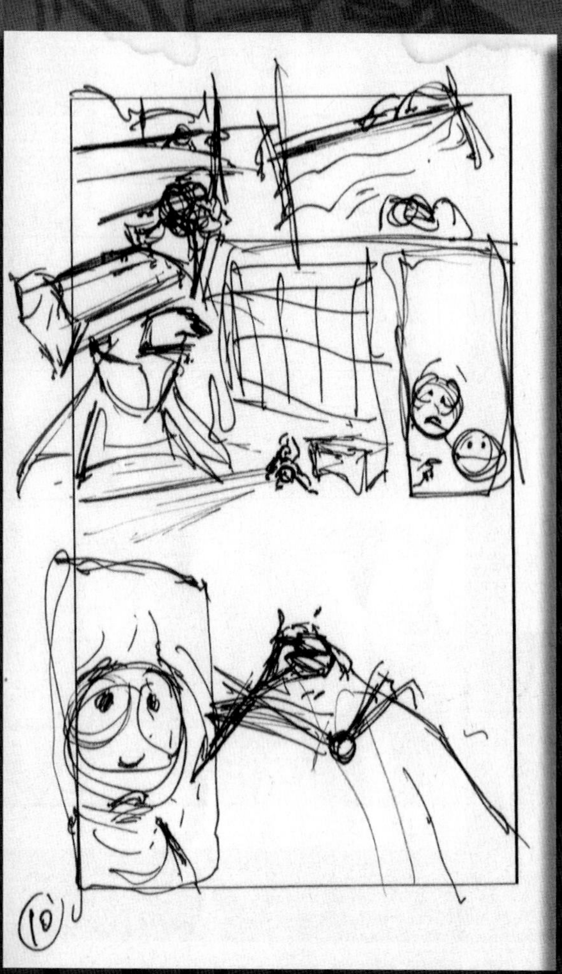
10

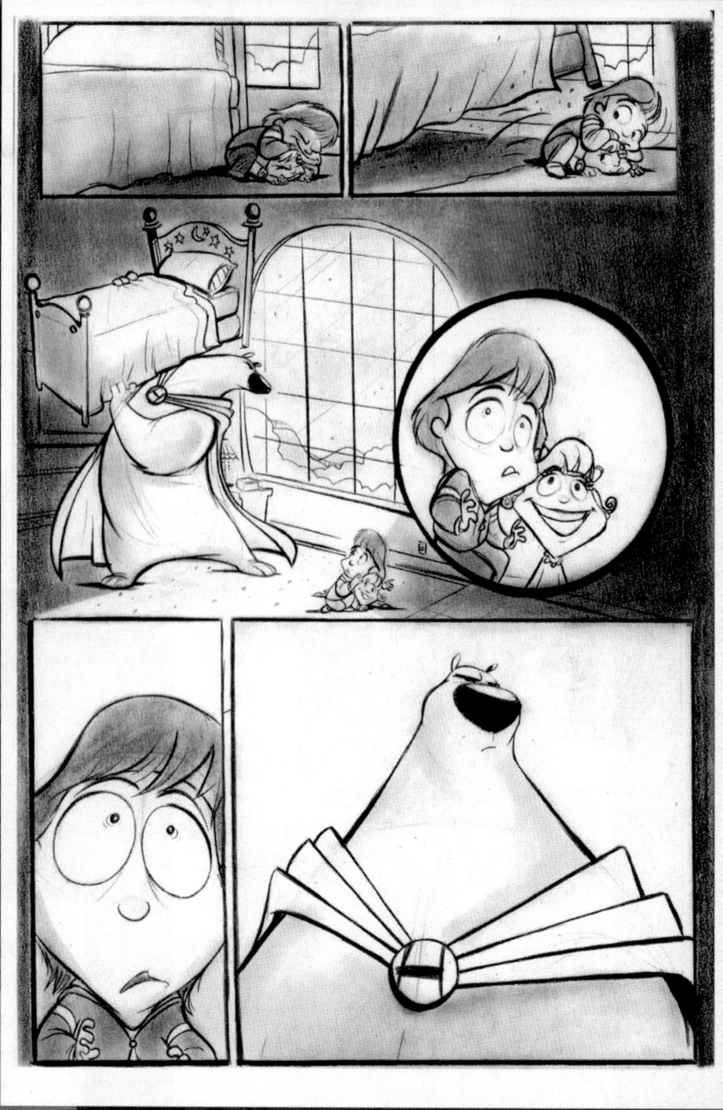

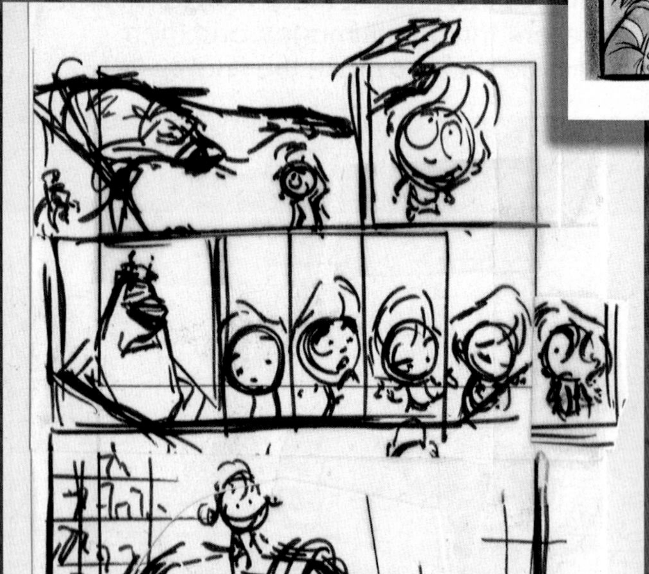

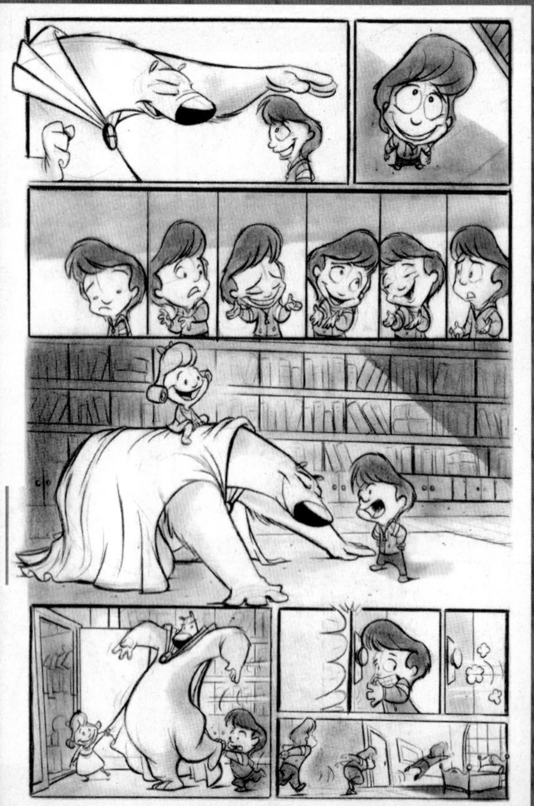
12

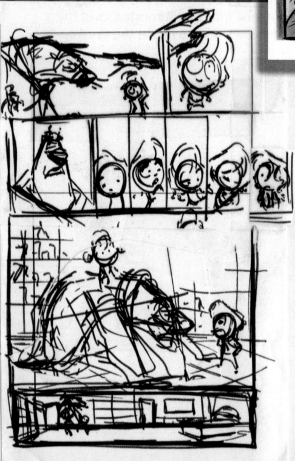

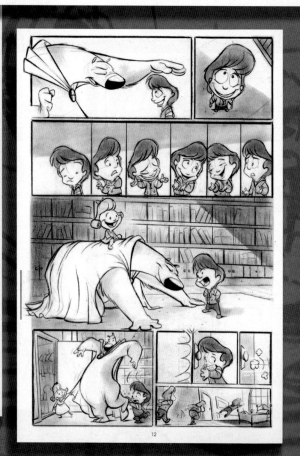

I'll often write script sections next to the thumbnails. For me, the script is an everchanging flow of the story that works hand in hand with the pictures. You have to be willing to adjust either the image or the word to fit each other.

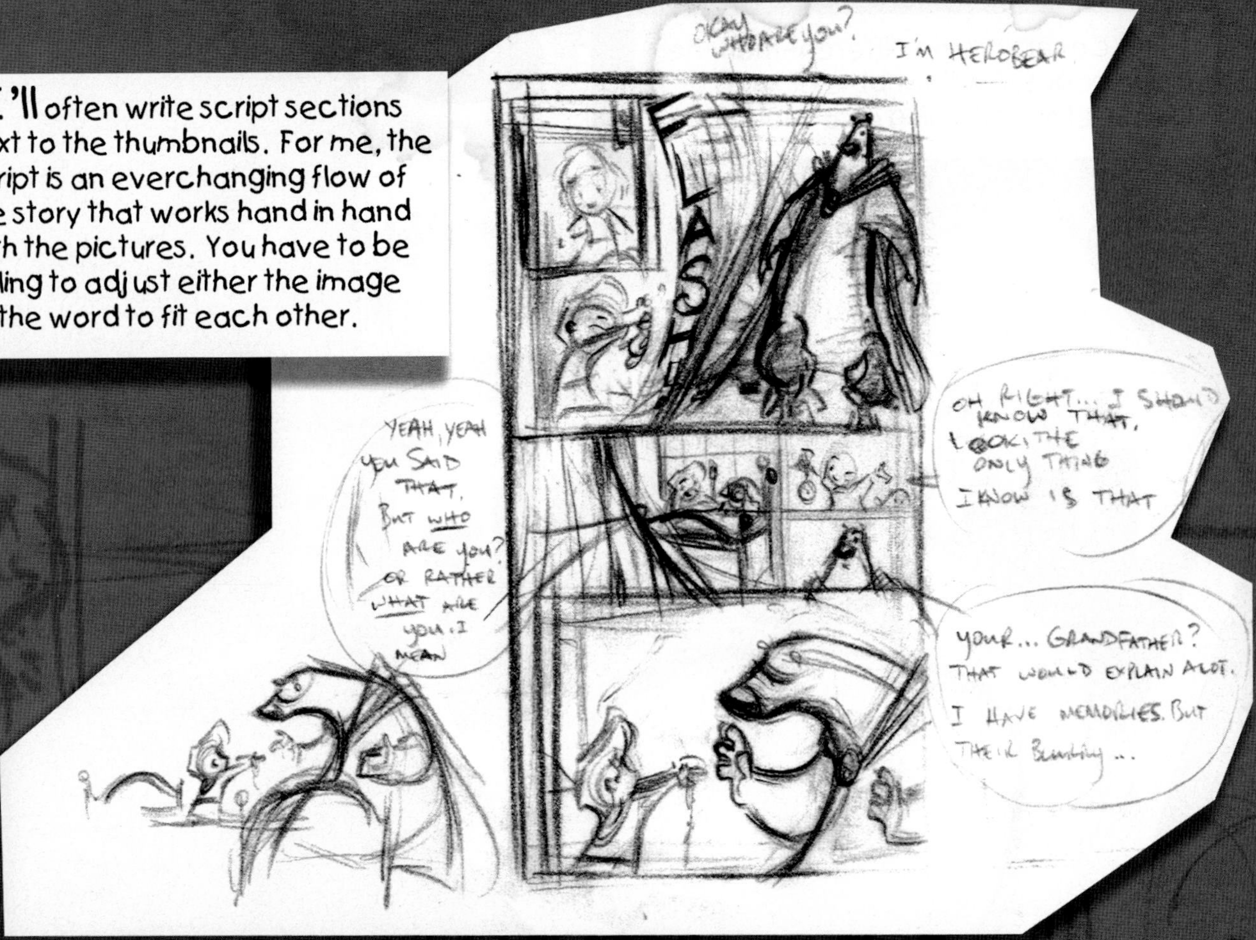
OKAY WHO ARE YOU?
I'M HEROBEAR
FLASH
YEAH, YEAH YOU SAID THAT. BUT WHO ARE YOU? OR RATHER WHAT ARE YOU. I MEAN
OH RIGHT... I SHOULD KNOW THAT. LOOK, THE ONLY THING I KNOW IS THAT
YOUR... GRANDFATHER? THAT WOULD EXPLAIN ALOT. I HAVE MEMORIES. BUT THEIR ...

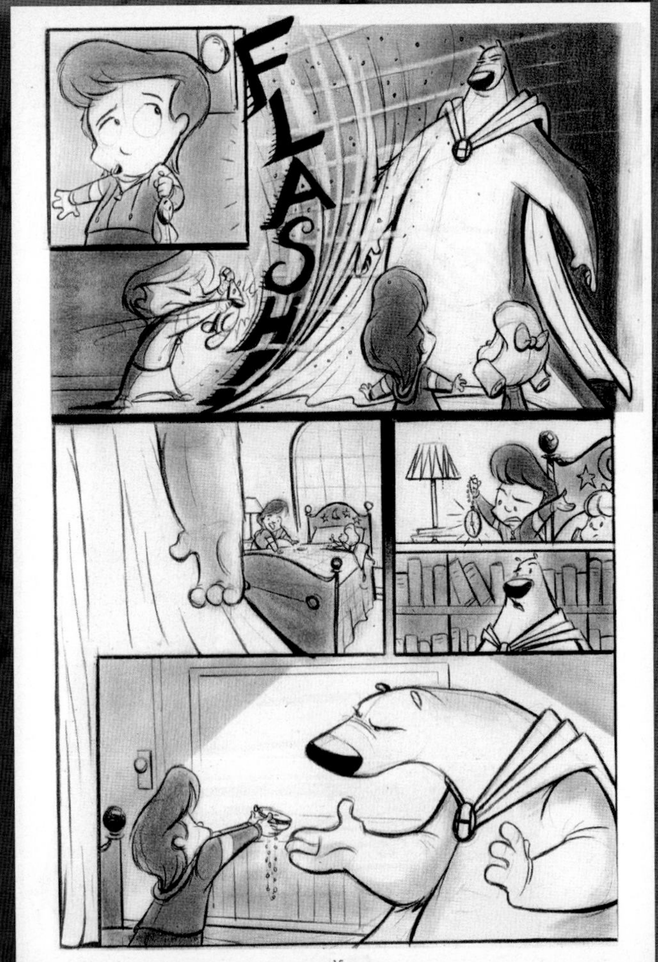
FLASH!
15

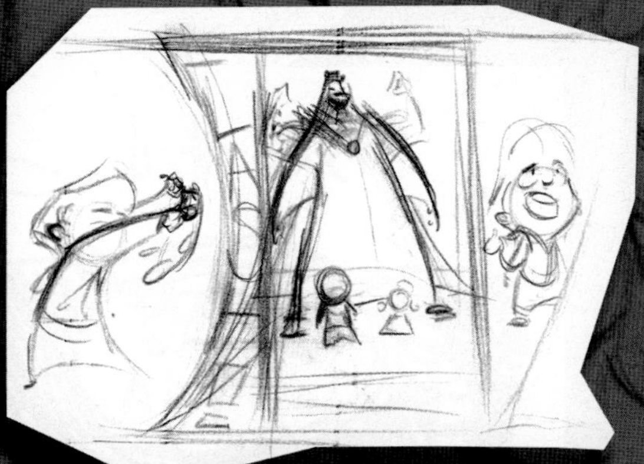

The process of thumbnailing has always been a big influence on the way I draw. I have all of these pages of tiny little drawings with writing next to them. I can see my thoughts as I search for the right pose or composition for the story.

The covers are no different than the inside pages. I will scribble all kinds of ideas before deciding on a final image.

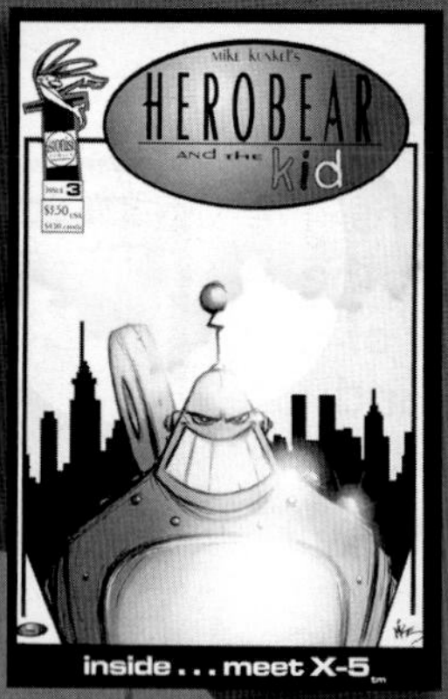
MIKE KUNKEL'S
HEROBEAR
and the kid
inside . . . meet X-5™

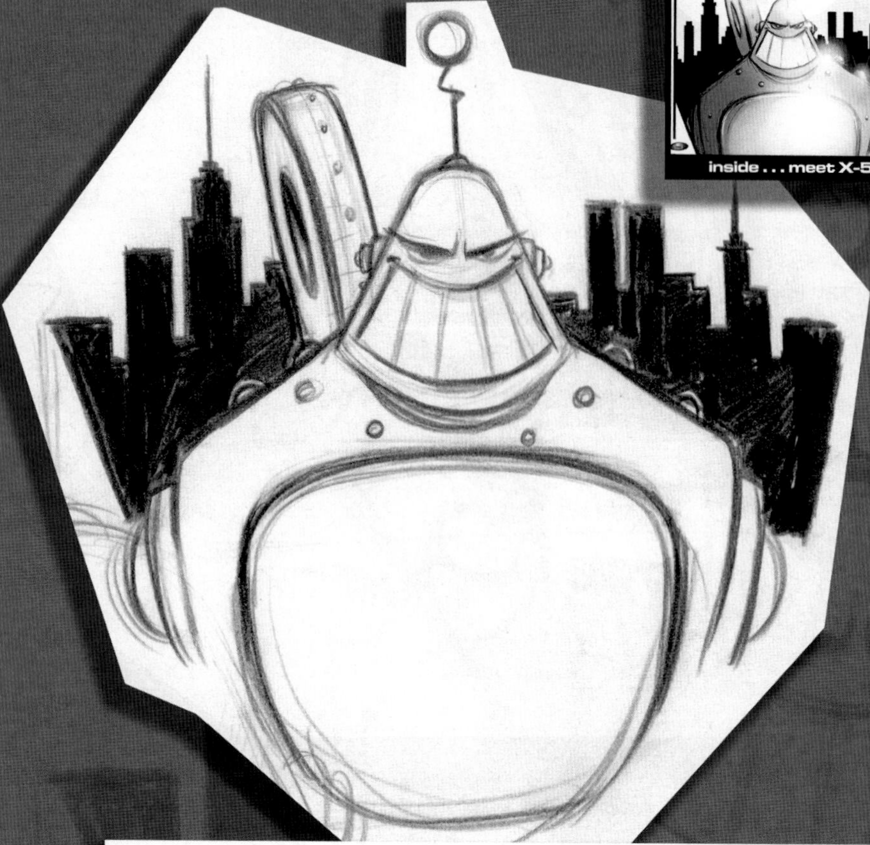

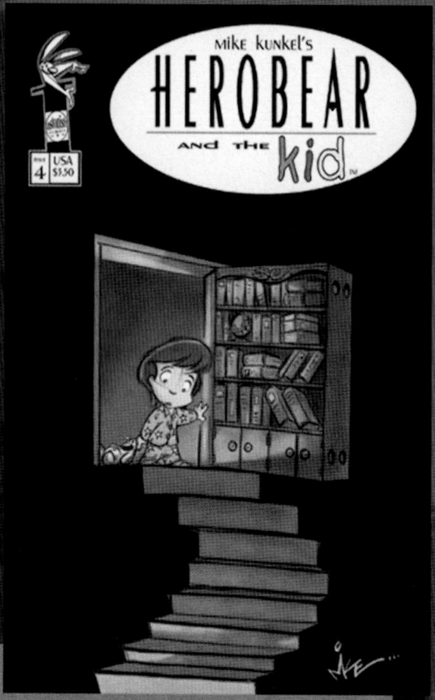
MIKE KUNKEL'S
HEROBEAR
AND THE kid™
4 USA $3.50

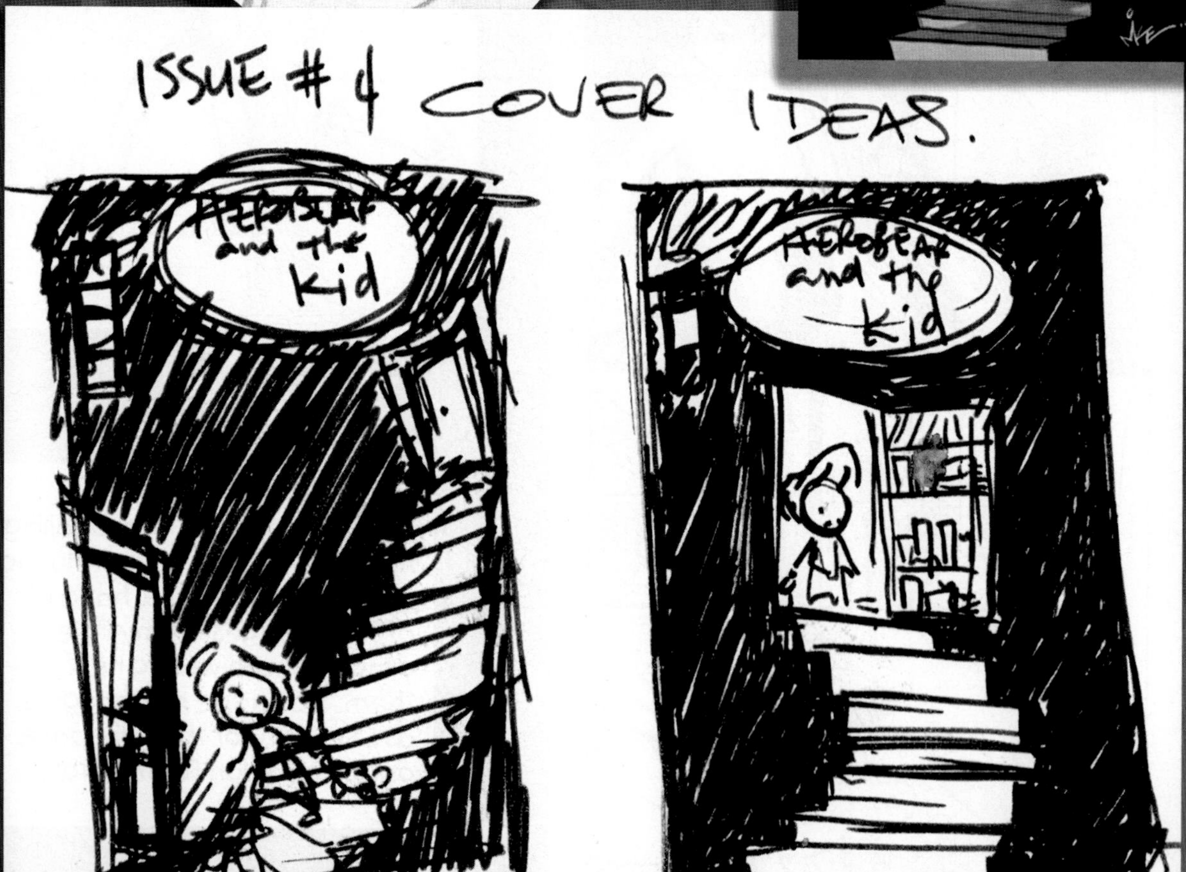
ISSUE # 4 COVER IDEAS.
HEROBEAR and the kid
HEROBEAR and the kid

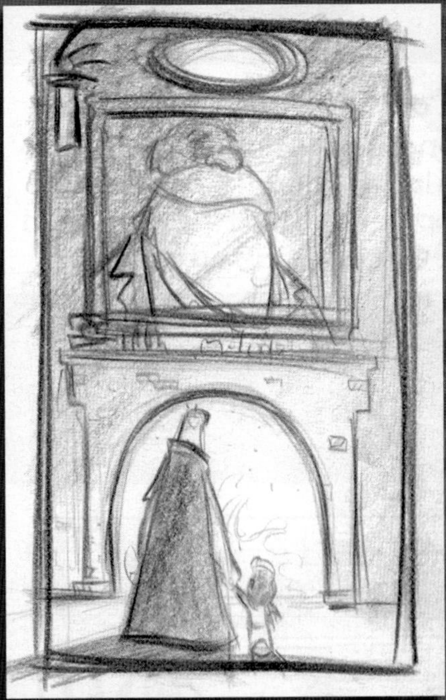

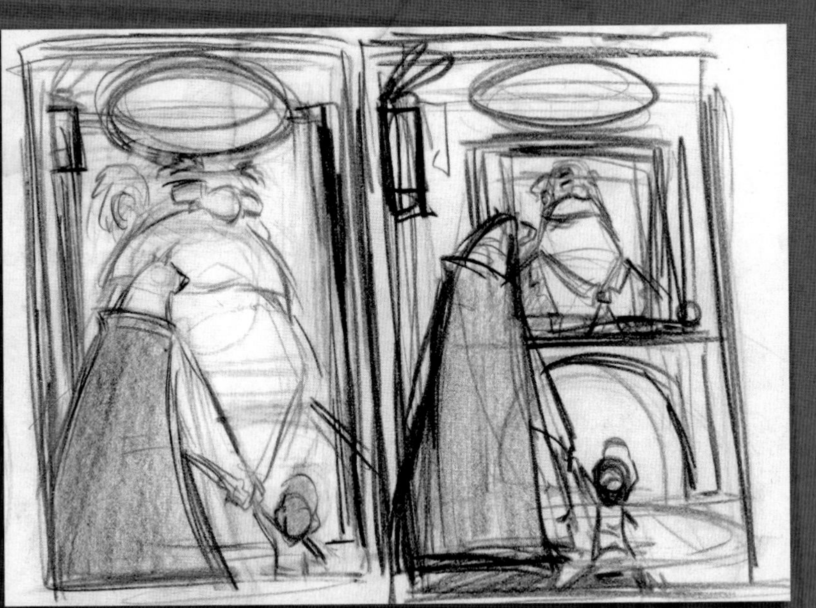

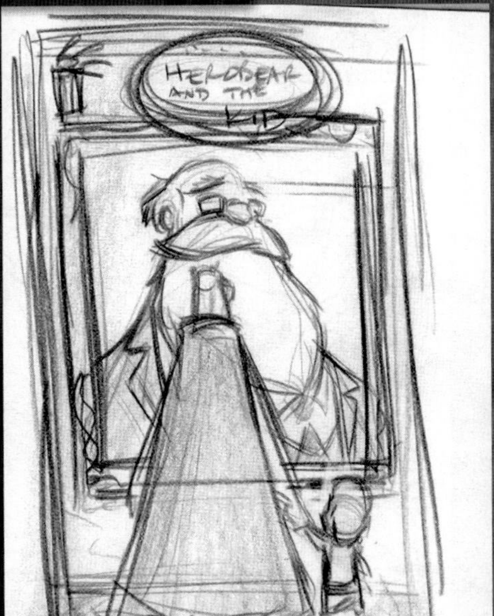
HEROBEAR AND THE KID

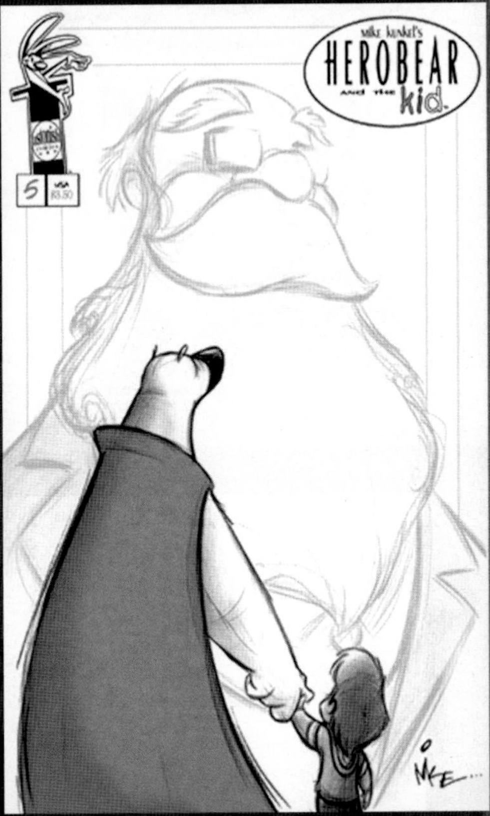
mike kunkel's
HEROBEAR
and the kid.
5

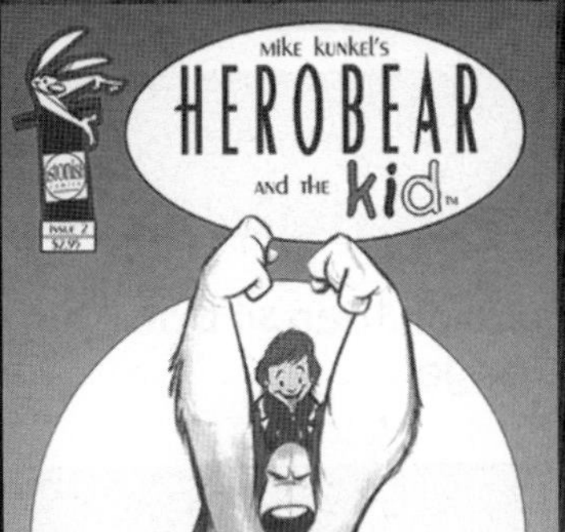
MIKE KUNKEL'S
HEROBEAR
AND THE kid™
ISSUE 2
$2.95

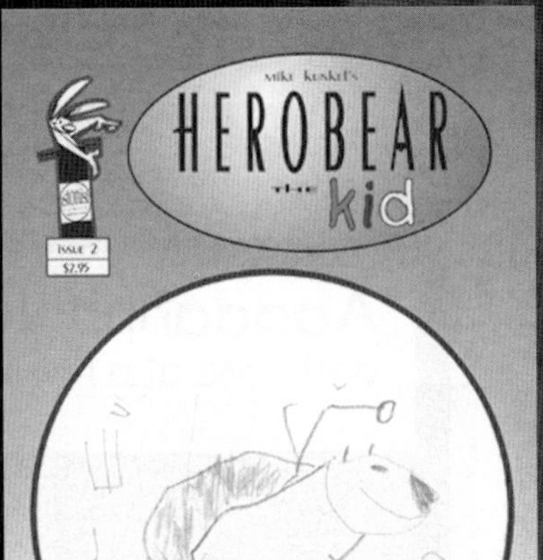
mike kunkel's
HEROBEAR
kid
ISSUE 2
$2.95
ISSUE NUMBER TWO

As with everything with this book so many amazing people have helped. Nothing would exist without them. My son even helped me to do this alternate cover for the second printing of issue number two.

Finally, after all of the scribbles and thumbnails, I make my brain settle on a finished looking page. I then scan it into the computer and add the script and color for the ever-special red cape.

Aaaaahhhhhh, I can then sit back and smile at a finished page ...

Of course, then I remember that the book is late, and I still have 30 more pages to finish.

So, though it takes a while for the art and story to finally come together, I love the entire process. There's such a good feeling from getting a box of freshly printed new books back from the printer. And all of the ideas and hard work are now real and tangible in the form of a simple little book.

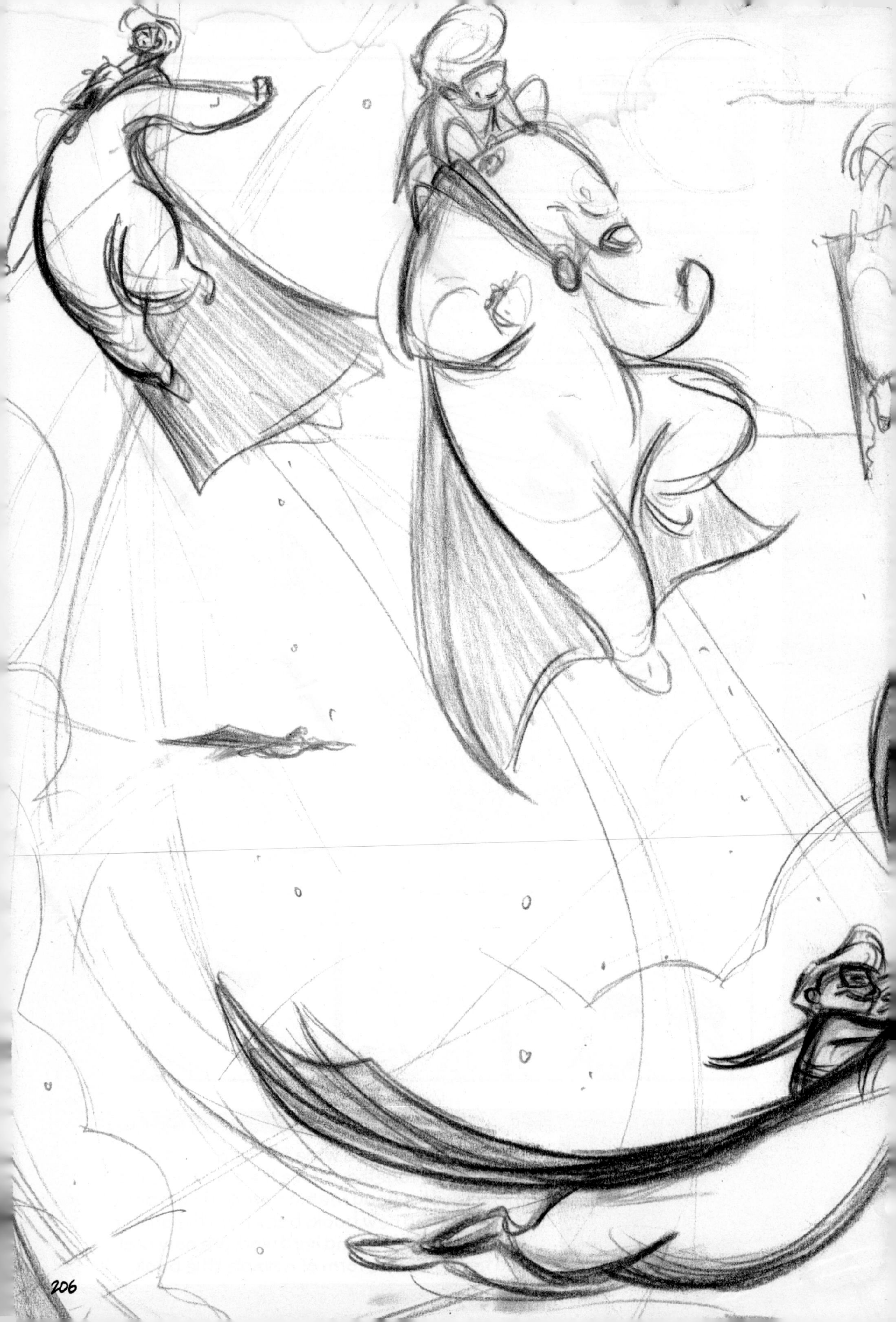

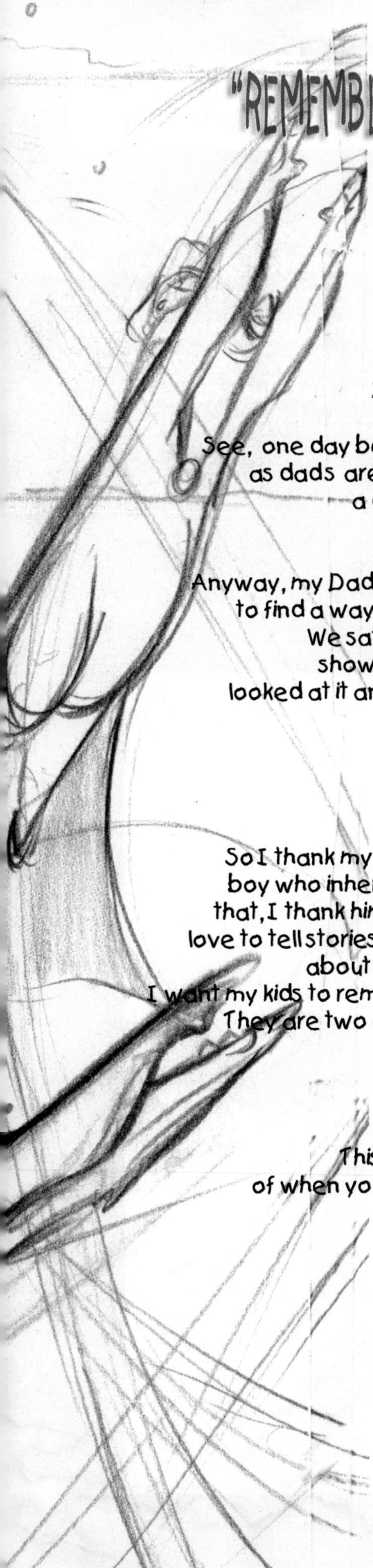

"REMEMBER YOUR CHILDHOOD ... AND PASS IT ON."

Ya know, I've had this phrase for a while.

A long while. But only half of it,
I only had "remember your childhood." So it only half worked.
I have my Pop to thank for the rest of it.
See, one day before issue #1 came out, we were talking about the story. And as dads are prone to do, he made a suggestion. I know this, now that I'm a dad myself, that this is just our way of passing on our wealth of knowledge to the ones that think they know more than us.
And probably do.
Anyway, my Dad is great with ideas. I have always respected him for his ability to find a way to enhance an idea. I think he's good at it because he cares. We sat and talked for a while, I showed him the drawings, and then I showed him the motto we were gonna use for Astonish Comics. He looked at it and then as if he'd been thinking about it for days, he said simply,
"You should say, 'and pass it on' at the end."
Now, my first thought was "darnit, why didn't I think of that." And then I smiled. It was perfect.
It felt right.

So I thank my Dad, for giving the right tag line to a nostalgic story of a young boy who inherits a stuffed bear and a broken pocket watch. But more than that, I thank him for reminding me to remember why I'm doing this, and why I love to tell stories. For he's passed on his care for his kids, and now, when I think about that phrase and my Dad, I think even more about my own kids.
I want my kids to remember their childhood as being a special and wonderful time. They are two of my most awesome inspirations. And I hope they are able to pass on a time of wonderment from when they were little.
I know I've been able to do that.
And it's made all the difference.

This book is for all of you who can reach back into your memories of when you were younger, to remember the fun times, the adventures, the events, the good feelings,
and remember a happy, simpler time.

And possibly... find a way to pass it on to others.

ONE MORE THING TO REMEMBER . .

I'd also like to remember that as with any project of love, it can't b
accomplished alone. No one can ever take credit fully for anything.
to remember that without God, this idea wouldn't have even existed
also remember that without my wonderful friends and family encour
and guiding, I wouldn't have been able to finish this story. The simple
of "thank you" can't possibly show my appreciation. But they do expr
much my heart is grateful for the involvement and input from all that
walked along with me in my life.

So, quite simply but most sincerely ... thank you for forever and a n

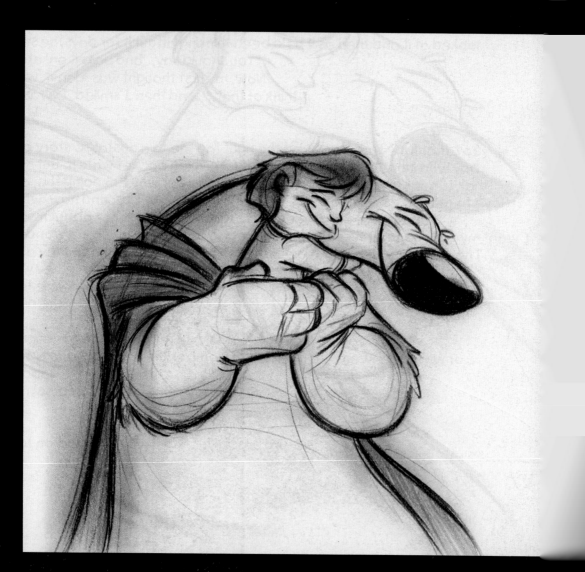

208